BEYOND THE FOUNDERS

BEYOND

THE

EDITED BY JEFFREY L. PASLEY,

ANDREW W. ROBERTSON,

AND DAVID WALDSTREICHER

FOUNDERS

New Approaches to the Political History
of the Early American Republic

The University of North Carolina Press, Chapel Hill and London

Designed by Jacquline Johnson
Set in Bembo
by Keystone Typesetting, Inc.

The paper in this book meets the guidelines for
permanence and durability of the Committee on Production
Guidelines for Book Longevity of the Council on Library Resources.

Library of Congress Cataloging-in-Publication Data
Beyond the founders : new approaches to the political history of the
early American republic / edited by Jeffrey L. Pasley,
Andrew W. Robertson, and David Waldstreicher.
p. cm.
Includes bibliographical references and index.
ISBN 0-8078-2889-0 (alk. paper)
ISBN 0-8078-5558-8 (pbk. : alk. paper)
1. United States—Politics and government—1783–1865—
Historiography. 2. Political culture—United States—Historiography.
3. Democracy—United States—Historiography. I. Pasley, Jeffrey L.,
1964– II. Robertson, Andrew W. (Andrew Whitmore), 1951–
III. Waldstreicher, David.
E302.1.B495   2004
973.4—dc22
2004007408

cloth   08 07 06 05 04   5 4 3 2 1
paper   08 07 06 05 04   5 4 3 2 1

To Marion Nelson Winship

who asks great questions

Contents

Illustrations

Acknowledgments

The editors would like to thank those who facilitated and contributed to the several conference sessions that went into the development of this volume, especially Marion Nelson Winship, Andy Burstein, John Murrin, Jack Rakove, Peter Onuf, Jim Banner, and Joanne Freeman. For helpful comments on the introduction and other parts of the manuscript we also thank Joyce Appleby, Scott Casper, Peter Onuf, and Al Young. And most of all we thank our contributors and the rest of the Society for Historians of the Early American Republic, who made it all so convivial.

David Perry of the University of North Carolina Press has stood by the project patiently; his editorial advice improved the manuscript at several stages.

We would like to pay tribute to the demographic expansion that has occurred in the authors' families during the gestation of this book. In order of their birth, they are Isaac Pasley, Isaac Huston, Owen Pasley, Rodda John, Angela Gormley, Laura Robertson, Emery John, Isaac Cotlar, Maya Waldstreicher, and Thad Robertson. We celebrate their appearance and acknowledge our families' support and assistance.

DAVID WALDSTREICHER,

JEFFREY L. PASLEY, AND

ANDREW W. ROBERTSON

Introduction

Beyond the Founders

The dawn of the twenty-first century has turned out to be a flush time for the founding fathers. Pundits celebrated their appearance on the best-seller lists, cited them as a tonic for contemporary disillusionment with politics, and got to work writing biographies themselves.

The founders' renewed popularity created opportunities for professional historians as well. Some dubbed "founders chic" a healthy antidote to academic attacks on the nation's "greatest generation." Joseph J. Ellis introduced his ensemble of paired founder studies with a "polite" but direct attack on social historians who vaulted "marginal or peripheral figures, whose lives are more typical" over "the political leaders at the center of the national story."[1] Critics, in response, decried "easy," conservative, or "lite" history, and the entire "greatness studies" approach, with its all-too-contemporary obsession with personalities and "character." As Alan Taylor pointed out, "In the recent spate of popular biographies of Founders, readers find one placed on a pedestal at the expense of foolish others."[2]

Was this all history had to offer: Jefferson down, Adams up? To a significant extent, this had always been precisely what the early republic offered. Comparative founder-worship and demonology helped inaugurate the American political tradition. Indeed, founders—or "Federalist"—chic and the works that have inspired it develop an important and long-lasting argument about the early national past, an interpretation that might be called neo-Federalist for the ways in which it appreciates what the Federalists were about, what they contributed to the survival of the United States as a nation, and how they were (rudely) knocked off their aristocratic pedestals after just a decade in national power.

Most compellingly laid out by Stanley Elkins and Eric McKitrick in the *Age of Federalism* (1993), and given an eloquent personal cast more recently by Ellis in *Founding Brothers*, this interpretation stresses the weakness of the national government after the ratification of the Constitution. The statesmen who came to the capitol seized the mantle of a new national politics; their actions, contests, and debates secured the legacy of the Revolution and shaped the political alternatives available to the following generations. Insofar as political parties and ideologies came into existence, they mainly reflected the personalities and practices of this small group.[3]

The 1790s succeeds the 1780s as, paradoxically, a golden age of statesmanship and a second infant stage in national politics. Fittingly, given the mix of celebration and condescension with which it is described, politics in the 1790s has an ironic, if not tragic, outcome, as the epic contentions of that brief moment are swept away by the modernizing and democratizing forces of the nineteenth century (in some versions as early as the election of 1800). The rest becomes, as they say, history—perhaps social, as opposed to political, history, but certainly another story. The gap between national, political history and social history, described by Ellis in terms of subjects or kinds of people, becomes a rigid chronological barrier as well when self-described historians of the founding era define a brief, Camelot-like early republic, when high politics ruled the day—a last bastion, apparently, of history as the interactions of great men. Only in this embattled context (embattled for the subjects if not also for its historians) could Ellis's stark opposition between a social history without politics and a political history without the people seem to be the only available options.

Meanwhile, others had moved on. These newest political historians of the early republic are heavily informed and sometimes inspired by post-1960s social and cultural history, not the vanguard of a backlash against it. Very much aware of the difference intellectual and political leadership made, they look beyond the founders to find a larger and richer political landscape during a longer early republic (1780s–1840s). While they do not reject the founders as a subject, they do insist that neither the invention of American politics nor the significance of the early republic can be grasped solely, or even mainly, from the top down.

The historians represented in this volume recognize both the power the founders had to shape subsequent American history and the importance of the political showdowns of the 1790s. Nevertheless, they emphasize how in an era of postrevolutionary ferment and retrenchment, uneven and contradictory democratization of public life, geographical expansion, and economic upheaval, politics took multiple shapes at interlocking local, state, regional, and national levels. The task of constructing (and for some, contesting) relatively new political institutions hardly ended with the ratification of the Constitution or with the turbulent 1790s. Beyond the founders, in terms of people and in terms of time, lay struggles to demarcate the identity of the citizen, the modes of political action, and the changing nature of the political itself.

THE NEWEST POLITICAL HISTORY AND THE PROBLEM OF THE EARLY REPUBLIC

The need for a broader approach to the early republic and its politics has been recognized by leading historians since the late 1970s. In the keynote address to the first conference of the Society for Historians of the Early American Republic (SHEAR), which became the first article published in the organization's new *Journal of the Early Republic* (1981), Edward Pessen observed the striking "continuities and similarities" in the "Federal" and "Jacksonian" eras. Research into the formation of classes and the exercise of power during the four decades before the Civil War had revealed a society much less democratic and egalitarian, and thus perhaps more old-fashioned, than previously believed. Meanwhile, the historians of the earlier early republic (ca. 1789–1820) had found vibrant partisan political cultures and extensive social change—both key harbingers of modernity. Enough changes did occur between 1820 and 1850 to warrant, perhaps, the continued use of the term "Jacksonian" for that period, but the attentive historian could no longer assume that there were two completely different eras. Social history had implications for generalizations about Jacksonian democracy, and political history could challenge complacent generalizations about premodern "Founding Fathers" in wigs and short pants.[4]

Seven years later, Gordon S. Wood laid down an even more comprehensive challenge to overspecialization and the division between social and political history. Since the progressive history narrative stressing the "decline of aristocracy" and the rise of democracy fell out of favor, the period suffered from a lack of "overall themes." It was "slighted and scorned" by social and cultural historians interested in longer-term change. Studies of African Americans, women, and Indians had begun to appear, but they remained "isolated and unconnected, uninvolved as yet in any overall reinterpretation of the period." Wood wisely laid the blame not only on the new histories and their lack of interest in politics but also on the dominance of political history itself, and on the style in which it was usually written: "This fascination with the great and not-so-great men of the era has tended to further fragment our understanding of the period. We often see the early republic solely in terms of its individual political leaders. . . . But such biographies of leading political figures contribute little to a comprehensive understanding of the early republic. Indeed, they tend to aggravate the incoherence of the period." The real significance of the early republic lay in the confluence of political and social trends: the spread of entrepreneurship, the movement of people, the democratization of religion, a new appreciation of the malleability of culture itself. All this amounted to "a basic social revolution," the empowerment of ordinary people, and the emergence of the quintessentially American society. Ordinary white men did it—a fact that explained the peculiar postrevolutionary anxieties of the founding fathers, or at least those whose persisting republicanism made them living anachronisms by 1820, if not before.[5]

Wood answered his own call for synthesis with *The Radicalism of the American Revolution*, a Pulitzer Prize–winning triptych of the period from 1750 to 1820. The Revolution's radicalism, for Wood, consisted precisely in the tendency for elite or gentry republicanism to be appropriated by and on behalf of the middling sorts, who used it to promote their own economic interests and their new political power. The early republic becomes the culmination of a long transition from republican "benevolence" and natural aristocracy to brash capitalism and "middle-class democracy," a gradual but real social revolution fought out simultaneously in the realms of politics and culture. The book has been criticized for painting the colonial "monarchy," revolutionary "republicanism," and early national "democracy" with overly broad strokes, and especially for doing little to integrate women, African Americans, or Indians into the story.[6] Wood certainly makes the early republic derivative of the Revolution, and politics itself derivative of social and cultural change, so that in the end it does not greatly matter where the one starts and the other ends, or what role actual political events might have played in the great transformation. Yet in light of the seeming rise of Founders Chic (which he has celebrated in a characteristically ironic mode), it is important to note that even where Wood tended to conflate the experience of many different groups in *Radicalism of the American Revolution*, he at least inquired into the particular relationship between elites and ordinary people, and indeed made that relationship central to his understanding of an expanded Revolutionary era. There was a generational experience, but it was not limited to the national leadership class. If anything, the experience of leaders was one of losing traditional perquisites of leadership.

With somewhat different emphases, Joyce Appleby has also brought together the dynamic changes of the late eighteenth and early nineteenth centuries under the twinned rubrics of capitalism and democracy. Although Appleby was one of Wood's critics in the republicanism versus liberalism debates which so occupied the field in the late 1970s and the 1980s, she, like Wood, argues strongly for the wide extent and fast pace of democratic change and fully justifies careful attention to a broad generational experience in an expanded early republic (1790–1830). For Appleby, the victories of the Jeffersonians in 1800, which she sees in a positive light, were only the beginning of the Revolution's modernizing, democratizing thrust. Yet Appleby too has trouble accounting for dissenting voices, for the multiplicity of subcultures, for seemingly counter-progressive trends, and for women and African Americans when they did not join in the entrepreneurial spirit.[7] As in Wood's synthesis, shifts in mainstream ideology are convincingly given their due. A new generation emerges, thanks in part to subversive tendencies in a new politics. But the actual battles and practices of post-revolutionary politics are subordinated. They become mere beginnings, derivative ultimately of more lasting changes in ethos and experience, as Appleby demonstrates the reality behind the rhetoric of capitalist democracy through the reminiscences of the successful self-made men and women of the era.

Democratization may or may not be a sufficient rubric for organizing the history of the early republic and its politics. We will not know, however, until we pay closer attention to the emergence and development of democratic political practices and to the consequences of broadened participation in politics for the political system as well as for the society. The work represented here turns to forms of culture, as much as to the ideological shifts that Wood and Appleby address, in search of political change. Influenced by a larger trend toward cultural history, younger political historians have broadened the study of political culture beyond the partisan persuasions and other "isms" they had read about as students.[8] The effects of an ascendant cultural history seems as diverse in this field as in others, signifying for some a revised yet vigorous social history, for some a broadened history of ideas or meanings, and sometimes a rejection of social history and its subjects.[9] Where it succeeds in connecting elites and plebeians and middling sorts along various trajectories of thought, experience, and political action, however, the editors believe that the "newest" political history has synthetic potential, and begins to answer the call of Pessen and Wood for a more integrated understanding of the early republic.

Three important precedents have shaped the style and substance of the cultural turn in recent scholarship. The first was the emergence in the 1960s and 1970s of what might be called social histories of politics in the age before the modern "mass" political party. "Neo-progressive" historians of the Revolutionary era like Alfred F. Young and Rhys Isaac pioneered local studies that took seriously such phenomena as street theater, tavern and meetinghouse rituals, millenarian movements, and even the rites of the colonial rebellion itself. Their influence on the work in this volume is not only methodological, in the sense of taking popular culture and its forms seriously, but also resides in a sense that the serious student of the period must not choose between a focus on groups or social movements and attending to the evolution of the political system. The larger story—indeed, the connecting tissue that continues to make the period from the 1760s to the 1810s seem like "an unusually long revolutionary period"—is the increased public activity of a widening variety of actors. Elites and the people in the streets respond to each other in these works, and the result is a potent mix of radicalism and reaction that set the stage for peculiarly American social relations.[10]

It is less easy to track the relationship between emerging work and the second important precedent, the older "new political history" that also emerged in the 1960s and 1970s. Much of this work concentrated so resolutely on parties, voting, and other quantifiable phenomena as to limit the reach of political history and to favor the mid-nineteenth-century party systems and their dynamics at the expense of the earlier period.[11] Yet the new political historians' interest in constituents as well as leaders, and their use of the concepts of ideology and political culture, clearly paved the way for a more explicit, expansive, and rigorous cultural approach to politics in the early republic.[12]

Political culture—defined most commonly as the set of assumptions (and less commonly as the set of methods or practices) that people brought with them into the political realm—enabled new political historians (sometimes referred to as the "ethnocultural school") to remain in a creative dialogue with intellectual history at a time when intellectual historians began to move away from their postwar rejection of the progressive school's insistence on class conflict as the dominant theme in U.S. history. This concern with variant, shifting, and contested political meanings in the nineteenth century helped set the stage for the more general rise of cultural history in the later 1980s.[13]

The new political history's search for *causes* of specifically political phenomena shaped the contributions as well as the later crisis of "political culture" for historians.[14] New political historians helped bring "political culture" into fashion for its ability to explain the assumptions behind, for example, the American

Revolution, the Civil War, or the lack of socialism in the United States. It was another way to get at the dialectic of conflict and consensus, not to mention of ideas and material realities, in American history. This is why historians with a synthetic bent, like Richard Hofstadter, first found themselves drawn to the concept. Political culture was especially useful because it could address historically shifting relationships between the national polity and specific groups—the key agenda, despite differences in methods, of the 1960s' new political history.[15] Though those who dared to generalize about the American political tradition as a whole remained vulnerable to withering critiques inspired by progressive school skepticism and social science standards of rigor, studies of political culture often succeeded at showing how partisan subcultures drew on a common heritage (like republicanism), particularized it in a movement, and succeeded in leaving their imprint on American history. One historical era's minority movement could become the next generation's common sense, or general framework, as occurred with real whig (republican) ideology in the eighteenth century and with antislavery (and proslavery) in the mid-nineteenth century.[16]

Like so many explanatory schemes that preceded it, political culture failed to fully explain the Civil War, leaving that albatross of American historiography for the most dedicated new political historians to study with increasing sophistication at the state and party level.[17] What political culture, or at least a version of it, did do—at least to the satisfaction of a generation of professional historians (and perhaps their students)—was explain the American Revolution and, to a significant extent, the early republic. It did so as an especially potent early version of the "linguistic turn," the third important trend that set the stage for the scholarship in this volume. Bernard Bailyn, Gordon S. Wood, and a score of fellow travelers depicted the Revolution as an ideological transformation that could be discerned through close attention to changes in political languages over time. The profusion of words unleashed by the Revolutionary controversy emerged as something more than propaganda: it was the material through which the Revolution, and America itself, could be grasped.[18]

Soon the linguistic turn met the neo-progressive emphasis on studying particular constituencies, with especially fruitful results. Historians took Bailyn's emphasis on ideology seriously and melded it with the kinds of questions about crowd actions, popular political consciousness, and the successes and failures of social movements associated with the British Marxist historians led by E. P. Thompson. The study of Revolutionary politics and culture remained especially lively in the 1980s, with excellent writers regularly seeking to combine the different approaches and different methods and to apply them to the "critical period" of the 1780s and the frenzied national politics of the decade that followed.[19]

By the 1990s, efforts to find the republicanism and liberalism among various groups and constituencies provided a common framework for students of white working people, southerners, and women, as well as of partisan politics from the Revolutionary era through the nineteenth century.[20] The results were somewhat different for the early republic as a whole, or at least where the republic diverged from the lengthening "revolutionary" era without meeting up with the Jacksonian ferment increasingly described, despite Pessen's warning, as having its roots wholly in post-1815 social change.[21] The debate concerning the relative power of persistent republicanism and emergent or latent liberalism preserved the tendency for political culture to mean ideas, idioms, or sustaining frameworks, not practices or institutions. As a result the debate could only selectively address political events, policies, or power. At best, political culture-qua-republicanism provided a bridge, or a backdrop that studies of the era after the War of 1812 could use as ideological background.[22]

At worst, the profusion of studies claiming to see republicanism everywhere in the nineteenth century only added to the confusion about what the early republic—or republicanism—had been. Meanwhile, the history of events and great personages continued to be written as usual, with occasional nods to important "isms."[23] In 1993, Elkins and McKitrick could define *The Age of Federalism* as composed of a very small group of national politicians, with hardly any protest from reviewers, who praised their magisterial narrative of diplomacy, politics, and thought at the seat of government. The very republicanism of early national politics, in other words, had made it a field unto itself: foundational and yet somehow unlike everything that came after.[24]

While the notion of the early republic before 1815 or even 1800 as a time of great creativity in political culture helped raise the profile of the period for American historians and the public, it has had its costs. By relying as much as they have on ideology, on language, and political culture, students of the early national period's political history made a Faustian bargain. They traded longitudinal impact, a role in an origins story about American politics, and the possibility of an interpretive reach greater than merely explaining the battles between Jeffersonian Republicans and Hamiltonian Federalists, for a huge debt to intellectual history and to a biographical style of political history. This debt mortgaged the quest for a more encompassing synthesis of the era and its politics. As a result, the only syntheses published during the 1990s either described high politics in a microscopic fashion or dissolved politics altogether into proto-bourgeois social revolution. Social history had not, in fact, been integrated into the story. And despite Pessen's 1981 cry of "a pox on stultifying periodizations," Jacksonian-era historians continued to see that period as fundamentally different, thanks largely to a socioeconomic shift they dubbed "the market revolution" and credited with causing the unprecedented plebeian anger that got the masses interested in organized politics (they imply for the first time).[25] The door was left open for "founders chic" 2000-style to utterly ignore the implications of the older and more recent work on late-eighteenth-century popular politics, and get the founders back up on their now somewhat more human-scaled pedestals.

POLITICAL CULTURE AND CULTURAL POLITICS

If the possibilities and limits of the political culture concept help to clarify where the "newest" political historians of the early republic depart from their forebears, the emergence of "cultural politics" and culture wars as subjects of scrutiny within and beyond the academy would seem to be an obvious point of departure for younger scholars. Yet it has not truly provoked most of the contributors here, for reasons that are also worthy of reflection. At first glance, one might think that the tendency for "cultural politics," and especially the interdisciplinary cultural studies movement, to make everything from classic literature to popular music to comic books political would endear it to the project of a renovated political history. The cultural politics approach to contemporary society and to history, however, derives in part from an extremely deep disaffection with mainstream or party politics, to such an extent that ordinary politics takes on the status that everyday life has for students of politics: it is the thing given, rather than the thing to be explained.[26] Cultural politics has the virtue of seeing the political aspects of other social phenomena, of seeing conflict as well as consensus in them, and, most of all, of bringing other actors into the political field. It does so, however, at the price of ignoring ordinary, official, politics—or worse, imagining that the formal, institutionalized political system has had no meaningful connection with the rest of the culture or no real impact on the daily lives of regular people.

Because of its bias toward the study of the present and its origins, as well as its oppositional, disillusioned stance toward mainstream politics, cultural politics has not often inquired into the changing historical relationship between politicized culture and ordinary politics, being content, instead, to "theorize" its operations in the present. Practitioners are often content to call cultural politics a phenomenon of modernity or even postmodernity, leaving the subject of the early republic's politics in the familiar terra incognita of that which is foundational and yet simultaneously irrelevant to later developments.[27] Ironically, it was the new political historians who also expended much energy in trying to place the Jeffersonians, Federalists, Jacksonians, or Whigs into regnant models of "modern" American (party) political development, only to declare the earlier period's politics "incomplete" or saddled (the terms were usually pejorative) with "proto-parties" at best.[28]

And yet we see intimations, in the essays by John Brooke, Saul Cornell, David Waldstreicher, and Nancy Isenberg, that approaches to cultural politics, if not cultural studies itself, may help us understand the ways in which extra-partisan strategies shaped American politics. Taken together, these essays suggest that even in relatively settled (postrevolutionary) times, cultural politics—and the pushing of the accepted boundaries of the public sphere—is the resort of both the high and the low when ordinary or official politics remains, on certain key issues, intractable. For the early republic, there are reasons to believe that this was much if not all of the time. The relationship between postrevolutionary U.S. political culture and the politics of everyday life was more intricate and recipro-cal than proponents of either orthodox political science or newfangled cultural studies allow.

The essays in this volume depict a deeply politicized culture and an indefati-gably cultural politics. As Jeffrey L. Pasley points out in "The Cheese and the Words," the period's partisan yet relatively uninstitutionalized popular politics encouraged creative gestures like making, carting, and commenting on a giant fromage. Nonvoters participated enthusiastically and often effectively in crowds, in taverns, and at celebrations. These and other cultural forms became clearing-houses for the invention and revision of political attitudes, rhetoric, and identi-ties. The rude insistence of ordinary Americans on voicing their opinions— which Wood, looking backward toward a colonial era marked by "deference," summarizes as the rout of aristocracy—probably added up to something more complicated: a way of addressing the persistence of class hierarchies, economic inequalities, and cultural differences amidst the emergence of relative white male equality in the official polity.

Ordinary people may have seized popular politics—and cultural politics— precisely because real power and real economic resources were not so easily to be had. The Revolution made politics free (and, in terms of the press, literally subsidized) at a time when capitalism was making everything else a commodity. It has been suggested that politics became divorced from matters of substance— such as the regulation of the economy—during these years when traditional elites lost their power truly to control the system.[29] We do not know what the concrete effects of politicization were; we do know, however, that by the 1830s a professional class of politicians had begun to systematize and rationalize the system anew, claiming "democracy" for the party system itself, and in the process inspiring incredible loyalty and profound disillusionment—the love-hate relationship with the parties that continues to this day. As Huston suggests, it is time to move beyond either normalizing or dismissing the claims of party managers, to take seriously the relationship between partisanship and its others—between political culture and cultural politics.[30]

If historians do not, others will. Historically oriented political theorists have been paying renewed attention to problems of representation, of voice, and of public identities in the early United States. Some have expanded their archive to include the kinds of documents that formerly interested only historians, subjecting them to fruitfully close readings that yield rich, complex conceptions of the political and of the citizen.[31] Meanwhile, literary critics have been poaching on the classic texts of politics, developing startlingly expansive interpretations of key political figures and sometimes even crafting new narratives of American political and cultural development in the process.[32] Representation (broadly conceived) and the problems of citizenship in the new nation are the most obvious common ground between political theorists, students of cultural politics, and the political history of the early republic. As political theorists have always reminded us, the first or ultimate subject of politics is often politics itself: the struggle to define the political, to identify political actors, and to set the agenda for political action.[33] This was especially true in a republic with aspirations to democracy—even, perhaps especially, if the ultimate result was the cordoning of "real" economic or social power from the electoral process.

The limits of a culturally oriented political history remain to be seen; in the meantime, we have sought to limit and specify our claims. *Beyond the Founders* includes a variety of work more and less "cultural" in orientation, in recognition of the fact that current debates reflect more the division between social history and "founders" or high political history than any sustained or rigorous discussion about the relative importance of policy, institutions, ideas, and cultural practices (though we hope and expect to see more such debate in the future).[34] Besides, as the essays show again and again, it is the transgression of those categories of politics and culture, along a variety of trajectories high and low, that we find most striking.

PRACTICES, IDENTITIES, NORMS, AND STRUCTURES

Beyond the Founders is organized to reflect the future prospects as well as the current achievements of the newest political histories. The first section, "Democracy and Other Practices," emphasizes the ubiquity and the importance of popular politics. The political arena was subject to multiple and intense negotiations for many decades after the institution of the federal government in 1788. The older "new" political history stressed a process of democratization within the two-party system that occurred primarily with the rise of the Jacksonians in the 1830s. The essays by Pasley and Andrew W. Robertson point to an expanding roster of participants who felt that more and more was at stake in public debates, in local affairs, and in national politics after 1789. Many of the innovations in political practice traceable to the first two decades after ratification can be explained in light of both the real stakes of the new American national politics, and the simultaneous struggle to ensure that the political system would be open to various kinds of people at different levels of government.

A proliferation of print mediated between diverse groups and across wide spaces in the expanding nation. Historians have generally been content to treat newspapers, pamphlets, and broadsides as windows onto events and the ideas of political actors. In doing so, they missed one of the striking phenomena of the age: the complex and pervasive mediation of American politics by the press, without which neither the emergent "party system" nor its reformist alternatives would have been possible. The historians here begin the process of understanding political practice as pursued through cultural forms that cannot be reduced to political "languages." Print shaped American politics (and connected it to American society and culture) in ways that more traditional approaches have had a hard time seeing. Indeed, the print theme is one of the most important examples of what we hope will be a major project for this new wave of political history: the detailed study of political practices as concrete social activities and economic enterprises, rather than simply as disseminating mechanisms.[35]

The essays by Pasley, Robertson, and Waldstreicher also share a desire to connect the rituals of public life as closely as possible to the substance of politics— outcomes, events, and policies—as well as to ideologies. Cultural approaches to politics are sometimes criticized for substituting mere "pomp" for policy, and rhetoric for realities.[36] Pasley argues that the mammoth cheese mattered because its very cheesiness, and the labor of carting it to the capital and consuming it, signaled relationships dear to Jeffersonians. Detailing how "voting rites" of the eighteenth century opened the door to expanded participation, Robertson breaks down any simple division between premodern political rituals and modern electoral procedures—and with it, the sectionalized interpretations of early national political culture which have experienced a renaissance of late.[37] Waldstreicher attends to the symbolics of clothing but also argues that clothing mattered culturally and politically because it mattered so much economically. As in most studies of political culture, part of the payoff lies in the appreciation of new realms of political practice, better attuning our ears and eyes to the modes of political action in a given era. More important, however, are the links sought here between the informal and formal political realms of politics, in this case between disenfranchised blacks and the statesmen of the new republic.

The creation of a formal political system also clarified what stood outside it while also, as Waldstreicher argues, suggesting politicizing strategies to compensate for the system's limits or boundaries. More than a quarter century ago, Alan Dawley called the ballot box the coffin of American class-consciousness. A broadened popular politics could just as easily be called the crib of gender and racial consciousness, indeed of all the nineteenth-century struggles for workers', women's, and civil rights.[38] Waves of popular interest and enthusiastic participation spurred emulative and innovative maneuvers by those at the edges of the system. The results of various compromises threatened the power of some of the white male leaders whose political interests and activities, it is often asserted, had nothing to do with their race or gender.

The essays in the second group, "Gender, Race, and Other Identities," suggest that the politics of identity is as much a legacy of the early republic as it is a late-twentieth-century phenomenon, and that white males of different classes in fact led the way. Class itself came to mean something somewhat different, as white men learned to couch their claims in the idioms of republican citizenship. Gender became an especially significant axis of political struggle during this period, for men as well as women. Phenomena as diverse as women's participation in politics, Federalist young men's habits of association, the Alien and Sedition Acts, the lure of the frontier, the Jeffersonian understanding of political economy, and the cultural use made of celebrities and treason trials in the period turned on gendered language and ideas about men, women, and sex roles. Rosemarie Zagarri's essay on women and politics demonstrates not only that party politics mattered to women, but that the idea and reality of female presences mattered to parties. A political history that takes gender and its meanings for granted will miss much of the content, as well as the symbolic forms, of the early republic's political battles.

The era's deeply gendered politics had uneven results for individual women and individual men, for women as a group and for men as a group. Women's rights and men's prerogatives were to a significant extent up for grabs and could be played on as part of other political battles. Albrecht Koschnik's interpretation of Thomas Pleasants's diary suggests that once politics is restored to its rightful places in everyday life, categories of individual experience like gender identity no longer seem nonpartisan, and politics no longer appears to proceed without gender trouble, or gender struggle. Gender even gains explanatory power in the exploration of political motivation. Koschnik's approach echoes earlier social-scientific appeals to "status anxiety" as a mobilizing factor in political movements, but in a new key with occupational and group identities revealed in their fully gendered nature. The example of the War of 1812 may also remind us of the need to consider the links between the early republic's periodic wars and war scares, and its political culture. Military mobilization and the politics of the militia linked the local, the national, and the international. "Young men" played particularly important roles, not just militarily but also culturally and in street-level party politics, during the years 1797–99, 1812–14, and 1845–48. War and the threat of war allowed people like Pleasants to become adults, political actors, and men, in what was becoming the fullest sense of that word. These cultural dynamics, in turn, made war more likely to occur.

We need to get more specific about gendered political strategies as well as outcomes, realizing that gender could shape both short-term political change and long-term political structure. Nancy Isenberg casts new light on the significance of Aaron Burr in his time, and on the rather dismal turn of his career after 1800, by bringing issues of sex and gender to the forefront of the story. She also makes effective use of theories and techniques borrowed from literary studies and social theory to read Burr as a kind of cultural text. Burr was the sex symbol of his age, Isenberg argues, a highly disturbing figure who fascinated legions of young men and women, but produced in many of his fellow politicians, including men as diverse as Thomas Jefferson and Alexander Hamilton, deep, uncontrollable fear and loathing. To those political historians prone to be skeptical of literary theory and cultural studies, we submit that one founder (Hamilton) died and another (Jefferson) abandoned his principles wholesale because of what they read in this particular cultural text.

Race, too, emerged as a major fault line in the new republic's politics, partly as a result of the democratization of politics for white men, partly because of the contradictory effects of the American Revolution on slavery North and South, and partly because territorial expansion further undermined the "middle ground" on which a relatively stable, mutual Indian-white politics had been conducted in colonial times. Woody Holton has written that "it is not sufficient to say . . . that slaves and Indians were denied the fruits of Independence. To a large extent, in 1776 as in 1861, slaves and Indians—or more precisely, the Indians' land and the slaves' labor—*were* the fruits of Independence."[39] A similar sensitivity to the relationship between racial politics and the rest of politics can be applied to the years in between the Revolution and the Civil War. As the early republic moved toward its Jacksonian phase, the seemingly weak federal government showed striking power and diligence where it came to extinguishing Indian land claims. Revitalization movements sparked Indian wars that affected regional and national politics, creating Indian-fighting political heroes like Andrew Jackson and William Henry Harrison who used their official influence to transfer more Indian land into the hands of their white constituents. Meanwhile, the campaign against Indian removal helped set the stage for abolitionism and women's rights. In the same period, debates over slavery shaped diplomacy, the emergence of the second party system, and different versions of romantic nationalism. Black and white abolitionists began to rock the boat of the mass parties.[40]

The essays by Richard Newman, Waldstreicher, and Andrew R. L. Cayton suggest that it would be fruitful to explore the reciprocal influence of "racial" issues for whites and the political actions of Indians and slaves and free blacks themselves. Causation seems to have run in both directions. Historians have rarely considered the strategies of African American activists—from petitions to parades to rebellion—to have existed in a creative dialogue with changes in the political system. Richard Newman's essay boldly insists on a fundamental shift in black politics during the 1820s and 1830s, coincident with the Jacksonian moment. Black politics became more aggressive, less deferential—more insistent on citizenship rights and more committed to "group tactics and confrontational conduct" to achieve its goals. Indeed, if the essay had been written a few decades ago, when racism itself was not considered a significant aspect of Jacksonian politics, it might have been called "The Black Jacksonians." This is not a criticism; in our view, a fully integrated political history will reveal that a great deal of mutual strategic, rhetorical, and methodological borrowing and imitation occurred between party politicians and the many other politicians, black, Indian, female, and radical, who were excluded from the party system.

The third group of essays, "Norms and Forms," builds on the achievements of intellectual historians, political theorists, and constitutional scholars. The continuing contest for participation made political language and its codification in constitutions and law just as important as it had been during the more carefully studied Revolutionary era. As Brooke points out in his tour de force on the public sphere, theoretical categories that conceptualize this middle ground between debate and law emerged during this very period in history. Even to describe this middle ground, then, requires both the historian's traditional empiricism and the theorist's openness to concepts and categories. Saul Cornell likewise finds ample middle ground between concept or norm-driven constitutional scholarship and the quest for a more grounded history of the period. Profound disagreement, widespread interest, and change over time characterized constitutional debate over the right to bear arms, for example.

Seth Cotlar's essay reminds us that the political culture of the early republic was decidedly more cosmopolitan, or international, than many of our recent histories indicate. Older narratives of the early republic at times went so far as to mock Americans of the 1790s for their passionate hatreds of things British or French. The community studies that characterized the new social and the new political histories in the 1960s, 1970s, and 1980s had no place for international-ism and hardly any for even the economic upheavals wrought by foreign wars and the new nation's place in the world-system. Political biographies of the founders often reduce cosmopolitan projects to matters of individual taste and experience. A newer political history, of a sort exemplified by Cayton's essay in this volume, will explore the tendency of many politically active early national Americans to be simultaneously provincial and international in outlook and interests. An international perspective had deep roots and was not merely the province of the elite. This was a time when even many northern European Protestant Americans were first- or second-generation immigrants. Rather than being a bar to a more cosmopolitan approach to American history,[41] the political history of the early republic can help show us the way beyond narrowly na-tionalistic understandings of the past—an especially necessary goal in consider-ing an era when nationalism was both rising around the world and still quite weak at the borders of the expanding United States.[42]

The last section, "Interests, Parties, and Other Structures," may be said to represent the least realized promise of the new work, informed as it is more by cultural history than political science: to incorporate policy outcomes, events, and institutions as well as meanings, identities, and practices. Matters of state, including diplomacy and the execution of domestic laws and powers, require reconsideration in light of the transformative changes that occurred in different sectors of society and different locations of politics in a complex federal system. Since the 1950s, historians have been so concerned with intellectual precondi-tions and electoral results that they have often underestimated governmental institutions, as well as constitutions and courts, as sites of struggle and even as "agents of change."[43] Resolutions in law could determine social development and what was culturally permissible, as well as the rules of political participation. Everywhere we look in the early republic we see different kinds of institutions being created, either through politics or with substantial effects on what was possible in politics. Richard R. John's essay shows that early American views on the competence, capacities, and proper sphere of government were not only expansive, but largely positive, to the point that the emergence of a private com-munications system was greeted with wide opposition and almost failed to take hold. So much for the laissez-faire orthodoxy of nineteenth-century America!

Cayton's essay here is a particularly fruitful exercise in bringing together things that are usually kept apart, thus making an impressively new and more holistic sort of political history. Drawing on studies in Texas social history, Native American history, and Spanish frontier history, Cayton finds southern planters, Connecticut Congregationalists, Cherokees, and Mexicans all participating in a common political world and reacting to common, or at least cognate, political trends, while each following their own distinctive course and arriving at their own distinctive destiny. He shows how seemingly mundane administrative matters that touched on land policy became concrete factors driving the movement of populations and the terms of individual labor, while also showing how such intimately social matters as the structure of patriarchal families could influence the high politics of elections and diplomacy. Ideology—in this case liberalism and nationalism—becomes more than the cement of party or the explanation of revolutionary commitment: it is expressive of material demands and a whole range of institutional commitments.

With Reeve Huston's case study of party and popular politics in antebellum New York, we come full circle—to both the basic concerns of the older new political history focused on parties and the rituals that have fascinated recent scholars. Huston proposes a "dialectical" approach to the mass parties and social movements of the Jacksonian era. The language and methods of the Democrats and Whigs informed insurgents like the Anti-Renters even as these activists distinguished themselves from the major parties as means of redress. The parties, in turn, responded to the ideas and actions of such groups.

Future explanations of antebellum politics will have to take account of both partisan enthusiasm and the profound disillusionment social historians have described, in both activists who worked outside the system and in ordinary Americans who expressed their skepticism of professionalized and ritualized partisanship. In light of Huston's account of the back-and-forth between anti-renters, Democrats, and Whigs, that disillusionment looks less like the "engaged disbelief" posited by Glenn Altschuler and Stuart Blumin than a kind of engaged ambivalence. Disbelievers, after all, are not personally invested. The ambivalent keep changing their minds, looking for the new movement or reforming faction to address the vices of the system, to renew and purify the party and the system. Party loyalty was real, and Jacksonian Americans relied on it, but they also appreciated the power of insurgents, conservative or radical, to redefine a debate.[44]

The process has implications for how we think about the role of the state and institutions like the law in an increasingly elaborated and popular political system. Not everyone stood with Abraham Lincoln, who in his Lyceum address of 1837 affirmed the essential purity and beneficence of constitutionalism. Others, like the Anti-Renters, defined the legacy of the Revolution as popular sovereignty in the hands of the legitimate crowd. That style of disbelief in partisan and electoral procedures signified not mere disillusionment or skepticism but also persisting traditions and a parade of organizational and associational innovations (including parades). If Huston is right, the history of Anti-Rent shows how an extralegal movement that significantly challenged both state law and an existing social order also contributed to the development of a more activist state. The dialectic of parties and popular movements, in other words, is also a dialectic between the state and the public sphere. Attempts to do it justice must in the end pay attention to political results as well as ideas and practices.

The founders, in sum, are only the beginning. Beyond the founders lies a complex and important story about how recognizably American political institutions and practices actually emerged from the top down, from the bottom up, and perhaps especially from the middle out in every direction. It is a story about leaders and followers together, about Americans simultaneously unified and divided by partisanship, by gender, by race, by class, by region, by nationalism, and by localism. Nothing about these categories keeps it from being a story about the making of the American republic, a story about the making and remaking, through politics, of the United States.

NOTES

1. Jay Tolson, "Founding Rivalries," *U.S. News and World Report*, February 26, 2001, 51–55; Evan Thomas, "Founders Chic: Live from Philadelphia," *Newsweek*, July 9, 2001, 48–49; David Broder, "Founders and Foibles," *Washington Post*, July 4, 2001; Joseph J. Ellis, *Founding Brothers: The Revolutionary Generation* (New York, 2001), 12–13; Gordon S. Wood, "The Greatest Generation," *New York Review of Books*, March 29, 2001, 17–22; John Ferling, *Setting the World Ablaze: Washington, Adams, Jefferson, and the American Revolution* (New York, 2000), ix–xi; Don Higginbotham, "Washington and the American People," in *George Washington Reconsidered*, ed. Higginbotham (Charlottesville, 2001), 327–29.

2. Sean Wilentz, "America Made Easy: McCullough, Adams, and the Decline of Popular History," *New Republic*, July 2, 2001; Andrew Burstein, "The Politics of Memory: Taking the Measure of the Ever More Popular Demand for Historical Greatness," *Washington Post Book World*, October 14, 2001; Jeffrey L. Pasley, "Federalist Chic," *Commonplace*, April 2002 <http://www.common-place.org/publick/200202.shtml>; David Waldstreicher, "Keeping It in the Family, Post-DNA," *Reviews in American History* 29 (2001): 198–204; David Waldstreicher, "Founders Chic as Culture War," *Radical History*

Review 84 (Fall 2002), 185–94; Alan Taylor, "Poor Richard, Rich Ben," *New Republic*, January 13, 2003, 34.

3. Robert H. Wiebe, *The Opening of American Society: From the Adoption of the Constitution to the Eve of Disunion* (New York, 1984), Part 1; Stanley Elkins and Eric McKitrick, *The Age of Federalism: The Early American Republic, 1788–1801* (New York, 1993); Ellis, *Founding Brothers*; Joanne B. Freeman, *Affairs of Honor: National Politics in the Early Republic* (New Haven, 2001). Some of the essays in Doron Ben-Atar and Barbara B. Oberg, eds., *Federalists Reconsidered* (Charlottesville, 1999), and James Horn, Jan Ellen Lewis, and Peter S. Onuf, eds., *The Revolution of 1800: Democracy, Race, and the New Republic* (Charlottesville, 2002), also contribute to a renewed appreciation of the Federalists.

4. Edward Pessen, "We Are All Jeffersonians, We Are All Jacksonians; or a Pox on Stultifying Periodizations," *Journal of the Early Republic* 1 (1981): 1–26.

5. Gordon S. Wood, "The Significance of the Early Republic," *Journal of the Early Republic* 8 (1988): 1–20.

6. Gordon S. Wood, *The Radicalism of the American Revolution* (New York, 1991); Barbara Clark Smith, "The Adequate Revolution," and Michael Zuckerman, "Rhetoric, Reality, and the Revolution: The Genteel Radicalism of Gordon Wood," *William and Mary Quarterly* 51 (1994): 684–92, 693–702; Alfred F. Young, "Introduction" and "Afterword: How Radical Was the American Revolution?," in *Beyond the American Revolution: Explorations in the History of American Radicalism*, ed. Young (DeKalb, Ill., 1993), 9, 333; Young, "American Historians Confront 'The Transforming Hand of Revolution,'" in *The Transforming Hand of Revolution: Reconsidering the American Revolution as a Social Movement*, ed. Ronald Hoffman and Peter J. Albert (Charlottesville, 1995), 481–90.

7. Joyce Appleby, *Inheriting the Revolution: The First Generation of Americans* (Cambridge, Mass., 2000); Gordon S. Wood, "The Enemy Is Us: Democratic Capitalism in the Early Republic," *Journal of the Early Republic* 16 (1996): 293–308; Joyce Appleby, "The Vexed Story of Capitalism Told by American Historians," *Journal of the Early Republic* 21 (2002): 1–18; David Waldstreicher, "Appleby's Liberal America," *Common-place* <http://www.common-place.org>, September 2000.

8. When Marion Nelson Winship asked fellow members of the H-SHEAR electronic discussion list whether they too had noticed a new kind of "cultural" political history emerging, mostly in not-yet-published work, there was some disagreement over what characterized the work Winship and others singled out. At least one participant in the ensuing discussions cited a common "cultural history" perspective. Some cited a concern with the diverse public *practices* of politics, elite and plebeian, as opposed to an earlier concern with party ideologies or with elections and regime changes. Winship acknowledged this by pointing to a tendency to write history less exclusively from the "top down" (the old political history) or the "bottom up" (the new social history) than from "the middle out," in all directions. These discussions, which began in January 1997, are archived at the H-SHEAR website: <http://www2.h-net.msu.edu/~shear/>.

9. Compare, for example, the following works: Simon P. Newman, *Parades and the Politics of the Street: Festive Culture in the Early American Republic* (Philadelphia, 1997); and Joanne B. Freeman, "Dueling as Politics: Reinterpreting the Burr-Hamilton Duel," *William and Mary Quarterly*, 3d ser., 53 (1996): 289–318. Other subsequently published works that are alluded to in this and subsequent exchanges include David Waldstreicher, *In the Midst of Perpetual Fetes: The Making of American Nationalism, 1776–1820* (Chapel Hill, 1997); Saul Cornell, *The Other Founders: Anti-Federalism and the Dissenting Tradition in America, 1788–1828* (Chapel Hill, 1998); Jeffrey L. Pasley, *"The Tyranny of Printers": Newspaper Politics in the Early American Republic* (Charlottesville, 2001); Freeman, *Affairs of Honor*; Marion Nelson Winship, "Enterprise in Motion in the Early American Republic: The Federal Government and the Case of Thomas Worthington," *Business and Economic History* 23 (1994): 81–91; Marion Nelson Winship, "The Land of Connected Men: A New Migration Story for the Early Republic," *Pennsylvania History* 64 (Special Issue, 1997): 88–104; Richard John, *Spreading the News: The Postal System from Franklin to Morse* (Cambridge, Mass., 1996); Albrecht Koschnik, "The Democratic Societies of Philadelphia and the Limits of the American Public Sphere, Circa 1793 to 1795," *William and Mary Quarterly* 58 (2001): 615–36; Susan Branson, *These Fiery Frenchified Dames: Women and Political Culture in Early National Philadelphia* (Philadelphia, 2001); Catharine Allgor, *Parlor Politics: In Which the Ladies of Washington Help Build a City and a Government* (Charlottesville, 2000); Andrew W. Robertson, " 'Look on This Picture . . . And on This!': Nationalism, Localism, and Partisan Images of Otherness in the United States, 1787–1820," *American Historical Review* 106 (2001): 1263–80. For two important attempts to assess the rise of cultural history, including its relation to social history, see Lynn Hunt, ed., *The New Cultural History* (Berkeley, 1989); and Victoria E. Bonnell and Lynn Hunt, eds., *Beyond the Cultural Turn: New Directions in the Study of Society and Culture* (Berkeley, 1999).

10. Alfred F. Young, *The Democratic-Republicans of New York: The Origins, 1763–1797* (Chapel Hill, 1967); Alfred F. Young, ed., *The American Revolution: Explorations in the History of American Radicalism* (DeKalb, Ill., 1976); Alfred F. Young, ed., *Beyond the American Revolution: Further Explorations in the History of American Radicalism* (DeKalb, Ill., 1993), quoted at 318; Rhys Isaac, *The Transformation of Virginia, 1740–1790* (Chapel Hill, 1982); Sean Wilentz, *Chants Democratic: New York City and the Rise of the American Working Class, 1788–1850* (New York, 1984); Thomas P. Slaughter, *The Whiskey Rebellion: Frontier Epilogue to the American Revolution* (New York, 1986); Alan Taylor, *Liberty Men and Great Proprietors: The Revolutionary Settlement on the Maine Frontier, 1760–1820* (Chapel Hill, 1990); Alan Taylor, *William Cooper's Town: Power and Persuasion on the Frontier of the Early American Republic* (New York, 1995), esp. 141–291.

11. By the 1980s they had pushed the beginning of the truly modern "party period" all the way back to the late 1830s. See William Nisbet Chambers and Walter Dean Burnham, eds., *The American Party Systems: Stages of Political Development* (New York, 1967); Ronald P. Formisano, "Federalists and Republicans: Parties, Yes—System, No," and William G. Shade, "Political Pluralism and Party Development: The Creation of a

Modern Party System, 1815–1852," in Paul Kleppner et al., *The Evolution of American Electoral Systems* (Westport, Conn., 1981), 34–76, 77–111. The work of Joel H. Silbey is both exemplary and representative. See Silbey, *The Partisan Imperative: The Dynamics of American Politics Before the Civil War* (Ithaca, 1985); Silbey, "The Incomplete World of American Politics, 1815–29: Presidents, Parties, and Politics in the Age of Good Feelings," *Congress and the Presidency* 11 (1984): 1–18; Silbey, *The American Political Nation, 1838–1893* (Stanford, 1991); Silbey, "Introduction," *The American Party Battle, 1828–1876* (Cambridge, Mass., 1999); Silbey, " 'To One or Another of these Parties Every Man Belongs': The American Political Experience from Andrew Jackson to the Civil War," in *Contesting Democracy: Substance and Structure in American Political History, 1775–2000*, ed. Byron E. Shafer and Anthony J. Badger (Lawrence, Kans., 2001), 65–92. The rise of the new political history overshadowed (and sometimes criticized) a series of "first party system" studies that appeared beginning in the late 1950s. While much less quantitative and obviously less dismissive of the earlier period, these studies nevertheless shared the new political history's commitment to parties and elections as the primary subject of political history. This fact left them vulnerable to the charge that they were exaggerating the significance and modernity of the early parties, which did operate quite differently from those that came later. See, for instance, Young, *Democratic-Republicans of New York*; Noble E. Cunningham, Jr., *The Jeffersonian Republicans: The Formation of Party Organization, 1789–1801* (Chapel Hill, 1957); Noble E. Cunningham, Jr., *The Jeffersonian Republicans in Power: Party Operations, 1801–1809* (Chapel Hill, 1963); Paul Goodman, *The Democratic-Republicans of Massachusetts: Politics in a Young Republic* (Cambridge, Mass., 1964); David Hackett Fischer, *The Revolution of American Conservatism: The Federalist Party in the Era of Jeffersonian Democracy* (New York, 1965); Carl E. Prince, *New Jersey's Jeffersonian Republicans: The Genesis of an Early Party Machine, 1789–1817* (Chapel Hill, 1967); James M. Banner, Jr., *To the Hartford Convention: The Federalists and the Origins of Party Politics in Massachusetts, 1789–1815* (New York, 1970); James H. Broussard, *The Southern Federalists, 1800–1816* (Baton Rouge, 1978). For recent reassertions of the importance and modernity of party politics on the state level, with all the rigor of the new political history, see William G. Shade, *Democratizing the Old Dominion: Virginia and the Second Party System, 1824–1861* (Charlottesville, 1996); Donald Ratcliffe, *Party Spirit in a Frontier Republic: Ohio, 1793–1821* (Columbus, 1998), and Donald Ratcliffe, *The Politics of Long Division, 1818–1828* (Columbus, 2000).

12. See especially Ronald P. Formisano, *The Transformation of Political Culture: Massachusetts Parties, 1790s–1840s* (New York, 1983); Eric Foner, *Free Soil, Free Labor, Free Men: The Ideology of the Republican Party Before the Civil War* (New York, 1970); Jean H. Baker, *Affairs of Party: The Political Culture of the Northern Democrats in the Mid-Nineteenth Century* (Ithaca, 1983).

13. John Higham and Paul Conkin, eds., *New Directions in American Intellectual History* (Baltimore, 1979); Peter Novick, *That Noble Dream: The "Objectivity Question" and the American Historical Profession* (Cambridge, 1988); Daniel Rodgers, *Contested Truths: Keywords in American Politics since Independence* (New York, 1987). The paradox is that even as

"political culture" became important as a synthetic device and a meeting ground for social historians, new political historians, intellectual historians, and cultural historians, some of the very new political historians who helped advance the political culture concept—especially those working on the early and mid-nineteenth century—began to notice that attention to culture seemed to take away interest from institutions, elections, and policy. As a result, and as William G. Shade's essay in this volume so compellingly demonstrates, the "new" and "newest" political historians find themselves looking on each other with the special regard and special suspicion of persons closely, but ambiguously, related.

14. For Ronald P. Formisano, a leading new political historian, recent studies of political culture display "excessive focus on the trappings of power—rituals, symbols, and other expressive mechanisms . . . at the expense of neglecting the material goals and consequences of power." These phenomena—power and policy—are ultimately reducible to "elites' competition for, and management of, tangible resources," in Formisano's view. Drawing on an important essay by the historical sociologist Richard Biernacki, Formisano rightly notes how the new cultural history makes "real" or foundational culture itself, vaunting it over other candidates for the (really) real. In doing so, cultural history makes the same move as social history did in its extended decades of ascension. Hence the slide from new social to new cultural history is a slide further and further away, Formisano implies, from a proper focus on "power" and "policy." Formisano, "The Concept of Political Culture," *Journal of Interdisciplinary History* 31 (2001): 393–426, quoted at 397; Richard Biernacki, "Method and Metaphor after the New Cultural History," in Bonnell and Hunt, *Beyond the Cultural Turn*, 62–92; Formisano, "The New Political History and the Election of 1840," *Journal of Interdisciplinary History* 23 (1993): 661–82; Formisano, "The Invention of the Ethnocultural Interpretation," *American Historical Review* 99 (1994): 453–77; Formisano, "The Party Period Revisited," *Journal of American History* 89 (1996): 93–120. See also Formisano, "State Development in the Early Republic: Substance and Structure, 1780–1840," in Shafer and Badger, *Contesting Democracy*, 7–35.

15. Lee Benson, *The Concept of Jacksonian Democracy: New York as a Test Case* (Princeton, 1961); Samuel P. Hays, "Politics and Society: Beyond the Political Party," in Kleppner et al., *The Evolution of American Electoral Systems*, 245–50; Formisano, "Invention of the Ethnocultural Interpretation"; Robert Kelley, "Ideology and Political Culture from Jefferson to Nixon," *American Historical Review* 82 (1977): 531–62. In this sense, the "cultural" moves of the "ethnocultural school" were of as much lasting importance as its seemingly counterprogressive insistence on ethnicity and religion (as opposed to class) as the primary basis of voting.

16. These studies were admirably dialectical in the ways they tracked the changing relationships between political subcultures and the larger culture. Many works could fit this description, but for particularly mature versions, see Baker, *Affairs of Party*; Ronald Walters, *The Antislavery Appeal: American Abolitionism after 1830* (New York, 1978); Drew Gilpin Faust, *The Creation of Confederate Nationalism: Ideology and Identity in the Civil War*

South (Baton Rouge, 1988). For a local synthesis covering an exceptionally long period, see John L. Brooke, *The Heart of the Commonwealth: Society and Political Culture in Worcester County, Massachusetts, 1713–1861* (Cambridge, 1989).

17. The two magisterial doorstops of this literature are William E. Gienapp, *Origins of the Republican Party, 1852–1856* (New York, 1987); and Michael F. Holt, *The Rise and Fall of the American Whig Party: Jacksonian Politics and Onset of the Civil War* (New York, 1999).

18. Bailyn and Wood (a student of Bailyn's) eloquently defended their methods as well as their interpretations in Bailyn, *The Origins of American Politics* (New York, 1968); Wood, "Rhetoric and Reality in the American Revolution," *William and Mary Quarterly* 32 (1966): 3–32; Bailyn, "The Central Themes of the American Revolution," in *Essays on the American Revolution*, ed. Stephen G. Kurtz and James H. Hutson (New York, 1973), 3–31; and Wood, "Intellectual History and the Social Sciences," in Higham and Conkin, *New Directions in American Intellectual History*, 27–41. See also Wood, "The Creative Imagination of Bernard Bailyn," in *The Transformation of Early American History: Society, Ideology, and Politics*, ed. James A. Henretta, Michael G. Kammen, and Stanley N. Katz (New York, 1989), 28–42.

19. Bernard Bailyn, *The Ideological Origins of the American Revolution* (Cambridge, Mass., 1967); Gordon S. Wood, *The Creation of the American Republic, 1776–1787* (Chapel Hill, 1969); Bernard Bailyn, "The Ideological Fulfillment of the American Revolution," in his *Faces of Revolution* (New York, 1990), 225–68; Wood, *Radicalism of the American Revolution*; Richard H. Buel, Jr., *Securing the Revolution: Ideology in American Politics, 1789–1815* (Ithaca, 1972); Pauline Maier, *From Resistance to Revolution: Colonial Radicals and the Development of American Opposition to Britain, 1765–1776* (New York, 1972); Lance Banning, *The Jeffersonian Persuasion: Evolution of a Party Ideology* (Ithaca, 1978); Drew R. McCoy, *The Elusive Republic: Political Economy in Jeffersonian America* (Chapel Hill, 1980); and Elkins and McKitrick, *The Age of Federalism*. Compare these works with Young, *American Revolution*; Young, *Beyond the American Revolution*; Eric Foner, *Tom Paine and Revolutionary America* (New York, 1976); Edward Countryman, *A People in Revolution: The American Revolution and Political Society in New York, 1760–1790* (Baltimore, 1981); Edward Countryman, *The American Revolution* (New York, 1985); Hoffman and Albert, *Transforming Hand of Revolution*; Young, *The Shoemaker and the Tea Party: Memory and the American Revolution* (Boston, 1999); Wilentz, *Chants Democratic*; Linda K. Kerber, *Women of the Republic: Intellect and Ideology in Revolutionary America* (Chapel Hill, 1980); Slaughter, *Whiskey Rebellion*; Taylor, *Liberty Men and Great Proprietors*.

20. See, for example, Bruce Laurie, *Artisans into Workers: American Labor in the Nineteenth Century* (New York, 1989); Kenneth S. Greenberg, *Masters and Statesmen: The Political Culture of American Slavery* (Baltimore, 1985); James Oakes, *Slavery and Freedom: An Interpretation of the Old South* (New York, 1990); Stephanie McCurry, *Masters of Small Worlds: Yeoman Households, Gender Relations, and the Political Culture of the Antebellum South Carolina Lowcountry* (New York, 1995); George C. Rable, *The Confederate Republic: A Revolution against Politics* (Chapel Hill, 1994).

21. Compare Harry Watson, *Liberty and Power: The Politics of Jacksonian America* (New

York, 1990); Sean Wilentz, "Society, Politics, and the Market Revolution," in *The New American History*, ed. Eric Foner (Philadelphia, 1990), 51–71; Charles Sellers, *The Market Revolution: Jacksonian America, 1815–1846* (New York, 1991); Richard E. Ellis, "The Market Revolution and the Transformation of American Politics, 1801–1837," Donald J. Ratcliffe, "The Crisis of Commercialization: National Political Alignments and the Market Revolution, 1819–1844," and Michael F. Holt, "From Center to Periphery: The Market Revolution and Major-Party Conflict," all in *The Market Revolution in America: Social, Political, and Religious Expressions, 1800–1880*, ed. Melvyn Stokes and Stephen Conway (Charlottesville, 1996), 149–76, 177–201, 224–58; Michael Morrison, *Slavery and the American West: The Eclipse of Manifest Destiny and the Coming of the Civil War* (Chapel Hill, 1998); John Lauritz Larson, *Internal Improvement: National Public Works and the Promise of Popular Government in the United States* (Chapel Hill, 2001).

22. For example, Kerber's defining study of "republican motherhood" provided a touchstone or framing device for studies of women in the nineteenth century, but only gradually inspired more work on women and politics before 1820. Kerber, *Women of the Republic*.

23. For critiques of the ideology school, and the use of republicanism in particular, see Joyce Appleby, "Republicanism in Old and New Contexts," *William and Mary Quarterly*, 3d ser., 43 (1986): 20–34; Ralph Lerner, *The Thinking Revolutionary: Principle and Practice in the New Republic* (Ithaca, 1987), 1–38; Richard L. McCormick, *The Party Period and Public Policy* (New York, 1986); Daniel Rodgers, "Republicanism: The Career of a Concept," *Journal of American History* 79 (1992): 11–38.

24. James Roger Sharp's *American Politics in the Early Republic: The New Nation in Crisis* (New Haven, 1993), which covered the same period, provided something of a neo-Jeffersonian bookend to Elkins and McKitrick's neo-Federalist tome. Sharp suggested the importance of Jeffersonian mobilization and the sectional basis of emerging political parties, but did not explore those transformations on local or regional levels.

25. Elkins and McKitrick, *Age of Federalism*; Sharp, *American Politics in the Early Republic*; Wood, *Radicalism of the American Revolution*; Appleby, *Inheriting the Revolution*; Sellers, *The Market Revolution*.

26. If contemporary political history and political science have their roots in the practice and celebration of mainstream party politics, particularly in its post–World War II heyday, then it should not be surprising that cultural studies should have its roots in the alternative political gestures of non-elites and youth in the 1960s and 1970s. Many of the criticisms flung back and forth between students of formal politics and proponents of cultural studies still invoke the language of that era: the previous generation decries the interests of the young as mere fluff or as dogma, while the younger scholars attack the establishment for marginalizing those who are not obedient. Of late, the conversation has become especially circular. See Joel H. Silbey, "The State and Practice of American Political History at the Millennium: The Nineteenth Century as a Test Case," *Journal of Policy History* 11 (1999): 5–9. For more tolerant and optimistic accounts, see Steven M.

Gillon, "The Future of Political History," *Journal of Policy History* 9 (1997): 240–55; Anthony J. Badger, "Introduction," in Shafer and Badger, *Contesting Democracy*, 1–6.

27. Jodi Dean, "Introduction: The Interface of Political Theory and Cultural Studies," and Barbara Cruikshank, "Cultural Politics: Political Theory and the Foundations of Democratic Order," in *Cultural Studies and Political Theory*, ed. Jodi Dean (Ithaca, 2000), 3–11, 77. For signs of change, however, see Lauren Berlant and Lisa Duggan eds., *Our Monica, Ourselves: The Clinton Affair and the National Interest* (New York, 2001).

28. Silbey, "Incomplete World of American Politics."

29. Wood, *Creation of the American Republic*, Part 5; John M. Murrin and Rowland Berthoff, "Freedom, Communalism, and the Yeoman Freeholder: The American Revolution Considered as a Social Accident," in Kurtz and Hutson, *Essays on the American Revolution*, 256–88; John M. Murrin and Gary Kornblith, "The Making and Unmaking of an American Ruling Class," in Young, *Beyond the American Revolution*, 27–79; Wiebe, *Opening of American Society*.

30. For the state of this (polarized) debate over party in the classical period, see Silbey, " 'To One or Another of these Parties Every Man Belongs' "; Formisano, "The Party Period Revisited"; Glenn C. Altschuler and Stuart M. Blumin, *Rude Republic: Americans and Their Politics in the Nineteenth Century* (Princeton, 1999); Michael Schudson, *The Good Citizen: A History of American Public Life* (New York, 1998); Jeffrey L. Pasley, "Party Politics, Citizenship, and Collective Action in Nineteenth-Century America: A Response to Stuart Blumin and Michael Schudson," *Communication Review* 4 (2000): 39–54.

31. This should not be surprising, given the roots of "political culture" histories in the engagement of intellectual historians with political theory and its categories. See Michael Paul Rogin, *Ronald Reagan, the Movie, and Other Episodes in American Political Demonology* (Berkeley, 1987); Anne Norton, *Alternative Americas: A Reading of Antebellum Political Culture* (Chicago, 1986); Norton, *Republic of Signs: Liberal Theory and American Popular Culture* (Chicago, 1995); Kimberly K. Smith, *The Dominion of Voice: Riot, Reason and Romance in Antebellum Politics* (Lawrence, Kans., 1999); Catherine A. Holland, *The Body Politic: Foundings, Citizenship, and Difference in the American Political Imagination* (New York, 2001).

32. Michael Warner, *The Letters of the Republic: Publication and the Public Sphere in Eighteenth Century America* (Cambridge, Mass., 1990); Thomas Gustafson, *Representative Words: Politics, Literature, and the American Language* (New York, 1992); Jay Fliegelman, *Declaring Independence: Jefferson, Natural Language, and the Culture of Performance* (Stanford, 1993); Priscilla Wald, *Constituting Americans: Cultural Anxiety and Narrative Form* (Durham, N.C., 1995); Dana D. Nelson, *National Manhood: Capitalist Citizenship and the Imagined Fraternity of White Men* (Durham, N.C., 1998); Robert Ferguson, *The American Enlightenment, 1750–1820* (Cambridge, Mass., 1998). Historians of women and gender have shown particular sensitivity to the intersections of recent literary criticism and political theory. Carroll Smith-Rosenberg, "Dis-covering the Subject of the 'Great Constitutional Discussion,' 1786–89," *Journal of American History* 79 (1992): 841–73;

Kathleen M. Brown, *Good Wives, Nasty Wenches, and Anxious Patriarchs: Gender, Race, and Power in Colonial Virginia* (Chapel Hill, 1998); Nancy Isenberg, *Sex and Citizenship in Antebellum America* (Chapel Hill, 1998).

33. For poststructuralist takes on the process, see Murray Edelman, *Constructing the Political Spectacle* (Chicago, 1988); Anne Norton, *Reflections on Political Identity* (Baltimore, 1988). The tendency of our leading historians, such as Wood and Appleby, to insist that such questions were fundamentally resolved by 1800 reveals both the continuing hold of traditional definitions of politics and the great difficulties in categorizing a polity that became more democratic in some ways, and for some people, but not others. For just a sampling of recent studies by historically oriented political scientists that, by contrast, stress the continuing sense of crisis over the definition of the citizen and the union, for example, see Rogers M. Smith, *Civic Ideals: Conflicting Visions of Citizenship in United States History* (New Haven, 1997); Mark Brandon, *Free in the World: American Slavery and Constitutional Failure* (Princeton, 1999); Rogan Kersh, *Dreams of a More Perfect Union* (Ithaca, 2001); Smith, *Dominion of Voice*.

34. For some beginnings, see Formisano, "Concept of Political Culture" and "State Development in the Early Republic"; Stephen Minicucci, "The 'Cement of Interest': Interest-Based Models of Nation-Building in the Early Republic," *Social Science History* 25 (2001): 247–74.

35. For more extended arguments of this point, see especially Waldstreicher, *In the Midst of Perpetual Fetes*; David Waldstreicher and Stephen R. Grossbart, "Abraham Bishop's Vocation; or, the Mediation of Jeffersonian Politics, "*Journal of the Early Republic* 18 (1998): 617–59, and Pasley, *"Tyranny of Printers."* On the mutual constitution of political oratory and print, see Andrew W. Robertson, *The Language of Democracy: Political Rhetoric in the United States and Britain, 1790–1900* (Ithaca, 1995).

36. See note 14.

37. Greenberg, *Masters and Statesmen*; Anne Norton, *Alternative Americas: A Reading of Antebellum Political Culture* (Chicago, 1986); Appleby, *Inheriting the Revolution*, 243–50, 261–62; John L. Brooke, "To Be 'Read by the Whole People': Press, Party and Public Sphere in the United States, 1789–1840," *Proceedings of the American Antiquarian Society* 110 (2002): 89–118.

38. Compare Alan Dawley, *Class and Community: The Industrial Revolution in Lynn, Massachusetts* (Cambridge, Mass., 1976); and Eric Foner, *The Story of American Freedom* (New York, 1998).

39. Woody Holton, *Forced Founders: Indians, Debtors, Slaves, and the Making of the American Revolution in Virginia* (Chapel Hill, 1999), 211.

40. Alexander Saxton, *The Rise and Fall of the White Republic: Class Politics and Mass Culture in Nineteenth Century America* (London, 1990), chaps. 2–3; David R. Roediger, *The Wages of Whiteness: Race and the Making of the American Working Class* (London, 1991); Gregory Evans Dowd, *A Spirited Resistance: The North American Indian Struggle for Unity, 1745–1815* (Baltimore, 1992); Michael D. Green, *The Politics of Indian Removal: Creek Government and Society in Crisis* (Lincoln, 1982); Waldstreicher, *In the Midst of Perpetual*

Fetes, chap. 6; James Brewer Stewart, "The Emergence of Racial Modernity and the Rise of the White North, 1790–1840," *Journal of the Early Republic* 17 (1998): 181–217; Stewart, "Modernizing 'Difference': The Political Meanings of Color in the Free States," *Journal of the Early Republic* 19 (1999): 691–712; Robert P. Forbes, "Slavery and the Meaning of America, 1819–1833" (Ph.D. diss., Yale University, 1995); William W. Freehling, *The Road to Disunion: Secessionists at Bay, 1776–1854* (New York, 1991); William W. Freehling, *The Reintegration of American History: Slavery and the Civil War* (New York, 1994); Leonard L. Richards, *The Slave Power: The Free North and Southern Domination, 1790–1860* (Baton Rouge, 2000); David Grinsted, *American Mobbing, 1828–1861: Toward Civil War* (New York, 1998); Mary Hershberger, "Mobilizing Women, Anticipating Abolition: The Struggle Against Indian Removal in the 1830s," *Journal of American History* 86 (1999): 15–40; Patrick Rael, *Black Identity and Black Protest in the Antebellum North* (Chapel Hill, 2002); David Waldstreicher, "The Nationalization and Racialization of American Politics: Before, Beneath, and Between Parties, 1790–1840," in Shafer and Badger, *Contesting Democracy*, 37–63; Pasley, "Party Politics, Citizenship, and Collective Action," 40–41; Matthew Mason, "The Battle of the Slaveholding Liberators: Great Britain, the United States, and Slavery in the Early Nineteenth Century," *William and Mary Quarterly*, 3d ser., 59 (2002): 665–96; Don E. Fehrenbacher, *The Slaveholding Republic: An Account of the United States Government's Relations to Slavery* (New York, 2001).

41. Just this was recently suggested in Joyce E. Chaplin, "Expansion and Exceptionalism in Early American History," *Journal of American History* 89 (2003): 1431–55.

42. Despite interesting recent work in diplomatic history, few recent studies we know of besides those of Cayton and Cotlar have tied internationalism or transatlanticism to popular or partisan movements. For beginnings, see Newman, *Parades and the Politics of the Street*; Branson, *Those Fiery Frenchified Dames*; Michael Durey, *Transatlantic Radicals in the Early American Republic* (Lawrence, 1998); Robertson, *Language of Democracy*; Douglas R. Egerton, *Gabriel's Rebellion: The Virginia Slave Conspiracies of 1800 & 1802* (Chapel Hill, 1993); Peter Linebaugh and Marcus Rediker, *The Many-Headed Hydra: Sailors, Slaves, Commoners, and the Hidden History of the Revolutionary Atlantic* (Boston, 2000); and Matthew Rainbow Hale, " 'Many Who Wandered in Darkness': The Contest over American National Identity, 1795–1798," *Early American Studies* 1 (Spring 2003): 127–75. The new wave of scholarship on the "Atlantic World" has thus far been too preoccupied with the negotiation of identities within the British empire to focus much on the international political connections of the postrevolutionary United States. For an overview of the burgeoning field of Atlantic World studies, see David Armitage and Michael J. Braddick, eds., *The British Atlantic World, 1500–1800* (Basingstoke, Eng., 2002). Many older and more traditional histories of political ideology and diplomacy are actually much better at placing the early American republic in transatlantic context. For two excellent examples, see Robert Kelley, *The Transatlantic Persuasion: The Liberal-Democratic Mind in the Age of Gladstone* (New York, 1969); and George Dangerfield, *The Era of Good Feelings* (New York, 1952). For an analysis of how scholars might link domestic and international politics in U.S. history that is attentive to an older historiography and also to the early

republic, see two essays by Ira Katznelson, "Rewriting the Epic of America" and "Flexible Capacity: The Military and Early American Statebuilding," in *Shaped by War and Trade: International Influences on American Political Development*, ed. Ira Katznelson and Martin Shefter (Princeton, 2002), 3–23, 82–110.

43. Richard R. John, "Governmental Institutions as Agents of Change: Rethinking American Political Development in the Early Republic, 1787–1835," *Studies in American Political Development* 11 (1997): 347–80.

44. Altschuler and Blumin, *Rude Republic*; Mark Voss-Hubbard, "The 'Third Party Tradition Reconsidered': Third Parties and American Public Life, 1830–1900," *Journal of American History* 86 (1999): 121–50.

DEMOCRACY
AND OTHER
PRACTICES

PART ONE

JEFFREY L. PASLEY

I

The Cheese and the Words

Popular Political Culture and Participatory Democracy in the Early American Republic

President Thomas Jefferson and his guests rang in the new year of 1802 as many later generations of Americans would celebrate New Years' Day, by consuming some snacks and watching a spectacle. In this case, however, the snack *was* the spectacle: the long-awaited "Mammoth Cheese" from Cheshire, Massachusetts, four feet in diameter, eighteen inches tall, 1,200 pounds, and already an American icon.[1]

The cheese and its saga were several months old by the time they reached President Jefferson. The "Ladies of Cheshire" had made the cheese back in August as "a mark of the exalted esteem" in which Jefferson was held by a small Berkshire County farming community that was monolithically Baptist in religion and Democratic Republican in politics. The Cheshire Baptists' esteem for Jefferson was especially exalted, and his accession to the presidency especially sweet, because they were members of an embattled religious minority in New

England, at odds with the Congregational establishment that still reigned and collected tax money in most of the region. Exalting God even above Jefferson (most of the time), the Baptists of Cheshire believed that no government or other human institution should have authority over matters of faith, which were God's alone. Allegedly following the example of a similar large dairy product made in Cheshire, England, to celebrate George III's recovery, they had gathered "the milk of 900 cows at one milking" in a vat six feet wide and used a giant cider press to actually create the cheese. A few weeks later, a bemused but admiring newspaper report of the project appeared in Rhode Island, where most of the Cheshire Baptists were born. It ended with the warning that "if some of the high toned Adams men do not soon turn and become friendly to Jefferson and the ladies," they might "have to eat their bread without cheese" in the future.[2]

The reporting newspaper was a strongly Republican one, but it was the Federalist press opposing Jefferson that was most active in spreading word of the cheese. Embittered by defeat but convinced that Jefferson's manifest unfitness and incompetence would soon drive him from public favor, Federalists could not believe their luck. "If we were not convinced of the stupidity of the Jacobin encomium-mongers," wrote one editor, "we should imagine the whole intro-duction to the *cheese vat* to be conceived in a vein of irony." In a seemingly endless stream of reports, comments, and satirical poetry that continued long after their subject was delivered and consumed, Federalist writers lampooned Cheshire's gift as the "Mammoth Cheese," after the mastodon bones that Charles Willson Peale had unearthed in New York during 1801 with aid from the Jefferson administration. It was considered a devastating stroke to link Cheshire's trib-ute to Jefferson's well-known interests in natural history and scientific re-search, which Federalists considered intolerably frivolous and had often satirized before.[3]

The leader in cheese-bashing seems to have been Joseph Dennie's prestigious Federalist literary journal, the Philadelphia *Port Folio*.[4] Dennie and his contribu-tors did some clever send-ups, especially "Reflections of Mr. Jefferson, Over the Mammoth Cheese," a poem in which Jefferson is depicted as seeing his "life and fortunes in this useless mass. / I curse the hands, by which the thing was made, / To them a cheese, to me a looking-glass." Federalists saw particular significance in the fact that the Mammoth Cheese, as unsealed, unrefrigerated foods will, attracted an appropriately mammoth share of insects and spoilage. (Republican papers responded with satirical charges that the Federalists now feared a "MAG-GOT INSURRECTION" along with their other worries about Jeffersonian rule.) In the *Port Folio*, the decaying cheese became a metaphor for Jefferson's hypocrisy and inner turpitude. "Like to this cheese," says the poem's Jefferson, "my outside [looks] smooth and sound / . . . When nought but rottenness within is found / . . . midst this shew of greatness and of ease, / Ten thousand vermin gnaw this wretched heart."[5] More often, the *Port Folio* simply spat contempt on "the mummery of the *Cheshire* simpletons," suggesting on at least two occasions that the cheese was really "made of *asses'* milk." Eventually Dennie tired of "cheese-communications," and tried to stop printing them, apparently to little avail as far as his contributors were concerned.[6]

It soon became apparent that the mammoth joke was really on the Federalists, as both the word "mammoth" and the mammoth tribute caught on with the populace. Giant foodstuffs and fossils seemed to communicate in some democratic, patriotic idiom that the Federalists did not understand. Their ridiculing publications introduced a new adjective into the English language, one that connoted nationalistic pride more than the wooly pretentiousness that they intended. A copycat baker in Philadelphia advertised "Mammoth Bread" for sale; a "Mammoth Eater" in Washington downed forty-two eggs in ten minutes; and two admiring Philadelphia butchers sent what Jefferson himself referred to as a "Mammoth veal," a hindquarter of the largest calf "we remember to have seen in this part of the country," 436 pounds at only 115 days old. Far from finding Jefferson's scientific investigations silly, butchers Michael Fry and Nathan Coleman had actually been inspired by Jefferson's much-twitted debate with European naturalists over the size and vitality of American fauna. They expressed joy "in being enabled to place confidence in the Man who while a private citizen laboured . . . to remove the European prejudice that animals were inferior & Degenerated in the New World." Sadly, despite Fry and Coleman's promise that the cool weather would allow their historic veal to arrive in Washington as fresh "as if it had been dressed this day," Jefferson declined to dine on the gift, though he did agree that it was a most impressive example of "enlarging the animal volume."[7]

A much more successful display of animal volume took place at Charles Willson Peale's museum in Philadelphia, where the eponymous Mammoth bones went on public display in December. The artist and his sons had spent several months piecing the bones together into a full skeleton, making some unintentional (but not unwelcome) anatomical errors that made the beast even more mammoth than it should have been. After a VIP showing Christmas Eve, there was a gala opening and parade replete with a trumpeter and an actor in Native American costume (keying into a Shawnee legend used in Peale's advertising). Crowds thronged the "Mammoth Room," paying an additional fifty cents a head over and above the Peale museum's usual twenty-five-cent admission price. The Pennsylvania state legislature was so thrilled that it soon allowed Peale to move his museum into larger quarters at the city and state's most prominent building, the former State House, now better known as Independence Hall.[8]

However, mere bread, meat, eggs, and bones could not begin to rival the half-ton appetizer from Cheshire. While originally planned as a spring gift, the extreme weight of the Mammoth Cheese dictated that it be delivered in winter, when as every good northern farmer knew, the snow and ice made it infinitely easier to haul heavy goods to market. The assigned deliverymen were John Leland and Darius Brown, Cheshire's leading Baptist divine and the son of his leading parishioner, respectively. The two men were on the road with the cheese for a month, traveling by sled, boat, and wagon, and creating a sensation wherever they appeared. A Stockbridge newspaper reported that twenty cheese-loaded wagons escorted Leland and Brown to their embarkation point on the Hudson, and even greater throngs seem to have materialized for their later stops. A prolific evangelist and the New England clergy's most radical exponent of religious freedom, Leland happily accepted the sobriquet "Mammoth Priest" and preached frequently along the way. The cheesemongers stopped just short of letting the tour become an actual circus: Leland turned down a thousand dollars to use the cheese in a show for twelve days in New York.[9]

Even the ceremony-averse Jefferson, whose typical manner on public occasions was low-key to the point of sedation, appeared "highly diverted" by the arrival of the cheese.[10] He stood in the doorway of the presidential mansion to receive the emissaries and their cargo, which was presented in "plain republican form" but announced as bearing the inscription "THE GREATEST CHEESE IN AMERICA—FOR THE GREATEST MAN IN AMERICA." Leland read Jefferson a message from the people of Cheshire, likely penned by the parson himself, that cast the freethinking president in the unlikely role of God's chosen instrument: "The supreme Ruler of the Universe . . . has raised up a JEFFERSON for this critical day to defend Republicanism and baffle all the arts of Aristocracy."

The message laid out the ideological grounds for the cheesemakers' veneration of Jefferson, giving the typical Jeffersonian themes of strict construction and limited government a northern, Baptist, and democratic spin. They considered the constitution "a description of those *Powers* which the people have submitted to their Magistrates, to be exercised for *definite* purposes, and not a charter of favors granted by a sovereign to his subjects." Among the frame of government's most "beautiful features" were the "right of free suffrage, to correct all abuses" (something actually not guaranteed by the Constitution in terms of its extent or form, but more and more widely claimed as a right after Jefferson's "Revolution of 1800") and "the prohibition of religious tests," which was alleged to "prevent all hierarchy." Perhaps most remarkably, given the modern view of Jefferson as an avatar of slavery, the cheese producers of Cheshire went out of their way to boast that their gift had been made "by the personal labor of freeborn farmers"—more accurately of freeborn farmers' wives and daughters—"(without a single slave to assist)."

On the spur of the moment, Jefferson decided to deliver his written reply to the message as a speech, making appropriate pronoun changes as he went. Declining to accept the messianic mantle offered by Leland, Jefferson praised the Cheshireites for their constitutional theory and pronounced himself particularly grateful for the nature of the gift, a "mark of esteem from freeborn farmers, employed personally in the useful labors of life" who expressed themselves through the medium of the goods that they produced.[11]

Visiting Federalist congressmen were not impressed by this democratic love-feast. The Reverend Manasseh Cutler of Massachusetts and several other New England solons went to the presidential mansion that morning intent on tweaking the head of the household. Upset at Jefferson's studied efforts to reduce the formalities surrounding the presidential office, they "were determined to keep up the old custom, though contrary to what was intended, of waiting on the President with the compliments of the season." An aggressively genteel man who delighted in reviewing the social performances of others in his diary, Cutler grudgingly admitted that he and his friends were "tolerably received, and treated with cake and wine." With the Federalist delegation thus lulled into a false sense of gentility, it was Jefferson's turn to tweak: he invited them to "Go into the mammoth room" (now the East Room) to see what Cutler regarded as a "monument of human weakness and folly," the Mammoth Cheese.[12]

Two days later, on January 3, the Mammoth Priest himself preached the sermon at Sunday services in the House of Representatives chamber, with Cutler and other pious Federalists among the captive audience. Though wildly popular with rural congregations, the rough-hewn, poorly educated Leland was considered something of an embarrassment even by some of the more polished clergymen in his own denomination. Besides alienating many of them with his uncompromising religious and political views, he was given to such colorful eccentricities as recounting his triumph over the "groaner," an evil spirit lurking in the Leland family home that he claimed to have exorcised through forceful prayer. (One can imagine Leland's fellow clergy cringing when he performed his blood-curdling impression of the demonic shrieks with which the groaner fled his house.) As a preacher, Leland was much closer to a political stump speaker in style than the elegant, erudite homilist that genteel churchgoers expected. Never a man to shy away from hyperbole, Leland took as his text "And behold a greater than Solomon is here," almost sacrilegiously applying the sentiment to

Jefferson (who sat in the audience) instead of Christ. No full record of Leland's sermon has survived, but it is apparent that he gave the assembled statesmen a relatively full-strength dose of backwoods preaching. "Such a farrago," Cutler reported, "bawled with . . . horrid tone, frightful grimaces, and extravagant gestures . . . was never heard by any decent auditory before."[13]

Federalists apparently did not speak the homely language of popular political bombast, evangelical religion, and compressed milk curds. The honorary *philosophe* Thomas Jefferson did not exactly *speak* this language either, but he understood it well enough to know how to respond. Jefferson may never have given a real stump speech in his life and typically preferred his religion more abstract and his cheese more French than what was offered in Cheshire. Yet he treated Leland as an honored dignitary and paid him two hundred dollars to reimburse some of his travel expenses. Jefferson also chose the very day of the cheese's arrival to issue his most important statement on the issue of greatest concern to the Cheshire Baptists, the separation of church and state. Jefferson thus scored points both with a key constituency and against his Federalist opponents. Nor did Jefferson drop the mammoth theme after Leland's visit. While the cheese's final fate cannot be definitely ascertained, indications are that it was kept in the White House and served, with the occasional pruning of rotten bits, for at least two years.[14]

Besides the probable disposal of the cheese, 1804 also saw another mammoth democratic event. As the first session of the Eighth Congress neared its end, Jefferson likely gave his blessing to the official Navy baker's creation of a "Mammoth Loaf," made from an entire barrel of flour and baked in a specially built oven. On March 26, the loaf was covered in white linen and carried on the shoulders of decked-out bakers to the Capitol, where it was placed in a committee room off the Senate chamber along with plenty of roast beef, hard cider, wine, and whiskey. A wild all-city party ensued, with (as one disapproving observer put it) "people of all classes & colors from the President of the United States to the meanest vilest Virginia slave" crowding into the Senate to enjoy the victuals and offend gawking New England Federalists. Jefferson himself was there "in the midst of the motley crew," reportedly eating beef and bread off his pocket knife and doing some justice to the liquor as well. Shocked Federalists claimed to have heard the president "sneeringly" compare "the unhallowed bread and wine" at "this disgraceful entertainment" to the elements of the Christian communion, which rumor was hotly debated in the press. Nor was Jefferson's comment the only political event of the day. Some members of the crowd brought large prints caricaturing certain senators who had proposed moving the government out of the city, and a large number of the partygoers lingered loudly in the chamber for the rest of the afternoon. The sergeant at arms tried and failed to eject them, and even when he later did get the floor cleared, the revelers only moved to the public gallery. At one point, Senator James Jackson of Georgia paused in mid-speech to threaten the unruly citizens of Columbia with violence if they ever behaved so badly again: "You shall be punished—I will inflict it—The navy shall be brought up & kill you outright." One assumes that Jefferson had gone home by this point, but then he did write an unusually small number of letters that day.[15]

However much Jefferson may have drunk on the occasion of the Mammoth loaf, his personal attitude toward such cheesy shenanigans was a little ambiguous. While publicly cordial in response to the public stunts in his honor, he also distanced himself in subtle but key respects. In January 1802, both presidential sons-in-law received letters that testified to Jefferson's enthusiasm for *le grand fromage*—he included its exact measurements—but also to a hint of condescension for its authors. The cheese was "an ebullition," or boiling over, Jefferson wrote, "of the passion of republicanism in a state where it has been under heavy persecution." While released to coincide with the presentation of the Mammoth Cheese, the influential letter on religious freedom was addressed not to the famed congregation in Cheshire, but to a more obscure and respectable Baptist association based in Danbury, Connecticut.[16]

Most aspects of the Mammoth Cheese story have been told many times before by historians, journalists, local colorists, and fiction writers, often with additional invented details that I have left out. The Mammoth Cheese seems to have been particularly well known during what Sean Wilentz has recently called the "golden age of historical popularization," the 1930s and 1940s. During those years of intense anxiety over the fate of middle American values in the face of depression, radicalism, and world war, thousands of historical novels and films, popular biographies, and folksy local histories were produced, and hundreds of museums and memorials were created (including the Jefferson Memorial in Washington and the Jefferson National Expansion Memorial, home of the Gateway Arch, in St. Louis). Most of these productions were done in a spirit of nostalgia and celebration more calculated "to fend off the intense insecurities of the day" than spread a deeper understanding of history.[17]

A politically somewhat bowdlerized version of the Mammoth Cheese incident was a natural anecdote for that period, and it was remembered often enough in western Massachusetts to inspire an act of commemoration by the Sons of the American Revolution in 1940. A life-size concrete "replica" of the cider press used to make the cheese was erected on a street corner in the middle of town. A metal plaque featuring the face and a capsule biography of Elder John

Leland was affixed to the front. The president of North Adams State Teachers College keynoted the dedication ceremony and managed to find in the once-radical cheese a comment on the corruption of American life by the politics and policies of the New Deal: "We need in America communities like the Cheshire of a century ago, independent and undominated by groups. In addition to the need of having the faith of the early people of Cheshire, there is the need for work for there is no way of getting something for nothing. We cannot save democracy by a life dwelt on race-tracks and bingo games." Unfortunately, reverence for Leland and the cheese in Cheshire appears to have grown less than mammoth in later decades. Though easily America's least prepossessing monument to begin with, it now sits in a state of profound disrepair, secluded behind a bus stop bench in the side yard of what appears to be a day-care center. Missing is the protruding screw on top that once clarified exactly what was being represented, though that must never have been an easy task; the visitor's sense of history is further impaired by the unprintable word that some vandal has etched across Elder Leland's forehead.[18]

Luckily, others outside of Cheshire have carried on the work. When I was first thinking about this essay, my elder son brought home a recent children's book called *A Big Cheese for the White House*. While a charmingly illustrated book, and considerably more sprightly than the bedraggled concrete cheese press, the authors also thoroughly updated the incident for the hypercapitalist 1990s. Instead of religious freedom or Democratic-Republican politics, the largely invented tale depicts the cheese as an advertising stunt, undertaken by a town of aggressively commercial cheesemakers trying to maintain their market share in the face of competition from other towns that were coloring and flavoring their cheeses.[19]

This story is as wrong-headed in spirit as it is inaccurate in its details. Though cheese was indeed sold for cash in the early republic, the commercialism involved in cheesemaking was rudimentary at best; an entire year's production was typically sold all at once for a price that was set throughout a neighborhood regardless of cost, decoration, or even quality. Only much later in the nineteenth century would cheesemaking become an aggressively competitive business, and "Mammoth Cheese" only went commercial when some factory dairy of the 1870s used it as a brand name.[20]

The disheveled Cheshire monument and the misguided children's book illustrate the fact that, making a partial exception for a few works on the church-state issue, neither the Mammoth Cheese nor the ideas and emotions behind it have been taken very seriously. Few accounts of Jefferson's presidency fail to mention it, but usually deploy the story only as a humorous example of just how darn popular Jefferson was with those wacky common folk. This would not matter much in itself if were not indicative of a general failure to understand the political culture of which Cheshire's gift to Jefferson was an unusual but nevertheless characteristic product.

Popular politics in the early republic was necessarily creative, adaptive, and variable. Because the early political parties were organizationally almost nonexistent, the work of building support for them was conducted by scattered groups of local activists, with little centralized direction or funding. Necessarily reliant on local resources and personnel, these typically self-appointed activists simply made partisan use of whatever existing traditions, institutions, and practices they could, including many that were longstanding features of Anglo-American culture. Among these were holiday celebrations, parades, taverns, toasts, songs, town meetings, petitions, militia company training days, and various products of local printing presses, including broadsides, handbills, almanacs, poems, pamphlets, and, especially, the small-circulation local and regional newspapers that sprang up everywhere after the Revolution.

Some of the most interesting political artifacts of this type are the plethora of songs published on the back pages of partisan newspapers and sometimes as sheet music or in songbooks, many of which were sung in taverns or at partisan gatherings. The musical output included not only "Jefferson and Liberty" and "The People's Friend," but also such unlikely numbers as "Adams and Liberty," "Huzzah Madison Huzzah," and even "Monroe Is the Man." Especially popular among local partisans were innumerable sets of new lyrics to popular tunes such as "Yankee Doodle," "Hail Columbia," and the "Anacreonic Song," better known today as the melody to "The Star-Spangled Banner."[21]

Each region of the country had its own particular local practices that were drawn into partisan politics and became part of a distinctive regional political culture. In the South, the famous court-day barbecues were transformed from rituals of noblesse oblige into competitive partisan debates, initiating the southern stump-speaking tradition. In the cities and larger towns, fraternal orders, voluntary associations, and militia companies were politicized, with the so-called Democratic-Republican societies and the Tammany Society being two of the best-known examples on the Republican side. These groups formed the beginnings of the highly disciplined neighborhood-based political organizations that would in time become known as urban political "machines."[22]

In New England, where churches and the clergy had always played an unusually prominent role in public life, many aspects of religious culture were adapted to partisan use. The Congregational establishment was heavily and intemperately Federalist, and its members did not hesitate to put partisan political instructions into their sermons. Around 1800, these instructions usually followed the formula published in the Federalist newspapers: Would the people choose "GOD—AND A RELIGIOUS PRESIDENT; Or impiously declare for JEFFER-SON—AND NO GOD!!"? At the same time, the traditions of the jeremiad and the publication of sermons gave rise not only to a large number of published political pamphlets and books by the clergy, but also the practice of secular politicians giving and publishing formal orations that often took on a distinctly homiletic tone. Elder John Leland's prominent role in Cheshire politics was just a more bumptious and aggressive version of what many other New England divines were doing.[23]

While always locally controlled and thus highly varied in tone and content, certain practices were nearly universal in this political culture. Among the most important were the holiday celebrations that dotted the civic calendar, each of which brought many of the elements mentioned above together into a single po-litical event.[24] For Republicans, the most important day was the Jefferson-centric Fourth of July, which they had championed as a more republican and democratic alternative to Washington's Birthday or government-declared thanksgiving and fast days. The festivities typically began with a parade or procession in which townsmen would march by trades, militia companies, and other groupings to a church, meeting hall, or public square. There a lengthy program would be held, featuring political and patriotic music (usually including at least one song written for the day), a reading of the Declaration of Independence, a prayer or sermon, and an oration by some local political activist. (Elder John Leland gave Cheshire's Independence Day oration in both 1801 and 1802, as well as in many later years. The Mammoth Cheese is said to have been first suggested by Leland at the 1801 celebration.) Finally the assembled group would retire to a hotel, tavern, or outdoor space, depending on the prosperity and location of the organizers, for a community banquet. Shady bowers on some prominent Republican's property seem to have been popular banquet spots in the Berkshires.[25]

The highlights of such banquets were the toasts, drunk at the end and accom-panied by cheers or cannon blasts if possible. At least fifteen or sixteen toasts were usually prepared in advance of the celebration, and those who could still speak after fifteen or sixteen belts could then offer "volunteers" from the floor. After-ward, an account of the celebration would be published in a sympathetic local newspaper, including a verbatim transcript of the toasts. No mere drinking game, political banquet toasts served, and were intended to serve, as informal platforms for the community, party, or faction that held the gathering. Pointed and quite specific political sentiments were expressed, and even the patriotic boilerplate was calibrated to reflect the values of the toasting group. So the Republicans of

Tyringham, Pittsfield, and Lenox, Massachusetts, all toasted the memory of George Washington, but worked into their salutes fairly bitter criticisms of the Federalist proposal to build a giant pyramid-shaped crypt for the first president. As the Tyringham celebrants put it, "8. *The memory of* WASHINGTON—More durably embalmed in the affections of *Republicans*, than in the most costly *Mausoleum.*—3 cheers." Not surprisingly, the cheesemaking Republicans of Cheshire were especially pugnacious. Three Federalist statesmen were given the toast, "From such supporters of the Constitution good Lord deliver us." To the federal judges who lost their positions in the Republican repeal of the Federalist Judiciary Act of 1801, they sent the message, "*Sixteen Dead Judges*—As Judges may they sleep in eternal peace."[26] Accounts of celebrations were often reprinted far outside their home region, and the toasts they contained were carefully parsed for the subtle and not-so-subtle indications they gave as to the balance of political forces and the state of public opinion in a given area. Toasts were also taken seriously enough to sometimes warrant follow-ups, reviews, and rebuttals.[27]

Another common denominator of this political culture was the use of newspapers as partisan political weapons. Indeed, newspapers were so central that, as I have argued elsewhere, we might well consider the parties of this period to be newspaper-based. Federalists commonly blamed Jefferson's election on the loose national network of Republican newspapers led by the Philadelphia *Aurora*, and Republicans tended to agree. After 1800, no serious political activist thought that anything could be accomplished without newspaper support in as many places as possible, and at times they equated the maintenance of a newspaper with the actual existence of a party, faction, or movement.[28] Aaron Burr's chief political henchman wrote in 1805 that "the instant" the Burr faction's tottering newspaper, the New York *Morning Chronicle*, failed, "*the Burrites would become 'uninfluential atoms,'* there would be *no rallying point*," and, even worse, their popularity and organizational vigor would be judged contemptibly weak because they were "*incapable any longer of supporting a press.*"[29]

Newspapers not only communicated party ideas, they represented and *embodied* these loosely organized parties in quite literal ways. Only in the pages of a partisan newspaper was a particular set of ideas, attitudes, policies, and candidates packaged together under the party label. Regular readers got a corporeal link to the party that they had few other ways of obtaining, and more important, they could learn, week to week, election to election, and public event to event, what it meant and how it thought to be a follower of that party. Many printers and editors became leading party activists and chief party spokesmen in their communities, and their offices were often unofficial party clubhouses.

As David Waldstreicher has argued, newspapers and other productions of the same partisan printing presses were critical to making the various elements of this political culture work as politics.[30] Since public events could be only be held intermittently, and attended only by a minority of the population of one small region at any given time, even an extremely well attended celebration or a particularly eloquent oration could have few wide-reaching or lasting political effects unless an account was printed in a newspaper. This was particularly true given the vast geographic extent of the nation and even of some states and individual congressional districts, such as the rugged First Western District of Massachusetts, where Cheshire was located. In such a situation, Alexis de Tocqueville noted, members of a party or any other political group needed "some means of talking every day without seeing one another and of acting together without meeting."[31]

Print transformed toasts, holiday celebrations, and parades from quaint local customs into vital forms of political communication. The whole practice of holding political banquets culminating in carefully worded toasts would have been politically meaningless without the newspaper report that allowed a few booze-soaked phrases to become a community's testament to the world. The Mammoth Cheese would have been nothing more than a hefty hors d'oeuvre without the newspaper publicity that grew up around it.

If words helped make the cheese, the cheesemakers were also involved with the printed end of the early republic's political culture on a much broader scale. The Republican newspaper network first established itself in Cheshire's region, the Berkshire mountains of western Massachusetts, in September 1800, when a newspaper called the *Sun* dawned in Pittsfield.[32] Though the Berkshires were far less hostile to Republicans than most of the rest of New England, its previous newspapers had all been short-lived, blandly commercial or Federalist-controlled. The area's most prominent journal, the Stockbridge *Western Star*, was under the influence of the area's arch-conservative Federalist congressman, Speaker of the House Theodore Sedgwick.[33] The effect of being presented with serious political choices was electric, the actual metaphor used in an 1801 Pittsfield Fourth of July toast to describe the changes in the "political Thermometer" of Berkshire County since Jefferson's victory and the *Sun's* appearance.[34] "I have lived in a Town, where none but *Federal* Newspapers have been taken, until lately, and we all believed them," wrote one of the *Sun's* readers, but upon actually reading a Republican journal, "I was astonished to find the sentiments of that party so different from the representations given of them by their enemies. I begin to suspect I have been deceived and imposed upon."[35] The people of Cheshire, who never needed to have their minds changed but were glad for the company, wished in a toast that "the splendour of the *Republican* Sun" would "continue to eclipse the *twinklings* of the *Western Lightning Bug*" (the Stockbridge *Western Star*).[36]

The *Sun's* editor, Phinehas Allen, was a practical printer just graduated from his apprenticeship with the Northampton *Hampshire Gazette*. He was one of a new generation of young printers who started their occupational lives expecting to be active politicians rather than mere mechanics who sometimes served politicians. Allen and many other printers who started Republican newspapers after 1798 were outraged by the Sedition Act's effort to force their trade into submission and were attracted by the opportunity, rare for young artisans, to exercise independent influence in their communities. A eulogist described the teenage Allen saving his earnings to buy printing equipment, with the dream of making his living by "advocating the political principles which *he* believed right." Allen would be the unbending chief tribune of the Berkshire Democracy until the Civil War, serving several terms in the state legislature and enjoying a national audience for his writings.[37]

The cheese story was originally broken by another newspaper founded at nearly the same time, and under the same impulses, as Allen's *Sun*. Despite its name, the Providence *Impartial Observer* was actually a much more radical paper than the *Sun*; a lengthy motto on its masthead proclaimed, among many other sentiments, that "a true history of the times, forebodes the entire downfall of all the inveterate enemies of true republican principles."[38]

Elder John Leland became the Pittsfield *Sun's* most "efficient" supporter, contributing articles and, more importantly, encouraging his parishioners, listeners, and acquaintances to subscribe. The relationship would continue for the remaining forty years of the Elder's life.[39] Though a considerably staider man than Leland, editor Phinehas Allen fully understood the power of festive politics, at one point helping start a Democratic hotel—and, in effect, a Democratic function hall—when the local innkeeper refused to let the Jeffersonians hold their Fourth of July banquet at his establishment.[40] Allen did not exactly *promote* the Mammoth Cheese in the *Sun*, but he did vigorously defend it, holding the project to be "not only *innocent*, but *laudable* and *patriotic*, the opposition of the *Federalists* to the contrary notwithstanding." The *Sun* also used the long Federalist obsession with the cheese to lampoon the hysteria and conspiracy theories with which they had filled the political air since the late 1790s. Though "the Cheshire Cheese has not yet been seriously represented to be in itself a violation of the Constitution," Allen wrote semi-facetiously, it was certainly regarded as stemming from "an alarming principle of disorganization and modern philosophy." Moreover, it was "shrewdly suspected that Albert Gallatin, the Genevan instigator of Whiskey Insurrections, instigated the good women of Cheshire to enter into the *Cheese-Plot*, the particulars of which may be expected in the *Appendix* of Dr. Morse's next *Thanksgiving Sermon*."[41] (Rev. Jedidiah Morse of Charlestown was the leading American promoter of the idea of the Illuminati conspiracy, of which Jefferson and his allies were thought to be card-carrying members.)[42]

One final aspect of the early republic's political culture may help explain the particular form that Cheshire's political statement took. This was the producerist language in which ordinary Americans often expressed themselves on public occasions, the tendency for people who made things to speak through the medium of the things they made. This language has been most frequently noted in the case of urban artisans, who marched in civic processions by trades and held periodic trade festivals. These performances often combined some demonstration of the craft or display of its products with slogans asserting its members' political virtue and contribution to the strength of the nation or some other formulation of the common good. Believing that their trades supplied needful community services as much as commodities to be sold in the market, producers thought it made perfect sense to ground their claims to citizenship at least partly on the utility, quality, and, sometimes, the size of their productions.[43]

The most famous example was the "Grand Federal Procession" held in Philadelphia (along with similar events in Boston and New York) to celebrate and legitimize the ratification of the Constitution. In Philadelphia, the potters had a horse-drawn float carrying a potter's wheel and men making actual cups, mugs, and bowls during the parade. A flag carried the motto, "*The potter hath power over his clay*," referring to the idea that a man with a trade could make his own independent livelihood and thus controlled his own mind and destiny. The cabinet and chair-makers also had a rolling workshop, with the slogan "*By unity we support society*," a double- or triple-entendre, taking in the solidarity of the craft, the actual crafting of devices to hold up the human bottom (chairs), and the great value to society of a craft that could meet so basic a need as sitting. The bricklayers contented themselves to march with their trowels, aprons, and a banner that made a straightforward link between their pride as tradesman and as republican citizens: "*Both buildings and rulers are the works of our hands*."[44]

These sentiments formed part of the complex of practices and ideals that Sean Wilentz has called "artisan republicanism." A similar complex seems to have existed in the realm of food production. Certainly the makers of mammoth veals and loaves thought so, as did the bakers, brewers, and "victuallers" who marched in the Grand Federal Procession. Such demonstrations did not and could not happen often in rural areas: farmers lacked organized craft traditions and geography made it impossible for them to assemble according to their specialities and march. Yet in some ways the Mammoth Cheese was a tribute by the farm people of Cheshire to themselves as much as to Jefferson, a testimonial to their prodigious ability to help feed the republic and serve as independent, active, and necessary members of the national community. While there does not seem to be any evidence of a direct connection to the cheese, it is intriguing to note that Berkshire County is widely regarded as the originator of that typical rural production festival, the American county fair. The event generally recognized as the first county fair was organized at Pittsfield by Elkanah Watson in 1810, and heavily promoted in Phinehas Allen's *Sun*.[45] At the very least, we know that the mixture of cheese and politics remained viable in Cheshire. In 1829, two of the 1801 curd suppliers, Israel and Molly Cole, sent another new Democratic president another congratulatory cheese, along with a cover letter inquiring about the new administration's naval policy. At one hundred pounds, however, Andrew Jackson's cheese was only big, not mammoth.[46]

It follows from this line of reasoning, then, that the Mammoth Cheese was not merely a colorful stunt. It was instead a natural by-product of a political culture that could not stray far from the fabric of everyday life, and that often asked people to exercise their political rights purposefully for the first time, to make a choice between alternatives rather than merely give assent. While an outsized version of a humble household foodstuff was a gross intrusion of plebeian specificity into what was often idealized as an impersonal public sphere of competing ideas, it was one of many such "intrusive" elements that helped allow for the political expression and mobilization of people who would never write a philosophical essay or give an oration.[47]

Perhaps the most important aspect of this variegated, festive, cheese-producing mode of conducting politics is that it worked. It is rare for historians to write about "Jeffersonian Democracy" or a democratic "Revolution of 1800" anymore unless to debunk or invert them,[48] and the rise of mass participatory democracy is now often delayed in historical interpretations until the 1830s or later.[49] Yet I would argue that this early partisan political culture—which developed during the 1790s, fully emerged after Jefferson was elected in 1800, and faded only after the parties became better organized in the 1830s—was one of the most participatory and transformative that the United States has ever experienced, despite its utter lack of many elements that came to define party politics later. Nationally, this political culture not only elected Thomas Jefferson in the face of government repression, but in doing so, fundamentally revised the nature of the United States as a political regime, unofficially but effectively rewriting the Constitution to incorporate organized competition for popular majorities. The founders had created "a republican Constitution, imposing salutary checks on the popular will," wrote the Jacksonian-era conservative Calvin Colton, but from 1800 on, "the popular will in the shape of a dynasty of opinion, has habitually triumphed over these provisions. The government has been republican in form, but democratic in fact."[50]

Remarkable changes can also be detected on the level of political behavior. Though dominant interpretations have long brushed the information aside, statistics gathered by J. R. Pole and Richard P. McCormick in the 1950s and 1960s, now buttressed by the work of the American Antiquarian Society's First Democracy Project, found an "extraordinary surge" of voting over the period 1800–1816. Voter participation approached 70 percent of adult white males during the campaigns of 1799 and 1800 in heavily politicized states such as Pennsylvania (see Figure 1.1), and trended up to those levels elsewhere a bit later. The surge was especially notable in New England, where Federalist-Republican competition was particularly intense after 1800, as the Federalists suddenly became vulnerable in places they once dominated with little challenge and the Republicans made strong efforts to win over the one region where they were defeated in 1800. According to the numbers generated by McCormick and Pole, it was not until 1840 or so that the better-organized parties of the Jacksonian era managed to match that record.[51]

Nowhere was the surge in voting more pronounced than in the cheese- and word-producing region of Cheshire and Pittsfield, Berkshire County, Massachusetts (see Figure 1.2). Before Jefferson's election, voter turnouts had rarely risen above 40 percent of the estimated number of adult white males and usually stayed well below 30 percent. The Berkshire numbers rocketed up immediately after the two major local political events of 1800, Jefferson's victory in the national election and the founding of the *Sun*. In a special congressional election held a few days after Jefferson's inauguration (not shown in the figure), more than 51 percent of the voters turned out countywide and an incredible 79 percent in Cheshire. Voting in elections for governor ramped up quickly in Pittsfield and countywide, crossing more or less permanently into the 60–80 percent range by 1805. In Cheshire itself, voting reached maximal levels, and sometimes beyond maximal. After 1800, Cheshire's turnout for governor went above 60 percent immediately, was usually more than 80 by 1805, and often above 90 thereafter. In the bitter near-war and war years of 1810 and 1815, Cheshire actually recorded more votes than there should have been voters, according to my estimates. Cheshire elections were not only very well attended, but nearly unanimous. In 1801, they voted for Republican candidate Elbridge Gerry 175–0, and in most other elections the Federalists would get perhaps two or three votes if they were lucky. In the more-than-full turnout years of 1810 and

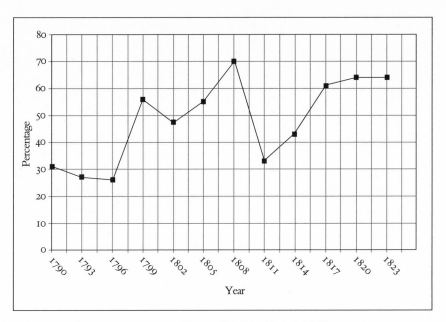

FIGURE I.I. Estimated Percentage of Adult White Males Voting in Pennsylvania Gubernatorial Elections, 1790–1823. Voting statistics courtesy of First Democracy Project.

1815, there was heavier opposition but even more crushing margins: 244–5 and 253–8. Was it Elder Leland's sermons? The strength of their Baptist identity? The rollicking Fourth of July celebrations? Something in the cheese? Whatever the combination of factors, the early republic's political culture had turned a sleepy farming town into one of the most politically energized places on the planet.[52]

The political culture of the Jefferson era not only maximized voting in Cheshire and elsewhere, it also mobilized the nonvoting population as well. Calling the cheese a gift from the ladies of Cheshire, as the *Impartial Observer* originally did, was no mere rhetorical device. Cheesemaking on preindustrial dairy farms was indisputably women's work, albeit a form of women's work that produced a commercial product and enjoyed an unusually high level of acknowledgment and esteem from the world of men. While the idea of making a giant cheese has traditionally been assigned to Leland, such a massive project could not have contemplated, much less accomplished, without the enthusiastic support of Cheshire's entire female population.[53]

The role of women in creating the cheese became a major point of ridicule by Federalists, who lashed out at any example of democratization or the expansion of political participation that came to their attention. The *Port Folio* cracked that

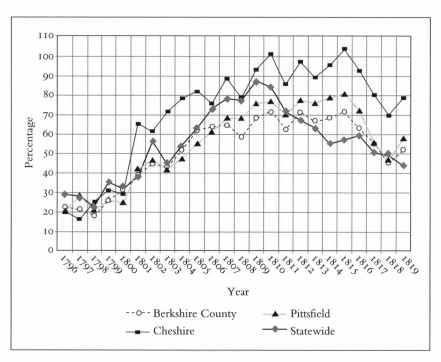

FIGURE 1.2. Estimated Percentage of Adult White Males Voting in Massachusetts Gubernatorial Elections, 1796–1819

the cheese was the effort of "some silly dairy-women, in one of the nooks of our countryside" to "amuse themselves." Later the paper published a satire involving a fictitious new tribute to Jefferson "consolidated by the female patriots of Massachusetts . . . in concert with their acquiescent husbands." To some Federalists, it seems, the politicization of dairy women threatened to unman the American husband and undermine his authority. The satirist also made his position on the intellectual capacities of women clear with an irony-soaked reference to the humorous monument as "this concentration of female genius."[54]

Though voting was limited largely to adult white males, there is much evidence that a lack of voting rights did not prevent women from developing strong and partisan political interests and opinions. Moreover, the festive, community-based political practices of the era afforded particularly wide opportunities for not only women but also other legally disfranchised groups, including children, African Americans, new immigrants, and propertyless white males, to participate in political events. Not everyone was invited to sit at one of those banquet tables or hand in a ballot, but just about everyone could and did attend the civic celebrations, listen to the speeches, or read or hear what was in the newspapers. Nonwhite groups also had political celebrations of their own.[55]

In accordance with the "separate spheres" stereotype of later generations, the role of women in the Mammoth Cheese incident was reduced in the semi-legendary accounts that developed later. Following the account often repeated in Federalist satires, these stories often credited the authorship of the project to Leland alone (a claim that the parson himself did not make) and emphasized the more masculine and technological aspects of the actual cheesemaking, such as the use of the cider press and the creation of a giant cheese hoop by the town blacksmith.[56]

Acknowledging democratization in the wake of Thomas Jefferson's "Revolution of 1800" does not mean we should minimize the damage done to African and especially to Native Americans or ignore the exclusions and limitations that the American form of party politics ultimately entailed. We do not even have to give Jefferson and his policies much credit. His primary contribution may have been the image he projected, or had projected on him, as "The People's Friend," a great statesman who nevertheless respected the values and intelligence of ordinary citizens and was willing to graciously accept their cheesy gifts. As a volunteer toaster at Lenox expressed this widespread perception, Jefferson had "virtues, and believes in the virtues of his fellow citizens."[57]

While strange and often rather ridiculous to modern eyes (and greatly lacking in the kind of uniformity and consistency that some social scientific scholars would like to see in a party "system")[58] this political culture was successful precisely because it was *not* a standardized national system. Instead, it was thoroughly embedded, and built out of, the culture of everyday life. Holidays, newspapers, barbecues, and cheese had all long existed in these local cultures. What early American party politicians did was adapt these local customs into something that was politically usable. There were no prefabricated posters and pamphlets mailed from the national party office, no celebrity candidate with entourage and security sweeping in for appearances, nothing but local people devising their own means of building support for the party with their own local resources. While historians have tended to emphasize the torch light parades, marching companies, and mass rallies of the mid-nineteenth-century as democratic ideals, it might be argued that many such practices were merely holdovers from earlier decades that had become routinized and bloated from too many injections of money. The summit of participatory party democracy may have been reached in the age of the Mammoth Cheese, when the major threat of bloat at political events came from good old fashioned mold.

1. The two standard scholarly works on the cheese incident are C. A. Browne, "Elder John Leland and the Mammoth Cheshire Cheese," *Agricultural History* 18 (1944): 145–53; and L. H. Butterfield, "Elder John Leland, Jeffersonian Itinerant," *Proceedings of the American Antiquarian Society* 62 (1952): 154–252. Both works are thorough but not particularly analytical. The most recent study, focusing more on the surrounding issues of religious freedom than the cheese itself, is Daniel L. Dreisbach, "Mr. Jefferson, a Mammoth Cheese, and the 'The Wall of Separation Between Church and State: A Bicentennial Commemoration,'" *Journal of Church and State* 43 (2001): 725–45.

2. Pittsfield *Sun*, November 16, 1801; Providence *Impartial Observer*, August 8, 1801, also reprinted in Butterfield, "Elder John Leland," 219–20; Boston *Columbian Centinel and Massachusetts Federalist*, August 12, 1801.

3. Pittsfield *Sun*, November 16, 1801; Butterfield, "Elder John Leland," 220–22; Charles Coleman Sellers, *Charles Willson Peale, Volume II: Later Life (1790–1827)* (Philadelphia, 1947), 127–48. The Federalist quotation is from Boston *Columbian Centinel*, August 12, 1801. The latest anti-cheese rant that I have found is the entire seventh chapter of William Fessenden, *The Political Farrago, or a Miscellaneous Review of Politics in the United States* (Brattleboro, Vt., 1807). The best treatment of Federalist satire on Jefferson remains Linda K. Kerber, *Federalists in Dissent: Imagery and Ideology in Jeffersonian America* (Ithaca, N.Y., 1970).

4. Philadelphia *Port Folio*, August 22, November 7, 1801, January 21, 23, 30, March 6, 13, 20, August 3, 1802.

5. Ibid., March 20, 1802; Boston *Republican Gazetteer*, June 26, 1802; Boston *Independent Chronicle*, July 8, 1802; Portsmouth *Republican Ledger*, July 13, 1802.

6. Philadelphia *Port Folio*, August 22, 1801, January 23, March 6, 1802.

7. Sellers, *Peale II*, 142–43; Thomas Jefferson to John Beckley, [October 22, 1801], Michael Fry and Nathan Coleman to Thomas Jefferson, October 17, 1801, Jefferson to Fry and Coleman, October 22, 1801, Jefferson Papers, Library of Congress; Dumas Malone, *Jefferson the President: First Term, 1801–1805* (Boston, 1970), 107.

8. Sellers, *Peale II*, 143–45, 148–53.

9. L. F. Greene, ed., *The Writings of the Late Elder John Leland, Including Some Events in His Life, Written by Himself, With Additional Sketches, &c.* (New York, 1845), 32; Stockbridge *Western Star*, December 5, 1801; Thomas Jefferson to Thomas Mann Randolph, Washington, January 1, 1802, Jefferson Papers, Library of Congress. On Leland's radicalism compared to the rest of New England's dissenting clergy, see William G. McLoughlin, *New England Dissent, 1630–1883: The Baptists and the Separation of Church and State* (Cambridge, Mass., 1971), 2:928–35.

10. Jefferson's expression is described in Benjamin Robinson to D. Robinson, January 1, 1802, ms. letter in a private collection, reprinted in Browne, "Leland and Cheese,"

151; and in *Springfield Union and Republican*, January 15, 1933, clipping in Local History file, Berkshire Athenaeum, Pittsfield, Mass.

11. *Washington Federalist*, January 2, 1802; Boston *Mercury and New-England Palladium*, January 12, 15, 22, 1802; New York *Evening Post*, January 7, 1802; Thomas Jefferson to Daniel Brown, Hezekiah Mason, et al., January 1, 1802, Jefferson Papers, Library of Congress; Washington *National Intelligencer*, January 20, 1802.

12. William Parker Cutler and Julia Perkins Cutler, eds., *Life, Journals, and Correspondence of Rev. Manasseh Cutler, L.L.D.* (Athens, Ohio, 1987), 2:65–66. For more on Cutler and gentility, see Jeffrey L. Pasley, "Private Access and Public Power: Gentility and Lobbying in the Early Congress," in *The House and the Senate in the 1790s: Petitioning, Lobbying, and Institutional Development*, ed. Kenneth R. Bowling and Donald R. Kennon (Athens, Ohio, 2002), 57–99.

13. Cutler and Cutler, eds., *Journal and Correspondence of Manasseh Cutler*, 2:58, 66–67; Greene, ed., *Writings of Elder John Leland*, 44–45. For a very useful delineation of the elements of self-conscious gentility, see Richard L. Bushman, *The Refinement of America: Persons, Houses, Cities* (New York, 1993), 30–99. For aspects of John Leland's characterization in this paragraph, see Nathan O. Hatch, *The Democratization of American Christianity* (New Haven, 1989), 95–101, 138; and McLoughlin, *New England Dissent*, 2:931–32.

14. Butterfield, "Elder John Leland," 227–28. The cheese-religious freedom connection is most strongly made in Dreisbach, "Jefferson, Mammoth Cheese, and Wall of Separation."

15. Everett Somerville Brown, ed., *William Plumer's Memorandum of Proceedings in the United States Senate, 1803–1807* (New York, 1923), 179–80; Norristown *Register*, May 10, 1804; Cutler and Cutler, eds., *Journals and Correspondence of Manasseh Cutler*, 2:170.

16. Thomas Jefferson to Thomas Mann Randolph (quoted), January 1, 1802, Jefferson Papers, Library of Congress; Jefferson to John Wayles Eppes, January 1, 1802, Jefferson Papers, University of Virginia; Jefferson to Nehemiah Dodge, Ephraim Robbins, and Stephen S. Nelson, "a committee of the Danbury Baptist association in the state of Connecticut," January 1, 1802, draft and final version, Jefferson Papers, Library of Congress, microfilm frames 20593–94. The letter to the Danbury Baptists, which originated the famous "wall of separation" metaphor used by twentieth-century jurists to explain the religious "establishment clause" of the First Amendment, has been analyzed in numerous books and articles, including most of the cheese-related works cited above. Recently, this debate has been rejuvenated by the restoration of the scratched-out portions of Jefferson's original draft of the letter. See James H. Hutson, "Thomas Jefferson's Letter to the Danbury Baptists: A Controversy Rejoined" and the forum that follows, *William and Mary Quarterly*, 3d ser., 56 (1999): 775–824.

17. Quotations from Sean Wilentz, "America Made Easy: McCullough, Adams, and the Decline of Popular History," *New Republic*, July 2, 2001, 35–40. Colonial Williamsburg and the restoration of Monticello date to just before the same period. An excellent

discussion of Jefferson memorialization in the mid-twentieth century appears in Merrill D. Peterson, *The Jefferson Image in the American Mind* (New York, 1960), 347–442.

18. The information on the memorializing of the cheese in Berkshire County and the dedication of the Cheshire monument comes from various clippings in the Local History file, Berkshire Athenaeum, Pittsfield, Massachusetts. The quotations and the description of the monument in its original condition come from "Leland Monument Dedicated by S.A.R. in Cheshire Rites," *Springfield Republican*, September 2, 1940; and "Cheshire Cheese Monument to Honor Elder John Leland," *Springfield Republican*, August 20, 1940. The author personally inspected its present condition in May 2001, photographs from which expedition have been posted at <http://jeff.pasleybrothers.com/images/cheese.htm>.

19. Candace Fleming and S. D. Schindler, *A Big Cheese for the White House: The True Tale of a Tremendous Cheddar* (New York, 1999). A more accurate fictional rendition, reflecting the present author's interpretation via some email exchanges and an internet version of this chapter, appeared in historical novelist Sheri Holman's largely modern-day story, *The Mammoth Cheese* (New York, 2003).

20. Sally McMurry, *Transforming Rural Life: Dairying Families and Agricultural Change, 1820–1885* (Baltimore, 1995), 43–61; X[erxes] A. Willard, *Willard's Practical Dairy Husbandry* (New York, 1877), 380.

21. Early political songs can be sampled in Vera Brodsky Lawrence, *Music for Patriots, Politicians, and Presidents: Harmonies and Discords of the First Hundred Years* (New York, 1975); *The Democratic Songster: Being a Collection of New Republican Songs, Mostly Originals* (Baltimore, 1801); [William Duane, comp.], *The American Republican Harmonist; or, A Collection of Song and Odes: Written in America, on American Subjects and Principles* (Philadelphia, 1803); James J. Wilson, comp., *A National Song-book, Being a Collection of Patriotic, Martial, and Naval Songs and Odes, Principally of American Composition* (Trenton, 1813); Carl Brand, *Presidential Campaign Songs, 1789–1996* (1999), Smithsonian Folkways CD 45051; Chestnut Brass Company and Friends, *Hail to the Chief! American Political Marches, Songs & Dirges of the 1800s* (1996), Sony Classical CD SFK 62485.

22. Charles S. Sydnor, *Gentlemen Freeholders: Political Practices in Washington's Virginia* (Chapel Hill, 1952); Daniel Dupre, "Barbecues and Pledges: Electioneering and the Rise of Democratic Politics in Antebellum Alabama," *Journal of Southern History* 60 (1994): 479–512; Kim T. Phillips, "William Duane, Philadelphia's Democratic Republicans, and the Origins of Modern Politics," *Pennsylvania Magazine of History and Biography* 101 (1977): 365–87; Jerome Mushkat, *Tammany: The Evolution of a Political Machine, 1789–1865* (Syracuse, 1971); Eugene Perry Link, *Democratic-Republican Societies, 1790–1800* (1942; reprint, New York, 1973); Philip S. Foner, ed., *The Democratic-Republican Societies, 1790–1800: A Documentary Sourcebook of Constitutions, Declarations, Addresses, Resolutions, and Toasts* (Westport, Conn., 1976).

23. The partisan political activities (as opposed to the ideologies, theologies, rhetorical strategies, or professional lives) of the New England clergy in the early republic still await

a full modern history. An excellent start has recently been made in Jonathan D. Sassi, *A Republic of Righteousness: The Public Christianity of the Post-Revolutionary New England Clergy* (New York, 2001), especially chapter 2, "The Two Kingdoms in Concert." For present purposes, the best single work on New England political practices in this period is David Waldstreicher and Stephen R. Grossbart, "Abraham Bishop's Vocation; or, the Mediation of Jeffersonian Politics," *Journal of the Early Republic* 18 (1998): 617–57. The background can be filled in with William A. Robinson, *Jeffersonian Democracy in New England* (1916; reprint, New York, 1968); James Truslow Adams, *New England in the Republic, 1776–1850* (Boston, 1926); Richard J. Purcell, *Connecticut in Transition, 1775–1818* (Washington, D.C., 1918); Christopher Grasso, *A Speaking Aristocracy: Transforming Public Discourse in Eighteenth-Century Connecticut* (Chapel Hill, 1999). Authors of multiple political orations include the Republican Abraham Bishop and the Federalists David Daggett and Theodore Dwight. The authors of published political sermons are far too numerous to catalog here, but two random examples would be Rev. Stanley Griswold for the Republicans and Rev. Jedidiah Morse for the Federalists. A collection of such sermons covering this period can be found in the second volume of Ellis Sandoz, ed., *Political Sermons of the American Founding Era, 1730–1805* (Indianapolis, 1991). John Leland was an especially mammoth producer of political sermons, and much of his output is collected in Greene, ed., *Writings of Elder John Leland*. Another less heavily published but equally significant political preacher in the Berkshires was Thomas Allen (uncle of the Pittsfield *Sun* printer mentioned below), a rare Republican among the Congregational clergy. Allen's church actually split into two over the political content of his sermons; a eulogy that Allen gave his son, a Republican state legislator, was a particular catalyst. See Thomas Allen, *Submission to the Will of God: A Discourse Occasioned by the Death of Thomas Allen, Jun. . . . .* (Pittsfield, 1806). Quotation is from Noble E. Cunningham, Jr., ed., *The Making of the American Party System, 1789 to 1809* (Englewood Cliffs, N.J., 1965), 154.

24. The discussion of "celebratory politics" in the next few paragraphs draws heavily on David Waldstreicher, *In the Midst of Perpetual Fetes: The Making of American Nationalism, 1776–1820* (Chapel Hill, 1997), except for the separately noted examples from western Massachusetts. For other works covering aspects of this festive political culture and its precursors, see Simon P. Newman, *Parades and the Politics of the Street: Festive Culture in the Early American Republic* (Philadelphia, 1997); Len Travers, *Celebrating the Fourth: Independence Day and the Rites of Nationalism in the Early Republic* (Amherst, Mass., 1997); Peter Thompson, *Rum Punch and Revolution: Taverngoing and Public Life in Eighteenth-Century Philadelphia* (Philadelphia, 1999); Susan G. Davis, *Parades and Power: Street Theatre in Nineteenth-Century Philadelphia* (Philadelphia, 1986).

25. For examples of Republican Fourth of July celebrations in the Berkshires, see Pittsfield *Sun*, July 7, 14, 21, 1801, July 12, 26, 1802. The *Sun's* account of the 1802 Cheshire toasts can be viewed at <http://jeff.pasleybrothers.com/images/cheese.htm>.

26. Ibid., July 14, 1801 (quoted), July 12, 26 (quoted), 1802. On the Republicans' principled objections to the Federalist efforts to turn Washington into a sanctified,

kinglike figure, see Simon P. Newman, "Principles or Men? George Washington and the Political Culture of National Leadership, 1776–1801," *Journal of the Early Republic* 12 (1992): 477–507.

27. For an index of how seriously celebrations and toasts were taken in the early republic, see the book *An Historical View of the Public Celebrations of the Washington Society, and Those of the Young Republicans* (Boston, 1823), a compilation of all the toasts given at the celebrations of a particular group of Boston Republicans over a seventeen-year period.

28. For elaboration and documentation on the general interpretation presented in this and the following paragraphs on newspapers, see Jeffrey L. Pasley, *"The Tyranny of Printers": Newspaper Politics in the Early American Republic* (Charlottesville, 2001), especially chaps. 1 and 9; Jeffrey L. Pasley, "The Two National Gazettes: Newspapers and the Embodiment of American Political Parties," *Early American Literature* 35 (2000): 51–86.

29. Matthew Livingston Davis to William P. Van Ness, August 15 (quoted), 28, 1805, August 1, 1809, Davis Papers, New-York Historical Society.

30. See Waldstreicher, *Perpetual Fetes*; Waldstreicher and Grossbart, "Abraham Bishop's Vocation."

31. Alexis de Tocqueville, *Democracy in America*, ed. J. P. Mayer, trans. George Lawrence (New York, 1969), 518.

32. J. E. A. Smith, *The History of Pittsfield (Berkshire County), Massachusetts, From the Year 1800 to the Year 1876* (Springfield, Mass., 1876), 82–83.

33. Ibid., 24–29; Richard E. Welch, Jr., *Theodore Sedgwick, Federalist: A Political Portrait* (Middletown, Conn., 1965), 97, 113–14, 122, 233–34.

34. Pittsfield *Sun*, July 7, 1801.

35. "A Plough-Jogger," ibid., July 28, 1801.

36. Ibid., July 26, 1802.

37. On Phinehas Allen, see Smith, *History of Pittsfield*, 82–84; "Death of the Senior Editor," Pittsfield *Sun*, May 10, 1860; John Todd, *The Old Man to Be Honored: A Sermon in Pittsfield, May 13, 1860, on the Death of Hon. Phinehas Allen* (Pittsfield, 1860), quotation on 20. On the new generation of Republican printers that took up the pen in the late 1790s, see Pasley, *Tyranny of Printers*, chaps. 6, 7.

38. Providence *Impartial Observer*, March 21, 1801; Clarence S. Brigham, *History and Bibliography of American Newspapers, 1690–1820* (Worcester, Mass., 1947), 1011–12. Most partisan newspapers carried such mission-defining mottos, but the *Impartial Observer's* is easily the longest I have found: "The intrigues of designing men will never deprive a wise and enlightened people of their rights. The wish of every good man must be, that republicans should so guard their rights, as to put it out of the power of Miscreants and Demagogues to destroy or even abridge them. The people of the United States fought for Liberty; they obtained it. They have agreed upon and established a free elective government; and they will support it, the wiles of Speculators and Peculators not withstanding. The honourable zeal which pervades the breast of every true republican in search of understanding, wisdom, and knowledge, and a true history of the times,

forebodes the entire downfall of all the inveterate enemies of true republican principles. Any person, who may be able, at any time, to communicate any information which will aid in the support of the rights of the people, and of good government, is requested to forward it for publication."

39. "Death of the Rev. John Leland," Pittsfield *Sun*, January 21, 1841.

40. Smith, *History of Pittsfield*, 185–87.

41. Pittsfield *Sun*, January 18, 1802 (quoted), November 16, 1801 (quoted), July 26, 1802.

42. David Brion Davis, ed., *The Fear of Conspiracy: Images of Un-American Subversion From the Revolution to the Present* (Ithaca, 1971), 35–54; Vernon Stauffer, *New England and the Bavarian Illuminati* (New York, 1918).

43. This is an elaboration on the seminal discussions in Sean Wilentz, "Artisan Republican Festivals and the Rise of Class Conflict in New York City, 1788–1837," in Michael Frisch and Daniel J. Walkowitz, eds., *Working-Class America: Essays on Labor, Community, and American Society* (Urbana, 1983), 37–77; and Sean Wilentz, *Chants Democratic: New York City & the Rise of the American Working Class, 1788–1850* (New York, 1986).

44. Quotations from Whitfield J. Bell, Jr., ed., *Francis Hopkinson's "Account of the Grand Federal Procession Philadelphia, 1788"* (Boston, 1962), 16, 20, 17–18.

45. Smith, *History of Pittsfield*, 316–51.

46. A. B. Whipple, "Town of Cheshire," in *History of Berkshire County, Massachusetts, With Biographical Sketches of Its Prominent Men* (New York, 1885), 622–23.

47. My sense of eighteenth-century ideals regarding public debate is most heavily influenced by Michael Warner, *The Letters of the Republic: Publication and the Public Sphere in Eighteenth-Century America* (Cambridge, Mass., 1990).

48. The current trend is to depict Jefferson's victory as a non-event or even counter-revolution against the rights of blacks, Indians, and women. For examples, see Doron Ben-Atar and Barbara B. Oberg, eds., *Federalists Reconsidered* (Charlottesville, 1998); and James Horn, Jan Ellen Lewis, and Peter S. Onuf, eds., *The Revolution of 1800: Democracy, Race, and the New Republic* (Charlottesville, 2002). Separate essays by the present author and Joyce Appleby defended the "Revolution of 1800" concept in the latter volume.

49. This was the conclusion of the "new political history" of the 1960s and 1970s. For overviews, see Paul Kleppner et al., *The Evolution of American Electoral Systems* (Westport, Conn., 1981); Ronald P. Formisano, "Deferential-Participant Politics: The Early Republic's Political Culture, 1789–1840," *American Political Science Review* 68 (1974): 473–87; Ronald P. Formisano, *The Birth of Mass Political Parties: Michigan, 1827–1861* (Princeton, 1971); Ronald P. Formisano, *The Transformation of Political Culture: Massachusetts Parties, 1790s–1840s* (New York, 1983); William E. Gienapp, " 'Politics Seem To Enter into Everything': Political Culture in the North, 1840–1860," in *Essays on American Antebellum Politics, 1840–1860*, ed. Stephen E. Maizlish and John J. Kushma (College Station, Tex., 1982), 14–69; Joel H. Silbey, *The American Political Nation, 1838–1893* (Stanford, 1991), 5–32.

50. Peterson, *Jefferson Image in the American Mind*, 89.

51. Richard P. McCormick, "New Perspectives on Jacksonian Politics," *American Historical Review* 65 (1960): 288–301; J. R. Pole, *Political Representation in England and the Origins of the American Republic* (Berkeley, 1971), 543–64; David Hackett Fischer, *The Revolution of American Conservatism: The Federalist Party in the Era of Jeffersonian Democracy* (New York, 1965), xiv–xv. The Pole data was originally published in a series of articles in the late 1950s and early 1960s.

52. The voting statistics are drawn from official state tallies available on microfilm in the Lampi Collection of Early American Electoral Data, American Antiquarian Society, Worcester, Mass. Turnout rates were calculated by the author based on federal census data and should be considered general estimates only. Since the censuses occurred only once every ten years and did not break down their data in a way that exactly matches the voting population, several calculations had to be performed to arrive at each yearly estimate of adult male population. "Adult" was defined as twenty-one and over.

53. McMurry, *Transforming Rural Life*, 62–99; and Joan M. Jensen, *Loosening the Bonds: Mid-Atlantic Farm Women, 1750–1850* (New Haven, 1986).

54. Philadelphia *Port Folio*, August 22, 1801, March 6, 1802.

55. See the works on celebratory politics cited in note 21 above, along with the following: Susan Branson, *These Fiery Frenchified Dames: Women and Political Culture in Early National Philadelphia* (Philadelphia, 2001); Ronald J. Zboray and Mary Saracino Zboray, "Political News and Female Readership in Antebellum Boston and Its Region," *Journalism History* 22 (1996): 2–14; Elizabeth R. Varon, *We Mean to Be Counted: White Women and Politics in Antebellum Virginia* (Chapel Hill, 1998); Thomas C. Leonard, *News for All: America's Coming-of-Age With the Press* (New York, 1995); and Catherine Allgor, *Parlor Politics: In Which the Ladies of Washington Help Build a City and a Government* (Charlottesville, 2000).

56. See "Rev. John Leland," *The Berkshire Hills* 1 (February 1801): 84–87; and most of the twentieth-century newspaper clippings on the Mammoth Cheese and John Leland in the Local History File, Berkshire Athenaeum, for instance, *Springfield Republican*, April 11, 1943, and *Berkshires Week*, August 30, 1985. More surprising, perhaps, is that the first scholarly piece on the incident, Browne, "Leland and Cheese," committed and fostered the same error. Two female local historians got the story basically right in Ellen M. Raynor and Emma L. Petticlerc, *History of the Town of Cheshire, Berkshire County, Mass.* (Holyoke, Mass., 1885), 85–88.

57. Pittsfield *Sun*, July 12, 1802.

58. For instance, see Ronald P. Formisano, "Federalists and Republicans: Parties, Yes—System, No," in Kleppner et al., *Evolution of American Electoral Systems*, 33–76.

ANDREW W. ROBERTSON

2

Voting Rites and Voting Acts

Electioneering Ritual, 1790–1820

One of the benefits of recent scholarship in the early republic has been a more profound understanding of political celebrations and festivals. With the exception of Alan Taylor and David Waldstreicher, and, in a later period, Mary Ryan and Jean Baker, historians have not paid explicit attention to electioneering rituals themselves.[1] In the 1950s and 1960s, historians described polling rituals metamorphosing from "deferential" politicking to a full-fledged "party system" by 1800.[2] In the late 1970s, Ronald Formisano coined the term "deferential-participant" political culture for this era.[3] Since then, historians have not really considered the ways in which "deferential" political rituals gave way to, or paved the way for, the mass-based politics that followed. This is particularly important, since we have solid empirical evidence indicating that between 1808 and 1814 upwards of 70 percent of all adult males in Pennsylvania and New Hampshire and all adult white males in North Carolina were voting.[4] Perhaps this is the time to look beyond Formisano's intriguing formulation and think about how the elements of "deference" and "participation" clashed and blended to form a unique political culture in the early republic.

In his consideration of deference in a democratic society, J. R. Pole wondered how we might explain "the paradox of popular consent to a scheme of government which systematically excluded the common people from the more responsible positions of political power."[5] Pole and Formisano understood that deference and popular participation were paradoxically linked together in the early republic. Pole observed that deference does not seem "a very secure cement to the union of social orders. Yet to those who live under its sway, it can be almost irresistible."[6] Why was this "irresistible" force so closely linked to a pattern of political behavior that would seemingly ensure its destruction? Perhaps it was because deferential political rituals by their very nature often enabled and sometimes encouraged the imaginary exercise of power by those who were marginalized in the community. This may explain why in the early republic, participant forms of electioneering frequently overlaid, exploited, and extended deferential forms of voting rituals.

In this essay, I propose to sketch out the layering of ritual behavior that occurred in early republican politicking. Understanding the interaction between ritual, rhetoric, and voting gives us the key to understanding why so many Americans in the early republic sought to participate in some form of politics. To describe this interaction I have concentrated on two states: Virginia, which preserved many aspects of a "deferential" political culture well into the nineteenth century; and Pennsylvania, which seemingly led the way toward organized mass partisanship. In fact, these distinctions between "old" and "new" political cultures generate as much confusion as clarity. In Virginia and Pennsylvania, as elsewhere during this period, mass politicking used both traditional and innovative rhetoric and practices to enlist the audience.

What was "deferential" about early republican electioneering? Perhaps J. G. A. Pocock in "The Classical Theory of Deference" has offered the clearest definition of political deference in the eighteenth century.[7] Pocock adopted his definition of eighteenth-century deference from the work of seventeenth-century English radical James Harrington, in the *Oceana*. According to Pocock, eighteenth-century politicians and voters had accepted Harrington's notion that the polity was divided between those who exercised a "deliberative" function and those who exercised a "verdictive" function. According to Harrington, these functions required very different orders of time and preparation, but they were equally important. The deliberative function was the prerogative of the few, in the legislature and in the law. Those with sufficient property, education, and leisure had the opportunity to debate important questions of policy as representatives of the many. This larger group exercised a likewise critical function, to render a verdict on aspiring members of the elite who would best represent the interest of the community.[8] The verdictive function of the electorate was analogous, and equal in importance to, the role of the jury in a court trial. Deferential electioneering ritual marked the intersection between the many and the few, the verdictive and the deliberative sections of the polity.

In the American colonies and the early years of the republic, the rulers accepted the verdictive function of the ruled insofar as the criterion for judgment was the character of men, not the substance of measures.[9] In the view of elites, ordinary voters did not have the intellectual capacity—and thus should not attempt—to exercise prospective power over policy; however, they could exercise the moral judgment inherent in all men to rule retrospectively on a candidate's character. In 1811, "AN OLD VIRGINIA PLANTER AND FARMER" provided a summary of the criteria that deferential electioneering rituals sought to promote in candidates for office. Membership in the propertied patriarchal order was required. Beyond that, voters should ask: "Is he honest? Is he free from addiction to drunkenness and gaming, and vice and immorality? If not, reject him. . . . Is he an honest, sober, industrious, humane moral intelligent planter or farmer with a wife and children?—Embrace him, vote for him, 'grapple him to your bosoms with hooks of steel.'"[10]

Particularly in Virginia, being a "planter or farmer with a wife and children" was important: a man of the soil with a freehold and a family offered the strongest pledges that he would represent the community to the best of his ability, since his life and livelihood were at stake. As James Barbour wrote in an 1805 letter to his Virginia constituents, a tiller of the soil would not make a profession of "flying false colors" and engaging in "sophistry" as would a "practising [sic] Lawyer." Electing a "Doctor of Physic" would do "injury to the neighborhood" by sending a doctor beyond the boundaries of his community. Barbour offered his family and property as hostages to his conduct: "I am a father, I am a husband, these are the pledges of citizenship I tender—& if so melancholy an occurrence should happen in my life I should forget what was due my conscience, my character, and my country, these ties are guarantees to your safety."[11]

Finally, deferential political culture emphasized not only a candidate's own character, but also his family's status and his ties to a particular community. Without the support of a party structure, only a man of some means could take on the considerable expense of campaigning among his neighbors at election time, and only a man of social prominence would have enough recognition to be elected. By recruiting candidates among the families long settled in the community, the process insured that any likely contender would be a known quantity: the candidate's bloodlines might be as important a topic of public discussion as the pedigree of a racehorse.[12]

But how were voters to judge *among* members of the propertied elite? How were they to determine which candidates had the moral and personal qualities—including courage, frugality, honesty, temperance, learning, and wit—necessary to represent the community's interests? Deferential electioneering as practiced into the early nineteenth century in both Virginia and Pennsylvania had two key elements. Candidates "spouted," or made literate and decorous speeches designed to impress the lower orders with their knowledge.[13] Such speeches were intended to soothe the voters, while steering away from any discussion of policy. At the same time, candidates "courted" voters, wooing them with elaborate flattery delivered either in person or in letters published in newspapers. At election time, such courtship must have appeared as a departure from the "condescension" that eighteenth-century gentlemen typically displayed in mixing among the common people. Taylor describes this as "a certain affability carefully modulated between reserve and familiarity."[14]

The rituals of "spouting" and "courting" highlight the Janus-faced nature of deference in the early republic. When listening to candidates "spout," voters paid overt deference to their social superiors. At the same time, would-be representatives practiced inverted deference when they "courted" their masters, the freeholders.[15] The very word "courting" draws a parallel between electioneering ritual and another ritual involving transposed deference. In patriarchal societies, courtship involves an extended display of flattery, humility, and protestations of worthy conduct on the part of the suitor, who will, if successful, exercise considerable authority over his intended. In colonial America, for example, husbands had the right to wield complete authority over their wives' property by virtue of the laws of coverture.[16] In such a society, a woman and her family have only the determinative power of refusal. If she would marry wisely, a woman must confer her consent on a worthy suitor. The greater the authority the suitor will exercise after the wedding ceremony, the greater his need to persuade his intended bride by an elaborate display of words and gestures that he will worthily exercise that authority. A similar dynamic applied in eighteenth-century politics: the greater the authority a candidate might wield after being elected, the more he had to flatter and cajole the freeholders.[17]

In Virginia such flattery occurred primarily during oral speeches and voice voting. In Pennsylvania in the 1780s and 1790s, candidates conducted their electioneering through printed letters and written ballots. Print politics involved its own form of role reversal. Before the polling, a candidate for election might publish a letter in the newspaper that would "respectfully request," "beseech," "entreat," or "beg" the constituents to vote for him. Such letters were signed by the candidate himself or by his "friends," who might go on to praise the candidate for his "honesty," "independence," "integrity," and "fidelity."[18] A letter often concluded with the candidate offering something similar to this ornamental closing of Arthur Lee, a candidate for Congress in Tidewater Virginia, in 1788: "I have the Honour to be, with the greatest Respect, GENTLEMEN, Your most obedient Servant."[19]

In the words of "Wou'dbe" a character in Robert Munford's 1770 play *The Candidates*, a contestant had to "cajole, fawn, wheedle" the electioneering audience.[20] The object was to please everyone and promise little in the way of specifics.[21] Lee, the Virginia candidate, said coyly, "It may be permitted me to hope, that I, in some Measure, merit the Confidence of my Country, both as to Discernment of what is useful to the Public, and [the] Integrity to pursue it."[22] Or, as one Pennsylvania Republican candidate declared as late as 1796, "I do not mean to make a parade of what I will do."[23]

If deferential electioneering partook of both conventional and inverted deference, it also marked the convergence of two very different kinds of public behavior—what Susan Davis has called "elite spectacle" and lower orders' "festivity."[24] In elite spectacle, events such as street processions or highly ornamental orations took place in an orderly or regimented fashion. Such spectacles reinforced the idea of hierarchy and elite rule. "Festivity," on the other hand, was usually a spontaneous public display, erratic, disorderly, and sometimes violent, that gave vent to potent popular sentiment. Before and during polling days, while candidates engaged in elaborate speechmaking and flattery of assembled voters, audiences were permitted, and sometimes even encouraged, to mock candidates. In both Pennsylvania and Virginia, deferential electioneering summoned the power of the audience to help determine the fittest representative.

As Wou'dbe observed, candidates were always "subject to the humours of a fickle crowd."[25] Polling rituals made broad allowances for merriment and dissipation, and sometimes even melee . . . and riot. Close contests might generate insults, intimidation, and brawling. A candidate's "friends" might verbally or even physically assault an opponent's supporters or even the opposing candidate. While most of the candidates escaped this fate by what Wou'dbe called "practising the grimace and compliments" among the freeholders, candidates still risked reputation and livelihood because the crowd exercised the real power of ridicule.[26]

The crowd played its role in a Darwinian process of selecting among contending elites. Although only white male property holders exercised formal voting power, candidates also faced unpropertied white men, women, children, free blacks, and convicts. Such crowds intermittently exercised influence through their "rough play" on polling days. Perhaps because of his hotheaded temperament, haughty demeanor, high-pitched voice, and flair for dramatic oratory, John Randolph of Roanoke seemed to invite such behavior.[27] At a Buckingham County gathering in 1811 a "dense throng gathered around" as Randolph "mounted the hustings." On the outskirts of this assemblage "there hung a lowering and sullen crowd that evidently meditated insult or violence at the first opportunity."[28] In 1813, Randolph reported that "a notorious villain" named Tom Logwood, earlier convicted of forgery, "undertook to speak to me impertinently" while Randolph was making a speech. Logwood had been seen "laughing, talking, and drinking" with Randolph's opponent, John W. Eppes. Randolph was not easily intimidated, however. "The scoundrel was obliged to take to his heels and make his escape home," reported Randolph indignantly, "or he would have been beaten to a jelly."[29]

In both their displays of inverted deference and their general rowdiness, polling days had much in common with inversion festivals in early modern Europe: the hierarchical order was symbolically overturned for a day and then reaffirmed. In the festival of carnival, for example, the "king" and "queen" of "mis-Rule" emanated from the lower orders to exert their sway over their "courtiers," often including the social elite. The license of carnival was followed by the peaceful restoration of the social order.[30] Something similar occurred in eighteenth-century Virginia. After much ridicule of the candidates, extended drinking, and a few threats of brawling in the last act of *The Candidates*, Captain Paunch announces, "We have done as we ought, we have elected the ablest," and all assembled freeholders shout huzzas for candidates "Wou'dbe and Worthy!"[31]

Nevertheless, as Natalie Davis notes, such role reversal, whether in "an Ashanti ceremony, a Christian sect, or a teenage street gang," may actually loosen "the rigors of a structured society."[32] Inversion festivals, she argues, can give those with the least power momentary access to "a second reality" removed "from power and the state but still public and perennial."[33] In Davis's view, some rituals of role reversal "do not merely reinforce the 'serious' institutions of society, they may work to alter them."[34] Historians have already applied this insight to one important American example of the powerless burlesquing the exercise of power: the "Negro Elections" held by African American communities in New England from colonial times until the eve of the Civil War. During these events, a slave or free person of color was proclaimed "king" or "governor" in a real election procedure, often limited to blacks that mirrored the official election rituals.[35] Recent scholarship has viewed these rituals as evolving toward an affirmative public political role for African Americans.[36] In Newport, Rhode

Island, Portsmouth, New Hampshire, and Hartford, Connecticut, the African American "Governor" rendered judgments on important disputes involving African Americans and meted out punishments. The election of black governors survived in Hartford until 1820 and "Negro Election" rituals survived elsewhere until the 1850s.[37]

Role reversal in actual elections also offered the lower orders momentary access to a "second reality." In the "practise of grimace and compliments" extended by their social betters, voters and onlookers could easily envision a world in which ordinary people mattered. Thus, deferential electioneering ritual, with its "courtship" of the voters and incorporation of the marginalized, paved the way for an extended mass-based participatory politics. This explains why many election rituals that arose in the fiercely competitive, partisan politics of the Jeffersonian era imbibed so heavily from earlier deferential practices. This new participant politics soon included unpropertied white males, and offered a vision of an even more extended participatory politics in the future.

Nevertheless, in the deferential political culture of the 1780s and 1790s, both the formal and informal powers of the ruled proved evanescent. In Virginia, where polling was conducted by voice vote, voters felt themselves vulnerable to pressure. Until the early 1790s, in both Virginia and Pennsylvania, elections were often lightly contested, and both voters and audience lost some of their political leverage. And even in a competitive election, crowd action, if it got "out of hand," could be reined in by force. In any event, the crowd lost its informal power once voters exercised their verdictive power and cast their votes.

In the end, polling ritual was designed to exert coercion toward local consensus and to favor the restoration of the status quo once the polling days were over. "Spouting" and "courting" made freeholders feel that they were a valued part of the community. Electioneering "festivity" gave the audience as a whole some license to vent their antagonisms against their betters without seriously disrupting the locality. Oral politics enlisted voters and nonvoters to attend the polling rituals, but because the elite sometimes closely monitored these actions, those in attendance often felt subtle or unsubtle pressure to sustain the existing order. At the conclusion of the poll, moreover, calm was usually successfully restored and the vestiges of community "consensus" reappeared. These electioneering rituals thus set out to confer upon a favored candidate the imprimatur of the community.

This winnowing process of electioneering, in which the "best" member of the elite was selected to represent a community, served neither the aggregate interests of the voters nor any single elite individual's interest. Rather, it served the propertied interest of the community. It encouraged temporary social upheaval in the name of consolidating the power of established interests. The point of this unruly selection method was to obtain a representative with long-standing personal ties to the community who was predictable in conduct, persuasive in speech, and nimble in wit.

While these practices continued in both Virginia and Pennsylvania until the 1820s, a new set of consonant electioneering practices appeared, often "under the radar" of contemporaries and many later scholars. One of the reasons we have not fully understood the political culture of the early republic is because we have not seen how "deferential" practices often combined with, and paved the way for, democratic politics. Participatory politics did not immediately supplant deferential electioneering: rather competitive, partisan, mass-based politics both exploited the old rituals and created new ones to form a more durable sense of party in the electorate.

The best example of an emerging political culture constructed in part on the persistence of old forms derives from a very famous example of "deferential" Virginia politics. This example of polling ritual comes to us from George Wythe Munford, who recounted experiences in Virginia politics from the end of the eighteenth century to the antebellum era, including the 1799 congressional contest between Federalist John Marshall and Republican John Clopton. Charles Sydnor and, more recently, Daniel Jordan have quoted extensively from Munford's account of this election, describing the ritual as a sterling example of deferential electioneering. If we look beyond Sydnor's and Jordan's narrative interpretations to the original source, however, we also see the emergence of new practices and an entirely different range of concerns initiated by the voters.[38]

Let us first consider the Sydnor-Jordan narrative. These two eminent Virginia historians note the "liquor in abundance," the "shoutings and hurrahs" and the "knock-down and drag-out" affrays that attended the polling.[39] The polling itself was being conducted in the presence of both Marshall and Clopton by the Henrico County sheriff.

> "Mr. Blair," said the sheriff, "who do you vote for?" "John Marshall," said he. Mr. Marshall replied, "your vote is appreciated, Mr. Blair." . . . "Who do you vote for, Mr. Buchanan?" "For John Clopton," said the good man. Mr. Clopton said, "Mr. Buchanan, I shall treasure that vote in my memory. It will be regarded as a feather in my cap for ever." The shouts were astounding. Hurrah for Marshall! Hurrah for Clopton![40]

In this oft-quoted example, both Marshall and Clopton exercised the obsequious flattery toward voters that was characteristic of "deferential" electioneering. Yet if we examine the latter portion of Munford's original account, a very different picture emerges. The parties, their leaders, and their "business committees" had become the prime agents in scripting election behavior. Every living voter, even if barely breathing, was pressed into service: "It was believed the contest would be very close. The parties were drilled to move together in a body; and the leaders and their business committees were never surpassed in activity and systematic arrangement for bringing out every voter. Sick men were taken in their beds to the polls; the halt, the lame and the blind, were hunted up, and every mode of conveyance was mustered into service."[41] Parties "drilled" their members for this election, mustering them out of their sickbeds for this closely contested vote.[42]

Moreover, Munford's account suggests that issues began to rival character as the most salient feature of an election contest. As Munford wrote, the success or defeat of each candidate in the portentous year of 1799 involved what each party believed was "the wellbeing and future prosperity of the country." This was a time of war hysteria against the French. It marked the peak of Federalist popularity in Virginia, partly because of President John Adams's popularity in the Quasi-War with France, and partly because of anti-Jacobinism fanned by the Federalist press. In this example we see how Virginia electioneering ritual remained consistent to its deferential form, even as an entirely new focus—the future of the country—motivated the sick, the halt, the lame, and the blind to turn out on polling day. Divergent ideological and partisan concerns, of Anglomanes and Gallomanes, had seized the imaginations of the voters, taking precedence over community interest, in these highly competitive congressional elections.

Another example of old forms and new practices occurred in Martinsburg, Berkeley County, Virginia (in what is now West Virginia), in 1808. The Republicans held a meeting in which they extolled their candidate for Congress in the old style: "That the Honorable *John Morrow*, our present representative, in consideration of his sound moral and political principles, and undeviating conduct, his intelligence, firm patriotism, long tried and faithful services, is justly entitled to our fullest approbation; and we do therefore, nominate him accordingly."[43] The Martinsburg Republicans then resolved, however, to select "a *Committee of Vigilance*" with the responsibility to "enjoin" their fellow citizens not to "imbibe ill-founded prejudices" or "erroneous impressions" about public measures.[44] This was clearly an attempt to promote policy-based campaigning and organize the party at the polls.

New forms and old practices also coexisted in Augusta County, Virginia, in 1811. Augusta County was in the Shenandoah Valley, and tended to be politically competitive throughout the first decades of the nineteenth century. In a county history, Joseph Waddell describes electioneering in 1811.

Party spirit ran high in those days. [Jacob] Swoope was the leader of the Federalists, and Judge Stuart of the Republicans. Both parties had balls in Staunton, to which their adherents in the county were invited, with their wives and children. Each also had street processions, headed by its chief. Mr. Swoope's competitor, when he was elected, was Daniel Smith, then a young lawyer in Rockingham. Swoope could speak German, while Smith could not, and the German people of the district generally voted for the former.[45]

The fact that candidate Swoope and Judge Stuart held balls for their partisans seems like a continuation of the old form of treating. The fact that wives and children were explicitly invited is another indication of an older form of electioneering ritual, where nonparticipants were enlisted as spectators. At the same time, the reference to street processions indicates that newer forms of partisanship were combined with the old forms of electioneering festivities. The Republican candidate, Jacob Swoope, also addressed the voters in German, an indication of the emergence of competitive ethnic politics.

Thanks to data now available from the First Democracy Project, we know that Virginia was not a placid one-party state from 1795 to 1799, but a hotbed of partisan competition in congressional races. In some areas like the Shenandoah Valley, such competition lasted into the first sixteen years of the nineteenth century. Between 1800 and 1816, national concerns, often cleverly linked to narrower geographical, economic, and religious interests, proved a durable motivating force to mobilize a mass electorate.

During this period, the wooing of divergent economic, geographic, and religious interests became an end in itself. Only a few years earlier, such blatant "pledging" by candidates to particular policies or interests had been roundly condemned as political corruption. Being a "slave to party" had once been among the most damning charges made by candidates who wrapped themselves in the mantle of anti-partisanship. In Richmond by 1808, however, party had not only achieved legitimacy, it had achieved dignity (at least among Republicans). As the Republican *Argus* noted, "the disproportion between" the Republicans and the Federalists "is so excessive that the latter scarcely claim the dignified appellation of a *party*."[46]

Deferential politicking made local elite interest its principal public concern, but it enforced a consensual representation of this "interest." Participant electioneering made use of the newfound concern with "interest*s*" and exploited local rivalries and conflicts to a partisan advantage. One Richmond Republican editorial even sought to win over local Federalists in 1808, by arguing that they would be better off if their "local interest*s*" were effectively represented. "FEDER-

ALISTS! Consider the *local interests* of this city and the importance of having in the Legislature a representative *well qualified* to *advocate*, as well as *zealous* to promote them."[47]

If the purpose of the deferential electioneering process was to obtain an effective, reliable representative for a locality's propertied interest, the purpose of partisan electioneering was to maximize votes for the party by aggrandizing diverse economic, religious, and ethnic interests. What was true in Virginia was even more evident further north. In many states, participant political culture emerged from strenuous party competition. The Republicans and then the Federalists struggled to gain the maximum number of votes against their partisan opponents.[48]

The transformation of electioneering reflects a larger transformation of American political identity that occurred in the late 1790s. In the middle of that decade, what had been a factional struggle among the national elite in Philadelphia became a full-fledged party struggle, first in Congress and then at the state level. Party competition in Congress begot the mobilization of a mass electorate. Before the 1790s were over, the partisan contagion had spread to the masses, first to propertied and then to unpropertied white males. The property restrictions on suffrage were only the first to come under attack. The lifting of suffrage restrictions eventually spilled over beyond race and gender boundaries to include many free blacks in the North and propertied female heads-of-household in New Jersey. Both parties came to support elimination of some suffrage restrictions, first in the West and some Middle States, then in New England and the South.

The principal vehicle for conveying the rhetoric and practice of mass partisanship was a growing network of newspapers and an expanding republic of letters.[49] Newspaper editors, party organizers, letter correspondents, the expanding postal system, and a growing readership were creating a newer and more abstract sense of community by means of the printed word.[50] Where the deferential political culture relied on personal relationships set within a localized, physical community, the participant political culture was sustained by a print community based on abstract relationships—ideology, interest, and common affiliation—among individuals. In New England and the Middle States, the web of relationships between editors, correspondents and readers grew and thickened.[51] The editors of these newspapers corresponded with one another, copied one another, praised and attacked one another and formed alliances with the postmasters. The parties had only begun to develop a permanent organizational base. This print community, however, "embodied partisanship" and allowed partisans to speak of and treat the parties as real things worthy of loyalty or opposition.

Printed forms of information generated a different sense of identification on the part of the readers—with parties rather than with personalities. Newspapers, party broadsides, and other printed communications provided an independent arena for posting information about political assemblies, mobilization efforts, and issues. Print provided the means for political reflection on the part of the individual and coherence on the part of the group. An individual, reading at leisure and in solitude, could form his opinion with more independence from his superiors and with less pressure or distraction from his peers.

In Pennsylvania, and especially in Philadelphia, Federalists and Republicans initially viewed electioneering in different ways. In the late 1790s, Republicans embraced a larger role for the people than mere passive acquiescence in politics. After 1800, Federalists also gradually accustomed themselves to the idea of appealing to an ever-larger audience of "the people."[52] "WE hail" said the Federalist *United States Gazette*, the "animating proof that *the People* are beginning to think for themselves."[53] Many Federalists, however, continued to maintain the distinction between rulers and ruled. As the *United States Gazette* proclaimed, "Let the people, by a free exercise of their elective franchise, designate their rulers."[54]

Gradually, however, both Republicans and Federalists evolved a different set of electioneering rituals. Participant electioneering served the party's interest rather than the propertied interest of a particular local constituency. Maximizing votes for the party meant assembling and mobilizing an amalgam of diverse interests rather than creating, shaping, or coercing a community consensus around a single dominant interest. Candidates in urban areas in the 1790s began for the first time to speak of their constituents' interests, in the plural rather than in the singular. Participant electioneering promoted the differentiation of local interests, in economic, geographic, religious, and ethnic terms.

Beginning in the 1790s in the urban North, newspapers increasingly came to identify and court specific interests for their respective parties. In the less heterogeneous West and later in the South, these appeals often spoke explicitly to geographic interest. In Philadelphia, on the other hand, Republican newspapers were especially skillful in targeting local religious and ethnic communities. By 1800, moreover, these religious and ethnic groups were not only being targeted, they were being organized, drilled, mustered, and mobilized in their neighborhoods on election day. For example, in 1808 the Philadelphia *Aurora* printed appeals "To the People Called Quakers," "To the Society Called Methodists," "TO THE IRISH CATHOLICS," and, characteristically, to "ALIENS who are desirous of becoming citizens and are friendly to the election of James Madison." The last of these was a notice to aliens indicating when and where they should appear to secure their citizenship and instructing them on how to vote for the Republican slate of presidential electors.[55]

In those cases where participant electioneering did not target economic, religious, and ethnic minority communities specifically, Republicans constructed a resonant identity for their adherents that would lend legitimacy to their partisan endeavors. Republicans often attempted to link their electioneering rites with the principles of the American Revolution and to equate Federalism with "toryism." In ritual and in rhetoric, newspapers of both parties used an enduring Atlantic oppositional identity to mobilize their voters: Federalists thus became "Tories" and Republicans became "Jacobins," long after these terms shed their substantive meaning in the American political context.

In one typical example from 1808, the Virginia *Argus* called upon "Whigs" (i.e., Republicans) to rally to the polls by linking their Federalist opponents to the Tories of the Revolution. "Exert yourselves, therefore, like true Republicans and Patriots. . . . Let the triumph of *Whiggism* be complete and let the *Tories* hide their faces in confusion."[56] The Federalists, like the Loyalists, were "treacherous" and would betray the people's interest in the election as the Loyalists had betrayed the people's interest in the Revolution. "The proponents of whig triumph have driven the tories to desperation—their *old tricks* and many *new tricks*, have been already played off—they are now endeavoring *to prevent any election in this city*, preferring anarchy to submission to the will of the majority," said the Philadelphia *Aurora*. "The struggle is, as during the revolution, for liberty and independence. Will you become virtually the colonies of Great Britain again?" The *Aurora* also appealed to the naturalized voters, who, like native-born Americans, were addressed as "Whigs." "Are you *Americans, foreigners*, whigs, you who are so will give . . . the WHOLE democratic ticket, your suffrage."[57]

Participatory rituals often imitated the practices of deferential politics. One favorite persuasive practice of the urban elite in the 1780s had been orchestrating public spectacles such as the Grand Federal Processions that took place in Boston, New York, Philadelphia, Baltimore, and Charleston. On these occasions, members of the crafts as well as the bar, the bench and the clergy paraded to demonstrate their unity in support of the Constitution. These public spectacles supported hierarchy and the social order. Each profession, craft, and fraternal order had its place within an orderly procession, and as in the case of the Grand Federal Processions, the intention of the spectacles was to persuade the entire community to stand in unity behind essentially conservative positions. While the old deferential spectacles stressed unity, new participant festivities used the form of street processions, but the organizers emphasized the distinctiveness of each craft's interests as they played up social and economic conflict. In "CORD-WAINERS ATTENTION!" the *Aurora* drew distinctions between the "whiggish" behavior of the crafts and the "toryish" behavior of the lawyers and judges. "All the free and patriotic journeymen shoemakers in the city and county of Philadelphia—all who are averse to the reign of terror established by our tory councils—all who recollect the fines and imprisonment of the *craft* by tory judges and tory juries for asserting the rights of freemen—preventing a repetition of such conduct are expected to attend and *shew* themselves to be the friends of liberty and independence."[58]

If the Republicans linked their opponents in rhetoric and ritual to anti-republican Tories, the Federalists linked their opponents to the French "Jac-obins," thus creating an odious anti-religious association with "Gallic" Republi-cans. The *Gazette of the United States* phrased it thus in the election of 1800, to mobilize their voters before the crucial Pennsylvania congressional elections: "The Question will be seriously and strenuously made, whether the experiment of a federative republic, under religious, moral, and steadfast politicians, tracing the high road to order, dignity, glory, and independence, is still to be essayed; or whether we be willing to submit to the Gallic domination of an acknowledged Deist, and barter away our birthright for worse than a mess of pottage, for the delusive possibilities of French Jacobin amity." This "Jacobin faction," said the *Gazette*, were practitioners of "popular artifice, servile to France, foes to order, greedy of dishonest gain," who were anxious to live, "not only without govern-ment, but . . . '*without* GOD IN THE WORLD.' "

In the rituals of partisanship that followed, the opposing parties held for each other the invidious role that the British king had held in constructions of na-tional identity during the Revolutionary era and that the French had held before the Revolution in colonists' construction of Britishness.[59] The energy devoted to these antagonistic rites suggests that many ordinary Americans cared deeply about the differing versions of national identity offered by the two opposing parties. In an ironic editorial entitled "WONDERFUL PHENOMENA!" the Phila-delphia *Aurora* satirized the Federalists' propensity for party nicknames and the inconsistency in positions that the party had managed to adopt. "In America during a few years past," said the *Aurora*, the world has seen "*Federalists* labouring to dissolve the confederacy of the states! *Federal republicans* openly advocating monarchy! *Washingtonians* speaking and acting directly contrary to the principles of Washington!" The *Aurora* accused the Federalists, professedly fearful of the Republican "mob," of sponsoring mob behavior of their own. The "*Friends of order*" were "parading the streets . . . like quarrelsome boys with chips on their shoulders." Philadelphia had seen "*Friends of the people*, bestowing on the body of

American citizens the nouns of 'mob' and 'rabble.' " The city had witnessed
" '*Friends of the government*' reviling and abusing the constitutional authorities and
opposing every measure of government. *Preservers of the country openly* advocating
its foreign reveries, and abetting the domestic disturbers of its peace!" On the
other hand, said the *Aurora*, "*Jacobins* and disorganizers" were "rallying round the
government, ready to defend it, against the 'friends of government.' Surely this is
an age of wonders!"[60]

While Pennsylvania elections had once combined elite spectacle and the
lower order's festivities, participant rituals gradually evolved into festivities open
to all social strata: scions of the Federalist upper class, on the one hand, and
Republican journeymen on the other.

The partisan press fanned the excitement of political "festivity." By attempting to replicate in print the enthusiasm, the hortatory language, and the very
spontaneity of street politics, it constructed a kind of *virtual* politics "out of
doors." *Actual* politics "out of doors" nevertheless remained a staple of partisan
electioneering. By enlisting the energies of young white males in public meetings and militia formations, ritual became a bonding experience. Young Federalists and young Republicans each drilled, drank, and "serenaded" their fellows,
and on many occasions brawled or "battled" with their partisan opponents.
Albrecht Koschnik has described the palpable anxieties that attended young
Federalists in early manhood.[61] The fraternal organizations of both Federalists
and Republicans may have served to palliate the real anxieties that attended the
life of journeymen Republicans or status-anxious elite Federalists.[62]

Particularly in working-class neighborhoods, the Republicans adopted a mili-
tary form of organization for their young men affiliates at election time.[63] In
Philadelphia, one appeal in 1808 addressed to partisans in the workingmen's
Northern Liberties precincts, the "DEMOCRATIC committee of vigilance of the
Northern Liberties are requested to meet at the Cock and Lion, THIS DAY, the
third of October, at 7 o'clock." In the same issue the First Light Infantry was
called upon in the Aurora to "TAKE NOTICE, to attend a parade of the corps, THIS
DAY, the 3d of October, in clean and complete uniform, precisely at 1 o'clock at
the State House Yard, furnished with 15 rounds of blank cartridges."[64] The
committees of vigilance and the military guard must have had the intended
effect. The day after the balloting the *Aurora* crowed that "the election has been
conducted without a single broil or riot of any kind." "The *whigs* had been
very injuriously menaced the day before; but we are happy to say the menace
was all."[65]

The threat of Federalist mobbing worked well to mobilize Republican workingmen. The *Aurora* urged their readers to be on their guard. In an "Address of

the Committee of Correspondence of the 'Association of Democratic Young Men of Philadelphia' TO THEIR FELLOW CITIZENS," the young men asked,

> For whom will you vote, for our country, or for its enemies? Now or never my boys. To-morrow will crown you with laurels, or cover you with disgrace. . . . Beware of *traitors* and *apostates* among yourselves. There are some wolves in sheep's clothing—detect and scorn them. . . . Be not easily irritated—they will seek to make quarrels, and to cast the blame on you—hear and forbear—the man of true courage never fights but when justice and necessity requires it— your duty to-morrow is not to fight—but when your country calls, you will be as ready to fight as to vote in support of your rights—do not therefore suffer yourselves to be irritated—*foul words break no bones*—keep from violence—let not the sacred right of suffrage be made a matter of pastime for the enemies of our rights.[66]

Partisan clubs with exotic names became part of young men's urban affiliation. In 1808, the Republican young men of Philadelphia broke into factions as exotic sounding as the politics of a United Nations conference in the twenty-first century. One Northern Liberties poll near Philadelphia reported a clash between "Jacobins," "Arabs," and "democrats." As soon as the poll declaration was made, "the *Jacobin leaders* shouted like savages having scalped women and children."[67]

As these examples suggest, participant electioneering employed crowds, just as deferential electioneering had. Deferential electioneering had co-opted crowd action to ratify its Darwinian selection process. Participant electioneering relied on mass mobilization and military discipline to instill and sustain party victories. Participant electioneering exploited economic and ethnic diversity, and stimulated crowd action, not only among the lower orders but among the elite as well. The coercive consensus of the deferential order with its encouragement of "festival" behavior paved the way for participant "rough play" carried out as class skirmishing.

Deferential inversion rituals, with their fawning flattery of the lower orders, gave way to fierce attacks by the effete few on the vulgar many. The lower orders were particular targets of Philadelphia Federalist antagonism in electioneering. "AMERICANUS" complained that "On the day of the election . . . every kennel [and] every Hovel, the habitations of those creatures of filth was well ransacked, and vehicles [were] prepared at a place of general rendezvous to convey them to the election."[68]

Republicans as well as Federalists understood the attendant problems of mass mobilization and political discipline. Unlike deferential electioneering rituals, with their rigid distinctions between the few and the many, participant mobilization generated no inherent class, race, or gender boundaries. There was no clear line of demarcation in a politically mobilized society that delimited the full extent of democratization, as if to say, "Thus far shall you extend deliberation and no further."

The electioneering rituals of the deferential order had offered those at the margins and in the lower orders of the community the idea that their appearance at electioneering ritual mattered: they had the power of mockery, even if they could not vote. The ordinary inhabitants of the community, even those furthest from power, were flattered by the attention paid to them by the candidates in the rough and tumble play at the polls. Nevertheless, their moment of power was fleeting in the polling ritual, and as in all inversion rituals, the temporary overthrow of the ruling hierarchy preceded its inevitable restoration.

As the new and fiercely competitive rituals of partisan politics replaced deferential electioneering, the old forms of communitarian coercion dropped away. The established hierarchy had less opportunity to intimidate voters directly when ticket voting replaced voice voting. Adult white male voters thus gained autonomy, and this autonomy is reflected in the voting data.

Sustained party competition promoted mass mobilization in Pennsylvania and the elimination of property requirements. Pennsylvania turnout figures from the First Democracy Project show the effect of vigorous party competition, press proliferation, and mass mobilization. Gubernatorial elections, conducted across the state and held every three years in Pennsylvania, convey the dramatic change in levels of participation. In 1790, 31 percent of free adult males voted in Pennsylvania for governor; by 1799 the turnout level had risen to 56 percent of free white males. In the 1808 election, 70 percent of adult males voted, a level not surpassed until after 1840. As late as 1817, turnout for governor was 61 percent and in 1821 and 1824 it stood at roughly 64 percent of adult males.[69] While turnout levels fluctuated in Pennsylvania in the first two decades of the nineteenth century, two-party contests for governor brought more than half of the men over twenty-one to the polling places. Statewide results understate the dramatic surge in voter turnout among free adult males. The effect of these partisan practices was palpable on the audience and measurable in the results.

Even in Virginia, where slavery, racial restrictions on free black suffrage, and property restrictions on poor whites remained in force, party competition and contested elections generated higher turnout in the late 1790s than Virginia would see again until the 1830s. As J. R. Pole has pointed out, suffrage in Virginia "was often exercised by persons to whom it did not belong as a right under the law."[70] In 1797, when Federalists contested seventeen of nineteen congressional seats, turnout averaged 26 percent of adult white males in those contested seats. In 1799 the turnout measured 27 percent. With the exception of the presidential race of 1800, also competitive in Virginia, turnout never again rose as high as 20 percent until the election of 1828.[71]

If we look below the state level, however, a somewhat different pattern emerges in the voting data. Augusta County, Virginia, was in the congressional district of Jacob Swoope, the German-speaking Federalist, in the Shenandoah Valley. This congressional district remained highly competitive from 1797 to 1825, and the turnout figures from this heterogeneous county bear witness to the stimulative effect of new electioneering techniques—such as targeting the Shenandoah Germans—along with retention of the old electioneering rituals— such as holding balls in Staunton for loyal voters and their families. In 1797 turnout in Augusta County measured 21.8 percent of all white males over twenty-one years of age. By 1799, when the statewide turnout in Virginia reached its peak, Augusta County turnout in the congressional election reached 28.0 percent. Yet even as statewide turnout continued to decline elsewhere in Virginia throughout the next two decades, in Augusta County, turnout reached 32.3 percent of all adult white males in the 1803 congressional election, 38.5 percent in 1809, 34.4 percent in 1811, 32.1 percent in 1813, and 36.5 percent as late as 1815.[72] Other counties in the Shenandoah Valley which had strenuous two-party competition tell the same story, and even some counties south of the James River where congressional seats were contested (e.g., Brunswick County) saw voter turnout hovering around 30 percent of all adult white males.[73] All this indicates the importance of carefully examining voting data at the local level.

High turnout did not occur without careful preparation. As George Wythe Munford testified in the election of 1799, "the parties were drilled to move together in a body."[74] Participant electioneering thus required military precision in its ritual, not only because of the bonding effect of drilling and marching. Perhaps more important, military discipline imposed a rigorous order on the anarchic force of imagined affiliation. In an age of mass mobilization, the relationship between rhetoric and ritual decisively changed. Language, more than ritual, worked to align the hearts and minds of the audience. Ritual, on the other hand, while indispensable to mass politics, might get "out of hand" if not subjected to rigorous regimentation.

If print rhetoric promoted a sense of "virtual" political identity, electioneering ritual ratified "actual" identity. Although ritual increasingly took its cues from print, ritual also had its role in affirming new forms of mass politics. Electioneering ritual adapted familiar practices to serve new purposes. The role reversal practiced in deferential ritual was intended to uphold the established order, but it subverted itself by projecting a "second reality" of egalitarian inclusiveness. In this fashion, then, deferential politics was oftentimes an essential precursor for mass-based politics. Mass-based politics in Virginia, Pennsylvania, and elsewhere constructed their new ceremonies gradually by transforming the old.[75]

Regimented polling ceremonies, often confined to their own neighborhoods, included the most volatile and potentially dangerous participants in election day politics: young men. In a sense, all young white males of the upper, middle, and lower orders gradually found themselves recruited into a new form of electioneering "spectacle," a term that had previously meant an upper-class public display.[76] Gone were the aspects of public "festivity" that had once made electioneering ritual a form of imagined inclusion for those consigned to the margins. Those once struggling to be included—African Americans and women— were now formally excluded from all forms of this participatory "spectacle." They would need to script their own political practices to bring a day of new voting rites, when every election would be a "Negro Election" and all politics would be "petticoat politics."

NOTES

1. Alan Taylor, " 'The Art of Hook & Snivey': Political Culture in Upstate New York during the 1790s," *Journal of American History* 74 (1993): 1371–96; David Waldstreicher, *In the Midst of Perpetual Fetes: The Making of American Nationalism, 1776–1820* (Chapel Hill, 1997), esp. 179–202, 244–45; Mary P. Ryan, *Women in Public: Between Banners and Ballots, 1825–1880* (Baltimore, 1990); Jean H. Baker, *Affairs of Party: The Political Culture of Northern Democrats in the Mid-Nineteenth Century* (Ithaca, 1983).

2. William Nisbet Chambers, *The First Party System: Federalists and Republicans* (New York, 1972).

3. Ronald P. Formisano, "Deferential-Participant Politics: The Early Republic's Political Culture, 1789–1824," *American Political Science Review* 68 (1974): 473–87.

4. Philip Lampi Collection of the First Democracy Project at the American Antiquarian Society. See also J. R. Pole, *Political Representation in England and the Origins of the American Republic* (London, 1966), 543–64; Richard P. McCormick, "New Perspectives on Jacksonian Politics," *American Historical Review* 65 (1960): 288–301; Chilton Williamson, *American Suffrage from Property to Democracy, 1760–1860* (Princeton, 1960); David Hackett Fischer, *The Revolution of American Conservatism: The Federalist Party in the Age of Jeffersonian Democracy* (New York, 1965); David Bohmer, "Stability and Change in Early National Politics: The Maryland Voter and the Election of 1800," *William and Mary Quarterly*, 3d ser., 36 (1979): 27–50; Alexander Keyssar, *The Right to Vote: The Contested History of Democracy in the United States* (New York, 2000).

5. J. R. Pole, "Historians and the Problem of Early American Democracy," *American Historical Review* 67 (1962): 646.

6. Ibid.

7. J. G. A. Pocock, "The Classical Theory of Deference," *American Historical Review* 81 (1976): 516–23.

8. James Harrington, *The Oceana* (London, 1700), 48.

9. Adam Smith, *The Theory of Moral Sentiments* (1797; reprint, New York, 1966).

10. *Virginia Patriot*, March 29, 1811.

11. Richmond Virginia *Argus*, March 30, 1805.

12. Daniel P. Jordan, *Political Leadership in Jefferson's Virginia* (Charlottesville, 1983), 98–102.

13. Ibid., 109–13, 118–32, 163–64.

14. Ibid., 102–31; also Alan Taylor, *William Cooper's Town: Power and Persuasion on the Frontier of the Early American Republic* (New York, 1995), 143.

15. Peter Shaw, *American Patriots and the Rituals of Revolution* (Cambridge, Mass., 1981), 204–26.

16. Merrill D. Smith, *Breaking the Bonds: Marital Discord in Pennsylvania, 1730–1830* (New York, 1991).

17. Shaw, *American Patriots*, 204–26.

18. *Richmond Enquirer*, April 12, 1813; Charles Town, (Virginia) *Farmer's Repository*, September 30, 1808.

19. "To the Freeholders of the Counties of Gloucester, Middlesex, Essex, King and Queen, King William, Caroline, Westmoreland, Richmond, Northumberland, and Lancaster" (Fredericksburg, Va., 1788), American Antiquarian Society, Broadside Collection.

20. Robert Munford, *The Candidates*, act I, scene i, *William and Mary Quarterly*, 3d ser., 5 (1948): 231.

21. Pole, *Political Representation*, 94–108, 162–63, 233–38.

22. "To the Freeholders of . . . Gloucester."

23. Philadelphia *Aurora and General Advertiser*, September 24, 1796.

24. Susan G. Davis, *Parades and Power: Street Theater in Nineteenth-Century Philadelphia* (Philadelphia, 1986), 156.

25. Munford, *Candidates*, act I, scene i, 231.

26. Davis, *Parades and Power*, 158–59.

27. Hugh A. Garland, *Life of John Randolph of Roanoke, 1773–1833* (New York, 1851), 129.

28. Ibid., 310.

29. Randolph to Josiah Quincy, April 19, 1813.

30. Victor Turner, *The Ritual Process: Structure and Anti-Structure* (Chicago, 1969), esp. 166–203; Natalie Zemon Davis, *Society and Culture in Early Modern France* (Stanford, 1975), 97–123.

31. Munford, *Candidates*, act III, scene iv, 256–57.

32. Davis, *Society and Culture*, 103.

33. Ibid., 97–103.

34. Ibid.

35. Robert A. Warner, "Amos G. Beman—1812–1874: A Memoir on a Forgotten Leader," *Journal of Negro History* 22 (1937): 200–221.

36. Shaw, *American Patriots*, 204–26; Shane White, " 'It Was a Proud Day': African Americans, Festivals, and Parades in the North, 1741–1834," *Journal of American History* 81 (1994): 13–50; Joseph P. Reidy, " 'Negro Election Day' and Black Community Life in New England 1750–1860," *Marxist Perspectives* 1 (1978): 102.

37. Reidy, " 'Negro Election Day,' " 105–6.

38. George Wythe Munford, *The Two Parsons; Cupid's Sports; the Dream; and the Jewels of Virginia* (Richmond, 1884).

39. Sydnor, *Gentlemen Freeholders*, 21–22; Jordan, *Political Leadership*, 129–30.

40. Munford, *Two Parsons*, 208–10.

41. Ibid., 210.

42. Baker, *Affairs of Party*, 291–305.

43. Charles Town (Virginia) *Farmer's Repository*, September 30, 1808.

44. Ibid.

45. Joseph A. Waddell, *Annals of Augusta County, Virginia, from 1726 to 1871* (Staunton, Va., 1902), 383.

46. *Argus*, November 11, 1808.

47. *Argus*, April 3, 1808.

48. Fischer, *Revolution of American Conservatism*, 91–109.

49. Richard John, *Spreading the News: The American Postal System from Franklin to Morse* (Cambridge, Mass., 1995), 56–57.

50. Michael Warner, *The Letters of the Republic: Publication and the Public Sphere in Eighteenth-Century America* (Cambridge, Mass., 1990), 118–50.

51. Alfred McClung Lee, *The Daily Newspaper in America* (New York, 1937), 711.

52. Fischer, *Revolution of American Conservatism*, 29–49.

53. Philadelphia *United States Gazette*, October 13, 1814.

54. *United States Gazette*, October 11, 1817.

55. Philadelphia *Aurora*, September 29, 30, October 3, 10, 1808.

56. *Argus*, November 1, 1808.

57. Philadelphia *Aurora*, October 10, 1808.

58. *Aurora*, October 12, 1812.

59. Linda Colley, *Britons: Forging the Nation, 1707–1837* (New Haven, 1992); T. H. Breen, "Ideology and Nationalism on the Eve of the Revolution: Revisions *Once More* in Need of Revising," *Journal of American History* 84 (1997): 13–39.

60. *Aurora*, October 9, 1807.

61. Albrecht Koschnik, "Fashioning a Federalist Self: Young Men and Voluntary Association in Early Nineteenth-Century Philadelphia," *Explorations in Early American Culture* 4 (2000): 220–57, and his essay in this volume.

62. New York *Time-Piece*, August 1, 1798; New York *Spectator*, August 3, 1798.

63. Davis, *Parades and Power*, 49–72.

64. *Aurora*, October 3, 1808.

65. *Aurora*, October 12, 1808.

66. *Aurora*, October 10, 1808.

67. *Aurora*, October 1, 1810.

68. *Gazette of the United States*, October 20, 1800.

69. McCormick, "New Perspectives on Jacksonian Politics," 301.

70. Pole, *Political Representation*, 146.

71. Lampi Collection, American Antiquarian Society.

72. Ibid.

73. Ibid.

74. Munford, "Two Parsons," 210.

75. Douglas R. Egerton, "Gabriel's Conspiracy and the Election of 1800," *Journal of Southern History* 56 (1990): 191–214.

76. Davis, *Parades and Power*, 156.

3

Why Thomas Jefferson and African Americans Wore Their Politics on Their Sleeves

Dress and Mobilization between American Revolutions

WHY BOTHER RE-DRESSING POLITICAL HISTORY?

"As long as we are dependent upon Great Britain for our clothing and other necessities, we must be influenced by her baneful politics," wrote George Logan to President-elect Thomas Jefferson on the eve of his inauguration.[1] Hamiltonian commerce versus Jeffersonian self-sufficiency, Old World corruption versus New World independence: these were familiar gestures by 1801. But what if we take notice of Logan's example? Why did he mention clothing in particular, while summarizing everything else as "other necessities"?

Logan seems to have taken for granted that clothes were the truest example of political economy in everyday practice. Clothing did its necessary and expressive work at the crossroads of constraint and independence, volition and representation, in postrevolutionary America. Signifying many kinds of status, dress could equalize or obscure ascribed identities; but it could also reinforce those of gender, race, region, and class. And even when boycotts were not in effect, sartorial choices could make visible specific partisan allegiances. As a long-term trend, dressing up and dressing down brought together the self-assertiveness and entrepreneurial spirit so often noted as characteristic of early national Americans, with the expanded political possibilities of the era.

Like political language, clothing was both put on and regarded. It existed on the person of the wearer and in the eyes of the beholder, on the streets and in a profusion of printed and graphic images. Thus dress opened up reciprocal possibilities for expression, for judgment, and for identification. As with the economy and partisan politics more generally, expanding possibilities did not lead to consensus in these judgments: it led to controversy, and still more multiplicity. One man's strategy for success, or gesture of solidarity and belonging, was another's inappropriate grasping, a sign of disorder, the corruption of bodies and politics. The politics of clothing in America between the consumer revolution of the eighteenth century and the industrial revolution of the nineteenth was both a deep or latent and an overt or manifest kind of politics. It was symbol and action, example and framework—perhaps because clothing was, as it has continued to be, a necessity as well as a luxury.

And yet how many American historians have paid more than cursory attention to the relationship between clothing and politics in an era of boycotts and tariffs, of homespun, silk, and the cotton gin, of dressing up and dressing down, of dressing as Indian, of minstrelsy, of regular and periodic military outfitting, and the deployment of all manner of partisan badges, sashes, buttons, hats?[2] Like the parades that partisans dressed up for, it is time to think about whether there might have been more political substance in clothing than allowed for by its usual relegation to the illustrative vignette.

This essay intentionally takes a subject that might seem to be solely (and literally) the stuff of cultural politics—dress, that is—and argues that it can be a synthetic tool that helps us move beyond, while capitalizing on, the older synthetic devices derived from the categories of intellectual history, such as republicanism. At the risk of being crude, I am not interested in replacing the study of political thought or language, or of the political system as a set of institutions, with an interdisciplinary hybrid such as the "politics of clothing" or "dress politics," interesting as such an effort might prove. Rather I seek to tell the history of the early republic in ways that keeps politics central while demonstrating that the place of noncitizens in the republic—particularly African Americans, Native Americans, and women—was a primary source of conflict, consensus, and even of events (the "real" stuff of history). The actions of these seemingly marginal figures undergirded politics because their actions had economic effects. Control over blacks, Indians, and women could be the property, or interests, for which partisans contended.[3]

As a heuristic device added to the knowledge gained from other methods in political history, like studies of party formation and battles over policy, the politics of clothing can also helps us move beyond periodizations that overstress national political events and underestimate how quickly and ordinarily Americans turned economic realities into political gestures, in a dialectical relationship with their leaders. American producers and consumers of clothing did not obey academic distinctions, or definitions, of the political and the cultural, or of "political culture" and "cultural politics." They failed to do so precisely because the political, and the political system, was multileveled, or federal, and porous at the edges. As such, it invited seemingly "cultural" gestures, to accomplish things that could not easily be accomplished in national or local elections, in legislation, or by the courts.

The best way to demonstrate such a proposition is to show how it obtained for both politicians themselves and for those formally excluded from participation in electoral politics. Thomas Jefferson and some African Americans trucked in clothing to mix social identities with partisan ideologies. In the process they broadened politics beyond its structural limitations in the liberal republic.

DRESSING FOR AMERICAN REVOLUTIONS: THE CASE OF THOMAS JEFFERSON

I return to my original question. Why did the new president of the United States, in the wake of an extraordinarily divisive national election, receive a letter from an important supporter that equated the importation of clothing with the corruption of the political system and the loss of national independence?

Thomas Jefferson came into personal and political maturity in a world of dressing up and dressing down. By the time President Jefferson greeted the British ambassador in dirty underclothes and slippers conspicuously "down at the heels," he had been learning and practicing sartorial politics for almost forty years.[4] If T. H. Breen is right about the political significance of the consumer revolution of the eighteenth century, the continuation of such gestures by Jefferson into the nineteenth century suggests the continuing importance of the American Revolution and its conditions in the politics of the early republic—but in a more popular and economically significant way than allowed by the older literature on republicanism, or the recent stress by some historians on elite political "combat" and "character."[5] Jefferson's conspicuous refusal of finery as president was merely the tip of the iceberg. It was more than a symbol of republican simplicity: it was an example of material and political battles long waged and communicated through practices of dress. These practices connected local and domestic to regional and Atlantic economies, and in doing so integrated the personal and the political, the private and the public, in regular, compelling, and effective ways.

Jefferson's first extant letter, a 1762 missive home to a friend written from college at Williamsburg, is a revealing attempt to make meaning out of clothing. He compares himself, studying away in a garret while rats eat his pocketbook and silk garters, to his peers who are really happy in the world, attending a party where they compete to see who "embroiders most" their discourse. Shy Tom soon came out of his shell and, like most gentry of the era, began to spend more and more time and money attending to his clothing—a fact that makes his later play with dishevelment all the more revealing.[6]

In Williamsburg during the 1760s, Jefferson learned dress and republican politics at once. For the Virginia gentry, imported clothing—the most frequently purchased item at the stores of Scots factors—had become a key source of debt and a symbol of colonial dependency. By 1765 planters like George Washington were experimenting with domestic production of homespun, trying to make osnaburg (a cheap linen) from hemp, and agreeing not to kill local lambs for meat, saving them instead for wool. Four years later, elite Virginians enthusiastically adopted non-importation of cloth (with the revealing exception of coarse fabrics for slaves). One planter came to the capitol in a suit made wholly by one of his slaves. The "envy of Williamsburg," he fielded at least one offer to trade a silk suit for his homespun. During the years leading up to the Revolution, patriot gentry would pay close attention to the ups and downs of the non-importation movement as they planned their wardrobe, as Jefferson did in 1771 when he sent an order to London for silk stockings to be filled as soon as the colonial boycott expired.[7]

Unfortunately for the gentry, the non-importation movement made more sense for big planters who could afford to experiment with new modes of domestic production (by their surplus slaves), and for backcountry householders who did not produce for export, than for the majority of tobacco growers. For them, it was cheaper to import cloth than to make it at home—at least when tobacco prices were reasonably high. According to Bruce A. Ragsdale, the presence of Scots factors filling yeomen's orders during the boycotts made it clear that only independence could make non-importation a truly successful strategy for changing the rules of Atlantic political economy. Revolutionary efforts to jump-start commercial cloth production in Virginia "never filled the market demand nor laid a foundation for peacetime industry." The result was a series of severe shortages that would greatly constrain and embarrass Jefferson during his term as wartime governor of Virginia.[8]

Such conditions only further encouraged gentry attempts to inspire self-denying republican virtue through public displays of dress. Republicanism, it was hoped, would succeed where interest failed.[9] Precisely because the production and consumption of clothing so often embodied class differences in late eighteenth century Virginia, the gentry continued to use dress to try to unify themselves and Virginia's citizens in the resistance. Consider the politicization of the hunting shirt. The entry of backwoodsmen into the contest in early 1775 inspired the derisive British epithet of "shirtmen" for all the patriots. As Rhys Isaac points out, cosmopolitan patriots then reversed their earlier disdain for frontier style and gave positive meaning to hunting shirts and tomahawks. In the spring a published resolution urged members of the House of Burgesses to wear hunting shirts to the spring session, and some actually did so, menacing Lord Dunmore when he arrived to make a conciliatory speech.[10] There is no better example of the use of frontier, and even Indian, identity to unify otherwise divided Americans than the Virginia leadership's appropriation of deerskin and osnaburg. In an era when Indian identity was signaled visually by the depiction of fringed garments, and frontiersmen were thought to be expert marksmen, the appearance of this distinctive clothing apparently struck fear into British regulars, or so George Washington believed. In the case of sartorial politics as elsewhere, republicanism appears as much a political strategy as a political theory, a surprisingly successful attempt to make a virtue out of necessities, out of the very limits of policy—at least in the short term. To dismiss it as mere ideology, or show, would be a mistake the founders themselves refused to make.[11]

Jefferson the founder never stopped believing that culture and political action could remake allegiances, alliances, and policy. Simple clothing became, for him, the epitome of an American middle state, the path toward attainment of the republic. By the 1780s he began to depict an idealized Virginia, and America, of subsistence farmers who produced a small surplus for salt, sugar, coffee, "and a little finery for his wife and daughters." At a time when women's consumption of British manufactures was blamed for draining the new states of specie, Jefferson proposed as one solution a state-designed republican costume for women. He defensively asserted, in *Notes on the State of Virginia*, that during the war Virginians had mostly produced their own clothing. Admitting that the quality was poor, he predicted that Americans would return to importing clothing but defined it as a necessary result of their virtuous attachment to agriculture.[12]

Jefferson's years in Paris only reinforced his sense of the ideological, if not actual, difference between European and properly American attitudes toward dress. He may have struggled to match the sartorial splendor of French court society on a strained diplomatic budget, but the experience allowed him both to dress up and to identify against the European fashion, as Benjamin Franklin had before him. By the time he returned to the states Jefferson had developed a taste for "superfine French cloth," as his orders to tailors make clear.[13] Yet the refusal of such display soon came to have a renewed meaning in domestic politics. During the 1790s, Democratic Republicans objected strenuously to the "court" style of the Federalist administration, and objects of dress, such as hairstyle and the wearing of cockades, came to symbolize the opposed poles of aristocracy and democracy, especially in the wake of the French revolutionaries' spectacular politicization of fashions.[14] Such attitudes carried over into questions of policy. The Federalist cartoon "A Peep into the Antifederal Club" (1793) depicted Secretary of State Jefferson as an enemy of "dry goods." Jefferson himself had begun to believe that the only way to guarantee American freedom on the high seas was to "lay a duty on British oznabrigs."[15]

In this light, Jefferson's simple dress at his inauguration in 1801 signaled policy and strategy as well as psychology. The domestic fabrics and colors Jefferson wore in office, such as his green and brown inaugural suit, represented the American people who had triumphed in the election of 1800.[16] The gestures were symbolic, to be sure: with Jefferson the president dressing down for diplomats like Anthony Merry, we are certainly in the realm of cultural politics. Yet these maneuvers had simultaneously domestic and international meanings. This was completely appropriate given the importance of foreign affairs to the American economy and partisan politics during these years when Federalists dressed up in well-tailored military costumes to signify their class identities, the aristocratic pretensions of their party, and their enthusiasm for war against France. Refusing to don a ceremonial sword, as John Adams had, translated directly into a refusal of the Quasi-War and Federalist mobilization. A focus on Jefferson's personality makes him look like a sphinx, if not a hypocrite, for his obvious love of fashion and simultaneous refusal of it.[17] A wider view of his sartorial politics reveals a politician in search of constituencies and a public man particularly sensitive to the accretion of political and economic meaning to clothing since the 1760s.

The embargo years reveal Jefferson's politics of clothing at its most brilliant, most flexible, and, ultimately, most strained. By the latter part of his second term, Jeffersonians had embraced a distinction between an extended carrying trade and large-scale manufactures, on the one hand, and small-scale or household manufactures on the other, which they increasingly defended as implicit in the Revolutionary doctrine of self-sufficiency. Jefferson moved to co-opt Federalist critics of his ostensibly agrarian anticommercial stand. In November 1808 he wrote to Connecticut Republican Abraham Bishop, asking him to approach Federalist David Humphreys, who manufactured fine cloth in his New Haven establishment, for a new blue suit which he would presumably wear in public. By January he had the homespun, and made sure to spell out its political meaning in a letter to Humphreys: "Some jealousy of this spirit of manufacture [exists] among commercial men." But Americans could and should manufacture everything for which they possessed the raw materials, for domestic consumption. Coarse goods could be made at home, but finer stuff would be manufactured in towns. If Americans seized the opportunity, when the embargo was lifted the nation would import only half of what it had beforehand.[18]

That Jefferson's critics appreciated the meaning of these gestures is made clear by a satirical print on the Non-Intercourse Act of 1809 (see Figure 3.1). Jefferson is depicted in rags proclaiming, "What a fine thing it is to feel Independent of all Taylors! I have stript myself rather than submit to London or Parisian Fashions!" The cartoonist, though, implies that this refusal is not neutral: it takes a French, Napoleonic side, signified by Bonaparte's applause. "French" style suffuses the Jeffersonian refusal of imported style: a closed-minded Jefferson insists that the "London cut . . . never suited me.—They are always wrong in their measures."[19] There is no better example of the deep international structure of politics in the early republic, nor of its continual recurrence to the images and realities of dress at a time when clothing continued to be a major object of production and consumption. Both political parties lambasted the other as foppish products of imported (British or French) ideological fashions. Clothing had become a metaphor for political language itself: its deceptions appeared to cover over the ultimate social referents of politics, but also politics' origins, and impact, in the international struggles over political economy.

After 1809 Jefferson took his sartorial politics back to Virginia, where it had all begun. Much as clothing had provided him a bridge from education and private life into politics during the 1760s, the political economy of cloth enabled Jefferson to continue to be a political actor even in retirement. He participated enthusiastically in schemes to raise merino sheep. From 1812 to 1814 he bought carding machines and looms, writing to Philip Mazzei that "a million spindles"

FIGURE 3.1. "Non Intercourse or Dignified Retirement" (1809), Peter Pencill (pseudonym). Courtesy of the Houghton Library, Harvard University.

whirred in America, one hundred in "our own family." "Scarcely a family fails to clothe itself," he told du Pont de Nemours. He wrote enthusiastically to Lafayette about a "revolution in domestic economy . . . well worth a war."[20] These letters continue the public project of *Notes on the State of Virginia*: like that book, they seek to bring into being the republican America they seem to describe, through exhortation at home and good public relations directed at influential Europeans. Eighteen twelve for Jefferson truly represented the republic reborn, the return to revolutionary time, precisely insofar as Americans, more than ever, more than even during the Revolution, made (and talked incessantly about) their own clothing.

In this light, it is intriguing that Jefferson's famous rapprochement with his old friend and political enemy John Adams occurred after Adams, cheekily complimenting him as a "Friend to American Manufactures . . . of the domestic kind," sent him "two Pieces of Homespun": his son John Quincy Adams's leather-clad *Lectures on Rhetoric and Oratory* (1810). The package of books got separated from the letter, so Jefferson did not get the joke at first, thinking that there were actual textiles from Braintree on their way south. The thought inspired him to wax poetic about the "economy and thriftiness" that placed one sheep for every person on Virginia farms, increased production of cotton, hemp, and flax, and ultimately made "every family in the country a manufactory within itself." After Adams explained about the books, Jefferson apologized for his flight of rhetoric. Adams replied that such words had been exactly what he had wanted— suggesting that each man sought to continue a conversation that had always mixed national politics and the everyday.[21]

Yet Jefferson's story about clothing as politics should give us pause where he talks about his family's self-sufficiency. His language of family was the language of slavery: when he wrote to Kosciusko of needing "2000 yards of linen, cotton and woollen yearly, to clothe my family," he was referring to his quite extended *plantation* family. It was his slave women, for the most part, who learned to weave and produce more and better cloth during the War of 1812.[22] Domestic economy for slaveholders turned not just on their own but on their slaves' production and consumption of clothing, a fact that the Virginia associators had recognized when they exempted slave clothing from their non-importation resolves in 1771.

After his return to America in the early 1790s, Jefferson, like any good planter, spent as much time looking into the price and quality of "negro" cloth as for the finery he purchased for himself and his daughters.[23] Yet when he wrote letters abroad and to friends like Adams twenty years later, he did not specify exactly who was making the clothes, or wearing them, at Monticello, any more than he credited slaves for Virginian or American self-sufficiency in any of his political writings.[24] The politics of clothing help us see that a great part of Jefferson's appeal to contemporaries, and his historical significance, lay in his ability to dress politics, and politicize dress, in a way that simultaneously depended upon economically, but obscured ideologically, the importance of slaves to the U.S. economy in an era when slavery first came under widespread criticism. From the 1770s to the War of 1812, Jefferson artfully conflated the particular needs of slaveholders who wanted to flexibly employ their valuable laborers in both cash crops and domestic manufactures with the desires of yeomen for "competency" and independence. He sought to meld the "composite farm" and the enlightened plantation, the hardy yeoman and the gentleman planter.[25] Americans wearing what they *and their slaves* grew actualized this political alliance. Homespun made it material as well as symbolic. It was not pomp, but politics at a level as deep and as lasting as any election.

THE POLITICIZATION OF CLOTHING AND THE MAKING OF
POLITICAL SUBJECTS: AFRICAN AMERICANS

In 1769, in his first recorded public act, Thomas Jefferson signed a non-importation agreement enumerating eleven types of cloth, as well as hats and stocking, to be boycotted. The agreement also pledged its adherents in Albemarle County to "not import any slaves, or purchase any imported." The young man's first actual venture into print, that September, was a runaway advertisement in the *Virginia Gazette* for a shoemaker from his plantation, a mulatto whom he called "artful and knavish" for absconding with the tools of his trade. African Americans in Jefferson's Virginia did not have to be told about the value of the clothes they made or the political meanings that could be derived from them.[26]

For a very long time, any say that enslaved African Americans had over the clothing of their own bodies was likely to be taken as evidence of the benevolence of slaveholders. Or, in an even more unbroken tradition, slaves' appropriations of used garments was seen by whites as "unsuccessful attempts by an inferior group to imitate white ways." More recent scholarship stresses the remarkable ability of slaves and free African Americans to find in clothing "an often surprising degree of social and cultural space." Recent works on black style elaborate the many meanings of dress among African Americans in the eighteenth and nineteenth century, and certainly makes clear that it is possible to write a history of African American resistance, as well as African American experience, from the ground up, from sources which may at first seem to resist such use. In careful, contextual reinterpretations of evidence like court records and runaway advertisements, they reveal the politics that political history has ignored.[27]

And yet, because of their concern to highlight African Americans and their choices, such works have not seized upon the opportunity to reconsider "white" or mainstream political history in the light of their findings. Studies of black politics and culture sometimes address black appropriations of white rhetoric or political practices, but rarely assess the impact that such appropriations may have had on the practices and even the events of American politics. While it might be argued that black politics was necessarily more "cultural" than properly political in the era of slavery, when most blacks were not citizens, such a view is perhaps as much an artifact of divisions between political, social, or cultural history, or a misapplication of twentieth-century understandings of politics, as it is an accurate reflection of life in eighteenth- and nineteenth-century America. African Americans became political subjects in part through debates about the dress (or undress) of southern slaves, which suffused abolitionist literature; racist satires that mocked the use of finery by free blacks on the streets of the North; and, of course, the sartorial choices of blacks themselves, some of whom specialized occupationally in clothing production and care, and most of whom had from personal experience a profound understanding of how much of a statement can be made with, or made out of, a body's surface. The extreme politicization of clothing in the antebellum debate over slavery and race, understood in light of the use of dress in Revolutionary and early national politics, suggests that "cultural" subjects like clothing, as much as or more than abstracted "language" or "power," can help us reconnect subjects like Thomas Jefferson and African Americans, and modalities like politicization and policy, in a renewed political history.

For both economic and political reasons, by the mid-to-late eighteenth century most slaves could be identified by distinct types of clothing. Dressing chattels in cheaper clothes not only saved money, it made them more easily identifiable at a time when confusions of identity could work to the advantage of unfree peoples. And yet "dress and speech did not infallibly disclose social rank in [early] America," observes Michael Zuckerman. For this very reason, sumptuary laws had been an important part of efforts to codify slavery and other divisions of rank. The rise of fashion, and the eighteenth century consumer revolution more generally, might seem simply to have increased the difference between black and white, or free and unfree, sartorial possibilities.[28]

Yet advertisements for runaway slaves reveal that the proliferation of clothing, in amount and kind, also opened up more opportunities for those with a chance to practice disguise and self-fashioning. The clothing that slaves cleaned, repaired, stored, and sometimes displayed for their owners could also be stolen. Shirts, buckles, and coats could be sold. They could help make one free. The very material artifacts that could establish genteel or white identities were used to contest those attributes by fugitives who, in changing clothes, could begin a process in which they changed their names, their status, and even sometimes their race. During the Seven Years' War and the American Revolution, slaves and mixed-race people in servitude found that military uniforms could initiate a social leveling process. Most obviously, some earned their freedom by agreeing, or fleeing, to serve. Others, however, found that the ambiguity involved in wearing cast-off parts of uniforms could make them appear free.[29]

These latter developments were part of a striking seizure of partial autonomy by slaves in the changing late-colonial world. On the one hand, the growth of the empire and a rising demand for agricultural products spelled the further rise of slavery in the South and, initially, in the mid-Atlantic region. On the other hand, the value of increased production, and the conflicts within the empire that put a higher price on plantation self-sufficiency and on labor more generally, led some masters to rely on an incentive system that included slave market activity—especially barter for clothing. Thomas Jefferson rewarded his most productive nail-makers with a new suit of clothes; Charles Carroll imported felt hats from England for "some of my best Negroes in order to encourage them to do well." Henry Laurens traded waistcoats for grain his slaves grew on their own plots.[30] In the Chesapeake especially, as in urban areas, the slaves' informal economy made the relationship between clothing and freedom more explicitly material. The slaves at Jefferson's Poplar Forest plantation most commonly bought clothes and the items associated with clothing with income they derived from their market activities. The archaeological evidence also reveals "the importance of personal adornment among slaves and their awareness of and ability to keep pace with changing fashions." Clearly African Americans, like other colonials, became more and more sensitive to the status associated with finer fabrics. When the Philadelphia merchant Thomas Cope sent some unsalable corduroy to an iron-master, the slaves at the forge threatened an insurrection and refused to wear the goods.[31]

Certainly slaves translated power into clothing, and clothing into power, much as their masters did. Whites often found the ways in which African Americans dressed to be an affront to their sense of how black people should act in the slave society of the South and in the caste society of the North. By the 1810s, the pretensions of free blacks in the North had begun to be pictured graphically as the sartorial excesses of black dandies, a racist tradition that certainly continued into the twentieth century (see Figure 3.2).[32]

The story could be told in terms of "power," in a micropolitical analysis of racial oppression. Racism had hegemonic power, and like other ideas and languages is deserving of causal investigation. Yet the importance of clothing in revolutionary and postrevolutionary political economy suggests that it would be insufficient to reduce images of clothing to so many more words in the lexicon of race. The white women of Revolutionary America took up homespun and in doing so made a distinct ideological contribution, but they did not solve the problem of the trade deficit in textiles.[33] That change, if it was to happen, was going to depend more on slave women, and in the remaking of slaves' lives to include more cloth production. This is where Jeffersonian politics met the cultural, and racial, politics of clothing. Jeffersonian political economy, in other words, sought to domesticate the promiscuous buying, selling, and wearing of clothing that, arguably, was making some slaves more free, some masters more wealthy, and everybody more dependent upon Atlantic networks.

FIGURE 3.2. "The Fruits of Amalgamation" (1839), Edward W. Clay. Courtesy of the American Antiquarian Society.

Racist depictions of black dress, in such a light, denied not only black upward mobility in the North but also the very material of African American aspiration and assimilation in the South. It was becoming more and more attractive to whites to engage in racist denial and ridicule of black consumption and production precisely because slave artisans were fomenting rebellions and free blacks were beginning to mobilize against slavery.[34] Recall Jefferson's depiction of his runaway shoemaker as "artful and knavish." In doing so he denigrated the skills he encouraged and profited from. This variation on the Hegelian master-slave dialectic—the more the master depends on the slave, the more potential power the slave possesses, and the more the master must deny the nature of the relationship—became a central dynamic in American political culture even as gradual emancipation occurred in the northern states.[35] When blacks started acting like Jeffersonian agrarians by producing their own clothing, and when they began to both appropriate and reinvent the strivings (and excesses) of other American men and women who strove for both distinction and solidarity through dress, neither their push for autonomy nor their centrality in American life could be denied.

The Jeffersonian expansion of slavery in the age of cotton broke up established slave families and communities in places like Virginia and the lowcountry.[36] Yet it also made the cash crop–centered farms of the South more dependent on cheap woolens and cottons from English looms. The politics of the tariff in the 1820s and beyond was about nothing if not the price of cheap shoes and shirts for slaves. High tariffs on woolens, a perennial issue by the 1850s, made clothing more expensive: it did nothing for the producers of cotton or their owners but much for the manufacturers of cotton and woolen clothing in the North. As the cotton-driven industrial revolution got underway, the politics of clothing became more obviously a circle of production and consumption, in which the needs of consumers of cotton (North) and producers of clothing (North) conflicted with those of the producers of cotton (South) and consumers of clothing (South).

It is easy, however, to miss the presence of slaves as producers and consumers, and thus the politicizing potential of slave clothing as a flashpoint in antebellum political economy. The manufacturing, sale, and resale of cloth linked North and South, slave and free, black and white, whether the articles in question were made in factories, sewn at home, or—as increasingly likely—some of both. David Walker, the southern-born northern black revolutionary and used clothing dealer, capitalized on this situation. His contacts were black seamen who transported such goods, and who sewed copies of his inflammatory *Appeal* into coats.[37]

Abolitionists put the question of what blacks wore squarely into the realm of political debate. As early as 1754, Quaker John Woolman (who himself wore all white costumes) had pointed out how "dressing them in uncomely garments" had become a technology for naturalizing racism and slavery.[38] The famous slave-ship image of 1790, however, made African nakedness less a sign of difference, or savagery, as in traditional racist discourse, than a sign of slaves' victimization at the hands of slave traders. Classical slave imagery, like Josiah Wedgwood's "Am I Not a Man and a Brother" cameo and Hiram Powers's statue of *The Greek Slave*, tended to render blacks as passive, but such depictions also effaced race and turned loose drapery into a mark of virtue.[39] By the 1830s and the rise of Garrisonian immediatism, slave nakedness, and the inferior insufficient clothing foisted upon slaves, became a potent symbol of precisely what was wrong with slavery. White abolitionists especially depicted a forced immodesty on the part of slaves, a situation that, they insisted, encouraged the sexual predation of masters. The slave South was an erotic nightmare, where pubescent children were forced to expose themselves and to see their elders stripped and whipped. Frederick Douglass made just such a scene the climax of the first chapter of his 1845 *Narrative*. Part of the idea for women's antislavery fairs was that sewing and embroidering items for sale encouraged women to identify with their oppressed sisters. This was literally true, for several fugitive slave women who became activists, including Sojourner Truth and Harriet Jacobs, had found freedom by making dresses for northern white women.[40]

During the 1840s and 1850s abolitionists and their opponents engaged in a full-scale war of images over the question of black dress. Fugitive slaves and other black abolitionists literally dressed the part of free people, in their public appearances and in widely distributed graphic images. Their clothing is almost without exception formal and even genteel in an age when those standards had become available to more and more people. For many northerners, the possibility of dressing well had come to embody freedom. The extreme covering of the body in these images made the argument that dress, not color, made the man or woman. In recognition of the very different assumptions and arguments at work in divergent apparel and images of dress, abolitionists developed a visual trope of dress "before and after" slavery. One New Bedford girl fashioned the meaning of Frederick Douglass's life in two very differently turned-out dolls (see Figure 3.3). The frontispiece of kidnapping victim Solomon Northrup's slave narrative pictured him in his new "plantation suit" on the Red River. Even cross-dressing Ellen Craft's tuxedo had liberating potential.[41]

The battle over the meaning of dress had turned into a key location of the debate over regional virtues, racial character, and American progress. This debate entered ordinary politics fitfully but regularly, in controversies over tariffs and what to do about fugitive slaves. Proslavery advocates who naturalized race as destiny sought to have the clothes match the racialized men and women. In the illustrations of John Pendleton Kennedy's pro-southern *Swallow Barn* (second edition, 1853), slave dress is simple but modest, appropriate to a content, childlike people. House slaves are well dressed, and field slaves dress for work (though they seem more likely to play). Dress is a function of place and task; it is not a matter of aspiration or individual character.

More ambivalently, the minstrel show played out the question of black dress again and again. Its politics, as several important recent studies have shown, reflected that of its audience: sympathetic (at least initially) to oppressed slaves, but hostile to pretentious free blacks, whose sartorial choices were relentlessly spoofed. Minstrels enacted whiteness by taking on and off the mask of blackness, the rags of slaves, and the duds of the northern black dandy.[42] (In doing so, however, they suggested the potential of changes in clothes, and the actual mutability of race.) Abolitionists, in turn, reappropriated minstrel images, turning them into narratives of re-dress, racial uplift, and master class excess. In *Uncle Tom's Cabin*, Harriet Beecher Stowe both drew on and sought to refute the stereotype of the black dandy by suggesting that the St. Claires's house slaves who dressed up in their masters' cast-offs, like Adolph, were the real Uncle

FIGURE 3.3. Frederick Douglass dolls made by Cynthia Hill of New Bedford,
Massachusetts, during the late 1850s. Courtesy of the New Bedford Whaling Museum.

Toms, for aping foolish Deep South aristocratic habits. Her sartorial exemplars
are the modest, neat Kentucky slaves and the plain-dressing abolitionist Quakers,
the very people who helped politicize dress while seeming to withdraw from
ordinary politics in the seventeenth and eighteenth centuries.

African Americans had the last word, perhaps, a decade later when they
dressed in Union blue to help defeat the slave South. For a Democratic Party
newspaper, wartime emancipation conjured up "the prospect of elevating

millions of enthralled blacks to luxury, laziness and good clothes." Douglass saw the good clothes of the soldier as the literal wearing of citizenship: "Once let the black man get upon his person the brass letters U.S., let him get an eagle on his button, and a musket on his shoulder and bullets in his pocket, and there is no power on earth which can deny that he has earned the right to citizenship in the United States." The photographs black Union soldiers had taken, and the pervasive iconography of black soldiers in uniform during and immediately after the war, attest to the significance contemporaries attached to clothing (see Figure 3.4). That black Union League members in South Carolina kept wearing their uniforms to escort fellow voters to the polls after the war suggests that they appreciated the relationships between dress and ordinary politics that this essay has sought to recover.[43]

CLOTHING POLITICIZED AND DEPOLITICIZED

If the relationship between politics and clothing was as important as I have argued, how could it have been so resolutely forgotten, or displaced in historical memory?

For this we can look again to Thomas Jefferson himself. Jefferson, as I have argued, followed Revolutionary and postrevolutionary democratizing trends in attending to the politicized meanings of clothing. Yet he also could employ clothing to naturalize the very developments he celebrated, to remove them from politics. During the War of 1812, he wrote to John Mason to praise his wife's production of homespun as more impressive than anything he had seen during, much less since, the Revolution: "Mrs. Mason is really a more dangerous adversary to our British foes, than all our Generals. These attack the hostile armies only, she the source of their subsistence. What these do counts nothing because they take one say and lose another: what she does counts double, because what she takes from the enemy is added to us: I hope too she will have more followers than our Generals, but few rivals I fear."[44] In the War of 1812, Jefferson saw an opportunity to revisit revolutionary politicization. As usual, he located sites of improvement, or promises of a glorious, if modest and self-sufficient, future.[45] And yet, while he celebrated women's political action, he also marked it out as singular from and different than men's public, political activity. Jefferson contains the problem of everything being potentially political *by separating and denigrating the political public sphere* even as he reserved it for men.

There is still more to what Jefferson was doing in this letter of 1814 than his advancement of an understanding of sex roles that makes women everything and thus nothing. In light of the importance he placed on both slaves' manufacture

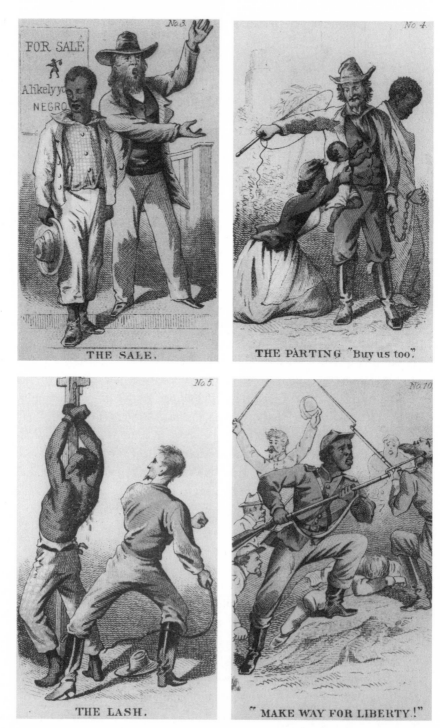

FIGURE 3.4. Four trading cards from a series of twelve issued by abolitionists to encourage African American men to enlist in the Union Army. Courtesy of the Library Company of Philadelphia.

of clothing and the need to keep down the price of his own slaves' clothing, his silence about slaves as sources of political weakness and strength circa 1814 suggests an important underlying reason for his comments regarding Mrs. Mason. Elite sewing women very usefully stood in for the entire realm of the domestic, his and America's "family."[46] Silence about slavery and its politics undergirds the celebration of a white woman's virtue. As such, Jefferson's theatricalities in and around clothing did not only address the symbolic meanings of clothing in the realms of political theory. They constituted a series of specific political strategies. They embodied the deeper structures of citizenship and political economy— most of all, the larger political compromise between slaveholders and middling white men and women that shaped American politics in its formative years.

It was this domestication of politics and clothing that African Americans and abolitionists turned inside out. Like the American revolutionaries, they politicized clothing because it was a necessity: a material basis of their lives, and an available resource when official or ordinary politics failed. The battle over clothing and its meanings, in fact, was a locus of the struggle to create, define, and limit the place of politics in the age of its democratization.[47] The explosion of "cultural politics" in the antebellum era simultaneously reflected the expansion of partisan cultures and responded to the limitations of partisanship in addressing matters of public import. Not the least because of what Jefferson and his constituents had done, keeping politics undressed may be a luxury that historians, like antebellum African Americans, cannot afford.

NOTES

1. Logan to Jefferson, February 27, 1801, quoted in Drew McCoy, *The Elusive Republic: Political Economy in Jeffersonian America* (Chapel Hill, 1980), 209.

2. Such work is starting to emerge, though it does not usually focus on explicit or manifest politics. Laurel Thatcher Ulrich, *The Age of Homespun: Objects and Stories in the Creation of an American Myth* (New York, 2001); Michael Zakim, "Sartorial Ideologies: From Homespun to Ready-Made," *American Historical Review* 106 (2001): 1553–86.

3. Historians of the South have made it much more difficult to define the "issues" as economic or "ethnocultural" while excluding the economically and culturally significant actions of women, African Americans, and Native Americans from consideration as political history. Stephanie McCurry, *Masters of Small Worlds: Yeoman Households, Gender Relations, and the Political Culture of the Antebellum South Carolina Lowcountry* (New York, 1995); Drew Gilpin Faust, *Mothers of Invention: Women of the Slaveholding South in the American Civil War* (Chapel Hill, 1996); Kathleen M. Brown, *Good Wives, Nasty Wenches, and Anxious Patriarchs: Gender, Race, and Power in Colonial Virginia* (Chapel Hill, 1996); James Sidbury, *Ploughshares into Swords: Race, Rebellion, and Identity in Gabriel's Virginia,*

1730–1810 (New York, 1997); Nancy Edwards, *Gendered Strife and Confusion: The Political Culture of Reconstruction* (Urbana, 1997); Woody Holton, *Forced Founders: Indians, Debtors, Slaves, and the Making of the American Revolution in Virginia* (Chapel Hill, 1999); Robert Olwell, *Masters, Subjects, and Slaves: The Culture of Power in the South Carolina Lowcountry, 1740–1790* (Ithaca, 1998).

4. Augustus John Foster, quoted in Henry Adams, *History of the United States of America during the Administrations of Thomas Jefferson* (1889–91; reprint, New York, 1986), 126–27. Adams, with his usual combination of brio and solid research, astutely observed that "Jefferson, at moments of some interest in his career as President, seemed to regard his peculiar style of dress as a matter of political importance, while the Federalist newspapers never ceased ridiculing the corduroy small-clothes, red-plush waistcoat, and sharp-toed boots with which he expressed his contempt for fashion."

Recently, Catherine Allgor and Joyce Appleby have called attention to Jefferson's efforts, as president, to republicanize, even democratize, American style. They make significant interventions by insisting on the "social" and "psychological" dimensions of Jefferson's campaign. Yet the direction of change, and the nature of politics in the early republic, seems to appear to them as essentially leader-driven. While Appleby (not unlike Adams) does suggest that Jefferson took his cues from the assertiveness of ordinary Americans, she does not attempt to prove the proposition, arguing instead that Jefferson "set in motion a variety of convention-shattering initiatives." Appleby, "Thomas Jefferson and the Psychology of Democracy," in *The Revolution of 1800: Democracy, Race, and the New Republic*, ed. James Horn, Jan Ellen Lewis, and Peter S. Onuf (Charlottesville, 2003), 156–59; Allgor, *Parlor Politics: In Which the Ladies of Washington Help Build a City and a Government* (Charlottesville, 2000), 4–47.

5. T. H. Breen, " 'Baubles of Britain': The American and Consumer Revolutions of the Eighteenth Century," in *Of Consuming Interests: The Style of Life in the Eighteenth Century*, ed. Cary Carson et al. (Charlottesville, 1994), 444–82; T. H. Breen, "Narrative of Commercial Life: Consumption, Ideology, and Community on the Eve of the American Revolution," *William and Mary Quarterly*, 3d ser., 50 (1993): 471–501; Joseph J. Ellis, *American Sphinx: The Character of Thomas Jefferson* (New York, 1996); Joseph J. Ellis, *Founding Brothers: The Revolutionary Generation* (New York, 2000); Joanne B. Freeman, *Affairs of Honor: National Politics in the Early Republic* (New Haven, 2001).

6. Jefferson to John Page, December 25, 1762, in *The Papers of Thomas Jefferson*, ed. Julian Boyd (Princeton, 1950–), 1:4–5; see also the orders for clothing articles in the same volume, pp. 11, 30, 44; Dumas Malone, *Jefferson the Virginian* (Boston, 1948), 48; Garry Wills, *Inventing America: Jefferson's Declaration of Independence* (New York, 1978), 15.

7. Bruce A. Ragsdale, *A Planter's Republic: The Search for Economic Independence in Revolutionary Virginia* (Madison, 1993), 14, 35, 57–58, 76–84; Lorena S. Walsh, "Slavery and Agriculture at Mount Vernon," in *Slavery at the Home of George Washington*, ed. Philip J. Schwarz (Mt. Vernon, 2001), 59; Jefferson to Thomas Adams, June 1, 1771, *Papers of Thomas Jefferson*, 1:71–72.

8. Ragsdale, *Planter's Republic*, 105, 236–38, 256; Jefferson to Baron von Steuben, December 8, 25, 1780, von Steuben to Jefferson, December 10, 1780, William Davies to Jefferson, February 8, 1781, Nathanael Greene to Jefferson, February 28, 1781, *Papers of Thomas Jefferson*, 4:187–88, 195–96, 5:23; Noble E. Cunningham, Jr., *In Pursuit of Reason: The Life of Thomas Jefferson* (Baton Rouge, 1987), 68–69.

9. Michael Zuckerman, "A Different Thermidor: The Revolution Beyond the American Revolution," in *The Transformation of Early American History*, ed. James Henretta, Michael Kammen, and Stanley N. Katz (New York, 1989), 170–93.

10. John E. Selby, *The Revolution in Virginia, 1775–1783* (Williamsburg, 1988), 42, 61; Rhys Isaac, *The Transformation of Virginia, 1740–1790* (Chapel Hill, 1982), 256–58. On revolutionary fashion more generally, see Ann Fairfax Withington, *Toward a More Perfect Union: Virtue and the Formation of American Republics* (New York, 1991).

11. Holton, *Forced Founders*, 104; General Orders, July 24, 1776, in *The Papers of George Washington: Revolutionary War Series*, ed. Philander Chase (Charlottesville, 1985–), 5:440.

12. John Chester Miller, *The Wolf by the Ears: Thomas Jefferson and Slavery* (New York, 1977), 83; *Papers of Thomas Jefferson*, 12:66; Jefferson, *Notes on the State of Virginia*, ed. William Peden (Chapel Hill, 1954), 164.

13. Jefferson to Christian Baehr, August 19, 1791, November 14, 1792, *Papers of Thomas Jefferson*, 21:39, 22:617.

14. Thomas K. Murphy, *A Land without Castles: The Changing Image of America in Europe, 1780–1830* (Lanham, Md., 2001), 43; Newman, *Parades and the Politics of the Street: Festive Culture in the Early American Republic* (Philadelphia, 1997); Lynn Hunt, *Politics, Culture, Class and the French Revolution* (Berkeley, 1984).

15. Jefferson to William Branch Giles, March 19, 1796, Thomas Jefferson Papers, Library of Congress.

16. Appleby, "Jefferson and the Psychology of Democracy."

17. Ellis, *American Sphinx*; Conor Cruise O'Brien, *The Long Affair: Thomas Jefferson and the French Revolution* (Chicago, 1998).

18. McCoy, *Elusive Republic*, 219–30; Jefferson to Abraham Bishop, November 13, 1808, Jefferson to David Humphreys, January 20, 1809, Jefferson Papers, Library of Congress.

19. Noble E. Cunningham, Jr., *The Image of Thomas Jefferson in the Public Eye: Portraits for the People 1800–1809* (Charlottesville, 1981), 119–22.

20. Jefferson to James Madison, May 13, 1810, in Jefferson, *Writings*, ed. Merrill D. Peterson (New York, 1984), 1223–25; Jefferson to Philip Mazzei, December 29, 1813, Jefferson to Marquis de la Fayette, November 12, 1814, Jefferson to James Ronaldson, January 12, 1813, Jefferson to E. I. DuPont DeNemours, December 25, 1812, Jefferson Papers, Library of Congress.

21. John Adams to Thomas Jefferson, January 1, February 3, 10, 1812; Jefferson to Adams, January 21, 23, 1812, in *The Adams-Jefferson Letters*, ed. Lester J. Cappon (Chapel Hill, 1959), 2:290–97.

22. James A. Bear, Jr., and Lucia Stanton, eds., *Jefferson's Memorandum Books* (Princeton, 1997), 2:1288, 1293; Lucia Stanton, *Free Some Day: The African-American Families of Monticello* (Monticello, 1999), 91–92.

23. Bear and Stanton, *Jefferson's Memorandum Books*, 2:832, 839, 887; Jefferson to Martha Jefferson Randolph, November 13, December 4, 1791, February 5, 1792, Jefferson to Bowling Clark, September 21, 1792, Jefferson to James Madison, May 15, 1794, Jefferson to John Barnes, November 20, 1794, *Papers of Thomas Jefferson*, 22:294, 377, 23:103, 24:409, 28:76, 204.

24. For the presence of slaves in Jefferson's family as a political problem as well as a fact of life, see Jan E. Lewis, " 'The Blessings of Domestic Society': Thomas Jefferson's Family and the Transformation of American Politics," in *Jeffersonian Legacies*, ed. Peter S. Onuf (Charlottesville, 1993), 109–46, and Jan E. Lewis, "The White Jeffersons," in *Sally Hemings & Thomas Jefferson: History, Memory, and Civic Culture*, ed. Jan Ellen Lewis and Peter S. Onuf (Charlottesville, 1999), 127–60.

25. McCoy, *The Elusive Republic*; Richard Bushman, "Markets and Composite Farms in Early America," *William and Mary Quarterly*, 3d ser., 55 (1998): 351–74. On the aspirations of yeomen see Daniel Vickers, "Competency and Competition: Economic Culture in Early America," *William and Mary Quarterly*, 3d ser., 47 (1990): 3–39; Allan Kulikoff, *The Agrarian Origins of American Capitalism* (Charlottesville, 1992); and Allan Kulikoff, *From British Peasants to Colonial American Farmers* (Chapel Hill, 2001). For enlightened planters, see Joyce E. Chaplin, *An Anxious Pursuit: Agricultural Innovation and Modernity in the Lower South, 1730–1815* (Chapel Hill, 1993); Jeffrey Robert Young, *Domesticating Slavery: The Master Class in South Carolina and Georgia, 1670–1837* (Chapel Hill, 1999).

26. *Papers of Thomas Jefferson*, 1:29–30; *Virginia Gazette*, September 14, 1769, in *Papers of Thomas Jefferson*, 1:33.

27. Shane White and Graham White, *Stylin': African American Expressive Culture from Its Beginnings to the Zoot Suit* (Ithaca, 1998), 5–36, quoted at 10, 16. See also Eugene D. Genovese, *Roll, Jordan, Roll: The World the Slaves Made* (New York, 1974), 550–61; Jonathan Prude, " 'To Look Upon the Lower Sort': Runaway Ads and the Appearance of Unfree Labor in America, 1750–1800," *Journal of American History* 78 (1991): 124–60; Helen Bradley Foster, *"New Raiments of Self": African American Clothing in the Antebellum South* (Oxford, 1997); Patricia K. Hunt, "The Struggle to Achieve Individual Expression Through Clothing and Adornment: African American Women Under and After Slavery," in *Discovering the Women in Slavery*, ed. Patricia Morton (Athens, Ga., 1996), 227–40; Stephanie M. H. Camp, "The Pleasures of Resistance: Enslaved Women and Body Politics in the Plantation South, 1830–1861," *Journal of Southern History* 68 (2002): 533–72.

28. White and White, *Stylin*, 5–36; Michael Zuckerman, "Tocqueville, Turner, and Turds: Four Stories of Manners in Early America," *Journal of American History* 85 (1998): 19; Philip D. Morgan, *Slave Counterpoint: Black Culture in the Eighteenth-Century Chesapeake and Lowcountry* (Chapel Hill, 1998), 14; Brown, *Good Wives*, 89–90.

29. Billy G. Smith, "Runaway Slaves in the Mid-Atlantic Region during the American Revolution," in *The Transforming Hand of Revolution: Rethinking the American Revolution as a Social Movement*, ed. Ronald Hoffman and Peter J. Albert (Charlottesville, 1995), 217, 219; David Waldstreicher, "Reading the Runaways: Self-Fashioning, Print Culture, and Confidence in Slavery in the Eighteenth-Century Mid-Atlantic," *William and Mary Quarterly*, 3d ser., 56 (1999): 243–72.

30. Morgan, *Slave Counterpoint*, 128–32, 186; Ann Smart Martin, "Complex Commodities: The Enslaved as Producers and Consumers in Eighteenth-Century Virginia," paper presented at the Omohundro Institute of Early American History and Culture Annual Conference, Winston-Salem, June 1997; Ronald Hoffman, *Princes of Ireland, Planters of Maryland: A Carroll Family Saga* (Chapel Hill, 2001), 257; Ira Berlin, *Many Thousands Gone: The First Two Centuries of Slavery in America* (Cambridge, Mass., 1998), 160, 166; E. M. Halliday, *Understanding Thomas Jefferson* (New York, 2000), 144.

31. Berlin, *Many Thousands Gone*, 137, 142, 168; Barbara J. Heath, *Hidden Lives: The Archaeology of Slave Life at Thomas Jefferson's Poplar Forest* (Charlottesville, 1999), 53; John Bézis-Selfa, "Slavery and the Disciplining of Free Labor in the Colonial Mid-Atlantic Iron Industry," *Pennsylvania History* 64, Supplement (1997): 282.

32. White and White, *Stylin'*, 106–24.

33. This point is well made in Dana Frank, *Buy American: The Untold Story of Economic Nationalism* (Boston, 1999), chap. 1, relying on the work of Mary Beth Norton and Barbara Clark Smith.

34. Douglas Egerton, *Gabriel's Rebellion: The Virginia Slave Conspiracies of 1800 and 1802* (Chapel Hill, 1993); Sidbury, *Ploughshares into Swords*; James Oliver Horton and Lois Horton, *In Hope of Liberty: Culture, Community, and Protest among Northern Free Blacks, 1700–1860* (New York, 1997); Shane White, *Stories of Freedom in Black New York* (Cambridge, Mass., 2002).

35. My use of Hegel's master-slave dialectic here, as indeed all my thinking on slavery, is indebted to David Brion Davis. See Davis, *The Problem of Slavery in the Age of Revolution, 1770–1823* (Ithaca, 1975), esp. 561–63.

36. For Jefferson's impact on American slavery see James Sidbury, "Thomas Jefferson in Gabriel's Virginia," in Horn, Lewis and Onuf, *Revolution of 1800*, 199–219.

37. Charles Wiltse, "Introduction," *David Walker's Appeal* (New York, 1965), ix.

38. Anthony Benezet, *A Caution to Great Britain and Her Colonies, in a Short Representation of the Calamitous State of the Enslaved Negroes in the British Dominions* (London, 1767), 10; John Woolman, *Some Considerations on the Keeping of Negroes* (1754; reprint, New York, 1976), 52, quoted in William B. Hart, "Black 'Go-Betweens' and the Mutability of 'Race,' Status, and Identity on New York's Pre-Revolutionary Frontier," in *Contact Points: American Frontiers from the Mohawk Valley to the Mississippi, 1750–1830*, ed. Andrew R. L. Cayton and Fredrika J. Teute (Chapel Hill, 1998), 96 n. 16.

39. On the image of the slave in visual culture see Jean Fagan Yellin, *Women and Sisters: The Antislavery Feminists in American Culture* (New Haven, 1989), 3–27, 99–123; Kirk

Savage, *Standing Soldiers, Kneeling Slaves: Race, War and Monument in Nineteenth-Century America* (Princeton, 1997), 3–51; Bernard F. Reilly, Jr., "The Art of the Antislavery Movement," in *Courage and Conscience: Black and White Abolitionists in Boston*, ed. Donald Jacobs (Bloomington, 1993), 47–74; Philip Lapsansky, "Graphic Discord: Abolitionist and Antiabolitionist Images," in *The Abolitionist Sisterhood: Women's Political Culture in Antebellum America*, ed. Jean Fagan Yellin and John C. Van Horne (Ithaca, 1994), 201–30; Marcus Wood, *Blind Memory: Visual Representations of Slavery in England and America, 1780–1865* (New York, 2000).

40. Harriet Jacobs, *Incidents in the Life of a Slave Girl*, ed. Jean Fagan Yellin (Cambridge, Mass., 1987); Nell Irvin Painter, *Sojourner Truth: A Life, A Symbol* (New York, 1996); Rafia Zafar, *We Wear the Mask: African Americans Write American Literature, 1760–1870* (New York, 1997), 172–73; Lee Chambers-Schiller, " 'A Good Work Among the People': The Political Culture of the Boston Antislavery Fair," in Yellin and Van Horne, *Abolitionist Sisterhood*, 269. For the "erotic south" of abolitionism, see Ronald Walters, *The Antislavery Appeal: American Abolitionism after 1830* (New York, 1978), 70–87; Theodore Dwight Weld, ed., *American Slavery as It Is* (Boston, 1839); Karen Sanchez-Eppler, *Touching Liberty: Abolitionism, Feminism, and the Politics of the Body* (Berkeley, 1991).

41. I have assembled these and a few similar images in "Slavery and Freedom: Dressing the Part," in *The Struggle Against Slavery: A History in Documents* (New York, 2001), 96–103.

42. Eric Lott, *Love and Theft: Blackface Minstrelsy and the American Working Class* (New York, 1993); W. T. Lhamon, Jr., *Raising Cain: Blackface Performance from Jim Crow to Hip Hop* (Cambridge, Mass., 1998); Dale Cockrell, *Demons of Disorder: Early Blackface Minstrels and Their World* (New York, 1998).

43. Mark Neely, *The Union Divided: Party Politics in the Civil War North* (Cambridge, Mass., 2002), 126; Susan-Mary Grant, "Fighting for Freedom: African-American Soldiers in the Civil War," in *The American Civil War*, ed. Susan-Mary Grant and Brian Holden Reid (Harlow, Eng., 2000), 197; Jackie Napoleon Wilson, *Hidden Witness: African American Images from the Dawn of Photography to the Civil War* (New York, 1999); Julie Saville, *The Work of Reconstruction: From Slave to Wage Laborer in South Carolina, 1860–1870* (New York, 1995), 146, 173.

44. Jefferson to John Mason, August 18, 1814, Jefferson Papers, Library of Congress.

45. Cynthia Kierner sees such celebrations of women's role by southerners as a temporary response to crisis, but nevertheless clearly documents its extent at such moments. Kierner, *Beyond the Household: Women's Place in the Early South, 1700–1835* (Ithaca, N.Y., 1998), 134–36.

46. The letter is thus a quintessential example of what Jan Lewis has called the domestication of American politics, and the concomitant domestication of slavery. See her essays cited above as well as her essay, "The Problem of Slavery in Southern Political Discourse," in *Devising Liberty: Preserving and Creating Freedom in the New American Republic*, ed. David Thomas Konig (Stanford, 1995), esp. 283–89. The phrase, and part of the idea, originates with Paula Baker, "The Domestication of American Politics: Women

and American Political Society, 1780–1920," *American Historical Review* 89 (1984): 620–47. Of course, what Jefferson did here is also analogous to what New Englanders did with homespun (Ulrich, *Age of Homespun.*)

47. Nancy Isenberg has addressed this phenomenon with respect to women and politics in *Sex and Citizenship in Antebellum America* (Chapel Hill, 1998), esp. 48–55.

PART TWO

4

Women and Party Conflict
in the Early Republic

The political history of the early republic has traditionally been written as the story of great white males. It is, of course, a tale well worth telling. Commanding figures such as George Washington, Thomas Jefferson, James Madison, Alexander Hamilton, and John Adams seized the moment of the nation's founding and forged the institutions and ideas that continue to shape our government even today. As majestic as it is, however, the traditional narrative seems to have no place for women. The American Revolution did not produce a collective movement for women's rights. Women could neither vote (except for a brief time in New Jersey) nor hold political office. Strong social strictures prohibited women from speaking in public or asserting themselves outside the home. On these terms, women seem not to have played any role in the creation of a national political culture, particularly in the emergence of the two great political parties of the time, the Federalists and the Democratic-Republicans.

More recent scholarship has refocused the traditional narrative in a way that does make room for women. Historians have come to understand that "politics" encompassed a much more capacious realm extending well beyond the confines of voting, electioneering, and the formal institutions of governance. A wide variety of informal norms, processes, and symbolic actions can be considered genuinely "political" in the sense that they influenced the structure of political power or the dynamics of political action. This was particularly true in the early republic. At the same time that Federalists and Jeffersonians faced off in Congress, politics spread to the streets. Patriotic rituals, parades, and celebrations as well as the growth of a partisan press politicized ordinary people—women as well as men—and inculcated loyalty toward one party or the other. As David Waldstreicher, Simon Newman, and Jeffrey L. Pasley have shown, long before the emergence of a modern party system, party politics thrived at the grassroots level.[1]

Other historians have sought to expand the compass of politics and broaden the definition of political action even further. Politics, they say, permeates all relationships, not just those involving governance, and should be interpreted, according to Joan Scott, to include all "unequal distributions of power."[2] The value of this approach is that it allows historians to show that even those who were marginalized by or excluded from official institutions possess demonstrable kinds of political influence or authority. Catherine Allgor, Susan Branson, and Cynthia Kierner have fruitfully used this notion to explore how characteristically feminine behaviors could be deployed for political purposes.[3] Allgor, in particular, demonstrates that women who lived in early Washington consciously used their role as society matrons to bolster their husbands' political careers, cement political alliances, and negotiate patronage for friends and relatives.

Valuable as these contributions are, it is important for some purposes to retain the boundary between formal and informal politics and not to exaggerate the extent to which the personal was political. As one historian has recently noted, "Once we assume power is everywhere, it usually turns out to be nowhere very much; if it is analytically directionless, it scarcely needs to be taken into account." In other words, if everything becomes political, then nothing is political. There is, however, "a middle ground" between a too-narrow focus on elite politics in which women play no role and an overly expansive approach that loses sight of formal institutions of governance.[4] With respect to the early republic, this means that we must analyze the emergence of the Federalist and Republican parties not only in terms of men's conflicts with each other but also with respect to the interactions between women and men. From the Revolutionary era through the War of 1812, women's actions, while less visible than men's, helped shape the structure of party organizations and influence the nature of political conflict.

Contrary to the traditional narrative, women's involvement was critical to the emergence of the first party system.

The American Revolution permanently altered women's relationship to the political community. In previous wars male political leaders assumed without question that women would support their husbands' decisions, even if they inconvenienced the family or caused suffering for the wife. Patriot leaders did not make that assumption. They understood that American women were not passive or quiescent. Beginning with resistance to the Stamp Act in 1765, they publicly appealed to women for their support in the fight against Britain. Newspapers, magazines, and broadsides urged women to boycott imported goods, produce homemade clothing, and, if necessary, sacrifice their husbands, sons, and brothers on the field of battle. Women responded to men's pleas. By taking on their husbands' responsibilities, they made it possible for men to leave home and serve their country, either in the armed forces, the state legislatures, or the new U.S. Congress.[5]

With independence achieved, men celebrated women's contributions and honored their sacrifices. Women as well as men, noted Richard Dinmore, "gloried in the appellation rebel."[6] Like men, women had felt the scourge of British tyranny. Like men, they had suffered a multitude of deprivations and hardships. "Though ruin and desolation pervaded your country, and those to whom you [women] were bound by the dearest ties were insulted, outraged and imprisoned," proclaimed John Fauchereaud Grimké, "still you remained firm and undismayed in the conscientious discharge of your duty."[7] Although female patriotism differed from men's—it was, as Keating Lewis Simons noted, more "of a kind entirely suited to their sex"[8]—women had fully earned the country's esteem. "Our heroines, in their place," concluded Solomon Aiken, "were not a whit behind our foremost heroes."[9]

This change in the perception of women's role provided an opening for women into the male political arena. Although women had not gained the vote (nor had they even demanded it), they were now considered political beings. They made political choices and exercised political judgments. Their actions were thought to have a profound effect on the country's welfare. This was especially true now that the country was a self-governing republic rather than a monarchy. As "republican mothers," to use Linda Kerber's term, women would inculcate virtue, promote patriotism, and encourage self-sacrifice in their husbands and children. Political leaders could ignore "the sex" only at their own peril.[10]

From the Revolution through the War of 1812 leaders continued to seek women's involvement in politics. Yet the political context in which women acted had radically changed. As is well known, the framers of the Constitution had not anticipated the growth of a two-party political system. Yet almost as soon as the first Congress met, profound differences emerged between two groups, which eventually coalesced into the Federalist and Democratic-Republican parties.[11] While lacking the institutional structure of modern parties, these groups nonetheless promoted distinctly different visions of society and government. Their policies as well as ideologies diverged. Whereas Federalists supported a fiscal-military state that preserved the privileges of the governing elite, Republicans advocated an agrarian republic that opened up voting and officeholding to whole new classes of white men. In fact, however, both groups operated in a climate that rejected the legitimacy of partisan divisions. Parties were considered factions, groups of selfish men who pursued their own interests at the expense of the common good. Each side considered itself to be the true heir of the American Revolution. Neither would acknowledge the validity of the other's existence—or even recognize the extent to which their own actions contributed to the creation of a party system.[12]

The emergence of parties shattered the illusion of consensus on a common national good. "In *theory*," noted a political tract published in 1812, "Patriotism signifies *the disinterested love of our country, and an earnest desire to promote its best interests. But, in practice*, it too often signifies nothing more than a flaming zeal to promote the ties of the *party to which one belongs*, and an ardent desire to *obtain or to keep an office*!"[13] Patriotism had become partisanship.

As they vied for popular support, politicians began to reach out not only to men who could vote but also to women who, by definition, could not. Ironically, women's lack of official political status made them a much sought-after prize. Female patriotism, according to Abigail Adams, was "the most disinterested of all virtues";[14] it was purer and nobler than men's, untainted by self-interest or the pursuit of personal gain. As such, women's approval transformed the dross of political machination into the gold of elevated principle.

But women did not remain above the partisan fray; they soon became a part of it. As with men, women first gained a strong sense of party identity in connection with the French Revolution. Beginning around 1792, women began to express definite party affinities. Women as well as men wore the tri-colored cockades of the Republicans or black badges of the Federalists. "With their delicate fingers," noted one commentator, the "fair sex" made "the emblems of the contending parties."[15] Women's fingers, however, were not always so delicate. One Congressman claimed that he saw women "meet at the church door and violently pluck the badges from one another's bosoms."[16] In Boston, French ideas about liberty and equality led to a leveling in nomenclature. While men were to be called "cits," women were to be addressed as "citesses."[17] Extremism infected women as well as men. In reaction to the Terror in France, Nelly Parke Custis, step-granddaughter of George Washington, proclaimed that she had become "perfectly Federal" and denounced the French as *democratic murderers.*"[18]

A play written in the mid-1790s, called *The Politicians; or, A State of Things*, reflects a certain acceptance of women's politicization. The female characters' names, Mrs. Violent and Mrs. Turbulent, suggest the depth of women's partisanship. Mrs. Turbulent, a Republican sympathizer, attacks the opposition as vociferously as any man. George Washington, she said, was "never equal to the situation he was placed in: vastly have his talents been over-rated." He and his "infamous party," she declared, "have been the ruin of our country."[19] The Federalist Mrs. Violent, on the other, hand, refers to the Republicans as "a wicked, restless, marplotting set" and tells her counterpart, "Your Jacobin faction are to be charged with all the evils that have beset us, and all the troubles that await our country: you have been abetting the French tyrants from the first to the present moment."[20] Significantly, the play's heroes are men named Conciliate and Dispassionate. Rejecting the evils of faction, they are the voices of reason and moderation who embrace a nonpartisan ideal. The play's depiction of men and women is significant. While the work criticizes the disruptive effects of partisanship on society, it does not disparage women for holding political beliefs. Women's enmeshment in the partisan frenzy was as bad as, but no worse, than men's involvement.

Party sentiment politicized everyday life. Independence Day, for example, became a partisan holiday. Federalists and Democratic-Republicans throughout the county held their own separate celebrations, parades, picnics, and orations.[21] While Jeffersonians sponsored public readings of the Declaration of Independence, Federalists avoided mentioning the Declaration, with its embarrassing references to "natural rights" and "equality," and toasted their hero, George Washington, instead. Women's actions, too, increasingly took on a partisan valence. In Caldwell, New Jersey, a Republican stronghold, citizens cheered as "sixteen young ladies uniformed in white with garlands in their hats" marched in parade, "bearing the Cap of Liberty, enwreathed in laurel, and all fingering *Columbia*, in concert with the German flute." In nearby North Farms, the women processed behind the men "round the Tree of Liberty, accompanied with music, both instrumental and vocal."[22] On the Federalist side, women in New Haven, Connecticut, joined their husbands in singing "Adams and Liberty" or presented flags to local militia groups in an elaborate ceremony.[23] Such scenes were repeated throughout the country.

National political events deepened women's political convictions. The Jay Treaty of 1795 created as much controversy among women as men. Mercy Otis Warren railed against Washington, accusing the president of having become an "idol of the people" who erred in "his *Indian war*, his British *treaty*, his coldness to the cause of France, his love of adulation, his favouriteism,—and in many instances his injudicious appointments."[24] On the other side, Federalist Judith Sargent Murray dreaded the consequences if the treaty were defeated. Congressional opposition sent her into the "depth of misery," in which she feared "impending darkness . . . [on] the political horizon." Only after it narrowly won approval could she confidently assert that "every well disposed American must felicitate himself that the eventful scale hath preponderated in favour of Order and good government."[25]

Jefferson's election in 1800 likewise provoked contrasting reactions. Margaret Bayard Smith, a convert to the Republican cause, described the president's inauguration in adulatory tones. "I cannot describe the agitation I felt, while I looked around on the various multitude and while I listened to an address, containing principles the most correct, sentiments the most liberal, and wishes the most benevolent, conveyed in the most appropriate and elegant language and in a manner mild as it was firm."[26] Dedicated Federalist women, however, felt alarm or disgust. Visiting New York City on March 4, 1801, Harriet Trumbull sourly noted that the day was one of "great rejoicings" for the Democrats. The presence of "so many disorderly creatures in the streets" had inconvenienced her, making it impossible for her and her sister to make their way home.[27] Rebecca Woolsey Hillhouse also hated the new president, but found some dim comfort in the fact that inauguration day had passed without incident. It was less likely, then, she said that Jefferson's supporters would be "takin up *arms* or cuting off *heads* [as] they have threatened."[28] Hannah Foster of Brookfield, Massachusetts, remained unrepentant. As she told her husband in 1802, she hoped that the Republicans "may be more and more Divided till there wicked plans are Done away."[29] Like men, female partisans saw party politics as a Manichean battle between good and evil.

Foreign policy provoked particularly intense responses among women. A state of near war had raged for years on the high seas. In 1807, a particularly nasty incident caused Congress, at Jefferson's behest, to pass the Embargo Law, which put an absolute ban on the export of American goods. As during the Revolutionary era, Americans were to put themselves on a war footing, returning to simple values, forgoing imported luxuries, and becoming economically self-sufficient. By mid-1808, however, the sanctions appeared to be hurting the United States more than Europe. The value of exports plummeted. Goods rotted aboard ships. Harbor life came to a standstill. Internal trade ground to a halt.[30]

Men had learned during the Revolution that women could make or break an embargo. But this time, men were bitterly divided. While Federalists denounced the measure, Republicans rushed to its defense. Accordingly, Federalist men did little to solicit women's support while Republican men urged women to boycott goods and make sacrifices for the common good. "Our women," opined the *Richmond Enquirer*, "should all learn to spin, card, weave, dye, and manufacture, in the various modes for flax, hemp, cotton and wool. We may not have open markets abroad for years, and our planters will want the aid of our manufactures to keep up the price of their produce, and to furnish supplies."[31] Reaching out to their female adherents, Jeffersonians stressed their common bonds with women. "[To] The Fair Daughters of Columbia," said Alexandria militia men. "—Should we draw the sword they must draw the thread."[32] Each sex would in its own way help make the program a success.

Because the Embargo was as much a propaganda battle as an economic policy, each party tried to lure women to its side. Women's approval represented a coveted prize, a moral edge in the contest for popular opinion. One Federalist broadside, for example, featured a woodcut of a Satanic figure, complete with devilish tail, trying to tempt a shapely woman into violating the ban.[33] Another Federalist broadside trumpeted women's purported disaffection with Jefferson's ("Tommy's") policy:

> Thus Tommy destroys,
> A part of our joys;
> Yet we'll not let the beautiful Fair go;
> They all will contrive
> To keep commerce alive,
> There's nothing they hate like Embargo.[34]

As the protectors of the "beautiful Fair," Federalist men claimed to have won the support of women who kept "commerce alive" and opposed the nefarious policy. Republicans responded in kind. Disparaging the opposition's claims, their broadside maintained.

> Thus Tommy destroys intriguers' chief joys;
>   But to ruin will not let the Fair go;
> For he will secure, our damsels so pure,
>   By keeping off rogues with EMBARGO.[35]

Whereas Federalist "intriguers" would allow "rogues" to prey on American women, Republicans would protect their purity through enforcement of the ban. They would be the true guardians of American womanhood.

Women's responses divided along party lines. Southern Republican women set to work, spinning, weaving, and making homespun clothing. "[A] hundred thousand spinning wheels put in motion by female hands," asserted one female author, "will do as much towards establishing our independence, as a hundred thousand of the best militia men in America."[36] On the Fourth of July in 1808, women in Richmond and elsewhere in the South displayed their sentiments by wearing homespun to the day's festivities.[37] Other women made preparations for war. "The Ladies of Norfolk," demonstrating "a patriotism which does them much honour," made cartridges for men's guns.[38] Richmond women mobilized themselves into a volunteer corps to show their support for the troops.[39]

Opponents of the Embargo could often do little more than express their dissatisfaction privately. Observing the disastrous effects on her community, Rosalie Stier Calvert of Maryland lamented, "This embargo is ruining a vast number of people. If it continues for some time yet, the consequences will be incalculable." Her next remark reveals just how deeply she felt her Federalism. "On the other hand," she maintained, "[the Embargo] is going to be the means of effecting a total revolution in popular opinion and of destroying the Democratic party."[40] A Republican woman living in Philadelphia detected a similar trend and found it disturbing. "The Embargo," said Maria Beckley, "is Federalizing all the eastern States."[41] In Federalist strongholds in New England, some women did more than just talk. In the fall of 1808, a group of women in Augusta in the district of Maine reportedly marched en masse to the local jail and "liberated several of the prisoners, confined there for breaches of the embargo laws."[42]

The coming of the War of 1812 tested the political convictions of women from both parties. They knew that even though they would not be called to take up arms, war could transform their lives. If their husbands or sons were called to the field of battle, they would bear the burden of caring for farms, families, and businesses without male assistance. At worst, it meant that their loved ones might be killed or maimed in action. Republican leaders tried to assuage women's fears and cultivate their support. They appealed to women to imitate their Revolutionary foremothers. Solomon Aiken reminded women that during the Revolution it was "the fire of *female patriotism*" that had stimulated men to go off to war. Unwilling to "submit to the degradation of becoming mothers of a progeny of slaves," the women had told their husbands, " 'Go! Go, under the protection of Heaven, and save our country.' "[43] Attempting to flatter feminine vanity, Ebenezer French observed, "Our women all know and value the blessings of INDEPENDENCE; value our fathers, who fought for it, and value the sons, who will strive to preserve it."[44] Anthony Haswell beseeched the "matrons" of Bennington, Vermont, to teach their daughters how to inspire military zeal in men, as they had during the Revolution.[45] While a woman's opposition might deter a man from enlisting, her vocal support might convince him to join the cause. "Urge then your husbands, your brothers, your sons, and your lovers, to those scenes where danger calls, and glory invites," insisted another speaker. "Bid them rally around the standard of liberty, planted by the hands, and watered by the blood of your fathers."[46] Leaders were not adverse to a touch of hyperbole. "Remember," declared Elias Glover, "that no heart can resist the voice of patriotism, when urged by the lips of beauty and innocence."[47]

In reaching out to a female audience, men acknowledged women's political role and influence. The war effort would be successful, they suggested, only if women as well as men rallied enthusiastically behind the cause. In a poem written in New York addressed to "the Patriotic Ladies of our Metropolis," one author stressed the importance of women's moral support.

Ye Fair of our city! To you we appeal,
Whose hearts are not wrapt in a casement of steel;
Ye who weep o'oer the soldier and share in his woe,
Whose tears for your fond-one in sympathy flow.

. . . To the forts on the heights of rough Brooklyn repair,
And with us the joys of our misery share,
How gladly we'd see you! we'd shout and declare,
"The Hero alone is deserving the fair!"[48]

The function of women was thus twofold: to encourage men to go off to war and to reward them upon their return. In both cases, they would provide the secret weapon that would help make victory over the British possible.

The actions of Republican women during the War of 1812 resembled those of their Revolutionary foremothers. In Charleston, they made shirts; in New York, they made socks; in New London, they made bedding.[49] Women, however, did not simply do men's bidding. They undertook activities on their own initiative. Just as Esther DeBerdt Reed led a campaign during the Revolution to collect money for the Continental Army,[50] so did the "ladies" of Frankfort, Kentucky, take it upon themselves in 1812 to take around a "subscription paper" soliciting funds for the troops. A newspaper reported that although "we have not understood what amount was subscribed," a "number of liberal donations [were] received."[51] In October 1814, thirteen New York women founded the Stocking

Society at the home of Mrs. General Lewis. Its purpose was to collect money and donations of wool for "Socks, Mockasins, Mittens, and Cloth Hoods" for American soldiers and the state militia. The printed subscription lists contained the women's call to action. "We whose names are underwritten, having long enjoyed the blessings of peace and national prosperity, and participating also in the calamities of war with which the Almighty has been pleased in infinite wisdom to visit the United States—are desirous, as far as possible of alleviating the sufferings to which our Fathers, Husbands, Brothers, and Friends are exposed in defence of their country."[52] Their creed reflected a sense of mutual participation and shared experience in the fate of the nation. Although the broadside referred to "their"—meaning men's—country, the Society's private correspondence spoke of "the future of *our* Country" (emphasis added). As during the Revolution, women would be patriotic in a manner befitting their sex.

Publicly at least, Republican women put the national cause above their personal reservations and fears. In 1812, *Niles' Weekly Register* printed the story of Mary Pruitt, wife of John Pruitt of Abbeville district, and the mother of two daughters and fourteen (!) sons. When a recruiter came though their community seeking enlistments, two sons decided to volunteer. Although the father demurred, he sent them to their mother. In contrast to the selfish father, she gave them her blessing, saying, "Be virtuous, faithful and honest, and my fears are at an end." The newspapers praised her conduct, admonishing readers, "Let those who think lightly of female virtue and patriotism read this and blush for shame."[53] Women's patriotism would again be an inspiration to men.

The story was different among Federalist women. Women, it should be noted, could express their political beliefs as much by what they did not do as by what they did do. Unlike their Republican counterparts, female Federalists during the War of 1812 did *not* make homespun or darn socks or collect money for the troops. Harriet Livermore, daughter of a Federalist congressman, recalled the summer of 1812 as a "melancholy season. . . . I abhorred the measures adopted by our rulers to secure sailors' rights, and avenge maritime affronts and injuries."[54] Livermore's precise formulation—a war to protect "sailor's rights" and to vindicate "maritime" interests—reflects her political sophistication as well as her intense partisanship.

Yet even women who opposed the war knew that they, too, might be asked to sacrifice their husbands or sons for the war effort. Federalist politicians and ministers fanned the flames of hostility. One minister, in fact, condemned from the pulpit "everyone who contributed the smallest degree of their influence to aid the unjust and unrighteous cause."[55] Sally Ripley of Massachusetts recorded the events of one "disorderly Sabbath" when her town received word that many of its men were drafted, effective immediately. "Public worship was this fore-noon suspended and instead was heard the beating of drums. . . . Many young men are thus called at short warning to leave their homes and families and quiet lives, for the din of war, the bustle of a camp and perhaps the battles' rage." Her objections were more political than personal, since her husband was "not liable to be called upon to serve in this inglorious cause." She was now enmeshed in the war because her friends and neighbors were at risk. Thus, her final thought was "May Jehovah be the God of our Armies and go with our troops whether to the field or to peace."[56]

Partisanship even tinged women's reactions to peace. In Richmond, a Re-publican center, the announcement of peace provoked, according to Julia Cabell Rives, a "universal rejoicing" expressed in "the thunders of innocent artillery, fire-works and illuminations [that] testified to the happiness and contentment of the inhabitants of our cities."[57] But Sally Ripley sounded a more cautionary note. "Many precious lives have been lost and much treasure wasted while the nation has won nothing but disgrace."[58] Far from fostering unity, the war exacer-bated political divisions among women as well as men.

Although the War of 1812 is sometimes called the second War for American Independence, it differed profoundly from the earlier conflict. After the Revolu-tion, the winners, the patriots, could define what patriotism meant without facing competing definitions from their loyalist adversaries. And when they recalled the war, they could be selective in their memories, stressing unity and minimizing dissent. In contrast, the War of 1812 wrenched the country in two, deepening the cleavage between parties. Even after the war ended, there was not—and would not be for many years—any clear victor in the contest between Federalists and Democratic-Republicans. Here an exclusive focus on national politics is misleading. Although the Federalists would never again win the presi-dency, and their power in Congress declined, they continued to display amazing resilience in state and local elections.[59] Federalist social organizations and benev-olent societies continued to flourish. Many individuals continued to identify themselves as Federalists. Thus factionalism continued to rear its ugly head, long after most Americans believed it would be extinguished. While it is true, as Richard Hofstadter has argued, that Americans did not regard parties as positive forms of political organization until at least the 1830s, party conflict had become an entrenched, though unwelcome, feature of political life.

The persistence of party conflict provided a new context for understand-ing women's political involvement. During the 1790s, both Federalists and Democratic-Republicans had solicited women's participation and involvement at party functions. They knew that women's presence helped broaden their party's appeal and widen its base of popular support. Moreover, in an era in which men themselves regarded partisanship as illegitimate, women's approval conferred moral sanction on men's somewhat suspect partisan activities. Yet once women became as partisan as men, they could no longer function as impartial symbols of moral authority. Before women had been trump cards, proving the superiority of one side over the other. Now they were wild cards, laughing reminders that neither side could claim an absolute moral or political edge. Patriotism had fractured and with it the belief that women could be patriotic without being partisan.

The extent of women's politicization, in fact, raised troubling questions about whether the country could withstand the assaults of partisan warfare on its social fabric. Partisanship was considered evil not only because it promoted self-interest but also because of its deleterious effects on society. Parties promoted a spirit of violence, an intolerance that undermined civility, harmony, and sociability. Factions were particularly dangerous in America. Unlike European nations whose inhabitants shared a long history and common traditions, the United States was a new nation, a heterogeneous society whose government was far off and at a distance. Differing economic interests, social patterns, and regional loyalties constantly threatened to tear it apart.

Party conflict further eroded the fragile bonds linking the states into a union and the people into a nation. Partisans embraced their views with an almost religious intensity. Party principles had the status of Truth. Just as established religions claimed to have a monopoly on religious truth, so each party—Federalists and Republicans alike—believed it possessed the one correct way to govern. "Truth," as John Taylor put it in his *Definition of Parties*, "is a thing, not of divisibility into conflicting parts, but of unity. Hence both sides cannot be right."[60] As long as party differences were cast in semi-religious terms as disputes over Truth, disagreements could never be simply a matter of differing opinions. Dissent was a kind of heresy; party conflict was tantamount to a holy war.

The results were disastrous for civil society. "Every social feeling, every generous emotion, every noble sentiment," noted one observer, "is usually sacrificed on the altar of *Party Spirit*."[61] Violence erupted in Congress. Discord ravaged communities. People stopped speaking to friends and neighbors. A New Yorker commented in 1804, "At no time since the revolution, has party spirit raged with such unbridled fury. . . . Party animosity swallows every social feeling. Neighbour looks at neighbour as an enemy . . . and each man regards his friend with a jealous eye." And lest the reader suspect exaggeration, the writer added, "Every man now conversant with society will bear witness that the above representation is *literally true*."[62] At many points from the mid-1790s through the War of 1812, Judith Sargent Murray and others repeatedly wondered whether the nation could withstand "the maddening rage of Party."[63]

The crisis in civility occurred simultaneously with the emergence of a new notion of womanhood, referred to variously as "the cult of domesticity," "the discourse of domesticity," or "separate spheres ideology."[64] Appearing in newspapers, ladies' magazines, and periodical literature, this discourse articulated an ideal in which men and women occupied separate but equal roles in society. As creatures of the domestic sphere, women were to confine their attentions to home, family, and religion; men were to venture into the corrupt and corrupting world of wage labor, business, and politics. Although a normative ideal rather than a description of actual behavior, separate spheres ideology increasingly dominated publications directed toward a female audience in the first decades of the nineteenth century.

Significantly, separate spheres ideology was radically at odds with the kind of political behavior in which women had engaged, with men's encouragement, from the time of the American Revolution. One recurrent theme within domestic discourse specifically addressed the question of women's political participation. The message was quite blunt: women should withdraw from party politics. Nothing less than the Union's survival was said to be at stake. Men had abdicated their role as mediators and peacemakers. Enmeshed in their factional struggles, men's emotions had become "*over-heated*." In fact, "the strength of their attachment to their party" had, according to one commentator, led to "the weakness, if not total demolition of their [men's] intellects."[65] Women must thus come to the rescue. As the guardians of society's morals and manners, they were, said the *Lady's Weekly Miscellany*, "beings of the highest consequence, and on them depends the healthiness or the contagion of social intercourse."[66] By exercising their influence on society, and removing themselves from politics, women could mediate between warring factions, ease social tensions, and mitigate the damage done to the polity. If politics had become a holy war, then women should assume the role of noncombatants.

Women, it was said, should themselves assume the role of peacemaker and mediator. "By the persuasive mildness of your conversation, and the sovereign influence of your example," a Massachusetts speaker told the "Columbian Fair" of Roxbury, you can "soothe party discord to friendship and unity."[67] Women's salubrious influence would contain partisanship's most divisive effects. Through "woman's kindness of heart," said the *Ladies' Magazine*, "political and polemical disputation might . . . be restrained within the limits of decency and propriety: local contentions [could] be charmed away, and men [might] be softened down into beings altogether better fitted for the great purposes of life."[68] *The Ladies'*

Visiter agreed: women's "benevolent affections" could "heal the dissentions of individuals and of society." In fact, "were commotions to arise from the feuds of faction, or the rancour of party spirit, that would threaten to embroil the state in civil discord, . . . [women] would be enabled . . . to unite the contentious, to heal the disaffected, and restore tranquility and peace to their country."[69]

Women's distinctively feminine traits would moderate factional strife. Rather than convince men through reason or logic, they should manipulate them with the power of their beauty, the "magic" of their smiles, the "threats" of their tears, or the virtue of their moral example.[70] Female indirection was said to magnify rather than lessen woman's power. The "stubbornness of party zeal," one woman noted, was "deaf to argument," but could be overcome if women used the "eloquence of tears" to "quell the opposition, disarming Fed. and Rep. and Demo. and reconciling man to man, and man to rule, and save the land from pending woe."[71]

Most significantly, women should abjure politics and focus on rearing a new generation of patriotic citizens. Women could, according to Asa Packard, "by guiding the inquiries, enriching the minds and forming the childish and youthful habits," shape the "future Citizens, future Legislators, Magistrates, Judges and Generals." But if, he said, women "like ardent politicians, assume a part in political disputes, on points where great and good cannot meet, . . . you will permit statesmen to *smile*."[72] As their (male) children's first teachers, they could promote intellectual openness and a tolerance of dissent. In a speech to the Harrisonburg Ladies' Academy, Daniel Bryan observed, "As man becomes more enlightened, the violence of party malignity, which is the offspring of prejudice, jealousy, avaricious competition, and conflicting pride, abates as liberality increases. . . . It is," he continued, "in the power of the well-educated and refined mother, to inspire the infant son with noble and expanded sentiments, to implant in his bosom correct views of an original diversity of the human mind, and convince him of the consequent impossibility for all men to think alike on subjects involving a complexity of interests."[73] Mothers could, in other words, teach their children that not every difference of opinion was a battle over Truth. If children grew up to be "men of moderation,"[74] they could settle disputes rationally, through negotiation and compromise rather than through violence and vituperation. "Liberality" and mutual respect would ameliorate party antagonisms.

Women might even be able to extinguish the flame of partisanship altogether. To achieve this, however, women would have to renounce their own partisan identities. For example, even when a woman agreed with her spouse's political ideas, she should refrain from engaging in political discussions. If, according to the *Monthly Magazine*, she allowed "her bosom . . . to swell with the turbulent spirit of party," then she would "agitate rather than soothe her husband." She should be a domestic pacifier. "When the harmony of [her husband's soul] is disturbed by political discord, she should be its regulator, and by her gentleness, attune it again to love and domestic delight."[75]

If women rejected the whole notion of factionalism, they could cultivate a disdain for partisanship in their children. In a piece called "Daughters of Freedom," originally written in 1809 for the *Scioto Gazette* and republished in an Indiana newspaper, "Laura" outlined her solution to the current crisis. Addressing other women as "The Daughters of Fredonia," she disparaged the influence of partisanship on American life. "Fed. and Rep. and Demo. ingrate to woman's ear, [and] cause dissention. Names how odious! Fie, Fie!" Although her husband was a Federalist, she herself spoke "without distinction of party . . . in the unbiassed language of a sister patriot." Other women, she insisted, should do the same. Although they should be committed to their country, they should stay aloof from party politics. Most especially, women should raise their children free from the taint of party labels and conflicts. Once this occurs, she said, "A race of heroes then may rise, not Fed. and Rep. and Demo. . . . Let men be brothers, women sisters; all Fredonians."[76] By positioning themselves and their children above the partisan fray, women would, in the words of Donald Fraser, "be the means of restoring peace to the world!"[77]

Domestic ideology, then, upheld the value of female nonpartisanship as a way to mitigate factionalism's most injurious effects. As long as women acted as the guarantors of social harmony, then men could engage in vicious partisan struggles without destroying their communities, undermining the social order, or destroying the union. Dolley Madison represented the new feminine ideal. As the wife of President James Madison, her charm and welcoming manner fostered an environment where, according to Margaret Bayard Smith, "*party* was lost in *social spirit*."[78] Quoting Jefferson's famous inaugural address, another author observed, "A politician of the present day, exclaimed on a memorable occasion, 'we are all federalists, we are all republicans.' In her intercourse with society, Mrs. Madison reduced this liberal sentiment to practice." Unlike her husband, whose partisan sentiments were unmistakable, Dolley Madison's gracious sociability prevented the contagion of party from spreading its divisive effects. "At a time when the restless spirit of party covered every path with thorns, this lady held the branch of reconciliation."[79] For her, a difference of opinion did not constitute a difference of principle. Or so it was said.

If domestic ideology provided a kind of theoretical solution to party conflict, it created other problems. The notion of gendered spheres gained prominence at the very time that women were participating in politics to a greater extent than ever before. The coincidence is not accidental. At the very least, the tension between an apolitical feminine ideal and the realities of partisan politics may account for the increasingly strident denunciations of "female politicians" found in the prescriptive literature of the early nineteenth century. If women had already ventured outside the home, invading—even at men's behest—the male realm of politics, it was all the more necessary to convince them to leave. One article attacking "female politicians," for example, concluded, "Within the domestic circle . . . every female should reside. There she may, if she will, find enough to fill the most capacious soul."[80] Another piece, criticizing the disagreeable effects of "female politicians" on domestic life, noted, "The eternal wrangling of discordant opinions about men and offices, and the petty details of elections and caucuses . . . may impair the harmony of one social circle, interfere with the domestic arrangements of one family, and drive from its intercourse all sensible company." The danger was as much for the individual woman as for society. "There can be no excuse for a female deserting her allotted privacy, and volunteering to encounter gladiators in the political arena. She has all to lose— nothing to gain." Such women should be shunned as "evil."[81]

Separate spheres ideology thus had profound political implications for women. It divided responsibility for the common good along gender lines: men would be responsible for politics; women would be responsible for society. This division of labor was part of a larger process of insulating society from politics. Just as the disestablishment of church from state enabled dissenting religious groups to peacefully coexist, so the separation of women from politics would allow competing political factions to indulge in their internecine battles without tearing society to pieces. As portrayed in the prescriptive literature, this arrangement appeared to enhance women's power and elevate their status. Women were depicted as vital players in the new republican order, crucial factors in maintaining social stability and political cohesion. From another angle, however, the new discourse represented an effort to diminish, or even thwart, women's growing political influence. Although women were still said to possess a political role, they were now supposed to exercise their influence only through indirection, by acting on husbands and children, rather than directly through their own participation in partisan causes and events. In effect, these strictures diminished the range of women's political choices.

Domestic ideology, moreover, blunted the impact of egalitarian ideology on the status of women. Rhetorically, at least, adjustments had been made to show the equivalence of men's and women's positions. If each sex occupied a role that was separate and equal, then no further social or political changes seemed necessary. Thus while historians usually portray separate spheres ideology as a tool that was used to prevent women from entering politics, it may in fact have represented something else: a conservative reaction against women's more extensive involvement in the nation's political life. Through their participation, women had helped create the problem of party politics. Now, by leaving, they would help resolve the conflict.

It is important to remember, however, that prescriptions against women's involvement in politics were just that, prescriptions. Women did not immediately or universally abandon politics. Even into the 1820s and 1830s, many white, middle-class women continued to read newspapers, inform themselves about political matters, and express their political opinions in letters, correspondence, and fiction.[82] During the 1840s, a group of women campaigned publicly in favor of presidential candidate William Henry Harrison.[83] Throughout the entire period, large numbers joined social reform movements, such as anti-slavery and temperance organizations, in order to eradicate the evils of American society. Some eventually turned to political action of various sorts, including petitioning and lobbying, in order to achieve their goals.[84] Thus even at the height of domestic ideology's influence, rhetoric had not completely constrained reality.

Yet a sea change had occurred. The new discourse about womanhood delegitimated what the American Revolution had opened up: norms sanctioning women's active involvement in politics. By the 1820s, firmer distinctions were made between women's social contributions, which were acceptable, and their political contributions, which were not. As patriots, women were to renounce their partisan allegiances for the sake of the common good. As peacemakers, mediators, wives, and mothers, they should use their feminine wiles and maternal solicitude to dampen party conflict among men. As a result, even as women in the temperance and abolitionist movements reentered politics through the back door of social reform, they denied that their actions should be construed as "political."[85] Now the barriers to women's participation in politics were more explicit, and perhaps even higher, than they had been before the American Revolution.

Sarah Josepha Hale's *Ladies' Magazine* published a fictional piece in July 1829 that epitomizes the new feminine ideal.[86] "Political Parties" tells the story of a Miss Pope, who recounts her youthful follies to her two young nieces. Her sin, it seems, was political rather than moral. Once, she said, she was engaged to a handsome young man named George Kendall. "This was," she noted, during the Quasi War with France in "the winter of '98 and 99—when party spirit raged so bitterly." Kendall went off to college, but returned a changed man. He was a Jeffersonian. "Strange as it may seem to you, strange indeed as it now seems to me," she told her nieces, "I did then believe that if the democratic party succeeded in electing their candidate, our liberty, laws and religion would all be sacrificed." Outraged and horrified, she tried to get him to recant his absurd notions. "I made the sentiments of my party the standard of rectitude, and had George committed a murder, I should hardly have been more shocked than when he declared himself a republican."[87]

At one point, Kendall accompanied her home, where he encountered her father, a died-in-the-wool Federalist. A heated argument ensued. Pope's father sent the young man packing. Naively, the young woman expected love to conquer politics. She fully expected her fiancé to see the error of his ways. He did not. He moved away, leaving his opinionated lady friend to live and die "an old maid."[88] Lest anyone miss the point, the woman warned her nieces: "I have told you this story that you may be warned against indulging the rancor of party feelings. I do not say ladies should abstain from all political reading or conversation. . . . But their influence should be exerted to allay, not to excite party animosities: their concern should be for their whole country, not for a party."[89] No other epitaph for "female politicians" was necessary.

NOTES

1. David Waldstreicher, *In the Midst of Perpetual Fetes: The Making of American Nationalism, 1776–1820* (Chapel Hill, 1997); Simon P. Newman, *Parades and the Politics of the Street: Festive Culture in the Early American Republic* (Philadelphia, 1997); Jeffrey L. Pasley, *"The Tyranny of Printers": Newspaper Politics in the Early American Republic* (Charlottesville, 2001).

2. Joan Scott, "Women's History," in *Gender and the Politics of History* (New York, 1988), 26.

3. Catherine Allgor, *Parlor Politics, in Which the Ladies of Washington Help Build a City and a Government* (Charlottesville, 2000); Susan Branson, *These Fiery Frenchified Dames: Women and Political Culture in Early National Philadelphia* (Philadelphia, 2001); Cynthia A. Kierner, *Beyond the Household: Women's Place in the Early South, 1700–1835* (Ithaca, 1998).

4. Susan Pedersen, "The Future of Feminist History," *Perspectives: American Historical Association Newsletter* 38 (October 2000), 22, 24.

5. Linda K. Kerber, *Women of the Republic: Intellect & Ideology in Revolutionary America* (New York, 1980); Mary Beth Norton, *Liberty's Daughters: The Revolutionary Experience of American Women, 1750–1800* (Ithaca, 1980); Alfred F. Young, "The Women of Boston: 'Persons of Consequence' in the Making of the American Revolution, 1765–76," in *Women & Politics in the Age of the Democratic Revolution*, ed. Harriet B. Applewhite and Darline G. Levy (Ann Arbor, 1990), 181–226.

6. Richard Dinmore, *A Long Talk, Delivered before the Tammany Society, of Alexandria, District of Columbia, at their First Anniversary Meeting, May 12, 1804* (Alexandria, 1804), 12.

7. John Fauchereaud Grimké, *An Oration, Delivered in St. Philip's Church, before the Inhabitants of Charleston, South-Carolina, on Saturday, the Fourth of July, 1807* (Charleston, 1807), 17.

8. Keating Lewis Simon, *An Oration delivered in the Independent Circular Church, before the Inhabitants of Charleston, South-Carolina, on Friday, The Fourth of July, 1806* (Charleston, 1806), 6.

9. Solomon Aiken, *An Oration, Delivered before the Republican Citizens of Newburyport, and Its Vicinity, July 4, 1810* (Newburyport, 1810), 13.

10. Kerber, *Women of the Republic*, 235–88. For a sense of a new, more political awareness among women, who referred to themselves as "the sex," see, for example, Judith Sargent Murray, *The Gleaner*, ed. Nina Baym (Schenectady, 1992), 702–9; *The Female Advocate* (New Haven, 1801), 10–21.

11. Richard Hofstadter, *The Idea of a Party System: The Rise of Legitimate Opposition in the United States, 1780–1840* (Berkeley, 1969), 40–73.

12. Ibid., 74–121; Joyce Appleby, *Capitalism and a New Social Order: The Republican Vision of the 1790s* (New York, 1984); Stanley Elkins and Eric McKitrick, *The Age of Federalism: The Early American Republic: 1788–1800* (New York, 1993); David Hackett Fischer, *The Revolution of American Conservatism: The Federalist Party in the Era of Jeffersonian Democracy* (New York, 1965); Linda K. Kerber, *Federalists in Dissent: Imagery and Ideology in Jeffersonian America* (Ithaca, 1970); Drew McCoy, *The Elusive Republic: Political Economy in Jeffersonian America* (Chapel Hill, 1980); James Roger Sharp, *American Politics in the Early Republic: The New Nation in Crisis* (New Haven, 1993).

13. [A Lay Preacher], *A Political Catechism, Intended for the Use of Children of a Larger Growth, and Respectfully Dedicated to the Republicans of the Counties of Morris, Essex and Sussex, in the State of New-Jersey* (Morris-Town, N.J., 1812), 15.

14. Abigail Adams to John Adams, June 17, 1782, *Adams Family Correspondence*, ed. L. H. Butterfield (Cambridge, Mass., 1963), 4:328.

15. John Morin Scott, *Oration delivered before the Philadelphia Association for Celebrating the Fourth of July, without Distinction of Party (July 4, 1833)* (Philadelphia, 1833), 8.

16. Cited in Alexander DeConde, *The Quasi-War: The Politics and Diplomacy of the Undeclared War with France 1797–1801* (New York, 1966), 82–83.

17. Charles Downer Hazen, *Contemporary American Opinion of the French Revolution*, Johns Hopkins University Studies in History and Political Science 16 (Baltimore, 1964), 214–15.

18. Eleanor Parke Custis to Elizabeth Bordley, November 23, 1797, and May 14, 1798, in *George Washington's Beautiful Nelly*, ed. Patricia Brady (Columbia, S.C., 1991), 41, 52.

19. [John Murdock], *The Politicians; or, A State of Things. A Dramatic Piece* (Philadelphia, 1798), 4.

20. Ibid., 4, 5.

21. Len Travers, *Celebrating the Fourth: Independence Day and the Rites of Nationalism in the Early Republic* (Amherst, 1997), 88–106; Newman, *Parades and the Politics*, 83–119.

22. Newark *Centinel of Freedom*, July 19, 1797.

23. Branson, *Fiery Frenchified Dames*, 82–87; Waldstreicher, *Perpetual Fetes*, 156–60.

24. Mercy Otis Warren to a Member of Congress, Plymouth 1795, Mercy Otis Warren Papers, Massachusetts Historical Society, Letterbook, 1:483.

25. Judith Sargent Murray to her brother, April 13, May 8, 1796, Judith Sargent Murray Papers, Mississippi State Archives, Jackson, Letterbook, 9:572, 583–84.

26. Margaret Bayard Smith to Miss Susan B. Smith, March 4, 1801, in *The First Forty Years of Washington Society in the Family Letters of Margaret Bayard Smith*, ed. Gaillard Hunt (New York, 1965), 25–26.

27. Harriet Trumbull to Daniel Wadsworth, May 6, 1801, in *A Season in New York 1801: Letters of Harriet and Maria Trumbull*, ed. Helen M. Morgan (Pittsburgh, 1969), 137.

28. Quoted in Karen Kauffman, "James and Rebecca Hillhouse: Public and Private Commitments in the Early Republic," *Connecticut History* 28 (Fall 1999): 116.

29. Rebecca Faulkner Foster to Dwight Foster, April 1, 1802, Foster Family Papers, American Antiquarian Society, Box 4.

30. Norman K. Risjord, *Jefferson's America, 1760–1815* (Madison, 1991), 268–70.

31. *Richmond Enquirer*, February 26, 1808; Kierner, *Beyond the Household*, 133–37; Louis Martin Sears, "The South and the Embargo," *South Atlantic Quarterly* 20 (1921): 254–65.

32. *Alexandria Daily Advertiser* [Virginia], July 6, 1808.

33. *The Embargo: A New Song—Tune 'Yankee Doodle'* (1808), broadside, American Antiquarian Society.

34. *The Embargo* (1808), broadside, American Antiquarian Society.

35. *The Sacred Refuge for Federalists* (1808), broadside, American Antiquarian Society.

36. Quoted in Kierner, *Beyond the Household*, 135.

37. Ibid.

38. *New-England Palladium*, July 14, 1807, reprinted in *New-York Weekly Museum*, July 18, 1807; *New-York Weekly Museum*, December 31, 1808.

39. *New-England Palladium*, August 7, 1807.

40. Rosalie Stier Calvert to H. J. Stier, July 9, 1808, in *Mistress of Riverdale: The Plantation Letters of Roslie Stier Calvert, 1795–1821*, ed. Margaret Law Callcott (Baltimore, 1991), 190.

41. Maria Beckley to Lucy Southall, June 8, 1808, Cutts Family Correspondence, Library of Congress.

42. *New-York Weekly Museum*, December 31, 1808.

43. Aiken, *Oration*, 13.

44. Ebenezer French, *An Oration, Pronounced July 4th, 1805, Before the Young Democratic Republicans of the Town of Boston in Commemoration of the Anniversary of American Independence*, 2d ed. (Boston, 1805), 22.

45. Anthony Haswell, "The Voice of Liberty," *Songs, Written for the Celebration of the 16th of August, 1810* (Bennington, Vt., 1810), 11.

46. Philip Mathews, *An Oration, Delivered on the 5th of July, 1813, in the Episcopal Church of Saint Helen* (Charleston, S.C., 1813), 27–28.

47. Elias Glover, *An Oration, Delivered at the Court-House in Cincinnati, on the Fourth of July 1806* (Cincinnati, 1806), 23–24.

48. *New-York Weekly Museum*, October 15, 1814.

49. Baltimore *Niles' Weekly Register*, July 2, 1814, 320; November 19, 1814, 168, supplement (1814), 188.

50. Norton, *Liberty's Daughters*, 178–88.

51. *Richmond Enquirer*, October 13, 1812.

52. Stocking Society Proceedings, Letter of November 1, 1814, and Subscription List (broadside), Papers of the Stocking Society, Luther Bradish Papers, New-York Historical Society.

53. Baltimore *Niles' Weekly Register*, August 22, 1812.

54. Harriet Livermore, *A Narration of Religious Experience* (Concord, N.H., 1826), 69.

55. Sally Ripley Diary, April 8, 1813, American Antiquarian Society.

56. Ibid., September 11, 1814.

57. Autobiography of Mrs. William C. Rives, William Cabell Rives Papers, Container 103, Library of Congress, 23.

58. Sally Ripley Diary, February 19, 1815, American Antiquarian Society.

59. Shaw Livermore, Jr., *The Twilight of Federalism: The Disintegration of the Federalist Party, 1815–1830* (Princeton, 1962), 265; Hofstadter, *Idea of a Party System*, 74–121; Pasley, *Tyranny of Printers*, 348–99; Andrew Robertson and Philip Lampi, "The Election of 1800 Revisited," paper presented at annual meeting of the American Historical Association, Chicago, January 9, 2000.

60. John Taylor, *A Definition of Parties; or the Political Effects of the Paper System Considered* (Philadelphia, 1794), dedication.

61. Joseph Bartlett, *Aphorisms on Man, Manners, Principles, & Things* (Portsmouth, N.H., 1810), 136.

62. Hudson (N.Y.) *Balance, and Columbian Repository*, April 24, 1804, 130–31.

63. Judith Sargent Murray to her brother, November 30, 1795, Judith Sargent Murray Papers, Letterbook, 9:495.

64. Nancy F. Cott, *The Bonds of Womanhood: 'Woman's Sphere' in New England, 1780–1835* (New Haven, 1977); Linda Kerber, "Separate Spheres, Female Worlds, Woman's Place: The Rhetoric of Women's History," *Journal of American History* 75 (1988): 9–39. In the second edition of *The Bonds of Womanhood* (New Haven, 1997), Cott uses the term "discourse of domesticity" in preference to her earlier usage, "cult of domesticity," xvii.

65. "For the Balance," *Balance, and Columbia Repository*, August 21, 1804.

66. New York *Lady's Weekly Miscellany*, December 13, 1806, 53.

67. "An Oration, Pronounced at Roxbury, July 4, 1800," *Columbian Phenix or, Boston Review*, July 1800, 425.

68. *Ladies' Magazine,* June 1831, 266.

69. Marietta (Pa.) *Ladies' Visiter,* May 27, 1819, 5.

70. *The Juvenile Port-Folio,* June 3, 1815, 86; *Literary Magazine and American Register* (Philadelphia), June 1806, 407.

71. Vincennes *Western Sun,* March 18, 1809.

72. Asa Packard, *An Oration, on the Means of Perpetuating Independence, delivered at East-Sudbury, July 4th, 1815* (Boston, 1815), 14–15.

73. Daniel Bryan, *Oration on Female Education, Delivered before the Visitors and Students of the Female Academy in Harrisonburg, August 4th, 1815* (Harrisonburg, Pa., 1816), 10.

74. *American Moral and Sentimental Magazine,* September 25, 1797, 217.

75. *The Monthly Magazine, and American Review* 3 (December 1800): 417–18, reprinted in New York *Lady's Monitor,* May 29, 1802.

76. Vincennes *Western Sun,* March 18, 1809.

77. [Donald Fraser], *Party-Spirit Exposed, or Remarks on the Times: to which is added Some Important Hints to the Ladies* (New York, 1799), 23.

78. *Ladies' Magazine, and Literary Gazette* 4 (December 1831): 530.

79. Philadelphia *Ladies' Literary Museum, or Weekly Repository,* February 7, 1818, 34. Of course, as Allgor points out, Dolley Madison's social charm was not as nonpartisan as it seemed. She was extremely successful in achieving partisan goals for herself and her husband. Allgor, *Parlor Politics,* 48–101. However, the contradiction between the rhetoric and the reality just goes to highlight the importance of the emerging discourse that attempted to depoliticize women.

80. *The Monthly Magazine, and American Review,* December 1800, 418; reprinted in *The Lady's Monitor,* May 29, 1802.

81. *The New York Mirror: A Repository of Polite Literature and the Arts,* September 25, 1830, 95.

82. See two articles by Ronald J. Zboray and Mary Saracino Zboray: "Political News and Female Readership In Antebellum Boston and Its Region," *Journalism History* 22 (1996): 2–14, and "Whig Women, Politics, and Culture in the Campaign of 1840: Three Perspectives from Massachusetts," *Journal of the Early Republic* 17 (1997): 278–315.

83. Elizabeth R. Varon, *We Mean to be Counted: White Women and Politics in Antebellum Virginia* (Chapel Hill, 1998), 74–84.

84. Lori D. Ginzberg, *Women and the Work of Benevolence: Morality, Politics, and Class in the Nineteenth-Century United States* (New Haven, 1990).

85. Ibid., 67–86. "Virtually all antebellum female activists, from ultraists to quite conservative women, recoiled from a public association with the potentially partisan nature of their efforts, but they lived with the contradictions of exerting their influence in decidedly political ways toward clearly political ends" (69).

86. *Ladies' Magazine,* July 1829, 299–307.

87. Ibid., 303.

88. Ibid., 299.

89. Ibid., 306.

5

The "Little Emperor"

Aaron Burr, Dandyism, and the
Sexual Politics of Treason

Lord Byron, as the story goes, identified three nineteenth-century men as truly great. Showing supreme humility, the poet placed himself third on the list, Napoleon Bonaparte second, and he humorously selected "Beau" Brummell, the cultural progenitor of the dandy, for the honored title of greatest man.[1] Whether he actually made this remark cannot be proven, but the statement is revealing for what it does say about masculine ideals. If Byron had added one American to his list, he might have chosen Aaron Burr. Nicknamed the "little emperor," and known for his unquenchable ambition, sexual exploits, small stature, elegant personal style, and hypermasculinity, Burr was thought to possess the dangerous yet fascinating qualities admired by Byron.

Burr's rather remarkable political identity deserves closer scrutiny. More than any other member of the founding generation, he has captured the literary and sexual imagination of all kinds of writers—biographers, confessional autobiographers, political novelists, writers of gothic romances, even pornographers. Yet his obvious sexual appeal has eluded historians. To date, no historian has explored the relationship between sexuality and politics in Burr's public career. More important, no one has asked what fiction writers long ago recognized: Does Burr's masculinity—his gender identity as a political figure—have a salient connection to the ways in which early Americans understood dangerous, scandalous, and even treasonous behavior?

I argue in this essay that Burr's dramatic career reveals the powerful role of gendered, sexualized discourses in constructing public identities and demolishing political reputations. From Burr's arrival on the national scene as a U.S. senator from New York in 1792, until his trial for treason fifteen years later, his political body became a terrain for debating partisan loyalty, which in a crucial way prefigured his later incarnation as a full-fledged traitor. Burr's identity, moreover, does not fit neatly into one simple category. While his contemporaries debated his alleged crimes, and his defenders sought to clear his name, Burr emerged as a hybrid figure, representing at once a ruthlessly ambitious, decadent, self-centered traitor, and the elegant emblem of an admirable masculine audacity. As his contested behavior moved to the center of two national scandals—the election of 1800, during which he was accused of trying to steal the election from Jefferson, and his treason trial in 1807—Burr's public persona was increasingly sexualized. Whether involving scurrilous rumors of his debauchery or praise of his virile masculine presence, Burr's gendered body affected how his political transgressions were exposed or refuted in the press.

To fully appreciate the political battle over Burr's scandalous and seductive masculinity, several key conditions of the political environment need to be explained. First, Burr's enemies and supporters recognized that within the vocabulary of republicanism, which celebrated moderation, virtue, and public service, lay its own antithesis: the subversive threat posed by the anti-republican sins of excess, vice, and self-interest. Second, the measure of a good republican involved public performance; representation required self-presentation in print and on the public stage.[2] This meant that political figures were expected to virtually embody the well-defined traits of republican virtue in their personal and public demeanor, speech, and lifestyle. In a climate in which individual men strove to protect their reputations, the emergence of partisan conflict, facilitating the role of nasty, often exaggerated, personal attacks, heightened the demands put on individual leaders: the "symbolic capital" of moral rectitude suddenly became subject to the demands of party.[3]

In defense of their party's aims, ambitious politicians and an equally ambitious press infused the language of partisan politics with irrational, indefensible attacks and outright lies. Recent scholarship has addressed the irrational in the "age of passion."[4] Scholars have paid less attention to the fact that the first American party system closely imitated the English political system. Partisan politicians and newspaper editors readily transferred grub-street tactics to the American scene. Indeed, partisan debates increasingly relied on hack writers who were versed in satire, slander, and innuendo. English historian Anna Clark has noted that eighteenth-century politics "mixed personal invective with political critique."[5] While the republican rhetoric of virtue demanded the moralizing exposure of dangerous and corrupting vice, heightened partisanship in the early republic inevitably promoted imaginative license, in which the distortion of truth, intentional misrepresentation, and character assassination were deemed permissible. Political satire, a genre that made sexual transgression its primary focus, contributed significantly to this volatile environment.

The press was instrumental in crafting Burr's identity through sexually ambiguous, politically charged allusions. He was, for instance, compared to Catiline, the notorious Roman conspirator, whose sexual debauchery matched his zeal for luxurious self-indulgence. Burr was called a "proteus," a term that had overtones of sexual instability found in the hermaphrodite; and he was invested with the hypnotic and seductive power of the rakish libertine of the moralist literature then in fashion. Drawing on the language of politeness and sociability, critical commentators portrayed Burr as the overly cultivated, suave courtier, a dandified figure who corrupted his young male admirers and the Republican Party at the same time.[6]

Within this partisan world, young men represented both political gains and dangers. Not surprisingly, young, unattached men in the city conjured fears of narcissism and effeminacy. Socially mobile young men throughout eighteenth-century England were regularly cast (in the terms then applied) as fops, beaus, bucks, fribbles, and dandies; they aroused classical republican concerns over *luxura* and *licentia*, and revived a masculine type that combined as one social fears of economic patterns of prodigal consumption and lurid images of sexual indulgence. By the 1790s, this idiom made its way from England to the United States.[7] This constantly recycled discourse was pointedly used to tar Burr's followers. Enemies labeled the New York–based "Burrites" childlike and effeminate, and associated Burr's faction with the sexual perversities of "strolling players." Indeed, as politically ambitious young men, Burr's followers were seen as dangerous because they symbolized the morally debased and illusionary world of the theater. Rather than honest republican men (whose words could be trusted), Burr's followers were accused of imitating the allure of actors, who were known to fascinate audiences and sexually manipulate men and women.

If, as Michel Foucault has suggested, the modern preoccupation with sex replaced the aristocratic obsession with blood lines, and if this transition occurred from the eighteenth to the nineteenth centuries, then the sexualized language of parties may have represented an intermediary step in a broadly based cultural and political transformation.[8] Current scholarship points in this direction: the new party system, as David Waldstreicher contends, centered on the "mobilization of young men."[9] The party system incorporated the older practice of patronage (with surrogate fathers), yet this evolving practice also unleashed tensions: Could improper political alliances form beyond the social control of kinship networks, and beyond community and partisan supervision? And did party passions raise the specter of a more sexualized style of relationships among men?

This discursive process served an obvious political purpose in nineteenth-century America.[10] By granting Burr's every action a symbolic value, those who scrutinized his political body, who pronounced on its qualities and flaws, its excesses and its exquisite perfections, gave important new meaning to the re-drawing of the moral parameters of acceptable partisan political behavior. Although Burr's career was destroyed, his reputation forever tarnished, the debate over his identity permanently joined an imaginary repertoire of sexual danger to growing political concern over partisan strife and dissension. As the first presidential candidate tried for treason, and the first traitor to his party, the scandal-bound Burr left a legacy that demonstrates the ways in which gender insinuated itself into the vocabulary of treason and created a new definition of party loyalty.

Born in 1756, Aaron Burr began life aiming for success in a world being transformed by the War for Independence. Like Alexander Hamilton, he was orphaned at an early age, and his maternal uncle, Timothy Edwards, served as his legal guardian. He attended Princeton in 1769, and though only thirteen, entered as a sophomore. There, his physical appearance already defined his reputation: he was known as "Little Burr," because of his extreme youth and small stature, delicate facial features, and glowing black eyes.[11]

While nineteenth-century writers invented Burr's legendary image as a libertine turned romantic hero, they drew upon rumor and folklore that celebrated Burr's coming of age during college. One tale told of Catherine Bullock, a young woman seduced by Burr while he was a student, whom he then abandoned, and who was to be remembered only for her lonely grave. This tragic tale had all the elements of a sentimental novel: Catherine was the forlorn "Charlotte Temple," Burr the guilty "Montraville." Yet it was not youthful indiscretions that would haunt his political reputation; he would be attacked for his supposed debaucheries as a mature rake, the alleged seducer of unsuspecting youth.[12]

At the age of nineteen he went to war. By joining the campaign to invade Canada in 1775, he quickly made a reputation for himself in the failed assault on Quebec. His commanding officer, General Richard Montgomery, was so impressed by Burr he made him a captain and aide-de-camp. He received a commission in the Continental Army as a lieutenant colonel in 1777.[13]

Burr enjoyed a successful military career, though unlike Hamilton, he did not become part of Washington's military family. He had no interest in making Washington into a surrogate or symbolic father figure, nor did he play the part of the pleasing courtier in Washington's presence. Later, he expressed contempt for the general's meager intellectual attainments and his colorless personality. Illness, at any rate, forced him to resign his commission in 1779, two years after meeting—while in uniform—his future wife, Theodosia Prevost, then the wife of an English military officer and the mother of five children.[14]

Burr's marriage in 1782 set him apart. Theodosia was ten years his senior, married when they first met, and later widowed. She also exhibited a cosmopolitan outlook and a refined education. Notwithstanding his later rakish reputation, Burr's bride was noted for neither her beauty nor wealth. When they met in 1777, Theodosia was thirty-one. In their correspondence, they discussed Voltaire, Rousseau, and Chesterfield. Theodosia's tone was decidedly that of a mature woman, capable of tempering Burr's youthful excesses. Their marriage allowed Burr, as he had done at every stage of his career, to gain in stature— manhood and respectability—at an earlier age than most. Burr had entered college at an early age; he had secured his inheritance and legal emancipation in his teens; and now, in 1782, he married and became the head of a family when only twenty-six.[15]

His only child, also Theodosia, was born in 1783. With his wife and child, Burr pursued his career as a lawyer in New York City. Though successful, he lived beyond his means, acquiring debts as he created important financial alliances with prominent political men. His wife died in 1794, two years after he began his term as U.S. senator from New York. It was during this turbulent decade that he earned the wrath of Alexander Hamilton, the politician most responsible for spreading malicious gossip about him.

Burr's troubled relationship with Hamilton has fascinated historians and popular biographers alike. All have seen Hamilton's dislike of Burr as something "pathological," or else they have imagined the two rivals as heterosexual competitors.

Their fateful duel has been explained in sexual terms: either they were fighting over a woman, or Burr wanted revenge for Hamilton's sexual slander against his good name. Novelist Gore Vidal inferred that Hamilton had spread a rumor of some unspeakable crime—possibly that Burr was having an incestuous relationship with his daughter.[16]

Hamilton and Burr were cut from the same cloth: both were small in stature, elegant and refined in their deportment, and ostensibly saw themselves as men of honor. Despite the outward civility they showed each other, they had different political styles. Hamilton disclosed all to his confidants, including his contempt for his enemies; he appeared completely self-assured when revealing his views to the reading public.[17] Burr, on the other hand, seemed to trust few people entirely, and revealed as little as possible, while maintaining an easy and pleasing conversational style. The consummate gossip, Hamilton was passionate and, at times, petulant. Burr was neither.[18]

They also acquired political influence in different ways. Hamilton's rise to power came from the patronage of his elders. Through his superior officer, George Washington, and his father-in-law, the New York manor lord and Revolutionary War general Philip Schuyler, he gained access to elite nationalist and Federalist circles and acquired unmatched influence first in New York politics and then in the first presidential administration. Hamilton was not, as generally assumed, Washington's protégé; rather, as he himself admitted at the time of Washington's death, Hamilton considered the commanding general an "aegis very essential" to his own success. Hamilton thus fashioned a role for himself as the president's precocious political adjutant—a Federalist prime minister who crafted speeches, devised policy, and shaped the identity of the Federalist Party.[19]

In contrast, Burr did not depend on the patronage of surrogate political fathers. He seems to have been far more willing to go it alone, skilled at making alliances across generations. Although Governor George Clinton aided his election to the Senate in 1792, he was never a true Clintonian; he was able to work, at different times in his career, with members of the two rival democratic family factions in New York, the Livingstons and Clintons. Burr mixed politics and economics: his political allies were often his financial partners, and his principal banking project touched a raw nerve in the Federalist-dominated financial world of New York City.[20]

Burr has often been called a "modern" politician because of his efforts in the election of 1800. At that time, he deftly orchestrated a temporary alliance with the two other Republican factions, convincing several prominent men to place their names on the slate of electors, and using their superior social reputation to defeat lesser-known Federalist candidates. He found a way to expand the electorate, extending suffrage to the "middling" and even "lower sorts" who tipped the balance in favor of the Democratic-Republican Party. His core of followers displayed a new kind of political discipline, a youthful vigor and a more visible presence, which caused the Federalists to resent Burr's skill at circumventing the tradition of deference in political affairs.[21]

Hamilton first voiced his disapproval of Burr in 1792. In personal correspondence, Hamilton derided his nemesis as "unprincipled, both as a public and private man," after Burr had defeated Hamilton's father-in-law Schuyler in the Senate race.[22] Over the course of the next twelve years, Hamilton attacked Burr in several carefully orchestrated letter campaigns; each time, Hamilton's mean-spirited comments were triggered by Burr's ambition for office. Hamilton could be circumspect or indiscriminate in leveling charges against Burr; he chose his words carefully, tempering or escalating his attacks in accord with the understood mood of the recipient of his letter.

Hamilton was skilled at invective. But if the language he used to describe Burr was rhetorical and hyperbolic, it was rarely original. His private correspondence took the same tone as his published letters and pamphlets. One code name for Burr was "Savius," later replaced by "Catiline," who was renowned for his ambition and treachery. Using Roman names was a common eighteenth-century practice for signing anonymously published letters, and this tradition continued into the nineteenth century. Hamilton signed his published essays in 1792 "Catullus" and "Metallus," identifying himself as the defender of republican virtue, while casting Jefferson as Caius Marius, another Roman general known for his factious designs. Hamilton continued to see Burr as his principal foe in this rhetorical battle, insofar as the fall of Marius made room for the greatest tyrant of all: Caesar. And Burr, for Hamilton, was an "embryo-Caesar" even in 1792.[23]

To call Burr "Catiline" or "Savius" was more than name-calling; these were unabashed verbal "cuts" at his character. The two Roman generals were depraved men, their careers stained by unspeakable acts of treason, murder, incest, and sodomy. The "serial killer" of his age, Catiline had a reputation that included slaughtering his son, wife, and brother, and sleeping with his sister and daughter.[24] He was, quite obviously, the antithesis of eighteenth-century republican virtue. Savius's less well known crime was even more disturbing—if known to Hamilton—for he had seduced and raped his own son.[25]

Savius, Catiline, and Burr all shared the same personal and sexual vices, according to Hamilton. In one of his harshest rebukes, Hamilton wrote in a letter to John Rutledge, Jr., in 1801, calling Burr a "dangerous man," "profligate," "with the cunning of Catiline," who was devoid of integrity and motivated by inordinate ambition. Like his Roman predecessor, Burr was "the haughtiest of men," aiming at nothing less than to establish "Supreme power in his own person." One of the most devastating insults contained in this letter was Hamilton's accusation that Burr's Catalinian cunning, like that of Savius, was based on his sexual power in "courting the young."[26] This reference to Burr's power over young men would prove to be a recurring refrain. More importantly, labeling Burr a bisexual seducer made his hypermasculinity dangerous in a distinctive sense: he had the power not only to captivate women, but he could entice (secure the personal devotion of) young, impressionable, vulnerable men.

In a famous handbill of 1801, Federalists accused Burr of debauchery and profligacy, seducing virgins, and populating the city with whores.[27] His Federalist enemies more typically represented Burr's libertine desires as a force contained within a self-consciously artificial but nonetheless refined presence. As Hamilton implied, Burr was a dangerous man because he adopted an elegant pose, fascinating others for blatantly political ends. A satire entitled "The Democratiad," published in 1795, showed the "courtly Burr" in this light. Aimed at senators who opposed the Jay Treaty, among whom Burr had assumed a leading role, this Federalist poem by Lemuel Hopkins highlighted Burr's physical appearance: "courtly" referred to his aristocratic dress and demeanor, while mention of his "haughtiness and scorn" and a "piercing look" conveyed his disdain and what became one of his most distinguishing traits—a cultivated theatrical art that enabled him to dismiss his foes with a penetrating glance. Overtones of Burr's pretensions as a *faux elite* appear in the final verse as "mad ambition in his bosom turn." It was understood that a man of such surface vanity could only be driven by vulgar passions.[28]

In 1804, New York's leading Federalist editor, William Coleman of the *Evening Post*, described Burr in a similar fashion. Writing after the duel with Hamilton, when New York Federalists' wrath toward Burr was at its peak, Coleman sketched a cold and selfish assassin. For Coleman, Burr's capacity to challenge and then kill Hamilton, tearing him from a loving family, evidenced "systematic selfishness" and "unprincipled ambition." Devoid of a real personality, Burr was an "*artificial self*," "an isolated being." As Coleman further explained, Burr's "exquisite hypocrisy can assume all forms and affect every virtue," and his "glossy duplicity can impose equally on the unsuspecting and on the incredulous." Burr's narcissism combined a constantly shifting, coldly detached identity, and an instinctively deceitful character that deployed his exquisite and glossy surface elegance to get his way.[29]

The highly moralistic tone of the Federalist critique is not surprising. Drawing his allusions from Roman satire, Hamilton saw Burr as an embodiment of the cognate vices of luxury and lust. He and other Federalists depicted Burr as a man whose appetites were out of control; his self-consuming passions were meant to have corrupted both his private behavior and his public ambition. Burr was both the ruthless libertine, roaming New York City for female victims of his lust, and the effeminate fop—the exquisite—whose allure extended to both young men and women. What is striking about Federalist invective and satirical style is the emphasis on Burr as a man of surfaces rather than substance. His power rested on an ability to fascinate others, to use his body to arouse, when he enlisted others in his aid. This echoes the classical Roman satirical harangue against actors. For the Romans, acting was incompatible with honor (*honesta*), transforming Burr's politics into pure style, and his dangerous potency into mere theatrics, symbolized by his fascinating demeanor and gaze.[30]

Coleman's attack added another interesting rebuke: Burr was an "isolated being," a man without a family. His status as a widower and father was erased from this political portrait, thus equating his role as an "assassin" (a trained killer devoid of national affections) with his antisocial personal life as an unattached man. Such a discursive distortion of Burr's actual family history had a purpose: Federalists sought to reassert their party's claim to moral superiority. By pronouncing on Burr's sexual flaws and turning him into a lecherous bachelor, Coleman, and other Federalists, energetically sought to rewrite Hamilton's political reputation in death. Surrounded by loved ones as he passed away, he could be memorialized as a devoted family man. Of course, though, it was Hamilton's scandalous past that had provoked this ironic death mask: in 1797, he had scarred the party and stained his reputation by admitting to an adulterous affair with a younger woman, Maria Reynolds. He was driven to publish a pamphlet, admitting to sexual misconduct in order to refute what he perceived as the more damaging charge of financial impropriety. In Republican newspapers, Hamilton was accused of hypocrisy—writers posed a common query: was adultery a lesser crime than embezzlement? He was mocked for the arrogance of his unrepentant confessional style, and he was charged with having abused his paternal role as the protector of a young woman in distress.[31]

As the martyr and loving husband and father, Hamilton achieved in death a political salvation that served the interests of his party. By deemphasizing his physical attributes, and inviting compassion for his family's loss, Coleman invented a moral posture for Hamilton that never existed in his lifetime. In a very real sense, Federalists hoped to transfer Hamilton's sins to Burr, cleansing the taint of immorality from their party, while smearing their rivals. Hamilton's redemption made his sexualized body invisible, so that Burr's dangerous and omnisexual potency could assume center stage for critics lodged within his own party.[32]

Political refugee turned scandalmonger James Callender was responsible for exposing Hamilton's "Reynolds affair," and his fellow British radical James Cheetham assumed a similar role in orchestrating Burr's fall from political grace. Cheetham arrived in New York in 1798, and two years later assumed the editorship of the *American Citizen*, a paper started with Burr's assistance. Despite this, he left the Burrite fold in 1801, claiming to have become suspicious of Burr's activities. He then embarked on a campaign to exile Burr from the Republican Party leadership. His attacks, which were probably instigated by the Clinton faction and likely encouraged by Jefferson, too, dogged Burr's every move. Cheetham's unrelenting assault in a barrage of pamphlets and daily articles led Burr and his supporters to establish another newspaper. In 1802, Peter Irving was persuaded to print the *Morning Chronicle*, as Burr's political organ in New York State.[33]

In May of that year, Cheetham initiated a pamphlet war, involving a series of accusations against Burr. The most damning of these was Cheetham's contention that the vice president had tried to steal the election from Jefferson. For months, Burr refused to respond. Then, in September, on the advice of a friend, Governor Joseph Bloomfield of New Jersey, he drafted a letter in which he called the charges "false and groundless." Predictably, his attempt to quell the controversy simply fueled further recriminations.[34]

Cheetham's story contained allusions to a rumored secret deal, veiled in mystery and intrigue, that concealed a dishonorable crime. He used the image of Burr's collusion with the Federalists to insinuate that the vice president—the *faux* republican—was living a double life. Because the transactions occurred in private, he did not have to provide any legal proof of his accusations. It was sufficient that circumstantial evidence existed. "Few men believe that Mr. Burr is innocent," the editor contended. "Many, very many, indeed, strongly suspect that he is guilty of the charge exhibited, but almost all are of the opinion that he has managed the negotiation with so much caution, dexterity, and art, as to defy the production of proof."[35]

The Federalists had set the tone for Cheetham's attacks, associating Burr with Catiline and attributing to him the finesse of the courtier and the effeminacy of the fop. Cheetham was more persistent and more explicit. He attacked Burr's vices and sexual pose by characterizing his relationships with other men in the party. He contended that Burr not only courted young men, but corrupted them. The Burrites all shared the weaknesses, submissiveness, and lusts of women or unevolved children. Cheetham directly raised the specter of a sodomite plot—a theme popularized in the conspiratorial satire of eighteenth-century England. In disparaging Burr, he invoked the fear that the Burrites symbolized a disruptive force within the party. They represented a destabilizing faction capable of polluting the manly homosocial bonds based on virtuous principles uniting the Republican Party.[36]

In August 1802, the month Irving began publishing the *Chronicle*, Cheetham described his new journalist rival as a "young man of handsome talents," but then went on to deride the editor as Burr's sexual pawn. "There is a softness," he claimed about Burr, "an insinuating deceitfulness about him admirably calculated to fascinate youth; to entrap the weary." He inferred that Irving, as well as Burr, exhibited womanish qualities, an enervated and alluring degeneracy, usually associated with sexual inversion. Irving—like a woman or child—lacked the manly strength to resist Burr's "flattering attentions," while Burr's softness endowed him with the seductive wiles of the sodomitical rake—the aristocratic debauchee who sexually enslaved women and boys.[37]

Cheetham's opening salvo was just the first of many insults. By October, he was attacking Irving's paper for its lack of "manliness," comparing it to a "Lady's Weekly Museum." He called Irving a "beau," who was issuing "effeminate attacks"; and he snidely implied that Irving might be a woman in disguise, his whining editorials a sign that he suffered from a "female complaint." Calling his rival "Miss Irving," and "Her Ladyship," the *Citizen's* editor derisively dismissed such "foolish satire" as "puerile and unmeaning frivolity," a tea-party style of prose that was best suited to the tastes of the "dandy."[38]

Youth marked the Burrites as amateurs and imposters. They were, in Cheetham's words, "an impotent faction," nothing more than "angry boys of a juvenile society." In one published letter to the editor of the *Citizen*, the author noted the political aberration of the underage Burrites in his self-description, stating, "I am old enough to be Republican, and too old to be a Burrite." Labeling Burr's followers as "boyish," or calling Irving a "child," Cheetham chose an insult that was plainly rhetorical. In 1802, he and his rival editor were both thirty—neither were children, nor was Irving the younger man.[39] Irving, however, was single, and like his more famous brother Washington Irving, who also supported Burr, he would never marry. In fact, what remains most striking about the Burrites is that they were literally a "band of brothers," for their inner circle was composed of cohorts of siblings.[40]

Sexual deviance obviously was the more scurrilous of Cheetham's charges. Burr's "precious band," as he called this unnatural faction, was "actuated by personal attachments"; they idolized Burr, and were "so extremely close," forming an emotionally intimate, sexually uncertain alliance. The homosexual overtones were intentional: like other all-male confederacies and combinations, Burr's band was united in either "vice" or "pleasure." Cheetham conjured clear images of elite dissipation from a knowledge of the sexual underworld of the theater, bawdy houses, and English mollyhouses (the worlds of "pleasure"), and the dark dens of secrecy and crime associated with pirates and banditti. By 1804, Cheetham was identifying the Burrites with "strolling players," continuing to associate the faction with sexual promiscuity and male prostitution.[41]

Burr's 1804 campaign for the governorship provoked Cheetham to publish vicious, pornographic satire. We should pay particular attention to two poems that appeared at the end of April, during the five-day period in which the polls were open. The first satire, "*Alba Lingustra cadunt dum nigra varcinia stent* [white-flowered shrubs fall while black varcinia stand], OR, AARON'S LAST SHIFT," charged that Burr had courted the black vote in the city. In the poem, Burr's slave tells his master, "Have I not ever faithful been, / Your pimp expert for many years?" His white supporters are wary of Burr's plan, warning that "blacks were faithless, never true, / Fond of deceit, of basest treason." Burr dismisses their concerns, stating, "I love blacks," and with this "motley crew," he toasts to a "*Union of honest* men."[42]

An explanation, probably written by Cheetham, followed the parody. At an actual gathering held the evening before the election, Burr had "assembled at his house, by special invitation, a considerable number of *gentlemen of colour*— upwards of twenty." The event involved a "ball and supper," in which Burr offered his guests "*elegant amusements.*" The so-called head of the black political faction was identified as "a celebrated perfumer in Broadway." Racist language combined with homosexual overtones, associating Burr's declaration of love for blacks with his eagerness to pimp for his guests by personally seeing to their "*elegant amusements.*" This was meant to constitute evidence that Burr was willing to prostitute himself for votes. What is even more striking is the description of the "*gentlemen of colour*," whose mock elegance suggests that, like Burr, they were a pretender class—a *faux elite.* Even more ridiculous than Burr himself, "*the gentlemen of colour*" were obviously dandified, their leader a "celebrated perfumer in Broadway."[43]

Another poem, published two days later, made punning capital with Burr's name. Like a plant bur, Burr's political machinations and his followers "stick to their folly, as close as a Burr." Three times, the poet repeats that there is "sting in a Burr," from "intrigue, art, oppression" and "deception." The thematic line of the poem employs sexual innuendo and a double entendre: "By a Man to be rul'd, or be prick't by a Burr." The word *prick't* simultaneously alluded to "prick," a vulgar term for penis, and "prick," a point or puncture. To be "prick't by a burr" crassly implied male sexual penetration of another male, and, conversely, sexual submission by a man. As revealing, the word pricket, according to Johnson's *Dictionary*, was slang for male buck, that is, a young male animal. And "buck," like another popular slang term, "puppy," referred to a dashing young fellow, or dandy.[44]

Both the Federalists and Cheetham drew on older notions of the dandy. Like the 1620 term *dandebrat* (perhaps the first usage of the slang), Burrites were indulged children (brats), scrambling for attention (puppies), and womanish in their devotion to fashion and grooming (pretty fellows).[45] Underneath this foppish exterior and glittering display, the modern political dandy, like its prototypes, concealed dangers more ominous. Here lurked the heart of an "assassin," the lusts of a rake or spoiled child, and the cunning, deceit, and dissimulation of the actor. Lift the veil from the dandy, and one might find other monstrous perversions: a woman in disguise, a black man pretending to be a gentleman or a party man, or a sodomite.

What did this dandified sexual pose mean for partisan politics? In the mid-nineteenth century, French poet and critic Charles Baudelaire would compare ancient prototypes of the dandy (Catiline, Caesar, and Alcibiades were his most "dazzling" examples) with dueling, one of the most crucial episodes in the construction of Burr's political identity. Both dandies and dueling, Baudelaire concluded, were institutions "beyond the laws," yet somehow ruled by their own internal "rigorous laws." At the heart of his observation was a provocative contradiction: dandyism, like dueling, was an aristocratic practice that still thrived in the anti-elite world of republics.[46] Burr's dangerous autonomy made him seem aristocratic yet subversive, and his faction represented a new political aristocracy, which was not based on inherited wealth and birth so much as the destabilizing force of political theatrics—the new culture of partisan performance. Glamorous leaders, surrounded by men with similar passions, were creating a culture in which "glossy" politicians could climb the partisan ladder, flaunting their seductive style for personal gain. As in the 1806 broadside "A Dandy Song," democratic politics was based on ruthless self-promotion, deceit and bribery, dazzling surface appeal, and vacillating principles—for the man who "gets the chair is dandy O."[47]

Burr's enemies repeatedly attacked his treacherous versatility, his ubiquitous appeal to young men and women, and his partisan instability. This composite view was evidenced by Cheetham's list of adjectives for Burr: he was a "proteus," "ambiguous," "mysterious"—a man whose genuine sentiments were inaccessible.[48] Federalist William Plumer recorded in his journal, in 1805, that he had spent an entire evening listening to Burr converse, assumed that he knew where Burr stood on the issues, and yet came away from the encounter finally uncertain of his views.[49] Critics painted Burr as a political hermaphrodite: he was not plainly attached to his party, nor committed to any single view. He seemed as indefinite politically as the dandy was sexually.[50]

As a man of fashion, the modern political dandy changed his clothes as easily as he changed his party affiliation. According to this critique, the dandy's narcissism and self-conscious artificiality bode ill for party politics.[51] The dandy's influence threatened to insulate the party machine from the reading and voting public. As William Charles, a Scottish émigré artist and engraver, captured in 1807, in one of the first caricatures of the dandy in the United States: a dandy was "a thing that loveth but himself," and a "cornstalk out of season."[52] As an aristocrat in a republic, or a traitor in a suave and seductive body, the dandy politician easily made a place for himself in the party. In an environment where political cornstalks—ambitious dandies or dueling men of honor—could grow and thrive, the party turned in on itself, relying on its own internal laws, enamored with its own surface image.

Burr's enemies relied on the well-established vocabulary of the dandified politician to expose his dangerous flaws. While his critics painted the Burrites as fops, and Burr himself was readily criticized for his "cunning" and "treachery," both those who admired him and those who detested him saw Burr's erotic appeal in terms of his refined hypermasculinity—his "audacity."[53] Hamilton understood the attraction of Burr's "audacity," a quality that expressed an admirable boldness and spirit, as well as impertinence. In the election of 1800, Hamilton was consumed with a genuine fear that many men in the Senate would be drawn to his "*dashing projecting* spirit."[54] "Dashing" implied an elegance of bodily deportment, a boldness of character, and an irresistible essence, which commanded respect and the approving gaze of male and female admirers.

Seven years later, Jefferson, too, was fully convinced of Burr's unparalleled audacity. "Burr's enterprise," he wrote in a letter to a friend, was "the most extraordinary since the days of Don Quixot[e]." His visions were "so extravagant," Jefferson confided, that he "meant to place himself on the throne of Montezuma, and extend his empire to the Allegheny."[55] Virginian William Thomson concurred: in his 1807 pamphlet on Burr's trial, this Jeffersonian explained that Burr had refused the Federalists' invitation to steal the election because he saw the presidency as "too limited to gratify inordinate ambition." The office was "only an object of contempt without the scepter." Burr exuded a dignified and impartial conduct in his political performances, Thomson added, because "his mind was too devoted to his own destiny, to be influenced by feelings of personal attachment for others."[56]

Bold, indifferent, and dangerous, Burr had not only placed himself outside his party, but above his peers. The new aristocrat had emerged as something ominous. After years of living outside the rules of society, in an enclosed and seductive world of fawning followers, Burr—the subversive and self-fashioned noble— now had come to imagine himself as a "despot." Burr was so "wrapped up in individual wishes," Thomson concluded, that he "feels the most perfect indifference for everything else."[57]

But what about Burr's devoted admirers? In heated exchanges with Cheetham, Irving and others had constantly praised his "open and manly" conduct, "his masterly displays of eloquence," and the "commanding dignity of his eye." Not afraid to call attention to Burr's physical body, they celebrated his "penetration, firmness, his assiduity." And rather than refute Cheetham's sexualized portrait of Burr, they embraced his highly masculine, cultivated style of self-presentation.[58]

They also praised his audacity. Burr the accomplished soldier, statesman, and lawyer exuded a bold, confounding "presence," which, they asserted, made weaker men shrink; that presence would make his accusers "melt before the lightening of his eye." Surrounded by the family-based factions of Clintons and Livingstons, Burrites described their candidate as a "self-made man." His rise to political acclaim rested on his remarkable presence, not a servile, effeminate dependency that came from family or political patronage. In a provocative defense of Burr, a writer in the *Chronicle* asserted that if Burr had projected a plan to steal the election as accused, given his superior talents, "he would have *secured his election and would have been your President.*" Far from embodying the treachery of a traitor, Burr deployed his skills with the incomparable mastery of an enterprising statesman.[59]

By emerging as national celebrities and scandalous figures in the same decade, Burr and Beau Brummell, the most celebrated dandy of the early nineteenth century, were alike in personal style. Unlike older satirical and sartorial versions of the dandy, Brummell was not effete, in the sense of dressing like a woman. Gone were the powdered wigs, lacy frills, outlandishly colored coats, perfume, and makeup—all the trademark excesses of fops and Macaronis. Brummell was, like Burr, small in stature. His pose was refined, in the style of a military man, and he wore a pristine, white, starched cravat and carefully polished, glossy, Hessian boots. There was an air of sober simplicity in his dress, a standard of elegance and impeccable attention to detail—what, in his time, described a pure masculine presence. Burr's daughter, Theodosia, called the Burrites the "Tenth Legion," drawing a connection to Brummell, whose rise to fame began while he was serving in the Prince Regent's (George IV's) own fashionable regiment from 1794 to 1798. They were known as the "Tenth Hussars," and nicknamed the "Elegant Extracts."[60]

Brummell was known for more than his dress. His meticulous control of every gesture matched his heroic insolence. Burr, like Brummell, gained a reputation for his powerful gaze. Each man had cultivated a penetrating stare that signified his conscious superiority as man in a world where performances mattered. A disciplined audacity, combined with flair and suave finesse, identified both with the ability to fascinate others. Called the "incomparable Burr"—just as Brummell was considered to be in a class of his own—the modern dandy symbolized an antidote to foppish fashion. He was always an irreproducible original, whose every performance set him apart from the crowd.[61]

Clothing by now represented more than style. Brummell was, as fashion historian Ann Hollander observed, a "new kind of hero made by tailoring." His heroism consisted in being completely himself; his superiority was entirely self-made and personal, "unburdened by any surface indices of worth attached to rank." A carefully tailored coat emphasized the natural elegance of the body; posture and graceful movement, which had to appear effortless, projected a refined male potency. Brummell's trademark—the "effortless effort"—was infused with a distinctive erotic attraction. This tension of opposites—ease and audacious flair—conveyed a new register of masculine prowess and personal character.[62]

In her letters to her father, Theodosia echoed this view, writing that his "presence threw a luster on everything around" him. She marveled at his extraordinary fortitude while in exile in Europe, his ability to transcend misfortune in an effortless manner. She saw such grace as something entirely unique to her father. She confided in 1809: "Often, after reflecting on this subject, you appear to me so superior, so elevated above all other men; I contemplate you with such a strange mixture of humility, admiration, reverence, love, and pride, that very little superstition would be necessary to make me worship you as a superior being; such enthusiasm does your character excite in me." Later, encouraging him to return to New York, she felt he should triumphantly make his stand there where the "fervency of surprise and delighted friendship" would allow for him to resume his station. No doubt his overwhelming presence would invite cabals to form. Yet, "in the midst of the tenth legion," she confidently assumed that his indisputable superiority would allow him to recapture the political stage.[63]

Burr's enemies responded by attempting to symbolically undress him before the public eye. One of the stranger exchanges between Cheetham and Irving focused on what Burr had worn during his duel with Hamilton. A rumor had circulated that Burr had worn black silk, an image that not only highlighted his glossy style, but implied cowardice (silk, it was believed, was better protection against bullets). Irving denied the story, only to find himself ridiculed again by Cheetham for his dandified expertise on the differences between silk and bombazin and cotton—the actual fabrics used in Burr's dueling attire.[64]

With unparalleled ease, if not heroic insolence, Burr proved more than once that he had the ability to remake himself. This was a skill that his supporters admired and his critics found incomprehensible. The July 1804 duel with Hamilton prompted more than snide comments about his clothing, of course. He was indicted for murder in both New York and New Jersey (the duel had taken place in Weehawken, New Jersey, across the river from New York City), and was forced to flee as a fugitive, traveling to Philadelphia, and then to Washington.

His reception in the national capital was mixed. He was shunned and reviled by Federalists, yet secretly admired by many Republicans. In one of his last duties as vice president, Burr presided over Judge Samuel Chase's impeachment trial, during which his "correctness and astonishing dignity" were warmly praised in the press. In March 1805, in another unusual turn of events, Burr's farewell speech to the Senate provoked a remarkable reaction: many of his colleagues found his words so moving—and filled with genuine sentiment—that they shed tears.[65] In this, seemingly his lowest moment, Burr accomplished what many promptly dubbed a sublime achievement. He had enacted an irreproducible performance, to belie the hatred and censure that the killing of Hamilton had brought to bear. A frustrated Cheetham complained that Burr was magically reinventing himself, surmounting the proofs, charges, and innuendoes that had combined to destroy his public career.[66]

Burr's arrest and trial for treason generated similarly conflicted reactions, invariably relating to Burr's masculine presence. Many who attended the trial were mesmerized by Burr's courtroom performance. A young Winfield Scott later wrote glowingly of Burr, confessing amazement and awe at the defendant's facility to teeter "on the brink of danger," but still appear "as composed, as immovable, as one of [Italian sculptor] Canova's living marbles."[67] Others were less impressed. Led to expect he would encounter the irresistible force of Burr's presence, one of the prosecutors and a devoted Jeffersonian, William Wirt, felt that the man paled in comparison to his larger-than-life reputation. In a letter to a friend, Wirt wrote, "Burr is certainly a man of talents—but not of that grand & overwhelming cast which I expected."[68]

Burr's masculine demeanor at the time of his arrest had by this time circulated through the gossip mill. The outfit he wore when captured seemed delightfully ironic to his enemies. Jefferson's allies wrote to the president about Burr's extraordinary getup: an "old white hat," a "country" jacket, a "pair of Virginia cloth pantaloons," and "old Virginia leggings."[69] The haughty, elegant Burr, once considered a dandified member of the New York *ton*, was now reduced to an uncouth bumpkin, with a tin cup and butcher's knife hanging from his belt. Nicholas Perkins, the federal land registrar responsible for his capture, stated that Burr's "keen" glance had given him away. Later embellished accounts similarly noted that Burr's dandified "tidy boot" had revealed his true identity. Perkins also testified that Burr had tried to escape in South Carolina en route to Richmond.[70] In this strange episode, which acquired mythic proportions years later, Perkins claimed to have put him back on his horse ("as though he was a child"), when Burr burst into tears, totally "unmanned" by the humiliating experience.[71]

Burr's sartorial image was restored in Richmond, however, even before the proceedings began. Two prominent Federalists loaned the ex-vice president $1000 for new clothes. He was tastefully attired in black silk for the duration of the trial.[72] One evening, he dined with the presiding Judge, Supreme Court Justice John Marshall, and his attorney, John Wickham, at Wickham's home. This unusual treatment quickly prompted Republicans to wonder if politeness had gone too far.[73] When he was finally housed in the penitentiary, he was given three large rooms, where he received adoring and curious visitors of both sexes, bearing fruit, candies, and other gifts. Harmon Blennerhassett, the Irish-born dilettante who was indicted along with Burr for conspiracy to commit treason, wrote in his journal: "Burr lives in great style, and sees much company within his gratings, where it is as difficult to get an audience as if he really were an Emperor."[74]

It is impossible to explain all the nuances in the events surrounding the trial. Yet a closer look at certain moments and key arguments will demonstrate how competing meanings of the dandy were insinuated into the actual proceedings. Calling Burr the "little emperor" registered this contradiction. During the trial, Blennerhassett expressed admiration and anger at Burr's heroic and insolent style. He marveled at his sexual finesse with women, observing that the former vice president's female visitors offered him more than their sympathy while he was on trial.[75]

For the prosecution to identify Burr as the "little emperor" linked him again to the lives of Catiline, Caesar, and even Bonaparte.[76] Like Cheetham before them, the prosecution relied on the image of Burr as inscrutable and dexterous, to assert that his actual crime might very well defy the production of proof; that is, all the proof the prosecution needed for conviction was apparent in Burr's purportedly scandalous behavior. His erotically charged body and unsavory reputation built from gossip and innuendo said it all.

This strategy was essential to the prosecution's case for two legal reasons. First, the indictment placed the criminal act of treason on Blennerhassett's Island, even though Burr was hundreds of miles away from the scene at the time of the alleged crime. Second, the prosecution felt it had to resort to defining "constructive treason," based upon the common law dictum: "In high treason each one is principal." Constructive treason allowed for the state to give evidence to the *appearance* of treasonous activities; with this strategy, Burr's scandalous reputation became pivotal. Either his intentions were proof of constructive treason, or Judge Marshall would rule that there could be no treason without proof that Burr had levied war—actually used military force to foment rebellion against the government.[77]

Virginia Republican George Hay, the district attorney in charge of the case, set the tone in his opening remarks. He argued that the state would prove that Burr had set in motion a "treasonable design" for "establishing an empire in the west," where he was to be "the chief." The prosecution's witnesses stressed Burr's insolence. Two of these repeated a dinner conversation, in which Burr boasted that "with two hundred men he could drive the president and congress into the Potomac." Testifying that Burr tried to recruit them using flattery and veiled propositions, John and Thomas Morgan revived the image of Burr as a sodomitical rake who rapaciously lured astray a "precious band" of underage men.[78]

Similar accounts had circulated in the newspapers before the trial, describing Burr's followers as "single men of conspicuous parentage," "enterprising young men," or "boys, young men just from school."[79] Another prosecution witness, Blennerhassett's gardener Peter Taylor, testified that Burr's young recruits were soft and refined, and did not work with their hands. Here the prosecution was trying to deflate one line of defense: that Burr had simply organized his expedition to establish a settlement on the Bastrop property, outside of New Orleans. Taylor's remarks made Burr's foppish followers appear to be ridiculously unsuited for the rigors of farming. His testimony also pointedly referred to Burr's imperial and, perhaps, incestuous designs, claiming that the defendant had told him "he [Burr] would be the king of Mexico," and his "daughter the Queen."[80]

The defense, which included Burr's "dream team" of John Wickham, Edmund Randolph, Benjamin Botts, and Charles Lee of Virginia, and Luther Martin of Maryland, made the reputation of the "incomparable Burr" integral to their case. Burr, himself a legal talent, oversaw his own defense. Before the prosecution even presented its witnesses, he asked the court for a subpoena *duces tecum*, requesting that President Jefferson provide papers considered relevant to the defense. Although Jefferson refused to respond, Burr's aggressive initiative nevertheless placed him in a valuable position.[81]

Luther Martin, known as the "federal bulldog," seized the moment and attacked Jefferson for hounding Burr, for abusing his executive power. This tactic dramatically shifted the terms of the debate away from Burr's so-called imperial designs, and pointed to the president's behavior as that befitting a ruthless tyrant or "Supreme Being."[82] The well-planned offensive was more than a grand gesture in that it clearly linked Burr's case to English treason trials like the 1793 case of Horne Tooke, who had subpoenaed the prime minister, William Pitt, to testify as a defense witness.[83] Martin went so far as to describe Burr as a persecuted patriot, a man trying to liberate Mexico from bondage—an heir to George Washington.[84] If a war had been declared against Spain, Burr's expedition would have encouraged a Mexican Revolution, and potentially the annexation of the territory to the United States. Despite his obvious hyperbole, Martin knew that many of Burr's supporters were openly in favor of a private filibuster, and such sentiments were published in the *Virginia Gazette* during the proceedings.[85]

The trial proved to be a tour de force of legal maneuvering, satirical wit, and live theater. At several crucial junctures, the defense made mocking references to the *faux* masculine bravado of the prosecution's star witness, General James Wilkinson. By informing on Burr, Wilkinson was praised in Republican newspapers as the man who had "saved the nation." Vain and pompous, known for his girth and lavish military dress, Wilkinson was an easy target in the courtroom. Edmund Randolph sneered at the excuses made for Wilkinson's delayed arrival, drolly explaining that his "gigantic bulk" had slowed him down. Rumored to have been Burr's co-conspirator, Wilkinson was also reviled by the members of the grand jury. Its outspoken foreman, Congressman John Randolph—who was a cousin of the defense attorney—was most open in his condemnation. He called the general a "mammoth of iniquity," the "most finished scoundrel," "from bark to core a villain." During the hearing, Randolph insisted that Wilkinson remove his sword, symbolically unmanning him in the courtroom. The public, too, had ample opportunity to snicker at Wilkinson: a caricature passed around Richmond cast him as Falstaff, the bumbling, rotund, and laughable sidekick of King Jefferson.[86]

In the theatrics of the courtroom, masculine presentation became part of the contest between Burr and Wilkinson. In one of the most memorable moments of the proceedings, Burr turned to look at the general, as he made his entrance. Washington Irving, sent to Richmond to report on the trial, described this exchange brilliantly, revealing Burr's fascinating power to trump an adversary with a well-timed glance. As Irving put it:

Wilkinson strutted into court, and took his stand in a parallel line with Burr on his right hand. Here he stood for a moment swelling like a turkey-cock, and bracing himself up for the encounter of Burr's eye. The latter did not take any notice of him until the judge directed the clerk to swear General Wilkinson; at the mention of the name Burr turned his head, looked at him full in the face with one of his piercing regards, swept his eye over his whole person from head to foot, as if to scan its dimensions, and then coolly resumed his former position, and went on conversing with his counsel as tranquilly as ever. The whole look was over in an instant; but it was an admirable one. There was no appearance of study or constraint in it; no affectation of disdain or defiance; a slight expression of contempt played over his countenance.

Of course, Wilkinson gave a completely different version of this event. David Robertson, one of the trial reporters and an ardent Jeffersonian, portrayed Burr's role in this exchange negatively: "On the appearance of the General in court, it was said that his countenance was calm, dignified, and commanding; while that of Burr was marked by haughty contempt." The essence of such performances was proving one's masculine superiority.[87]

The most crucial debate centered on constructive treason. Scholars have completely overlooked the brilliant way the defense relied on satire and wit to demolish the prosecution's argument that Burr was guilty of treason even if he had not actually levied war against the state. Wickham demonstrated why all accomplices were not necessarily principals, and pointed to the danger of imagining conspiratorial motives without material proof. He introduced a series of old English laws equating treason with seduction, alluding to the traditional understanding that sleeping with a relative of the King was considered an act of treason. By playing off Marshall's dictum that treason must be an openly visible and physical act, he showed the potential abuses of constructive treason. Suppose a female had acted as accomplice to a male traitor by participating in the treasonous act of defiling a royal personage. Not only was the female accomplice not present, Wickham said, she lacked the physical attributes to engage in the commission of the crime. Constructive treason suddenly seemed so outrageous that it defied nature and reason. Reliance on hearsay rather than visible evidence, and on the assumption that all are equal participants in the crime, allowed for what was unimaginable: a woman copulating with another woman.[88]

Wickham's bawdy allusion led Wirt to respond with his own sexual trope to explain the twisted definition of treason. His speech—later known as "Who Is Blennerhassett?"—proved to be the most remembered forensic display of the trial.[89] Wirt's narrative of seduction gained such acclaim because it evoked a recurrent motif in Burr's dandified identity: his potent ability to seduce men. Building on the testimony of Taylor and the Morgans, Wirt presented a convincing portrait of Burr as one who routinely lured young men of ambition and talent, men whose "youthful ardor" drew them "into a love of his person." As Cheetham had before him, Wirt noted how difficult it was to see into the "traitor's heart," to discover proof of his "secret intentions." It was Burr who had invaded the tranquil domestic retreat of Blennerhassett's Island; *he* was the aggressor, the principal, the "stranger," who found a way into the Irish dilettante's heart, "by the dignity and elegance of his demeanor, the light and beauty of his conversation, and the seductive and fascinating power of his address." As much as Blennerhassett was seduced, his island doubled as Eden, the symbol of Adamic and masculine innocence—and Burr, of course, was the "serpent." A man of intrigue, "elegant hypocrisy," and "glossy duplicity," a destroyer of the family hearth (a popular theme since Hamilton's death), he had now become, in Wirt's reconstruction, a dandified Satan.[90]

Who won this battle of wit and legal wrangling? Marshall decreed that the prosecution's evidence did not meet the constitutional standard for proof of treason, and thus he ruled its inadmissibility in this case.[91] Wirt wrote to his friend, Jefferson's nephew Dabney Carr: "Marshall has stepped in between Burr and death."[92] The case, however, had consequences beyond Marshall's ruling. Burr may have been acquitted, but his political career was permanently ruined. In 1809, at the age of 51, he left the country for Europe. By the time he returned in 1812, even his most strident defenders, like Luther Martin, had openly denounced him, while others privately shunned him.[93] Burr won the case, but he lost the battle—if the battle was for reputation—as he was forever branded as a traitor.

Burr's dandified style of treason, with its homosexual overtones, combined the trope of seduction with sexual perversion and conspiracy. His model of masculine prowess and seduction revealed treason to be a highly personal crime, and the traitor a lone mastermind. If seen as an arrogant manipulator who stood outside the system, narcissistically isolated and indifferent to others, he remained a potently dangerous sexual force by alluring followers through his refined but erotic surface style. Anticipating later psychologically laden images of the traitor, Burr's violent act—his crime—was against the social order. The proof of his deviant genius, his immoral desire for power, was skin deep—played out on the surface of his body. It was registered through the sexual tension felt by his audience: those who feared and adored his dashing enterprising spirit, his effortless and audacious masculine presence.

This portrait of the dandy as conspirator offered early republican audiences a frightening new kind of civic personality. It conjured an entire class of men, heretofore unknown: some were young and on the make, others older and perhaps more sinister, but all perceived as political outcasts, heading west to build their flagging careers. What changed was that male disorderly behavior now represented a threat to national security, and perhaps a sign of regional differences and growing conspiratorial discontents. This fascination with Burr thrived, and he bequeathed his dandified pose to another celebrated performer who scandalized the nation in 1865: John Wilkes Booth, handsome, elegant, insolent, and gifted in the arts of disguise and deceit, one with the audacity to match Aaron Burr. Booth resurrected what Burr began: an American version of treason, imagined nationwide as a personal crime carried out in the dark by a dandified and seductive hero, with grandiose plans to change the course of history.

NOTES

1. Ellen Moers, *The Dandy: Brummell to Beerhohm* (London, 1960), 22.

2. For the meaning of self-presentation (the capacity to appear in public, lead, judge others, and risk being judged by one's presence and words) and the public sphere, see Hannah Arendt, *The Human Condition* (Chicago, 1958), 32, 48–57, 176–86, 189, 198–99, 206.

3. For the notion of "symbolic capital," see Pierre Bourdieu, *Distinction: A Social Critique of the Judgment of Taste*, trans. Richard Nice (London, 1984), 291.

4. On the 1790s as the "age of passion," see Stanley Elkins and Eric McKitrick, *The Age of Federalism: The Early American Republic, 1788–1800* (New York, 1993); Marshall Smelser, "The Federalist Period as an Age of Passion," *American Quarterly* 10 (1958): 391–419. On the language of sexual deviancy in politics and the broader culture, see David Waldstreicher, "Federalism, the Styles of Politics, and the Politics of Style," in *Federalists Reconsidered*, ed. Doron Ben-Atar and Barbara B. Oberg (Charlottesville, 1998), 99–117, esp. 108, 116–17; Toby L. Ditz, "Shipwrecked; or, Masculinity Imperiled: Mercantile Representations of Failure and the Gendered Self in Eighteenth-Century Philadelphia," *Journal of American History* 81 (1994): 51–81, esp. 54–55, 58–59, 63; Mark E. Kann, *A Republic of Men: The American Founders, Gendered Language, and Patriarchal Politics* (New York, 1998), 3, 30, 52–78. On the importance of gossip, dueling, and honor among elite politicians, see Joanne B. Freeman, *Affairs of Honor: National Politics in the New Republic* (New Haven, 2001), esp. xv, xx, xxii, 62–104. Freeman, however, omits a gender analysis, which most other contemporary scholars on honor and dueling have stressed. See, for example, Robert A. Nye, *Masculinity and Male Codes of Honor in Modern France* (New

York, 1993); Pieter Spierenburg, ed., *Men and Violence: Gender, Honor, and Rituals in Modern Europe and America* (Athens, Ohio, 1998); and Irina Reyfman, *Ritualized Violence Russian Style: The Duel in Russian Culture and Literature* (Stanford, 1999).

5. Anna Clark, "The Chevalier d'Eon and Wilkes: Masculinity and Politics in the Eighteenth Century," *Eighteenth-Century Studies*, 32 (1998): 21.

6. See Catherine Edwards, *The Politics of Immorality in Ancient Rome* (Cambridge, 1993), 5, 68–71, 81; for "proteus," see James Cheetham, *On the Subject of Aaron Burr's Political Defection* (New York, 1803), 24.

7. For the pervasiveness of the "fop," "beau," and "dandy" types in English culture, see Michèle Cohen, *Fashioning Masculinity: National Identity and Language in the Eighteenth Century* (London, 1996), 37–41; Philip Carter, "Men about Town: Representations of Foppery and Masculinity in Early Eighteenth-Century Urban Society," in *Gender in Eighteenth-Century England: Roles, Representations and Responsibilities*, ed. Hannah Barker and Elaine Chalus (London, 1997), 31–57; Susan C. Shapiro, " 'Yon Plumed Dandebrat': Male 'Effeminacy' in English Satire and Criticism," *Review of English Studies*, new series 39 (1988): 400–412. For examples in American periodicals, see "Description of a BEAU," *The Weekly Museum* [New York], September 20, 1794; and *A Dictionary of Love; where in is the description of a perfect beauty; the picture of a fop or macaroni; and key to all the arch phrases, difficult terms, and peculiar idioms, used in that universal language* (Philadelphia, 1798); "Origin of a Beau," *Massachusetts Magazine* [Boston], June 1794; and *The Rural Magazine* [Newark], October 27, 1798.

8. Michel Foucault, *The History of Sexuality, Vol. 1: An Introduction*, trans. Robert Hurley (New York, 1978), 124–25.

9. Waldstreicher, "Federalism, the Styles of Politics, and the Politics of Style," 111, 114; also see Daniel A. Cohen, "Arthur Mervyn and His Elders: The Ambivalence of Youth in the Early Republic," *William and Mary Quarterly*, 3d ser., 43 (July 1986): 362–80, esp. 372, 379.

10. This newly created party system meant that "playing the party man" incorporated gender expectations into the informal rules of party membership and political practice. This development laid the foundation for a brand of masculinity that defined manhood suffrage and citizenship in the antebellum period. I discuss the importance of masculine definitions of civic identity in *Sex and Citizenship in Antebellum America* (Chapel Hill, 1998).

11. Nathan Schachner, *Aaron Burr: A Biography* (New York, 1961), 14, 17–22; Kline, ed., *Political Correspondence and Public Papers of Aaron Burr*, I, lvi.

12. Schachner, 23; see Susanna Rowson, *Charlotte Temple*, ed. Cathy Davidson (New York, 1986); the young woman actually died of tuberculosis—not a broken heart. See Samuel H. Wandell and Meade Minnigerode, *Aaron Burr: A Biography compiled from rare, and in many cases, unpublished sources* (New York, 1925), 31.

13. Schachner, *Aaron Burr*, 33–34; Kline, ed., *Political Correspondence and Public Papers of Aaron Burr*, 1:lxi–lxii.

14. Hamilton did play the courtier; see John Ferling, *The First of Men: The Life of George Washington* (Knoxville, 1988), 255, 257; Kline, ed., *Political Correspondence and Public Papers of Aaron Burr*, 1:lxiii–lxvi.

15. For correspondence with his wife, see Mathew L. Davis, ed., *Memoirs of Aaron Burr* (New York, 1836), 1:224–363.

16. Burr biographer Nathan Schachner saw Hamilton's "obsession" as "pathologic," and the recent study of Burr and Hamilton by Arnold Rogow continues to contend that Hamilton's hatred of Burr was "obsessive." See Schachner, *Aaron Burr*, 117, and Arnold A. Rogow, *A Fatal Friendship: Alexander Hamilton and Aaron Burr* (New York, 1998), 147, 228; Gore Vidal, *Burr* (New York, 1973), 356.

17. Freeman, *Affairs of Honor*, 161, 167, 170–71; Schachner, *Aaron Burr*, 249.

18. Burr did not resort to the style of personal attack used by Hamilton. Federalist Richard Peters of Pennsylvania remarked after the duel, "I never knew of Colonel Burr [to] speak ill of any man, and he had a right to expect a different treatment from what he experienced." See Kline, ed., *Political Correspondence and Public Papers of Aaron Burr*, 2:881–2; and Freeman, *Affairs of Honor*, 197.

19. Nathan Schachner, *Alexander Hamilton* (New York, 1946), 57, 125, 129, 247, 274, 348; Ferling, *First of Men*, 256–57, 376, 379–81.

20. Clinton had appointed Burr attorney general in 1789. When Burr ran for the U.S. Senate, he was "a tentative ally" of Clinton, but over the course of the next six years term, this connection proved to be less significant in defining Burr's political identity. See Kline, ed., *Political Correspondence and Public Papers of Aaron Burr*, I, 47, 92; also see Robert E. Wright, "Artisans, Banks, Credit and the Election of 1800," *Pennsylvania Magazine of History and Biography* 122 (1998): 211–39.

21. For Burr's political innovations, see Kline, ed., *Political Correspondence and Public Papers of Aaron Burr*, 1:419–25; and Schachner, *Aaron Burr*, 168–78.

22. Harold Syrett suggests that the strife between Hamilton and Burr can be traced back to 1789, when George Clinton appointed Burr state attorney general. Burr's decision to accept the position led to his victory over Philip Schuyler. To win the Senate seat, he had to secure the joint support of the Livingston and Clinton factions. See Harold C. Syrett and Jacob E. Cooke, eds., *The Papers of Alexander Hamilton* (New York, 1961–87), 12:480–81 and 26:238.

23. Mackubin Owens, Jr., "A Further Note on Certain of Hamilton's Pseudonyms: The 'Love of Fame' and the Uses of Plutarch," *Journal of the Early Republic* 4 (1984): 280–84.

24. In his seventeenth-century play *Catiline*, Ben Jonson highlights his crimes as incests with his sister and daughter, murders, rapes, and "parricide, late, on thine own only son." See Ben Jonson, *Catiline*, ed. W. F. Bolton and Jane F. Gardner (Lincoln, Neb., 1973), xix, 10.

25. Hamilton made this reference in 1792. Savius referred to Plautus Saevius, a Roman who was only known to history because he was charged with seducing his son. He lived

during the reign of Tiberius in the first century A.D. See Syrett, *The Papers of Alexander Hamilton*, 11:545–46; also see Milton Lomask, *Aaron Burr: The Years from Princeton to Vice President, 1756–1805* (New York: Farrar, Straus, Giroux, 1979), 160.

26. Hamilton included this description of Burr as an enclosure in his letter, calling it "a faithful sketch of Mr. Burr's character." See AH to John Rutledge Junior, January 4, 1801, in Syrett, ed., *Papers of Alexander Hamilton*, 25:293–98.

27. The handbill was titled "Aaron Burr!" and was first circulated by the Federalists in 1801, and later used by the anti-Burrite Republicans in Burr's campaign for governor in 1804. A copy of the 1804 handbill is in the New-York Historical Society; the content of the handbill was republished in James Cheetham's New York *American Citizen*, April 28, 1804. The handbill called Burr a "too successful DEBAUCHEE," and referred to his "ABANDONED PROFLIGACY." It claimed he had ruined dozens of women, including his most recent seduction of the daughter of a respectable tradesman who intended to seek revenge for his "family's DISHONOR."

28. Lemuel Hopkins, *The Democratiad: A Poem in Retaliation for the Philadelphia Jockey Club* (Philadelphia, 1795), 10–11. Another poem, *Aristocracy* (Philadelphia, 1795), also took Burr as its central character. See Charles E. Modlin, "Aristocracy in the Early Republic," *Early American Literature* 6 (1972): 252–57.

29. *New York Evening Post*, August 4, 1804.

30. Edwards, *Politics of Immorality in Ancient Rome,* 5, 99, 128.

31. Jacob Katz Cogan, "The Reynolds Affair and the Politics of Character," *Journal of the Early Republic* 16 (1996): 396–98, 400, 406–7.

32. Hamilton's apologia contributed to his postmortem image as the devoted family man, and the ultimate public servant, willing to die for the public good. See Freeman, *Affairs of Honor*, 163–66, 197.

33. Kline, ed., *Political Correspondence and Public Papers of Aaron Burr*, 1:645, 2:730 n. 3; and Cheetham to Jefferson, December 10, 1801, *Proceedings of the Massachusetts Historical Society*, 3d ser., 1 (1907–8): 46–52.

34. See Kline, ed., *Political Correspondence and Public Papers of Aaron Burr*, 2:641–46, 724–28, 737–39.

35. See "Letter Eight," New York *American Citizen*, October 12, 1802.

36. See Cameron McFarlane, *The Sodomite in Fiction and Satire, 1660–1750* (New York, 1997), 30–31, 37, 101–2, 111, 114.

37. New York *American Citizen*, August 16, 1802.

38. See New York *American Citizen*, October 18, 25, November 1, July 20, 22, 25, 1803. On Peter Irving's literary aspirations, see Stanley T. Williams, *The Life of Washington Irving* (New York, 1935), 1:25.

39. Cheetham and Irving were both born in 1772. *Dictionary of American Biography* (New York, 1930), 4:47. New York *American Citizen*, October 12, 1802, and January 21, April 20, June 20, 21, July 3, August 3, 20, 1803, and January 17, 1804.

40. Four families of brothers formed the core of the Burrites. Peter Irving (1772–1838)

recruited his brother Washington (1783–1859) to write for the *Morning Chronicle* and the *Corrector*. Burr stalwart Jonathan Swartwout (1770–1823) recruited Robert Swartwout and Samuel Swartwout (1783–1856). William P. Van Ness (1778–1823) and John Peter Van Ness (1770–1846) were lifelong friends and political allies of Burr. Mathew Livingston Davis (1773–1850) was considered Burr's political lieutenant. Davis's brother, William, and William's father-in-law, John Sanford (1752–1806), became active Burrites. See Kline, ed., *Political Correspondence and Public Papers of Aaron Burr*, 1:xxxi, 412, 584, 2:613, 894; B. R. Burnson, *The Adventures of Samuel Swartwout in the Age of Jefferson and Jackson* (Lewiston, N.Y., 1989), 1–2.

41. See New York *American Citizen*, February 1, 9, 1803. For references to enlisting young men in his "electioneering company," and "strolling players," see New York *American Citizen*, February 3, 24, 25, March 23, April 7, 21, 1804. Mollyhouses were located near the theater in London, and Peter Irving and his group "the Lads of Kilkenny" often gathered at a public house near Park Theater in New York. For the sexual underworld of English mollyhouses, see Tim Hitchcock, *English Sexualities, 1700–1800* (New York, 1997), 65–70; and for Irving's group, see Bruce I. Granger and Martha Hartzog, eds., *The Complete Works of Washington Irving: Letters of Jonathan Oldstyle, Gent. / Salmagundi* (Boston, 1978), xxiii.

42. New York *American Citizen*, April 28, 1804.

43. Ibid. Hair was a key cultural symbol of racial difference and acculturation. That one of the figures in this story was a hairdresser suggests this tension. For the cultural meaning of dress and race in New York City, see Shane White, *Somewhat More Independent: The End of Slavery in New York City, 1770–1810* (Athens, Ga., 1991), 185–87, 198–99. There is evidence to suggest that the Burrites were recruiting black voters. See Dixon Ryan Fox, "The Negro Vote in Old New York," *Political Science Quarterly* 32 (1917): 252–75.

44. New York *American Citizen*, April 30, 1804. See *Lexicon Balatronicum; A Dictionary of Buckish Slang, University Wit, and Pickpocket Eloquence* (London, 1811).

45. Shapiro, " 'Yon Plumed Dandebrat,' " 408–9.

46. See Rhoda K. Garelick, *Rising Star: Dandyism, Gender, and Performance in the Fin de Siècle* (Chicago, 1998), 32–33.

47. The earliest date for this broadside is 1806. See A. W., *A Dandy Song* (Boston?: s.n., between 1806 and 1826), Broadside Collection, American Antiquarian Society, Worcester, Mass.

48. Cheetham, *On the Subject of Aaron's Burr's Political Defection* (New York, 1803), 24; Charles Nolan, Jr., *Aaron Burr and the American Literary Imagination* (Westport, Conn., 1980), 50–51, 53. For similar allusions, see New York *American Citizen*, February 1, 1803.

49. Everett Somerville Brown, ed., *William Plumer's Memorandum of Proceedings in the United States Senate 1803–1807* (New York, 1923), 517–18.

50. Shapiro, " 'Yon Plumed Dandebrat,' " 406–8.

51. Garelick, *Rising Star*, 5.

52. William Charles, *Modern Dandy's*, colored engraving, 1807, American Antiquarian Society, Worcester, Mass.

53. For "audacity," see "The examination of Various Charges against Mr. Burr," New York *American Citizen*, December 17, 1803.

54. Syrett, ed., *Papers of Hamilton*, 25:305.

55. Thomas Jefferson to Charles Clay, January 11, 1807, Thomas Jefferson Papers, Library of Congress.

56. William Thomson, *A Compendious View of the Trial of Aaron Burr, (Late Vice-President of the United States) Charged with High Treason; together with Biographical Sketches, of Several Eminent Characters* (Richmond, 1807), viii–ix.

57. Ibid., xi.

58. See New York *Chronicle Express*, December 29, 1803, February 20, 1804; "Communication," January 30, 1804; "To the Republican Electors of the State of New-York," March 22, 1804.

59. "The Rights of Editors: No. XXXV," New York *Chronicle Express*, February 28, 1803, and "To the Republican Electors of the State," ibid., April 5, 1804. On accusers melting before his eye, see "Communication," ibid., February 20, 1804; and his confounding presence, see ibid., December 29, 1804; and on his ability to make his enemies tremble in his presence, see "To the Independent Citizens of the State," ibid., March 22, 1804; and "Who shall be our next President?: No. XVI," ibid., February 16, 1804.

60. George Bryan Brummell (1778–1840); Moers, *The Dandy*, 21, 24–27, 30–31, 33–36; Hubert Cole, *Beau Brummell* (New York, 1977), 44–45, 78–82; John Harvey, *Men in Black* (Chicago, 1995), 29–30; Schachner, *Aaron Burr*, 173; and for a discussion of these other male types, see *A Dictionary of Love*, 32–33, 35, 51, 53–54.

61. The phrase "incomparable Burr" appeared in a Kentucky newspaper to announce a ball in his honor after the first attempt to charge Burr with treason failed and the charges were dropped. See Ronald Rayman, "Frontier Journalism in Kentucky: Joseph Monfort Street and the Western World, 1806–1809," *Register of the Kentucky Historical Society* 76 (1978): 108; also see Garelick, *Dandyism*, 5.

62. Ann Hollander, *Sex and Suits* (New York, 1994), 92, 100.

63. Mark Van Doren, ed., *Correspondence of Aaron Burr and his daughter Theodosia* (New York, 1929), 255, 306, 326.

64. See New York *American Citizen*, August 7, 16, 1804.

65. Federalist William Plumer mocked Burr's insistence on proper procedure and etiquette, but recorded the tears shed during his farewell address; see Brown, ed., *Plumer's Memorandum*, 283, 285, 312–13. For a favorable account of Burr's speech, see "Extract of a Letter from a Member of Congress," New York *American Citizen*, March 11, 1805; and see Burr's descriptions of both events in a letters to his daughter, dated March 13, 1805, in Van Doren, ed., *Correspondence of Aaron Butt and His Daughter Theodosia*, 205; also Schachner, *Aaron Burr*, 261–638.

66. See "Communications," New York *American Citizen*, March 22, 1805.

67. See Winfield Scott, *Memoirs of Lieut.-General Scott, LL.D. Written by Himself* (New York, 1864), 1:13.

68. See William Wirt to Peachy Gilmer, July 18, 1807, William Wirt Papers, Manuscript Division, Library of Congress. Wirt, of course, fashioned himself as a "man of sentiment," and likewise had a more sentimental style of relationship with men his age. See Andrew Burstein, *America's Jubilee: How in 1826 A Generation Remembered Fifty Years of Independence* (New York, 2001), 34–58; and Anya Jabour, "Male Friendship and Masculinity in the Early National South: William Wirt and his Friends," *Journal of the Early Republic* 20 (2000), 83–111.

69. For the two descriptions sent to Jefferson, see William Tatham to Thomas Jefferson, March 27, 1807, and Caesar A. Rodney to Thomas Jefferson, March 27, 1807, Thomas Jefferson Papers, Library of Congress, Washington, D.C. John Randolph, who would serve as the foreman of Burr's grand jury, gave a similar account of him being "accouter in a shabby suit of homespun, with an old white hat flapped over his face, the dress in which he was apprehended." See John Randolph to John Nicholson, March 25, 1807, in Henry Adams, *John Randolph: A Biography by Henry Adams*, ed. Robert McColley (Armonk, N.Y., 1996), 147.

70. Nicholas Perkins to C. A. Rodney, relating to the capture of Aaron Burr, n.d., Nicholas Perkins Papers, Tennessee Historical Society, Nashville, Tennessee. In the trial report, Perkins affidavit mentioned Burr's eye as giving him away. See *Reports of the Trials of Colonel Aaron Burr (Late Vice President of the United States), for Treason, and for A Misdemeanor, in preparing the means of a military expedition against Mexico, A Territory of the King of Spain, with whom the United States were at Peace, in the Circuit Court of the United States, held in the city of Richmond in the district of Virginia, in the Summer Term of the Year 1807* (Philadelphia, 1808), 1:2–3. Burr's outfit was debated in the papers. See *Richmond Enquirer*, April 21, 1807.

71. For a later embellished account that emphasized Burr being "placed in his saddle as though he were a child," and Burr bursting into tears and being "unmanned," see Albert J. Pickett, *Arrest of Aaron Burr in Alabama in 1807* (Montgomery, Ala., 1850), 10; and for a portrait of his capture that highlights Burr's "tidy boot" as giving his away (a somewhat more dandified version), and his escape described as being "unmanned," see William H. Sanford, ed., *The Blennerhassett Papers* (Cincinnati, 1891), 215, 226.

72. See Ruth Doumlele, "Treasonable Doubt: Aaron Burr on Trial," *Richmond*, March 1995, 44; *Richmond Portraits: In an Exhibition of Makers of Richmond, 1737–1860* (Richmond, 1949), 74–75; Schachner, *Aaron Burr*, 409; Thomas Perkins Abernethy, *The Burr Conspiracy* (New York, 1954), 239.

73. New York *American Citizen*, April 16, 1807; *Richmond Enquirer*, April 28, 1807; *Reports of the Trials of Colonel Aaron Burr*, 1:58.

74. Doumlele, "Treasonable Doubt," 46; July 3, July 6, July 30, 1807, in *Correspondence of Aaron Burr to his Daughter Theodosia*, 222–24; Sanford, ed., *Blennerhassett Papers*, 324.

75. Sanford, ed., *Blennerhassett Papers*, 406.

76. Blennerhassett referred to Burr as the "little emperor," but it also appeared in the

press before and during the trial. See Sanford, ed., *Blennerhassett Papers*, 343, 461; *New York Herald*, October 1, 1807; "The Conspiracy," *Richmond Enquirer*, December 11, 1806; "An outlaw emperor," *Richmond Enquirer*, March 24, 1807; and New York *American Citizen*, December 20, 1806, January 6, 12, May 8, 1807.

77. Bradley Chapin, *The American Law of Treason: Revolutionary and Early National Origins* (Seattle, 1964), 103, 105; Mary K. Bonsteel Tachau, "Treason and the Whiskey 'Insurrection,'" in John Johnson, ed., *Historic U.S. Court Cases 1690–1990: An Encyclopedia* (New York, 1992), 9.

78. *Report on the Trials of Aaron Burr*, 494, 563.

79. See New York *American Citizen*, January 6, February 24, March 19, 1807; and *Richmond Enquirer*, November 14, 1806; "Burr Expedition," *Richmond Enquirer*, January 3, 1807; "Burr Conspiracy," *Richmond Enquirer*, January 15, 1807.

80. *Report of the Trials of Aaron Burr*, 2:517.

81. Chapin, *American Law of Treason*, 103–4.

82. Chapin, *American Law of Treason*, 104; *Reports of the Trials of Aaron Burr*, 1:113–14, 12, 128–31.

83. See Fintan O'Toole, *A Traitor's Kiss: The Life of Richard Brinsley Sheridan, 1751–1816* (New York, 1997), 300–301.

84. *Reports of the Trials of Aaron Burr*, 1:467.

85. This "vindication" was reprinted in New York *American Citizen*, July 2, 1807.

86. For Wilkinson's vanity, see Royal Arnan Shreve, *The Finished Scoundrel: General James Wilkinson, sometime commander-in-chief of the Army of the United States, who made intrigue a trade and treason a profession* (Indianapolis, 1933), 100, 133; and Nathaniel Weyl, *Treason: The Story of Disloyalty and Betrayal in American History* (Washington, D.C., 1950), 121; *Report of the Trials of Aaron Burr*, 1:69, 155; Sanford, ed., *Blennerhassett Papers*, 502; Adams, *John Randolph*, 147; Abernethy, *Burr Conspiracy*, 239.

87. A "piercing eye" reflected the current popularity of physiognomy and theatrical self-presentation. Brummell became famous for his dismissive look, something he used against the Prince of Wales after their falling out in 1811. See Moers, *The Dandy*, 19–20, 37. It was a gesture suggested for attorneys; see "Some Considerations on the viva voce Examination of Witnesses at the Bar," *New York Magazine*, May 1796, 230; See Irving's letter to James K. Paulding, June 22, 1807, in *Complete Works of Washington Irving: Letters*, 1:239–40; James Wilkinson to Thomas Jefferson, June 17, 1807, Jefferson Papers, Library of Congress, microfilm reel 38; *Reports of the Trials of Aaron Burr*, 1:197.

88. *Reports of the Trial of Aaron Burr*, 1:557, 559, 562–63.

89. *New York Herald*, October 3, 1807; New York *American Citizen*, October 5, 1807; Parton, *Life and Times of Aaron Burr*, 2:146.

90. *Report on the Trials of Aaron Burr*, 2:65–66, 96–98.

91. Chapin, *American Law of Treason*, 110–13; *Reports on the Trials of Aaron Burr*, 2:417–21.

92. William Wirt to Dabney Carr, September 7, 1807, in William Wirt Papers, Maryland Historical Society, Baltimore.

93. See *The Private Journal of Aaron Burr* (Rochester, 1903), 2:28–29.

ALBRECHT KOSCHNIK

6

Young Federalists, Masculinity, and Partisanship during the War of 1812

Until recently political historians of the early republic have paid little attention to the deeply gendered nature of male political socialization and the crucial role of gender in shaping the development of partisan politics. In this they have followed the biases of their sources, most of which were generated by male public figures who presented their identities as political actors and citizens as fully formed, self-contained, and unrelated to marriage and family life. Consequently, by concentrating on men's public representation of themselves as their object of study, historians have neglected the lives of husbands and fathers, of sons and suitors, and separated assertions of power from the social and cultural roots that shaped those claims. Similarly, most sources for political history also tend to obscure the gendered dynamics of male gatherings and associations. As I will argue here, by looking at a group of young Philadelphia Federalists, intense concern over gender issues permeated exclusively male realms such as voluntary associations, the legal profession, and the military. The male world of the young

Federalists was one of the locations where, in Toby L. Ditz's words, the "cultural production of gender categories" took place.[1]

The current interest in questions of gender and masculinity has grown out of the work on women's history done in the last three decades. That work has established several fundamental propositions, namely, gender categories were cultural, not biological, products; male and female identities always evolved in relation to each other; and no gendered terminology had a fixed meaning. Gendered language that distinguished between masculine and feminine qualities—for example, self-control and rationality versus passion and irrationality—did not invoke absolute characteristics, but desirable and undesirable qualities, respectively, which changed and took on meaning according to the perspective and needs of the author. Such distinctions paved the way for strategies of inclusion and exclusion, for men's exercise of social and political power, and for the denunciation of troublesome and undependable men.[2] While women's history has demonstrated the crucial role of gender in the political culture of the early republic, as well as the part women played in that culture, so far the emerging historiography on masculinity has not fully engaged men's position as gendered beings in early republican politics, or illuminated the political uses to which appeals to manhood could be put.[3]

Just as women's historians have called for a history of women and men written around the notion of gender relations, they have also called into question the analytical concept of separate public and private spheres. While recent works on postrevolutionary women's history have shown that this concept continues to be useful for describing a cluster of powerful contemporary propositions concerning appropriate male and female behavior, they also demonstrate—by highlighting women's involvement in electoral politics or activities which quickly assumed political dimensions, such as organized benevolence—that women's experience defied the mutually exclusive categories of public and private.[4] Historians of the early republic need to revisit the male worlds of work, politics, associations, and home in a similar fashion, and demonstrate how these realms informed each other in the creation of male identities and political personas.

Our related efforts to go beyond the language of public and private and introduce gender as a central category into the study of male partisanship have to be joined with a reconceptualization of what kind of actions we consider as political behavior. Once we define politics broadly—and go beyond a history of parties, elections, and ideologies—we are led exactly to those environments where cultural and gender imperatives interacted particularly powerfully and directly with politics. Like recent accounts of eighteenth-century club life that have pointed to the intermediate position of male sociability between private assemblies and the colonial public sphere, I argue that the young Federalists—in their associational life as well as their less formal gatherings—shifted effortlessly between different styles of political action, styles we cannot categorize as either exclusively public or private, political or nonpolitical. For that reason they have received very little attention from political historians.[5] For example, in his classic study of Federalism in this period David Hackett Fischer identified two generations of Federalists, "young" and "old," and demonstrated that the younger generation—including men in Philadelphia—tried to build up a Federalist partisan organization in response to Thomas Jefferson's presidential victory in 1800.[6] The young Philadelphians introduced here were not—with a few exceptions—part of Fischer's "young" Federalists. Younger than these men, less well established and connected, they formed a third generation of Federalists. More importantly, their activities—outside of Fischer's focus on electioneering and partisan organization—have remained largely unexplored.

My essay concentrates on the coming-of-age experience of this third generation to explore the interconnections between masculine identities and Federalist persuasion. It is based primarily on the diary of Thomas Pleasants, as well as the published and unpublished writings of his cohort. During the later stages of the War of 1812, Pleasants chronicled his contacts with male friends, his involvement in visiting and other mixed-sex entertainment, his fledgling attempts to establish himself as a lawyer, and his attendance at militia musters and the meetings of political societies. Pleasants's diary notes his conversations with his friends in considerable detail. As a result, even though the diary is first and foremost a record of his thoughts and observations, it reveals Pleasants as part of a network of like-minded men. It demonstrates that every facet of their lives proved to be an exceptionally competitive and judgmental environment and a testing ground for their evolving sense of themselves as men and Federalists. With their personal and political significance always at stake, they assessed and compared each other's comportment, actions, and oratory as indices of their manhood as well as their commitment to Federalism. Their ideal of republican manhood focused on a man's ability to achieve independence and professional success, defend his personal reputation, preserve social distinctions, and, during the War of 1812, defend American "national honor." In turn, the writings of Pleasants's peers show how their political and cultural socialization found expression in their assumptions about appropriate masculine, professional, and political behavior and beliefs—which in no small part evolved in reaction to their Republican opponents.

Pleasants's parentage, college life, professional choice, and literary and military aspirations made him representative of the Federalist young men who were moving from adolescence to adulthood at the beginning of the 1810s.[7] His father, Israel Pleasants, was the president of the United States Insurance Company in Philadelphia. Born in 1790, Pleasants had attended the University of Pennsylvania from 1805 to 1808, where he helped organize the Philological Society, a student debating club; in 1808 he also gave the anniversary oration before the Attican Society, a similar association. At least one of his literary efforts appeared in a local magazine ("The Ladies of Philadelphia," 1810). Pleasants read law with his uncle Walter Franklin in Lancaster, and gained admittance to the Philadelphia bar in February 1814. He continued to live with his parents and siblings, but opened an office to begin his law practice. In 1811 he joined a Federalist organization, the Washington Association; and during the war he helped to establish and eventually led a volunteer militia company, the Washington Guards, which identified itself strongly with Federalists politics.[8]

The peculiar position of Pleasants and his friends as young men created a set of specific pressures and concerns. Despite their different career plans—ranging from commerce, pedagogy, and theology to their most frequent choice, the law—all the men had yet to secure the status, rewards, and markers of full manhood they believed their social background, upbringing, and education entitled them to: economic independence, professional success, and public distinction. At the beginning of the nineteenth century, as Joseph F. Kett points outs, an adolescent moved from dependence within the family unit to a semi-dependent position once he entered college or an apprenticeship. Since arrangements regarding schooling and occupational and professional training varied widely, a young man could remain semi-dependent until his mid-twenties, if not later. He would not be considered as fully independent and an adult until he was self-employed, was married, and had set up his own household. Here organizations played a crucial role for young men: according to Glen Wallach, they helped the men to "articulate the significance they attached to their own youth and how they imagined themselves as men," and to create companionship in the face of their temporary marginality.[9]

There is strong evidence for the unsettled situation of most young Federalists. Even though most men had finished their formal professional education or apprenticeship—among lawyers, the average age of admittance to the Philadelphia bar was just under twenty-two—the first steps in their chosen occupation were not easy. The young men compared their fathers and employers' accomplishments and success with their own tenuous position. In fact, Pleasants's experience demonstrated that failure was a distinct possibility: his legal business floundered, and the end of the war terminated all prospects of receiving the appointment in the regular army he had sought. He eventually left Philadelphia to join a mercantile partnership in New Orleans. In a letter to a legal apprentice Nicholas Biddle reduced the hazards of professional life to a simple problem: "You have ceased to be a boy, you are now a young man, just beginning to have in your hands the government of your own conduct at a period the most difficult and trying. Your success in the world must indeed essentially depend on your first exertions, and perhaps the whole character of your future life may be decided by the manner in which you employ the next year or two."[10] For Biddle advancement depended on a single factor, individual hard work; he told the younger man to think of his own effort as the key factor determining his future success or failure in reaching full adulthood and manhood, and gaining the respect of his peers and the community.

Pleasants followed similar advice, offered by his uncle Walter Franklin, when he proceeded to establish himself as a lawyer. After he had opened his own office, he resolved in his diary:

> The following is the model of study I have prescribed for myself, which I am resolved to pursue as nearly as I can.
> Two hours before breakfast to read State Laws.
> Six hours in the rest of the day to Law.
> One hour to composition.
> One hour to other reading.
> If the hours appropriated to Law be otherwise employed, an equal portion of time taken from other pursuits must be devoted to it, unless some special reason should prevent.[11]

In committing a detailed plan of study to his diary and keeping a daily record of his reading, Pleasants followed common precepts concerning the larger purposes of a diary. Beyond creating an account of his thoughts and deeds, of his "conversations" and "opinions of characters and their views," Pleasants hoped to use the diary as a tool to further his self-improvement through self-scrutiny and observation. The daily account of time spent in "useful employment" or "trifled away" was always ready for his own consideration and forced him to face his shortcomings. Walter Franklin "approved of [keeping a diary] and recommended its continuance."[12]

Still, such scrutiny did not assure professional success. The leaders of the bar monopolized the most lucrative cases in Philadelphia, while a much larger number of lawyers, including Pleasants, struggled to make a living during their first years in the profession. At the beginning of his career even Horace Binney, one among a handful of lawyers who would dominate the profession in the nine-teenth century, had to "wait upon the courts" and "profess his readiness" to attract occasional clients, all the while living off his inheritance. Pleasants, how-ever, could not rely on his family's wealth. On the contrary: since his father's strained finances severely limited any help he could offer his son, Pleasants resolved to "be rigidly economical, laboriously industrious, and resolutely ab-stinent." Even though he determined to "make known [and] improve my law business" and attended circuit court in the counties surrounding Philadelphia, he received only a few cases.[13]

Pleasants's office became a preferred meeting place for the members of the Washington Association and Washington Guards. While frequent visitors added to his anxieties by interrupting his studies, their calls also offered the opportunity for diverting talk about legal and professional problems, politics, books, and the volunteer militia. Whether engaged in work, associational activities, or leisure, Pleasants spent a considerable amount of each day's time in his friends' company. Whereas his family appeared as no more than distracting dinner company, his friends shared in every aspect of Pleasants's life that defined him as a professional, partisan, citizen-soldier, and young man.[14]

Pleasants also violated his resolutions by visiting the Athenaeum. In Decem-ber 1813 half a dozen young Philadelphians, all in their early or mid-twenties, resolved to open a subscription for a library and reading room containing news-papers, books, and reference works. As one of the founders explained in retro-spect, they felt "the want of a convenient place of common resort, in which their leisure hours could be passed, without danger to morals or tastes." By 1816 close to three hundred and fifty shareholders and subscribers appeared in the minutes: the majority of the initial shareholders, officers, and directors were under thirty years old, described themselves as lawyers or merchants, and had joined Federal-ist associations in recent years. Even though Pleasants spent money for his militia uniform and equipment, he did not purchase a share in the Athenaeum (twenty-five dollars) or pay annual dues (three to five dollars). Instead, the shareholders among his friends introduced him as a regular guest. Initially at least, the same political views and a shared interest in the predominantly European and conser-vative publications to which the Athenaeum subscribed provided the main bond between its patrons.[15]

Pleasants's diary recorded his many visits to the Athenaeum. Between his office, the exercising ground, and frequent rounds of visiting and entertainment in mixed assemblies, the Athenaeum occupied a central place in Pleasants's life.

He spent evenings in the reading rooms, taking advantage of the extended opening hours, and caught up with recent publications, or tracked down articles other patrons had recommended to him. He welcomed the opportunity to network and to assimilate literature and learning in an informal setting. Aside from his office, Pleasants and his friends used the Athenaeum's conversation room as a convenient place to meet and exchange news and gossip. Here they talked about politics, especially the course of the war, and shared impressions about the dances, sleigh rides, and evenings at the theater of Philadelphia's social season.[16] Visiting the Athenaeum permitted the young men to create a common sensibility built around the patronage of high culture, which helped to ground and legitimate their claims to distinction and leadership.

Conversation at the Athenaeum and Pleasants's office occurred in an exclusively male environment. In contrast, visiting, dancing, and going to the theater brought Pleasants into contact with a considerable number of young women, and talk about courtship and possible companions and future spouses occurred frequently between him and his male friends and female relatives. However, Pleasants decided to terminate his courtship of the "angelic," "divine," and "bewitchingly sweet" Ann Coleman until he had acquired a "competency"— the means to maintain a household and support a family—a resolution that appears to have deepened his sense of unsettledness and marginality (and quite probably contributed to his decision to move to New Orleans).[17]

However, while such all-male or heterosocial gatherings provided important sites for informal learning, socialization, and pleasure, Pleasants's militia company created an environment in which questions of masculinity and its relationship with politics and class surfaced particularly frequently and urgently. The Washington Guards epitomized male sociability, embodied the young men's privileged access to public space, and constituted the ultimate vehicle for asserting their masculinity—as the defenders of home and nation. The athletic and martial competition of the militia muster received its especially intense gender dynamics from the simultaneous exclusion of women from military service and their inclusion as spectators of the militia on parade.[18]

Aside from such displays of manhood, joining a volunteer company also revealed genteel aspirations and demonstrated combative partisanship. Ever since the early 1790s the volunteer militia system was closely connected with partisan politics. Federalist and Republican companies used their parades on national holidays to demonstrate their political preferences. In 1814 several new volunteer companies, including the Washington Guards, quickly established their presence in Philadelphia. Pleasants took a serious interest in the militia: his position as sergeant and later as captain of the Washington Guards occupied him at least one afternoon every week. The Guards marched in the parades organized by Federalist associations, held separate public drills and musters, and published accounts of their dinners and toasts. The publication of the toasts in particular served to demonstrate the politics of a company. For example, on the Fourth of July in 1814 the Washington Guards gave twelve cheers to a toast written by Pleasants: "The Principles of Federalism: The political creed of the best and wisest men of our country—the safety and existence of the nation depend on their prevalence." Pleasants also started to write a "history of the war," in which he paid special attention to "the inadequacy of the militia," and tried to cast the Guards' volunteer effort in a decidedly partisan light. Submitted for publication, the essay was rejected "on acc[oun]t of its political nature."[19]

Beyond making such political statements, the volunteer system also raised questions of class. While men in the draft militia evaded service as best as they could, and many used muster days as an occasion for frolic and intoxication, ambitious young men in volunteer companies could turn martial exercise into a conspicuous display of uniforms, weaponry, and genteel and exclusive social intercourse. Although the state of Pennsylvania or the federal government paid the volunteers when they were on duty, they had to pay for their equipment and were expected to train regularly. As Pleasants's diary demonstrates, training could take up the better part of an afternoon, an investment most workingmen could not make, not to mention the expense of providing their own outfits. Consequently, volunteering mixed politics with the aspirations of young men to distinguish themselves as "gentlemen volunteers," as their commander called them.[20]

"TALENT," "VIRTUE," "KNOWLEDGE," "MANNERS"

The young Federalists came of age at a time when their social position and education no longer entitled them to political and civic leadership. Even though they claimed to possess skills, taste, and understanding far superior to those of the Republicans, such claims no longer went unchallenged. The image of an organic society structured by notions of hierarchy, deference, and civic virtue, and governed by the natural aristocracy, had lost much of its force since the time when George Washington presided over Federalist administrations, if not earlier. Even though the unity of social standing and political power had always been tenuous in Pennsylvania, the young Federalists tried to resist its complete disintegration. Accordingly, faced with an ever stronger egalitarian current, they continued to stress family background and an advanced education, not only as requisites for mastering the technical complexities of trade and the law, but as the indispensable foundations of civic leadership.

In joining the "legal fraternity" the young men consciously and enthusiastically entered a professional subculture that reinforced and heightened their sense of separation from democratic politics. In the new republic lawyers claimed social and professional preeminence as well as political influence by pointing to their position as the creators and interpreters of constitutions and laws, and as the conservative guardians of the new polity against the passions of ordinary citizens. As legal apprentices and young lawyers, Pleasants and his cohort received their training and socialization from a set of established practitioners who transmitted closely connected precepts concerning professional conduct, masculine identity, and especially their avowed Federalism to their students. Undoubtedly, the new lawyers' conservative politics were also a result of their background: as Gary Nash has shown, the majority of lawyers admitted to the bar in the early nineteenth century came from upper-class mercantile or professional families.[21]

The young men connected refinement and higher education with the ability to form a reasoned political judgment and engage in patriotic action. John Elihu Hall defended inequality based on differences in education: in contrast to "some of our young republicans" who asserted that "we all are created equal," Hall argued that "the man of education"—meaning somebody like himself—"whose mind is impressed with the soundest maxims essential to the existence of government, and whose prudence has taught him the propriety and necessity of obedience," was best qualified to be "the honest supporter of the interests of his country." Hall credited a classical education for establishing these skills. Only "he whose mind has been disciplined in the school of classical lore, whose taste has been refined by the example of Homer, and the precepts of Aristotle," can fully grasp and defend "the interests of his country." Conversely, Republican politicians and their supporters in Pennsylvania lacked such an education and, consequently, were unable to perform the same services.[22]

Similarly, the members of Pleasants's Philological Society defined the politically responsible individual in their own image, educated and able to distinguish between a "partisan spirit" and "the public good." Within the doors of the Society they had acquired the "knowledge and stability" that turned them into "useful and respectable" citizens. Consequently, since "virtue and knowledge are the only genuine distinctions which render one man superior to another," they were better equipped to lead the community than the "lawless mobs" they saw around them as the Republicans took over elective offices in Pennsylvania. As soon as the "ignorance and incapacities of the lower class of our cities" could be prevented from polluting the political process, men of talent would again assume their rightful place.[23]

The young Federalists saw a close connection between a lack of manliness and a lack of education, deportment, and "talent." They set high standards for themselves: speaking before the Philological Society in 1813 Robert H. Smith noted that their college education had filled them with "hopes of excellence and honor and usefulness." Based on such ideals, they set out to judge the men around them. During his year as a Pennsylvania legislator in 1810–11 Nicholas Biddle wrote a series of short assessments of a dozen Federalist and Republican legislators in the House of Representatives, evaluating each according to his merits on those counts. He noted that many of the Federalists were men with "an excellent education" or "good legal knowledge," and declared a representative as "a man of reading." At the same time, he found a general lack of "talent," education, and "liberal views" among the Republican legislators. About a papermaker, he wrote that "he has no education and I confess I almost blushed for the county when I observed on his files a note on the health law in which he mentions the frequency of 'yillor feaver.'" He also assessed the representatives' manners to judge their capabilities. While he praised the Federalists' "excellent sense and judgment," their "good temper[,] good manners, and plain strong understanding," and found them "manly and liberal both in public and private," he declared that almost all Republicans had neither the "manners" nor the "talents" to qualify them for public office. Biddle's appraisal of his fellow representatives created a triangular relationship between partisanship, manhood, and manners, and his judgment of one aspect determined his verdict on the other two.[24]

CITIZEN-SOLDIERS, PARTISAN POLITICS, AND
THE FATE OF THE REPUBLIC

Pleasants and his friends eventually made the transition from citizen-soldiers on the streets of Philadelphia to actual service in the War of 1812. For most of the war, Philadelphia and the Delaware River were under no direct threat from the British army and navy. However, after the burning of Washington and attempted conquest of Baltimore, an attack seemed likely, and a bi-partisan committee began to organize the defense of the city. Many young Federalists served in the "Advance Light Brigade," an umbrella organization for the volunteer militia companies of Philadelphia. Stationed in Delaware from late August until the end of November 1814, they never saw the enemy.[25]

The men's military service was part of a larger effort to come to terms with the shifting realities of officeholding and political power in early nineteenth-century Pennsylvania. Although resistance to the Embargo of 1808 and the war had allowed Federalist candidates to do well in state and local elections, even during the war years the young men continued to equate the Republican ascent in Lancaster, the state capital, with their substantially diminished prospects of access to those institutions that promised opportunities for distinguished public service. On the Fourth of July in 1814, Pleasants offered the following toast to the Washington Guards: "The state of Pennsylvania," he declared, "abounding with statesmen of exalted talents, unblemished fame, and just political views— she is disgraced by her cold neglect of them, and her misplaced confidence in demagogues of depraved principles—despicable for their meanness, and contemptible for their folly." While they offered their services in the defense of Philadelphia the young men also knew that they could no longer take a public career for granted.[26]

The young Federalists' concern over the distribution of public offices was part of their elaborate, if fanciful, story of the rise and decline of the American republic. Under the Federalists the new republic had experienced economic prosperity, domestic peace, international neutrality, and the protection of civil liberties; the Republicans had allowed these achievements to wither away. The young Federalists took this decline under the Republican administration as a sign of corruption and partisanship: unqualified Republicans had received positions as political rewards, while the Federalists, a meritocracy of capable, public-spirited men, had been chased out of office. The young men bemoaned the "systematic exclusion of the friends of Washington from the important offices of the state." Instead of "recompensing exalted merit," the Republicans forced "pre-eminent worth . . . to languish in obscurity and perish with neglect."[27] For Philadelphia Federalists, despair over the state of American and especially Pennsylvania politics and alarm over the Republicans' occasionally disastrous mismanagement of the war fused with their perception that almost all roads to distinction had been closed to them.

In this perspective, the young Federalists considered fighting in the War of 1812 as much an assertion of their worth as citizen-soldiers as a declaration of their continued political significance. While only a few of them had been able to secure a military position or other appointive office that had opened up as a consequence of the war, they could still volunteer on their own terms. Volunteering provided the opportunity to demonstrate their dedication to the republic as well as their military prowess—to themselves, their peers, and the American public.[28] Of course, the Federalists had opposed the declaration of war as a partisan adventure and explained its lackluster conduct as the logical result of giving commissions to incompetent men, but they also noted under what conditions they would be willing to contribute to the war effort. "Although the federal party have hitherto disdained to rally around the standard of [the] administration," explained Charles Caldwell in a Fourth of July address in 1814, once the prosecution of the war would be placed into "SUITABLE HANDS, [and] on that sacred spot, *the point of honour*," the Federalists would be ready to offer their services in the defense of their home state.[29]

After the war Nathaniel Chauncey offered an account of the local defense efforts in which he reiterated this point. As soon as the British army had burned Washington, "it was now seen that the people must defend themselves. That our rulers could declare war, but were unable to carry it on. That though they were bound by the constitution to protect the country, its deliverance was not to proceed from them." In contrast to the dubious invasions of Canada, "*the protection of our own soil*" became

> a cause in which our countrymen might *lawfully* display their courage. Numbers came forward, prepared to repel the enemy, and redeem the honour of the American name. Many who hear me, thus displayed their attachment to their country; and the name of 'Washington Guards' was assumed by a band of men, who were ready to prove that they were worthy of that honourable title. When the spirit of the people was thus roused, their real character appeared. They showed that they were true descendants of the men who, in the revolution, foiled the efforts of Great Britain. From the tameness with which we had endured insult, and injuries, and plunder, and confiscation from France, our character had miserably fallen: but it is now restored, and Americans are once more respected.

Chauncey carefully separated the national administration and its conduct of the war from the defense of Philadelphia. Since the national government was unable to provide for the defense of the city, the Federalists had to fulfill this task by themselves. In Chauncey's account, the Federalist display of courage had not only won the war, but saved American honor and independence.[30]

The memory of the American Revolution became the standard against which the young Federalists measured the success of their own coming-of-age. In their perspective, living in wartime, if not the actual experience of battle, and securing the creation of the republic had been the defining experience of the Revolutionary generation. In their Fourth of July toasts the young men told tales of struggle and sacrifice, and vowed to preserve "the memory of the heroes" who "died on the fields of Honor," and to ensure "the gratitude of posterity." Even though it seemed futile, young Federalists contemplated ways for their generation, "the descendants of those who were the associates in arms," to live up to the challenge of accomplishing something equal in scope and sacrifice. "A new succession of men," inspired by "the recital of [Washington's] glorious deeds," had to assume the responsibility of defending the country. This moment arrived during the 1814 campaign: while the volunteers did not see battle, their willingness to fight completed the transition. As Nathaniel Chauncey pointed out, the threat of invasion let "their real character appear," and by volunteering they had demonstrated that they were the "true descendants" of the Revolutionary generation.[31]

YOUNG MEN, MASCULINITY, AND THE REPUBLICAN POLITY

The young Federalists' struggle to gain independence and respect expressed itself not the least in their persistent concern over personal reputation and manly behavior. Gender historians conceive of manhood as a cultural "construct which is constantly being remade," rather than a biological fact.[32] Consequently, the young men's relentless attempts to assert, demonstrate, and defend their masculinity do not point to a crisis in manhood or gender relations at this time; instead, they direct our attention toward masculinity's performative character and toward the strategies gendered language offered these men to cope with the challenges they faced. By highlighting the young men's specific circumstances, in particular their ambiguous position and heightened sense of insecurity, I point to the social and cultural sources of their concern over manhood.

Pleasants and his friends carefully evaluated men's behavior to detect signs of a lack of manliness. In their judgment masculine conduct and "gentlemanly manners" became largely synonymous. This fusion highlights their social aspirations as well as the class dimensions of such gendered language. Assessing his acquaintances Pleasants noted their "politeness" and "liberality," both markers of and codewords for gentlemanly behavior. He thought of a friend he had sponsored for membership in the Washington Guards as "a man of good judgment and an improved mind," and "a sensible and agreeable companion." In another member of the Guard he discovered, to his dismay, "impudent" behavior, "uncouthness of manners, destitution of principles, and meanness of deportment." When Pleasants suggested electing more men to the Guards, his listeners voiced their concern that the company would be "filled with disagreeable members," and concluded it would be "necessary to exert ourselves to augment the number of respectable men."[33]

The young men chose to consider themselves insulted by careless words, the insistent stare of another man, or any other slight which might cast a shadow on their masculinity. In the course of six months, Pleasants recorded six confrontations framed as disputes over honor and involving talk about a possible duel, one conflict with a subordinate in the Washington Guards where Pleasants himself expected to be challenged, and one protracted honor proceeding in which he served as a second. The last incident occurred during Pleasants's service in Delaware: a misunderstanding over drill instructions turned into an exchange of epithets, and escalated into a challenge for a duel, pitting two captains of the Washington Guards against each other. Only the intervention of other officers prevented the duel and forced a settlement by a military "court of honor." After noting the news of an earlier challenge, Pleasants reflected on the pressures he and his peers subjected themselves to: "Should I ever be placed in a situation [where I would] be obliged to fight, I hope a consciousness of my standing in soc[iet]y, my military character, as well as innate courage, and a sense of the gulf of infamy in which cowardice would precipitate me, would make me act in a becoming manner."[34] As Pleasants and his friends knew very well, reputation and honor existed only in the eyes of others, and the pressure of living up to their peers' notions of manhood largely determined how they evaluated their own conduct.

The young Federalists saw politicians and political events through the lens of the gendered narrative they applied to themselves. By using a language that monopolized masculine characteristics for Federalists, while it associated the Republicans with unmanly behavior, the young men created a set of stories that allowed them to present themselves as the only men fit to govern. Describing the Republican administration as "weak and wavering" was an obvious partisan slogan, but gendered language appears so regularly in the young men's descriptions of Republican and Federalist conduct that we cannot dismiss it as mere rhetoric. The young Federalists' dependence on the language of masculinity also suggests that they used it to conceptualize their confusion over partisanship. At this point, neither the Republicans nor the Federalists were fully prepared to regard themselves as a party, or possessed the vocabulary to legitimate and talk about partisanship. Each side claimed universality against the other's partiality. The young men used a language that equated masculinity with nonpartisanship to explain Republican partisan behavior, and to rationalize their own partisan efforts as attempts to abolish partisanship.[35]

George Washington played a crucial role in the young Federalists' effort to conceptualize manly conduct and partisan politics. In Washington, as general and president, the young Federalists found the symbolic connection between the Revolutionary War, disinterested statesmanship, and Federalist politics. They described Washington as the patron saint of the virtuous, their own activities as the emulation of the "principles of the father of his country" (epitomized in the frequent reading of his farewell address), and explicitly denied the partisan character of this appropriation.[36] More significant, though, was the young men's use of Washington to establish a standard by which they judged the politicians and politics of their day. They spoke of Washington's perfect restraint, moderation, dispassionate decision making, lack of ambition, and his "dignified manliness of comportment" features that, inevitably, the Republicans lacked.[37]

While they considered Washington a nonpartisan president, they found the Republican administration and its measures unmanly, and in their judgment the Republicans' partisanship and lack of manhood determined each other. In their toasts the Washington Guards decried a war "conducted without vigour" and characterized the cabinet in Washington as cowardly, given to "tame and humiliating submission" when "manly actions" were needed to defend the United States. The Sons of Washington demanded in a Fourth-of-July toast that the American ambassadors in Europe would use "language in defense of their country's rights" that was "firm, dignified, and impressive." Similarly, Nicholas Biddle observed about the American navy that "the present administration found us possessed of a young and manly force able and willing to defend us, of seamen [as] active and intrepid as those of any country, of officers yielding the palm of courage and skill to none." This he contrasted with the lack of skills of the current secretary of the navy, whose "conduct . . . has been distinguished rather by the timid incapacity of a boy than the vigor or the candor of a man."[38] Boys, of course, should not have a hand in leading the country; on the contrary, defending American interests required strength, judgment, and determination only men could have—and Biddle implied that only the Federalists possessed those very qualities.

Faced with the uncertainties of their personal and political coming-of-age, the young Federalists used gendered language to express their concerns over character and social position, and to make sense of the political world they were growing into. The organization of the young men's social and political universe interacted with their concepts of manhood: they initiated each other into organized Federalism in several settings, ranging from casual socializing in Pleasants's office and the Athenaeum to their militia company and its political and military demonstrations. As I have demonstrated, these environments existed on a continuum which defies a clear division into public and private realms, or limits political action to the public sphere. The young Federalists' private activities had political meaning and prepared the ground for their future public and political involvement. Attention to the gender dimensions of this problem helps us go beyond the language of public and private. Young men in voluntary associations created a competitive yet companionable environment that encouraged them to consider what counted as manly behavior, and what mattered in politics. By contextualizing the young Federalists' political language, especially their persistent focus on manhood, and by revealing the sources of their partisan self-representation, we also begin to see how their combination of gender and politics originated in their private and social worlds.

NOTES

Parts of this essay previously appeared in "Fashioning a Federalist Self: Young Men and Voluntary Association in Early Nineteenth-Century Philadelphia," *Explorations in Early American Culture* 4 (2000): 220–57; I thank the editors for the permission to reprint here. I presented the core argument of this essay at the 1998 SHEAR meeting at Harper's Ferry.

1. Toby L. Ditz, "Shipwrecked; or, Masculinity Imperiled: Mercantile Representations of Failure and the Gendered Self in Eighteenth-Century Philadelphia," *Journal of American History* 81 (1994): 53. Kirsten E. Wood argues that politics can be understood only by linking gender, political culture, and everyday life (" 'One Woman So Dangerous to Public Morals': Gender and Power in the Eaton Affair," *Journal of the Early Republic* 17 [1997]: 240–41, 275). See also Judith A. Allen, "Men Interminably in Crisis? Historians on Masculinity, Sexual Boundaries, and Manhood," *Radical History Review* 82 (2002): 192; Michael Roper and John Tosh, "Introduction: Historians and the Politics of Masculinity," in *Manful Assertions: Masculinities in Britain Since 1800*, ed. Roper and Tosh (New York, 1991), 1, 13.

2. Susan Juster, *Disorderly Women: Sexual Politics and Evangelicalism in Revolutionary New England* (Ithaca, 1994), 138; Joan W. Scott, "Gender: A Useful Category of Historical Analysis," *American Historical Review* 91 (1986): 1054, 1067, 1070; Roper and Tosh, "Introduction," 4, 8; John Tosh, "What Should Historians Do With Masculinity? Reflections on Nineteenth-Century Britain," *History Workshop Journal* 38 (1994): 184; E. Anthony Rotundo, *American Manhood: Transformations in Masculinity from the Revolution to the Modern Era* (New York, 1993), 1, 300 n. 1; Carroll Smith-Rosenberg, "Dis-Covering the Subject of the 'Great Constitutional Discussion,' 1786–1789," *Journal of American History* 79 (1992): 844; Mary Poovey, *Uneven Developments: The Ideological Work of Gender in Mid-Victorian England* (Chicago, 1995), 7–8, 199.

3. On gender and political culture in the early republic see, in addition to the previously cited titles, Rosemarie Zagarri, "Gender and the First Party System," in Doron Ben-Atar and Barbara B. Oberg, eds., *Federalists Reconsidered* (Charlottesville, 1998), 118–34; Stephanie McCurry, *Masters of Small Worlds: Yeoman Households, Gender Relations, and the Political Culture of the Antebellum South Carolina Low Country* (New York, 1995), esp. 239–78; Norma Basch, "Marriage, Morals, and Politics in the Election of 1828," *Journal of American History* 80 (1993): 890–918; Anne M. Boylan, "Women and Politics in the Era before Seneca Falls," *Journal of the Early Republic* 10 (1990): 363–82;

Mary P. Ryan, *Women in Public: Between Banners and Ballots, 1825–1880* (Baltimore, 1990); Jan Lewis, "The Republican Wife: Virtue and Seduction in the Early Republic," *William and Mary Quarterly* 44 (1987): 689–721; Linda K. Kerber, *Women of the Republic: Intellect and Ideology in Revolutionary America* (Chapel Hill, 1980).

Representative works on masculinity include Rotundo, *American Manhood*; Anya Jabour, "Male Friendship and Masculinity in the Early National South: William Wirt and His Friends," *Journal of the Early Republic* 20 (2000): 83–111; Mary Ann Clawson, *Constructing Brotherhood: Class, Gender, and Fraternalism* (Princeton, 1989); Mark C. Carnes, *Secret Ritual and Manhood in Victorian America* (New Haven, 1989); Mark C. Carnes and Clyde Griffen, eds., *Meanings for Manhood: Constructions of Masculinity in Victorian America* (Chicago, 1990); Cecilia Morgan, *Public Men and Virtuous Women: The Gendered Languages of Religion and Politics in Upper Canada, 1791–1850* (Toronto, 1996); Amy S. Greenberg, *Cause for Alarm: The Volunteer Fire Department in the Nineteenth-Century City* (Princeton, 1998); Laura McCall and Donald Yacovone, eds., *A Shared Experience: Women, Men, and the History of Gender* (New York, 1998). Mark E. Kann deals with "gendered language" in an ideal-typical fashion that tends to obscure its specific meanings and uses in the early republic (*A Republic of Men: The American Founders, Gendered Language, and Patriarchal Politics* [New York, 1998]).

4. Linda K. Kerber, "Separate Spheres, Female Worlds, Woman's Place: The Rhetoric of Women's History," *Journal of American History* 75 (1988): 9–39; Scott, "Gender," 1056; Linda K. Kerber et al., "Beyond Roles, Beyond Spheres: Thinking about Gender in the Early Republic," *William and Mary Quarterly* 46 (1989): 565; Carol Pateman, *The Disorder of Women* (Stanford, 1989), 3–4; Karen V. Hansen, "Rediscovering the Social: Visiting Practices in Antebellum New England and the Limits of the Public/Private Dichotomy," in *Public and Private in Thought and Practice: Perspectives on a Grand Dichotomy*, ed. Jeff Weintraub and Krishan Kumar (Chicago, 1997), 268–302; Paula Baker, "The Domestication of Politics: Women and American Political Society, 1780–1920," *American Historical Review* 89 (1984): 620–47; Elizabeth R. Varon, *We Mean to Be Counted: White Women and Politics in Antebellum Virginia* (Chapel Hill, 1998); and, most recently, "Redefining Womanly Behavior in the Early Republic: Essays from a SHEAR Symposium," *Journal of the Early Republic* 21 (2001): 71–123.

5. David S. Shields, *Civil Tongues and Polite Letters in British America* (Chapel Hill, 1997), esp. 104–26, 175–208; Wilson Somerville, *The Tuesday Club of Annapolis (1745–56) as Cultural Performance* (Athens, Ga., 1996). See also Jeff Weintraub, "The Theory and Politics of the Public/Private Distinction," in *Public and Private in Thought and Practice*, 1–42.

6. Fischer, *The Revolution of American Conservatism: The Federalist Party in the Era of Jeffersonian Democracy* (New York, 1965).

7. For detailed evidence of the young Federalists' demographics, and documentation of college attendance, occupation, and multiple membership in associations, see my "Fashioning a Federalist Self."

8. Pleasants's manuscript diary is held by the Historical Society of Pennsylvania (here-

after HSP). Heavily edited excerpts appear in "Extracts from the Diary of Thomas Franklin Pleasants, 1814," *PMHB* 39 (1915): 322–36, 410–24; and see the use of Pleasants's account of the Washington Guards's Fourth of July celebration in 1814 in Len Travers, *Celebrating the Fourth: Independence Day and the Rites of Nationalism in the Early Republic* (Amherst, 1997), 107–9. "Minutes of the Philological Society, 11 April to 7 Nov. 1807," University Archives, University of Pennsylvania; Philological Society, Misc. Papers (1809–11), American Philosophical Society; Pleasants, anniversary oration before Attican Society of Philadelphia, November 12 1808, in Tench Coxe Papers, HSP; Attican Society Papers, HSP; [Pleasants], "The Ladies of Philadelphia," *The Port Folio*, December 1810, 604–7. Pleasants's presence in the Washington Association and the Washington Guard is documented in his diary as well as in *The Constitution and Laws of the Washington Association of Philadelphia* (Philadelphia, 1811); *Poulson's American Daily Advertiser* (hereafter *Poulson's*), August 1, 1811, February 26, 1812, February 23, 1813, March 2, 1815; [Condy Raguet], *A Brief Sketch of the Military Operations on the Delaware during the Late War; Together with a Copy of the Muster-Rolls of the Several Volunteer-Corps which Composed the Advance Light Brigade, As They Stood at the Close of the Campaign of 1814* (Philadelphia, 1820), 20, 51. Additional biographical information appears in "Extracts from the Diary of Thomas Franklin Pleasants," *PMHB* 39 (1915): 322.

9. Kett, *Rites of Passage: Adolescence in America, 1790 to the Present* (New York, 1977), 13, 18, 29–37; Wallach, *Obedient Sons: The Discourse of Youth and Generations in American Culture, 1630–1860* (Amherst, 1997), 56. See also Rotundo, *American Manhood*, 56–74.

10. Nicholas Biddle to R[oger] D[illon] Drake, Andalusia, October 11, 1816 (draft), Nicholas Biddle Section, Biddle Family Papers, HSP.

11. The outline of Pleasants's study plan appear in "Diary," April 7, 1814 (plan renewed on June 3, 1814). Pleasants reflected retrospectively on his uncle's advice on May 28, 1814.

12. Ibid.

13. Binney, "Autobiography," 3 ms. vols., I, n.p., HSP; Pleasants, "Diary," May 21, August 22, 1814. Pleasants also mentioned his financial concerns on June 18, August 22, September 14, 1814, February 6, 1815; notices of his legal practice appear on April 16, 18, 20, 26, 27, 28, 30, May 2, 3, 1814.

14. For his complaints about interruptions caused by visitors, or "loungers," as Pleasants usually called them, see, for example, "Diary," May 11, 12, 16, 1814. References to visitors and their conversations with Pleasants appear in the diary almost daily, and I will not cite them here. Aside from his office and the Athenaeum, Pleasants also met acquaintances at the Merchants' Coffee House. See April 29, May 13, June, 3, 8, July, 8, August 23, 1814; March 6, 7, 1815.

15. Thomas Isaac Wharton, *Address Delivered at the Opening of the New Hall of the Athenaeum of Philadelphia, on Monday, October 18th, 1847* (Philadelphia, 1847), 6; Arthur M. Kennedy, "The Athenaeum: Some Account of Its History from 1814 to 1830," *Transactions of the American Philosophical Society*, new ser. 43 (1953): 260, 263; Jill C. Meisner, "The Pursuit of Culture: The Athenaeum of Philadelphia, 1814–1847" (Mas-

ter's thesis, University of Delaware, 1986), 49 n. 20; "Minute Book, 1814–21," Athenaeum. A detailed profile of the men involved in the creation of the Athenaeum can be found in Koschnik, "Voluntary Associations, Political Culture, and the Public Sphere in Philadelphia, 1780–1830" (Ph.D. diss., Univ. of Virginia, 2000), chap. 6, and Meisner, "Pursuit of Culture."

16. Pleasants, "Diary," May 27, June 3, 8 July, 7, 8, August 10, 11, 23, December 16, 1814, January 2, February 6, 8, 23, 1815. Meisner, "Pursuit of Culture," 14, 51–52 n. 35–36.

17. Pleasants, "Diary," January 19, 20, 29, February 7, 23, 1815. On young men and courtship see Rotundo, *American Manhood*, 111–16.

18. Here I am influenced by Tosh, "What Should Historians Do With Masculinity?" 186–87; Nancy F. Cott, "On Men's History and Women's History," in Carnes and Griffen, eds., *Meanings for Manhood*, 208; Donald J. Mrozek, "The Habit of Victory: The American Military and the Cult of Manliness," in J. A. Mangan and James Walvin, eds., *Manliness and Morality: Middle-Class Masculinity in Britain and America, 1800–1940* (New York, 1987), 221; Kathleen M. Brown, *Good Wives, Nasty Wenches, and Anxious Patriarchs: Gender, Race, and Power in Colonial Virginia* (Chapel Hill, 1996), 279, 291.

19. Fourth of July toast in *Poulson's*, July 7, 1814. For the account of the Washington Guards celebration of Washington's birthday see *Poulson's*, March 1, 1814; there Pleasants gave a toast honoring "the memory of Alexander Hamilton." For the Guards' presence in celebrations organized and led by the Washington Benevolent Society see *Poulson's*, February 25, 1814; February 22, 24, 1815. In his diary Pleasants made frequent references to incidents revealing the Washington Guards as a decidedly Federalist organization; see especially June 21, 22, 27, July 4, 6, 11, 12, December 27, 1814; January 13, 1815. On the Guards' frequent public drills, musters, and parades see April 4, 7, May 4, 10, 13, 24, June 29, and especially July 4, 1814. Pleasants had to write the toasts to be given at the Guards dinner, a task he agonized over on June 23, 29, 30, July 2, 1814. For the composition of Pleasants's "history of the war" and its eventual rejection see April 23 to June 18, and August 1, 1814.

20. Thomas Cadwalader to Mary Cadwalader, Camp Dupont, October 4, 1814, Thomas Cadwalader Section, Cadwalader Collection, Box 7 T, HSP. See also Susan G. Davis, *Parades and Power: Street Theater in Nineteenth-Century Philadelphia* (Philadelphia, 1986), 49–72; Koschnik, "Voluntary Associations, Political Culture, and the Public Sphere in Philadelphia," chap. 3.

21. Gary B. Nash, "The Philadelphia Bench and Bar, 1800–1860," *Comparative Studies in Society and History* 7 (1964–65): 206–7, 214–19; Robert R. Bell, *The Philadelphia Lawyer: A History, 1735–1945* (Selinsgrove, Pa., 1992), 37–38, 40–41, 80–81; Robert A. Ferguson, *Law and Letters in American Culture* (Cambridge, Mass., 1984), 11–17; Samuel Haber, *The Quest for Authority and Honor in the American Professions, 1750–1900* (Chicago, 1991), 67–69; Lawrence M. Friedman, *A History of American Law*, 2d ed. (New York, 1985), 318–19; Michael Grossberg, "Institutionalizing Masculinity: The Law as a Masculine Profession," in Carnes and Griffen, eds., *Meanings for Manhood*, 134–39.

22. [Hall], "Sedley," *Port Folio*, October 4, 1806, 193.

23. Essay No. 15, "Observations on the State of Literature in the United States, With Some Ideas of the Advantages of Social Institutions"; Essay No. 2 [no title, on cities], both in Philological Society, Misc. Papers, American Philosophical Society.

24. Robert Hobart Smith, *An Oration Delivered Before the Philological Society of Philadelphia on the 16th of January, 1813* . . . (Philadelphia, 1813), 15; Biddle, untitled notebook, Nicholas Biddle Section, Biddle Family Papers, Box 28, HSP.

25. The most detailed military history of the Philadelphia volunteers remains [Raguet], *A Brief Sketch of the Military Operations on the Delaware during the Late War.*

26. *Poulson's*, July 7, 1814.

27. Richard Smith Coxe, *Oration Delivered before the Washington Association of Philadelphia, on the 22nd of February, 1814* (Philadelphia, 1814), 14–15. Here and below I draw on a wider range of sources generated by other Federalist organizations which attracted young men. For examples of the rise-and-decline narrative and of the complaints over incompetent and partial officeholders, see Washington Association, *Poulson's*, August 1, 1811; Charles Willing Hare, *Oration Delivered Before the Washington Benevolent Society . . . February 22nd, 1813* (Philadelphia, 1813), 6; Joseph Reed Ingersoll, *An Oration, Delivered Before the Washington Benevolent Society . . . July 5, 1813* (Philadelphia, 1813), 16–19; Condy Raguet, *Oration Delivered Before the Washington Benevolent Society . . . February 22, 1814* (Philadelphia, 1814), 9–10; Washington Association, *Poulson's*, August 19, 1813; Coxe, *Oration Delivered Before the Washington Association*, 7–11; John Morin Scott, *An Oration Delivered Before the Washington Benevolent Society . . . February 22nd, 1815* (Philadelphia, 1815), 23–24.

28. Correspondingly, a man's decision not to join the military effort in some way made elaborate explanations necessary, most often a "weak constitution of the body." See Robert Walsh, Jr., to James Monroe, Philadelphia, September 3, 1814, Gratz Collection, HSP; Edward Read to Thomas Cadwalader, March 20, 1813, Philadelphia, Thomas Cadwalader Section, Cadwalader Collection, Box 16 T, HSP.

29. Charles Caldwell, *An Oration, Commemorative of American Independence, delivered before the Washington Benevolent Society of Pennsylvania* . . . (Philadelphia, 1814), 50–52, emphasis in original.

30. Nathaniel Chauncey, *An Oration Delivered before the Washington Association of Philadelphia, and the Washington Benevolent Society of Pennsylvania, on the Fourth of July, 1815* (Philadelphia, 1815), 10–12, emphasis in original. For other expressions of concern over the Republicans' lackluster defense of America's "national honor" see, for example, Coxe, *Oration Delivered before the Washington Association*, 20, 21, Sons of Washington, *Poulson's*, July 7, 1810; Washington Association, *Poulson's*, August 19, 1813; Washington Guards, March 1, 1814; James Milnor to Samuel F. Bradford, Washington, December 11, 1811, Bradford Collection, HSP.

31. American Republican Society, *Poulson's*, July 7, 1809, July 7, 1810; Washington Association, *Constitution*, Preamble; Washington Association, *Poulson's*, August 1, 1811; Sons of Washington, *Poulson's*, February 27, 1811; Chauncey, *Oration Delivered Before the*

Washington Association, 11. See also Charles Caldwell, *An Oration, Commemorative of the Character and Administration of Washington, . . .* (Philadelphia, 1810), 4; Caldwell, *An Oration, Commemorative of American Independence*, 8; Sons of Washington, *Poulson's*, July 7, 1810. Whereas George B. Forgie sees the postrevolutionary generation struggling with, almost revolting against, the fathers' legacy, Glenn Wallach argues that young men embraced that legacy. The language of the young Federalists in Philadelphia supports Wallach's interpretation. Forgie, *Patricide in the House Divided: A Psychological Interpretation of Lincoln and His Age* (New York, 1979), 7–12, 20–26; Wallach, *Obedient Sons*, 6, 33, 66–67.

32. Bederman, *Manliness and Civilization*, 7, 10, quote on 11; Edward E. Baptist, "Revisiting the Historiography of Honor and Masculinity" (Paper, Brown-Bag Seminar, McNeil Center for Early American Studies, November 19, 1997), 5.

33. "Gentlemanly manners," in Pleasants, "Diary," June 25; "politeness," August 27; "liberality," October 9; "a man of good judgment and an improved mind" and "a sensible and agreeable companion," August 10; "impudent" behavior," September 13; "uncouthness of manners, destitution of principles, and meanness of deportment," June 24; company "filled with disagreeable members . . . ," "necessary to exert ourselves . . . ," July 2, 1814. See also May 13, June 27, July, 2, 4, 12, August 10, 12, 19, October 17, 18, November 20, 1814; January 9, 10, 11, 1815.

34. "Should I ever be placed . . . ," in Pleasants, "Diary," July 18, 1814. On insulting language: July 4, 15, 1814; on honor disputes: July 4, 18, 27, August 20, September 12, 1814; on Pleasants expecting to be challenged, November 9, 10, 1814; on Pleasants's service as second, October 7, 9, 12, 15, 17, 18, December 7, 8, 10, 1814.

35. James Milnor to Samuel F. Bradford, Washington, December 11, 1811, Bradford Collection, HSP.

36. American Republican Society, *Poulson's*, February 24, 1810; Sons of Washington, *Poulson's*, February 27 1811; American Republican Society, *Poulson's*, July 7, 1809. See also the oration of James Milnor before the Sons of Washington, *Poulson's*, February 26, 1810; American Republican Society, *Poulson's*, July 7, 1810; Washington Association, *Constitution*, Preamble.

37. "Dignified manliness of comportment," James Milnor, oration before the Sons of Washington, *Poulson's*, February 26, 1810. See also American Republican Society, *Poulson's*, July 7, 1809; February 24, July 7, 1810; Sons of Washington, *Poulson's*, February 27, 1811; Washington Association, *Constitution*, Preamble; Hare, *Oration Delivered Before the Washington Benevolent Society*, 13; Raguet, *Oration Delivered Before the Washington Benevolent Society*, 10–11; Scott, *Oration Delivered Before the Washington Benevolent Society*, 11; Caldwell, *Oration, Commemorative of American Independence*, 33.

38. Washington Guards, *Poulson's*, March 1, 1814; Sons of Washington, *Poulson's*, July 7, 1810; Biddle, untitled notebook. See also James Abercrombie sermon, described in Thomas Law to Phineas Bond, Philadelphia, October 20, 1812, Cadwalader Collection, HSP.

7

Protest in Black and White

The Formation and Transformation of an
African American Political Community
during the Early Republic

Politics has been defined as the art of the possible. For early black activists,
politics had the nearly opposite meaning—the art of the impossible. While free
blacks certainly voted in northern elections during the early national period, and
while many early state constitutions (New York, Massachusetts, and Pennsylvania) did not initially differentiate between black and white rights, most African Americans were completely excluded from the political process. Well over
90 percent of American blacks resided in the slave South though the 1860s. And
in the North and Midwest between the 1820s and 1860s, many states disfranchised black voters, with only a select few New England states maintaining
black access to the polls. In short, as James and Lois Horton have recently
written, antebellum black disfranchisement offers perhaps the most trenchant
counterpoint to any narrative of American political inclusion.[1]

Ironically, African American life and protest also provide an instructive guide to the expanding definition of politics during the early republic.[2] African American culture was a constant source of political debate, both in and beyond formal institutions of governance. How blacks dressed, how they talked or were depicted as talking, their leisure activities, religious observances, folkways, and interrelations with white citizens—all these issues became deeply politicized in early national society. African Americans in the emancipating North routinely faced a hostile racial climate when they ventured into the public adorned not in the rags of slavery but in those of a fashionably independent person. "For many whites," as Shane White and Graham White have put it in *Stylin'*, an insightful recent book on the politics of race and style, "a well-dressed black . . . [brought] an underlying sense of disquiet, a fretful complaint at the blurring of what had seemed relatively clear cut racial boundaries." Merely to live as a person of color, then, was to be involved in the broader politics of race, civic participation, and nationhood.[3]

As much as they were victims, however, African Americans fought back. If they were denied the vote and routinely fell under public scrutiny, African Americans attempted nevertheless to infiltrate public life in any manner possible—to claim city streets as their own, to protest disfranchisement in speeches and newspapers, to assume a public role in debates over race and African Americans' place in the republic. By the early nineteenth century, northern blacks routinely held parades to demonstrate their independence. "The attaining of freedom in the North," as White and White put it, "sparked an exuberant cultural display, as newly liberated blacks deliberately, consciously, and publicly tested the boundaries of freedom."[4]

Beyond such acts of defiance, African Americans created a broader political style by seizing print. Indeed, early black activists quickly recognized print as a most valuable political tool. Print could defeat problems of space and time, the former by means of distribution beyond a local community, the latter by allowing future generations a view of a neglected history. Print also provided a public voice to a politically powerless people. Where the rules of party politics and the very sites of political venues blocked black expression, the public sphere of print—decentralized, virtually impossible to shut down, and long enshrined in American culture as an open forum—offered room for black views. Southern legislators and politicians discovered this unpleasant fact in 1830, when crates of David Walker's famous "Appeal" appeared in their midst. Although published in Boston, Walker's work traveled to Richmond, Savannah, and other distant locales. Slaveholders put a bounty on Walker, pressuring northern politicos to round him up—but they could not silence his work.

This concept of occupying printed space as a political tactic was not unique to black activists. Borrowing theoretical concepts on public discourse and print from such figures as Jürgen Habermas and Benedict Anderson, and examining the expansion of letters in early national culture, scholars of early American life have come to view print as a revolutionary political forum for powerless groups. African Americans played a crucial role in defining the public sphere as a political realm. By the early 1800s, print became perhaps the central means of conducting black abolitionist politics. As Henry Louis Gates suggested long ago, black protest literature—newspaper essays, slave narratives, poetry, and pamphlets—combatted Enlightenment-era stereotypes of mentally inferior and subservient blacks. Mastering print thus allowed black views to be heard while also forcing white society at large to reconsider its justification of bondage. As a black convention put it boldly in 1847, "Our warfare lies in the field of thought. . . . In training our soldiers for the field, we need a Printing press. . . . [It] is the ruler of opinions." More recently, historians of early black activism have noted that print abetted African American autonomy, allowing black churches, community organizations and educational institutions to publicly proclaim their independence from white control.[5]

Cultural displays and printed matter were just part of African American efforts to forge a politics of their own in the early republic. First-generation black leaders created a rich and nuanced politics of accommodation and resistance. Often adhering to a model of deference tactics, they crafted careful written appeals to white elites calculated to gain access to institutions of power. In the Jacksonian world of mass democracy, market revolutions, and renewed racial polarization, however, many black activists embraced group-power tactics to press for racial justice—and they envisioned as their primary constituency African Americans themselves.[6] From this perspective, disfranchised African Americans may be viewed as participating in the same democratizing trends that were occurring in the larger world of American politics from which they were ever more aggressively excluded.

One place to begin an investigation of early black political conduct in the public sphere is in the postrevolutionary North. New York was the North's largest slaveholding polity at the close of the eighteenth-century.[7] Indeed, while the state assembly would pass a gradual abolition act in 1799, such legislation was slow in coming, with bills failing year after year despite the fact that prominent New Yorkers such as John Jay supported them and other northern states had already secured emancipation laws. But debate over abolitionism transcended formal political venues—and white authorities. A New Yorker writing as "Rusticus" discovered this when he penned an anti-abolitionist article for the *Gazette of the United States* in the spring of 1790. Arguing that blacks were inferior in mind, but superior in body, Rusticus labeled emancipation itself mere folly. Beyond Rusticus's ideas, his very tone suggested that the debate over slavery and race excluded African Americans themselves. If they were inferior, how could they even respond? Blacks, he concluded flatly, were the missing link between apes and man. A few days later, a self-proclaimed black writer calling himself Africanus issued a stirring reply, challenging the white writer's assumption that blacks played no role in public discussions over slavery. "I am a sheep hairy Negro," he proclaimed, "the son of an African man and woman, who by a train a fortunate events . . . was let free when very young . . . received a common English school education, and was instructed in the Christian religion." An independent tradesman and friend to many "generous Americans who are pleased to praise me for employing my time so much more rationally (as they say) than most white men in the same station of life," Africanus claimed an unqualified right to respond in print to the antiblack slanders of Rusticus and his ilk. "The American and the African are one species," he summed up, "and I, the son of a sheep hairy African Negro, being free and in some degree enlightened, feel myself equal to the duties of any spirited, and noble, and generous American Freeman."[8] According to Africanus, emancipation was not only righteous but blacks must be consulted about its political and social efficacy.

Throughout the early decades of the republic, a steady stream of black pamphleteers, essayists, and public speakers issued similar notices. If blacks could not vote, or their voting numbers were too small to prompt political change, they would nonetheless inject their views into the wider arena of debate over slavery and race. And in doing so, black activists would demolish racial stereotypes. In 1809, for example, New York's William Hamilton told a group of black congregants that he was honored to speak before them on the theme of African freedom in the American republic—but the group's request to publish the speech as a pamphlet was an even greater honor, for it would allow him to combat "opinions of learned men that Africans are inferior in mind."[9]

Print became a metaphor for black autonomy in the early republic.[10] As a technology, pamphleteering offered blacks control over their message and its distribution. Pamphlets were smaller, cheaper to produce, and thought to be more ephemeral documents than expensive leather-bound books. Thus, unlike the antebellum slave narratives, which reached a wider white audience but brought the potentially intrusive hand of white editors and philanthropists, black pamphleteers retained command of their documents. Moreover, the very process of getting a pamphlet published was evidence of a new black politics of public engagement. Beginning in the 1790s, black writers in Philadelphia, New York City, Boston, and other locales began searching for white printers who might publish their work. Most printers were simply hired guns: if an author had enough money, a printer would produce his or her product. But race somewhat changed the equation. Certain printers refused to publish African American works. Others published black pamphlets but refrained from inserting their names on the title page (which after all was free advertising). Neither of Prince Hall's pamphlets ("A Charge," 1792, 1797) carried his publishers' names, although both printing houses had longstanding liberal reputations in Massachusetts (both had printed documents for insurgent colonial and then independent state legislatures during the 1770's). When white ruffians attempted to intimidate free blacks like Prince Hall from stepping out into the civic arena, Hall stood firm. When white printers shied away from distributing his works, Hall sold copies from his masonic lodge.[11]

In this manner, African American writers' very act of bringing a pamphlet to fruition in the early republic was a political statement: it announced black independence and control, and, through efforts to secure printers, told white audiences that blacks were determined to enter the public sphere. In Philadelphia, Absalom Jones and Richard Allen searched through Philadelphia's dozens of printers to find William Woodward, an up-and-coming publisher during the 1790s who had a reputation for issuing documents of a reformist bent. Jones and Allen published the first patented pamphlet by blacks with Woodward, "A Narrative of the Proceedings of the Colored People During the Yellow Fever Epidemic." A vindication of the black community's conduct during the horrible summer of 1793, the pamphlet was also a challenge to the city's racial politics in which whites assumed blacks would not respond. Celebrated printer Matthew Carey had already published a critical account of African American behavior during Philadelphia's crisis. Would Carey's charge go unanswered? As important, who would print a rebuttal to this well-known printer and businessman? Jones and Allen declared that African Americans served ably and had been unjustly slandered by Carey. And by going out in the streets to find a printer, they acted assertively and proactively to make their views heard. In 1797, Absalom Jones would return to Woodward for the publication of the "friendly society" Constitution, a benevolent group at St. Thomas African church. In New York and Boston, black leaders forged similar relationships with white printers.[12]

Black activists disseminated their product through both black and white communities in hopes of shaping public discussions over racial issues. Jones and Allen's 1794 publication serves as a useful example. As their pamphlet indicated, blacks had been stung by white accusations that they ransacked Philadelphia homes and exploited sick families during the fever's worst moments. Despite the fact that African Americans had rendered aid as nurses and laborers, and despite a significant number of black casualties, many Philadelphia whites agreed with Matthew Carey's assessment that the black community deserved a large measure of condemnation. Jones and Allen objected to the charge, not simply because it was unfounded, but the more so because it had been published in a form, as they put it, that would now remain etched in people's minds as truth. Their own pamphlet, these black writers continued, would correct Carey's blasphemy and assume its own permanence as a written document. Jones and Allen went on to attack the foundations of Carey's charge: slavery. With bondage still part of the American landscape, African Americans would be viewed forever as unequal members of society. Get rid of slavery, however, and blacks would become valued citizens of the republic. In one of the earliest assertions of nurture over nature, Jones and Allen challenged white citizens locally and nationally to overcome their racial prejudice and support black uplift. If whites were enslaved, would they achieve much? African Americans expected no less equal treatment in a republic dedicated to freedom.[13]

Establishing autonomous institutions, claiming an independent voice in print, and securing the services of white printers all formed a critical part of early black politics. So too did the concept of black leadership. As the attempt to publish pamphlets indicated, early black leaders viewed themselves as spokesmen for the race. This elite status, they hoped, might become a bridge between black and white leaders working for racial justice. The nation's inaugural abolition group, the Pennsylvania Abolition Society (PAS), recognized the importance of black elites in Philadelphia. In 1790, the group (which was dominated by white elites) contacted the recently formed Free African Society and, as a black pamphleteer would recall, "inform[ed] us of [their] plan for improving the condition of the free blacks." White abolitionists had already established committees on "inspection, guardians, education and employment." To facilitate contact with the black community—which white reformers recognized as a rapidly changing entity— abolitionists asked the African Society to "accompany them in the business." A committee of eight blacks, including Absalom Jones, was then created. As two autonomous but interlocking groups, they researched Philadelphia's black community and issued a report.[14]

The relationship here flowed top to bottom, with elite white reformers serving as a link to political power and black elites serving as a link to African American masses. African American leaders' understanding of deferential politics informed their tactics. Indeed, the conduct of early national black politics was part and parcel of the world they inhabited. Deference may have been contested at the close of the eighteenth century but deferential political styles still mattered, especially among the white Federalists who were most sympathetic to the black cause.[15] According to John Salliant, black preacher Lemuel Haynes of Vermont "turned to Federalists . . . for protection against the white people" who denied African Americans' economic opportunity or social autonomy. In his public writings and personal contacts with various Federalists, Haynes "appeal[ed] to authority and patronage as a means of securing [black] freedom."[16] Although black leaders would decry early white reformers' racism—the PAS did not accept black members until the antebellum period—they exploited their connection to white elites to get petitions presented, to lobby against antiblack laws, to gain support for educational and religious institutions in the black community. A good example comes from the year 1799, when Philadelphia blacks attempted to petition Congress on ending the overseas slave trade. Signed (or marked) by over seventy blacks, the Philadelphia petition was written in deferential language. It addressed Congress as an honorable body and sought nothing more than was constitutional. But how would it be presented? The petitioners relied on white patronage. Pennsylvanian Nicholas Waln helped blacks bring the petition to Congress's attention. Deep South representatives expressed outrage. "We the people," one Georgian shouted, did not mean "them." While Congress ultimately returned the memorial to its presenters, black activists succeeded in one critical respect: reporters covered the event, telling readers in New York City, Boston, and Philadelphia about the petitioners' request and Congress's short but sharp debates over it (southern papers excised that day of congressional coverage).[17] Had black activists simply appeared outside of Congress with an anti–slave-trading memorial, or not consulted a trusted white figure, they might not have infiltrated government at all.[18]

In cases such as this, black elites used their position to issue calls for racial justice. In other instances, black leaders sought to demonstrate their command of the community. In 1809, for example, Philadelphia's black elite formed the "African Society for the Suppression of Vice and Immorality." Ostensibly aimed at black moral uplift, the African society appointed representatives "to visit the more dissipated parts of Philadelphia and offer advice, instruction and persuasive measures to produce reformations of manners." In a pamphlet advertising the society's formation, the group illuminated a deeper, perhaps less visible objective: to impress white leaders to support black uplift. The African Society sent missives to two of Philadelphia's leading citizens—William Tilghman, head of the Pennsylvania Supreme Court, and Jacob Rush, son of noted doctor and abolitionist Benjamin Rush. Tilghman wrote back with his blessings, saying the society's "object is highly commendable." Rush wished the group success, too. Both replies became part of the Society's official record. With two worthies on their side, Philadelphia blacks hoped to muster further elite support for racial justice.[19]

One might call this conduct patron-client politics. Black contacts with white elites connected African Americans to the world of laws, governance, and assembly-level debate from which they were formally denied access. Deferential tactics also appealed to white patrons who deemed them nonsubversive. James Forten perhaps best understood patron-client politics when he wrote to the only congressional official who supported the black petition of 1799. Discovering that James Thatcher of Massachusetts had tried unsuccessfully to uphold black petition rights, Forten praised his attempt to "unfetter" African American political speech. Forten knew full well that such patronage required him to appear humble before the Massachusetts man—even though by 1800, Forten was well on his way to becoming a wealthy member of Philadelphia society, having taken over George Bridge's sailmaking business. According to Forten, Thatcher must support his lesser clients, black as well as white. While his humble language mimicked that used by any lobbying gentleman of the age (suggesting Forten's keen understanding of how politics worked), it had a deeper, peculiarly racial meaning too, for he wrote as a man defined as "so much property, as a house, or a ship." "You, sir," he told Thatcher, "consider us part of the human race." Indeed, having supported black's attempt to "diffuse [antislavery] knowledge," Thatcher received heartfelt thanks from a black man who carried snuff, often refused to bow before white citizens and was described as having an almost regal bearing— but now spoke as a representative of "seven hundred thousand" oppressed people "concerned in our petition." To get a hearing before Congress, Forten understood that deference to a white leader had enormous tactical potential.[20]

In the same month that blacks used patron-client political connections to enter Congress, Richard Allen utilized this tactic to issue a national appeal to white statesman. In December 1799, Allen gave a complex eulogy of the recently deceased George Washington that caught the attention of white printers in Philadelphia and New York. While praising the General's decision to emancipate his slaves, the eulogy also criticized Americans for tolerating bondage. Allen's original eulogy at his AME Church is lost to history. Was it a celebration of Washington's emancipation act or a sarcastic portrait of the ex-president's delayed abolitionism? Whatever he told his congregation, Allen jumped at the chance to address a broader white public. His eulogy did not overtly condemn either Washington or the American people but still managed to rebuke American statesmen for not following Washington's "emancipatory zeal" with their own abolitionist measures. Allen's editor called his work evidence of blacks' patriotism, and he thereby endorsed emancipation. Allen knew this public support may not have followed if he had simply blasted the American people as hypocrites.[21]

African American leaders' tactical exploitation of client-patron politics flowed from a northern context of race relations. Over a decade of scholarship on northern bondage has exploded any remnants of the myth that it was a benign institution or insignificant to northern economies. Still, northern slavery's unique social dimensions among New World regimes (for instance, diversified labor usages, lack of large plantation settings, a smaller ratio of blacks to whites, and greater institutional access for blacks) offered African Americans relatively more room for overt political expression[22]—or rather, African Americans exploited whatever modicum of public space appeared to them in the North. Pinkster celebrations formed the root of such activity. Originally a European religious festival associated with Dutch and German colonists, Pinkster was claimed during the eighteenth century by black communities in New York and New Jersey who turned it into an African-centered holiday. Beyond a time for connecting with African folkways, however, enslaved black northerners viewed Pinkster as a right: Each spring around the time of Pentecost, masters must allow blacks to have their own holiday or festival time. Many northern masters complied. Similarly, Negro Election Day, which often occurred around white election time, became an African-centered festive day suffused with political meaning. Local blacks anointed a leader, staged skits poking fun at the master's pretensions, and reconnected with friends and loved ones. The master-slave dynamic of such festivals involved delicate negotiations of power, with blacks pushing and masters relenting in key instances.[23]

Anthropologist James Scott has argued that oppressed peoples everywhere have historically attempted to do what colonial blacks did via Pinkster: create a "hidden transcript" of protest (via song, dance, humor, and irony) that channeled subordinates' anger into an indirect challenge of masters' power.[24] Perhaps uniquely among pre-twentieth-century oppressed peoples, black northerners also created a formal public transcript of their struggle via print and other forms of direct protest. This struggle began during the Revolutionary era with blacks' explicit push for rights. As early as 1774, for instance, four enslaved African Americans petitioned the Massachusetts colonial assembly for freedom on the ground that they had been denied the inalienable rights of freedom and justice. Although the assembly did not act on the matter, it did accept the blacks' memorial, thereby validating their political protest. Moreover, the state's Supreme Court considered the freedom suit of Quok Walker in the early 1780s—

and it declared not only in favor of the enslaved man's freedom but also in favor of all slaves' liberty. Even Prince Hall, who jousted often with Bay State leaders (he started a school for free blacks in his own home when Boston officials demurred), found that he could present memorials and petitions to Massachusetts governments.

To be sure, white patronage and tolerance for African American political acts in the North could be capricious. In 1800, white sponsors of Philadelphia blacks' anti–slave-trading petition quickly caved in to Deep South opposition, adding their votes to an 84–1 dismissal of the memorial. But this differed from South Carolina, where in 1790 a white editor received so many complaints about a single black letter writer that he vowed never again to publish African American thoughts. Ironically, the letter writer had asked not for emancipation but for less punishment from southern masters. Yet that was enough of an indirect criticism of the state's slave regimes for South Carolina readers.[25]

To ensure a full hearing in the North, first-generation activists often couched their critiques in moderate appeals. William Hamilton celebrated New York's final emancipation decree in 1827 by observing that the state had "regenerated" itself, heralding a time of interracial harmony. From Albany, the Reverend Nathaniel Paul echoed Hamilton's thoughts, lauding each of the abolition bill's legislative sponsors. Interestingly, only a decade before both Paul and Hamilton had worried that white northerners might be losing their commitment to racial justice. In one pamphlet from 1815, Hamilton had declared Euro-Americans man-stealers for their longtime role in African slave trade. These conflicting public positions may have been nothing more than part of a political arsenal with which northern blacks armed themselves during the early national period. On some occasions, they emphasized activism and resistance to unjust laws or racial codes; on other occasions, they emphasized accommodation and deference to American political forms. In 1813, James Forten decried a proposed law stripping blacks emigrating to Pennsylvania of their civil rights. Writing as one of the nation's leading black citizens, Forten took the Quaker State to task for seemingly forgetting the cause of racial justice—a cause that Pennsylvania had led during the Revolutionary era by passing the world's first gradual emancipation act. As much as he hoped to stop the bill from being passed, however, Forten also told state officials that black Pennsylvanians "had no wish to legislate." Rather, he humbly but adamantly hoped to persuade the state's leaders to protect black interests.[26]

To further moderate their appeals before the 1820s, many black leaders called for gradual, not immediate abolition.[27] One of the most skillful examples came from the Reverend Daniel Coker, a leading member of the AME church and one of the only Southern black pamphleteers of the early republic. His 1810 essay, "A Dialogue Between an African minister and a Virginian," called for general but gradual (and uncompensated) emancipation of slaves. Knowing that Chesapeake masters were particularly wary of even this policy in the wake of two planned slave rebellions in the early 1800s, Coker cast his African minister as a deferential man. He never hectors or outright condemns the Virginia slaveholder; rather, he uses what the Virginia slaveholder terms a moderate tone. In one instance, when the master announces that he will attempt to persuade the black man of slavery's biblical and economic justification, Coker's minister states, "Sir, I will hear you with pleasure." But the black character replies to the Master's arguments by saying slaves have a better claim: the principles of universal justice and freedom. To make the case for a general emancipation, Coker's African minister concedes that "the immediate liberation of all the slaves may be attended with some difficulty." But, he continues, this should not be used as a reason against gradual abolition. The Virginia slaveholder departs as a supporter of emancipation. In the end, Coker's "Dialogue" serves as a metaphor for the conduct of black politics in a deferential age: blacks must skillfully exploit connections to white leaders to be successful quasi-politicians.[28]

Early black leaders may have made a final tactical calculation: that gradualist conduct and deferential appeals proved that African Americans could meld into the nation's civic culture. No mere assimilationist ethic, in which blacks simply dissolved racial identity altogether, this ideology assumed that once free from slavery blacks would become valued citizens while also maintaining an autonomous social and cultural identity. In one of the most forceful meditations on this subject, William Hamilton told members of the Free African Church in 1809 to maintain their independent society as a means of preserving black cultural space but also to keep their eyes on the prize of American citizenship. "Our advancement in every point of view depends much on our being united in social bodies," he called out. But (perhaps addressing white readers too) he also hoped that the future would bring blacks into the nation's political realm as equal citizens, for America was their country too. After all, did not blacks identify with the country's ideal of freedom and justice for all? "The sources of slavery are drying up," he went on, noting that African American literary production had already staked a claim to civic integration. "If we continue to produce specimens like these," he told his audience while holding up examples of black writing, "we shall soon put our enemies to the blush . . . and confounded, they shall quit the field and no longer urge their superiority of their souls."[29]

In an early national world where patronage and deferential political conduct were under attack but still the norm even for many white males with full political rights, African American leaders created a mode of political action well suited to their surroundings. Viewing the Republic as an organic whole, in which autonomous parts melded in the political or civic realm, they sought to create and exploit contact with white elites (mostly Federalists) who might strike at racial injustice via the courtrooms and legislative chambers where they dominated. They also utilized the press, broadly conceived, as a political instrument, one representing black autonomy at the same time that it promoted publicly notions of black equality and abolitionism.

Between the 1820s and the 1840s, amid a flurry of social and political changes in American culture at large, black activists transformed their political conduct. The patron-client activities suited to a deferential political age assumed less importance in Jacksonian America, which celebrated the common man generally and common white men in particular. Moreover, with economic and cultural changes pushing downward on black communities, African Americans were increasingly viewed as a threat to white labor.[30] In an important article, James Stewart has called this development "racial modernity": the hardening of racial lines and ideologies during the Jacksonian era. As gradual abolition laws and the migration of former slaves from the South swelled black communities in the North, a racial backlash occurred. Stewart argues that "the rise of the white North" effectively ended the tactics of "deference politics."[31]

Even black leaders' emphasis on community uplift via education, religious piety, and temperance made lower class whites nervous about free blacks rising above them. "In every northern city," Stewart notes, "African-American Sabbath observances and schoolday activities became targets for periodic white harassment."[32] Matters grew worse still: by the early 1830s, the free black population grew from 70,000 to over 200,000 but new laws restricting free black immigration were passed or debated in western, eastern, and southern states. In addition, while many states adopted new constitutions embracing expanded suffrage for white citizens, New York, Pennsylvania, and Ohio, among others, restricted black suffrage. Race riots occurred in Pittsburgh, Boston, Cincinnati, and New Haven. And, of course, slavery expanded territorially and demographically so that by the 1840s, the peculiar institution had rebounded completely from any losses incurred by northern gradual abolition laws.

Longtime black activists such as Connecticut's Hosea Easton openly expressed pessimism that America would ever embrace black equality. Where before Easton believed that black uplift and deferential politics would bring African Americans into the nation's civic culture, by the 1830s he saw an almost immovable racial wall separating black and white. His experiences lecturing on immediate abolition and full black equality in the Northeast informed his views, which

Easton put to paper in an 1837 pamphlet. In small towns and large cities, he confronted angry white mobs who challenged Easton's very right to speak. African Americans, he concluded, are "accounted as aliens and outcasts . . . identified as belonging to no country." James Stewart concludes that this was the new reality of "racial modernity"—black and white accepting racial polarization: "As people of differing classes and skin color clashed over the drawing of racial boundaries, animosity spilled into politics and into city streets."[33]

Yet black protesters responded by not merely intensifying their criticism of slavery and racial injustice, or by accommodating to racial polarization, but by entirely recasting black political culture. After 1820, African American reformers emphasized group tactics and confrontational conduct in the public sphere as a way to protect black interests in a country increasingly hostile to them. First-generation activists helped initiate change by serving as leaders of the black convention movement and articulating group responses to new racial codes. In 1830, the Reverend Peter Williams, Jr., of New York City announced that blacks "should [consider seeking] a convenient asylum to which we and our children may flee." Referring to new Cincinnati laws of 1829 that demanded that African Americans prove their freedom via documents signed by white officials and that they put up several hundred dollars to guarantee good behavior, Williams expanded his critique to all of American society. "We are NATIVES of this country, we ask only to be treated as well as *foreigners*. Not a few of our fathers suffered and bled to purchase its independence. . . . We have toiled to cultivate it, and to raise it to its present prosperous condition; we ask only to share equal privileges with those who come from distant lands, to enjoy the fruits of our labor."[34]

A new generation of black activists also emerged in northern communities—David Walker, Henry Highland Garnet, Maria Stewart, David Ruggles—arguing for a new type of black politics based on militant conduct and community mobilizing. Whether staging mass rallies, holding black conventions, or initiating daring public rescues of fugitive slaves, this new black political conduct turned increasingly away from the deferential tactics of the early national era. By the end of the 1830s, as the editors of the *Black Abolitionist Papers* have noted, "disillusioned blacks grew contemptuous" of old-style reform tactics, those that sought to persuade white Americans of blacks' virtue, patriotism, and industriousness. Even the emergence of radical white abolitionists could not conquer racial oppression, and indeed, even they harbored romantic racialist notions of "inferior blacks" in need of white assistance. "Growing discrimination, disfranchisement, loss of jobs, kidnapping, and racial violence convinced black leaders that moral reform had failed," they write.[35]

Legal and political venues appeared more tainted than ever. "When the laws of a country are equitably administered," New York's David Ruggles declared in the mid-1830s, "every member of the community feels a satisfactory assurance in the possession of that portion of right which the law has assigned to him." But many northern judges "are made the rendez-vous of oppression," he continued (offering the example of accused fugitive slaves), when they return blacks to bondage. Particularly in New York and Pennsylvania, northern free blacks found themselves being kidnapped or grabbed as fugitives. Northern jurists as often as not simply turned a blind eye to this wicked behavior. Thus, with few voices raised against such abusive action, Ruggles declared that free blacks had no choice but to form a vigilant force of their own, one that patrolled city streets and aided blacks who had no social, political, or legal allies.[36]

The transformation of black politics mirrored shifts in American politics and society at large, revealing just how in touch black activists remained with the larger political/social world they inhabited. Jacksonian politics broke from many aspects of early national political culture. Party systems were no longer denigrated as harmful to the nation but celebrated for clarifying issues for American voters. Media campaigns replaced the parlor culture maneuvers of the deferential age. Even reform groups got into the act: from new generations of abolitionists and temperance advocates to Bible tract societies and Sabbatarians, they hired traveling lecturers to mobilize the grassroots, published newspapers for a mass readership, and held large public rallies to influence political behavior. By the 1830s, American politics was more fragmented and explicitly partisan than ever before.[37]

How exactly did black politics come to embrace new action when one of its principal tactics during the early republic was political deference? The transformation was closely tied to the rise of colonization in the 1810s and 1820s. Formed in 1817 ostensibly to encourage private emancipation of southern slaves, the American Colonization Society sought to export free blacks. According to many ACS supporters, this plan would encourage masters to liberate their slaves, secure in the knowledge that free blacks had no place on the American continent. Because colonization's rise coincided with the first stirrings of the market revolution (as well as calls for relaxed voting standards for white males), white communities in the North as well as the South embraced the ACS as a means of solidifying a white America. During its inaugural decade and a half, the ACS attracted increasing support in the North, among non-elite whites as well as nationally known statesman and philanthropists. Auxiliary groups proliferated in Pennsylvania, Massachusetts, and New York; support came from the likes of Daniel Webster, Edward Everett, and a host of other worthies. Combined with the backing of James Madison, Henry Clay, and other eminent national figures from the South, the ACS posed a formidable obstacle to racial justice. Indeed, such was the power of colonization that even longstanding abolitionist groups, such as the Pennsylvania Abolition Society, refrained from publicly rebuking the ACS for fear of offending those political elites that white abolitionists had traditionally hoped to convert to their side.

It is important to underscore the national consensus on race afforded by the ACS. Not since the Revolution itself had northern and southern leaders found room for agreement on matters relating to race and slavery. Now both northerners and southerners seemed to agree that free blacks were a problem in what many believed to be a white republic. Many southern masters viewed free blacks as a threat to plantation security. As for northern politicians, colonization promised to expel what many considered a problematic class of people—free blacks. Blacks competed with white laborers for various jobs, and therefore posed a threat to community order. Evidence gathered by early abolitionists countered such claims in places such as Philadelphia. But these stereotypical views struck a chord with many northern supporters of colonization.[38]

With colonization ascendant by the 1820s—and the relatively black-friendly Federalists repudiated—African American leaders found themselves much less able to find patrons in politics and law. With economic competition between white and black laborers intensifying, and with white political enfranchisement being posed against black suffrage, many white elites came to see racial allegiance as more important than racial justice. Even white reformers thought twice before confronting the colonizationist consensus. Immediately upon the formation of the ACS, black reformers in Philadelphia petitioned the Pennsylvania Abolition Society, hoping that these venerable white activists would mobilize a thoroughgoing defense of their black clients. While sympathetic, and while certain PAS members privately criticized colonization, the group did not mount a public attack on the ACS until the late 1820s.

Writing in 1834, New York black activist William Hamilton would note that American society in his lifetime had become "divided into several parts . . . that of the white man, that of the slave, and that of the free colored men." "How lamentable, how very lamentable," he went on, "that there should be, anywhere on earth, a community of casts with separate interests!" Coming himself from slavery during the early republic, Hamilton had hoped that African Americans would slowly but surely become part of American society. Indeed, recalling the incredible debates on civic duty that defined the Revolutionary era, he asserted that "society must be the most happy, where the good of one is the common good of the whole. Civilization is not perfect . . . until the community shall see that a wrong done to one is a wrong done to the whole." No longer could this sentiment prevail in the American nation. As the culture at large frowned on black justice, African Americans must recast their political actions and act as a self-interested group.[39]

With many white leaders refusing to support black justice, it was clear that African Americans needed to "combine and closely attend their own particular interest." Society had shifted, and it appeared to Hamilton that white leaders would seek to solidify their own power by appealing to whites' racial prejudice. "They would sacrifice the free people of color," Hamilton argued. Colonizationists "have resorted to every artifice to affect their purposes, but exciting in the minds of the white community the fears of insurrection and amalgamation; by petitioning state legislatures to grant us no favors; by petitioning Congress to aid in sending us away." And what response did the ACS receive? "Such are the men of that society that the community are blind to their uncertainties, contradictions and paradoxes." But Hamilton also told his audience (both in person and in a pamphlet) to cheer up, because blacks had been fighting "the dragon" of colonization since its inception, and the development of group organizing tactics such as the black convention movement might well win the battle against prejudice.[40]

As Hamilton's pamphlet indicated, print continued to offer a political outlet, as it were, to African Americans challenged by the age rise of colonization and white man's democracy. Indeed, the formation of *Freedom's Journal* brought black printed protest into the age of mass politics. Not simply the first black newspaper in America, it was the first printed forum whose primary audience was blacks themselves. During its two-year run (1827–29), *Freedom's Journal* served as a forum for a black constituency now actively considering itself a nation within a nation. "The civil rights of a people being of the greatest value," the editors called out, "it shall be ever our duty to vindicate our oppressed brethren." Thus, they continued, the paper shall "bring together . . . from the different states" black activists who would urge united action shattering "the iron fetters of bondage." *Freedom's Journal* would also "urge our brethren to use the elective franchise [where possible]," and, lastly, to "lay our cause before the public."[41] The paper served as a stepping stone for key second-generation black activists, such as David Walker, who as a leader of Boston's General Colored Association already favored mass mobilization over the politics of deference.

The pamphlet literature of the Jacksonian era reveals the shifting conduct of black politics just as clearly.[42] Indeed, pamphlets became the critical means of disseminating more militant views and advocating more confrontational tactics. David Walker remains the preeminent black pamphleteer of the Jacksonian era.

A free black man who slowly journeyed from his North Carolina roots to Boston by the 1820s, Walker issued the most significant pamphlet in antebellum black society in 1829 and 1830: "An Appeal to the Colored Citizens of the World." Its denunciatory language surpassed that of any previous writer. Walker's call for blacks to mobilize themselves as a nation within a nation also heralded a new tactical direction for black activism. Walker's leadership role in Boston's General Colored Association prepared him for the new tactic. But his pamphlet itself served as a weapon for a revitalized black politics—one that pitted black justice against the American republic. Walker worked with black seamen to send crates of his pamphlet southward (a bounty was put on Walker's head by southern governors). He told blacks to read and perform the document for their illiterate brethren as a means of mobilizing all African-descended people, in the South as well as the North, slaves as well as free blacks. He used his clothing shop on Boston's waterfront as an antislavery depot, dispensing copies of the "Appeal," arguing on behalf of black justice, and plotting mass action. If only a fraction of "two million and a half of colored people in these United States" organized, he famously challenged, "what mighty deeds could [not] be done by them for the good of our cause?"[43]

In the wake of Walker's "Appeal," a host of new pamphleteers emerged, including female activists, former slaves, and unheralded community reformers. Not every pamphleteer echoed Walker's militancy, although many expanded upon his community mobilization tactics. In the pamphlet literature of the 1830s, it is the black constituency that assumes more importance than a white one, with pamphleteers emphasizing in myriad ways the ultimate goal of community mobilization. Boston's Maria Stewart stood out in this vein. A religious activist and educator, Stewart began speaking before black and interracial audiences in the early 1830s as colonization gained steam. Her pamphlets consistently emphasized mass mobilization as the means of achieving black justice. "Why sit each year and die?" she asked in one pamphlet. In an America where blacks—and now not slavery—seemed to be the main problem, Stewart called on the black community to follow the example of that "most noble, fearless, and undaunted" black abolitionist, David Walker. "I shall glory in being one" of the martyrs to freedom, "sacrificing my life for the cause of my brethren" if need be. Stewart argued that black women played critical roles as community activists and educators: "[I hope] the many powerful sons and daughters of Africa . . . [would] arise," she exclaimed, and demand "their rights" anew as a potent protest bloc. Stewart was not afraid to issue a darker warning to her white readers either. "If refused" freedom, she stated flatly, "I am afraid that they [mobilized blacks] will spread horror and devastation around."[44]

The year before Stewart published her collection, the African Female Benevolent Society of Troy (New York) issued a pamphlet making the same point in somewhat less confrontational language. The society formed in 1833 as a spiritual and educational endeavor. In one year, the group's twelve members blossomed to over sixty. On its first anniversary the Troy society asked one of its members, Elizabeth Wicks, to mark the occasion with a speech and pamphlet. Wicks heaped praise on Troy's black women for stepping beyond the household and helping the black community as a whole mobilize and achieve racial uplift. "Let me invite you to put your shoulder to the wheel and press foreword without delay," Wicks advised, adding that African American women of the North must always "let our minds travel south and sympathize with the present state of the two millions of our brethren who are yet in bondage." Where white colonizationists hoped to expel free blacks, and separate them from southern slaves, Wicks challenged her sisters to proclaim solidarity with southern slaves.[45]

Just under a decade later, Henry Highland Garnet made a more stirring appeal to national black unity. Where Wicks wanted northern black women to think always of the enslaved, Garnet addressed them directly. He counseled militant action at the southern grass-roots level: enslaved people must go to their masters and demand freedom. If not liberated, he said slaves would, and should, rebel. Northern blacks must aid their cause. "Remember you are two millions," he shouted, echoing his great hero David Walker. Garnet's "address to the slaves" prompted vigorous debate among his more immediate constituency of free black activists meeting in Buffalo in 1843. Among them, Frederick Douglass argued against the publication of the address in the official convention minutes. According to Douglass, the address contained "too much of the physical": both he and others believed it would lead to a bloodbath for southern slaves and, importantly, violent retribution against northern free blacks. Garnet thought confrontation the way to proceed, whatever the consequences. In his passionate defense of publishing the address in the Buffalo minutes, Garnet asked, "What more could be done [to end slavery]—if we have not waited long enough—if it were not time to speak louder and longer—to take higher ground and other steps." Great applause followed what the stenographer called "a masterly effort" by Garnet. Still, his speech was tabled and Garnet would have to self-publish it five years later, along with a new version of Walker's appeal.[46]

Black pamphleteers of the 1830s and 1840s reflected a political shift occurring at the street level among black activists. Working as educators, organizers, and speakers, Wicks and Stewart, Walker and Garnet, all realized that white political elites would no longer rush to blacks' defense in the age of colonization and racial mobbing. Activists must organize the black community just as a political party would mobilize a base of supporters.[47] Perhaps the best example of this strategy comes from New York City's David Ruggles. Ruggles published five pamphlets during the 1830s and inaugurated the *Mirror of Liberty* in 1838, the first quarterly magazine owned by an African American.[48] He also helped found the New York City Vigilance Committee, a group dedicated to rescuing fugitive slaves and kidnapped free blacks. Ruggles used the *Mirror of Liberty* to trumpet his street activism. As he put it, "the reader need not examine *The Mirror* for long and theoretical disquisitions on abstract questions." Ruggles demanded "full enfranchisement of my downtrodden countryman" and an immediate end to slavery everywhere in America. If such pronouncements seemed less than extraordinary at the close of the 1830s, Ruggles went on to define in practical terms what he meant by "equal Liberty." The very first edition carried Ruggles's story of liberating a female slave living with her South Carolina master in New York City. Ruggles recalled how he brashly entered the master's home, confronted the Master's daughter and declared not only that the enslaved woman had a right to freedom (because she resided in free New York) but that Ruggles himself would "carry her off."

Ruggles's act exemplified his Vigilance Committee tactics of physically standing up to white anti-abolitionists and slave catchers. The *New York Gazette*, whose editor Ruggles labeled "a notorious panderer for slaveholders," lashed out at Ruggles's intervention in the enslaved girl's behalf. This Ruggles, the editor stated, "is an insolent fellow. . . . He actually stayed [in the master's house] three hours on one occasion, to the great annoyance of the mistress of the mansion, who thought impossible to get him out of it alone and go to unprotected as she was." Ruggles refused to budge. "Let the rascal try his impudence again, if he thinks it would be conducive to human Liberty," the white editor challenged.

Ruggles met this challenge in print as well as on the streets, "pleading guilty to the charge" of rescuing the enslaved woman but relating his own version of events. As Ruggles recalled, he had heard that a South Carolina family resided in Brooklyn with their slaves for longer than nine months—a period that, according to New York's emancipation decree, allowed the slaves to go free. Ruggles appeared on the family's doorstep one day, confronting in turn the mistress, her daughter, a friend of the family, and the master. Each of these people rebuffed Ruggles's request to free the enslaved family, or to pay them just wages for their toil. Ruggles highlighted the moment when the family friend, a doctor and learned man, declared the black editor "an intruder, having no right in the house," especially the right to talk to the master's slaves without the master's permission:

Ruggles: "I charged *him* with being intruder, having no right to interfere there against Liberty and laws of the state."

Family friend: "I wish you would leave, sir."

Ruggles: "I wish *you* would leave, sir."

"The doctor," as Ruggles explained of the friend, "looking over and under his spectacles, viewing me from head to foot, as though he felt disposed to use his rattan, came to the conclusion I suppose [that] as I occupied some inches in height and in bulk more than himself, he would be *unsafe* to attend to an experiment" with his stick.[49]

Ruggles's rescue of the young woman was just one of the Vigilance Committee's hundreds of success stories.[50] Equally significant was Ruggles's broader political message that blacks owed deference to no one but themselves. Where first generation black leaders had for a time argued that the principles of racial justice and national harmony went hand-in-hand, now leaders from David Walker to David Ruggles asserted that national interest and black interest may well be incompatible—that black Americans might be the saviors of American democracy by becoming its most radical dissenters.

Black parades of the 1830s and 1840s expanded the meaning of Ruggles's street politics and provided a corollary to the more militant print addresses of the age. As Patrick Rael has noted, "the problem confronting black activists [by the 1830s] was [how] to pursue to freedom struggle by presenting blacks as a powerful public force. The answer lay in orchestrating "mass celebrations." Rallies were carefully planned and extensively reported on by black newspapers. At one event in 1837, New York's black community gathered a crowd of 3,500 people, white as well as black, to mark British emancipation in the Caribbean. Rallies in Philadelphia, Boston, and Cincinnati in that same decade attracted huge crowds as well—in some case, crowds larger than could be accommodated at a church or meeting house.[51]

African American rallies not only sought to register a more powerful image of black masses in the minds of American citizens; they established community networks that might be called upon to rescue a fugitive slave or stand up to white mobs. For example, black reformers in Harrisburg helped galvanize a crowd at a fugitive slave trial in 1837. When the judge released the accused fugitive (because of a lack of proof), black reformers drove a carriage to the courthouse and, as one newspaper put it, "ushered him away" before slave catchers could capture him. The final blow for slaveholders, however, came in an antislavery newspaper a few days later, in which a correspondent told northerners that the mobilizing efforts of the people, particularly those of local blacks, had liberated the accused fugitive and set a model of action for countless others.[52]

By the Jacksonian era, black writers viewed themselves as a legitimate constituency in the public sphere—a virtual political community—even if formal political institutions continued to disfranchise them. Of course, free black activists vigorously pressed for voting rights in northern and midwestern states prior to the Civil War, but usually to no avail. Nevertheless, in print as well as on city streets, by the 1830s and 1840s African Americans were recognizable players in public debates over slavery, race, and nation. A revealing portrait of their political identity comes from a man who figured in one of the best-known incidents involving sectional politics in the 1850s: Massachusetts senator Charles Sumner, who was infamously caned by South Carolina's Preston Brooks for defaming the South. Returning from Europe as a young man two decades earlier, Sumner hardly recognized his own country. Whereas before, union and patriotism carried the day, now Sumner confronted a political and social world pervaded by groups fighting for hegemony—not only "South vs. North," or "abolitionists vs. slaveholders," but "the slaves, colored men and women, and Africans" vs. the allies of racial subjection. Black abolitionist writings—slave narratives, pamphlets, reprinted sermons—and black civic action (slave rescues) framed political debates in Sumner's Boston as well as in the nation's Congress. Who could reclaim a fugitive in the North, he asked a British Lord, when the citizenry increasingly frowned on such action? Whether or not they could vote, then, Sumner knew that African Americans were shapers of his political world.[53]

Even slaveholders acknowledged blacks' membership in the American political community, broadly conceived. While black and white abolitionists attracted only a "miserable handful at the ballot box," Georgia's Thomas Cobb sneered at a secessionist convention of 1861; northern public culture had nevertheless been thoroughly "abolitionized." "The pulpit, the press . . . popular assemblages all belched forth nothing but imprecations on the South," added Georgia lawyer Robert Toombs. If they exaggerated northern support of abolitionists, both of these men recognized correctly that abolitionists (black as well as white) operated in a world of political action whose boundaries were much wider than the formal institutions of government and the party system. In that broader public sphere of print and street protest, as opposed to in Congress, black activist writers and speakers claimed legitimacy and made themselves a political force that slaveholders ignored at their own peril.[54]

The process of becoming a virtual political community via print and public action was arduous and anything but complete in the Jacksonian era. Indeed, the formation and transformation of black politics between the 1790s and 1840s occurred in a dynamic political and social world in which African Americans not only thought politically but paid constant attention to shifting political styles as well as how to reformulate their own political tactics. It all came back to print. Absent the right to vote, James Forten stated in his 1813 pamphlet decrying a proposed anti-black law in Pennsylvania, "an appeal to the heart is my intention."[55] His pamphlet helped mobilize opinion against the law, which was never passed. Generations of activists, black and white, followed Forten's lead, relying on print to exert political influence. Any list of major antebellum events would certainly include either works by black writers (Frederick Douglass's *Narrative*, say, or David Walker's "Appeal"), or works deeply indebted to black public protest, from Harriet Beecher Stowe's *Uncle Tom's Cabin* (with its appendix of black sources) back to William Lloyd Garrison's radical abolitionist newspaper, *The Liberator* (which, in its very first year, relied on black authors for one-fifth of its editorial content).[56] Black votes may not have counted much before the Civil War but black public protest most assuredly did.

NOTES

1. James Oliver Horton and Lois E. Horton, *In Hope of Liberty: Culture, Community, and Protest among Northern Free Blacks, 1700–1860* (New York, 1987), 167–68.

2. For a sense of the latitude of black politics, see Walter Johnson, *Soul by Soul: Life Inside the Antebellum Slave Market* (Cambridge, Mass., 1999); Shane White and Graham White, *Stylin': African American Expressive Culture from Its Beginnings to the Zoot Suit* (Ithaca, 1998); Robert S. Levine, *Martin Delaney, Frederick Douglas, and the Politics of Representative Identity* (Chapel Hill, 1997); and Mia Bay, *The White Image in the Black Mind: African-American Ideas about White People, 1830–1925* (New York, 2000).

3. White and White, *Stylin'*, 1–19.

4. Ibid, 7.

5. Henry Louis Gates, *The Signifying Monkey* (New York, 1987); *Proceedings of the National Convention of Colored People* (Troy, N.Y., 1847), reprinted in *Pamphlets of Protest: An Anthology of Early African American Protest Literature, 1790–1860*, ed. Richard Newman, Patrick Rael, and Philip Lapsansky (New York, 2000), 167–77.

6. On Jacksonian politics' social dimensions, see especially William W. Freehling, *The Road to Disunion: Secessionists at Bay, 1776–1854* (New York, 1990); also Julie Roy Jeffrey, *The Great Silent Army of Abolitionism: Ordinary Women in the Antislavery Movement* (Chapel Hill, 1998); and Donald Jacobs, ed., *Courage and Conscience: Black and White Abolitionists in Antebellum Boston* (Bloomington, 1993).

7. On emancipation and free black life, see Gary Nash, *Forging Freedom: The Formation of Philadelphia's Black Community, 1720–1840* (Cambridge, Mass., 1988); Shane White,

Somewhat More Independent: The End of Slavery in New York City, 1770–1810 (Athens, Ga., 1991); Julie Winch, *Philadelphia's Black Elite* (Philadelphia, 1988).

8. *Gazette of the United States*, March 31, April 7, 1790.

9. Hamilton, *An Address to the New York African Society for Mutual Relief* (New York, 1809), reprinted in *Early Negro Writing, 1760–1837*, ed. Dorothy Porter (Boston, 1971), 33–41.

10. See, in particular, Elizabeth McHenry, "Dreaded Eloquence: The Origins and Rise of African American Literary Societies and Libraries," *Harvard Library Bulletin* 2 (Spring 1995): 32–56, and Richard Newman, Patrick Rael, and Philip Lapsansky, "Introduction," *Pamphlets of Protest*, 1–15.

11. Thomas and John Fleet published Hall's 1792 pamphlet; Benjamin Edes printed Hall's 1797 edition.

12. William Woodward published St. Thomas's "Friendly Society's" Constitution in 1797. He also published reform essays, such as William Brown's *An Essay on the Natural Equality of Men* (1793).

13. Absalom Jones and Richard Allen, *A Narrative of the Proceedings of the Black People During the Late Awful Calamity in Philadelphia* (1794), reprinted in Newman, Rael, and Lapsansky, *Pamphlets of Protest*, 32–43.

14. See the anonymous pamphlet Philadelphia's African Church (Philadelphia, 1860), 50–65.

15. For recent work on postrevolutionary challenges to deferential political culture, see Michael Merrill and Sean Wilentz, eds., *The Key of Liberty: The Life and Democratic Writings of William Manning, "a Laborer," 1747–1814* (Cambridge, Mass., 1993); and Jeffrey L. Pasley, *"The Tyranny of Printers": Newspaper Politics in the Early American Republic* (Charlottesville, 2001).

16. John D. Salliant, *Black Puritan, Black Republican: The Life and Thought of Lemuel Haynes, 1753–1833* (New York, 2003), 119–20.

17. See Porter, *Early Negro Writing*, 330–32, for a reprint of the petition.

18. For information on congressional reaction to black and white petitions in the 1790s, including the 1799 petition, see Richard Newman, *The Transformation of American Abolitionism: Fighting Slavery in the Early Republic* (Chapel Hill, 2002), chaps. 2 and 4.

19. See the pamphlet history of this institution, *The African Society for the Suppression of Vice and Virtue* (Philadelphia, 1809).

20. James Forten, "Letter Addressed to the Honorable George Thatcher, Member of Congress," in Porter, *Early Negro Writing*, 333. Also see Julie Winch's fantastic biography, *A Gentleman of Color: The Life of James Forten* (New York, 2002).

21. Allen's eulogy is reprinted in *Lift Every Voice: African American Oratory, 1787–1900*, ed. Philip S. Foner and Robert James Barnham (Tuscaloosa, Ala., 1998), 56–58.

22. Lorenzo Greene once stated that "the condition of Negro, then, in colonial New England was primarily that of a chattel . . . but slavery was so conditioned and modified . . . that in reality it was an admixture of bondage and indentured service." See Greene, *The Negro in Colonial New England, 1620–1776* (New York, 1942), 290–315.

23. On Pinkster's radical dimensions, see Sterling Stuckey's classic treatment in *Slave Culture* (New York, 1987), 141–42.

24. James C. Scott, *Domination and the Arts of Resistance: Hidden Transcripts* (New Haven, 1990).

25. *Columbia Herald*, August 12, 14, 1790.

26. Hamilton, "O! Africa," January 2, 1815, in Foner and Barnham, *Lift Every Voice*, 91–97; Paul, *Address . . . on the Celebration of the Abolition of Slavery in . . . New York* (1827) in *Negro Protest Pamphlets*, ed. Dorothy Porter (New York, 1969), 1–24; Forten, "Series of Letters by a Man of Color" (1814), in Newman, Rael, and Lapsansky, *Pamphlets of Protest*, 66–73.

27. On deference politics, see Gordon S. Wood's provocative article, "Interests and Disinterestedness in the Making of the Constitution," in *Beyond Confederation: Origins of the Constitution and American National Identity*, ed. Richard Beeman, Stephen Botein, Edward C. Carter II (Chapel Hill, 1987), 69–112.

28. Daniel Coker, *A Dialogue Between a Virginian and an African Minister* (1810), in Newman, Rael, and Lapsansky, *Pamphlets of Protest*, 52–65.

29. Hamilton, *Address Before the African Society*, in Porter, *Early Negro Writing*, 33–41.

30. On the economic and cultural consolidation of "whiteness," see Alexander Saxton, *The Rise and Fall of the White Republic: Class Politics and Mass Culture in Nineteenth-Century America* (New York, 1990); David R. Roediger, *The Wages of Whiteness* (New York, 1991); Noel Ignatiev, *How the Irish Became White* (New York, 1995).

31. James Brewer Stewart, "The Emergence of Racial Modernity and the Rise of the White North 1790–1840," *Journal of the Early Republic* 18 (1998): 181–217, and also the reply from James Horton, 220–25.

32. Stewart, "Emergence of Racial Modernity," quotation on 192.

33. Ibid; see also George R. Price and James Brewer Stewart eds., *To Heal the Scourge of Prejudice: The Life and Writings of Hosea Easton* (Amherst, 1999).

34. Williams's speech became a pamphlet. See Foner and Barnham, *Lift Every Voice*, 114–21.

35. C. Peter Ripley, et al., eds, *The Black Abolitionist Papers* (Chapel Hill, 1985–93), 3:19–20.

36. Ruggles, "New York Committee of Vigilance for the Year 1837" (New York, 1837), in Newman, Rael, and Lapsansky, *Pamphlets of Protest*, 144–55.

37. On antebellum political fragmentation, see Freehling, *Road To Disunion*, 1, "The Reorganization of Southern Politics"; Richard R. John, *Spreading the News: The American Postal System From Franklin to Morse* (Cambridge, Mass., 1995); and Harry L. Watson, *Liberty and Power: The Politics of Jacksonian America* (New York, 1990).

38. See Newman, *Transformation*, chap. 5.

39. William Hamilton, *Address to The National Convention* (New York, 1834) in Newman, Rael, and Lapsansky, *Pamphlets of Protest*, 110–13.

40. Ibid.

41. *Freedom's Journal*, October 27, 1827.

42. See Newman, Rael, and Lapsansky, *Pamphlets of Protest*, 1–31.

43. See Peter P. Hinks, ed., *David Walker's Appeal to the Coloured Citizens of the World* (University Park, Pa., 2000), 4–82.

44. Stewart, "Productions" (Boston, 1835), reprinted in Newman, Rael, and Lapsansky, *Pamphlets of Protest*, 122–30.

45. Elizabeth Wicks, *Address Delivered Before The African Female Benevolent Society of Troy* (Troy, N.Y., 1834), ibid., 114–21.

46. Garnet, *Address to the Slaves of the United States of America* (New York, 1848), ibid., 156–64.

47. Wilson J. Moses, *The Golden Age of Black Nationalism* (New York, 1987).

48. Graham Hodges of Colgate University is currently working on the definitive Ruggles biography.

49. *Mirror of Liberty*, August 1838. I am indebted to Phil Lapsansky and the Library Company of Philadelphia for the citation.

50. Ruggles, *New York Committee of Vigilance for the Year 1837* (New York, 1837), in Newman, Rael, and Lapsansky, *Pamphlets of Protest*, 144–55.

51. Patrick Rael, *Black Identity and Black Protest in the Antebellum North* (Chapel Hill, 2001), 55–57, 72–79.

52. See Newman, *Transformation*, chap. 9.

53. Richard Sewell, *Ballots for Freedom: Antislavery Politics in the United States, 1837–1860* (New York, 1976) and Vernon Volpe, *Forlorn Hope of Freedom* (Kent, Ohio, 1990).

54. William Freehling and Craig Simpson, eds., *Secession Debated* (New York, 1992), 25–29.

55. Forten, "Letters," in Newman, Rael, and Lapsansky, *Pamphlets of Protest*, 66–73.

56. For expanded treatment of this issue, see Newman, *Transformation*, chap. 5.

PART THREE

JOHN L. BROOKE

8

Consent, Civil Society, and the Public Sphere in the Age of Revolution and the Early American Republic

While historians instinctively avoid theory, we necessarily attempt an exploration where imagination, fact, and theory all come to bear, as we attempt to visualize the spaces in which our historical subjects engaged with one another. Over the past decade, a new understanding of public space has begun to provide a more precise structure and coherence to that difficult visualization. First proposed in 1962 by the German philosopher Jürgen Habermas, in a book published in English in 1989 as *The Structural Transformation of the Public Sphere*, the concept of "public sphere" has emerged as a formal, even technical, term for historians of the early modern and modern epochs, defining a specific space in civil society for discourse, communication, and association, mediating between the state and the people in their private capacities.[1] Habermas's great contribution has been to allow us to visualize more clearly—or at least to argue more specifically about—the place where matters of shared importance unfold in early

modern and modern societies. First taken up by historians of the French Enlightenment and of American women, the concept of a public sphere has helped
to establish an increasingly broad definition of the nature of "the political", and
may well provide a useful framework in which to situate the newest political
history of the early and antebellum American republic. Beyond the problem of
visualizing the past, the public sphere as a theoretical question is thus a matter of
considerable interpretive consequence in its own right.

Historians' first encounter with Habermas's public sphere came at the height
of a grand generational struggle between older and newer histories, histories that
give essential priority to law and to language, respectively, as competing outcomes of ultimate significance in the experience of "the political." Thus the
older political history would posit the enactment of statute and constitutional
law as the ultimate manifestation of power; the newest cultural-political history
would posit subtle but profound shifts in cultural meaning as fundamentally
determinative. This essay explores the boundary between the old and new histories, between these priorities of law and language, while recognizing the slippery
middle ground where they meet. I will suggest that these histories share far more
than many of their practitioners will admit, and that Habermas's notion of public
sphere, and its essential framing corollaries of consent, legitimacy, and civil
society, can comprise a common meeting ground. If historical thinking about
the public sphere in early America has been almost entirely restricted to the
domain of language and cultural history, it stands available as the ground upon
which to rebuild a relationship between the old political history of law and the
new cultural history of language.

This is especially so since the appearance of Habermas's massive new synthesis, *Between Facts and Norms*, published in English in 1996.[2] Here he offers an
extended model of the ideal constitutional and political conditions of liberal
democracy, in which the procedures guaranteeing deliberation stand as the foundation of consent and legitimacy. As a philosopher, however, Habermas is interested in ideal conditions, not messy realities. He still has little specific to say in his
new book about the complexities of culture, of what I shall call the domain of
persuasion, which cultural historians are showing to be equally fundamental in
building of consent. But he does leave room for such persuasion, couched as
"distorted communicative discourse" undermining the free flow of deliberation.
Suitably dissected, qualified, stretched, and amplified, his framework allows us to
begin to visualize in a single interpretive field the requirement and variants of
consent, the domains of state, public sphere, and civil society, and the various
overlapping agencies of deliberation, persuasion, and force, which I will propose

encompass a vast field of intersection between the old and the new histories, as they bear on the problem of power. The shape of this field bears particular importance for historians of the early and antebellum American republic, where bizarre extremes along a spectrum of civil condition made the question of consent especially problematic and volatile.

DELIBERATION AND PERSUASION

In great measure the boundary between older and newer histories involves this distinction between these two modes of purposeful communication: deliberation and persuasion. How should we define these terms? I define deliberation as the structured and privileged assessment of alternatives among legal equals leading to a binding outcome, perhaps a law, perhaps a contract or covenant, in the wider sense. The essential circumstances here are equality of condition and formality of outcome. Traditional political historians are fundamentally interested in the processes and outcomes of deliberation, as are a growing number of political scientists and philosophers, seeking to understand the basis of the legitimacy of the modern liberal polity in the procedures that set the terms of deliberative outcomes, procedures that are the essential topic of constitutional history.[3]

And what is persuasion? Perhaps I am artificially and arbitrarily restricting the definition of the word, since in common understanding the persuasive use of language is fundamental to deliberation. But such a violation may help to highlight a series of essential contrasts. If the circumstances of deliberation are necessarily an equality of condition and formality of outcome, those for my definition of persuasion are often an *inequality* of condition and necessarily an *informality* of outcome.[4] Thus if deliberation requires equality, persuasion often unfolds in circumstances of inequality as measured by a command of economic, social, or cultural resources. And rather than formal, legal, and binding, a persuasive outcome is informal and often imperceptible. I can actively try to persuade you to change your opinion, perhaps in anticipation of a formal deliberation, but I can also shape, and be shaped by, a host of cultural signals—most powerfully language itself—that set boundaries on the possible. Most important, persuasion can be either hegemonic or it can be subversive, and it works most effectively when its operation is invisible to the persuaded. The explication of this entire realm of the persuasive comprises the agenda of cultural history as practiced today. And if Habermas in *The Structural Transformation* would have separated rigidly any element of the public sphere from the market, in *Facts and Norms* he now concedes that a domain of persuasion in an expanded public sphere is literally co-extensive with the market in all its dimensions.[5] He would also concede that this persuasive domain is the site of contest among many competing voices and "publics."[6]

Thus both deliberation and persuasion take place in the public sphere in Habermas's most recent formulation, a formulation that has not yet received the attention that it deserves. More precisely, deliberation is to unfold in two distinct public spheres, linked by important exchanges. In a first stage of deliberation, opinion is formed in the public sphere of civil society, shaping the second stage of "will-formation," including lawmaking, administration, and justice, all unfolding in a formal public sphere internal to government, in which deliberation is tightly bound by constitutions, statute law, and legislative rules.[7]

Opinion formation unfolds in a chaotic, anarchic, but productive public sphere of civil society, where a contest of ideas leads to the strategic coalescence of opinion. Elections, and communication with officeholders, mediate between this and a second tier of the deliberative public sphere, closely regulated by constitutions and rules, operating inside governments themselves, in legislature, committees, and commissions, in courts and bureaucracies. Information about process and outcome is then fed back into the open public sphere, completing a cycling of power and legitimation. At each point around the cycle there is ample opportunity for violation and breakdown: elections can be rigged, legislators bribed, information withheld, and circumstances distorted. And all around this lawmaking cycle, nondeliberative discourses—what I will call persuasion—work various, less direct political purposes, profoundly shaped by the inequalities of the market economy.[8]

Here lies an irony, and a profound disagreement, that I am attempting to resolve in this essay. Cultural historians, with literary theorists and historicists, have seen in Habermas's almost material concept of a public sphere a "hard" and socially real space in which to visualize the creation and consumption of cultural forms and literary texts. But, fundamentally committed to an analysis of persuasive action, they have rejected Habermas's original and ongoing insistence that the public sphere *should* be a site of rational discourse and deliberation, while ignoring his implied understanding that things are not always so neat and tidy. Traditional political historians, conversely, fundamentally committed to the outcome of deliberation in law (rational or not), have by and large avoided any encounter with the concept of the public sphere.

This irony is compounded because political and cultural historians of the early American republic are engaged in a remarkably similar project. Both the old and the new histories, as they examine the wider transformations starting with the age of revolution, ultimately are concerned with the conditions and practices of consent. Ideally, modern governments and the policies they enact are subject to the consent of the people; they are to be open to inspection and criticism and routinely renewed in elections. Citizens engage in that inspection, criticism, and renewal, and their participation in these processes of deliberation conveys their grant of *express* consent to that government. To be legitimate, this grant of consent must be uncoerced by violence or intimidation, and protected by constitutional procedure.

But what about that slippery, complex field of persuasion where all do not speak with voices of equal power and authority, where culture and language shape and limit the outlines of the possible? Traditional political historians have little to say here, viewing the deliberative outcome in law, grounded in express consent, as the fundamental measure of legitimate and illegitimate force. Cultural historians see the persuasive qualities of language and cultural formations as determinative of a pervasive field of *tacit* consent, and indeed as a coercive force as powerful as overt violence itself. Each subdiscipline may well seek to maintain its intellectual priorities. But increasingly, some scholars may well find it fruitful to transcend these priorities, and to consider the relationships among deliberation and persuasion, express and tacit consent, law and language, within the Habermasian framework of the public sphere.[9]

LEGITIMACY AND THE AGE OF REVOLUTION

At the center of this discussion so far and of Habermas's understanding of the public sphere lies the foundational problem of legitimacy and the way in which it was transformed in the wider age of revolution. Before the great liberal revolutions of the eighteenth century, the legitimacy of law and the state lay in "metaphysical" codes, the sacred qualities of kingship and the moral purposes and religious underpinnings of the medieval and early modern state, which lay beyond the reach of rational discourse.[10] Where lies the legitimacy behind the coercive force of law in the modern state as transmitted from the age of revolution? Our traditional answer is that this legitimacy lies in the "people," in popular sovereignty. A more precise answer would be to argue that the age of revolution brought a fundamental restructuring of the circuitry connecting people and the state, circuitry comprised primarily of consent and civil society. First, the era of the American and French Revolutions redefined conceptions of the consent of the governed around the Atlantic world. Once at best assumed to be simply a passive grant made in the face of metaphysical claims to divine authority, the consent of the people became not just necessary but the very basis for legitimate lawmaking powers in the constitutional liberal polity. Not longer simply "tacit," consent was to be "express." Second, notions of "civil society" were making a broader transition from a diffuse and inclusive "political society" toward a new understanding of distinct and discrete institutions mediating between state and the people. In express consent and in the new institutions of civil society lay a new circuitry of liberal politics that relocated the source of the legitimacy of the state and its lawmaking and administrative powers in popular sovereignty.

Such is the classical account of the age of revolution, to which one might add the corollary that it was in the United States that the circuitry of consent and civil society was most fully developed, most fully subordinating the power of the state to the will of the people. Many contemporary historians have their doubts about this account as a narrative of what did happen in the late eighteenth century. But arguments about its central premises run deep in our historical writing and research and are as important to the writing of social and cultural history as they are to an older, sometimes celebratory, political history. Social historians have often asked fundamental questions about the extent of inclusion in citizenship and civil society; cultural historians are now asking equally fundamental questions about the terms and practices of consent in its widest sense. If our narrative is not an account of achieved transformation in these circuits of consent and civil society, it often is one of struggle toward that transformation, a struggle that can fairly be called the mainspring of American history.[11]

This then opens to a wider proposition: since the age of revolution, the legitimacy of the liberal state is grounded in consent *enacted* in civil society. To say that legitimacy is grounded in consent is not particularly controversial. But to argue that consent is "enacted in civil society" leads to an open-ended set of questions. How were consent and civil society understood in the eighteenth century? How do we know if someone has granted their express consent or their tacit consent? How, when, where, do these things happen in civil society? And what are their implications for the state?

Some of the paradoxical tensions embedded in the notion of the public sphere as the evolving meeting place of consent and civil society become apparent if we conduct a brief survey of a few of the north Atlantic polities in the age of revolution. Struggles over public space, inclusion, and citizenship took different configurations around the north Atlantic. If we narrow our vision to the 1790s, radical notions of consent espoused in France contended with conservative understandings of civil society defended in Great Britain. Between these two extremes lay the young United States, with its commitments both to express consent and to the institutions of civil society. The contradictions between consent and civil society in the early and antebellum republics meant that persuasion would be intermixed with deliberation in American politics, and with the field of coercion and force that lay beyond their domain.

CIVIL SOCIETY

"Civil society" is a notoriously protean term with evolving and overlapping meanings that make its analytical use complex at best. Most broadly, and minimally, civil society has long defined the space subject to and protected by formal national codes of law as opposed to the customary law of "uncivil" lineage societies. Beyond civil society as protected by formal law lies a field of seemingly unregulated force. In this minimal sense, ancient empires and medieval kingdoms encompassed civil societies, in which legitimacy of formal legal codes was grounded in what Habermas calls "metaphysical authority." Its sacred qualities thus put this metaphysical authority beyond the marketplace; it was manifested in a mobilization of resources in ritual and bodily symbolism that Habermas summarized in 1962 as "public representation." (Figure 8.1 is an attempt to graphically represent this ancient model of state and law-protected civil society as it was beginning to be reformulated in the early eighteenth century.) From ancient to early modern times, civil society might also more expansively be synonymous with a deliberative "political society" and difficult to disaggregate from the state.[12] "Civil society as political society," classically manifested in the Greek polis and the Roman republic, consisted of the entire domain of public deliberation, lawmaking, and governance outside the privacy of the household. As such, the state and civil society were continuous and inseparable. The agents of civil life were independent property holders, men of virtue and *virtu*, whose dependents—women, children, servants, and slaves—had no legitimate place in public.

Colonial America, it can be said only very briefly, comprised a complex amalgam of these definitions. Metaphysical authority rested distantly in the person of the monarch and more immediately in the Reformed Puritan and Anglican religious establishments variably granted religious hegemony in New England, New York, the Chesapeake, and the Carolinas. And if Parliament was the model of a state deliberative body separated from society at large, it too was distant and inaccessible, while the colonial assemblies, with their traditions of direct representation and constituent instruction, functioned almost on the model of "civil society as political society," as did the vast array of local governments and Protestant churches that governed ordinary life. This concept of civil society as political society, transmitted in the form of theories of classical

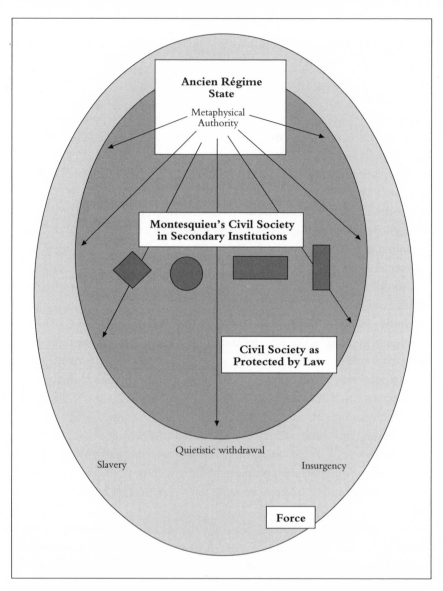

FIGURE 8.1. Civil Society and the Late Ancien Régime State

republicanism, had powerful influences in Revolutionary and postrevolutionary America well into the nineteenth century.[13]

But at the turn of the eighteenth century two new understandings of civil society were developing in Great Britain and on the continent, challenging the austere vision of a corporate society and a virtuous republic, each both extending and departing from older conceptions of civil society. Some of these departures were grounded in fears that the civil and religious violence of the seventeenth century might explode anew, and worked to fuse a mannered civility with the complex new forces of commercial capitalism. This early eighteenth-century revisioning of civility altered the traditional priority of "political society" in which state and civil society occupied a coterminous and seamless continuum. Working from the framework established by Hobbes, Locke, and Shaftesbury, the Scottish Common Sense philosophers Adam Ferguson and Adam Smith described civil society as a domain distinctly separate from the state, a world of refinement, politeness, and mannered civility, of commercial enterprise. In this definition, civil society was epitomized by the refined sensibilities and rational achievements of a rising bourgeoisie, contrasted with the violent behavior of both the "rude" and the noble, and with the dangerous enthusiasms of the seventeenth-century sects. The state provided legal guarantees of property and contract, but made few demands upon this private domain of property and prosperity.[14]

A second and related redefinition emerged from concern about the powers of a centralizing state, leading directly to the modern definition of civil society mediating *between* the state and the general domain of private life. This understanding was first articulated by Montesquieu in *The Spirit of the Laws*, which posed the necessity of intermediate or "secondary" bodies of authority intervening between the state and the people. Montesquieu's intermediate authorities were aristocratic and benevolent and acted to thwart the rising power of French royal absolutism.[15] (Figure 8.1 depicts the "moment" when Montesquieu's "secondary institutions" were recognized as intervening in the ancient relation of state-in-monarchy and a minimal, law-protected, civil society.) He had spent a formative period in England between 1729 and 1731, and much of his thinking was grounded in his admiration for the British "mixed constitution"; the English returned the favor in a wild admiration for *The Spirit of the Laws* and in a disciple, Edmund Burke. Burke published early justifications of party politics as a member of the Chatham administration in the 1760s, describing the solidarity of members of Parliament, placeholders, and ministers in a party as a defense against royal intrusion.[16] His understanding of the necessity of a bulwark against absolute power brought him to sympathy with the American Revolution but to opposition to the French Revolution. For Burke, as it might well have for Montesquieu, French Revolutionary Jacobinism threatened to sweep away all the enduring structures of intermediary civil society and leave the individual powerless in the face of the modern state.[17]

Alexis de Tocqueville carried on this conservative tradition by modernizing Montesquieu and extending Burke's analysis of the French Revolution. Ruminating on both his American experience and recent French history, Tocqueville saw the fantastic elaboration of voluntary association and the press in America as bulwarks against the tyranny that he feared from the postrevolutionary state. "I firmly believe," he wrote at the end of the second volume of *Democracy in America*, "that an aristocracy cannot be founded again in the world, but I think that private citizens, by combining together, may constitute bodies of greater wealth, influence, and strength, corresponding to the persons of an aristocracy."[18] In essence, then, liberal democracies could and would be stabilized by intermediate institutions, standing between state and the people, protecting society at large but most particularly the interests of property from an aggrandizing government and the unmediated sovereignty of the people. The institutions of an independent civil society stood as the structural heirs to the privilege and obligation that powerful aristocracies had once derived from and owed to a wider society.

Tocqueville, however, did see some new functions for civil society that Montesquieu could not. Civil society for Montesquieu was a jealous monitor of the state, defending the liberties of the people. For Tocqueville, civil society in antebellum America was a vehicle of constructive social and economic development, a vital means of improvement in the context of a weak and powerless state. Democratic Americans could achieve "great undertakings" through the proliferation of civil institutions. "Americans of all ages, all conditions, and all dispositions constantly form associations," he wrote in his classic summary. "Wherever at the head of some new undertaking you will see the government in France, or a man of rank in England, in the United States you will be sure to find an association. . . . If they never acquired the habit of forming associations in ordinary life, civilization itself would be endangered."[19]

Modern neo-Tocquevillians, most notably Robert Putnam of the "Bowling Alone" thesis, follow this thread of Tocqueville's analysis, describing the private institutions of civil life as fundamentally empowering, building "social capital" and extending the efficacy of the engaged citizen.[20] But if modern Tocquevillians find public benefit in Tocqueville's articulation of the private power of civil society, many others have a far more negative view. American populists and Italian Marxists have variously seen the organized power of discrete groups in civil society, whether capitalist, cultural, or sporting, as barriers to a full and free participation in society and indeed to the equitable working of the modern state.[21] Another important school of thought, including Putnam's Harvard colleague Theda Skocpol, sees association and communication in the public sphere as symbiotic with and indeed dependent upon the democratic state, empowering citizens by forging connections through, rather than in resistance to, the liberal state. Here a strong and responsive state is a necessary corollary, rather than the antithesis, of a strong and democratic civil society.[22]

CONSENT

The radical critics of neo-Tocquevillian thinking are some of the intellectual descendants of the radical opposition of the eighteenth century. Where Montesquieu, Burke, and Tocqueville defended the institutions of civil society against both king and people, Rousseau, Paine, and Price championed the radical notion of the primacy of popular consent in government. The doctrine that government rests in the explicit consent of the people was forged in the greater age of revolution, grounded more distantly in the Reformation. It was fundamental to the Glorious Revolution against the Stuarts, to American independence from an imperial Britain, and to the French Revolution against absolutism. Over the course of the eighteenth century John Locke's contractualism was extended by Jean-Jacques Rousseau into a utopia of republican virtue and announced as a founding principle in the American Declaration of Independence.[23] Behind a doctrine of popular consent to government lay the ahistorical "fiction" of the state of nature in which people in a condition of natural right contracted among one another to establish governments.

The nature of this grant of consent is, however, fundamentally problematic. In a constitution-making moment, one can enter directly into the founding contract of a given polity. But most modern experience has been with the long epochs of political routine separating one transforming constitutional moment from another.[24] Grants of consent at revolutionary or constitutional moments and in ensuing epochs of routine politics are very different in assumption and structure. In the revolutionary moment consent is grounded in active participation in a bilateral horizontal contract among putative equals; the founding generation in taking up arms or voting in constitutional meetings could express their consent in direct and tangible fashion. In the routine politics that follow the revolutionary moment, consent involves a more vertical and often unilateral relationship between the individual and the lawmaking state.[25] In the condition of political routine, John Locke and most subsequent theorists have differentiated between express consent and tacit consent. In routine post-founding politics the enfranchised exercise their express consent or enact "political obligation" in many layers, from office holding to participation in deliberative public debate to voting in representative elections. Others, perhaps paying taxes, or simply—in Locke's classic example—walking on the public roads, give only their tacit consent to the public benefits of the polity.[26] Consent is tied to obligation, the most onerous task of which is military service in defense of the polity, onerous in some measure since—until recent times—it was required of men too young or too poor to enjoy the privilege of expressing their consent by voting. For many centuries, then, military service marked an ambiguous halfway house between tacit and express consent.[27]

Among the eighteenth-century philosophers Rousseau and Paine were the standard-bearers advancing the doctrine that political legitimacy lay in express popular consent; Montesquieu, Hume, Blackstone, Burke, and Tocqueville all variously stood against this "popular rage." David Hume saw the legal structures of civil society as a cultural "artifice" designed to ensure individual rights in property; in this construct assumptions about ancient foundational contracts and ongoing popular consent were delusional and even dangerous.[28] William Blackstone's legal synthesis of monarchy, parliament, and church established a foundation of unified sovereignty that admitted no place for popular deliberation and express consent.[29] Burke declared an ideological war on Thomas Paine and Richard Price, radical contractarians who threatened to undermine the enduring fabric of the British nation. Rousseauian notions of contract, consent, and universal, ahistorical individual rights, Burke argued, would sweep away the traditional institutions and practices mediating between state and people. But Burke, as had Hume, left room for consent of the tacit variety. Between the 1770s and the 1790s he moved from more express to more tacit definitions. He had supported the Americans in their defense of consent to taxation but had hoped for Parliamentary concessions that would avoid an overt struggle over rights. But well before the French Revolution, which he critiqued so famously in his *Reflections*, Burke was propounding a vision of enduring stability and order in which civil society, grounded in church and state, was divinely ordained. "The people, indeed," he argued, "are presumed to consent to whatever the legislator ordains for their benefit; and they are to acquiesce in it."[30]

Thus the late eighteenth-century political philosophers leave us with a series of paradoxes. In Burke and Rousseau we can posit (perhaps deceptively) neat oppositions. Burkean reverence for the institutions of civil society was grounded in an assumption that popular consent would only be of the tacit variety; a Rousseauian destruction of those institutions would unfold on the authority and in the interest of the express consent of the people at large. Burkean civil society was thus put to the "persuasive" purposes of convincing the great majority to "acquiesce" in their station in life; Rousseauian doctrine of express consent in the will of the people assumed a grand national forum of "deliberation," unsullied by intermediate institutions. For conservatives and radicals alike, complex civil society and the abstractions of contract and consent were mutually exclusive categories, pitted against one another in epochal struggle. In France consent of the most radical kind trumped civil society; in Great Britain civil society trumped consent.

In France the result was a failure to arrive at a stable revolutionary settlement. Modern historians of the French Revolution have arrived at the Tocquevillian judgment of its outcome. In François Furet's paradigm-shaping analysis, monarchic absolutism was replaced by republican absolutism; a royal will was replaced by the general will comprised of the unanimous voices of the people in their natural right to govern.[31] More effectively than had the absolute monarch, the revolutionaries condemned the established and emerging structures of civil society as vestiges of a feudal past. The resulting reduction of civil life to the general will brought political paralysis and an enduring crisis in revolutionary settlement. Lynn Hunt, among others, has stressed the failure of the French Revolution to produce a working and legitimate pluralism of opinion, association, and party, with the result that within a decade the revolutionary republic had given way to Napoleonic dictatorship and the various empires. Far into the nineteenth century, as late as the founding of the Third Republic in 1870, unions were banned and the press was censored; associational life was regulated until 1901.[32]

At the other extreme, while it shaped an enduring stability in Britain, the Burkean veneration of the living structures of civil society slowed the reform of suffrage and the extension of the principle of the express consent of the British people in their government. Defeat in the American Revolution and the emergence of a truly military British empire in India enhanced hierarchical definitions of civil society while damping down old Whiggish traditions of British liberties. Although there is some debate as to whether British civil life through 1832 partook more of bourgeois commerce or of an enduring and vital *ancien régime*, the expansion of the bounds of the British political nation would be a painfully long and drawn-out affair. Ironically, both Britain and France would ground the terms of national citizenship in a culture of arms: through the nineteenth century mass military mobilization for Napoleonic war served these European opposites as the foundational experience of collective, national identity.[33]

AMERICA

The new United States sits at the third corner of this interpretive triangle. The American Revolutionary settlement was compounded of both conservative understandings of civil society and radical notions of consent. In some measure, the survival of the American republic was grounded in the cross-fertilization of civil society and consent, of institutions and transcendence. But this American settlement was not quite as immaculate as European comparisons would suggest, and these categories did not migrate across the Atlantic in quite their European configurations. More generally, American difficulties lay—and still lie—in the inherent contradictions involved in this cross-fertilization, this attempt to balance between equally elaborated notions of structure and equity. This tension between the abstract equality of consent and the selectivity and hierarchy of civil institutions, the struggle to achieve equal voice in civil society, is perhaps the central problem in American history and indeed in contemporary American public life.

Tocqueville's distance from Burke and Montesquieu helps to map out the American distinction in greater specificity. While Tocqueville made no overt attacks on doctrines of natural right and consent, he worked assiduously to develop a theory of civil society as comprised of such intermediate institutions, or secondary powers, that would stabilize emerging democracies, serving as buffers between the people in civil equality and a centralizing state.[34] Where Rousseau, Priestley, and Price celebrated the politics of an equality of condition and the requirement of political consent, Tocqueville braced himself against this new order of things. But despite his anxiety about the future, Tocqueville recognized in American civil institutions a place for enacting express consent, rather than simply enforcing tacit consent. The "great undertakings" that Americans achieved in their antebellum associations—"to found seminaries, to construct churches, to diffuse books," to charter banks and build railroads—involved both deliberation and persuasion, law and language. The work of these associations—and the press—shaped realities through both deliberative pursuit of outcomes in statute law and persuasive efforts at cultural definition. Shorn of the thin and tattered layer of "metaphysical authority" embodied for the colonies in a distant king and a Protestant establishment, America would have to find its way in a frenzy of political and cultural action unfolding in a public sphere broadly defined. The requirements of the republican experiment, and paradoxical extremes in civil condition, meant that both deliberative and persuasive politics in the public sphere would be elaborated on a scale never before imagined.

Before turning to the early and antebellum republics, I need to briefly consider an array of interpretations of civil life in colonial and Revolutionary America. Here I also want to suggest, perhaps with tongue in cheek, that the warfare of the eighteenth-century philosophers has its echoes in the analytical approaches, if not the actual politics, of our contemporary historians. Burke and Rousseau live on in our twenty-first century interpretations of consent and civil society in the age of revolution.

Three distinct positions about the nature of civil society and consent in early

America compete for primacy in contemporary historical analysis. The first, and perhaps the oldest, traces their linked roots to the religious culture of radical Protestant dissent, to the personal, vertical relation of the individual with the Calvinist God, and the collective, horizontal relation of membership in the church covenant. This argument is traditionally discussed in reference to Puritan New England, but the explosive growth of Presbyterian, Baptist, and Methodist congregations throughout the colonies in the second half of the eighteenth century, followed by the even more dramatic developments of the Second Great Awakening between the 1790s and the 1830s, points to the fundamental importance of religious culture in shaping American public life.[35] At the same time, there is an inherent paradox here, as yet not adequately explored: this mass experience was grounded in the sectarian struggles of the seventeenth century against which the new European civility was designed to inoculate. Timothy Breen, Timothy Hall, and Frank Lambert offer to solve this paradox in arguing that religion and commerce began to flow together in the forging of a distinct religious public sphere, laying the ground for the massive outpouring of religious print culture that David Nord and many of the authors of the first volume of the *History of the Book in America* have described in great detail.[36]

It remains something of a challenge to spell out the ways in which the culture of sensibility increasingly tied together secular and religious imperatives, taming and channeling sectarian imperatives of the seventeenth century.[37] Similarly, the relationship between religious culture and the structures of secular politics has yet to be sketched in detail. Such an argument might begin with the religious imperatives driving the disestablishment of religion and the separation of Habermas's metaphysics from the state. It would then pursue the proposition that partisanship in the early republic roughly followed denominational lines and that the acceptance of political difference was built gradually upon an emerging toleration of religious difference.[38]

Jack P. Greene has been developing another grand approach to civil society in colonial America. Fundamentally interested in the continuities of law and economy, but recently branching out into cultural history, Greene downplays religious institutions and grounds colonial civil society in secular and constitutional development, observed and ratified by transatlantic intellectual inquiry. Greene, I would suggest, is virtually Burkean in his emphasis on steady social development, the forging of a social capital in civil experience, and approvingly cites Burke on both the growth of the colonies and his efforts at imperial conciliation.[39] Even more Burkean is Greene's account of the role of the American Revolution in shaping American civil society.[40] "Some scholars," he writes in a recent essay on "Social and Cultural Capital in Colonial British America," "have been so intent upon assimilating the American Revolution to the great European revolutions—emphasizing its revolutionary character and radical discontinuity with the American past—that they have largely neglected to explore the bearing of earlier American social experience upon the events and developments of the American Revolution."[41]

Here Greene's nemesis is Gordon Wood, the leading figure among contemporary scholars emphasizing the liberal "radicalism of the American Revolution."[42] For the narrow proposes of this essay, I again will stretch things a bit, and call Wood a follower of Rousseau. His book *The Radicalism of the American Revolution* can partially ground a third essential approach to American civil life in the eighteenth century, that which sees fundamental and decisive changes flowing from the consequences of the Revolution. In Wood's account, the Revolution brought the destruction of a hierarchical society shaped by an ethos of patriarchy and monarchy and the emergence of a democratic society grounded in individual gain and in the new associativeness that Tocqueville would remark upon. If Wood does not dwell on political consent in *Radicalism*, his argument there and in *The Creation of the American Republic* is consistent with J. R. Pole's formulation of thirty years ago. During the Revolution, Pole wrote, " 'consent' was being turned into something far more active than the tacit acceptance of the law which it had meant to Locke, and which it had usually meant even in the American colonies. . . . The transformation of passive consent into something resembling active, even continuous participation, was a direct result. . . . [Americans] had charged the old notion of 'consent' with a more democratic connotation than it had ever born before."[43] And beyond Wood and Pole lies the Neo-Progressive tradition, led by Gary Nash and Alfred Young. If Wood is an optimistic Rousseauian, celebrating the civil outcomes of the Revolution, the neo-Progressives are pessimistic Rousseauians, seeing the potential for liberating change blocked by the very elaboration of civil society that Wood celebrates.[44]

It may well be that each of these three proposals—a religious grounding of American civil society, a steady development of social capital, or a revolutionary transformation—are each equally valid, each describing a different part of the larger elephant. But if we want to focus on the associations and print culture that comprised the core of Habermas's public sphere, it is increasingly clear that—given the gradual emergence of secular print from the 1690s—the Revolution and the events leading up to it were of paramount importance. A decade ago Michael Warner, in his *Letters of the Republic*, argued that the print culture of the mid-eighteenth-century colonies already comprised a functioning public sphere.[45] But David Hall, summarizing the themes developed in the *History of the Book in America* volume on the colonial era, finds it impossible to use the framework of the public sphere: "On this side of the Atlantic, social and political criticism were never fully differentiated from the languages and practices of radical Protestantism. . . . Political, religious, and social authority was remarkably local and decentralized." Arguing that the "broad distribution of printed matter" required in the public sphere was never apparent in the colonies, Hall prefers to speak of the "republic of letters" and "a ethos of 'free inquiry'" in colonial learned culture.[46] The findings of this first volume on *The History of the Book*, of the subsequent volume in preparation on the period 1790–1840, and of Christopher Grasso's *A Speaking Aristocracy* all point to decisive moments of change for the volume of print in the 1760s, as the revolutionary crisis got under way, and in the 1790s, when a national politics emerged.[47] Similarly, the work of Richard Brown, Steven C. Bullock, Peter Clark, and others reveal the same trajectory in associational life, with an expansion in the 1760s followed by an explosion in the 1790s and the decades following.[48]

It seems reasonable to suggest that the experience of the French and Indian War, and especially the ensuing imperial crisis, played a fundamental role in expanding association and print in colonial America. Here, it might be added, there is a common theme that stretches around the Atlantic world: eighteenth-, even seventeenth-century expansions of the imperial state—and the levying of taxes to fund those expansions—were met by popular response framing and driving the emerging forms of "public sphere." Historian Michael Kwass has argued that in mid-eighteenth century France the increasing scale and penetration of royal taxation led to foundational developments in the critical public sphere of the French Enlightenment, which the wider Tocqueville-Furet school in turn sees as the ground of the Revolution.[49] Obvious parallels can be seen both in England in the 1640s, where David Zaret has proposed the emergence of a precocious public sphere, and in the British North American colonies in the 1760s.[50] And it was Spanish efforts in the 1760s to reform their American empire that contributed to the forging of Benedict Anderson's imagined communities among Latin "creole pioneers" and the foundations of nationalism in Spanish American colonies.[51] This was civil society in Montesquieu's sense, emerging to monitor the state and to mediate as an intermediate power between the fiscal demands of state and empire and the interests of the people in their private households. Thus the American Revolution was both consequence and cause of a widening domain of print and association: the public sphere.

The reciprocal relationship between the revolutionary crisis and the expansions of public print and association in the North American colonies in the 1760s inevitably provokes the insidious and delicious counterfactual: What if the imperial crisis had been resolved quickly and durably in 1765–66? How would public life in America have differed without the parliamentary crisis and the revolution? One has to suggest that European civil forms of print and association would have grown more steadily, but more slowly. And they would never have assimilated the political shock of the revolutionary demands for allegiance to provisional governments and of the moments of constitution making, which dramatized the new order of popular sovereignty and express consent.[52]

THE EARLY REPUBLIC AND JÜRGEN HABERMAS

What, then, of the Habermasian public sphere, civil society, and consent in the early American republic, as it emerged from revolution? I will organize my remarks around two larger propositions, posing problems that might be addressed through Jürgen Habermas's conceptions of communicative rationality and the public sphere. These two propositions are really standard fare: (1) something did indeed happen as a consequence of the Revolution, but (2) that change was paradoxically flawed and incomplete.

Despite the importance of Protestant beginnings and Anglo-American continuities, something did indeed happen as a consequence of the American Revolution beyond simple independence. The Revolution powerfully accelerated trajectories toward expectations of democracy, toward the incorporation of larger numbers into the political process, toward the explosive elaboration of civil associationalism. Colonial political cultures, however autonomous, were subject to a monarchy and stood exposed to the potential threat of imperial authority. During the crisis and in the war itself these colonies declared themselves republics, and the language of republican virtue provided a central benchmark of collective purpose during both the Revolution and the decades following. If the American republic was rapidly developing into a liberal polity in which representatives were elected to achieve distributive ends for the interests of their constituents, the language of virtue and morality did not disappear from American public discourse. Increasingly sharply differentiated from practical politics, moral impulses found expression in public in the proliferation of denominational organizations and individual churches, in massive ventures in religious print, and in the emerging organizational structures of moral reform. If they were separate entities, interest politics and organized morality by the 1830s danced to the same tune of public and plural competition in which they competed for public opinion, for participation, for consent.

And obviously this change was limited and incomplete. By the 1830s, even in the 1770s, the United States was an amalgam of extremes possibly unique in human history; a bizarre spectrum of civil condition running from democracy to slavery. While white men of some property could participate directly and fully in the debating and making of laws in state and nation, persons of African descent stood either in slavery, outside civil society in a state of undeclared war,[53] or on the fringes of civil life, free barely to form families and households and to own property. Well before David Walker raised his *Appeal* in 1829, the paradox of slavery and other inequities in a land of freedom was beginning to be apparent to many, perhaps in some way to practically everyone. Between these extremes of deliberation and slavery a majority of adult Americans stood on a steep—and stepped—gradient of civil status occupied by white men of lesser property and by women of all conditions. Where some could claim the fullest privileges of deliberation and express consent, others were beyond the pale of even persuasion and tacit consent, directly subject to force. More ambiguously, others occupied the intervening space, included in civil society but excluded from its deliberative core. American life between the Revolution and the Civil War was grounded both more fully and more problematically in the dynamics of consent and civil society than anywhere else in the world. This mosaic in civil condition has contributed to the uses that American historians have found for Jürgen Habermas's notion of the public sphere, and to the arguments that they have had with his notion, particularly as originally formulated in *The Structural Transformation*.

The Habermasian public sphere has shaped the recent avalanche of work among cultural and literary historians. It has also been subjected to withering critiques. As defined in *The Structural Transformation*, the key participant in the public sphere was an autonomous, independent man of middling property, and Habermas argued that this quality of autonomy was eroded with the growth of nineteenth-century capitalism, and with it the rational public sphere. He has since conceded the point,[54] and where in 1962 he described the public sphere as a historical grounded arena of bourgeois rationality, in his 1996 *Between Facts and Norms* the public sphere is open to competing voices. But more broadly there is the inevitable tension between philosophical idealism and historical realism: Habermas described a polity that ought to be, historians describe polities as they have functioned in real time. Written as an abstract analysis of the ideal liberal polity, Habermas assumes that a universal citizenship and suffrage, and an essential personal autonomy, are established facts, not the ground of historical struggle.

Driven by a mandate to describe real life, many historians are particularly dubious about Habermas's apparent emphasis on deliberation and rationality. Communication in public occurs in modes other than rational deliberation— literary, artistic, and performative modes that are cognitively emotional, symbolic, or emotional rather than rational-critical.[55] And cultural historians in particular, so attuned to the artificial and constructed qualities of culture, are pessimistic about the human autonomy and agency assumed in Habermas's model of rational deliberation. In great measure the project of cultural history has been to demonstrate the embedding of the human experience in the invisible webs of power that are language and culture. Maybe it is too much to call them Burkean, but, in their pessimism about the reach and range of deliberative discourse, culture theorists and cultural historians do echo Burke's analysis of the human condition.[56] A prime example may be found in Edmund Morgan's opening to *Inventing the People*, where he invokes David Hume's query about "the easiness with which the many are governed by the few"; the Gramscian notion of cultural hegemony is explicit in Morgan's premise that "the success of government requires the acceptance of fictions"—including those of consent and popular sovereignty.[57] At this juncture I cannot resist the observation that cultural historians can be viewed as Burkean and conservative in their pragmatic realism, seeing the popular voice limited to tacit consent; and traditional political historians as Rousseauian and naively utopian, in their willingness to take the institutional structures of deliberation and lawmaking at face value.

In essence, cultural historians have tackled the unpacking of two key problems: first, the operation of "tacit consent" and second, the alternative avenues to the expression of consent and dissent, avenues by which those excluded from deliberation can turn the tables on the dominant culture. Cultural historians are asking an ever-widening array of questions about the cultural dimensions of power—about the deployment of language and imagery in public forms in ways that limit, constrain, or advance the circumstances and fortunes of individuals and groups in the social and political spaces of civil society. Here we have an account of the wider practices of tacit consent in civil society, what I call the arena of cultural persuasion. Cultural studies historians have made persuasive discourse the primary ground of a new cultural history of the political. They have by and large rejected the idea of deliberation as a realistic account of government in the liberal polity.

In his new synthesis, *Between Facts and Norms*, Habermas placed the deliberative in relation to both the persuasive and the violent. He is fundamentally concerned with establishing the basis for the making of law, which without legitimacy is simple force. In what he calls "metaphysical" societies, where law and morality are linked in a single sovereignty, the legitimacy of law is grounded in the morality encoded in sacred texts. But where lies the legitimacy of law once it is divorced from morality, as was decisively the case in the American Revolutionary disestablishment of religion? Habermas proposes that this legitimacy be grounded not in any specific content but in procedures that protect the right of every citizen to participate in the rational deliberation that will lead eventually to the framing of law. Here he sees himself mediating between inadequate liberal and republican solutions to the postmonarchical polity. In his reading, liberalism limits the political role of the individual to the vote; republicanism reintroduces metaphysics in its demand for consensus and moral virtue as the ground for political action. His procedural and discursive polity is designed to steer between these extremes.[58] Habermas is—in my terms here—a Rousseauian optimist on the question of express consent,[59] but he departs from Rousseau in constructing a model of rational deliberation by individuals in the public sphere operating on the process of lawmaking in the state.[60]

Though his ideal is rational deliberation, Habermas in *Between Facts and Norms* accounts for the operation of persuasion and force in brief but fundamentally important discussions of the "distortions" of communication enabled by "social power." The public sphere of civil society, he argues, is "vulnerable to the repressive and exclusionary effects of unequally distributed social power, structural violence, and systematically distorted communication."[61] These forces are the social "facts" that Habermas counterposes to collective "norms" in his title, literally the tension between the structures of civil society and the ideals of consent. Democratic societies after the age of revolution, he argues, have been faced with this fundamental contest of social facts: the realities of unequal "social power" versus the ideals of equal right and participation that underlie consent and legitimate social peace.[62] The Habermasian procedural ideal of equal access to deliberative discourse is the fundamental vehicle for resolving this tension and arriving at legitimate social peace. But beyond the ideals of rational deliberation, and the boundaries of legitimacy that Habermas seeks to describe, he sees the messy realities of cultural persuasion and even physical violence.

A REVISED MODEL OF THE PUBLIC SPHERE

All these considerations suggest the possibility of an expanded approach to the Habermasian paradigm of the public sphere and its relationship with the liberal state. Such a revised model is visualized in Figure 8.2 as a series of concentric circuits intersecting with the state, the constitutional locus of lawmaking and administration and the vehicle of legitimate force. The domain of civil society, with its public sphere of opinion-formation divided into interpenetrating zones of deliberation and persuasion, virtually encircles—and perhaps restrains—the state. Legislatures and courts in the constitutional state share a field of political deliberation with this open public sphere, linking state and civil society in a

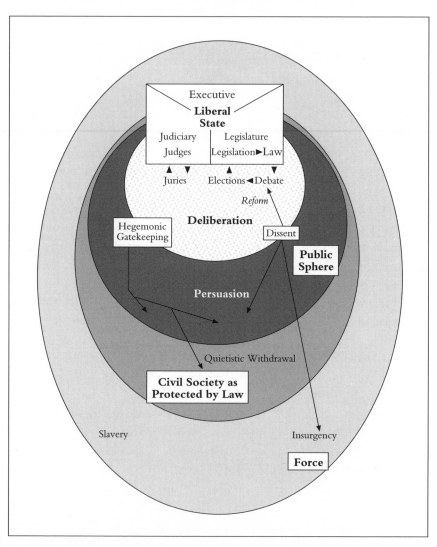

FIGURE 8.2. The State, Civil Society, and the Public Sphere in the Early American Republic

cycling of power. Here the enfranchised are supposed to enact their express consent in the formal politics of debate, election, legislature, and courtroom: the constitutional-bound arenas of the making and administration of law.[63]

Formal "rational" deliberation is intermingled in the public sphere with a much more pervasive, informal, cultural persuasion.[64] Each acts on the other: deliberation through formal political outcomes in law, and persuasion in informal political outcomes in language. Cultural persuasion involves both tacit consent and the various forms of cultural dissent. This is a fluid world of communicative power and authority, subject to systematic distortion by social and economic inequalities by the very marketplace that carries its meaning in saleable commodities.[65] If only the enfranchised are involved in deliberation, almost everyone of some civil status is affected in some way by persuasion. This is the funhouse of cultural politics, what Habermas calls distorted, chaotic, and anarchic, what Gramsci called hegemonic. Where entry into deliberative politics is the franchise, entry into the domain of persuasive politics is simply the possession of human faculties of sight, hearing, and speech, greatly augmented by literacy. For the most part the field of persuasion is the field of tacit consent: language and symbols establish the boundaries of the possible in a particular historical context and are deployed by cultural gatekeepers to the ongoing end of maintaining those boundaries. Some of this persuasion perhaps lies outside Habermas's definition of the public sphere in a residual arena of "public representation," in which the symbols of power represent themselves in display and ritual unmediated by commodified text.[66] Tacit consent is achieved in the passive acceptance of the subject of deliberation and persuasion.[67] Everyone is affected by this persuasion, but it bears particular salience for the dependent and disenfranchised, standing beyond the sacred circle of enfranchised deliberation. Cultural persuasion to tacit consent might be seen as a cheap, perhaps guilt-free, vehicle for the social control of the disenfranchised. Inside the bounds of civil society, constitutions and laws protect the law-abiding from the violence of both the arbitrary state and the outlaw individual. But beyond the field of persuasion in civil society lies that threat of force, justified by express consent of the deliberative enfranchised and wielded by the state.

If the field of cultural persuasion is the field of tacit consent, its open, accessible, unregulated nature means that it is also open to voices that are other than tacitly consenting. Many, of course, are the voices of gatekeepers, maintaining the persuasive, symbolic order enforcing that tacit consent. But others can also be contrary voices, speaking a gradient of *dissent*. Herein lies the special complexity of the cultural arena, since admission is not necessarily wholly controlled, and contrary voices and interpretations can slip out. Habermas touched on this slippage in *The Structural Transformation*, when he distinguished between the sociological "bourgeois," the propertied member of the public sphere, and the universal "homme," the inclusive referent to the "people" at large in the discourse of the public sphere.[68] If participation in the deliberative process is constitutionally limited to the enfranchised, participation in the persuasive process is open to anyone; if a privileged and authorized "web of significance" woven by cultural gatekeepers in the public sphere works to establish the boundaries and layers of civil participation, conversely, unauthorized discourses of subversive meaning develop to challenge these boundaries. Thus dissent in the outer circle of persuasion in the public sphere can drive interventions building toward deliberation, law, and restoration of consent. This cultural expression of dissent would only be the edge of a wider zone of danger for the lawmaking center, a zone in which consent, express or tacit, is progressively withheld, and in which this dissent is manifested in a progression of strategies, including subcommunal withdrawal, criminal activity, and outright insurgency and rebellion. Thus beyond both the state and the constitutionally protected space of civil society lies the arena of force: civil outlaws withhold both express and tacit consent, their political voice is violence, and in turn they are met with state-sanctioned force.

Across these concentric circles we can identify a stepped series of gradients marked by sharp boundaries between inclusion and exclusion in the civil process, between civil and "uncivil," between the "refined" and the "rude," to apply the language of eighteenth-century sensibility. And fundamentally, this gradient of participation in civil life can be mapped onto a gradient of consent, from express to tacit, to alienated and withheld. Civil society, and particularly the play of deliberation and persuasion in the public sphere, was the site where the terms of consent and participation were negotiated and where the practices and outcomes of consent and participation, of citizenship, were enacted—and struggled over. And it was on the boundaries between state and civil society, between civil deliberation and civil persuasion, and between constitutionally protected civility and extra-constitutional violence, that many of the great struggles of American history have unfolded.

THE REVISED MODEL APPLIED

The extremes in American civil condition and their contradiction with announced ideals have driven the uses that American historians of the period between the Revolution and the Civil War have found for Habermas's notion of the public sphere. If this epoch began with the violent overthrow of a metaphysically grounded polity and the establishment of a constitutional polity seemingly grounded in civil discourse, its public struggles unfolded in every conceivable domain in and beyond civil society. I would like to close by reviewing some of the implications of the notion of public sphere as I have proposed revising it here for several strands of contemporary historical writing on the United States in the wider age of Revolution. Though some might well object, I would suggest that this revision does capture and connect important themes in what historians have been writing about early America.

JOHN L. BROOKE

I will start with a background condition, the emergence of civil discourse in Habermas's postmetaphysical age. The fundamental precondition for Habermas's deliberative legitimacy is that the basis of "norms" can no longer be religious or metaphysical; mutable civil discourse would replace immutable sacred text. We might go back to Machiavelli to chart the larger contours of the transition from sacred to secular norms. But in early American historiography it suffices to note that a cultural history of secular culture roughly tracks the trajectory of the public sphere from its putative origins in the coffee houses and clubs of Restoration England. While we see hints of secular persuasion in the closing chapters of David Hall's *Worlds of Wonder, Days of Judgment,* for example, this and the other leading examples of cultural history in seventeenth-century America are necessarily religious in theme.[69] But from the turn of the eighteenth century we now have a new and vibrant literature on the shape and culture of public life in colonial America that barely touches on religion. Though its argument is under challenge, Michael Warner's *The Letters of the Republic* was the first of a generation of books positing the emergence of a print-based secular public sphere in the eighteenth-century colonies, establishing an imagined community of readers who already formed an American nation by 1776. Warner's work was followed by David Shields's *Oracles of Empire,* charting a language of commerce and politics in belles lettristic manuscript poetry, and David Conroy's *In Public Houses,* describing the rise of the tavern as secular public space in eighteenth-century Massachusetts. A secular language of refinement and sensibility, and a considerable amount of deliberative discourse, was being moved by new vehicles: the club, the lodge, the novel, the newspaper.[70]

Whether this constituted a coherent "Habermasian public sphere" may be debated. But it did slowly construct the ground of a civil secular discourse running in parallel and intermingled with the religious. The Revolutionary crisis, fundamentally and classically about the nature of consent, can be understood as the epoch of the decisive emergence and consolidation of an American public sphere, both deliberative and persuasive. The essential issue of representation and taxation involved the right relation of civil society and the state and led to an explosion of deliberative print.[71] As deliberation failed and the legitimacy of the imperial polity fell into question, a secular politics of persuasion emerged for the first time in the political culture of the Sons of Liberty and the wider early revolutionary movement.

This street politics of symbol, ritual, and riot, effecting the crisis of legitimacy and the transfer of allegiance to the American cause, has been the topic of a number of remarkable books and articles on the Revolution and the early republic.[72] Certainly this persuasive politics, whether on the printed page or in the streets, was filled with religious references and undertones, but its essential thrust was secular. The more recent of these are grounded in Benedict Anderson's understanding of the relationship of nationalism to vernacular reading developed in *Imagined Communities* and introduced to the American literature in Warner's *Letters of the Republic*. Here the readers of print vicariously experience, indeed consume, a cultural production that builds a new identification with a new imagined community, a new nation. In these more recent books, this cultural action is transpiring entirely in the persuasive field of the newly emerging secular public sphere, a persuasion made all the more salient as the deliberative process stalled and failed in the Revolutionary crisis.

The new cultural history of the Revolution has, with its counterparts in other fields, recaptured the persuasive at the considerable cost of foreshortening the wider arena of historical analysis. In pursuing the insight that "language is power," cultural historians typically leave unattended the traditional problems of deliberation, law, and force. It will be one of the challenges of the coming decades to reintegrate these artificial polarities. The promise of this challenge is best suggested in a brief review of how several generations of historians have treated the boundaries between state and civil society, between deliberation and persuasion, between civility and violence.

An older literature on charivari, riot, and rebellion in the eighteenth century, traditionally identified with the work of George Rudé, E. P. Thompson, and Emanuel Le Roy Ladurie, is notable for the manner in which it crossed these thematic boundaries.[73] Here the disenfranchised on the edges and margins of civil society, excluded from any role in deliberation in the early modern polity, used ritualized violence to assert a claim in the field of persuasion to the right of consent and dissent. Routinized in carnival and Christmas riot, as Stephen Nissenbaum has cogently argued, the inversion of civil and uncivil both challenged and reinforced the social order. But during the Revolutionary crisis it was put to specific political purposes in a substitution of ritual force as deliberation failed.[74] Here the symbolism of disguise provides another perspective: Boston Tea Party rioters dressed as Mohawks in part—as Timothy Breen suggests—because Indianness was a European code for Americanness. But the survival of Indian disguise among land rioters in Maine described by Alan Taylor, and the Anti-Renters in New York described recently by Reeve Huston and Charles McCurdy, has to suggest that "Indianness" stood for the status of being outside civil society and in rebellion against the state.[75] Though an option taken up by the Virginia volunteer rifle companies, George Washington decisively avoided any hint of such "Indianness" in modeling the Continental Army, an army that was defending a refined civil society in the name of a new state.

JOHN L. BROOKE

If some white men found themselves outside the privileges of civil society by virtue of a lack of property, many others, a numerical majority, endured more extreme forms of civil exclusion. The entire history of American slavery can be read in terms of an exclusion from consent and civil society literally written into the provisions of the 1787 United States Constitution. Orlando Patterson has described slavery as "social death," a term that might be amended to "civil death"; Peter Onuf has reminded us that Jefferson followed Locke in seeing the state of slavery as a continuing state of war, slaves as chattels denied any status in civil society other than minimal rights to life. Sally Hadden and Christopher Waldrep have recently fleshed out Onuf's insight in detailing the legal structure of this violent exclusion from civil life. Resistance and rebellion were the obvious outcomes of this exclusion, a natural recourse to force in self-defense amplified by the slaves' inevitable exposure to the revolutionary doctrine of consent.[76] On the other hand, we can think about the process of slave accommodation in terms of the carefully orchestrated—or ignored—movements of slaves across this boundary into the shadows of civil status. In Eugene Genovese's account of the master-slave relation, the force of public opinion played this role. The neighborhood's enforcement of legal limits on the master's power, providing the most minimal civil protections for the slave, confirmed the essential structure of the relationship.[77] So too the considerable access to the market that Philip Morgan describes among slaves in the South Carolina task system suggest that a certain slippage across the line into civil society worked toward slave accommodation.[78] The role of religion among slaves is also fraught with questions about the boundary of civil society; by 1830 slave preachers were establishing the beginnings of the autonomous black church—and thus a form of recognized civil life—only to subsumed within the structures of the white evangelical church in the ensuing thirty years.[79] Willie Lee Rose's *Port Royal Experiment* and the various works of Eric Foner on Reconstruction revolve around the terms and conditions under which freed slaves would enter civil society, either fully included in the deliberative center or excluded from deliberation and subject to the cultural persuasion and the legal force and illegal violence of Redemption and Jim Crow. Here it is Foner's great contribution to pinpoint the unique circumstances of American slavery and emancipation, compared to the British empire and elsewhere. The stakes were high, leading to all-out civil war, because freed slaves could and did demand entry into the deliberative public sphere, to the rights of voting office-holding. And as Willie Lee Rose made very clear, military service and sacrifice were the half-way house to citizenship for African Americans of the Civil War generation.[80]

If the experience of race and slavery in America can be fit into the framework of civil society, the historians of women in the United States between the Revolution and the Nineteenth Amendment were the first American scholars to explore the interpretive possibilities of the Habermasian public sphere. They also objected to his limiting definition of the public sphere as a domain of rational deliberation, and by more than implication only male. But this tension with Habermas's formulation has contributed some of the most creative departures in recent historical writing, exploring the boundaries in civil life proposed here.

For decades historians of American women have been carefully examining female political action in the persuasive domain and the trajectory of this work into the deliberative public sphere of civil society. Excluded from deliberation and the franchise, and at the same time vulnerable to physical force, women's public life was one fundamentally configured by boundaries in civil society. Such is the central theme of Linda Kerber's *No Constitutional Right to be Ladies*, which examines the problem of American women's citizenship in terms of the obligations that adhere in a male definition of consent and rights. Nancy Isenberg, exploring the discourses of early feminism in *Sex and Citizenship in Antebellum America*, explicitly defines the boundary in Habermasian terms: excluded with children beyond a claim to express consent, women had no claim to deliberative politics and lesser rights in law, but they could act under "the ideology of publicity or the public sphere." Excluded from deliberative rights, women used persuasion in public to build a case for inclusion in those rights. The persuasive powers of the "literary public sphere" and the "religious public," both inside civil society but outside the boundary of formal deliberation, were mobilized to build a case for women's suffrage.[81] Though she wrote over fifteen years ago in a perhaps pre-Habermasian age, Paula Baker's "The Domestication of American Politics" is perhaps the paradigmatic essay in this exploration. Women's exclusion from deliberation meant that they constructed an entire politics of reform in the persuasive domain, a politics that was gradually inserted into the deliberative domain.[82] Eventually the priorities of the Progressives and the New Deal would emerge out this nineteenth century politics of reform. The work of Isenberg and Baker will have to stand here for the work of an entire generation of scholarship on the central role of women in antebellum reform movements, including Mary Ryan, Nancy Hewitt, Julie Roy Jeffrey, and Lori Ginzberg, whose abolitionist women finally decided in the 1850s, usefully for my purposes here, that "moral suasion was moral balderdash."[83]

Nineteenth-century women's trajectory across the boundary between persuasion and deliberation constitutes one of the fundamental lessons of the historiography of the past quarter century. An emerging literature at the intersection of women's history and literary studies is beginning to situate the origins of this persuasive politics in the eighteenth-century culture of sensibility. Traditionally reform has been seen as emerging solely from the imperatives of evangelical religion, but the new work on sensibility has made it clear that secular reading, situated in a emerging middle-class culture, played a fundamental role. The rise of a sense of sympathy for others, and other's vulnerabilities, over the course of the eighteenth century, was grounded in the transformation of manners and the rise of the novel. George Barker-Benfield's *Culture of Sensibility*, examining this process in England, depicted the rise of sensibility and sympathy as political in the broader meaning and essentially persuasive. Women deployed this culture as a vehicle for the reform of men's manners, and succeeded in achieving a broad transformation of the public climate.[84] Most recently, in *The Consent of the Governed*, literary scholar Gillian Brown has developed an argument about the relationship of sensibility and consent in early America. She suggests that the accounts of the afflictions of the vulnerable woman—"stories of compelled consent"—that so dominated the novels of sensibility were essentially an extended consideration of the boundary between consent and force. "For late eighteenth-century America," she writes, "the image of women's fates exemplified the anxieties attendant upon consent. . . . Images of the disenfranchised keep present the state of existence that individuals must always avoid and reject. . . . Disenfranchised women suggest that individuals must continue the labor of consent throughout adult life."[85] Sensitivity to coercion and the denial of consent, it has been argued by Thomas Haskell, Karen Halttunen, Elizabeth Clark, Markman Ellis, and David Gellman, were foundational to the wider Atlantic movement to abolish slavery and to associated efforts for charity and humanitarian reform.[86]

The federal cities of Philadelphia and Washington have been the sites of yet another—and quite different—approach to women on the boundary between persuasion and deliberation in the early republic. Rather than a theme pervading and changing an entire culture driven by print in the persuasive public sphere, this literature is focusing on the face-to-face specifics of life in the nation's center of formal deliberation. Fredrika Teute, Jan Lewis, Catherine Allgor, and Susan Branson have collectively rediscovered the unique role of women in a "Republican Court," beginning with the French Revolution and coming to a crisis with the accession of Andrew Jackson and the Peggy Eaton affair. Variously describing a social sphere, informal sphere, or private sphere, these historians see women playing a fundamental role in national politics between 1789 and

1828. During these four decades, always limited by their constitutional constraints, they actively scouted and probed the boundary between persuasion and deliberation.[87]

Finally, the historiography of national politics is deeply shaped by assumptions about deliberation, persuasion, and force.[88] If we begin chronologically in the 1780s, historians of the ratification place the shape of deliberation in the press and in convention at the center of the story. Recent work describes the Democratic-Republican societies of the mid-1790s as working to forge a deliberative space in the public sphere.[89] Jeff Pasley's *Tyranny of Printers* describes the role of the political editors in building an audience for political reading and an electorate for the polls. His new book will be read with Richard John's *Spreading the News*, which sees the federal postal system as an active agent in building a national public sphere in the 1790s.[90] Andrew Robertson's essay in this volume, with the recent work of Pasley and Waldstreicher, has reasserted that the early republic saw a real democratization of polity.[91] These recent interventions are reopening consideration of a grand, if sometimes celebratory, tradition—perhaps running back to Schlesinger's *Age of Jackson* and George Bancroft himself—focusing on the deliberative qualities and substantive outcomes of American politics. In doing so, they are challenging even these great figures by reaching back before the Jacksonian era to find the age of political democratization. While this recent work stress the importance of the shape and form of political participation, Richard McCormick has led an effort to stress the content of political outcomes, maintaining that voters were directly engaged with issue-based deliberation of a distributive politics from the Jacksonian period forward.[92]

If McCormick's thesis asserts the role of the deliberative, however, it stands as a reaction to an earlier shift toward the persuasive. Beginning in the late 1950s the ethno-cultural school of "new political historians" led by Lee Benson were early explorers of the persuasive in American politics. Convinced that American politics was not fundamentally and expression of class interest, the ethno-culturalists explored the ways in which cultural persuasion rather than substantive deliberation shaped the response of American voters to political parties. Convinced that substantive deliberation unfolds only behind closed doors, the ethnoculturalists were as pessimistic and Burkean in their own way as cultural historians are today; despite their differences both generations would agree that the American polity is held up by tacit rather than express consent.[93]

The American voters, in the ethnocultural view, were at least enthusiastic. Glenn Altschuler and Stuart Blumin, in their recent book *The Rude Republic*, have argued that American political parties were not necessarily great engines of either deliberation or persuasion. Rather the American voter increasingly saw parties as irrelevant to their lives and treated politics with a range of disengagement, disaffection, and "suspended disbelief." Altschuler and Blumin are mischievous subversives in the house of American political history, because they strike an optimistic note in their recovery of a skeptical and wily American public, unduped by scheming pols.[94]

But Blumin and Altschuler's thesis may well be limited in its application to the decades just before the Civil War. The work of the historians of the "newest political history" suggests that partisanship was a vibrant fusion of deliberation and persuasion in the half century following constitutional ratification. Where resent work has described Democratic-Republican efforts to forge a deliberative public space, Seth Cotlar's essay in this volume demonstrates that the Federalists saw 1798 as the moment to launch a cultural "counter-revolution" that would have powerful persuasive effects far into the coming century. Cotlar's analysis, with work by David Waldstreicher, Rosemarie Zagarri, Ronald and Mary Zboray, Jeff Pasley, and Daniel Walker Howe, highlights the essential truth that the Federalists, and later the Whigs, were far more adept than their opponents in mobilizing resources to pursue a cultural, persuasive strategy, a strategy that would come to include virtually the entire institutional and publication armature of the evangelical empire.[95] In this regard it is well worth noting that conservative American Whigs, in Daniel Walker Howe's reading, were ardent followers of that theorist of the cultural basis of tacit consent, Edmund Burke.[96] If Whigs dominated in institution building and persuasive, putatively nonpolitical print, their Democratic-Republican and Democratic opponents prevailed in the genre of popular political print and perhaps in persuasive performance of stump and stage.[97]

Finally, we should return briefly to political violence: the riot. In the eighteenth century, the violence of the riot gave disenfranchised outsiders a voice in governance. By the 1830s the story was quite different. Antebellum rioting in great part was aimed by insiders against outsiders; a great number of antebellum riots involved a patrolling of the boundaries of civil society against those attempting to change its definition, abolition and slave insurrection being the most obvious. But violence in the antebellum decades was also centered on problems of legitimacy and constitution; the Buckshot War in Pennsylvania, the Dorr War in Rhode Island, even the Mormon Wars in Missouri and Illinois and the Anti-Rent Wars in New York: each involved in some way crises of constitution and procedure that overwhelmed routine deliberation and threatened the legitimacy of state governments. All in turn were set in the context of a wider constitutional crisis over slavery, consent, and the slave power in which sectional persuasion overwhelmed duly constituted deliberation.[98] As it had in the Revolution, a routine deliberative process collapsed as a wave of persuasive culture set the stage for Civil War.

What this brief review suggests is not an answer, but a framework for discussion. Scholarship runs in cycles and generations with attention shifting from topic to topic in a very imperfect reflection of wider cultural and intellectual currents of an age. Recent memory has seen an American history centering on political institutions and ultimately the making of law challenged by a call to include the excluded, as New Left, new social, and new political histories explored lived experience and the politics of raw force. These "new" histories have been in turn been pushed off center stage by a revived cultural history invigorated by critical approaches to symbols, to language, to discourse. I have tried to suggest here that all of these histories engage with the problems of legitimacy and consent; all of these histories can be read in terms of a triptych of relations between the state, civil society, and the outlaw "uncivil" in terms of the agencies of lawmaking deliberation, cultural persuasion, and physical force. If a cultural history focused on the domain of persuasion has gripped the imaginations of a strategic group of rising and established historians there are also signs of a new integration.[99] Just over the horizon and in some of the most noted work that we have available to us lies a creative interpretive slippage across these domains of law, language, and force, and a history centering on the problem of consent in American civil life.

NOTES

The author is indebted to the editors and to Michael Les Benedict, Saul Cornell, Ronald Formisano, Stephen Kern, Ben Mutchler, Michael Neblo, Peter Onuf, Andrew Schocket, Dale Van Kley, and Peter Way variously for readings and conversations that have contributed to this essay, which has been presented in the "American Culture and Politics Series" at Oregon State University; at the SHEAR Annual Meeting, 2001; as a Humanities Inaugural Lecture at Ohio State University; and at the Policy History Seminar at Bowling Green State University.

1. Jürgen Habermas, *The Structural Transformation of the Public Sphere: An Inquiry into a Category of Bourgeois Society*, trans. Thomas Burger (Cambridge, Mass., 1989).

2. Jürgen Habermas, *Between Facts and Norms: Contributions toward a Discourse Theory of Law and Democracy*, trans. William Rehng (Cambridge, Mass., 1996).

3. Here I hope to address the concerns about the lack of attention given to policy and lawmaking in recent writing, articulated by Ronald P. Formisano in "The Concept of Political Culture," *Journal of Interdisciplinary History* 31 (2001): 393–426, and Joel H.

Silbey, "The State and Practice of American Political History at the Millennium: The Nineteenth Century as a Test Case," *Journal of Policy History* 11 (1999): 1–30, while at the same time maintaining equal attention to the cultural history of politics.

4. An important political mode not discussed here involving formal outcomes and unequal relations would be one of "petition," deference, and noblesse oblige. While such "petition"-deference politics might take place in "civil society," very broadly defined to include medieval forms, it would violate the terms of the "public sphere," as defined by Habermas and any of his critics.

5. See Habermas's discussion of "social power" in *Between Facts and Norms*, especially 307–8, 327–31, and 441–42. In *The Structural Transformation*, of course, Habermas describes the market economy, especially in its advanced corporate stage, as undermining a "classical" deliberative public sphere. In his less historical and more normative *Between Facts and Norms* the threat of the market to the deliberative public sphere is still real, but he is willing to concede a greater plurality of voices. For a fuller discussion of his position in *Between Facts and Norms*, see John L. Brooke, "Reason and Passion in the Public Sphere: Habermas and the Cultural Historians," *Journal of Interdisciplinary History* 29 (1998): 43–67.

6. See Habermas, *Between Facts and Norms*, 307. For critiques of his original formulation, see the essays by Nancy Fraser, Mary Ryan, and Geoff Eley in *Habermas and the Public Sphere*, ed. Craig Calhoun (Cambridge, Mass., 1992), 109–42, 259–339, and Habermas's own self-critique, in the same volume, 422–27. For an important response, see Harold Mah, "Phantasies of the Public Sphere: Rethinking the Habermas of Historians," *Journal of Modern History* 72 (2000): 153–82. For a sociological literature that is developing this discussion, see Jeffrey C. Alexander, "Theorizing the 'Modes of Incorporation': Assimilation, Hyphenation, and Multiculturalism as Varieties of Civil Participation," *Sociological Theory* 19 (2001): 237–49; Agnes S. Ku, "Revisiting the Notion of 'Public' in Habermas's Theory—Toward a Theory of Public Credibility," *Sociological Theory* 18 (2000): 216–40; and Eyal Rabinovich, "Gender and the Public Sphere: Alternative Forms of Integration in Nineteenth-Century America," *Sociological Theory* 19 (2001): 344–70.

7. The briefest examination of the published and unpublished records of a state or federal legislature or court makes the complexity of this intra-government deliberative public sphere fully apparent. For examinations of workings of this governmental deliberative public sphere, see William Lee Miller, *Arguing About Slavery: The Great Battle in the United States Congress* (New York, 1996); and L. Ray Gunn, *The Decline of Authority: Public Economic Policy and Political Development in New York, 1800–1860* (Ithaca, 1988). More broadly, it needs to be said that this essay neglects a fuller discussion of the state in relation to the public sphere. Here see the arguments developed in Richard R. John, "Governmental Institutions as Agents of Change: Rethinking American Political Development in the Early Republic, 1787–1835," *Studies in American Political Development* 11 (1997): 347–80; and Michael Schudson, "The 'Public Sphere' and Its Problems: Bringing the State (Back) In," *Notre Dame Journal of Law, Ethics, and Public Policy* 8 (1994): 529–46.

8. My discussion here is shaped by Habermas's procedure analysis of democracy, civil society, and the public sphere, in *Between Facts and Norms*, 287–387. For an important discussion of the "ambiguities" of the early modern public sphere, see James Van Horn Melton, *The Rise of the Public in Enlightenment Europe* (New York, 2001).

9. This bridging is of course already underway in the entire project of the cultural history of American politics, and most explicitly, for my dichotomy of law and language, in Robert Ferguson, *Law and Literature in American Culture* (Cambridge, Mass., 1984).

10. For Habermas's analysis of the transition from "metaphysical" societies, in which legitimacy is grounded in "authoritative norms and values," to modern, "post-metaphysical" societies, in which legitimacy is grounded in communicative discourse, see *Between Facts and Norms*, 23–26, 36–38, 71–72, 97–99, 408; which should be read in relation to his discussion of "representative publicness," in *The Structural Transformation*, 5–14.

11. Judith N. Shklar, *American Citizenship: The Quest for Inclusion* (Cambridge, Mass., 1991); Eric Foner, *The Story of American Democracy* (New York, 1998); Alexander Keyssar, *The Right to Vote: The Contested History of Democracy in the United States* (New York, 2000).

12. Here I follow the very useful discussion by John Ehrenberg in *Civil Society: The Critical History of an Idea* (New York, 1999), 1–54.

13. For the social grounding of a classical republican definition of civil society in one part of early America, see John L. Brooke, *The Heart of the Commonwealth: Society and Political Culture in Worcester County, Massachusetts, 1713–1861* (New York, 1989).

14. Marvin B. Becker, *The Emergence of Civil Society in the Eighteenth Century* (Bloomington, 1994); J. G. A. Pocock, "Conservative Enlightenment and Democratic Revolutions: The American and French Cases in British Perspective," *Government and Opinion* 24 (1989): 81–105.

15. Judith N. Schlar, *Montesquieu* (New York, 1987), 79–83.

16. Cecil P. Courtney, *Montesquieu and Burke* (Oxford, 1963), 58–82; Richard Hofstadter, *The Idea of a Party System: The Rise of Legitimate Opposition in the United States, 1780–1840* (Berkeley, 1969), 29–35.

17. Richard Boyd, "The Unsteady and Precarious Contribution of Individuals: Edmund Burke's Defense of Civil Society," *The Review of Politics* 61 (1999): 465–91; Courtney, *Montesquieu and Burke*, 142–66.

18. Alexis de Tocqueville, *Democracy in America*, ed. Phillips Bradley (New York, 1945), 2:342. See the discussion in Ehrenberg, *Civil Society*, 167–68.

19. Tocqueville, *Democracy in America*, 2:114–15.

20. Most recently, see Robert D. Putnam, *Bowling Alone: The Collapse and Revival of American Community* (New York, 2000), and *Making Democracy Work: Civic Traditions in Modern Italy* (Cambridge, Mass., 1993).

21. Joseph V. Femia, *Gramsci's Political Thought: Hegemony, Consciousness, and the Revolutionary Process* (Oxford, 1981); Ehrenberg, *Civil Society*, 233–50; Grant McConnell, *Private Power and American Democracy* (New York, 1966); Sidney Verba et al., *Voice and*

Inequality: Civic Voluntarism in American Politics (Cambridge, Mass., 1995); and Theda Skocpol, "Unraveling from Above," *American Prospect* 25 (March–April 1996): 20–25.

22. Theda Skocpol et al., "How Americans Became Civic," in *Civic Engagement in American Democracy*, ed. Theda Skocpol and Morris P. Fiorina (New York, 1999), 27–80; Schudson, " 'Public Sphere' and Its Problems"; and Bob Edwards, Michael W. Foley, and Mario Diani, eds., *Beyond Tocqueville: Civil Society and the Social Capital Debate in Comparative Perspective* (Hanover, N.H., 2001).

23. On Rousseau and virtue, see Carol Blum, *Rousseau and the Republic of Virtue: The Language of Politics in the French Revolution* (Ithaca, 1986).

24. My thinking here is shaped by Bruce Ackerman, *We the People. 1: Foundations* (Cambridge, Mass., 1991).

25. Carole Pateman, *The Problem of Political Obligation: A Critical Analysis of Liberal Theory* (New York, 1979), 22, 70–71, 172–78; Harry Beran, *The Consent Theory of Political Obligation* (London, 1987), 154.

26. Pateman, *The Problem of Political Obligation*, 62–76; P. H. Partridge, *Consent and Consensus* (New York, 1971), 21–25, 49–70; Beran, *Consent Theory*, 7–8, 28–29, 54–55, 101–2, 150–55; Don Herzog, *Happy Slaves: A Critique of Consent Theory* (Chicago, 1989), 182–84; Stephen Holmes, *Passions and Constraint: On the Theory of of Liberal Democracy* (Chicago, 1995).

27. Michael Walzer, *Obligations: Essays on Disobedience, War, and Citizenship* (Cambridge, Mass., 1970), 77–166; Linda Kerber, *No Constitutional Right to Be Ladies: Women and the Obligations of Citizenship* (New York, 1998), 221–302; Keyssar, *The Right to Vote*, 37–38, 104–5, 215–17, 246–51, 253–356, 277–81.

28. David Hume, "Of the Original Contract," in *David Hume: Political Essays*, ed. Knud Haakonssen (New York, 1994), 186–201; Adam B. Seligman, *The Idea of Civil Society* (Princeton, 1992), 36–41; Becker, *Emergence*, 60.

29. Gordon S. Wood, *The Creation of the American Republic, 1776–1787* (Chapel Hill, 1969), 264–65; J. C. D. Clark, *The Language of Liberty, 1660–1832: Political Discourse and Social Dynamics in the Anglo-American World* (New York, 1994), 75–93.

30. Courtney, *Montesquieu and Burke*, 144, 157; Boyd, "The Unsteady and Precarious Contribution," 473–81; Jim McCue, *Edmund Burke and Our Present Discontents* (London, 1997), 17, 71–73; Michael Freeman, *Edmund Burke and the Critique of Political Radicalism* (Chicago, 1980), 18–19, 108; J. G. A. Pocock, "Empire, revolution, and an end of early modernity," in *The Varieties of British Political Thought, 1500–1800*, ed. Pocock (New York, 1993), 302–4; R. R. Fessessy, *Burke, Paine, and the Rights of Man: A Difference in Political Opinion* (The Hague, 1963), 108–55; Robert R. Palmer, *The Age of Democratic Revolution* (Princeton, 1959), 1:308–17.

31. François Furet, *Interpreting the French Revolution*, trans. Elberg Forster (New York, 1981); Lynn Hunt, *Politics, Culture, and Class in the French Revolution* (Berkeley, 1984); Keith Michael Baker, *Inventing the French Revolution: Essays on French Political Culture in the Eighteenth Century* (New York, 1990).

32. Lynn Hunt, David Lansky, and Paul Hanson, "The Failure of the Liberal Republic

in France: 1795–1799: The Road to Brumaire," *Journal of Modern History* 51 (1979): 734–59. On Rousseau's rejection of pluralism, see Jules Steinberg, *Locke, Rousseau, and the Idea of Consent: An Inquiry into the Liberal-Democratic Theory of Political Obligation* (Westport, Conn., 1978), 81–102. See also Patrice Higonnet, *Goodness Beyond Virtue: Jacobins During the French Revolution* (Cambridge, Mass., 1998); Isser Woloch, *The New Regime: Transformations of the French Civic Order, 1789–1820s* (New York, 1994), 74–94, 104–12; and Anne Sa'adah, *The Shaping of Liberal Politics in Revolutionary France* (Princeton, 1990). On the French state, association, labor, and academies, see Stanley Hoffman, "Paradoxes of the French Political Community," in Hoffman et al., *In Search of France* (New York, 1963), 1–18; Steven M. Beaudoin, " 'Without Belonging to Public Service': Charities, the State, and Civil Society in Third Republic Bordeaux, 1870–1914," *Journal of Social History* 31 (1998): 671–99; Emmet Kennedy, *A Cultural History of the French Revolution* (New Haven, 1989), 188–92.

33. Pocock, "Empire, revolution, and an end of early modernity," 297–98; J. C. D. Clark, *English Society, 1660–1832*, 2d ed. (New York, 2000); Linda Colley, *Britons: Forging the Nation, 1707–1837* (New Haven, 1992); Kathleen Wilson, *The Sense of the People: Politics, Culture, and Imperialism in England, 1715–1785* (New York, 1995). For the roots of this British culture of arms in the 1757 Militia Act, see Eliga H. Gould, *The Persistence of Empire: British Political Culture in the Age of the American Revolution* (Chapel Hill, 2000), 72–105; Woloch, *The New Regime*, 280–426; Alan Forrest, "Citizenship and Military Service," in *The French Revolution and the Meaning of Citizenship*, ed. Renee Waldinger et al. (Westport, Conn., 1992), 153–65.

34. Alexis de Tocqueville, *The Ancien Régime and the French Revolution*, trans. Stuart Gilbert (New York, 1955); Larry Siedentop, *Tocqueville* (New York, 1994), 24, 140.

35. Timothy H. Breen, *The Character of the Good Ruler: Puritan Political Ideas in New England, 1630–1730* (New Haven, 1970), 14–34, 136–37, 154–57, 266–67; Stephen Innes, *Creating the Commonwealth: The Economic Culture of Puritan New England* (New York, 1995); Seligman, *The Idea of Civil Society*; Gillian Brown, *The Consent of the Governed: The Lockean Legacy in Early American Culture* (Cambridge, Mass., 2001), esp. 31–56; Clark, *Language of Liberty*, 141ff. On the Second Great Awakening, see the classic article by Donald G. Mathews, "The Second Great Awakening as an Organizing Process, 1780–1830: An Hypothesis," *American Quarterly* 21 (1969): 23–43.

36. Timothy H. Breen, "Retrieving Common Sense: Rights, Liberties, and the Religious Public Sphere in Late Eighteenth Century America," in *To Secure the Blessings of Liberty: Rights in American History*, ed. Josephine F. Pacheno (Fairfax, Va., 1993), 55–65; Timothy H. Breen and Timothy Hall, "Structuring Provincial Imagination: The Rhetoric and Experience of Social Change in Eighteenth-century New England," *American Historical Review* 103 (1998): 1411–39; Frank Lambert, *Peddler in Divinity: George Whitefield and the Transatlantic Revivals, 1737–1770* (Princeton, 1994); David P. Nord, "Teleology and News: The Religious Roots of American Journalism, 1630–1730," *Journal of American History* 77 (1990) 9–38; Nord, "The Evangelical Origins of the Mass Media in America, 1815–1835," *Journalism Monographs* 88 (1984): 1–31; Nord, "Religious Read-

ing and Readers in Antebellum America," *Journal of the Early Republic* 15 (1995): 241–73; Hugh Amory and David D. Hall, eds., *The Colonial Book in the Atlantic World*: Vol. 1 of *History of the Book in America* (Worcester and New York, 2000); see also Mark S. Schantz, "Religious Tracts, Evangelical Reform, and the Market Revolution in Antebellum America," *Journal of the Early Republic* 17 (1997): 425–66.

37. Here see G. J. Barker-Benfield, *The Culture of Sensibility: Sex and Society in Eighteenth-Century Britain* (Chicago, 1992); 250–79; Richard Bushman, *The Refinement of America: Persons, Houses, Cities* (New York, 1993); 313–52.

38. Here Madison's role both in religious disestablishment and in forming the Jeffersonian Republican opposition can be set into a much larger picture. For one corner of the country, see Brooke, *The Heart of the Commonwealth*, 158–88, 247–59, which should be read in tandem with Breen and Hall's analysis of the Great Awakening and the Land Bank in "Structuring the Provincial Imagination."

39. Jack P. Greene, *Pursuits of Happiness: The Social Development of the Early Modern British Colonies and the Formation of American Culture* (Chapel Hill, 1988); Jack P. Greene, *The Intellectual Construction of America: Exceptionalism and Identity from 1492 to 1800* (Chapel Hill, 1993); Jack P. Greene, "Social and Cultural Capital in Colonial America: A Case Study," *Journal of Interdisciplinary History* 29 (1999): 491–509; Jack P. Greene, "The Colonial Origins of American Constitutionalism," in *Negotiated Authorities: Essays in Colonial Political and Constitutional History* (Charlottesville, 1994), 25–42; Jack P. Greene, "From the Perspective of Law: Context and Legitimacy in the Origins of the American Revolution," in *Interpreting Early America: Historiographical Essays* (Charlottesville, 1996), 467–92.

40. Further grounds for labeling Greene "Burkean" lie in his opposition to the argument advanced by J. C. D. Clark that the American Revolution was in some measure a religious civil war between a Blackstonean Anglican establishment and the wider community of British Protestant dissenters. See Jack P. Greene, "The Revolution Revisited," in *Interpreting Early America: Historiographical Essays* (Charlottesville, 1996), 493–507.

41. Greene, "Social and Cultural Capital," 501–2.

42. Gordon S. Wood, *The Radicalism of the American Revolution* (New York, 1992); for specific critical references to Wood's thesis, see Jack P. Greene, "The American Revolution," *American Historical Review* 105 (2000): 93–102, esp. 100–102.

43. J. R. Pole, *Political Representation in England and the Origins of the American Republic* (New York, 1966), 343–44. Here I am sidestepping, for the moment, the old and important issue of deference in colonial politics. If I were to take a stand on this issue, it would be to argue that, while colonial Americans were probably *not* as behaviorally deferential as some have made them out to be, outside of the New England town meeting and the standing practice of instruction, they did not have the institutional vehicles (in the public sphere) that would allow them to engage their anti-authoritarian attitudes with the deliberative process. The building of these institutional vehicles, namely press and party, is a big part of the story of the Revolution and the early republic. On the issue of deference, see Michael Zuckerman, "Tocqueville, Turner, and Turds: Four Stories of Manners in Early America," *Journal of American History* 85 (1998): 13–42,

and the commentaries by Kathleen Brown, John Murrin, and Robert Gross following in that issue, 77–97.

44. See Gary B. Nash, "Also There at the Creation: Going Beyond Gordon S. Wood," *William and Mary Quarterly*, 3d ser., 46 (1987): 602–11; Barbara Clark Smith, "The Adequate Revolution," and Michael Zuckerman, "Rhetoric, Reality, and the Revolution: The Genteel Radicalism of Gordon Wood," both in the *William and Mary Quarterly* 51 (1994): 684–702; Alfred F. Young, "American Historians Confront the Transforming Hand of Revolution," in Ronald Hoffman and Peter J. Albert, eds., *The Transforming Hand of Revolution: Reconsidering the American Revolution as a Social Movement* (Charlottesville, Va., 1996), 346–494.

45. Michael Warner, *The Letters of the Republic: Publication and the Public Sphere in Eighteenth-Century America* (Cambridge, Mass., 1990).

46. Amory and Hall, *Colonial Book in The Atlantic World*, 10. I would argue that if there was no "colonial public sphere," the rudiments of urban public spheres were emerging in Boston by 1690 and in New York and Philadelphia by the 1720s. See John L. Brooke, "Ancient Lodges and Self-Created Societies: Voluntary Association and the Public Sphere in the Early Republic," in *Launching the "Extended Republic": The Federalist Era*, ed. Ronald Hoffman and Peter J. Albert (Charlottesville, 1996), 284–88.

47. Christopher Grasso, *A Speaking Aristocracy: Transforming Public Discourse in Eighteenth-Century Connecticut* (Chapel Hill, 1999).

48. Richard D. Brown, "The Emergence of Urban Society in Rural Massachusetts, 1760–1820," *Journal of American History* 61 (1974): 29–51; Stephen C. Bullock, *Revolutionary Brotherhood: Freemasonry and the Transformation of the American Social Order, 1730–1820* (Chapel Hill, 1996); Brooke, "Ancient Lodges and Self-Created Societies"; John L. Brooke, "To Be 'Read by the Whole People': Press, Party, and Public Sphere in the United States, 1790–1840," *Proceedings of the American Antiquarian Society*, 110 (2000): 41–118; Peter Clark, *British Clubs and Societies, 1580–1800: The Origins of an Associational World* (Oxford, 2000), 388–420; David Copeland, "America, 1750–1820," in *Press, Politics and the Public Sphere in Europe and North America, 1760–1820*, ed. Hannah Barker and Simon Burrows (Cambridge, 2002), 145–46. The classic text here may well be Richard L. Merritt, *Symbols of American Community, 1735–1775* (New Haven, 1966).

49. Michael Kwass, "A Kingdom of Taxpayers: State Formation, Privilege, and Political Culture in Eighteenth-Century France," *Journal of Modern History* 70 (1998): 295–339.

50. For England, see David Zaret, *Origins of Democratic Culture: Printing, Petitions, and the Public Sphere in Early-Modern England* (Princeton, 2000). For an early argument of this position, see Mervyn James, *Family, Lineage, and Civil Society: A Study of Society, Politics, and Mentality in the Durham Region, 1500–1640* (Oxford, 1974). For a comprehensive critical overview, see Ian Atherton, "The Press and Popular Opinion," in Barry Coward, ed., *A Companion to Stuart Britain* (Malden, Mass., 2003), 88-110.

51. Jaime E. Rodríguez O., *The Independence of Spanish America* (New York, 1998), 19–36; Lester D. Langley, *The Americas in the Age of Revolution, 1750–1850* (New Haven,

1996), 147–65; Benedict Anderson, *Imagined Communities: Reflections on the Origins and Spread of Nationalism*, rev. ed. (New York, 1991), 47–65.

52. James Kettner, *The Development of American Citizenship*; Michael Kammen, "The American Revolution as a *Crise de Conscience*: The Case of New York," in *Society, Freedom, and Conscience: The American Revolution in Virginia, Massachusetts, and New York*, ed. Richard M. Jellison (New York, 1976), 125–89; Anne Fairfax Withington, *Toward a More Perfect Union: Virtue and the Formation of American Republics* (New York, 1991).

53. On slavery as a state of war, see Peter S. Onuf, " 'To Declare Them a Free and Independant People': Race, Slavery, and National Identity in Jefferson's Thought," *Journal of the Early Republic* 18 (1998): 1–46.

54. Jürgen Habermas, "Further Reflections on the Public Sphere," in Calhoun, *Habermas and the Public Sphere* (Cambridge, Mass., 1994), 421–61, esp. 422–27. See above, note 6.

55. Most important here, see Kimberley K. Smith, *The Dominion of Voice: Riot, Reason, and Romance in Antebellum Politics* (Lawrence, Kans.), 1999. There is an emerging countervailing position, arguing that Habermas never intended deliberation to be exclusively rational. This position blurs but does not erase my distinction between deliberation and persuasion in the public sphere. Here see the work of Michael A. Neblo and Michael Steffen, presented at the Ohio State Political Science Seminar, November 27, 2001: "Impassioned Democracy: The Role of Emotion in Deliberative Theory."

56. For an often caustic critique of cultural studies on related grounds, see Steven Watts, "The Idiocy of American Studies: Poststructuralism, Language, and Politics in the Age of Self-Fulfillment," *American Quarterly* 43 (1991): 625–60.

57. Edmund S. Morgan, *Inventing the People: The Rise of Popular Sovereignty in England and America* (New York, 1988), 13–15. On Gramscian notions of hegemony, I find Femia, *Gramsci's Political Thought*, most useful; see also T. J. Jackson Lears, "The Concept of Cultural Hegemony: Problems and Possibilities," *American Historical Review* 90 (1985): 567–93.

58. Habermas, *Between Facts and Norms*, 295.

59. For Habermas and Rousseau, see Douglas Kellner, "Habermas, the Public Sphere, and Democracy," in *Perspectives on Habermas*, ed. Lewis Edwin Hahn (Chicago, 2000), 259–88, esp. 261; Kenneth Baynes, "Democracy and *Rechtsstaat*: Habermas's *Faktizität und Geltung*," in *The Cambridge Companion to Habermas*, ed. Stephen K. White (New York, 1995), 201–32, esp. 201.

60. Habermas, *Between Facts and Norms*, 100–103; Thomas McCarthy, "Practical Discourse: On the Relation of Morality to Politics," in Craig Calhoun, ed., *Habermas and the Public Sphere* (Cambridge, Mass., 1994), 54, 59.

61. Habermas, *Between Facts and Norms*, 307–8.

62. Ibid., 288.

63. In this discussion I am eliding the complexities of the federal structure of American politics in the interest of simplicity. A full discussion of state and civil society in America, particularly in light of Tocqueville's famous assumption of a weak American state and a

strong civil society, would have to spell out the interrelationships of persuasion, delibera-tion, and "the state" at the level of both the federal government and the state govern-ments, as well as primate cities and rural county seats, all of which had their particular but interlocking articulation with the public sphere.

64. Here it might be noted that throughout this paper I have avoided the dichotomy between "public" and "private," mostly by abandoning the idea of the "private." It may be that the boundary between deliberation and persuasion is more useful than that between "public" and "private." Here I have been influenced by the ways in which Karen Hansen and Catherine Allgor have discussed a "social sphere" intervening between the formal public sphere and the private sphere of domesticity. I would suggest that the "social sphere" and the private domestic sphere should be seen as protected spaces in civil society, embedded in—and perhaps the main context of—the domain of persuasion in the public sphere. See Karen V. Hansen, *A Very Social Time: Crafting Community in Antebellum New England* (Berkeley, 1994), and Catherine Allgor, *Parlor Politics: In Which the Ladies of Washington Help Build a City and a Government* (Charlottesville, 2000).

65. Habermas, *Between Facts and Norms*, 307–8.

66. Habermas, *The Structural Transformation*, 5–14.

67. Carroll Smith-Rosenberg's "Discovering the Subject of the 'Great Constitutional Discussion,' 1786–1789," *Journal of American History* 79 (1992): 841–73, is virtually the paradigmatic essay in the analysis of the deployment of culture to forge tacit content in the early republic.

68. Habermas, *The Structural Transformation*, 55–56.

69. David D. Hall, *Worlds of Wonder, Days of Judgment: Popular Religious Belief in Early New England* (New York, 1989). For an exception to this rule, see Philip H. Round, *By Nature and By Custom Cursed: Transatlantic Civil Discourse and New England Cultural Production, 1620–1660* (Hanover, 1999).

70. Warner, *The Letters of the Republic*; David Shields, *Oracles of Empire: Politics and Empire in British America* (Chicago, 1990); David W. Conroy, *In Public Houses: Drink and the Revolution of Authority in Colonial Massachusetts* (Chapel Hill, 1995). See also Steven C. Bullock, *Revolutionary Brotherhood: Freemasonry and the Transformation of the American Social Order, 1730–1840* (Chapel Hill, 1996); Peter Thompson, *Rum Punch and Revolution: Taverngoing and Public Life in Eighteenth-Century Philadelphia* (Philadelphia, 1999); Charles E. Clark, *The Public Prints: The Newspaper in Anglo-American Culture, 1665–1740* (New York, 1994); Ian K. Steele, *The English Atlantic, 1675–1740: An Exploration of Communication and Community* (New York, 1986); David Shields, *Civil Tongues and Polite Letters in British America* (Chapel Hill, 1997).

71. Edmund S. Morgan, *The Stamp Act Crisis: Prologue to Revolution* (Chapel Hill, 1953); Bernard Bailyn, *The Ideological Origins of the American Revolution* (Cambridge, Mass., 1967).

72. Merritt, *Symbols of American Community*; Peter Shaw, *American Patriots and the Rituals of Revolution* (Cambridge, Mass., 1981), Anne Fairfax Withington, *Toward a More*

Perfect Union: Virtue and the Formation of American Republics (New York, 1991); T. H. Breen, "Narrative of Commercial Life: Consumption, Ideology, and Community on the Eve of the American Revolution," *William and Mary Quarterly* 50 (1993): 471–501; Jay Fliegelman, *Declaring Independence: Jefferson, Natural Language, and the Culture of Performance* (Stanford, 1993); Christopher Looby, *Voicing America: Language, Literacy Form, and the Origins of the United States* (Chicago, 1996); David Waldstreicher, *In the Midst of Perpetual Fetes: The Making of American Nationalism* (Chapel Hill, 1997).

73. George Rudé, *The Crowd in History: A Study of Popular Disturbances in France and England* (New York, 1964), E. P. Thompson, *Customs in Common: Studies in Traditional Popular Culture* (New York, 1991); and Emanuel Le Roy Ladurie, *Carnival in Romans* (New York, 1979).

74. Stephen Nissenbaum, *The Battle for Christmas* (New York, 1996); Sterling Stuckey, "African Spirituality and Cultural Practice in Colonial New York," in *Inequality in Early America*, ed. Carla Gardina Pestana and Sharon V. Salinger (Hanover, N.H., 1999), 160–81; Peter Stallybrass and Allon White, *The Politics and Poetics of Transgression* (Ithaca, 1986), 171–90.

75. T. H. Breen, "Ideology and Nationalism on the Eve of the American Revolution: Revisions Once More in Need of Revising," *Journal of American History* 84 (1997): 13–39; Alan Taylor, " 'A Kind of Warr': The Contest for Land on the Northeastern Frontier, 1750–1820," *William and Mary Quarterly*, 3d ser., 46 (1989): 3–26; Reeve Huston, *Land and Freedom: Rural Society, Popular Protest, and Party Politics in Antebellum New York* (New York, 2000); Charles W. McCurdy, *The Anti-Rent Era in New York Law and Politics, 1839–1865* (Chapel Hill, 2001). McCurdy's book, it should be noted, argues that New York land law was sealed off effectively from either deliberation or persuasion.

76. Orlando Patterson, *Slavery and Social Death: A Comparative Study* (Cambridge Mass., 1982); Onuf, " 'To Declare Them a Free and Independant People' "; Sally E. Hadden, *Slave Patrols: Law and Violence in Virginia and the Carolinas* (Cambridge, Mass., 2001); Christopher Waldrep, *Roots of Disorder: Race and Criminal Justice in the American South, 1817–1880* (Urbana, 1998); on rebellions, see Douglas R. Egerton, *Gabriel's Rebellion: The Virginia Slave Conspiracies of 1800 and 1802* (Chapel Hill, 1993); Stephen B. Oates, *The Fires of Jubilee: Nat Turner's Fierce Rebellion* (New York, 1975). The term "civil death" was first applied to the legal condition of women in the nineteenth century.

77. Eugene D. Genovese, *Roll, Jordan, Roll: The World the Slaves Made* (New York, 1974), 25–49. Genovese's analysis, and its implications for defining and extending the boundaries of civil society, can be compared with the careful attention to the technicalities of the law that Edward P. Thompson found in the enforcement of the Black Act: *Whigs and Hunters: The Origins of the Black Act* (New York, 1975).

78. Philip D. Morgan, *Slave Counterpoint: Black Culture in the Eighteenth-Century Chesapeake & Lowcountry* (Chapel Hill, 1998), 358–72.

79. Genovese, *Roll, Jordan, Roll*, 49–70, 202–9; John Blassingame, *The Slave Community: Plantation Life in the Antebellum South*, 2d ed. (New York, 1979), 77–80, 344–60;

Sylvia R. Frey, *Water From the Rock: Black Resistance in a Revolutionary Age* (Princeton, 1991), 243–83; Sylvia R. Frey and Betty Wood, *Come Shouting to Zion: African American Protestantism in the American South and British Caribbean to 1830* (Chapel Hill, 1998).

80. Willie Lee Rose, *Rehearsal for Reconstruction: The Port Royal Experiment* (Indianapolis, 1964); Eric Foner, *Reconstruction: America's Unfinished Revolution, 1863–1877* (New York, 1988); Eric Foner, *Nothing but Freedom: Emancipation and Its Legacy* (Baton Rouge, 1983).

81. Nancy Isenberg, *Sex and Citizenship in Antebellum America* (Chapel Hill, 1998), 33–34, 43, 55–56.

82. Paula Baker, "The Domestication of Politics: Women and American Political Society, 1780–1920," *American Historical Review* 89 (1984): 620–47. See also Glenna Matthews, *The Rise of Public Woman: Women's Power and Women's Place in the United States, 1630–1970* (New York, 1992); Michael McGerr, "Political Style and Women's Power, 1830–1930," *Journal of American History* 77 (1990): 864–85.

83. Mary Ryan, *Women in Public: Between Banners and Ballots: 1725–1880* (Baltimore, 1990); Nancy A. Hewitt, *Women's Activism and Social Change, Rochester, New York, 1822–1872* (Ithaca, 1984); Julie Roy Jeffrey, *The Great Silent Army of Abolition: Ordinary Women in the Antislavery Movement* (Chapel Hill, 1998); and Lori D. Ginzberg, *Women and the Work of Benevolence: Morality, Class, and Benevolence in the Nineteenth-Century United States* (New Haven, 1990), 98. Recently Elizabeth R. Varon has extended this essentially northern literature to southern women, in *We Mean to Be Counted: White Women and Politics in Antebellum Virginia* (Chapel Hill, 1998), 10–70. See also Nancy Isenberg, "The Personal is Political: Gender, Feminism, and the Politics of Discourse Theory," *American Quarterly* 44 (1992): 449–58; Rabinovich, "Gender and the Public Sphere"; and Carol Lasser, "Beyond Separate Spheres: The Power of Public Opinion," *Journal of the Early Republic* 21 (2001): 115–24.

84. Barker-Benfield, *The Culture of Sensibility*; see also John Brewer, *The Pleasures of the Imagination: English Culture in the Eighteenth Century* (New York, 1997), esp. 113–22.

85. Brown, *Consent of the Governed*, 112, 123, and 177–78.

86. Thomas L. Haskell, "Capitalism and the Origins of Humanitarian Sensibility, Parts 1 and 2," *American Historical Review* 90 (1985): 339–61, 547–66; Karen Halttunen, "Humanitarianism and the Pornography of Pain in Anglo-American Culture," *American Historical Review* 100 (1995): 303–24; Elizabeth R. Clark, " 'The Sacred Rights of the Weak': Pain, Sympathy, and the Culture of Individual Rights in Antebellum America," *Journal of American History* 82 (1995): 463–93; Markman Ellis, *The Politics of Sensibility: Race, Gender, and Commerce in the Commercial Novel* (New York, 1996), 49–128; and David N. Gellman, "Race, the Public Sphere, and Abolition in Late Eighteenth-Century New York," *Journal of the Early Republic* 20 (2000): 607–36. These themes were broached in Winthrop D. Jordan, *White over Black: American Attitudes Toward the Negro, 1550–1812* (Chapel Hill, 1968), 365–72.

87. Fredrika J. Teute, "Roman Matron on the Banks of the Tiber Creek: Margaret

Bayard Smith and the Politicization of Spheres in the Nation's Capital," and Jan Lewis, "Politics and the Ambivalence of the Private Sphere: Women in Early Washington, D.C.," both in *A Republic for the Ages: The United States Capitol and the Political Culture of the Early Republic*, ed. Donald R. Kennon (Charlottesville, 1999), 89–151; Allgor, *Parlor Politics*; Susan Branson, *These Fiery Frenchified Dames: Women and Political Culture in Early National Philadelphia* (Philadelphia, 2001).

88. I give no consideration here to the thesis that we ought to "bring the state back in." In its starkest form, this thesis argues for the full autonomy of the state, and thus—in the terms developed here—for an impermeable boundary between the American state and civil society. Whatever the problems of defining the state in the United States, here utterly neglected, I have my doubts about the legitimacy of an autonomous state. This issue becomes of considerable importance in the mid-to-late twentieth-century era of the "imperial presidency." Any judgment about state autonomy is a judgment about one of the boundaries in the model proposed here.

89. Waldstreicher, *In the Midst of Perpetual Fetes*, 131–33, 136; Saul Cornell, *The Other Founders: Anti-Federalism and the Dissenting Tradition in America, 1788–1828* (Chapel Hill, 1999), 173–74, 195–99; Albrecht Koschnik, "The Democratic Societies of Philadelphia and the Limits of the American Public Sphere, circa 1793–1795," *William and Mary Quarterly*, 3d ser., 58 (2001): 615–36. See also Brooke, "Ancient Lodges and Self-Created Societies," 309–16.

90. Jeffrey L. Pasley, *"The Tyranny of Printers": Newspaper Politics in the Early American Republic* (Charlottesville, 2001); Richard R. John, *Spreading the News: The American Postal System from Franklin to Morse* (Cambridge, Mass., 1995).

91. Pasley, *"The Tyranny of Printers"*; Waldstreicher, *In the Midst of Perpetual Fetes*; Waldstreicher and Steven R. Grossbart, "Abraham Bishop's Vocation; Or, the Mediation of Jeffersonian Politics," *Journal of the Early Republic* 18 (1998): 617–57.

92. Richard L. McCormick, *The Party Period and Public Policy: American Politics from the Age of Jackson to the Progressive Era* (New York, 1986); Gunn, *The Decline of Authority*; John Ashworth, *"Agrarians and Aristocrats": Party Political Ideology in the United States, 1837–1846* (New York, 1987).

93. Lee Benson, *The Concept of Jacksonian Democracy: New York as a Test Case* (Princeton, 1961).

94. Glenn C. Altschuler and Stuart M. Blumin, *Rude Republic: American and their Politics in the Nineteenth Century* (Princeton, 2000).

95. David Waldstreicher, "Federalism, the Style of Politics, and the Politics of Style," and Rosemarie Zagarri, "Gender and the First Party System," both in *Federalists Reconsidered*, ed. Doron Ben-Atar and Barbara G. Oberg (Charlottesville, 1998), 99–134; Ronald J. and Mary S. Zboray, "Whig Women, Politics, and Culture in the Campaign of 1840: Three Perspectives from Massachusetts," *Journal of the Early Republic* 17 (1997): 277–315; Pasley, *"The Tyranny of Printers,"* 248–57; Daniel Walker Howe, "The Evangelical Movement and Political Culture in the North during the Second Party System," *Journal of*

American History 77 (1990): 1216–39. One might go back to articles written in the 1930s by Evarts B. Greene and Dixon Ryan Fox describing the Second Great Awakening as a "Counter-Revolution," to reach the historiographical roots of the argument.

96. Daniel Walker Howe, *The Political Culture of the American Whigs* (Chicago, 1979), 227–37.

97. Here I am drawing on Waldstreicher, *In the Midst of Perpetual Fetes*; Pasley, *"The Tyranny of Printers"*; Jean H. Baker, *Affairs of Party: The Political Culture of the Northern Democrats in the Mid-Nineteenth Century* (Ithaca, 1983); and Heather Nathans, personal communication, August 8, 2001.

98. David Grimsted, *American Mobbing, 1828–1861: Toward Civil War* (New York, 1998); Leonard L. Richards, *The Slave Power: The Free North and Southern Dominion, 1780–1860* (Baton Rouge, 2000); Smith, *Dominion of Voice*.

99. For only one example, published while this essay was in the final stages of revision, see Liette Godlow, "Delegitimizing Democracy: 'Civic Slackers,' the Cultural Turn, and the Possibilities of Politics," *Journal of American History* 89 (2002): 922–57; see pages 927–29 for a particularly useful theoretical-thematic discussion.

9

Beyond the Myth of Consensus

The Struggle to Define the Right
to Bear Arms in the Early Republic

The political history of the early republic has undergone an impressive renaissance in recent years. One of the distinguishing features of this newest version of a "new political history" has been the way it has self-consciously shifted its focus away from the elite world of the founders. The impact of the new scholarship has profoundly altered the intellectual landscape of early American history. Americans from all walks of life have been restored to their proper place as actors in the dramatic political life of the new nation. It would be unfortunate, however, if the move beyond the founders led historians to abandon constitutional thought in this vital and formative period of American history. In the rush to reconstruct the elaborate rituals of political life in the early republic, constitutional questions can easily be shunted aside.

Constitutional history is at much greater risk of being neglected than political history. As long as biographies of leading founding fathers top the best-seller lists it is unlikely that the political history of the early republic will ever lack attention. Indeed, despite jeremiads lamenting the plight of political history in a profession now dominated by social and cultural history, the number of dissertations in political history has almost kept pace with newer fields such as gender history or cultural history. The same cannot be said about the number of dissertations completed in legal and constitutional history, which continue to trail far behind political history.[1] For some younger scholars constitutional history is tainted by its allegedly elitist orientation.[2] The one notable exception to this rule is the constitutional history of race and gender, which continues to enjoys some cachet. More traditional topics in constitutional history—issues such as federalism or the right to bear arms—have been largely neglected by younger historians. While a number of eminent senior scholars remain active in the field of constitutional history, a new generation of constitutional historians has not emerged to take their place in history departments.[3]

Meanwhile, the world of the founders continues to be an immensely important subject for legal academics.[4] Much of this legal scholarship has been driven by the desire to identify the original meaning of various provisions of the Constitution. Originalist legal scholarship, like all exercises in law office history, has little to offer scholars working on the early republic. By contrast, the new constitutional historicism that has emerged within legal scholarship can illuminate a number of important issues of interest to historians.[5] In contrast to the static quality of originalist constitutional theory, which is obsessed with the founding moment and is based on a notion of consensus that few historians would accept, the new constitutional historicism stresses the contingent and contested nature of early American constitutionalism and recognizes the importance of the early republic as a transitional period in which competing constitutional visions of law vied for dominance.[6]

It would be a mistake to return to a model of constitutional history focused entirely on a handful of texts written by members of a small elite. Yet simply casting these constitutional texts aside because of their allegedly elite bias leads to another type of historical distortion. The structure of the early American public sphere, particularly its printed dimensions, meant that many of these texts were available to a broad audience. Although one cannot assume that everything written by Federalists and Anti-Federalists was equally influential, particularly among non-elites, one cannot simply dismiss such texts as irrelevant. Rather, one must try to reconstruct the diverse patterns of reading and uncover which, if any, of the texts produced by elites did influence popular thought. Equally important, one must pay attention to how texts produced by ordinary citizens may have shaped the ideas of elites and influenced other groups in American society. Only by analyzing the process of intertextual reading and writing, the circulation of texts and ideas, can historians appreciate the role of constitutionalism in the early republic. To do so one must unite the traditional top-down perspective of constitutional history with the bottom-up perspective of social and cultural history. Only when these two halves are reunited can a comprehensive history of early American constitutionalism be written.[7]

Constitutionalism was essential to American political culture in the early republic. In the period between 1776 and 1828, Americans from all walks of life were drawn into a wide-ranging debate about the nature of constitutional government. In 1787 Americans were called upon to deliberate on the merits of a new federal constitution that would replace the old Articles of Confederation with a more powerful central government. Building on a public debate that had begun in 1776, Americans entered into lively discussion over the nature of government and the best means to secure the blessings of liberty. The Constitution was debated in newspapers, taverns, and town squares. It is impossible to understand early American political life outside of the context of these discussions.

In the view of poet, politician, and essayist Joel Barlow, a properly framed constitution "ought to serve not only as a guide to the legislative body, but as a political grammar to all the citizens. The greatest service to be expected from it is, that it should concentrate the maxims, and form the habits of thinking, for the whole community." Barlow's statement captures an important element of elite constitutional thought. Constitutionalism was no less important to the Massachusetts tavern keeper William Manning. "I have," Manning wrote, "been a constant reader of public newspapers and have closely attended to men and measures ever since—through war, the operation of paper money, framing constitutions, and making and construing laws." Manning's belief in the centrality of constitutionalism to political life is evidenced in his recommendation that the very first issue of a monthly magazine he hoped to start to rally together the "farmers, mechanics, and laborers" would have reprinted "both the state and federal constitutions, complete with all their amendments, and some of the principles on which they were founded." The fact that the Constitution provided a common language for all Americans should not obscure the fact that Americans continued to speak that language with a variety of accents that reflected the persistent regional and class divisions in American society.[8]

The ratification debates focused elite and popular attention on constitutional issues and resulted in a remarkable outpouring of writing on this subject. After the Constitution was ratified, Federalists celebrated its genius, while others continued to harbor suspicions about the new frame of government. In the view of William Manning, the Constitution "appears too much like a fiddle, with but few strings, but so fixed as that the ruling majority may play any tune they please upon it."[9] Manning's image captured the contingent and open-ended quality of America's new constitutional text. Although the cultural divide separating Barlow from Manning was significant in many respects, both men were steeped in America's evolving culture of constitutionalism. Neither man was a passive consumer of constitutional ideas. Both eagerly read the writings of others writers, particularly the many newspaper essayists who rushed forward to offer their views on the new Constitution. The line separating readers and authors was easily crossed by individuals who shifted from being the consumers of constitutional texts to the producers of their own constitutional commentaries. Although American public discourse was cast in a constitutional idiom, this language was not hegemonic. Rather, as Barlow's metaphor suggested, it functioned as a flexible conceptual vocabulary and grammar for Americans. To return to Manning's own musical metaphor, one might describe the constitutional discourse of the new republic as polyphonic. Although constitutionalism certainly set limits on the range of political action, it also facilitated and energized various groups to articulate their aspirations.

Historians have come to recognize that the founders were deeply divided over many basic constitutional questions such as the meaning of federalism or the nature of freedom of the press.[10] Given the tensions that characterized these questions, it seems odd that so much modern scholarship would view something as potentially revolutionary as the right to bear arms in consensual terms. Given the intensity of political conflict in the decades after ratification, it would be astonishing if there were no disagreement over the meaning of this right. Current scholarship on the Second Amendment would have us believe that the people who opposed each other over the meaning of the First Amendment during the Alien and Sedition Crisis had somehow reached a consensus on the meaning of the Second Amendment. Such a view ought to strike anyone with even the slightest familiarity with this period as a deeply problematic assumption. As is so often true with so many of the claims made in modern Second Amendment scholarship, this assumption turns out to have little to do with the complex history of the founding era, and owes more to the contemporary dynamics of the debate over gun control in American politics.[11]

A fresh examination of the Second Amendment seems particularly important for scholars interested in the early republic. A serious historical exploration of the Second Amendment provides a fresh way of examining a variety of topics, ranging from the consolidation of the early federal system to the tensions between elite and popular constitutional thought in the years after ratification. Indeed, no topic in early American constitutionalism better illuminates the complex nature of early American constitutional history than the Second Amendment.

CONSTITUTIONALISM AND THE RIGHT TO BEAR ARMS
IN THE FOUNDING ERA

Americans feared standing armies and venerated the ideal of the militia. The militia not only provided a means of checking the danger posed by a powerful standing army, but it was viewed by many as an institution absolutely essential to the survival of a virtuous republic. Although there was considerable disagreement over how much virtue was necessary for the survival of a republic, at a very minimum there was a broad consensus that a republic had to possess enough virtue to ensure that its citizens would take up arms when necessary to meet internal and external threats. A republic could only survive if citizens were willing to bear arms in defense of the state and their communities. In an age without organized police forces and when the specter of slave rebellions and popular insurrections haunted the imaginations of many of the founders, the importance of a well-regulated militia could not be understated. Historians have long recognized that the right to bear arms reflected the influence of civic republican ideals in the founding era. In addition to this vital political context, bearing arms must understood in a legal context. Bearing arms was not only a right, but it was a legal obligation.[12] Thus, the 1776 Pennsylvania Constitution affirms

> That every member of society hath a right to be protected in the enjoyment of life, liberty and property, and therefore is bound to contribute his proportion towards the expence of that protection, and yield his personal service, when necessary, or an equivalent thereto: But no part of a man's property can be justly taken from him, or applied to public uses, without his own consent, or that of his legal representatives: Nor can any man who is conscientiously scrupulous of bearing arms, be justly compelled thereto, if he will pay such equivalent: Nor are the people bound by any laws, but such as they have in like manner assented to, for their common good.[13]

In exchange for the protection provided by the rule of law, citizens were expected to "bear arms for the defence of themselves and the State." Bearing arms as part of a well-regulated militia was in essence a form of taxation. While Pennsylvanians explicitly prohibited government from taking private property without consent, the state specifically exempted militia service from this prohibition. The state could require individuals to outfit themselves with muskets and ammunition and had no legal obligation to compensate citizens for their expenditures. Perhaps the best way to translate this conception into modern terms would be to describe it as a civic right.

In contrast to genuinely individual rights such as freedom of speech, civic rights such as bearing arms were far more limited in scope. While citizens can be compelled to bear arms, they cannot be compelled to publish or speak. The only other provision that bears a close analogy to bearing arms is jury service. Both are rights exercised by citizens in a collective manner for a distinctly public purpose and require the sanction of the state to enjoy legal force. Guns and words were different in other ways. While prior restraints on the press were unacceptable to the founders, certain restrictions on gun ownership were not.[14] Americans of the founding era showed no hesitation in using loyalty oaths to disarm large portions of the population, but they were unwilling to impose prior restraints on political speech or publishing. Even the infamous Sedition Act did not act as a prior restraint. Laws requiring that gunpowder be safely stored posed no constitutional problem. It is impossible to think of a similar type of legal restraint on print.[15] Achieving the ideal of a well-regulated militia required extensive government involvement in the lives of citizens. The effectiveness of the militia meant that governments could require citizens to participate in mandatory musters. Fines might be imposed for failing to report to muster. Militia returns were compiled to keep track of the militia's armaments. Government prescribed the type of weapons it required of members of the militia. The regulatory framework necessary to create a well-regulated militia makes any comparison with freedom of the press seem even more far-fetched.[16]

Constitutional thought in the founding era was perfectly compatible with a variety of ascriptive limits on citizenship. Not every individual was a citizen in the republican polity. The differences between the rights accorded citizens and those accorded individuals could be quite significant in the founding era.[17] In contrast to a fundamental individual right such as freedom of religion, a civic right such as bearing arms could be restricted to a portion of the citizenry deemed virtuous enough to exercise that right in a responsible manner. While women, or free Africans, might claim certain individual rights, they were not usually accorded civic rights. Defining the portion of the polity who would be accorded such civic rights was a political, not constitutional, question.[18]

The fear that the Constitution would allow the federal government to create a powerful standing army that might become a tool of tyranny was frequently voiced during ratification. It is impossible to understand the argument between Federalists and Anti-Federalists over the meaning of the right to bear arms without noting that this issue was closely connected to the larger debate over the meaning of federalism. Anti-Federalists believed that the new Constitution threatened the survival of the state militias. As Luther Martin, a leading Maryland Anti-Federalist, noted, "When a government *wishes* to deprive their citizens of freedom, and reduce them to slavery, it *generally makes use of a standing army* for that purpose, and *leaves the militia in a situation as contemptible as possible, [lest] they might oppose its arbitrary designs*."[19] In contrast to a standing army, Anti-Federalists championed the ideal of a militia drawn from the ranks of citizens, at least those judged to have sufficient virtue to bear arms. Such a militia would never threaten liberty because it would always be composed of independent yeomen who would only take up arms when the good of society demanded that they leave their families and farms to defend liberty.

The Anti-Federalist claim that the Constitution threatened to undermine the state militias was vigorously disputed by Federalists who asserted that the states would continue to retain significant control of their militia. Although some Federalists doubted its effectiveness, a number of Federalist writers continued to praise the ideal of the militia. This view was concisely stated by Federalist Tench Coxe: "THE POWERS OF THE SWORD ARE IN THE HANDS OF THE YEOMANRY OF AMERICA."[20] Federalist Noah Webster echoed these sentiments: "Before a standing army can rule, the people must be disarmed; as they are in almost every kingdom in Europe. The supreme power in America cannot enforce unjust laws by the sword; because the whole body of the people are armed, and constitute a force superior to any band of regular troops that can be, on any pretence, raised in the United States."[21]

None of the major spokesmen for either side in the debate over ratification argued against the idea that the states ought to retain some measure of control of the militia. Anti-Federalists articulated a strong states' rights conception of the militia, while Federalists believed in a weak version of states' rights, a view that acknowledged a limited role for the states in maintaining the militia, but ceded ultimate control over the militia to the federal government.[22] The main disagreement between Federalists and Anti-Federalists during ratification was over the impact that the Constitution would have on the militia.[23] As was true for nearly every point of contention between Federalists and Anti-Federalists, the issue of federalism was entangled with the debate over the militia.

In the Virginia ratification convention, George Mason captured the essence of the Anti-Federalist fears about the danger posed by the Constitution to the right to bear arms when he wrote, "The militia may be here destroyed by that method which has been practised in other parts of the world before; that is by rendering them useless—by disarming them."[24] Mason's primary fear was not that government would seize arms, but that government would fail to arm the people. The same theme was sounded by Patrick Henry when he asserted that "the great object is that every man may be armed." It is important to place Henry's and Mason's fears in context. Henry not only believed in an armed citizenry; he also bewailed the fact that Virginians had failed in their effort to arm the people. "We have learned, by experience," he lamented, "that necessary as it is to have arms, and though our Assembly has, by a succession of laws for many years, endeavored to have the militia completely armed, it is still far from being the case."[25] Henry's perception of the failure of Virginia to adequately arm its citizenry provides an indispensable context for understanding the origins of the Second Amendment. For Henry and Mason, the great danger of disarmament came not from potential government action, but rather from government inaction. Although Henry and Mason believed that many militia men would supply their own weapons, each realized that simply depending on citizens to meet this obligation would not be sufficient. If the ideal of a citizen militia was to be realized, it would require government to supply weapons to those who could not arm themselves.[26] "Say that Congress shall not arm or discipline them till the states shall have refused or neglected to do it," proclaimed Henry.[27] He feared that congressional inaction might lead to the militia being effectively disarmed. His discussion of the right to bear arms occurred in the context of his defense of the militia, and he affirmed the need to give the primary responsibility of arming and disciplining the militia to the states. Although this right was phrased in a civic republican idiom, the conception of republicanism that Henry defended was tied to a distinctive theory of federalism. Henry linked the idea of an armed citizenry with state control of the militia, and he would have been puzzled by modern efforts to separate the two. Republicanism and federalism were not easily disentangled in the constitutional thought of the founding era. Nor can one ignore the sense in which bearing arms was as much an obligation as a right. The right Henry defended was linked to a civic obligation. Not only could the state force individuals to bear arms, but it could effectively tax them by requiring that they provide their own weapon and shoot their own ammunition. [28]

Two issues were central to the Anti-Federalist theory of the right to bear arms: state control of the militia and the inclusion of a declaration of rights that would explicitly affirm the right of the people to bear arms as part of a well-regulated militia. The right esteemed by modern gun rights advocates and scholars, an essentially private right severed from any connection to the militia and devoid of any sense of public obligation, shares little with Henry's civic understanding of arms bearing.[29]

Although there are many examples of Anti-Federalists invoking the ideal of an
armed citizenry and the interconnected idea of a well-regulated militia, there are
relatively few statements about the right to own weapons outside of the context
of militia service. The absence of evidence does not mean that Anti-Federalists
did not believe that citizens had a right to own weapons for hunting or personal
protection, but it does suggest that this issue was not at the core of the debate
over the Second Amendment.[30]

In the vast corpus of writings produced during ratification, there is only one
example in which the term "bearing arms" was used outside the context of
militia service: the Anti-Federalist Dissent of the Pennsylvania Minority.[31] Here
is what the Dissent said about arms bearing:

> That the people have a right to bear arms for the defense of themselves and
> their own state, or the United States, or for the purposes of killing game; and
> no law shall be passed for disarming the people or any of them, unless for
> crimes committed, or real danger of public injury from individuals; and as
> standing armies in the time of peace are dangerous to liberty, they ought not
> to be kept up; and that the military shall be kept under strict subordination to
> and be governed by the civil powers.[32]

The hastily assembled Dissent blended together two different rights protected
by the Pennsylvania Constitution, a right to bear arms and a right to hunt.
Although the Dissent was widely reprinted, no other state ratification convention opted to follow its novel formulation of the right to bear arms. While
historians cannot afford to dismiss the Dissent, which was an important statement of Pennsylvania Anti-Federalist ideas, they must acknowledge that in many
ways the Dissent was atypical. The Dissent explicitly granted the federal government the right to disarm citizens when they posed a threat to public safety. The
authors of the Dissent, members of the Pennsylvania Constitutionalist Party,
were hardly modern civil libertarians. Pennsylvania Constitutionalists had enacted a stringent loyalty oath that gave the state sweeping powers to disarm
citizens who refused to swear an oath of allegiance to the state. While Anti-
Federalists were perfectly comfortable allowing states to disarm citizens when
they posed a potential threat to public order, granting such a power to the federal
government was something quite out of character for ardent Anti-Federalists.
Indeed, New Hampshire's ratification convention, which contained a number of
vocal Anti-Federalists, suggested a constitutional amendment that would have

explicitly prevented the federal government from disarming citizens except in time of rebellion, a view far more typical of Anti-Federalists. Given that the Dissent was assembled in a hasty manner, employed a number of unusual arguments, and was not emulated by any other state ratification convention, its language regarding the right to bear arms cannot be taken as widely representative.

There is considerable evidence that not even all the signers of the Dissent were entirely comfortable with its language. A number of the signers of the Dissent were present in the convention that revised the Pennsylvania state constitution in 1790. That convention did not copy the anomalous language employed by the Dissent, but chose to describe bearing arms in language very similar to that employed in Pennsylvania's 1776 Constitution. Further evidence that the Dissent was not viewed as an appropriate guide to the original understanding of the Constitution is provided by a comment made by William Findley, another signer of the Dissent, during the debate over the Jay Treaty several years later. Findley dismissed the arguments of the Dissent and suggested that Congress would be ill advised to put much stock in a text that had been thrown together at a time of heightened political passions.[33]

The Dissent had almost no impact on the deliberations of the First Congress that drafted the Second Amendment. Pennsylvania Anti-Federalists were routed during the first federal elections. Not only did the signers of the Dissent not participate in the First Congress, but the Federalist Frederick Muhlenberg, who represented the state in Congress, disparaged the extremism of the Dissent in a letter to Federalist Benjamin Rush. Nor is there any evidence that Madison consulted the Dissent when he proposed his own draft of the Bill of Rights.[34]

The subject of the militia was widely discussed during ratification, and there were a small number of statements about the need to protect the right of citizens to keep those arms that were required to meet their militia obligation. Apart from the Dissent, there were no discussions of a personal right to own weapons outside the context of militia service. In the founding era, bearing arms was understood to refer to weapons carried in a military capacity. A religious pacifist might bear a gun to kill a deer, but he would never "bear arms." No one in the founding era would have doubted that individuals retained a right of personal self-defense. The meaning of self-defense had developed under common law, and the rules governing the ownership or storage of weapons were regulated by the states under their police powers.[35]

The attention lavished on the Dissent of the Minority by modern Second Amendment scholarship ultimately has little to do with a desire to understand the role of this text in the public debate over ratification of the Constitution and far more to do with Anti-Federalism's appeal to modern conservatives, particularly those of a libertarian bent. The rediscovery of Anti-Federalism has tended to obscure the voices of Federalists. While modern scholarship continues to place Publius at the center of the debate over the Constitution, relatively little attention has been devoted to other Federalist authors who may have been more influential at the time and can tell us more about how typical Federalists interpreted the arguments of their Anti-Federalist opponents. Rather than focus on those aspects of the Dissent that seem most interesting to the modern debate over gun control, it makes more historical sense to reconstruct how Federalists responded to its argument. When the Dissent and the Federalist rejoinders are read together, intertextually, it is clear that the personal right to own guns was simply not at issue in the ratification debate. One of the most vocal Federalist critics of the Dissent was Tench Coxe, who authored two detailed attacks on this Anti-Federalist text.[36] Coxe viewed the argument of the Dissent as entirely specious. There is nothing in Coxe's response to the Dissent that speaks to the issue of an individual right to own guns outside the context of militia service.[37] If such an argument had been central to the critique of the Constitution framed by the Dissent, then one would expect Coxe to have tried to rebut this contention. Yet Coxe focused his attention squarely on the Dissent's charge that the Constitution posed a threat to the militia. Naturally, as was true for all Federalists, he viewed this fear as utterly without foundation. "Who are these militia?" Coxe asked readers. "*Are they not ourselves?*" Coxe went further, declaring that Congress have no power to disarm the militia. "Their swords, and every other terrible implement of the soldier, are *the birth right of an American*." [38] The military focus of dispute between Coxe and the Dissenters is underscored by his claim that it was the "implements of the soldier" that were the birthright of Americans, not firearms intended primarily for private use, such as fowling pieces. While the most comprehensive study of gun ownership in the founding era places ownership at slightly more than half of the households probated, many of these guns were fowling pieces and not "the implements of the soldier" referred to by Coxe. Bearing arms required ownership of muskets, not fowling pieces. Coxe's response to the Pennsylvania Dissent adopted the more orthodox notion that bearing arms was a military function.[39]

When the Bill of Rights was being debated in Congress, Coxe sought to assure the public that "the right of the people to keep and bear their private arms" would be protected by the Second Amendment. Individual rights theory has interpreted this claim as a strong statement of an expansive individual right to own arms for private purposes.[40] Yet when read in the context of his own earlier response to the Anti-Federalist Dissent of the Minority, Coxe's reference to private arms is best read as a defense of the weapons essential to a well-regulated militia: privately owned military-style weapons intended for a distinctive public purpose. The scope and limits of individual ownership of firearms outside the context of the militia were not a constitutional matter, but a subject to be regulated as part of the state's police power. Does this mean that Coxe believed that there was no right of self-defense or a right to own weapons for hunting? Here again it is important to distinguish between arms intended for personal self-defense and those employed for public self-defense. A Quaker pacifist might own firearms for the former purpose but would be religiously scrupulous about using weapons for the latter purpose. Writing as "a Freeman," Coxe noted that the states will "regulate and administer the criminal law" and "regulate the police; and many other things of the utmost importance to the happiness of their respective citizens. In short, besides the particulars enumerated, every thing of a domestic nature must or can be done by them."[41] The authority to regulate firearms for nonmilitary purposes fell under the police powers of the state.[42] Although it is hard to imagine the state disarming a large segment of the population under ordinary circumstances, the power to do so was clearly something within the power of the state. This is precisely what Pennsylvania had done with its own Test Acts.[43]

Although Coxe and the authors of the Dissent clearly agreed that the right to bear arms was a civic right, a huge gulf separated them about how they understood the vital question of how the right to bear arms would fit into the structure of federalism. The most articulate voices within the ranks of the Federalists, including Coxe, were willing to concede that the states had to have some control over the militia. This weak version of the states' rights view of the militia was rejected by most Anti-Federalists who continued to clamor for greater state control over the militia. As was true for so many constitutional ideas debated during ratification, the potential implications of their arguments about the militia were not fully appreciated by either side at the time. Did the logic of the Anti-Federalist position mean that states could resist federal authority with force? Could the federal government use the state militia against a state that defied federal authority? No clear consensus emerged out of the debate over the Constitution or the more limited discussion of the Second Amendment. Conflicts over control of the militia in the years following adoption of the Constitution suggest that the more assertive version of states' rights championed by some Anti-Federalists continued to attract some support.[44]

A RIGHT OF REVOLUTION?

The middling democrats who authored the Dissent of the Minority were ardent supporters of a states' rights vision of federalism. Protecting the ability of the states to maintain their militias was essential to preserving this conception of federalism. A different conception of the militia and the right to bear arms inspired the most radical wing of Anti-Federalism, plebeian populists. For these radicals the militia was not an agent of the states, but an expression of the voice of local communities. Plebeian populists were simple majoritarians who embraced an extreme form of local democracy. In contrast to most members of the Federalist and Anti-Federalist elite, plebeian populists believed in a continuing right of revolution. The tension between this radical conception of the right to bear arms and the more conservative doctrine embraced by elites on both sides of the ratification controversy has not attracted sufficient attention from modern scholars.

The most serious outbreak of violence during ratification occurred in Carlisle, Pennsylvania. When Federalists gathered to celebrate their recent victory in the Pennsylvania ratification convention, Anti-Federalists attacked their opponents, effectively denying them the right to assemble. Anti-Federalists believed that they were justified in preventing such a celebration if it offended the views of the local community. While assembling to seek redress of grievances may have been constitutionally protected, street revelry apparently was not. Nor did plebeian Anti-Federalists feel any qualms about confiscating a cannon that Federalists procured to salute the new Constitution. The behavior of Anti-Federalists in the streets of Carlisle illustrates how limited their view of the right of assembly was and how narrowly they viewed the right of dissent from community values. Interestingly, plebeian populists showed far greater latitude to political speech in print. Although annoyed by the politics of the *Carlisle Gazette*, the local newspaper that leaned toward the Federalist side, plebeian populists refrained from attacking its printer.[45]

Further evidence of the strongly localistic and communitarian views of Carlisle Anti-Federalists can be obtained from their response to the arrest of several of the rioters who had attacked Federalists in the streets of the town. Anti-Federalists saw nothing wrong with organizing themselves into local militia units outside state control and marching on the town jail to liberate the prisoners. For plebeian populists the release of the prisoners was an example of direct democracy in action. Events in Carlisle vindicated their radical conception of constitutionalism and strengthened their resolve to oppose the new government. Middling Democrats such as the authors of the Dissent of the Minority viewed such actions as examples of mob rule. The Carlisle Rioters did not fear the mob and saw the militia's actions as an authentic expression of the will of the people. William Petrikin, a rioter who became a spokesman for plebeian populist ideas in Carlisle, attacked Federalists, accusing them of trying to disarm "farmers, mechanics, labourers." According to Petrikin, Federalists thought "it would be dangerous to trust such a rabble as this with arms in their hands." Petrikin's assault on the Federalists' notion of the militia reveals an important aspect of plebeian thinking about this issue. These Anti-Federalists rejected the notion that one had to be a member of the solid yeomanry to vote, serve on juries, or participate in the militia.[46]

The notion that the militia was literally the entire body of the people in arms, and that it might spontaneously organize to resist tyranny, inspired backcountry Anti-Federalists in Pennsylvania to constitute themselves as militia units outside the control of the state. As one anonymous author noted, "The counties of Cumberland, Dauphine, and Franklin, appear to take the lead, and have been long since repairing and cleaning their arms, and every young fellow who is able to do it, is providing himself with a *rifle* or musket, and ammunition." This author went on to echo a common plebeian Anti-Federalist criticism of the Constitution, charging that "the *lawyers*, &c. when they precipitated with such fraud and deception the new system upon us, it seems to me, did not recollect, that the militia had arms." Anarchy was not something to be dreaded if the alternative was despotism. "A *civil war* is dreadful, but a little blood spilt now, will perhaps prevent much more hereafter."[47]

Additional evidence that plebeian populists were not particularly concerned about preserving a states' rights conception of arms bearing is provided by their reaction to Pennsylvania's effort to recall public arms for cleaning and inspection in the midst of the heated struggle over ratification, a move that aroused considerable suspicion. When the Supreme Executive Council issued the repair order, a number of Anti-Federalists attacked the plan, charging that it was designed to effectively disarm the backcountry. While such a plan would have seemed perfectly reasonable to the authors of the Dissent, it alarmed plebeians. This alarm provides additional evidence that disarmament was more likely to be accomplished by simply failing to take positive steps to arm citizens. A recall of *state-owned weapons* would essentially have left large segments of the backcountry with too few firearms to arm the militia.[48]

The right to bear arms defended in the Dissent of the Minority was far too limited for plebeian populists. Their conception of arms bearing had little to do with well-regulated militias or a right to hunt. Plebeian populists championed the right of local communities to organize themselves into militia units and take up arms whenever government threatened liberty. The conception of bearing arms defended by plebeian populists was genuinely an insurrectionary right.[49] For mainstream Anti-Federalists and Federalists, this radical conception of the right to bear arms was essentially mobocracy, not democracy. Members of both the Federalist and Anti-Federalist elites believed that the Constitution and the Bill of Rights had been adopted to rid America of the danger of mobocracy, not enshrine its localist majoritarian ideology into the highest law of the land. For many in the founding generation, particularly members of the established political elites, a well-regulated militia was far more likely to be used to put down a slave insurrection or popular tumults than to foment revolution.[50]

THE CHANGING MEANING OF THE ARMED CITIZEN
IN THE EARLY REPUBLIC

Although much modern scholarship on the right to bear arms has treated this right in static terms, a profound transformation in the history of the right to bear arms occurred in the early Jacksonian era, when several state constitutions abandoned the distinctive eighteenth-century formulation, "the right of the people to keep and bear arms in defense of themselves," in favor of a much more unambiguously individual right, "every citizen has a right to bear arms, in defence of himself and the State."[51] The changes in constitutional discourse evidenced in state constitutions written after the War of 1812 are profound.[52] A transition from an older republican conception of the right to keep and bear arms to a new, more liberal conception occurred in several states. One can easily track this transformation if one considers the following state constitutional provisions pertaining to the right to keep and bear arms enacted between 1776 and 1820:

1776, Virginia: That a well regulated militia, composed of the body of the people, trained to arms, is the proper, natural, and safe defense of a free State; that standing armies, in time of peace, should be avoided, as dangerous to liberty; and that in all cases the military should be under strict subordination to, and governed by, the civil power.

1776, Pennsylvania: That the people have a right to bear arms for the defence of themselves and the State; and as standing armies, in the time of peace, are dangerous to liberty, they ought not to be kept up; And that the military should be kept under strict subordination to, and governed by, the civil power.

1780, Massachusetts: The people have a right to keep and to bear arms for the common defence. And as, in time of peace, armies are dangerous to liberty, they ought not to be maintained without the consent of the legislature; and the military power shall always be held in an exact subordination to the civil authority, and be governed by it.

1817, Mississippi: Every citizen has a right to bear arms, in defence of himself and the State.

1819, Maine: Every citizen has a right to keep and bear arms for the common defence; and this right shall never be questioned.

1820, Missouri: That the people have the right peaceably to assemble for their common good, and to apply to those vested with the powers of government for redress of grievances by petition or remonstrance; and that their right to bear arms in defence of themselves and of the State cannot be questioned.[53]

Before simply assuming that republicanism was swept away by an emerging liberal constitutionalism, it is important to look closely at the actual language of these constitutions. There was no uniform pattern of constitutional change across America in the period between 1776 and 1820. While the 1817 Mississippi state constitutional convention adopted more liberal, individualistic language, the Maine and Missouri constitutions chose the older, more republican formulation that clearly persisted well into the nineteenth century. The Missouri constitution is fascinating because it asserted that the right to assemble was designed to promote the common good, an explicitly republican formulation, and it directly juxtaposed the right of assembly with the right to keep and bear arms. In its 1790 Constitution, Pennsylvania had considered a similar juxtaposition of bearing arms and assembly but ultimately abandoned this novel formulation. The right to assemble for redress of grievances provides another example of a right that does not fit easily into the sharp individual/collective rights dichotomy that shapes modern constitutional debate over the Second Amendment. An individual cannot assemble; only groups of individuals assemble. The purpose of assembling in the eighteenth century was also tied to a distinctive public purpose, to seek redress of grievances.[54]

The changes evident in the language of state constitutionalism can be discerned in other aspects of American culture. The shifting meaning of the armed citizen can be demonstrated by comparing two of the most important pieces of public sculpture commissioned in the early republic: Jean-Antoine Houdon's eighteenth-century statue of George Washington in the Virginia state capitol and Enrico Cauisici's nineteenth-century relief depicting the "Conflict of Daniel Boone and the Indians" in the U.S. Capitol. The two sculptures present radically different conceptions of the armed citizen.

In Houdon's work, Washington is cast as the ultimate example of the virtuous citizen soldier, the modern embodiment of Cincinnatus. In this rendering of the armed citizen, Washington is shown with a sword, not a musket.[55] The contrast between the Washington and the Boone sculpture is dramatic. Not only is the musket placed at the center of the Boone sculpture, but the subject matter of the work is a life-and-death struggle for individual self-preservation rather than an abstract conception of virtue. Self-defense, not public defense, had come to represent the ideal of the armed citizen.

Although modern Second Amendment scholarship has generally portrayed the founding era and the early republic as a time of consensus, the reality is far more complex and contested. From the radical localist Carlisle rioters to the more nationalist-minded Federalists, Americans from all walks of life were participants in a spirited—and in many cases discordant—debate over the meaning of the right to keep and bear arms in the early republic. Reconstructing the perspectives of the Federalist and Anti-Federalist elites is a necessary first step in any effort to understand the original meanings of the right to bear arms. It is also important to move beyond the familiar range of voices from within these elites and try to understand how the militia and the right to bear arms were understood by the middling democrats who authored the Dissent of the Minority and the radical localists who took to the streets in Carlisle.

Recognizing that there was a range of views on the meaning of the right to keep and bear arms is a necessary first step in moving beyond the limits of both the individual and collective rights paradigms, each of which has been imbued with a strong dose of consensus history. It is also important to abandon the static ahistorical account of the meaning of this right in early American history that has been associated with so much originalist legal scholarship. Change, not stasis, characterized thinking about the right to bear arms in the early republic. The shift in constitutional language regarding the right to bear arms in the decade after the War of 1812 is perhaps the most dramatic example of this transformation.

It is somewhat ironic that Anti-Federalist ideas once esteemed by left-leaning Progressive historians at the start of the twentieth century have now been appropriated by right-leaning legal scholars at the dawn of the twenty-first century. If Americans do wish to go in search of a usable past, it is important that they understand something of the complexity of that history. While a better historical understanding of the disputed nature of the right to bear arms in the early republic may not help resolve the modern debate over gun control, it does serve as a useful reminder of the dangers of ceding the study of the constitution to lawyers and activists.

1. The *Journal of American History*'s list of new dissertations for the period between 1996 and 2001 clearly demonstrates a pronounced decline in interest in constitutional and legal topics among historians.

2. Terry Bouton, "Whose Original Intent: Expanding the Concept of the Founders," *Law and History Review* 19 (2001): 661–771; Marcus Daniel, "The Economic Origins of Anti-Federalism?," <http://www.h-net.msu.edu/reviews/showrev.cgi?path=1379897 1448317>, February 5, 2004.

3. For a thoughtful review essay demonstrating the vitality of gender as a category for constitutional history, see Rosemarie Zagarri, "Gender and the New Liberal Synthesis," *American Quarterly* 53 (2001): 121–30. Among the senior scholars who have recently entered the Second Amendment debate are Don Higginbotham, "The Federalized Militia Debate: A Neglected Aspect of Second Amendment Scholarship," *William and Mary Quarterly*, 3d ser., 55 (1998): 39–58; Jack N. Rakove, "The Second Amendment: The Highest Stage Of Originalism," *Chicago Kent Law Review* 76 (2000): 103–66; Paul Finkelman, " 'A Well Regulated Militia': The Second Amendment in Historical Perspective," *Chicago Kent Law Review* 76 (2000): 195–236. One of the few younger scholars to enter the Second Amendment fray is Robert Churchill, " 'The Highest and Holiest Duty of a Freeman': Revolutionary Libertarianism in American History" (Ph.D. diss., Rutgers University, 2001).

4. Laura Kalman, "Border Patrol: Reflections on the Turn to History in Legal Scholarship," *Fordham Law Review* 66 (1997): 87–124; Barry Friedman, "The Turn to History," *NYU Law Review* 72 (1997): 928–65; G. Edward White, "The Arrival of History in Constitutional Scholarship," *Virginia Law Review* 88 (2002): 485–683.

5. For a defense of originalism, see Randy Barnett, "The Original Meaning of the Commerce Clause," *University of Chicago Law Review* 68 (2001): 101–47, and more generally his "An Originalism for Nonoriginalists," *Loyola Law Review* 45 (1999): 611–54. Barnett's "original meaning" refers to the "meaning a reasonable speaker of English would have attached to the words, phrases, sentences, etc. at the time the particular provision was adopted." Barnett believes that such meaning "is objective insofar as it looks to the public meaning conveyed by the words used in the Constitution, rather than to the subjective intentions of its framers or ratifiers."

6. The most important exponent of the new constitutional historicism among legal scholars is Larry Kramer. See Kramer, "What's a Constitution for Anyway? Of History and Theory, Bruce Ackerman and the New Deal," *Case Western Reserve Law Review* 46 (1996): 885–933; Kramer, "Putting the Politics Back into the Political Safeguards of Federalism," *Columbia Law Review* 100 (2000): 215–93; Kramer, "Madison's Audience," *Harvard Law Review* 112 (1999): 611–79; Kramer, "The Supreme Court 2000 Term Foreword: We the Court," *Harvard Law Review* 115 (2001): 4–169.

7. For an illustration of this method, see Saul Cornell, *The Other Founders: Anti-Federalism and the Dissenting Tradition in America, 1788–1828* (Chapel Hill, 1999), 8–12.

8. Joel Barlow, *A Letter to the National Convention of France, on the Defects of the Constitution of 1791* (New York, 1793), 30; William Manning, *The Key of Liberty*, ed. Sean Wilentz and Michael Merrill (Cambridge, Mass., 1993), 126, 125, 122. See also H. Jefferson Powell, "The Political Grammar of Early Constitutional Law," *North Carolina Law Review* 71 (1993): 949–1009.

9. Manning, *Key of Liberty*, 148.

10. For discussions of the founders' views of federalism, see Samuel Beer, *To Make a Nation: The Rediscovery of Federalism* (Cambridge, Mass.,1993); Forrest McDonald, *States Rights and Union: Imperium In Imperio, 1776–1876* (Lawrence, Kans., 2000). On divisions over the meaning of freedom of the press, see Norman J. Rosenberg, *Protecting the Best Men: An Interpretive History of the Law of Libel* (Chapel Hill, 1986).

11. Andrew McClurg, "The Rhetoric of Gun Control," *American University Law Review* 42 (1992): 53–113

12. For the republican origins of the right to bear arms, see Robert E. Shalhope, "The Armed Citizen in the Early Republic," and Lawrence Delbert Cress, "A Well-Regulated Militia: The Origins and Meaning of the Second Amendment," in *Whose Right to Bear Arms Did the Second Amendment Protect?*, ed. Saul Cornell (Boston, 2000).

13. *The Constitution of the Commonwealth of Pennsylvania* (Philadelphia, 1776), 7, 9.

14. Saul Cornell, "Commonplace or Anachronism: The Second Amendment, The Standard Model and the Problem of History in Contemporary Constitutional Theory," *Constitutional Commentary* 16 (1999): 221–46.

15. For additional examples of restrictive firearms regulation, see William Novak, *The People's Welfare: Law and Regulation in the Nineteenth Century* (Chapel Hill, 1996). For a modern argument that guns ought to be treated like words that rests on a problematic reading of the founders' views, see L. A. Scott Powe, Jr., "Guns, Words, and Constitutional Interpretation," *William and Mary Law Review* 38 (1997): 1311–1403, and William Van Alstyne, "The Second Amendment and the Personal Right to Arms," *Duke Law Journal* 43 (1994): 1236–55.

16. For a discussion of gun regulations in the founding era and early republic, see Saul Cornell and Nathan DeDino, "Well-Regulated Right: The Early American Origins of Gun Control," *Fordham Law Review*, forthcoming.

17. To acknowledge the important civic republican dimensions of the Second Amendment need not require treating it as part of a hegemonic republican ideology. For an ambitious effort to deal with the multiple ideological strains of constitutionalism in the founding era, see Rogers Smith, *Civic Ideals: Conflicting Visions of Citizenship in U.S. History* (New Haven, 1997).

18. On the similarity between bearing arms and jury service, see Akhil Reed Amar, *The Bill of Rights Creation and Reconstruction* (New Haven, 1998).

19. [Luther Martin], "Genuine Information," in *The Complete Anti-Federalist*, ed. Herbert J. Storing (Chicago, 1981), 2:58–59, 71.

20. Tench Coxe, "A Pennsylvanian, III," *Pennsylvania Gazette*, February 20, 1788;

"John De Witt," Boston *American Herald*, December 3, 1787; "A Militiaman," Philadelphia *Independent Gazetteer*, June 7, 1788.

21. Noah Webster, "Leading Principles of the Constitution," in *Friends of the Constitution: Writings of the Other Federalists, 1787–88*, ed. Colleen A. Sheehan and Gary L. McDowell (Indianapolis, 1998), 398.

22. Higginbotham, "Federalized Militia Debate."

23. Richard H. Kohn, "The Constitution and National Security," in *The United States Military under the Constitution of the United States, 1789–1989*, ed. Kohn (New York, 1991).

24. George Mason, "Speech in Virginia Convention," in *The Complete Bill of Rights*, ed. Neil H. Cogan (New York, 1997), 193.

25. Patrick Henry, "Speech in the Virginia Convention," ibid., 198.

26. On this point, see Jack N. Rakove, "Words, Deeds, and Guns: *Arming America* and the Second Amendment," *William and Mary Quarterly* 59 (2002): 210.

27. Henry, "Speech in the Virginia Convention," 198.

28. David Williams, *The Mythic Meaning of the Second Amendment: Taming Political Violence in a Constitutional Republic* (New Haven, 2003), approaches republicanism as a monolithic ideology and ignores the connection between the right to bear arms and federalism. It is impossible to understand the function of the militia as a check on tyranny without understanding the founders' views of federalism.

29. The modern individual rights view of the Second Amendment is effectively summarized by Glenn Harlan Reynolds, "A Critical Guide to the Second Amendment," *Tennessee Law Review* 62 (1995): 461–512.

30. Don Higginbotham, "The Second Amendment in Historical Context," *Constitutional Commentary* 16 (1999): 263–68.

31. Modern gun-rights scholarship has used the example of the Dissent to support the claim that the phrase "bearing arms" could be used outside the context of the militia or public defense; see Nelson Lund, "The Ends of Second Amendment Jurisprudence: Firearms Disabilities and Domestic Violence Restraining Orders," *Texas Review of Law & Politics* 4 (1999): 157–90; and Barnett, "Is the Right to Keep and Bear Arms Conditioned on the Militia?" For evidence to the contrary, see David Yassky, "The Second Amendment: Structure, History, and Constitutional Change," *Michigan Law Review* 99 (2000): 588–668; and Michael C. Dorf, "What Does the Second Amendment Mean Today?," *Chicago Kent Law Review* 76 (2000): 291–347.

32. [Samuel Bryan], *Dissent of the Minority*, in Storing, *Complete Anti-Federalist*, 3:151. For an effort to totally dismiss the argument of the Dissent, see Garry Wills, "To Keep and Bear Arms," in Cornell, *Whose Right to Bear Arms*.

33. Cogan, *Complete Bill of Rights*, 181. On Findley's reaction during the Jay Treaty, see Cornell, *Other Founders*, 225–26. For a rare statement that employed different language but was close in spirit to the Dissent, see the comments made by Maine Anti-Federalist Samuel Nasson during the debate over amendment during the First Congress, in Cogan, *Complete Bill of Rights*, 204. Nasson's defense of a right to hunt was not framed in terms of bearing arms, and there is no evidence that Nasson's letter to George Thatcher had any

influence on congressional deliberations on the Bill of Rights. It is hardly surprising that Nasson, a middling Anti-Federalist from the Maine frontier, would view the right to hunt in terms similar, if not exactly the same, as the middling backcountry Anti-Federalists who wrote the Dissent of the Minority.

34. Frederick A. Muhlenberg to Benjamin Rush, August 18, 1789, in Helen E. Veit et al., *Creating the Bill of Rights* (Baltimore, 1991), 280.

35. Higginbotham, "Second Amendment in Context," argues that explicit statements supporting an individual right to gun ownership apart from the context of militia service were rare in constitutional writings from this era. For a similar argument, see Rakove, "The Second Amendment: The Highest State of Originalism." On regulation, see Cornell and DeDino, "Well-Regulated Right." For a discussion of the evolution of the right of self-defense, from a limited right to a more expansive one, see Richard Maxwell Brown, *No Duty to Retreat: Violence and Values in American History* (New York, 1991). During the Paxton uprising, Quakers armed themselves, implicitly asserting a right of self-defense even as they continued to oppose bearing arms. See [David James Dove?], *The Quaker Unmasked or Plain Truth* (Philadelphia, 1764).

36. Randy E. Barnett and Don B. Kates, "Under Fire: The New Consensus on the Second Amendment," *Emory Law Journal* 45 (1996): 1139–59.

37. For an effort to press Coxe's thought into service in the cause of gun rights, see David Kopel and Stephen Halbrook, "Tench Coxe and the Right to Keep and Bear Arms, 1787–1823," *William and Mary Bill of Rights Journal* 7 (1999): 347–99. Unfortunately, this essay does not examine the debate between Coxe and the Dissent of the Minority.

38. [Coxe], "A Pennsylvanian III," *Documentary History of the Ratification of the Constitution*, ed. Merrill Jensen et al. (Madison, 1976–), 2, microform supplement, 1779.

39. On the prevalence of fowling pieces and other sorts of weapons intended primarily for hunting and pest control in the hands of private citizens, see Randolph Roth, "Guns, Gun Culture, and Homicide: The Relationship between Firearms, the Uses of Firearms, and Interpersonal Violence," *William and Mary Quarterly* 59 (2002): 230; see also James Lindgren and Justin L. Heather, "Counting Guns in Early America," *William and Mary Law Review* 43 (2002): 1777–1842. Taken together these two essays have effectively discredited the much lower levels of gun ownership suggested by Michael Bellesiles, *Arming America: The Origins of a National Gun Culture* (New York, 2000).

40. Tench Coxe, "A Pennsylvanian," Philadelphia *Federal Gazette*, June 18, 1789.

41. [Tench Coxe], "A Freeman," *Friends of the Constitution*, 95–96.

42. On this point, see Rakove, "Highest State of Originalism."

43. Cornell, "Commonplace or Anachronism."

44. One problem with modern legal scholarship on the Second Amendment derives from the desire to seek a level of intellectual coherence from the founders that may not have existed at the time. Don Kates and Glenn Harlan Reynolds, "The Second Amendment and States' Rights: A Thought Experiment," *William and Mary Law Review* 36 (1995): 1737–68, argue that the states' rights view leads to what they call the absurd

conclusion that the states may use their militias to resist federal authority. Kates and Reynolds do not seem to have consulted the standard narrative histories before publishing their ill-thought-out experiment. During the 1790s, Pennsylvania and Virginia did in fact contemplate using their state militias against the federal government. James Rogers Sharp, *American Politics in the Early Republic: The New Nation in Crisis* (New Haven, 1993); Joanne B. Freeman, "The Election of 1800: A Study in the Logic of Political Change," *Yale Law Journal* 108 (1999): 1959–94.

45. Cornell, *Other Founders*, 112. Pennsylvania Anti-Federalists also draw a distinction between political speech and artistic speech and were inclined to give the former far greater protection than the latter. On this distinction in Anti-Federalist thought, see Cornell, "Commonplace or Anachronism."

46. For a more detailed discussion of Petrikin and the Carlisle Riot, see Cornell, *Other Founders*, 108–20.

47. "Extract of a letter from Franklin County 24th April 1788," *Documentary History of the Ratification of the Constitution* 17, 252. The Supreme Executive Council had directed militia officers "to collect all the public arms of the city and several counties" and repair them. Carlisle Anti-Federalists viewed the Council's action as an effort to disarm the people. The actions of the Council and the response of some Anti-Federalists only underscores the contested nature of the right to bear arms in Pennsylvania.

48. Most of the documents related to this incident have been collected by the *Documentary History of the Ratification of the Constitution*, 2, Microform Supplement, pp. 1361–73. There was a contradiction in this position. Plebeians wished to remain autonomous but still believed that government ought to help them.

49. Sanford Levinson, "The Embarrassing Second Amendment," *Yale Law Journal* 99 (1989): 637–59.

50. The term insurrectionary right is borrowed from Dennis Henigan, "Arms, Anarchy, and the Second Amendment," *Valparaiso University Law Review* 26 (1991): 107–29; Carl T. Bogus, "The Hidden History of the Second Amendment," *University of California Davis Law Review* 31 (1998): 309–408; Higginbotham, "Federalized Militia Debate."

51. For a static portrait of state constitutional law in this period that ignores the profound changes in conception of provisions for the right to bear arms in the decades following adoption of the first state constitutions, see Eugene Volokh, "The Commonplace Second Amendment," *New York University Law Review* 73 (1998): 793–821. The static and ahistorical approach of much recent scholarship is evident in the overview presented in Reynolds, "Critical Guide."

52. For an argument that the War of 1812 marked a watershed in the evolution of the transition from republicanism to liberalism, see Steven Watts, *The Republic Reborn: War and the Making of Liberal America, 1790–1820* (Baltimore, 1987). The literature on the debates over the relative importance of republican and liberal ideas in American life is enormous. For a useful overview of the historiography, see Daniel T. Rodgers, "Republicanism: The Career of a Concept," *Journal of American History* 76 (1992): 11–38.

53. Francis Newton Thorpe, ed., *The Federal and State Constitutions, Colonial Charters,*

and Other Organic Laws (1909; reprint, Buffalo, 1993), 7:3814; 3:1892, 1648; 4:2034, 2163; David B. Kopel, "The Second Amendment in the Nineteenth Century," *Brigham Young University Law Review* 4 (1998): 1359–1545.

54. *The Proceedings Relative to Calling the Conventions of 1776 and 1790 and the Minutes of the Convention that Formed the Present Constitution of Pennsylvania* (Harrisburg, 1825), 163. For a discussion of the original conception of the right to assemble, see Richard Primus, *The American Language of Rights* (Cambridge, 1999).

55. On Houdon's Washington, see Garry Wills, *Cincinnatus: George Washington and the Enlightenment* (New York, 1984). For a general discussion of the role of the Boone myth in the political culture of the early republic, see Richard Slotkin, *Regeneration through Violence: The Mythology of the American Frontier, 1600–1860* (Middletown, Conn., 1973). On Cauisici's Boone sculpture, see Vivien Green Fryd, "Imaging Indians in the United States Capitol during the Early Republic," in *Native Americans and the Early Republic*, ed. Frederick E. Hoxie et al. (Charlottesville, 1999) and J. Gray Sweeney, *The Columbus of the Woods: Daniel Boone and the Typology of Manifest Destiny* (St. Louis, 1992).

SETH COTLAR

10

The Federalists' Transatlantic Cultural Offensive of 1798 and the Moderation of American Democratic Discourse

In late 1798 two radically different publications—Britain's arch-conservative *Anti-Jacobin Review* and Boston's staunchly democratic and pro-French *Independent Chronicle*—found some rare interpretive common ground. In the opening article of its first edition, the *Anti-Jacobin Review* commented favorably on the American activities of Federalist printer and writer William Cobbett, remarking that the pieces he had written during the diplomatic crisis with France had given "a proper tone to the public spirit in America."[1] While the *Anti-Jacobin Review* celebrated the rise of anti-Jacobin conservatism in the United States, a writer in the *Independent Chronicle* decried the spirit of 1798. From his perspective, the war scare and the torrent of antidemocratic print that it had unleashed had "enabled . . . the friends of aristocracy and monarchy [such as William Cobbett] . . . to propagate principles which were once heard with disgust and horror, and it has enabled them to accomplish designs which could not have been attempted two years ago without producing an immediate and universal insurrection of the people."[2] Although one author celebrated the American developments of 1798 and the other lamented them, these two pieces shared an important but largely forgotten interpretation of the Alien and Sedition Acts, an interpretation that stressed the extent to which they moderated the tone and content of public political discourse in the new nation.

In hindsight, the claim that the Alien and Sedition Acts accomplished any of the Federalists' goals is a difficult one to make.[3] The Federalists lost the national election of 1800 and within a decade would no longer be an effective political force outside a few areas in New England. The Federalists' attempts to restrict the freedom of the press provoked a new cadre of Jeffersonian printers to establish scores of effective, explicitly partisan newspapers throughout the nation in 1799 and 1800.[4] The legal proceedings under the Acts that the Adams administration pursued produced more unrepentant and vocal martyrs than it did silenced victims. And the broader, outraged response that the Acts generated would severely limit the power of the government to take similar actions in the future. That said, we should perhaps pause to take seriously the claims (put forward by Federalists and democrats alike) that the remarkable outpouring of anti-French and antidemocratic print that accompanied the political crisis of 1798 had a profound impact on how Americans publicly discussed politics. Indeed, this essay will argue that the events of 1798 created a unique opportunity for conservatives to float antidemocratic ideas that had gained little public hearing in previous years. With a surge of intellectual creativity, Federalists reconfigured older, Revolutionary-era ideas and appropriated the works of contemporary European conservatives in a fairly successful effort to undermine the utopian, democratic discourse that had recently flourished in the midst of the excitement over the radical transformations promised by the French Revolution.

The need to delegitimate the radical example of the French Revolution was particularly urgent in America, a nation whose own revolution had only recently and tenuously been declared over. Throughout the 1790s, the American democratic opposition seized upon French ideas and actions in order to justify their calls for an ongoing revolution that could establish a more egalitarian and radically democratic polity. These democrats called upon ordinary Americans to reimagine themselves as revolutionary citizens of the world, rational actors authorized to criticize their nation's policies from the perspective of universal justice. In this spirit, many American democrats experimented with ideas such as those in Thomas Paine's *Agrarian Justice* where he advocated a plan for creating a more equal distribution of property. These 1790s democrats also drew inspiration from the Jacobin clubs and similar British and Irish societies where ordinary citizens claimed a right to shape law and policy in more substantive ways than merely voting a representative into office. Many had also embraced Paine's plebeian variety of deistic anticlericalism, drawing public attention to the ways that clerical and political leaders cynically used religious doctrines to defend a wide range of hierarchical social relationships. Throughout the new nation, traditional ideas about politics, economics, and religion came under severe attack from those who followed Thomas Paine and the French Revolutionaries' call to rethink the first principles that undergirded their societies and polities.[5]

Where such radical experimentation had once been carried on in mainstream prints under the mantle of Jeffersonian Republicanism, the Federalists' cultural offensive in the spring and summer of 1798 effectively reframed such democratic experimentation as the sinister machinations of dangerous "foreign disorganizers." Just as the Pitt administration's Sedition Bill of 1795 had the desired effect of truncating an emerging British democratic movement by driving its most radical elements underground and out of public debate, so America's almost identically worded bill and the barrage of antidemocratic print it legitimated had a similar, if more limited, effect on American political discourse. Where the Pitt administration had used its formidable powers of physical intimidation, imprisonment, and deportation, American Federalists' turned to the cultural arena, particularly the worlds of print and oratory, in their effort to drive radically democratic ideas to the margins of public political discourse.

In the face of this xenophobic and antidemocratic language, Jefferson and his respectable supporters were forced to reformulate their public persuasion. As they attempted to defend themselves against the charges of Jacobinism, atheism, levellerism, and the whole panoply of late eighteenth century political epithets that came into such frequent use in 1798, prominent Jeffersonians jettisoned many of their most transformative ideas and distanced themselves from the more radically "democratic" elements in their coalition. Indeed, it could be argued that Jefferson the centrist—the Federalist and the Republican, to quote his inaugural speech—was one product of the Alien and Sedition Acts. This moderate, anti-revolutionary tradition of Jeffersonian democracy could successfully push other visions of democracy to the margins of political discourse only once the most radical connotations of the term "democracy" were shorn from that protean term and shunted into a newly fashioned compartment of political discourse, the "Jacobinical" and "Atheistic" radical fringe. What had once been an emergent, transatlantic, radical democratic tradition was, in the midst of the diplomatic crisis of 1798, successfully refigured in America as an illegitimate, alien import. Washington's famous call in his 1796 farewell address for no foreign diplomatic entanglements had been by 1798 transposed into an injunction to reject the "foreign" ideology of the French Revolution, a bundle of ideas that many Americans continued to find compelling.

Put another way, the Alien and Sedition Acts moved popular anti-Jacobinism into the center of the American political self-conception. Where most historians have tended to regard "fear of Jacobinism" as one of the "chief support[s] for the Alien and Sedition Acts,"[6] the argument here turns this traditional account on its head. Seventeen ninety-eight's cultural assault on all forms of democratic utopianism (French and otherwise) did not tap into a widespread, deep-seated, and preexisting animus toward such ideas. Rather, it led to the rapid crystallization of a xenophobic and explicitly anti-revolutionary vision of American politics, a vision that was widely disseminated for the first time in the crucible of that year's diplomatic crises. The Alien and Sedition Acts were thus a crucial moment in American political (and nationalist) discourse in that they sped the growth of a new self-congratulatory narrative of national identity that framed America not as part of a radical European political tradition, but as luckily isolated from it. As anti-French Americans successfully took control of the dominant interpretation of the revolutionary events of the early 1790s, they rendered suspect the utopian, democratic aspirations those events had generated in the minds of many Americans. The exceptionalist and anti-revolutionary American political tradition that Federalists and moderate Jeffersonians worked to construct would force all but the most strident of America's radical democrats (in 1798 and for years to come) onto the defensive whenever they floated their ideas in public forums.

By pushing radical interpretations of the American and French revolutionary traditions into the recently invented, marginalized category of Jacobinism, Federalists were able to put forward quasi-Tory visions of American political life without the fear of being branded traitorous monarchists. Capitalizing upon the stories about Jacobin conspirators that they effectively disseminated, Federalist orators called upon American citizens to reject popular politicization and embrace a virtuously passive conception of citizenship. Where pro-French democrats had envisioned a nation composed of explicitly political voluntary societies where ordinary citizens engaged in political discussions on a regular basis, Federalists urged Americans to reject such Jacobinical ideas, focus on election day as the primary moment of political action, and leave the decision making up to their more qualified, chosen leaders. In place of the constant political debate and action that Thomas Paine and the French Revolutionaries had advocated, Federalists encouraged citizens to focus on private institutions—families and churches—as the primary arenas of virtuous action. This focus on the private (or domestic) roles of citizens was supported by a conservative gender ideology that framed political action as a threat to virtuous womanhood, and as a dangerous distraction for upstanding male citizens. Put most simply, where the French example had once legitimized the idea of an ongoing revolution in America, the creation and dissemination of stories about the "Jacobin menace" in 1798 lent more credence to the claims of those who sought to bring that ongoing process of radical democratization to a close.

The claim that the Alien and Sedition Acts worked to de-legitimate previously uncontroversial ideas and thus change the general tenor of American public discourse is not an original one, for this is how 1790s democrats interpreted and experienced them. Connecticut democrat Abraham Bishop, for example, described the spirit of 1798 thus: "If a man says to his neighbors . . . in the language of our declaration of independence, 'that all men are created equal . . .' he is denounced by the modern friends of order as an anarchist [or a] Jacobin."[7] Writing to their friend Mathew Carey from Chambersburg, Pennsylvania, in July 1798, the recently transplanted Philadelphia printers Snowden and McCorkle complained that anti-French hysteria had forced them to keep their criticisms of Adams's policies to themselves. "To deny the presidential infallibility seems equally as heinous as to deny the existence of a god. We are, therefore, obliged to bend a little to the storm." A handbill critical of Philadelphia's leading democratic newspaper editor Benjamin Bache had been "pasted all over town; and, no one has candour enough even to hear his vindication read. For our parts, we have so much to do to defend ourselves, that we dare not say anything about him."[8] Another democratic friend of Carey's, Robert Maxwell, complained that his neighbors had likewise jettisoned their critical faculties in the face of the Federalists' rhetorical onslaught: "The taste for reading that once prevailed has certainly declined very rapidly of late—notoriously discountenanced by a certain description of people; nothing except on one side, is fashionable to read, consequently the light is half put out."[9]

As such testimonials suggest, Federalists responded to the diplomatic crisis of 1798 by embarking on a concerted effort to shape the way ordinary Americans discussed political matters. The Alien and Sedition Acts were merely the legal manifestation of this broader project, a project whose cultural front was more effective than its legal front.[10] Indeed, while only a handful of people were ever physically silenced or expelled by the legal mechanisms of the acts, the cultural manifestations of the Acts worked to render a broad swath of the population suspicious in the eyes of their fellow citizens. With a series of vituperative orations, public meetings, pamphlets, and newspaper pieces in the summer of 1798, the Federalists made a fairly compelling case that Americans should view any criticism of their government as a dangerous, if not treasonous, act. Describing their opponents as "vipers in our bosom" and "vultures preying on our bowels," Federalist orators called for the American people to "silence" and "set our faces against" this dehumanized opposition.[11] By erasing the distinction between political opposition and violent rebellion, the Federalists raised the stakes for those who voiced even mild doubts about the administration's policies. As they saw more and more of their formerly sympathetic readers acquiesce to this rhetoric, democratic writers throughout the nation complained, largely in vain, about how Federalists used the "bugbears" of Jacobinism and atheism to avoid rational debate.[12] Many Federalists, meanwhile, wrote gleeful letters to each other commenting on "the wonderful and happy change in the public mind."[13] As would happen many more times in American history, a diplomatic crisis created the ideal conditions for both the formal and informal silencing of radicals and their sympathizers.

In the summer of 1798, these efforts often took the form of a public meeting held to draft and send an address of support to John Adams. Throughout the country, local elites organized approximately 300 such events in their efforts to banish the political divisions supposedly fomented by French operatives and to foster a spirit of American unanimity. At the end of each of these meetings, the organizers had the audience approve a prewritten address that was then sent to John Adams. Remarkably, the president responded to each address personally, and newspaper editors across the nation then printed these petitions and responses in great numbers. The *Gazette of the United States*, for example, reprinted eighty-seven of them, nearly one a day for the entire summer. One printer even went so far as to collect these highly repetitive addresses and responses into a 360-page book.[14] This barrage of patriotic print took these hundreds of discrete, well-orchestrated moments of local patriotism and reflected them back to an American audience as evidence of a preexisting spirit of national unity.

Historian Thomas Ray, in the only extended analysis of this phenomenon, argues that the Federalist version of events was correct, that these petitions show that "a highly polarized American public began to develop a consensus on certain key issues in domestic and foreign affairs, and approached a degree of unity unknown in the previous decade." The case could be made, however, that these petitions did not reflect some strong, preexisting, and widely shared spirit of nationalism as much as they were efforts to generate and enforce the appearance of local unity by means of a socially intimidating public ritual. An analysis of the geographical distribution of these meetings supports this alternate interpretation. Ray found (to his surprise) that "the generally Republican areas of the Middle Atlantic and southern states outstripped Federalist New England in numbers [of petitions]."[15] The locations of the addresses look less surprising, however, if they are regarded not as a sign of unanimous local support for Adams,

but as a means by which a local Federalist group could try to silence the previously vocal Republicans in their midst. Where there was minimal democratic
opposition (e.g., much of Federalist-dominated New England), there was no
need for a proclamation. Where unanimity really did exist, there was less need to
draw up a petition attesting to it, because the gesture was about reclaiming the
Federalists' lost sense of control over local, public discourse. The petitions and
their frequent republication around the nation created a compelling image of a
spontaneously assenting nation perfectly contented with its leadership. In this
way, the authors and disseminators of these petitions sought to create the pre-
rational, affective nationalism that they thought had been so lacking in the
preceding years.[16]

While the petitions drafted at these public meetings were largely formulaic
and repetitive, they drew on a body of more fully developed arguments that had
been articulated and disseminated in the unusually large number of Federalist
orations that appeared in the spring and summer of 1798. These orators went to
great lengths to warn their fellow citizens about the dangers of French-inspired
utopianism, and in the process gave a new conservative twist to the narrative of
American distinctiveness that had emerged out of the Revolution. Rather than
framing America as a nation in the vanguard of a worldwide process of political
reconfiguration, Federalist orators crafted a vision of American politics as wholly
cut off from the age of democratic revolutions' spirit of experimentation.[17] By
insisting that questions about the fundamental principles and institutional structures of the American system had been successfully settled, they refigured America's polity as a static ideal that the rest of the world should emulate, rather than as
one local manifestation of an ongoing international process of democratization.
Where the exceptionalism of the Revolutionary era conjured up an open-ended
future of continued change for the better, the Federalists' narrative of distinctiveness suggested that any future changes could only bring declension from an
already achieved ideal rather than progress toward an ever-evolving one. This
narrative justified the Federalists' attempts to convince American citizens that
they had no legitimate grounds for criticizing their exceptional system. Instead,
they should be thankful for it.

This was Noah Webster's goal when he stood before the citizens of New
Haven on July 4, 1798: "[Asia and Africa are] overspread with ignorance and
despotism; [Europe] is agitated by an inveterate contest, between the advocates
of the old systems and the delirious projectors of visionary schemes of reformation." After thus framing the rest of the world as utterly unworthy of emulation,
Webster was able to claim that "America alone seems to be reserved by Heaven
as the sequestered region, where religion, virtue and the arts may find a peaceful

retirement from the tempests which agitate Europe." America prospered because it had neither European "kings," "hierarchies," and "mobs," nor their
"visionary theorists." Webster thus situated America between two equally unat-
tractive forms of Europeanness. America's uniqueness lay not just in its rejection
of monarchy and aristocracy, but also in its refusal to "exchange our civil and
religious institutions for the wild theories of crazy projectors; or the sober,
industrious moral habits of our country, for experiments in atheism and lawless
democracy." America's greatness, in other words, rested in large part upon the
citizens' rejection of cosmopolitan universalism, "of that false philosophy which
has been preached in the world by Rousseau, Condorcet, Godwin and other
visionaries. . . . In all ages of the world, a political projector or system-monger
of popular talents, has been a greater scourge to society than a pestilence."[18]
America, according to Webster, should forever serve as a refuge from European
ideologies.

In this oration Webster mingled two different arguments against the utopian
radicalism generated by the French Revolution. The most straightforward one
claimed that events in Europe had demonstrated that their democratic thinkers
had nothing to offer Americans who wished to live in a peaceful, ordered
society. The second argument was aimed less at particular Europeans and more at
the universalistic mode of political discourse that had legitimated the democratic
movements throughout Europe. This cosmopolitan subjectivity, Webster argued, threatened to undermine the ties of nationhood that preserved order.
Where radical democrats called for citizens to feel allegiance to principles of
liberty, equality, and universal justice, Webster urged his fellow citizens (whom
he explicitly defined as male) to identify themselves as part of a historical, blood-
rooted community of patriarchs. "Our fathers were men—they were heroes and
patriots—they fought—they conquered—and they bequeathed to us a rich inheritance of liberty and empire. . . . We have an excellent system of religion and
of government—we have wives and children and sisters to defend; and God
forbid that the soil of America should sustain the wretch, who wants the will or
the spirit to defend them."[19] Such discussions of America as a community of
blood (as opposed to a voluntary collectivity held together by rational consent)
translated the cold legal language of the Alien and Sedition Acts into a culturally
powerful force capable of transforming how ordinary Americans felt about and
treated their more radically minded neighbors.[20]

On the same day in Philadelphia, the Volunteer Company of Grenadiers made
a series of toasts that echoed Webster's call for patriarchal patriotism. These
armed Federalists took a clear stand in the present crisis of foreign and domestic
affairs, disparaging the "crowing of the Gallic Cock," praising Adams and Wash-

ington, imagining the day when "The Opposition" would be "crushed under [the] wheels . . . of government," and putting forward the wish that "the soil of our country [would] become poisonous to traitors, and cease to nourish men animated by foreign predilections." The toast that got the most cheers, aside from the ones to Washington and Adams, was to "the American Fair: May the leap of ten thousand swords from their scabbards, to protect them, prove that the spirit of chivalry is not gone."[21] Such talk of taking up arms to protect "our" nation and defend "our" women, such appeals to martial manhood in other words, had been standard fare during the Revolutionary War, but had largely dropped out of American public discourse once the military conflict ceased. What made this toast particularly remarkable in the context of the 1790s was its positive appropriation of Edmund Burke's veneration of the "Age of Chivalry," a phrase that had been frequently ridiculed and rarely defended in American print culture. In the hands of the Philadelphia Grenadiers, Burke's lamentations for the passing, aristocratic order became the centerpiece of an appeal for American political mobilization. Unlike Paineite forms of politicization, however, these toasts did not claim to mobilize abstract, rational-critical citizens. Rather, they invoked a nation of patriarchal, nativist men who wanted to deny citizens the right to openly oppose governmental policies. In other words, these toasts imagined a nation of passively obedient citizens and active, patriotic patriarchs—and those two character types were melded inseparably together.

Virtually all the orations of 1798 made the case for the supposedly natural ties of nationhood, "social order," and "domestic happiness" by framing them in opposition to the dangerous artificiality of "European connections."[22] Theodore Dwight's July 4 oration, for example, suggested that Americans should be "ashamed" that many "foreigners" held public office. "Where is our national spirit! Where is our pride!" Such sham "patriots" had recently emigrated to America, "holding the rights of man in one hand, and the seeds of Rebellion in the other, they harangue the mob, preach against the oppression of the laws, [and] rail at all good men." Americans should have been wary from the start of these people because they had learned "the principles of rational liberty . . . among the savage hordes of 'United Irishmen,' or in the Jesuitical schools of Geneva." In contrast to these untrustworthy foreigners, "With our own countrymen, we are acquainted, and run no risque of being imposed upon by the patriotism of knaves . . . traitors, thieves, and pickpockets." In this oration, Dwight blamed all domestic discord on the influence of foreigners. Native-born Americans, he suggested, framed "wholesome laws" and supported "our excellent Constitution," while émigrés invariably sought to undermine them.[23] Having thus reduced the matter of political virtue to a question of the place of one's birth, Dwight was able to claim that the survival of the nation depended upon the expulsion of foreigners and the rejection of foreign influences.

Orators used such xenophobic language to encourage American citizens to root out and destroy those dangerous foreigners and American democrats who were supposedly insufficiently dedicated to the preservation of their newly created nation. In a Connecticut fast-day oration, Hezekiah Packard told his auditors, "If you love your country, you will . . . not only discard with abhorrence French principles and French influence, but look with a frown upon those who act in character of French Americans."[24] In Pennsylvania Alexander Addison argued that "to remove danger, we must . . . set our faces against . . . those lying newspapers, lying pamphlets, lying letters, and lying conversations, with which the country has been filled." Those who criticized the current administration were "vipers in our bosom, vultures preying on our bowels, and fatal instruments of . . . our enemies."[25] In Massachusetts Jedidiah Morse argued, "If we love . . . our country . . . let us shun the philosophists of Europe, and their hosts of emissaries in America, and discard and detest their baneful principles."[26] Another orator offered a comparison between a Moses-like Washington, who had given "us to eat of the trees of liberty, in this political paradise," and "American Traitors and French Jacobins," who had tempted Americans with "forbidden fruit . . . which, whoso eateth, merits literal death and perdition!"[27]

As this biblical language suggests, many of the arguments against utopian visions of political regeneration linked them to a Protestant narrative about the ongoing struggle against Satan. In a May 1798 oration, for example, David Osgood described European democrats "as so many infernals, broken loose from their chains in the pit below, and now appearing in this upper world under the shape of men, but still thinking and acting as demons." America's community of pro-French democrats thus became newly recognizable as merely the most recent manifestation of satanic deception. This interpretation inverted Paine's optimistic narrative about universal, political regeneration and reread the popular politicization of the previous years as a sign of declension rather than progress. "In a manner most alluring, they professed principles of liberty and philanthropy; and invited all nations to fraternize with them in schemes of universal benevolence. By these arts they imposed upon the ignorant mass of their own nation, and upon the ignorant of all other nations, a deception similar to that of the arch fiend, when, under the delusion of making them gods, he seduced our first parents into apostasy." Osgood ended with an injunction to his auditors and readers: "If you would not be ravished by the monster, drive her panderers from among you." In this and many other orations in 1798, audiences were encouraged to look suspiciously upon anyone who criticized the government, for "in this good land, there are no . . . grounds for complaint or disquietude."[28]

What legitimated this persecution, more than anything else, was the widespread assumption that American democrats were engaged in an international conspiracy, headed by the Bavarian Illuminati, to overthrow all government and religion.[29] The talk of an international Jacobin conspiracy began in 1797 in Europe with the publication of John Robison's *Proofs of a Conspiracy against all the Religions and Governments of Europe* and the Abbé Barruel's *History of Jacobinism*. These exhaustive, multivolume histories arrived in America at an auspicious moment, precisely as the nation's Federalist leaders were trying to convince their fellow citizens of the danger of French principles. On May 9, 1798, Jedidiah Morse excitedly summarized Robison's new book on "THE ILLUMINATED" for audiences in Boston and then Charleston. According to Morse, members of this clandestine group "abjure Christianity . . . call patriotism and loyalty narrow minded prejudices, incompatible with universal benevolence—declaim against the baneful influence of accumulated property . . . decry marriage, and advocate a promiscuous intercourse among the sexes." Morse thus found in Robison's text a coherent narrative that could explain why pro-French democrats posed such a threat to American society. Drawing the parallel between Robison's account of Europe and recent political events in America, Morse warned that it was "not improbable that the affiliated Jacobin Societies in this country were instituted to propagate here the principles of the illuminated mother club in France."[30]

Robison's book became the proof text for scores of Federalist orations in the summer of 1798 because it seemed to provide "authentic and uncontrovertible" evidence of the conspiratorial designs of supposedly patriotic democrats.[31] Not since Paine's *Rights of Man* appeared in 1791 had one book garnered so much attention. When William Linn quoted Robison in his May 9 oration he made the unusual gesture of informing his readers when and from whom they could purchase Robison's book.[32] Likewise, Morse suggested that Robison's book "ought to be read by every American."[33] Robison's text so effected John Lathrop that it led him to look upon his democratic neighbors as "noxious . . . frogs" who were "croaking and spawning in every lake and fen, vexing the air with their noise, and poisoning the waters with their slime. These spirits of devils are gone into all the world, corrupting the religious principles, and breaking the political peace of the nations."[34] For Timothy Dwight, Robison's book conjured up a future in which "our sons [will] become the disciples of Voltaire, and the dragoons of Marat; [and] our daughters the concubines of Illuminati."[35] Robison's comprehensive account framed the Illuminati as the group behind virtually every contemporary form of social disruption in Europe. The orators of 1798 extended this analysis to America, raising the specter of Jacobin conspiracy to tap into every fear that a property-owning patriarch could harbor—of losing one's property, of losing control over one's wife and children, of churches being abolished, or of seeing the nation descend into anarchy.

According to the orators of 1798, American citizens could play an important role in thwarting Jacobin conspirators. They must first be wary of the means by which the Illuminati disseminated their ideas, through "the reading and debating societies, the reviewers, journalists or editors of newspapers and other periodical publications, [and] the book sellers."[36] Second, citizens had to realize that "personal obedience and reformation is the foundation, and the sum, of all national worth and prosperity." Citizens needed to focus less on grand matters of politics and religion in order to make themselves and their families more virtuous and obedient. As Timothy Dwight put it on July 4, 1798: "Few persons can be concerned in settling systems of faith, moulding forms of government, regulating nations, or establishing empires. But almost all can train up a family for God, instil piety, justice, kindness and truth, [and] distribute peace and comfort around a neighbourhood."[37] Dwight encouraged his audience to channel their world-changing energies toward their families and their localities and leave complicated matters of politics and religion to their leaders. When ordinary people began thinking and talking about universal justice and the rights of man, Dwight suggested, they risked being duped by foreign conspirators who sought to enlist them in an international conspiracy against all government and religion.

All these paeans to an explicitly anti-French variety of popular patriotism, or what the democrats called (in a reference to George III) "passive obedience," opened new space in American political discourse for a brand of conservatism that had previously found little public expression. Indeed, the Alien and Sedition Acts, along with the war crisis of which they were a part, created a new market for British anti-Jacobinism that printers such as William Cobbett and Cornelius Davis soon tapped with great success. In Britain, Thomas Paine's *Rights of Man* had provoked a voluminous counterattack almost as soon as it appeared in 1791. Anti-Paineites responded with hundreds of pamphlets aimed at Paine's audience—the poor and middling folk who had traditionally been defined as outside the political nation.[38] These cheap pamphlets with titles like *Reasons for the Contentment of the Poor* greatly outnumbered pro-Paine productions in Britain, but in America, virtually none of these unapologetically propagandistic tracts saw the light of print during the early 1790s.[39] That omission was remedied in 1798 as printers around the country sought to promote the backlash against "foreign principles," and also profit from it, by reprinting several British anti-Paineite political tracts.

The key purpose of most of these productions was to model a passive version of virtuous citizenship for non-elites. They mercilessly ridiculed the attempts of educated reformers to politicize the people, as well as attempts on the part of laborers to educate themselves on political matters and discuss them with their peers. Such productions meshed perfectly with the pro-Adams discourse of 1798 that stressed the need for Americans to leave political decision making up to their chosen leaders and support their decisions without question. The exigencies of impending war made many influential Americans particularly interested in those Britons who had made a compelling case against democratic calls for popular politicization.

It was in this context that Boston printer and staunch Federalist Cornelius Davis reprinted the apotheosis of British anti-Jacobinism, the Cheap Repository Tracts.[40] This series of approximately sixty short stories, written primarily by Hannah More between 1795 and 1798, was inspired by the King's proclamation calling for the suppression of vice and immorality among the lower orders in Britain. Most British historians agree that the purpose of this proclamation and the publications it inspired and funded was to generate a "voluntary" Church and King backlash against Paineite radicalism. The advertisement for these widely disseminated tracts freely admitted that their purpose was "to improve the habits, and raise the principles of the common people, at a time when their dangers and temptations, moral and political, were multiplied beyond the example of any former period. . . . And as an appetite for reading had . . . been increased among the inferior ranks in this country, it was judged expedient . . . to supply such wholesome aliment as might give a new direction to their taste, and abate their relish for those corrupt and inflammatory publications which the consequences of the French Revolution have been so fatally pouring in upon us."[41]

As this self-description indicates, the mission of the Cheap Repository was to change the reading habits, and thereby the political practices of ordinary Britons. The protagonists of these stories were usually the same: pious, happily poor or middling, deferential ordinary people who did not worry about foreign or even domestic politics but rather preferred to exercise their virtue at the familial and parish level. A frequent antagonist was the "modern philosopher" who talked about universal benevolence, or the untrustworthy, politically ambitious non-elite who prattled on about liberty and equality. One story, for example, described Mr. Fantom, "the new fashioned philosopher," as one of those people who "despised all those little acts of kindness and charity which every man is called to perform every day. . . . And while he was contriving grand schemes which lay quite out of his reach, he neglected the ordinary duties of life which lay directly before him." When Fantom tells his neighbor—the subtly named Mr. Trueman—that he is preparing a political essay for publication in a newspaper, Trueman replies, "I had rather not distinguish myself, unless it was by leading a better life than my neighbours. There is nothing I should dread more than being talked about. I dare say now heaven is in a good measure filled with people whose names were never heard out of their own street or village." Fantom scorns Trueman's provincialism: "I despise a narrow field. O for the reign of universal benevolence! I want to make all mankind good and happy."[42] Mr. Trueman simply replies that Fantom should start with a town or parish first, and then leaves his neighbor to revel in his abstract speculations. With stories such as this, the Cheap Repository tracts saturated the world of cheap print with images of a happily localist, plebian identity, and coupled this image with arguments about the undesirability, and the practical impossibility, of cosmopolitan citizenship. A nation of Mr. Truemans would be invulnerable to the threat of Jacobin conspiracy.

The first American to reprint the Cheap Repository, New York's Cornelius Davis, freely admitted his intentions to transform the reading practices of ordinary Americans. He wrote to Mathew Carey in August 1798 offering to sell him 500 copies, noting that "I mean to sell them low, because the work is excellent—calculated to be useful to that class of people who have little money and less inclination to buy and read good books." It is not surprising that Davis liked the political message of these tracts, for, as he admitted to Carey, a United Irishman and a democrat, "We are not well pleased with the conduct of that party in Politicks which you are said to side with."[43] Like many of his Republican counterparts, Davis thought of his printing business as a means of fomenting political change. Along with three editions of the Cheap Repository, he also published Barruel and Robison. Whereas these latter two texts were written and priced for elite consumption, the Cheap Repository tracts (sold at four cents apiece) echoed many of the same themes, only they presented them in the form of short, moralistic tales designed to influence the less literate segments of the population.

The anti-Jacobinism of 1798—the orations, the Cheap Repository Tracts, and the Federalist addresses and toasts—demonized all things "foreign" by framing them as a threat to the "natural" ties of nation and family. Anti-Jacobins frequently used the highly suggestive term "disorganizer" to describe their enemies, thus intimating that the nation, the family, and the locality were preexisting, natural forms of social organization. When Paineite democrats urged people to measure all political institutions and relationships against the egalitarian dictates of universal justice, they challenged the supposedly "natural" status of every form of authority. While their goal was to reorganize rather than disorganize, their opponents succeeded in erasing the constructive component of radical enlightenment political theory. Accounts of French events like those by Robison and Barruel claimed to demonstrate that a universalist political language could only destroy and never reconstruct social ties. The world of popular print in 1798 was saturated with talk of impending war, detailed accounts of foreign conspiracies against the nation, and panicked claims that foreign incendiaries and their American minions sought to eliminate all religion and break apart families. In such an atmosphere, what was once a relatively uncontroversial choice to identify as a Paineite friend to universal justice became suddenly freighted with an imposing host of negative connotations. According to Timothy Dwight, "multitudes" of Americans, "heretofore attached to France with great ardour, have, from full conviction of the necessity of changing their sentiments and their conduct, come forth in the most decisive language, and determined conduct, of defenders of their country. . . . Almost all native Americans will, I doubt not, speedily appear in the same ranks."[44] Perhaps some ordinary citizens scaled back their utopian political visions in the rational and voluntary manner that Dwight described in his supposedly objective account of 1798; yet his final, insistent prescription for behavior suggests that many Americans needed to be persuaded by influential men like Dwight, men who could use their access to public forums to turn the disapproving gaze of their listeners toward their "disorganizing" neighbors.

It is ironic that the form of "disorganization" that seemed to most alarm Federalist orators in 1798 was actually a form of organization—that is, the attempts on the part of ordinary citizens to build informal institutions through which they could influence the political process. Orators repeatedly singled out for criticism the radically active notions of citizenship that had emerged in 1790s Europe and offered their listeners an alternative, passive vision of the virtuous, American citizen. Obedience, they argued, rather than critical engagement, was the primary duty that all citizens owed their government. Thus, Hezekiah Packard followed a formulaic account of the unique virtues and extreme piety of the nation's current leaders with a stern reminder that "citizens have a place and a sphere in which to act as well as their rulers."[45] In Wrentham, Massachusetts, Nathanael Emmons echoed this sentiment: "The People have nothing to do, in the affairs of government, but merely to chose [their leaders]." Indeed, Emmons argued that the more active a nation's citizens were the more unstable it would be. "Just so far as any civil constitution allows the people to assist or control their Rulers; just so far it is weak, deficient, and contains the seeds of its own dissolution."[46] At Harvard College, John Thornton Kirkland made a similar claim, distinguishing "between the right to protection and the right to govern the state. . . . The share which each member shall have in the management of public affairs, is a matter of convention and expediency, and not an original universal right of man."[47] Before the diplomatic crisis and war scare of 1798 such explicit calls for a passive citizenry and arguments about the unavoidably exclusionary nature of American politics would have appeared far too aristocratic and reactionary to be unapologetically advocated in most public forums. After supposedly unmasking democratic theories as smokescreens for traitorous plots to overthrow the American government, however, Federalists could depict their antidemocratic arguments not as un-American, but as the only ideas that could save the republic from destruction. While they framed themselves and their sympathetic auditors as the true protectors of the republic, they also sought to legitimate and disseminate a vision of that republic's political system that was less participatory and more exclusive than what seemed to be emerging in the mid-1790s.

To put this point in slightly different terms, Federalist orators capitalized on the diplomatic crisis of 1798 to shore up the boundary that excluded ordinary Americans from what John Brooke has called the "deliberative" public sphere.[48] They continually emphasized the distinction between the active role of the leadership class (or "the political nation") and the passive role of the rest of the citizenry (or "the nation"). This was a difficult case to make, however, writing as they were in the wake of the American and French Revolutions, with their stirring rhetoric about the role of "the people" in governing themselves. Hyperbolic stories about bloodthirsty Jacobins culled from Robison and Barruel helped, as did Hannah More's didactic tales about happily apolitical plebes.

In 1798 Richard Dobson published one more anti-Jacobin pamphlet, adding another dimension to the assault on utopian visions of popular politicization—the argument that political action drew men away from their more important roles as fathers and husbands. William Brown's *Look before ye Loup; or, A Healin' sa' for the Crackit Crowns of Country Politicians, by Tam Thrum, an Auld Weaver* had first appeared in Edinburgh in 1793 in an effort to combat the political clubs that had formed there. At the time, no American printer had deemed it worthy of an American edition, but in 1798, Federalists hoped that the American audience was ready to hear Brown's message. Brown speaks through Tam Thrum, a working man who attends a meeting of the local political club but finds himself utterly unpersuaded by their efforts to turn ordinary people into political activists. "To be plain wi' ye, lads, you have ta'en us aw frae our ploghs, our shuttles, an' our needles, to mak' constitutions, an' mend governments; you've deprived us of our innocence, our happiness an' contentment." Throughout the pamphlet, wise commoners chastise their compatriots for abandoning their duties to their wives and children in pursuit of something that is beyond their ken. Harry Heeltap's "rusty-cat" wife Jenny, for example, intrudes into one of his political meetings, asking him to come home and make money to help support his starving family. "Leave your speeches an' your nonsense about the rights o man to them that can afford to fool awa their time in sic a way. Come awa home, an' mind your family." In the same vein, Tam Thrum tells his readers the tragic story of Davie Deal, a wright, who had a beautiful wife and children and lived in a clean house with plenty of work. Once he started going to clubs and reading Tom Paine, however, things changed: "Now, if I gang to Davie wi' ony little job, O, 'tis club night, Davie has the affairs o' the nation to settle." Meanwhile, Davie's wife sits at home crying while his children go hungry.[49] The moral of this tale was unmistakable—political deliberation should be left to those with the wisdom and wealth to do so responsibly.

Texts like *Tam Thrum* and the *Cheap Repository Tracts* framed private, domestic bliss as the more virtuous alternative to public political participation. Such portrayals offered ordinary citizens an important role to play in preserving social harmony and national prosperity; only that role was a profoundly nonpolitical one. The collective life envisioned in these texts involved the family and the church. When men strayed into other venues—the tavern, the coffee house, or the political club—they risked being pulled into a world where they could become the tools of powerful demagogues, and where their productive energies would be channeled in irresponsible, socially disintegrative directions. It is in these anti-Jacobin juxtapositions of politics and virtuous domesticity that we can find some of the origins of a relatively new vision of the model American citizen that emerged in the early nineteenth century—the modest farmer or artisan who minded his own business (literally and figuratively), enjoyed domestic tranquility, and picked the proper leaders to govern him. This image meshed perfectly with a discursive shift that occurred throughout the Atlantic world as the age of revolutions faded into memory, that is, a rebifurcation of the world into the active "political nation" and the passive "nation." With the heightened discourse of popular sovereignty inspired by the French Revolution in the early 1790s, this distinction (that had been so important to Burke and provided one of the major themes of his *Reflections*) came under severe attack. The events of 1798 gave new life to this beleaguered distinction that was then reasserted and naturalized in the figure of the virtuous, locally minded yeoman, a figure to which both Jeffersonians and New England Federalists appealed, although to different ends.

The hyperbole and hysteria that marked the orations of the summer of 1798 becomes more understandable when we appreciate both how essential and how difficult it was for the Federalists in the late 1790s to craft an intellectually satisfying distinction between dangerously active and virtuously passive forms of citizenship. Having recourse to few widely accepted arguments against utopian visions of a perpetually participatory citizenship, Federalists repeatedly returned to salacious stories about bloodthirsty and immoral Jacobins in order to take what was once an inspirational vision of "the people" reconstituting their political institutions in order to more literally govern themselves and turn it into a nightmare scenario that would result instead in the destruction of all "natural" forms of social order. Harvard orator John Thornton Kirkland, for example, suggested that ideas like "liberty and equality" or universal manhood suffrage "contributed . . . to pull down the fabric of social order" because they disregarded "the gradations and distinctions of nature and society . . . placing the young on a level with the old, the child with the parent, and the pupil with the instructor, annul the claim of age to respect, and of authority to submission." Preserving a place for these "natural" ties of hierarchy and submission in the American political language of the late 1790s, however, still required some rhetorical manipulation. Indeed, Kirkland admitted that every citizen equally possessed certain rights such as "the right to life and personal security, the right to acquire, hold, and transmit property, the right to liberty of action, the right to reputation, the right to liberty of opinion, of speech, and of religious profession and worship." His task was to explain why this list did not contain the equal right to participate actively in political matters. To make this claim he shifted the tone of his discussion, turning to a playful discussion of "the new theory of the Rights of Women" intended to draw complicit laughs from the Harvard men who made up his audience. Kirkland insisted that although the writings of Mary Wollstonecraft had made the exclusion of women from the political process seem "selfish, illiberal, and tyrannical," the American women he knew were happy to play their allotted role as the governors of "society," thus leaving the "drudgery and vexation" of politics to the men. So while "modern philosophers" may have spoken about liberty and equality in expansive and radical ways, Kirkland assured his audience that the objects of liberation were quite content to let the traditional rulers of society continue to govern the political world unmolested.[50]

Kirkland's speech partook of a powerful configuration in American political discourse that had existed since the revolution but had been reconfigured and newly crystallized into an easily referenced, conservative orthodoxy in the late 1790s—that is, the distinction between two theoretically discrete realms denoted politics and society that roughly corresponded with the distinction between the political nation and the nation. Whereas the world of politics was composed of only those theoretically equal (that is, white, male, and, in most states, proper-tied) citizens who had a right to participate actively in the deliberative process, "society" included everyone, yet the terrain of the social, unlike that of the political, was decidedly uneven. Indeed, as used by the Federalists of the 1790s and their nineteenth-century heirs, the category of the social became the reposi-tory of the supposedly "natural" hierarchies of race, class, and gender that were so frequently glossed over by the seemingly universalistic and inclusive language of late eighteenth-century politics. This radical separation of the social from the political differed dramatically from how American revolutionaries had used the term in the 1770s. In one of the most familiar lines from *Common Sense*, Thomas Paine had denoted "society" as a blessing and "government" a "necessary evil." This veneration of society over politics may at first seem comparable to Kirkland and other Federalists' use of those concepts, but one crucial difference remains. Where Paine evoked society as a means to inspire citizens to engage in political action against an unjust government—to, in essence, reclaim their natural right to govern themselves—the Federalists in 1798 used the concept of "society" to encourage citizens to avert their eyes from political matters. Indeed, by the late 1790s more and more Americans regarded the realm of society not as the seed-bed of politics, but rather as a refuge from it. Perhaps because the political valence of the term "society" was in the midst of this transformation in the mid-1790s, Paineite democrats in that decade rarely used the concept of the social, tending instead to interpret most social relations (and especially those between white men) as political and hence subject to renegotiation. For such thinkers, the public sphere provided the arena in which these negotiations over just and unjust authority should be contested.

Wanting to squelch what they perceived to be Paine's calls for endless conver-sations about the implications of republican political ideology for household, neighborhood, and workplace relations, Federalists like Kirkland chose to view society as a fairly static realm of life set apart from the political changes of the late eighteenth century. Encompassing religious institutions, education, the market, manners, and morals, this vision of society appealed to such thinkers because it provided them with a compelling way to frame existing inequality as a function of "natural" social differences. These differences theoretically preceded political arrangements, and were thus not subject to change through collective human action or rational investigation. Used this way, the notion of society gave ordi-nary citizens, men and women, an important though indirect part to play in sustaining political tranquility, for their actions as fathers, mothers, and economic producers indirectly benefited the nation by generating virtuous and law-abiding citizens.[51] If citizens agreed to think of themselves as social actors rather than political actors, this would also serve the purpose of muting the rancorous partisan divisions of the late 1790s. Kirkland's was just one of many orations in the summer of 1798 that used this strategy of dividing the social from the political as a means to justify a highly passive and exclusive conception of American citizenship. While Federalists often used humorous discussions of women's rights or bumbling apprentices to blunt the force of their explicitly exclusionary arguments, behind their jovial tone lay a degree of legitimate anxiety about their ability to control the course of popular politics in the midst of worldwide revolution.

These anxieties were well grounded. As recent studies of popular politics and party formation in the early republic suggest, more and more non-elite white men became involved in formal politics in the years following 1798. And despite the Federalists' rhetorical onslaught in the summer of 1798, Jefferson captured the presidency in 1800 and the Democratic Republicans dominated national politics for over two decades. While it must be acknowledged that these political victories profoundly democratized the electoral process, this does not mean that the anti-Jacobin onslaught of 1798 failed to transform the way Americans publicly discussed their possible political futures. The Federalists' cultural offensive rendered suspect the spirit of intellectual experimentation that had marked the revolutionary 1790s, refiguring the most utopian aspirations of the early 1790s as dangerous and perverse. This move enabled Federalists to mark off a segment of the political nation as the "un-American, radical fringe" and drive the most "democratic" components of the Jeffersonian coalition into that fenced-off area. In this way, the pro-Adams rhetoric of 1798—the orations, the public meetings and addresses, the sudden proliferation of anti-Jacobin tracts like Barruel, Robison, and the Cheap Repository—worked together to transform an abstract spirit of patriotism into the local policing mechanism of ridicule and shame. They encouraged readers to translate the abstract foreign disorganizer or atheist infidel into concrete figures such as the local tavern owner who continued to keep Paine's works on his tables and had refused to cancel his subscription to the *Independent Chronicle* or the *Aurora*. Around the country, simultaneously in hundreds of discrete locations, this process occurred—ruining reputations, silencing nettlesome Jacobins, discrediting the religiously unorthodox, and training the suspicious eyes of ordinary readers on anything that appeared tainted by an association with the democratic radicalism of the Atlantic world's 1790s. It was in these subtle yet pervasive ways that the cultural front of 1798 altered the tone of local and national political discourse.

Archival evidence of this informal squelching of dissent is difficult to find for many reasons. In the case of Irish-American democrat Mathew Carey, it appears that in 1798 he destroyed much of his correspondence relating to the United Irishmen, thus obliterating the evidence of his past radicalism.[52] In February of that year, after residing in America for fifteen years, he took a public oath to the United States for the first time, presumably with the intention of combating charges that he was a foreign incendiary. Likewise, his correspondence from the summer of 1798 suggests that the Federalist-dominated Bank of the United States had singled him out for financial persecution. Carey himself never wrote about how the events of 1798 changed his political activities, but this fragmentary archival evidence perhaps explains how this former United Irishman and radical democrat was transformed into a moderate Jeffersonian by 1800.[53]

The American career of the radical émigré printer Daniel Isaac Eaton followed a similar trajectory. Having escaped prosecution for treason in England, Eaton arrived in Philadelphia in early 1797 and immediately began selling scores of radical pamphlets that he had printed in Britain. He took out regular ads in Philadelphia's main democratic newspaper, the *Aurora*, listing the political tracts he had for sale in his small bookshop. By mid-1798, however, Eaton's American career was severely jeopardized by the Alien and Sedition Acts. According to William Cobbett, "the Alien Law soon made him withdraw both his advertisement and himself from the notice of the public." By September 1798 he was reportedly evicted from his home once his landlord discovered "what gentry he had got for tenants." Within a few years Eaton would return to England to renew his political career there.[54] Despite experiences like Carey's and Eaton's, many transatlantic radicals, including such major figures as William Duane, James Thomson Callender, and James Cheetham, refused to bend to the storm. In the years following 1800, however, it quickly became apparent that the Republican leaders who gained power under President Jefferson were mostly moderates intent on distancing themselves from the radical democrats in their midst, all in the interest of constructing a more respectable and electable coalition.[55]

Meanwhile, at the level of political discourse, the link that emerged during the war crisis of 1798 between a sentimental rhetoric of domesticity and a narrowly nationalistic, patriarchal conception of "patriotism" became an even more central aspect of public political discourse in the nineteenth century. Indeed, 1798 was arguably America's first experience with its own variant of the radical John Bullism that British historian Linda Colley and others have discussed.[56] But where British nationalism had several relatively stable objects to use as its central focus—the King, the ancient constitution, the figure of John Bull as the anti-gallican—the American "character" was a much fuzzier figure. Because it was so hard to define, it had been easy for Paineite radicals and other opponents of the status quo throughout the early and mid-1790s to legitimately claim the mantle of true Americanism for themselves. In the summer of 1798, however, through sheer repetition of a mantra of national unity, a very different conception of the American character came into wide usage. In scores of public sermons and orations, Americans heard the changes rung on two themes: the need for virtuous patriarchs to rebuff "foreign influence" and the need for a resurgence of Christian faith in order to combat the French poison of atheism and excessive democracy that threatened to undermine all morality and government. Put most bluntly, this was an only slightly transformed version of British anti-Jacobin nationalism transposed into an American idiom. The American "we" was contrasted to the French, non-Protestant other. And what made this persuasion seem even more convincing in the summer of 1798 was the perception—derived largely from Robison and Barruel—that this alien walked amongst us in the form of democratic newspaper editors, itinerant Jacobins, experimenting free thinkers, and United Irishmen on the lam.

No matter how loudly "democrats" cried out against this witch hunt, they were still forced to defend themselves on terms not of their own choosing. Throughout the republic, many radical democrats faced a choice between either changing their intellectual course or losing their audience.[57] The truncation of radical conversations described here occurred throughout the Atlantic world in the late 1790s, and America did not escape this process. While the actual legal mechanisms of the Alien and Sedition Acts either disappeared or passed into disuse, their broader cultural impact was reflected later in the unapologetically chauvinistic and romantic nationalism of the mid-nineteenth century, and in the increasingly bourgeois discourse of American "democracy" and domesticity that went to such great lengths to distance itself from foreign levellerism, atheism, immorality, and Jacobinism. One small indicator of this persisting link between the anti-Jacobinism of the 1790s and the domestic ideology of the nineteenth century is the fact that Hannah More, the author of the Cheap Repository Tracts, would become one of America's most popular authors of children's books in the 1810s. As More's increased popularity suggests, the romantic and evangelical reactions against radical Enlightenment political theory that shaped British and French politics in the early nineteenth century also shaped American politics—only America's more moderate reaction came to be called democracy.

1. *Anti-Jacobin Review*, July 1798, 7.

2. Boston *Independent Chronicle*, December 31, 1798.

3. On the Alien and Sedition Acts see John C. Miller, *Crisis in Freedom* (Boston, 1951); James Morton Smith, *Freedom's Fetters* (Ithaca, 1956); and Leonard Levy, *The Emergence of a Free Press* (New York, 1985).

4. Jeffrey L. Pasley, *"The Tyranny of Printers": Newspaper Politics in the Early American Republic* (Charlottesville, 2001).

5. These American manifestations of transatlantic, Paineite radicalism are discussed at greater length in Seth Cotlar, "In Paine's Absence: The Trans-Atlantic Dynamics of American Popular Political Thought, 1789–1804" (Ph.D. diss., Northwestern University, 2000).

6. Miller, *Crisis in Freedom*, 143.

7. Abraham Bishop, *Oration Delivered in Wallingford. . . .* (New Haven, 1801), 19.

8. Letter to Mathew Carey, July 8, 1798, Lea & Febiger Correspondence, Historical Society of Pennsylvania (hereafter HSP).

9. Letter to Mathew Carey, July 25, 1798, Lea & Febiger Correspondence, HSP.

10. The term "cultural front" is borrowed from Michael Denning, *The Cultural Front: The Laboring of American Culture in the Twentieth Century* (London, 1996).

11. These quotations come from Alexander Addison, Esq., *An Oration on the Rise and Progress of the United States of America, to the Present Crisis; and On the Duties of Citizens* (Philadelphia, 1798).

12. Thomas Cooper, a radical émigré who had experienced a great deal of political harassment in Britain before emigrating to America in 1794, claimed that the Federalists were merely copying their Anti-Jacobin compatriots in Britain when they began using "cant terms" like Jacobin and "Disorganizer" with such frequency: "Those who are but slightly read in European politics know the origin, and the use of these words; and the insidious purposes to which they are applied." *Political Essays, Originally Inserted in the Northumberland Gazette, with Additions* (Northumberland, Pa., 1799), 16.

13. Jedidiah Morse to Oliver Wolcott, May 21, 1798, quoted in Vernon Stauffer, *New England and the Bavarian Illuminati* (New York, 1918), 130.

14. William Austin, ed., *A Selection of the Patriotic Addresses, to the President of the United States, Together with the President's Answers* (Boston, 1798).

15. Thomas M. Ray, " 'Not One Cent for Tribute': The Public Addresses and American Popular Reaction to the XYZ Affair, 1798–1799," *Journal of the Early Republic* 3 (1983): 393, 400.

16. In March 1797 one Federalist, Elihu Hubbard Smith, complained to Senator Uriah Tracy, "We have suffered, from the want of a common, national sentiment. . . . It is time for us to call to mind that we pretend to be a people. . . . The people are almost ripe for entire conviction; & the moment must be seized to press it upon them." Smith's use of the term "conviction" here—a term with religious connotations—is significant. The variety

of nationalist sentiment that Smith (and many other Federalists) longed for was more akin to religious faith than rational consent. Elihu Hubard Smith to Uriah Tracy, March 31, 1797, in *The Diary of Elihu Hubbard Smith*, ed. James E. Cronin (Philadelphia, 1973), 303–4.

17. David Brion Davis has discussed this "anxiety of influence" in *Revolutions: Reflections on American Equality and Foreign Liberations* (Cambridge, Mass., 1990), chap. 2.

18. Noah Webster, *An Oration Pronounced Before the Citizens of New Haven on the Anniversary of the Independence of the United States, July 4th 1798* (New Haven, 1798), 6–7, 15, 12. Similar arguments about America's lucky isolation from Europe appear in many other orations from 1798. For one example see Josiah Dunham, *An Oration on the Fourth of July, 1798*, 2d ed. (Hanover, N.H., 1798), 6–8.

19. Webster, *Oration*, 16.

20. Many of the petitions to John Adams (and many of his responses) deployed similarly organic, familial language in order to encourage ordinary citizens to use the force of social ostracization against the supposed Jacobins in their midst. See for example John Adams's response to the citizens of Weston, Massachusetts, in which he congratulates them "on their signal felicity, in having no disorganizers. Two or three of this description of characters are sufficient to destroy the good neighborhood, interrupt the harmony, and poison the happiness of a thousand families." Boston *Columbian Centinel*, August 15, 1798.

21. Philadelphia *Gazette of the United States*, July 5, 1798.

22. Samuel Miller, *A Sermon, Delivered May 9, 1798* . . . (New York, 1798), 40.

23. Theodore Dwight, *An Oration Spoken at Hartford . . . on the Anniversary of American Independence, July 4th, 1798* (Hartford, 1798), 20–22.

24. Hezekiah Packard, *Federal Republicanism, Displayed in Two Discourses, Preached on the Day of the State Fast at Chelmsford, and on the day of the National Fast at Concord, in April, 1799* (Boston, 1799), 19.

25. Addison, *Oration on the Rise and Progress of the United States*, 22.

26. Jedidiah Morse, *A Sermon Preached at Charlestown, November 29, 1798* . . . (Boston, 1798), 21–22.

27. Dunham, *Oration on the Fourth of July, 1798*, 12.

28. David Osgood, *Some Facts evincive of the atheistical, anarchical, and in other respects, immoral Principles of the French Republicans, Stated in a Sermon Delivered on the 9th of May, 1798* . . . (Boston, 1798), 10–11, 13, 22.

29. The best account of the Illuminati scare of 1798 is still Stauffer, *New England and the Bavarian Illuminati*.

30. Jedidiah Morse, *A Sermon, Delivered at the North Church in Boston, in the Morning, and in the Afternoon at Charleston, May 9th, 1798* . . . (Boston, 1798), 20–21, 24–25.

31. John Lathrop, *A Sermon on the Dangers of the Times, from Infidelity and Immorality; and Especially from a Lately Discovered Conspiracy against Religion and Government* . . . (Springfield, Mass., 1798), 13.

32. William Linn, *A Discourse on National Sins: Delivered May 9, 1798* . . . (New York, 1798), 23.

33. Morse, *Sermon, Delivered at the North Church*, 25.

34. Lathrop, *Sermon on the Danger of the Times*, 20.

35. Timothy Dwight, *The Duty of Americans, at the Present Crisis* (New Haven, 1798), in *Political Sermons of the American Founding Era, 1730–1805*, ed. Ellis Sandoz (Indianapolis, 1991), 1383.

36. Morse, *Sermon, Delivered at the North Church*, 20.

37. Dwight, *Duty of Americans*, in Sandoz, *Political Sermons*, 1378, 1380.

38. On this phenomenon in Britain see Mark Philp, "Vulgar Conservatism, 1792–1793," *English Historical Review* 101 (1995): 42–69.

39. Gayle Pendleton, "Towards a Bibliography of the *Reflections* and *Rights of Man* Controversy," *Bulletin of Research in the Humanities* 85, no. 1 (1982): 65–103.

40. Harry B. Weiss, "Hannah More's Cheap Repository Tracts in America," *Bulletin of the New York Public Library* 50 (1946): 539–49, 634–41. One of More's biographers claims that "large orders [for the Cheap Repository Tracts] came from America, accompanied by letters of congratulation on 'the uncommon success' of the Tracts." M. G. Jones, *Hannah More* (Cambridge, 1952), 144.

41. *The Works of Hannah More* (New York, 1848), 190. For secondary work on the politics of the Cheap Repository Tracts see David Eastwood, "Patriotism and the English State in the 1790s," in *The French Revolution and British Popular Politics*, ed. Mark Philp (Cambridge, 1991), 146–68; Robert Hole, "British Counter-revolutionary Popular Propaganda in the 1790s," in *Britain and Revolutionary France: Conflict, Subversion and Propaganda*, ed. Colin Jones (Exeter, 1983), 53–69; and H. T. Dickinson, "Popular Conservatism and Militant Loyalism, 1789–1815," in *Britain and the French Revolution*, ed. H. T. Dickinson (New York, 1989), 103–26.

42. Hannah More, *The History of Mr. Fantom, the New Fashioned Philosopher and his Man William*. (Philadelphia, 1800), 2–8.

43. Letter to Mathew Carey, August 23, 1798, Lea & Febiger Correspondence, HSP.

44. Dwight, *Duty of Americans, at the Present Crisis*, in Sandoz, *Political Sermons*, 1387.

45. Packard, *Federal Republicanism*, 28.

46. Nathanael Emmons, *A Discourse, Delivered May 9, 1798. Being the Day of Fasting and Prayer throughout the United States* (Wrentham, Mass., 1798), 15, 6.

47. John Thornton Kirkland, *An Oration, Delivered, at the Request of the Society of Phi Beta Kappa, in the Chapel of Harvard College . . . July 19, 1798* (Boston, 1798), 10.

48. See John L. Brooke's essay in this volume.

49. [William Brown], *Look before ye Loup; or, A Healin' sa' for the Crackit Crowns of Country Politicians, by Tam Thrum, an Auld Weaver* (Philadelphia, 1798), 5–9.

50. Thornton, *Oration*, 5–21. For fuller discussions of the relationship between gender, the political, and the social in the late eighteenth century see Rosemarie Zagarri, "The Rights of Man and Woman in Post-Revolutionary America," *William and Mary Quarterly*, 3d ser., 55 (1998): 203–30, and Jan Lewis, " 'Of Every Age, Sex, & Condition': The Representation of Women in the Constitution," *Journal of the Early Republic* 15 (1995): 359–87.

51. With the rise of women's reform movements in the 1830s and 1840s, this notion of women's "social" role became the launching pad for more explicitly "political" activity. In the 1790s, however, the unintended democratic possibilities of "the social" were still a long way off.

52. I discuss the process through which many 1790s radicals disavowed their earlier activism in order to integrate more effectively into the moderate Jeffersonian party of the early 1800s in "Joseph Gales and the Making of the Jeffersonian Middle Class," in *The Revolution of 1800: Democracy, Race, and the New Republic*, ed. Peter S. Onuf, Jan E. Lewis, and James Horn (Charlottesville, 2002), 331–59.

53. Carey's biographer, Edward C. Carter III, carefully avoided the question of whether he actually was a United Irishman in the mid-1790s ("The Political Activities of Mathew Carey, Nationalist, 1760–1814" [Ph.D. diss., Bryn Mawr, 1962]). James Green, who has done extensive research on Carey's career as a bookseller and printer, has speculated that Carey indeed destroyed some of his papers to cover up his past radicalism (conversation with author, June 1998.) Evidence of Carey's difficult dealings with the Bank of the United States can be found in much of his correspondence from 1798. See Lea & Febiger Letter Books, HSP.

54. Very few archival records of Eaton's experience in America exist. This description is based on a brief biographical sketch of Eaton in Michael Durey, *Transatlantic Radicals in the Early American Republic* (Lawrence, Kans., 1997) and an account in William Cobbett, *Porcupine's Works*, 9:258. While Cobbett's portrayals of radicals are generally far from reliable, there is no evidence to disprove this description of Eaton's fate.

55. For a detailed examination of how this process worked out in Pennsylvania see Andrew Shankman, "Malcontents and Tertium Quids: The Battle to Define Democracy in Jeffersonian Philadelphia," *Journal of the Early Republic* 19 (1999): 43–72.

56. Linda Colley, *Britons: Forging the Nation, 1701–1837* (New Haven, 1992).

57. On April 19, 1798, Joseph Priestley wrote to his friend and fellow British émigré Benjamin Vaughan, complaining about how Americans had become intensely "jealous . . . of the interference of foreigners. I keep out of the way of all Politicks, and yet I meet with more and more coarse abuse here, than in England, and in a Newspaper most patronized by the governing people. . . . The zealous friends of the revolution here are in general out of favour now, and the tories are courted and popular." Benjamin Vaughan Papers, American Philosophical Society.

PART FOUR

ANDREW R. L. CAYTON

II

Continental Politics

Liberalism, Nationalism, and the Appeal of Texas in the 1820s

In the 1820s, Texas attracted the attention of citizens of the United States, Mexico, and the Cherokee Nation interested in improving the quality of their lives. We tend to think of these people as settlers rather than émigrés and to assume that they went to Texas to replicate rather than revise familiar worlds. Yet more than a few Americans considered migration because they felt constrained, in part by personal economic difficulties and in part by related fears, real or imagined, of powerful national governments. Uncomfortable with the correspondence between politics and society they saw emerging in the new republics of North America, they envisioned Texas as an opportunity to redress the balance between public and private power upset by the creation of liberal nation-states. The postcolonial character of the continent in the 1820s exacerbated their concern, because ideological as well as territorial borders were everywhere in flux in the aftermath of the independence of the United States and Mexico.

What men wanted, and how they went about pursuing their desires, depended largely on their perception of what was best for them in a particular place at a particular time. If their behavior seems inconsistent, even contradictory, in retrospect, it is because they believed that North America offered more than one definition of liberty and more than one path to autonomy.

This tension was uncommonly dynamic in Texas. Part of Mexico, which declared its independence from Spain in 1821, but enticing to both white men and Indians, especially Cherokees, living in the United States, Texas was one of the last great borderlands in North America, a place literally in between two imperial federal republics with divergent colonial pasts.[1] Its future was uncertain: we cannot assume the inevitability of the creation of the Republic of Texas in 1836 any more than its annexation by the United States in 1845. Neither should we assume that people interested in Texas wanted to transform it into a perfected version of the world in which they lived. Many Americans, Mexicans, and Cherokees were unhappy with North American governments in the 1820s. Seeing themselves as brothers to other men on a public, national level, they considered themselves fathers to women, children, and enslaved African Americans on a personal, local level. Indeed, they sometimes perceived a liberal, national authority as pitting public power against private power. Men who were happy to see themselves as democratic brothers united in a nation centered on Washington D.C. or Mexico City also wanted to see themselves as benevolent patriarchs whose authority within the confines of families and local communities was absolute.

Looking at the ways in which early nineteenth century North Americans imagined the possibilities of life in Texas helps us understand better the complex evolution of political authority in North America as a whole. Politics in the United States, Mexico, and the Cherokee nation occasionally intersected, rather than paralleled each other, because North Americans argued across national boundaries as well as within them, projecting their hopes and fears onto each other.[2] In Texas, the existence of two competing centers of political authority— the United States and Mexico—enabled men unhappy with the direction of one government to contemplate a better relationship between public and private power under the other, and thereby to contribute to one of the most enduring stories in North American political history: the all-consuming desire of local patriarchs to limit the influence of revolutionary national governments.

LIBERALISM AND NATIONALISM IN THE UNITED STATES

"Americans born after independence became the self-conscious shapers of a liberal society."[3] Free to govern themselves, white men and women were perpetually in motion, dreaming of a hitherto unimaginable world of material and moral progress. In this new world, politics was increasingly separated from the rest of people's lives. Until the democratic revolutions of the late eighteenth century, the structures of public power reflected the structures of private power. Monarchies were patriarchal households writ large. Gentlemen who governed their families and their localities governed larger communities as well. The democratization created by both political and commercial revolutions severed that connection. In the United States, virtually all adult white males, regardless of their social standing, participated in their own government. As thousands of new men from all kinds of backgrounds sought office and gentlemen retired from the rough and tumble of partisan competition, politics itself became a career. At least in the North, patriarchal gentlemen whose authority rested on their local status were suddenly anachronisms.[4] The loss of power was private as well as public. Both the market revolution and evangelical Christianity empowered women to express political opinions, even as courts challenged the autonomy of unitary patriarchal households by defining families as consisting of "distinct members, each with his or her own legal rights."[5]

Many white men resisted these changes, especially as they were embodied in the growing power of a United States government guided by men from the northeastern states. Anti-Federalists and later Jeffersonian Republicans championed the authority of local democratic patriarchs against the perceived power of the federal government created by the Constitution of 1787 and elaborated on by the Federalist administrations of the 1790s.[6] Although the largely pragmatic presidency of Thomas Jefferson and the rapid decline of the Federalists in the early 1800s calmed critics, concerns about defining the United States in national and liberal terms revived after the War of 1812. White male southerners in particular were worried about their futures in an American republic committed to national liberalism. Between 1819 and 1829, the power of the national government appeared to pose a more serious threat to the sanctity of patriarchal households and local autonomy—particularly with regard to land, slaves, and taxes—than at any other time between the 1790s and the 1850s. Not coincidentally, it was the longest extended period without a strong national party system. Lacking partisan organization to organize and temper divisions, Americans were free to indulge their ceaseless fear of a tyrannical central government. Governments, some argued, existed to protect local and private autonomy, not threaten them. According to J. Mills Thornton, men who would rally to the banner of Andrew Jackson "emphasized the notion that freedom is autonomy: that is the absence of external forces manipulating one's life." As late as the 1850s, argues Stephanie McCurry, virtually all white males in South Carolina remained committed to "the virtually unlimited right of an independent man to mastery over his own household and the property that lay within its boundaries."[7]

White émigrés to Texas in the 1820s tended to be men who believed that such a world was under serious threat in the United States. Of course, Americans went to Texas for a variety of reasons, many of them idiosyncratic and prosaic; some were "failures," "drifters almost by nature," "fugitive[s] from justice," or "misfits." But the majority of the 10,000 or so migrants were undoubtedly ordinary southern white men, most of whom had neither a family nor owned enslaved African Americans.[8] Not all were poor, single men, however. Forty years old in 1822, a native of Virginia who had lived in Georgia and Alabama, Jared E. Groce migrated in style. His household traveled in fifty covered wagons and "included the women and children of his family [his oldest son rode a horse like his father], more than ninety slaves, furniture, spinning wheels, looms, clothing, farming equipment for a large operation, and food to feed his entourage along the way. A train of livestock, including mules, cows, sheep, hogs, and extra horses, followed the wagons."[9] Many others moved in families, although few did so in the grand manner of Groce.

Rich or poor, emigrants were primarily interested in protecting the interests of their household or prospective household, something they saw as increasingly difficult in the United States. The 1820s began ominously with a national economic depression caused by the Panic of 1819. Particularly in trans-Appalachia, men who purchased thousands of acres in the late 1810s with generous credit from the Bank of the United States and the federal government found their dreams of landed independence shattered by economic contraction. Together, they owed almost $23 million to the United States. Some men worried about imprisonment—a physical loss of independence—because they lacked the money to pay off their creditors.[10] In 1824, Charles Douglas of Murfreesborough, Tennessee, complained that "the people are heels over head in debt. . . . Although our legislature has from time to time been trying to relieve the people, yet all their plans have the effect of plunging them still further into difficulties. So much for legislative relief systems in time of pecuniary embarrisment."[11]

Congress did not seem any more responsive than state legislatures. It established cash-only sales and minimum purchases and loosened rules for paying off debt. While these relief measures revealed the government's desire to sell public lands as quickly and cheaply as possible, not everyone saw them that way at the time. In fact, a widespread sense that the federal land business was corrupt was rooted in reality. Until the mid-1820s, "the administrators of the public domain were unable to prevent disorganization, confusion, uncertainty, favoritism, fraud, and exploitation from permeating the land business."[12]

Meanwhile, Americans heard that land was easier to acquire in Texas. Stories abounded that settlers would receive around 4500 acres of land (subject to a delayed tax and the fees of the *empresario*) and full riparian rights to all water within or next to their property. In 1825, the *Missouri Advocate* saw the difference between Mexico and the United States as "a republic which gives first-class land gratis and a republic which will not sell inferior land for what it is worth."[13] The *Nashville Republican* reprinted an 1825 letter from a Texas settler extolling not just the quality of the land, but the terms under which it could be gained. Settlers would receive land just for settling it. As an added bonus, their "land will be exempt from Taxation for the term of ten years." Even then, taxes would probably "be merely nominal for many years to come" because "the principal source of revenue" in Mexico was "derived from the *Mines*."[14] Americans also applauded the federalism of the Mexican land system. Unlike in the United States, noted Stephen Fuller Austin, the most prominent American émigré to Texas in the 1820s, "The States of the Mexican Confederation never did cede any portion of their vacant Lands to the General Government. The right to sell or grant them to individuals resides with the state to which they belong."[15]

The combination of cheap land and local autonomy made Texas more than just another place to settle. In many ways, it represented an alternative world, free from the centralization of political power many southern white men feared was becoming more pronounced in the United States. Stephen Austin suggested in 1830 that "the greatest misfortune that could befall Texas at this moment" would be for the United States "Govt" to "get hold of us and introduce its *land system*." This "would be a sudden change by which many of the emigrants would be thrown upon the liberality of the Congress of the United States of the North—*theirs would be a most forlorn hope*."[16]

Born in Virginia in 1793, Austin was the descendant of Connecticut Congregationalists. His father, Moses, possessed in ample measure the entrepreneurial energy of Americans in the early republic, and devoted his life to the pursuit of the main chance.[17] In 1798, the Austins moved to Upper Louisiana, now the state of Missouri, where they became, albeit briefly, subjects of Spain and then, in 1800, the French leader, Napoleon Bonaparte. Moses did not take his obligation to become a Catholic too seriously, but he did accommodate himself to the legal and social structures of a Spanish colony without much complaint. Moses thrived in culturally diverse Missouri, owning lead mines, a dry-goods store, and shares in the Bank of St. Louis.

The Austins suffered severe financial constrictions in the late 1810s. In tandem with his sister and her husband, Stephen moved to Arkansas Territory in 1819. He and his brother-in-law got involved in an ill-fated land speculation, which resulted in a debt of $9,000 that took him years to erase.[18] Contemplating a career as a lawyer, Stephen ended up working for and boarding with Joseph H. Hawkins, a former congressman, who had a legal practice in New Orleans. Meanwhile, Moses set out to reverse his financial problems by negotiating to buy land in Texas. He made a deal with the governor of Texas in San Antonio to locate 300 families in the Mexican province, then returned to Missouri where he promptly died. Stephen rushed home to take over the family business and proceeded with the Texas migration, bolstered by a $4,000 loan from Hawkins that entitled his former employer to one-half interest in all of Austin's Texas lands.

Among other things, the Austins' story demonstrates the weakness of national loyalty in the early American republic, especially in the trans-Appalachian region where hundreds of men from William Blount and James Wilkinson to Daniel Boone, Aaron Burr, and Andrew Jackson had flirted with the Spanish authorities west of the Mississippi River. Patriotism was negotiable.[19] Men such as the Austins cared about the United States to the extent that it enhanced their local authority. They knew that government could be an ally as well as an enemy; what mattered most was the power of nation-states to advance or retard the interests of a brotherhood of democratic patriarchs intent upon dominating the southern and western regions of the new republic. Because the primary goal of the Austins was to protect their household, territorial boundaries were not as important as the security of their property.

Land was not the only form of property in need of protection. The Austins owned slaves in a place that was at the center of contemporary controversy about the institution. In Missouri, economic depression in 1819–1820 coincided with the first major political crisis over slavery under the Constitution. Northern congressmen objected to admitting Missouri as a slave state. While this dispute was resolved with a compromise that divided the North American continent along the 36° 30' parallel, it reinforced fears that the U.S. government was as unreliable in its protection of human property as it was in its guarantees of natural property.

These doubts about the centralizing tendencies of liberal northerners intensified during the administration of John Quincy Adams. Elected by the House of Representatives after he had garnered less than a third of the popular vote, Adams drew support primarily from the Northeast, although one crucial vote came from Missouri. Once in office, his contention that "liberty is power," and his insistence on an activist role for government in doing good in the world, frightened many Americans. Supporters of Andrew Jackson, who had polled more votes than Adams in 1824, saw the president's government as corrupt and illegitimate. Disturbed by economic depression, land laws, and attacks on slavery, white men in the trans-Appalachian South had good reason to wonder about their futures in the United States.

Tariff controversies confirmed these doubts. In 1824 and 1828, Congress raised the rates on a protectionist tariff passed originally in 1816, largely in response to the demands of northeasterners for protection from ruinous foreign imports. Outraged southerners, who wanted to buy European goods and exalted the principle of free trade, denounced the 1828 tariff as one of "Abominations," evidence of undue northeastern influence in the national government. The American "Tariff System," complained Austin in 1829, "will make this country [Texas] prosper—The men of '76' are sinking into the grave—and I do seriously fear that the bonds of national union will decay and rot with them—."[20] No wonder Americans worried that agriculture was "fast declining in all the Middle and Southern region of our country, oppressed with heavy duties on imports from abroad and taxes at home, and the people burthened with debts," and envied those whose "happy star had conducted them to a country blessed with the finest soil in North America, with plenty, health, peace and happiness."[21]

Austin was not alone in fretting about whether the United States could long survive. The Nullification Crisis was a "most gloomy cloud" hanging "over our native land." If Virginia, North Carolina, and Georgia joined South Carolina in defying the federal government's tariff policy, "the union is at an end, & it is not very improbable that it may split into three parts. God help them—*they are all mad—.*"[22] There was no better place to escape such madness, according to Austin, than Texas.

LIBERALISM AND POLITICS IN THE CHEROKEE NATION

The citizens of the United States were not the only North Americans debating the revolutionary impact of liberalism or considering life in Texas. Cherokees who lived in the western Carolinas and Georgia were also working through the implications of the new order. Cherokee politics had long reflected Cherokee society, an extension of a world in which harmony took precedence over all other values. Nothing mattered more than sustaining kinship ties, mutuality, and the authority of clans. Law and politics were about restoring balance to the world; personal and direct, they required few intermediaries or institutions. If someone killed someone, the punishment was retaliation in kind. Political leaders, moreover, were generally men of status within their communities who emphasized the importance of consensus and expected those who failed to carry the day in tribal councils to withdraw from them rather than persist in opposition.

The emergence of the United States threatened the destruction of this world. East of the Mississippi River, the American victory in the War of 1812 marked the end of serious military resistance to the republic. In the 1830s, American governments would forcibly remove most Indians to land west of the Mississippi. In the interim, however, under pressure from whites, a minority of elite men of mixed race origins began to move toward a modified liberal conception of their political order. They created a strikingly independent judiciary with a supreme court. In July 1827, a constitutional convention devised a government that emulated that of the United States in terms of a separation of power among three distinct branches and the establishment of a legal system that superseded village and family control. Women lost influence that they had once exercised in local councils. And while these changes sparked considerable controversy, they occurred within the parameters of a public conversation about the past and the future. By 1828, a Cherokee named Elias Boudinot, educated by missionaries and trained at a college in New England, was editing a bilingual newspaper, supported by the nation and utilizing the written version of the Cherokee language devised by a man named Sequoyah.

The reordering of Cherokee society was a creative response to an increasingly desperate situation. As pressure from Americans mounted, the Cherokees sought to use their institutions to protect their autonomy. The adoption of liberal values and institutions did not mean that they lost a sense of themselves. To the contrary, many Cherokees became more conscious of the ways in which race, religion, and history differentiated them from Americans. Treaty commissioners appointed by the United States in 1822 reported that the skillful Cherokees would not part with more land largely because of "the fondness with which they cherish the feeling of National pride" and "a determination to perpetuate their National Character." They did not want to become part of the United States, subject to its laws. They wanted autonomy.[23] If necessary, they would eventually come into the republic on their own terms. Soon, predicted the young Cherokee David Brown in 1823, there would soon be "an aborigine in congress who will act in the capacity of a representative of the Cherokee Nation."[24]

As in the United States, however, a considerable number of the members of the Cherokee Nation resisted this transformation. As individualism, commercialism, and patriarchy increasingly displaced local communalism and matrilinealism, as more and more Cherokees became farmers, merchants, innkeepers, and slave-owners, as the Nation upheld competition, monogamy, and self-discipline, some Indians decided that migration to another place was preferable to life in an increasingly liberal society. Like many white Americans dissatisfied with the power of the United States government in the 1820s, they found the Texas region especially attractive.

Starting in the early 1790s and growing in the 1820s, thousands of Cherokees (many of mixed-race ancestry) who were committed to traditional forms of social and political organization migrated across the Mississippi River. The Western Cherokees settled first in Arkansas, where they lived in villages by hunting and some farming. At the end of the first decade of the nineteenth century, they were seeking permission to move into Spanish Texas. Meanwhile, the Cherokee National Council, worried that they would continue to deal with the United States for land in Arkansas, condemned the migrants as "Stragglers" who should be treated as expatriates. The council made citizenship a reflection of residence, not kinship. "The Cherokee Nation was not simply a people; it was a place," writes McLoughlin.[25]

As long as they stayed near Americans, émigrés found life difficult. In the Arkansas River Valley, Indians' insistence on consensus and retaliation created tension with American officials committed to individualism, capitalism, and the rule of formal law. Led by the chief Duwali, dozens of Cherokees and some Delawares, Creeks, and Chocktaws moved in the winter of 1819–20 into the Great Bend region of the Arkansas River. There they and their predecessors were regularly at odds with Americans. Most problematic were legal issues, especially cases of murder. American officials, such as Indian agent Dr. John Sibley, insisted on handling crimes with European notions of justice. That is, they wanted judges and juries to hear evidence, listen to arguments, and decide on an appropriate punishment in accordance with customary practice. Indians, for their part, demanded immediate retribution. The death of one person should result in the death of another person. The needs of the group took precedence over the rights of an individual. When Sibley asked a Coushatta village to turn over an Indian who had killed an American, apparently in retaliation for the murder of an Indian by a white man, the village refused. Soon, the residents had packed up and migrated into Spanish Texas.

By the 1820s there was a steady stream of Alabamas, Coushattas, and Cherokees, as well as a few Delawares and Shawnees from north of the Ohio River into Texas. The land was immensely appealing. So, too, was the prospect of an imperial government that might balance the burgeoning power of the United States. Worried about the American expansion, the Spanish began in the late 1810s to woo Indians with presents and trading privileges. Seeking to create a spirit of respect and mutuality, Spanish officials hoped to make the Indians a buffer against further American settlement.[26] Eager to make up for their dilatoriness in mastering borderland politics, the Spanish highlighted the bad behavior of Americans and invited Indians to settle in Texas.

Harassed by Americans, Indians as well as whites sought permission to settle in Texas in the 1820s. Not only did they know the land to be fertile and well watered, they expected life with Europeans to be less chaotic. The government in Mexico City might well be prevailed upon to offer protection in return for loyalty and goods. Cherokees and other Indians envisioned a traditional world in which politics worked best when the group played one set of Europeans against another. In or near the United States, Indians had no way short of violence or withdrawal to resist assimilation into a liberal state that valued individualism, competition, and private property. In Texas, at least, there was hope of an alternative. Here, they suggested, was an alternative to the United States. It was a siren song that many discontented North Americans, both white and Indian, found immensely attractive.

LIBERALISM AND NATIONALISM IN MEXICO

Created in 1821, the independent nation of Mexico, which governed Texas, was distinctly different from the United States. For a variety of reasons, localism and patriarchy were more entrenched in Mexico and all efforts to liberalize and centralize first the colony of New Spain and then the new nation provoked strong resistance.

In the second half of the eighteenth century, the Spanish empire implemented a series of reforms growing out of its defeat in the Seven Years' War. On the one hand, the Bourbon Reforms were designed to reduce the privileges or liberties of corporate bodies within the empire, fully in keeping with the eighteenth-century transformations of *anciens régimes* in Great Britain, its North American colonies, and France. They included an assault on the Roman Catholic Church, whose officials not only held secular offices but controlled the wealthiest institution in New Spain. They also tried to revitalize the economy by promulgating a policy of *comercio libre*, or free trade, within the empire. Rather than destroy the inefficient system of viceroys and *audiencias* that had governed the empire for centuries, the Spanish created an alternative governmental structure. French-style *intendants* were appointed with commissions to improve judicial systems and streamline government activities.

Although these proto-liberal policies stimulated economic growth and the expansion of an urban bourgeoisie, New Spain remained overwhelmingly a society of institutions and privileges in which *criollos* (people of European descent born in the Americas) and *mestizos* (people of mixed-race ancestry) saw government less as a *threat* to their liberty than as the *source* of their liberties. Even the Bourbon reforms reflected this. While adopting *comercio libre*, the Spanish empire sought to revitalize economic production by offering important concessions to mining guilds. Most characteristic of the Bourbon Reforms was the widespread granting of the *fuero militar*. Designed to enroll criollos in the defense of the empire as cheaply as possible, the fueros were privileges (exemptions from taxes, the right to be tried by special military courts, the right to wear uniforms) that attracted the attention of certain kinds of men and attached them to the empire. Criollos never completely associated the idea of liberty with freedom from government. They and their superiors generally considered liberties as privileges, grants of freedom to certain bodies of men in return for their service to the state as a whole.

The army was the classic example. Unlike in the British colonies, where colonists served in locally organized militia units, often with contracts that limited both their obligation to governments and governments' power over them, criollos in New Spain looked to the imperial government's power to grant privileges as a guarantee of social status. Nothing reflected this more than the fact that Carlos III (1759–88) gave twenty-three titles of nobility to Mexicans (there were another eighteen before independence).[27] Much as the Bourbon Reforms sought to revitalize the empire, the Spanish retained the core conception of their society as a collection of corporate bodies rather than individuals.

Reinforcing this notion among criollos was a combination of race and ideology. As in the United States, color mattered immensely in Mexico. But unlike the United States, where it sharply divided one group from everyone else, race in Mexico created a kaleidoscope of identities. Because Indians and whites (and Africans) intermingled with each other sexually far more than in British North America, Mexico was a baroque profusion of racial categories. Race and status were closely related, but they often had a fictive quality to them, with people working hard to construct facades of racial purity. Criollos obsessed with the privileges of whiteness could buy special certificates of whiteness that attested to their pure backgrounds.

More important, racial mixture meant that even many criollos had a dual heritage. Many liked to speak of their Spanish fathers and Indian mothers, to see themselves as the children of conquest and rape. Mexicans were far more conscious of their dramatic history than British North Americans were of their more prosaic beginnings. In the early nineteenth century, many Mexican gentlemen romanticized precontact history, disparaged the European conquest, and developed notions of a Mexican nation that both antedated and survived the colonial era.[28] Social revolution was not what they had in mind. It is entirely consistent that their initial government was a constitutional monarchy (with Agustín de Iturbide on the throne) designed to protect institutions and privileges while ensuring national autonomy. And it is entirely consistent that the supporters of the monarchy refused to tax themselves to pay for it.

In fact, Mexican independence followed from a loss of faith in an imperial government that was increasingly liberal. The revolutions of Miguel Hidalgo y Costilla and José María Morelos originated in response to the collapse of the empire (with the fall of Spain to Napoleon in 1808), and they failed, suppressed by a combination of *peninsulares* (Europeans in the Americas who were born in Spain) and criollos who feared revolution from below more than they feared revolution from above and used the army to achieve their ends. When Mexico finally declared independence in 1821, it did so because Royalist officers in the powerful army were reacting to the institution of a liberal government in Spain. They believed their interests, their rights, their liberties were threatened by an imperial regime that promised to destroy the corporate privileges that were the bedrock of criollo life in New Spain. The leaders of Mexican independence were more interested in autonomy than in independence.[29]

Several Americans were in Mexico City during the reign of Agustín I. The one we know the most about was the South Carolinian Joel Poinsett who would soon become a meddling American ambassador. Less well known are the experiences of other Americans, including *empresarios* Stephen Austin and Robert Leftwich. The latter was fascinated by the coronation of the emperor and empress on July 21, 1821. He described the throne, its surroundings, the way in which the seats for the Congress grew shorter from front to back, the music, the religious ceremonies, and the great excitement of the residents of the city.[30]

Leftwich and his colleagues knew they were in a foreign place, and not just territorially. Craving local autonomy, they feared not monarchy, but a strong central government. Within months of Iturbide's coronation, they were certain that they would get their wish, although they remained fearful of the army. Argued Leftwich in February 1823: "The public opinion is in favour of a republic but the people in this country are almost a Cypher. The army is the *Sovereign*[.] [W]hat they order the people obey[.]"[31] Still, in July 1823 Austin was certain that opposition to "the federated system" had dissipated. While Mexicans ought to recognize "a center of the union, without which nothing can save us from anarchy," they would place real power in the states.[32]

Also in Mexico City in 1823 was Richard Fields, a representative of the Texas Cherokees. Born in 1780 in Tennessee, Fields was one-eighth Cherokee and had migrated to Texas with others after the War of 1812, in which he had fought as a member of Andrew Jackson's army. Probably chosen by a council representing several villages in 1822, Fields had begun lobbying Antonio Martínez, governor of Texas, for land, with the question, "What is to be done with us poor Indians?"[33] In the fall, a new governor had agreed to allow the Cherokees to stay in Texas (and more to join them) in return for organizing militia units to protect the state and stop cattle-rustling. The Indians were to "be considered Hispano Americans, and entitled to all the rights and privileges granted to such."[34] With this agreement in hand, Fields and several other Cherokees traveled to Mexico City.

Fields never met Agustín I because the latter's reign ended almost as soon as it began. Mexico was moving toward the kind of decentralized government the empresarios sought. The Bourbon Reforms and the long, nasty war in the 1810s (in which one out of every ten Mexicans died and their economy was virtually destroyed) had reinforced a regionalism founded in part of geography and economic development. Far more than the United States, Mexico was a collection of distinct areas that saw themselves as coherent, powerful, and privileged regions. The persistence of regional, class, and racial identities made a centralized national government virtually impossible. After the overthrow of Iturbide in 1823, the Mexican Congress adopted a staunchly federal constitution, which would be the basis for government in Mexico for more than a decade. The Constitution of 1824 created a federal government in which the power of states was much stronger than that of their counterparts in the United States.

From the long perspective, the federalism of the 1820s was short-lived. Conservatives constantly attacked and undermined the authority of the new constitution and by 1829 Mexico was awash with the *caudillismo* and instability that would last until the 1860s. However fleeting, the liberal moment of the 1820s was not unimportant. It was a decade of intense political and intellectual excitement in Mexico, comparable in many ways to the 1790s in the United States. And there were significant reforms. The Mexican nobility supported the ending of entail (as a way to turn assets into cash) and the abolition of titles of nobility in 1826. Congress forbade the use of the titles "*don*" and "*doña*," suggesting the use of "*ciudadano*" and "*madama*" in their place. States wrote their own constitutions, claiming a high degree of political and economic autonomy. Many outlawed slavery.[35]

Radical as these measures were, they should not be confused with the kind of liberal revolution that was transforming the United States. Liberalism did not take hold as an organizing principle in Mexican society. Indeed, Mexican political history between the 1820s and the 1860s was a struggle between conservative and liberal forces, between those who remained committed to the importance of privileges, ranks, and institutions and those who wanted to privilege individualism and a negative definition of liberty. These issues would not be resolved in any serious fashion until the triumph of the liberal Reforma in the late 1860s.

Meanwhile, Mexicans joined the Colombian Simón Bolívar in rejecting the universality of the political system of the United States. To be sure, the Mexican Congress hung a portrait of George Washington in the gallery of heroes and the newspaper *El Sol* in 1823 called the American Constitution of 1787 "one of the perfect creations of the human spirit" and "the base on which rests the most simple, liberal, and happy government that we know in history." But even republican enthusiasts such as Servando Teresa de Mier Noriega y Guerra recognized important differences between Mexico and the United States. By the 1830s, Lorenzo de Zavala, a strong advocate of the federal constitution of 1824, knew that while Mexico had assumed "the formulas, the phrases, the words, the names, the titles, in short all the outward constitutional effects of the United States . . . much was lacking in order that the substance, the essence of the system, that reality itself corresponds to the principles professed."[36]

Mexico, in short, could not—and should not—replicate the political culture of the United States. Neither Spanish nor Mexican efforts to centralize authority could overturn the entrenched power of local leaders whose political power corresponded directly with their social and economic standing. By the middle of the nineteenth century, what Florencia Mallon has called a "democratic patriarchy," or horizontal relationships among men based upon their vertical position within their households and local communities, flourished in Mexico.[37] For both American and Indian émigrés to Texas in the 1820s, Mexico seemed much more supportive of local autonomy and patriarchal power than the United States. At precisely the same time many Americans were worrying about the centralizing tendencies of the Adams administration, Mexico offered a clear-cut alternative.

PATRIARCHY AND FEDERALISM IN TEXAS

The Mexican Constitution of 1824, which located power primarily in the states, was a boon to potential settlers in Texas because real authority lay with the nearer government of Coahuila y Texas. The National Colonization Law of August 18, 1824, prevented the national government from interfering with settlements on Mexican territory.

Indians benefited directly from this development. Mexican officials in the state government were happy to welcome Cherokees, along with Alabamas and Coushattas. They hoped the Indians would serve as a buffer against American immigrants as well as Comanches and other Indians to the west. Cherokee and other Indians were now living under a government that of necessity was eager to protect their local worlds as long as their interests overlapped. The colonization law of the state of Coahuila and Texas permitted "Indians of all nations bordering on the state, as well as wandering tribes that may be within its limits" to trade and apply for land grants if they supported Mexico's religious and legal institutions.[38]

Indians made up a sizable number of émigrés to Texas in the 1820s. When Cherokees, Delawares, Shawnees, and Kickapoos, many of them from north of the Ohio River, rallied against other Indians, nervous officials demanded an explanation. Fields and other Cherokee leaders took the opportunity to declare their independence. They had "nothing to do with the Anglo Americans here, and we will not submit to their laws, or dictates, but we do, and always will, submit to the laws and orders emanating from the Mexican nation."[39] Mexico, however, was far less of a threat to Indians than the United States. In Texas, maintained a more traditional political structure. The visitor Jean Louis Berlandier noted that while young men were often insubordinate, decisions were made collectively. There was no acceptance of permanent opposition. Generalizing broadly, Berlandier observed that Indians lacked institutional Ameans, "particular or general, for obliging citizens to perform any of their duties." Instead of "power" residing "in the law, among these natives . . . *the law resides in power.*" Because crime and punishment were personal issues and lay "in each individual . . . neither superstitions nor the expressed will of their assemblies can impose punishment." The idea was "to live in the closest and most perfect unity."[40]

White Americans in search of similar local autonomy also had reason to look favorably on life in Texas. After Austin, succeeding *empresarios* negotiated with the state of Coahuila y Texas. Its colonization law, dated March 24, 1825, announced that "All foreigners" who wished to settle in compliance with the provisions of the national act of 1824 were "at liberty to do so," provided that they could produce certificates attesting to "their christianity, morality, and good habits." All *empresarios* were to receive "a premium" for each 100 families (up to 800) of five *sitios* of grazing land and five labors of land. Land was granted to each family who farmed, with more to those who raised stock. Unmarried men received their share when they took a wife and one quarter more if she was Mexican. But "those who are entirely single, or who do not form a part of some family whether foreigners or natives" received only a quarter share "until they marry." People who wished to join settlements later were also eligible for grants.[41]

Under challenge in the United States, patriarchy remained supreme in Mexico. Indeed, the government encouraged *empresarios* to act paternally. Green De Witt, one of the most successful *empresarios*, received a grant in 1825 from the state of Texas and Coahuila for a substantial amount of land adjacent to the Austin grant. In return, he promised to settle 400 families within six years. De Witt was obliged to respect the property rights of people already residing within his grant. Otherwise, however, his primary responsibilities were to the government rather than his settlers. He had to demonstrate that they were Catholic, that they were of "good moral character"; he had to refuse, and even forcibly expel, "vagrants, or persons of bad morals." De Witt was made commanding officer of the local militia, which he was to organize. It was his "duty" to inform the proper officials of the arrival of 100 families so that a properly appointed commissioner could create towns, to communicate with Mexican officials in Spanish, to establish schools (with the Spanish language), and "to erect churches in the new towns; to provide them with ornaments, sacred vessels, and other adornments dedicated to divine worship; and to apply in due time for the priests needed for the administration of spiritual instruction."[42]

In other words, De Witt was responsible for assuring the Mexicanizing of his settlers through language, religion, and governmental organization. Of these, the most problematic for most settlers was religion. Or so it seemed initially. The establishment of the Catholic Church in Mexico did not mean that it was a significant presence in Texas. In fact, there were only two secular priests in Texas in 1835, and there was no bishop in the diocese of Linares (with its see in Monterey) between 1821 and 1836. According to Howard Miller, the closest student of the Americans and Catholicism, "the Catholic requirement was by and large ignored by Anglo-Texans and unenforced by Mexican officials."[43] For the most part, Americans ignored religion altogether, rarely mentioning it or freedom of conscience in public documents and petitions until 1835.

Meanwhile, *empresarios* were autonomous benevolent patriarchs. Stephen Austin invariably treated his settlers like children, or dependents who needed his patronage to succeed. In 1823, he told his colonists that he felt "almost the same interest for their prosperity that I do for my own family—in fact I look upon them as one great family who are under my care."[44] He learned Spanish so that he could communicate with Mexican officials; he studied the judicial system and structures of local government. He had no hesitation in addressing his superiors as "Your Lordship."[45] While he never married, he planned an elaborate mansion to share with his sister Emily and her husband, James Perry.[46]

Private and public realms blended in the actions of *empresarios*. In 1827, Austin noted that he did far more with new emigrants than his contract required. He often had "to receive in my house most of those who come to see the country preparatory to moving, entertain them, spend days and weeks going over the land to instruct and inform them as newcomers of their situation." He had to explain Mexican laws and customs and translate documents. He had to supervise surveyors and explain the questions of Americans to Mexican commissioners. Austin complained that these chores reduced him to the "work of a pack mule who carries all the load and receives none of the benefit."[47]

Austin nevertheless enjoyed acting as a patron to his client settlers. There was simply little that they could accomplish without his knowledge and connections in Saltillo and Mexico City. When settlers arrived in his domain, they had to register with Austin and swear loyalty to the Mexican and Coahuila y Texas constitutions. The *empresario* could turn them away if they lacked the proper character. As supreme judge, as distributor of land, Austin and other *empresarios* were acting as the agent of the state as well as that of the settlers. He was not just a friendly face and a familiar facilitator; he was the visible embodiment of the Mexican government.

While Austin took his fee in kind (usually animals or corn) and offered a deferred payment plan, many early colonists objected to it. They believed that he had already received remuneration with huge grants of land from the government. Why should they pay him, too? Austin dismissed this discontent as typical of Americans, especially frontiersmen. "It is innate in an American to suspect and abuse a public officer whether he deserves it or not," he wrote in September 1825. Too many of them were licentious, wild, and greedy. Indeed, "to the ignorant part of the Americans independence means resistance and obstinacy, right or wrong."[48] Or, as he put it in 1829, people "growled and grumbled and muttered, without knowing why, or without being able to explain why" because of "a principle which is common to all North Americans, a feeling which is the natural offspring of the unbounded republican liberty enjoyed by all classes in the United States; that is, jealousy of undue encroachment on personal rights and a general repugnance to everything that wore even the semblance of a stretch of power."[49]

A Mexican official, José Antonio Saucedo, intervened in this early dispute by establishing a fee schedule more in keeping with custom. His endorsement of Austin explained the nature of authority in the colony. Saucedo explained that "Austin is completely authorized by the Supreme Government to found this colony and unless he forfeits the good opinion that is now entertained of him he will continue to exercise the Civil and Military powers he now has until the organization of this colony is completed."[50] In other words, Austin derived his power from above. It was not clear whose "good opinion" mattered, but the implication is that it was that of the government in Mexico City. Settlers could protest Austin's actions, they could receive redress from them, but he remained the supreme figure. Moreover, Austin worked out a solution to his dilemma that was unlikely to have passed muster in the United States. He arranged with the Mexican land commissioner to get one-third of his $127 per league fee.[51]

Despite his complaints, Austin considered himself the head of an extensive household with hundreds of dependents. "North Americans [were] the most obstinate and difficult people to manage that live on earth."[52] But it was easier to do so in Texas, where the nature of government and society were more amenable to patriarchy. There he could "treat the settlers as my children and Brothers" and "exercise that firmness and energy which my duty to the Government of my adoption, to the common good of the Colony, and to my own family require."[53]

Disgusted by the influence and ubiquity of lawyers in the United States and implicitly by the power of banks, Austin in 1832 proposed that credit be based on "moral character alone, and not upon wealth and coersive [sic] means—or, in other words, to annul all laws (avoiding unjust retroactive effects) for the coersive collection of debts, all landed or personal securities, all imprisonment or process against the person or property for debts."[54] This proposal reflected the experience of many western Americans in the 1820s. It also, however, spoke to a larger question of human relationships. Austin wanted to eliminate property and money as the basis of social ties and replace them with character.

More practically, Austin hoped for better emigrants. In 1829, he sought more of "that class of emigrants who deserve the appellation of Southern Gentlemen, whose fortunes are independent but not overgrown, whose judgment has been enlightened by education and matured by experience, and who have families to keep the intemperate, wild, ambitious passions of the human heart within the circle of prudence."[55] Austin was always more a paternalistic variation on democracy. In 1829, he laughed at his colonists' behavior in the election of the local *alcalde*. While "The Sovereigns" were initially pleased with their choice, within "*one month* [they] reversed the thing, tho for no other reason than because it is an act of *high Sovereignty* to curse those who are in office—right—or wrong."[56] In Mexico, popular sovereignty counted for far less than in the United States, which meant that *empresarios* could function more like the fathers than the brothers of their clients.

Coahuila y Texas offered a major concession to settlers by exempting them from taxes (except those raised in case of an invasion) and tariffs for a period of ten years. In the towns to be formed by the state and its commissioners, free lots were available to contractors and "artists of every class." When the population reached forty families, they could form their own government; they would elect an *ayuntamiento* when there were two hundred families. The last article was the most ambiguous, stating that with regard to slavery, "the new settlers shall obey the laws already established, and which hereafter may be established on the subject."[57]

Slavery was a key ingredient, for many of the white Americans and some Indians, most notably Cherokees, wanted to own slaves. The Mexican government, while committed in principle to the abolition of slavery, remained ambiguous on the subject. In 1824, the national Congress forbade "Commerce and traffic in slaves, proceeding from any country and under any flag whatsoever . . . in the territory of the United Mexican States."[58] These antislavery provisions of the Mexican constitution should not be interpreted as an endorsement of liberal notions of social equality. Mexicans may have been against slavery, but they were not against a society of castes and ranks. Moreover, the national government made virtually no effort to enforce its general emancipation. The act was a statement without force. Indeed, it was up to the individual states to decide what to do about slavery within their borders. Coahuila y Texas was so anxious to attract Americans that it was willing to adjust the general ban on slavery. Its 1827 constitution allowed the importation of slaves for six months after its promulgation. A year later, the state congress voted to allow émigrés to bring slaves when they called them indentured servants. Debt peonage was an acceptable form of dependence. Compensated with low annual wages, they had to pay for their food, housing, and clothing as well as the costs of their transportation to Texas. Typical was Marmaduke D. Sandifer of San Felipe de Austin's 1833 agreement to take care of Clarissa, "a girl of color," in return for her promise to "conduct & demean herself as an honest & faithful servant, hereby renouncing and disclaiming all her right and claim to personal liberty for & during a term of ninety-nine years."[59] Nationally, President Vincente de Guerrero exempted Texas from a general emancipation decree in 1829. Austin was sure that as a "Slave State," Texas would eventually become "the best State in the Mexican Union."[60] The newspaper in his town announced with delight that Texicans had achieved their fondest wishes—"the SECURITY of our PERSONS and PROPERTY."[61] By 1834, there were reportedly 2,000 slaves in a total Texas population of 21,000. As early as 1825, slaves constituted almost one quarter of the population of Austin's tract, with sixty-nine families owning slaves.[62]

The foundation of white Americans' hopes about Texas was a local political structure that shielded them from the power of both other governments and excessive democracy. Most important was the *ayuntamiento*, or city councils, as the colonial *cabildos* were now called. Under the Coahuila y Texas Constitution of 1827, *ayuntamientos* consisted of one to three *alcaldes* (depending on the size of the city) and several *regidores*, or councillors, and *syndicos*. Established by both custom and law, the duties of the *ayuntamiento* were extensive. The council was responsible for administering justice and governing the town in accordance with orders it received from above. Meeting once a week, it supervised the fiscal health of the community and collected customary taxes.

Coahuila y Texas appointed commissioner(s) to direct the establishment of cities for American settlers. They created a square plat with a plaza or town square in the middle connected to the peripheries by perpendicular streets. The width of streets was standardized, as were the locations of ecclesiastical and government buildings, the size of common lands. Aside from the organization of space, the most marked differences from the American system was the strong and specific role of government and law. After creating the town, the commissioners presided over the first elections to the *ayuntamiento*. Voters were "citizens enjoying their rights, domicilated and resident within the limits of the respective Ayuntamientos." But, unlike in the United States, citizens were required to vote, and by *viva voce*. Suffrage was not simply a right; it was a responsibility owed to the corporate body of which you were a member. So, too, was service on the *ayuntamiento*. Such "offices shall be municipal charges, which no one can decline."[63] In short, Mexican citizenship legally created obligations as well as freedom, entailing service to the state as well as freedom from it.

Obviously, Americans did not embrace every aspect of Mexican law. They were principally troubled by the lack of trial by jury in a world in which *alcaldes* had extraordinary adjudicatory powers. Even more disturbing was the Spanish tradition of trial by conciliation. Still, if some parts of the Mexican system of local government horrified Americans, others were quite appealing. More than anything else, the centrality of towns and alcaldes reinforced the corporate and patriarchal character of life in Texas. *Empresarios*, who usually functioned as a kind of all-powerful judicial figure before the creation of towns, were often elected *alcaldes* when the government created *ayuntamientos*. In practice, Austin delegated authority over most conflicts to others. But he retained enormous power. The thirty articles of his straightforward Civil Regulations reflected concessions to both the situation and patriarchal authority. Ignoring the existence of trial by jury, Austin established the system of *conciliacion* for disputes ranging from ten to two hundred dollars. Above that amount, Austin himself was the "judge of the colony."[64] He retained this position until 1828, when he refused to seek election as an *alcalde* because he was tired of dealing with trivial disagreements. The regulations also adopted the Mexican principle of detaining alleged criminals until they could be tried by proper authorities and with proper procedures.

In the spring of 1836, as Texans fought for independence against Mexico, Stephen Austin traveled across the United States to obtain military and financial aid for the beleaguered rebels. Everywhere, Austin insisted that the cause of Texas was the cause of the United States. He wanted his "countrymen" to understand that "*we*, the Texians [are] obeying the dictates of an education received here: from you the American people, from our fathers, from the patriots of 76?" If only the citizens of the United States would realize that the Texans' struggle against Mexico was "*a national war* in defence of national rights interests and principles and of Americans,"[65] "a war of barbarism and of despotic principles, waged by the mongrel Spanish-Indian and Negro race, against civilization and the Anglo-American race."[66] The United States did not declare war on Mexico. But the Texans' victory at San Jacinto meant that it did not really matter. Texans, most of whom had arrived in the 1830s, governed themselves until they agreed to annexation by the United States in 1845.

When we take for granted Austin's assertion in 1836 that Texas was the epitome of an American nationalism rooted in race and religion, we fail to appreciate the novelty of his assertion and accept a decidedly teleological reading of the history of the North American continent in the early nineteenth century. The expansion of the United States, fueled by remarkable demographic and economic growth, did not have to happen the way it did. No one knew in 1821 that in 1836 Texans would proclaim themselves proud Americans. What seems so inevitable in retrospect was highly contingent in the event. Only six years earlier, Austin had assumed that "the settled policy of Mexico was to make Texas a state as soon as possible and [that] it will be the best, the brightest star in the Mexican constellation."[67] Like others, he had imagined the creation of an alternative world within the borders of a truly federal Mexican republic, a world that would follow a different path than the one taken by the United States. The fact that it did not happen that way reflected political decisions made in both nations, decisions about how to organize and exercise power, as well as political decisions made in the borderlands between them. To look at the continent as a whole is to highlight the importance of national politics, not subsume them.

Austin and others looked to the United States in the mid-1830s because the political situation in both countries had changed. The northern republic's president was Andrew Jackson, a southern slaveholder who had decisively defeated John Quincy Adams in the election of 1828. Meanwhile, Mexican vice president

Anastasio Bustamante became president in 1830 as the result of a military revolt. Bustamante's chief minister, Lucas Alaman, led an attack on the rights of the states. While the new regime was overthrown in 1832, a period of intense liberal reform proved no more stable. A new constitution of 1836 transformed self-governing autonomous states into administrative departments run by centrally appointed governors and councils. Meanwhile, previous governments had not only abolished slavery; they had placed control of colonization in the hands of the central government and encouraged Mexicans to settle in Texas. As important, Mexico opened a customs house in Anahuac (Galveston) in 1832 to collect duties on imports. Closed because of American opposition, it reopened in 1835. By then, concessions from the government of President Antonio Lopez de Santa Anna, including more town councils, the use of English in official matters, and trial by jury, could not reverse the growing fears of American settlers that Mexico had become what the United States had threatened to become in the 1820s.

Only then did Texans move toward a romantic identification with the United States. Only then did they begin to move to subjugate or remove the Cherokees and other Indians. But, as always, their national loyalty remained a function of their commitment to local, democratic patriarchy. In that cause, their ancestors had created the United States in 1776 and their descendants would create the Confederate States in 1861. National loyalty mattered to the extent that their chosen nation embodied liberty defined as the protection of the autonomy of democratic patriarchs rather than as an assertion of the universal freedom of individual human beings.

NOTES

An earlier draft of this essay was prepared for a working group sponsored by the Woodrow Wilson Center and benefited from the suggestions of Mike Lacey and the members of the seminar (Colleen Dunlavey, Hendrik Hartog, James Henretta, Daniel Walker Howe, Richard John, John Larson, and Gordon Wood), as well as comments from Fred Anderson and Mary Kupiec Cayton.

1. Jeremy Adelman and Stephen Aron, "From Borderlands to Borders: Empires, Nation-States and the Peoples in Between in North American History," *American Historical Review* 86 (1999): 841–44; D. W. Meinig, *The Shaping of America: A Geographical Perspective on 500 Years of History. Volume 2: Continental America, 1800–1867* (New Haven, 1993); and David J. Weber, *The Spanish Frontier in North America* (New Haven, 1992).

2. This comes as no news to comparative and diplomatic historians, although they have not much exploited the insight beyond major political events. See James E. Lewis, Jr., *The American Union and the Problem of Neighborhood: The United States and the Collapse*

of the Spanish Empire, 1783–1829 (Chapel Hill, 1998), and Lester D. Langley, *The Americas in the Age of Revolution, 1750–1850* (New Haven, 1996).

3. Joyce Appleby, *Inheriting the Revolution: The First Generation of Americans* (Cambridge, Mass., 2000), 11. See also Daniel Walker Howe, *The Political Culture of the American Whigs* (Chicago, 1979); Howe, *Making the American Self: Jonathan Edwards to Abraham Lincoln* (Cambridge, Mass., 1997); Peter S. Onuf, *Jefferson's Empire: The Language of American Nationhood* (Charlottesville, 2000); David Waldstreicher, *In the Midst of Perpetual Fetes: The Making of American Nationalism, 1776–1820* (Chapel Hill, 1997); Steven Watts, *The Republic Reborn: War and the Making of Liberal America, 1790–1820* (Baltimore, 1987); and Gordon S. Wood, *The Radicalism of the American Revolution* (New York, 1992).

4. Alan Taylor, *William Cooper's Town: Power and Persuasion on the Frontier of the Early American Republic* (New York, 1995).

5. Michael Grossberg, *Governing the Hearth: Law and the Family in Nineteenth-Century America* (Chapel Hill, 1985), 25, 26, xii.

6. Saul Cornell, *The Other Founders: Anti-Federalism and the Dissenting Tradition in America, 1788–1828* (Chapel Hill, 1999).

7. J. Mills Thornton III, *Politics and Power in a Slave Society: Alabama, 1800–1860* (Baton Rouge, 1978), xviii; Stephanie McCurry, *Masters of Small Worlds: Yeoman Households, Gender Relations, and the Political Culture of the Antebellum South Carolina Low Country* (New York, 1995), 6.

8. Mark E. Nachman, "Anglo-American Migrants to the West: Men of Broken Fortunes? The Case of Texas, 1821–1846," *Western Historical Quarterly* 5 (1974): 443–46.

9. Elizabeth Silverthorne, *Plantation Life in Texas* (College Station: Texas A & M University Press, 1986), 12.

10. See Austin quoted (1828) in Nachman, "Anglo-American Migrants," 448.

11. Charles Douglas to Austin, February 26, 1824, in *The Austin Papers*, 3 vols., ed. Eugene C. Barker (Washington, D.C., 1924), 1:745–46.

12. Malcolm J. Rohrbough, *The Land Office Business: The Settlement and Administration of American Public Lands, 1789–1837* (New York, 1968), 143.

13. Quoted in Gerald Ashford, "Jacksonian Liberalism and Spanish Law in Early Texas," *Southwestern Historical Quarterly* 57 (1953): 7.

14. "The Province of Texas," *Nashville Republican*, January 14, 1826, in *Papers Concerning Robertson's Colony in Texas*, 18 vols., ed. Malcolm D. McLean (Fort Worth and Arlington, 1974–93), 2:432, 433.

15. "Extract of a letter from a highly intelligent source," *Nashville Whig*, March 11, 1826, ibid., 2:438.

16. Austin to James F. Perry, March 28, 1830, in Eugene C. Barker, *The Life of Stephen F. Austin, Founder of Texas, 1793–1836* (Nashville, 1925), 315.

17. See David B. Gracy II, *Moses Austin: His Life* (San Antonio, 1987); Gregg Cantrell, *Stephen F. Austin, Empresario of Texas* (New Haven, 1999).

18. Joseph W. McKnight, "Stephen Austin's Legalistic Concerns," *Southwestern Historical Quarterly* 89 (1985–86), 242.

19. Andrew R. L. Cayton, "'When Shall We Cease to Have Judases?': The Blount Conspiracy and the Limits of the 'Extended Republic,'" in *Launching the "Extended Republic": The Federalist Era*, ed. Peter J. Albert and Ronald Hoffman (Charlottesville, 1996), 156–89.

20. Austin to David G. Burnet, May 29, 1829, in *Fugitive Letters, 1829–1836: Stephen F. Austin to David G. Burnet*, comp. Jacqueline Beretta Tomerlin (San Antonio, 1981), 14.

21. Ellis to Austin, January 3, 1828, in Barker, *Austin Papers*, 2:148.

22. Austin to Burnet, January 27, 1833, in Tomerlin, *Fugitive Letters*, 29.

23. Quoted in William G. McLoughlin, *Cherokee Renascence in the New Republic* (Princeton, 1986), 306.

24. Ibid., 324–25.

25. Ibid., 163.

26. Daniel Jacobson, "Written Ethnological Report and Statement of Testimony: The Alabama-Coushatta Indians of Texas and the Coushatta Indians of Louisiana," in *(Creek) Indians: Alabama-Coushatta* (New York, 1974), 49–55.

27. Doris M. Ladd, *The Mexican Nobility at Independence, 1780–1826* (Austin, 1976), 17.

28. Jaime E. Rodriguez O., "From Royal Subject to Republican Citizen: The Role of the Autonomists in the Independence of Mexico," in *The Independence of Mexico and the Creation of the New Nation*, ed. Jaime E. Rodriguez O. (Los Angeles and Irvine, 1989), 19–44.

29. Barbara A. Tenenbaum, "Taxation and Tyranny: Public Finance during the Iturbide Regime, 1821–1823," ibid., 201–14.

30. "The Robert Leftwich Diary and Letterbook, 1822–1844," in McLean, *Papers Concerning Robertson's Colony in Texas, Introductory Volume*, 306–16.

31. Leftwich to John P. Ervin, February 19, 1823, ibid., 430.

32. Austin to J. M. Guerra, [ca. July 18, 1823], in Barker, *Austin Papers*, 1:113.

33. February 1822, quoted in Everitt, *Texas Cherokees*, 27.

34. November 8, 1822, ibid., 27.

35. Stanley C. Green, *The Mexican Republic: The First Decade, 1823–1832* (Pittsburgh, 1987), 5.

36. Quoted in Charles A. Hale, *Mexican Liberalism in the Age of Mora, 1821–1853* (New Haven, 1968), 194, 195, 198.

37. Florencia E. Mallon, *Peasant and Nation: The Making of Postcolonial Mexico and Peru* (Berkeley, 1994), 74–88. See also Michael P. Costeloe, *The Central Republic in Mexico, 1835–1846: Hombres de Bien in the Age of Santa Anna* (Cambridge, 1993); and Steve J. Stein, *The Secret History of Gender: Women, Men, and Power in Late Colonial Mexico* (Chapel Hill, 1995).

38. Quoted in Everitt, *Texas Cherokees*, 31.

39. Quoted in ibid., 37.

40. Ibid., 41, 40, 41.

41. "The Coahuila-Texas State Colonization Law," March 24, 1825, in *Documents of*

Texas History, 2d ed., ed. Ernest Wallace, David M. Vigness, and George B. Ward (Austin, 1994), 48–50.

42. "De Witt's Empresario Contract," April 15, 1825, ibid., 59.

43. Howard Miller, "Stephen F. Austin and the Anglo-Texan Response to the Religious Establishment in Mexico, 1821–1836," *Southwestern Historical Quarterly* 91 (1987–88): 290.

44. Austin to the colonists, August 6, 1823, in Barker, *Life of Austin*, 272.

45. See, for example, Austin to Ramon Muzquiz, [February 12, 1828], in Barker, *Austin Papers*, 2:15.

46. Silverthorne, *Plantation Life in Texas*, 17.

47. Austin to Saucedo, May 8, 1826, in Barker, *Life of Austin*, 155n.

48. Austin to Edwards, September 15, 1825, ibid., 122, 123.

49. Austin to White, March 31, 1829, ibid., 272–73.

50. Saucedo to the Colonists, May 20, 1824, ibid., 114.

51. Ibid., 119.

52. Austin to Leaming, June 14, 1831, ibid., 276.

53. Austin to Josiah H. Bell, August 6, 1823, in Barker, *Austin Papers*, 1:682.

54. Austin to [Edward Livingston], June 24, 1832, in Barker, *Life of Austin*, 228.

55. Austin to William H. Wharton, April 24, 1829, ibid., 251.

56. Austin to Burnet, May 29, 1829, in Tomerlin, *Fugitive Letters*, 13.

57. "The Coahuila-Texas State Colonization Law," March 24, 1825, in Wallace, Vigness, and Ward, *Documents*, 50.

58. Quoted in Randolph B. Campbell, *An Empire for Slavery: The Peculiar Institution in Texas, 1821–1865* (Baton Rouge, 1989), 17.

59. Ibid., 24.

60. Austin to James F. Perry, March 28, 1830, in Barker, *Austin Papers*, 2:352.

61. Texas *Gazette*, quoted in Campbell, *Empire for Slavery*, 27.

62. Ibid., 31, 13, 14, 18, 19.

63. Andrés Tijerina, *Tejanos and Texas under the Mexican Flag, 1821–1836* (College Station, 1994), 35, 36.

64. McKnight, "Stephen Austin's Legalistic Concerns," 250.

65. Austin to Andrew Jackson et al., April 15, 1836, in Barker, *Austin Papers*, 3:332, 333.

66. Austin quoted in Weber, *Spanish Frontier in North America*, 339.

67. Austin to David G. Burnet, January 16, 1830, in Tomerlin, *Fugitive Letters*, 17–18.

RICHARD R. JOHN

12

Private Enterprise, Public Good?

Communications Deregulation as a National Political Issue, 1839–1851

In June 1847, Supreme Court Justice Levi Woodbury delivered a remarkable paean to the regulatory powers of the federal government. "To dream," Woodbury declared, that the Post Office Department might be supplanted by "individual enterprise" was to "dream as wildly as in the tales of the Arabian Nights." Private enterprise might conceivably meet the needs of a compact territory that was densely settled and bustling with commercial activity: "But what could it do for the county of Coos, or Tioga, or for Iowa, and Florida, and Oregon?"[1]

Woodbury's remarks had been occasioned by one of the many lawsuits in the mid-1840s that pitted the federal government against a parcel delivery company. Beginning around 1840, these companies, known popularly as private expresses, challenged the various legal restrictions on private mail delivery by providing postal patrons with a low-cost alternative to the Post Office Department on many lucrative routes in New England and the mid-Atlantic states.

Supporters of the private expresses included David Hale and Gerald Hallock, the editors of the influential New York *Journal of Commerce*. Beginning in 1840, Hale and Hallock editorialized in support of the establishment of "free trade" in mail delivery in the conviction that this would foster a salutary competition.[2] "Private enterprise carries the letters *better*, as well as cheaper, than the government mails," Hale and Hallock declared, in a typical column in February 1844.[3] Hale and Hallock went so far as to proclaim the postal monopoly unconstitutional, and to endorse the unsuccessful attempt of postal reformer Lysander Spooner to bring the issue before the Supreme Court.[4]

Woodbury was well aware of the challenges to the postal monopoly that its critics had raised, and met them head-on. His critique was at once historical and normative. To contend that the postal monopoly lacked a constitutional warrant was to ignore the circumstances that had existed seventy years earlier, when the federal Constitution had been originally drafted. At that time, Woodbury observed, no one could have envisioned that the Post Office Department might one day face private competition. On the contrary, such a situation had become conceivable only in the relatively recent past, with the improvement of the road network, the coming of railroads and steamboats, and the rise of "greater private enterprise and capital."[5]

Normative considerations underlay Woodbury's historical argument. The elimination of the postal monopoly, Woodbury warned, would benefit the few at the expense of the many. Should the courts dismantle the "great central regulations" that the federal government enforced, this would severely disadvantage the two-thirds of the American people who lived in the seven-eighths of the country that lay outside of the major commercial centers. No longer would these Americans be able to enjoy the postal cross-subsidies that the postal monopoly underwrote. While some contended that Congress might choose to fund these cross-subsidies out of the general treasury, Woodbury did not: like most public figures, he considered it axiomatic that the Post Office Department should, at the very least, break even. As a consequence, he considered the postal monopoly an indispensable mechanism for transferring the surpluses generated in the major commercial centers to the thousands of towns and villages in the interior. In its absence, there would be no way to subsidize the circulation of the myriad newspapers, magazines, pamphlets, and government documents that crowded the mails. The subsidized delivery of such an enormous volume of printed matter was, Woodbury argued, one of the "great peculiarities" of the American government. Without it, Americans would be deprived of intelligence of every kind, including "food for the public mind, new views, new helps, new discoveries of inventions, new principles, new reforms—in short, new improvements in everything that strengthen or adorn society."[6]

Woodbury found the rationale for the federal regulation of communications so compelling that he extended it to embrace even the electric telegraph, a means of communication unknown to the framers of the federal Constitution. Woodbury was well aware that, for some time, a small but articulate group of promoters, newspaper editors, and congressmen had been advocating the commercialization of the telegraph as a private enterprise. Here, once again, Woodbury demurred. Under no circumstances, Woodbury warned, should the government permit "private experiments" with the new technology to override the "welfare and wants of the whole community."[7]

Woodbury's remarks provide a vantage point from which to explore the movement that flourished between 1839 and 1851 to limit the involvement of the federal government in mail delivery and telegraphy—at the time, the two principal forms of long-distance communication. This essay is neither a full history of this movement nor a survey of its relationship to the wider currents of American reform. Rather, it highlights certain features of its history in order to document the emergence in American public life of a new, and distinctive, understanding of the advantages and disadvantages of what we today would call communications deregulation, or what contemporaries called private enterprise.

For over fifty years, historical accounts of nineteenth-century public life have downplayed the importance in national politics of issues involving the regulatory powers of the federal government. Beginning in the 1940s, with Thomas C. Cochran's critique of the "presidential synthesis," and accelerating in the 1960s, with the rise of the "new" social history, it has been customary to dismiss federal regulation—along with most governmental institutions—as irrelevant to the larger drama of social and cultural change.[8]

Curiously enough, this neglect of federal public policy has extended even to political historians. Intent on exploring the social dimensions of public life at the grass roots, the so-called "new" political historians often ignored national political issues altogether. Preoccupied with why voters voted, they only rarely pondered what the government did. And when political historians did turn their attention to federal public policy, they typically reduced it to nothing more than a distributive struggle over discrete and often highly particularistic outcomes, such as a land sale or a political appointment. As a consequence, a host of regulatory and redistributive issues were assumed away.[9]

This essay points historians of the early republic in a different direction. Building on recent scholarship on social relationships and cultural norms, it shows how the study of national political issues can raise larger questions about American public life. In particular, it reveals that, even in the supposed heyday of laissez-faire, private enterprise remained a contested ideal. Not until the 1840s would public figures begin even to acknowledge the possibility that large-scale, nationwide enterprises, such as the postal system or the telegraph network, could be coordinated by institutions other than the federal government. The significance of this perceptual shift is often overlooked. To borrow a phrase from Eric Hobsbawm, private enterprise was an invented tradition, a late-Jacksonian era response to prior developments in American public life.[10]

The novelty of the idea that large-scale ventures could be coordinated by non-governmental institutions is underscored by the infrequency with which the phrase "private enterprise" occurred in the writings of the founders of the American republic.[11] The phrase was rarely used in early congressional debates, and appeared but once in the published edition of the journals of the Continental Congress. In the half-century between the adoption of the federal Constitution and the Panic of 1837, the only president to invoke the phrase in a public address was Thomas Jefferson, who used it once in his 1806 message to Congress.[12] Jefferson's use of the phrase was revealing. In his address, Jefferson proposed that the federal government support the establishment of certain scientific institutions that private groups lacked the resources to endow. "Education," Jefferson observed, "is here placed among the articles of public care, not that it would be proposed to take its ordinary branches out of the hands of *private enterprise*, which manages so much better all the concerns to which it is equal."[13]

Though Jefferson acknowledged the superiority of private enterprise in "all the concerns to which it is equal," he implicitly conceded that public support would be imperative in certain realms, such as the funding of scientific institutions. Nowhere did Jefferson imply—as would later government critics—that even complex and costly ventures were best coordinated by organizations other than the federal government. Indeed, it would be a mistake to assume that Jefferson accorded the phrase any special significance. If he had, he could have been expected to have repeated it in a variety of contexts. In fact, in a lengthy address he used it but once, as a felicitous counterpoint to "public care."

The phrase private enterprise remained somewhat exotic until the 1830s.[14] A few public figures, like Jefferson, invested it with positive meaning. The Post Office Department, observed New York *Evening Post* editor William Leggett in 1835, did not own the means of conveyance upon which it relied to transmit the mail. Why, then, might not the legal restrictions on private mail delivery be abolished, and the business "safely trusted" to "private enterprise"?[15] Others considered it something of a put-down. The "grander cosmopolitan project" of a government-funded ship canal across the isthmus of Panama, one essayist warned in 1839, might well be stymied by small-scale ventures that were hostile to the "common interest of the world at large" and that could be consummated "*even* by private enterprise."[16]

Historians of the United States often assume that, in the United States, in contrast to Europe, big business preceded big government.[17] From the standpoint of the Progressive era, this generalization is understandable. After all, by the early twentieth century, no public agency could match the administrative capacity of private corporations such as the Pennsylvania Railroad or American Telephone and Telegraph.

In the early republic, a different situation prevailed. While most businesses remained small, the government—including, above all, the federal government—was enormous. Within the federal government, no public agency could match the size or geographical reach of the Post Office Department. No institution of any kind employed more people, deployed more complex managerial techniques, or operated on a comparable scale. Few commanded a comparable measure of trust.[18]

The large size and expansive mandate of American governmental institutions—at the state as well as the federal level—owed much to their genuine popularity. Ordinary Americans coveted a vast panoply of public works—including canals, roads, and improved mail delivery—and legislators responded.[19]

Prior to 1851, Congress mandated that improvements in mail delivery be funded out of postal revenue, without recourse to the general treasury. While this requirement was occasionally relaxed, it was rarely ignored. To fund popular, though expensive services—such as the low-cost circulation of newspapers and the extension of postal facilities into thinly settled regions—legislators established an ingenious regulatory regime. To keep the Post Office Department self-sustaining, postal administrators used the surplus generated on letter postage to cover the cost of transmitting newspapers and other kinds of printed matter, and the surplus generated in the major commercial centers to maintain postal facilities in the rest of the country. In no sense were these cross-subsidies merely distributive, in the sense of providing easily divisible benefits to particular claimants. Rather, they had structural biases that reflected—and, indeed, helped to promote—policy goals that were widely shared.[20]

Prior to steam-powered transportation, this regulatory regime worked reasonably well. In large measure, this was because postal administrators retained a great measure of control over the stagecoach proprietors and post riders upon whom they relied to transport the mail. Postal administrators set the schedules that stagecoach proprietors followed, and had little trouble discouraging post riders—who they themselves had appointed—from circulating mailable matter on their own private account.

With the advent of steam-powered transportation—steamboats, railroads, and ocean-faring steamships—the situation grew more complex. By greatly increasing the facilities for travel, these new means of conveyance enormously expanded the opportunities for travelers to carry small packages—including letters—on their persons, or, as the phrase went, "outside of the mail." No longer was the mail carriers' carrying capacity confined to the stage drivers' baggage rack and the post riders' saddlebags. And no longer did postal administrators set the schedules for the means of conveyance on which the mail carriers relied.

This novel situation created a market niche that was quickly exploited by the enterprising group of young men who founded the parcel delivery industry. The first successful parcel delivery company was established in 1839 by William Harnden, a twenty-five-year-old former railroad conductor. Harnden set himself up in business by advertising that, for a set fee, he would carry newspapers and small parcels by railroad and steamboat between Boston and New York. For a time, Harnden also carried letters under a special arrangement with the Post Office Department. Harnden's success was assured when, following a tip from the New York newspaper vendor James W. Hale, he coordinated his trips to meet the heightened demand for high-speed communication that followed the establishment by Samuel Cunard of ocean-faring steamship service between Liverpool and Boston.[21]

Harnden's innovation led to the establishment of similar parcel delivery companies throughout much of New England and the mid-Atlantic states. Like Harnden, these companies often carried letters, which as a consequence of the existing regulatory regime they could transmit for substantially lower rates than the federal government. To avoid running afoul of the laws prohibiting competition in the letter-mail business, Harnden took various precautions. "Keep good friends with the Post Office folks," Harnden wrote a business associate in 1841, after his original contract with the Post Office Department had expired: "Gain and keep their confidence. Receive nothing mailable. . . . You will have no small number of Post Office spies at your heels. They will watch you very closely. See that they have their trouble for their pains."[22] Harnden's competitors ignored his warnings and quickly became major competitors of the Post Office Department in the lucrative letter-mail business throughout much of the Atlantic seaboard and upstate New York. By 1845, private expresses and ordinary travelers were together diverting from the Post Office Department as much as two-thirds of all the correspondence in the country.[23]

The rise of the parcel delivery industry raised basic questions about postal policy. If the private expresses could make large profits by underbidding the Post Office Department, why did the basic letter rate remain so high? Between 1840 and 1845, this question received a great deal of coverage in the press. During this period, individuals from throughout the country flooded Congress with petitions for "cheap postage"—including, as its centerpiece, a major reduction in the basic letter rate. Few of the major political issues of the day boasted a broader base of support. Perhaps the best measure of the popularity of cheap postage was the willingness of so many Americans to patronize the private expresses— mounting what was, in effect, a massive boycott of the federal government.

Many congressmen opposed the letter-rate reduction that the petitioners sought. They feared, not implausibly, that such a radical change would significantly reduce the revenue that postal administrators relied upon to maintain the existing regulatory regime. Echoing their misgivings were Postmaster General Charles Wickliffe and the Washington *Madisonian*, the official organ of the Tyler administration.[24] Taking to the offensive, Wickliffe intensified the legal campaign that postal administrators had long waged against their competitors. By 1845, Wickliffe's subordinates had instituted hundreds of lawsuits against individual companies. This prosecutorial crusade was so elaborate that, at its height, James W. Hale, now the proprietor of his own letter-mail company, quipped that he was the "most arrested" man in the world.[25]

This combination of popular defiance and governmental intransigence occasioned a searching reevaluation of the possibilities of private enterprise. Initially, as maverick expressman Lysander Spooner would later reminisce, his critics derided the mail delivery company that he had established as "destitute of all patriotic or moral principles." Gradually, however, they came to dignify it as "private enterprise."[26] No longer did contemporaries assume—as had, for example, Thomas Jefferson—that private enterprise must necessarily be restricted to commercial ventures that were relatively small in scale. With the rise of the private expresses, it was now plausible to envision—for the first time in American history—that even the mail delivery business might be entrusted to private companies. At the height of the private mail delivery boom, one of Harnden's former agents, Henry Wells, was reputed to have offered to take over the entire mail delivery business and run it himself.[27] Prior to the boom, such a proposal would have been quite literally inconceivable. In a similar spirit, political economist Amasa Walker offered Congress $1 million in 1844 for the rights to the postal monopoly for twenty years on the condition that he maintain the existing level of service while significantly reducing the basic letter rate.[28]

Several public figures followed the lead of the *Journal of Commerce* and called for the outright repeal of legislative prohibitions on private competition. Yet such appeals were relatively rare. More characteristic was the response of a special committee of the New York Chamber of Commerce. In August 1844, this committee presented the postmaster general an open letter on postal reform. Unsurprisingly, the committee endorsed a major reduction in the basic letter rate. Yet the committee *also* supported new legislation to *tighten* the laws prohibiting private mail delivery, on the grounds that the present conveyance of letters by private expresses—"even if legal"—was not a proper source to be permanently relied on for "so responsible a trust."[29]

Public sentiment, so far as it can be gauged from petitions to Congress, expressed similar misgivings. In the early 1840s, thousands of Americans petitioned Congress to lower the basic letter rate. Yet few regarded the private expresses as anything more than a temporary expedient, even though many recognized that, by successfully underbidding the Post Office Department, these companies had provided a major impetus to the rate reductions that the petitioners desired. Should the Post Office Department match its competitors, predicted the Illinois General Assembly in 1843, the whole people might soon secure a level of service that, at present, was confined to a few: "Under a just and reasonable rate of postage, this successful competition with the public mail could never succeed."[30]

Newspaper editors voiced related concerns. Arunah S. Abell of the Baltimore *Sun* prided himself on being the first editor south of the Hudson to champion the cause of postal reform.[31] Yet Abell had little patience with what he derisively termed the "daily increasing activity and efficiency" of the private expresses, and urged Congress to reduce the basic letter rate so that these "evils" might be averted.[32] The mail delivery business, reflected Horace Greeley in the *New-York Daily Tribune*, had for many years exceeded the "powers" of private enterprise. Now the situation had changed and the federal government should respond by lowering the basic letter rate. Greeley deplored the prosecution of the private expresses: "No government is in the discharge of its rightful duty while thus seeking to repress private enterprise and industry."[33] Yet Greeley regarded private competition as a mere temporary expedient that would hasten the long-hoped-for postal reform: "We believe *one* mail establishment can serve the people of the whole Union better and cheaper than a thousand warring concerns."[34]

Greeley's straddle was typical of many city editors. Private enterprise, declared an editorialist in the *Buffalo Commercial*, would hasten postal reform. And when it did, the authority to transmit letters and other mailable matter should be "exclusively vested in the government."[35] What would happen, wondered the editors of the Washington *Daily National Intelligencer*, if the Supreme Court declared the postal monopoly unconstitutional? Without that "great regulator," the Post Office Department, how would the public be guarded from the exorbitant charges that a private combination might levy? And who would guarantee the sanctity of the mails?[36]

Even Hale and Hallock of the *Journal of Commerce* recognized that certain private expresses might endanger the public good. The occasion for this remarkable departure from free trade orthodoxy was the establishment by a consortium of merchants in January 1845 of a private horse express between Covington, Georgia, and Montgomery, Alabama. Such an express, Hale and Hallock warned, might well give a half-dozen men in New Orleans advance knowledge of a sudden rise in the markets in Liverpool—a valuable asset, should the New Orleans market be glutted with cotton, wheat, and other sought-after goods. Hale and Hallock found the merchants' "private enterprise" commendable, yet considered it a "nuisance" to the mercantile interests and urged that it be swiftly "countervailed" with the establishment by the Post Office Department of a competing government express.[37]

Private mail delivery fared little better in Congress. Between July 1842 and March 1845, postal reform was the subject of several long and sometimes contentious debates. Though several congressmen questioned the propriety of prosecuting the private expresses, none hailed them as commendable examples of private enterprise or urged the abolition of the postal monopoly—as, for example, one congressman had in 1839.[38] On the contrary, everyone affirmed the indispensability of the existing regulatory regime. The crux of the matter, explained Congressman James Buchanan of Pennsylvania, was to protect postal revenue from outside assault. What would happen, Buchanan asked, if the private expresses rendered profitless the very routes postal administrators relied on to keep the institution from running into debt? To pose the question was to answer it. Under no circumstances, Buchanan declared, should Congress permit its "unquestionable constitutional power" to be defeated by the "lawless action of individuals."[39] Some congressmen favored stiff new penalties to frustrate private enterprise in mail delivery; others advocated a major reduction in the basic letter rate. Still others favored some combination of the two. On one point, everyone agreed. The private expresses must be stopped.[40]

Few congressman attacked private enterprise in mail delivery with more ingenuity than Maryland senator William Merrick. It was "indispensably necessary," Merrick declared, to prevent by suitable legislation the "great and alarming frauds" that the private expresses had perpetrated.[41] After all, the proprietors of these companies were nothing but mere "private competing individuals" actuated by the "cupidity of gain": the public good was far above such "mere" pecuniary considerations. Merrick conceded that an exclusive reliance on restrictive legislation could never solve the problem that the private expresses posed. In addition, he believed, Congress should curry public favor by lowering the basic letter rate. Mollified by the rate reductions, the public would once again sustain the government's legal campaign against the private expresses and perpetuate the regulatory regime.[42]

Merrick's compromise became a cornerstone of the Post Office Act of 1845, which simultaneously reduced postal rates while strengthening legal prohibitions on private mail delivery. The popular response to this legislation, however, fell short of Merrick's hopes. Though Congress had substantially reduced the basic letter rate, the new rate remained *higher* than that charged by many of the private expresses. Predictably, a few decided to risk prosecution and remain in business. "Private expresses," reported one New Hampshire newspaper editor shortly after the new law went into effect, "*have not* been discontinued in this quarter. Far from it. They are now doing as large a business as ever, carrying letters at half the government rates. . . . The new postage act did not abate what is called 'private enterprise,' and the act itself, it is thought, will soon be found to be insufficient."[43]

Within Congress, the failure to suppress the private expresses led a growing number of legislators to call for the outright privatization of the Post Office Department. In the near future, speculated the chairman of the House post office committee in June 1848, the public good might well be better served if Congress replaced the postal monopoly with a competitive "system" that encouraged "individual enterprise." Under such an arrangement, Congress could retain the power to designate post routes and set maximum postal rates. The conveyance of the mail, however, would become the prerogative not of salaried dependents but of the same kind of energetic individuals who were running the private expresses and the nascent telegraph industry.[44] It would not be long, declared one senator a few months later, before the "present post office system" would cease to exist, with its "duties" taken over by private enterprise.[45] It was only a matter of time before legislators took the logic of privatization to its extreme and proposed—as did Gerrit Smith of New York in 1854—the outright abolition of the Post Office Department.[46]

In the end, however, all proposals to deregulate the Post Office Department failed. In an era that witnessed the defeat of John Quincy Adams's national program of internal improvement and the triumph of Andrew Jackson's war on the Bank of the United States, this failure is worth underscoring. How can it be explained?

The failure of postal deregulation owed something to the role that postal patronage had come by the 1840s to play in campaign finance. For the party workers who rallied voters to the polls, postal contracts and jobs were a highly coveted reward. For postal reformers Joshua Leavitt and Barnabas Bates, this simple fact doomed any thoroughgoing reform. The "naked truth," Leavitt editorialized in 1845, was that Congress perpetuated the postal monopoly neither for the benefit of the people, nor by virtue of any constitutional authority, but to provide party leaders with jobs for their supporters.[47] Political exigency, Bates confided to one-time expressman Lysander Spooner in 1851, derailed Bates's attempt to secure from the federal government an exclusive franchise to transmit the mail. Bates had failed—or so Bates assumed—because Congress insisted on maintaining the Post Office Department for "electioneering purposes."[48]

Partisan imperatives furnished postal reformers like Leavitt and Bates with a convenient explanation for their inability to secure the reforms that they sought. Yet they cannot explain the failure of postal deregulation. Far more important was the reluctance of Congress to buck public opinion and dismantle the existing regulatory regime. Though thousands of Americans had patronized the private expresses in the early 1840s, only a few joined Hale and Hallock of the *Journal of Commerce* in championing private enterprise as a permanent alternative to the Post Office Department. Of the hundreds of petitions on postal topics that found their way to Congress during the 1840s, for example, few praised the private expresses, while none called for the outright abolition of the Post Office Department. What petitioners sought, instead, was the elimination of special privileges for government officials, improvements in the level of service, and, most important of all, a major reduction in the basic letter rate. Popular pressure proved so compelling that, in 1851, Congress lifted a major constraint upon postal expansion. Henceforth postal revenue no longer had to cover postal expenses, making it possible for Congress to cut postal rates—as it did in 1851—without a countervailing reduction in the level of service.[49]

Postal improvements, in short, were popular, while private mail delivery was not. Should Congress permit private competition, explained Missouri congressman Willard P. Hall in 1851, it would be well advised to get out of the mail delivery business altogether. Yet such a radical proposal, Hall added, had the support neither of Congress nor of the "people of the country."[50] The existing regulatory regime, lawyer Charles M. Ellis declared at about the same time in an unusually forthright statement of a common view, was not a monopoly in its "odious sense." In a "democratic state of society," Ellis posited, a monopoly deprived the people of the ability to control the means of communication through "united and efficient action." In no sense was this true of the Post Office Department. For reasons vital to the public welfare, the federal government had an obligation to put everyone on an equal footing in the "transmission of intelligence" by making it "as free, as quick, as sure and as cheap as the light of day." Should a private mail delivery company ever rival the federal government in its "completeness," it would be the "most dangerous power in the State."[51]

A comparable faith in the regulatory power of the federal government shaped the initial public response to telegraphy. Electric telegraphy was new in the 1840s, and it was by no means obvious to contemporaries how it was going to be commercialized, or even whether it would promote the public good. These anxieties are worth underscoring, since they are often forgotten. From the outset, newspaper editors, merchants, and public figures from almost every corner of the United States hailed the new technology as the greatest invention of the age. Almost no one questioned the desirability of facilitating high-speed— and, at least in theory, instantaneous—communication between far-flung localities.[52] Accompanying this euphoria, however, was a strong undercurrent of concern. The new technology was so powerful, its critics warned, that were it not properly regulated, it might well prove less of a blessing than a curse.

The appeal of federal control helps explain why the first telegraph line in the United States to be open to the public—a forty-mile line between Washington and Baltimore—was financed out of general revenue and administered during its first two years by the Post Office Department. Among the most tireless champions of federal control was Samuel F. B. Morse, the painter-turned-inventor whose ownership of a majority share in a key telegraph patent gave him a major voice in the early history of the industry. Morse fervently believed that the federal government should own the rights to his patent—which, with a self-confidence bordering on arrogance, he presumed to cover every important feature of the new technology. In pursuit of this goal, Morse secured federal support for experiments that culminated in 1844 with the successful demonstration of the commercial possibilities of electric telegraphy and in 1845 with the opening of the Washington-Baltimore line.

Morse's faith in federal control antedated by almost a decade the commercialization of the new technology. "It would seem most natural," Morse observed in 1837, to "connect a telegraphic system with the Post Office Department; for, although it does not carry a mail, yet it is another mode of accomplishing the principal object for which the mail is established, to wit: the rapid and regular transmission of intelligence."[53] Morse predicated his postal analogy on the expansive role that the Post Office Department had come to assume since the 1820s in the circulation of time-specific information. Beginning with Postmaster General John McLean, a succession of postal administrators had proclaimed that the federal government had an obligation to transmit information faster than any possible rival. In an age when merchants could make fortunes overnight by running private horse expresses to outpace the mails, this federal guarantee was vital to the thousands of planters and farmers who were dependent on foreign markets for the sale of their crops. Federal control, Morse predicted, would prevent the few from defrauding the many. Should Congress leave telegraphy to speculators to monopolize for themselves, Morse warned, it might easily become the means of enriching a single corporation while causing the "bankruptcy of thousands."[54]

Equally disturbing for Morse was the possibility that the federal government might monopolize the new technology by itself. Such an arrangement, Morse warned, might well work "vast mischief." The optimal form of federal control, instead, was a mixed enterprise in which the federal government retained the exclusive right to the new technology by virtue of its ownership of the key patents—including, of course, Morse's own. Under such a scheme, the federal government could designate a number of lines for its own use. The core of the network, however—the "private telegraphs," as Morse termed them—would be built and maintained by investors upon payment to the federal government of a licensing fee that granted them exclusive rights to specific routes. In this way, the federal government would possess the communication facilities it needed, while encouraging a general competition among investors governed by whatever regulations legislators might think proper. Such "checks and preventives of abuse," Morse predicted, would harness this "otherwise dangerous power" to the public good. Given the enterprising character of Americans, Morse predicted, it was "not visionary" to suppose that before long the whole surface of the country would be "channeled" for those "*nerves* which are to diffuse, with the speed of thought, a knowledge of all that is occurring throughout the land; making, in fact, *one neighborhood* of the whole country."[55] Prior to 1847, every contract that Morse entered into specified that Congress retained the right to purchase his patent for a mutually agreed upon sum. After 1847, Morse and his business associates struggled doggedly—though, ultimately, with limited success—to exploit the new technology in an orderly fashion by using their ownership of Morse's patent to enforce common procedures for companies wishing to enter the market.

Similar, though usually less elaborate, plans for federal control had broad support in the press. Early on, many editors regarded a federal buyout of Morse's patent as inevitable, if only because, like the private expresses, private telegraph companies threatened to deprive the Post Office Department of a great deal of revenue. Others looked to federal control as a safeguard against speculative fraud and abuse. Private enterprise, declared James Gordon Bennett of the *New York Herald* in April 1845, was fast erecting telegraph lines in many directions, yet the public interest would be much more securely promoted should the federal government undertake the arrangement.[56] It must be "clear to every one," declared James Watson Webb of the *Morning Courier and New-York Enquirer*, at about the same time, that no private enterprise should be permitted to use the new technology for "private and exclusive purposes." On the contrary, the federal government should control it and make "such a disposition of its vast powers as should most conduce to the public welfare."[57] So enormous were the dangers of speculation, editorialized William M. Swain of the Philadelphia *Public Ledger* the following October, that the federal government might even find it advisable to prohibit anyone other than a government official from transmitting a message over the wires. "Perhaps the best security," Swain speculated, "would be in the prohibition of all private correspondence. Some will say that this would render the telegraph nearly useless. We grant that it would—to speculators, and we add that for mercantile speculations only will it be much used in private correspondence, excepting during elections."[58]

Some contemporaries openly doubted whether telegraphy could be administered as a public-private joint venture, as Morse had hoped. Congress had erred in permitting the new technology to be commercialized by a "private company," warned a New York newspaper correspondent in 1845 who styled himself "Mercator," since no governmental body could devise regulations sufficiently stringent to "shut out the chance, not to say probability, of its abuse." Should the "vast monopoly" fall into the hands of speculators, Mercator warned, an indignant public could be expected to rise up and destroy its property immediately after it learned of the first major speculation to have made use of its "agency."[59]

The merits of federal control were recognized even by stalwart champions of private enterprise. Should telegraphic promoters refuse the "privilege" of sending and receiving telegraphic dispatches to anyone willing to pay a reasonable fee, Hale and Hallock reflected in the *Journal of Commerce* in January 1845, private control of an "instrumentality so powerful" would be a "public nuisance" that should not be tolerated.[60] And were speculators to gain control of the new medium, Hale and Hallock warned in November of the following year, this would be an "evil of no ordinary magnitude" that would require the prompt intervention of the strong arm of the law. The reluctance with which even such fervent champions of private enterprise endorsed the privatization of telegraphy was perhaps the most telling evidence of the extent to which its future remained contested. Nineteen months after the telegraph had made its commercial debut, the editors of one of the most influential commercial newspapers in the country remained uncertain as to whether the new technology would be a "public blessing" or a "public nuisance."[61]

Editorial support for federal control owed a good deal to the uneasiness with which editors contemplated the disruptive effects of telegraphy on their own news-gathering efforts. Some editors worried that private telegraph companies might discriminate against their newspaper in ways that would benefit their rivals. Others worried that the new technology would raise the cost of news gathering. Telegraphic dispatches were expensive, and, at least initially, it was far from self-evident that newspapers would receive favorable rates. At present, observed the editor of the Baltimore *Patriot*, newspaper editors enjoyed under federal law the right to exchange with each other an unlimited number of newspapers free of charge. These exchanges, in turn, provided editors with the bulk of the news that they relied on to fill their columns. Should the Post Office Department retain control of the new technology, this policy would presumably be maintained; if it devolved upon private enterprise, however, it might well be abandoned. In either event, the postmaster general should work with the private telegraph companies to ensure the free circulation of all information "important or interesting to the whole people." The cost of this information, in turn, should be borne by those individuals who used the telegraph for "*private* benefit or speculation"—by analogy with the longstanding presumption that the postage on merchants' letters subsidized the exchanges upon which editors relied for their news: "This will be found, we are sure, to be the true policy of the telegraphs, whether regard be had to their profits or to their use." Should this policy be adopted, editors would continue to receive news broadcasts free of charge "as in the case of the exchange papers in the ordinary mail."[62]

This constellation of concerns helps explain why federal control of telegraphy had the backing of four of the most widely circulated newspapers in the country—the New York *Sun*, the *New York Herald*, the Baltimore *Sun*, and the Philadelphia *Public Ledger*.[63] The editors of the "penny press," as these newspapers would come to be known, had been quick to fault the Post Office Department for high rates and poor service. Indeed, they were among the leading champions of postal reform. These criticisms notwithstanding, they remained skeptical of all proposals to privatize the new technology. It was not hard to see why. In contrast to their more expensive, better-established rivals—

such as the *Morning Courier* and the *Journal of Commerce*—the penny papers were dependent for revenue on daily sales rather than annual subscriptions. As a consequence, their editors were extremely sensitive to anything that might affect their access to a steady stream of cheap and abundant up-to-date news.

Editorial support for federal control persisted even after private companies had begun to extend lines to the major commercial centers. "Public opinion," declared the editor of the Philadelphia-based *Pennsylvania Inquirer* in June 1846, was "decidedly in favor" of a federal takeover of the various telegraph lines that private individuals had established. A federally owned and operated telegraph, the editor predicted, would reduce rates and improve service. The many individuals who had built up the telegraph industry during the past year deserved great credit for their "enterprise and perseverance," yet such a "vast engine of communication" should be in the hands of the federal government under proper regulations.[64]

Even critics of federal control acknowledged its popularity. Though he himself favored the commercialization of the telegraph as a private enterprise, Jeremiah Hughes of *Niles's National Register* acknowledged that his views were unique, at least within the press. "All the other public journals that expressed opinions," Hughes observed in September 1846, "appeared to urge the government to make the telegraph a government monopoly." Impatience with private enterprise, Hughes inferred, was a logical counterpart of the universal desire to expand the telegraph network rapidly, since it was taken for granted that the federal government could construct new lines faster than even the most enterprising of private companies.[65]

Perhaps the most careful student of popular sentiment on the telegraph issue was Morse's business agent, Amos Kendall. Federal control—or so Kendall reported to Morse's business partner, Francis O. J. Smith, in a series of confidential letters in 1845—was broadly popular, making it imperative that the patentees not foreclose the possibility of a government sale. It was "all important," Kendall lectured Smith shortly after the opening of the Washington-Baltimore line, to keep "public opinion with us."[66] Most telegraph investors, Kendall explained in 1846 to the chairman of the House post office committee, opposed such a sale of Morse's patent to the government. Nonetheless, Kendall added, the owners of Morse's patent felt themselves "called upon" by public opinion to "hold this great instrument of wealth and power" at the disposition of the federal government for a "reasonable consideration."[67]

Federal control even received the formal endorsement of one group of prominent merchants. It was simply unacceptable—declared the influential Baltimore mercantile house of Alexander Brown & Co. in November 1846, in heading up a petition to Congress signed by many of the city's leading merchants—for the federal government to permit the private expresses to beat out the Post Office Department day after day. Should Congress purchase Morse's patent, this evil could be avoided. "The control of the entire commercial and news correspondence of the country," the merchants explained, was a "tremendous power" that ought to be possessed exclusively by the "most responsible public agents." The "obvious fact" that the new technology gave telegraph managers control over the interests of merchants, the press, the government, and indirectly of the whole people was sufficient to "show the danger" of leaving it in private hands.[68]

Federal control also had the support of Whig presidential candidate Henry Clay. Should the new technology remain in private hands, Clay warned in a letter to one of Morse's business partners during the height of the 1844 campaign, speculators would be able to "monopolize intelligence": "I think such an engine ought to be exclusively under the control of government."[69]

One of the most elaborate appeals for federal control took the form of a report to Congress in March 1845 by Georgia Whig Absalom Chappell. Enamored, like Morse, with the postal-telegraphic analogy, Chappell tried unsuccessfully to persuade legislators to extend Morse's telegraph from Baltimore to New York. Chappell conceded the dangers of most projects to augment federal power, yet regarded the telegraph as an exception. "The great and fundamental principle" upon which the Post Office Department operated, Chappell postulated, was the presumption that the federal government not be "outstripped" in the circulation of "correspondence and intelligence." In support of this principle, Chappell observed, Congress had recently awarded lucrative mail contracts to several railroad corporations. It was with "equal certainty," Chappell predicted, that Congress would adopt for postal purposes any other "newly discovered agency or contrivance" that offered a "decided advantage of celerity."[70]

Chappell's logic failed to sway prominent Democrats in Congress, and had little effect on the Democratic president, James K. Polk, who does not seem to have left any record of his views on the subject. The Polk administration's official organ, the Washington *Union*, took no position on the telegraph issue, though it did run a letter from a supporter of federal control as late as December 1846.[71] Given the traditional Democratic hostility toward governmental activism, this was perhaps not surprising. More intriguing was the fact that federal control did win the approval of several Democratic-leaning newspapers, including the New York *Evening Post*, the Philadelphia *Pennsylvanian*, and the Washington *Constitution*. Federal control also had the support, at various times, of a number of nationally prominent Democrats. These included Polk's postmaster general, Cave Johnson; two former Democratic cabinet members, Levi Woodbury and Amos Kendall; Morse himself; and former Democratic congressman Francis O. J. Smith. To be sure, none but Woodbury were disinterested: Johnson stood to gain in power and prestige should the telegraph remain under his control; Smith owned a percentage of Morse's patent; and Kendall was Morse's business agent.

Smith made the case for federal control in an essay on postal reform that he published in the February 1845 issue of the *Merchants' Magazine*. Federal funding for the rapid extension of telegraphy, Smith contended, was far preferable to the "odious system" of harassing the private expresses in the courts. Smith doubted that the Post Office Department could ever underbid the private expresses, given the constraints that the regulatory regime imposed. Were the federal government to establish its own telegraph network, however, the challenge posed by the private expresses would disappear. "Can any one believe," Smith asked rhetorically, that if Congress lowered the basic letter rate and the Post Office Department established a low-cost telegraph on the Washington–New York route, the private letter-mail companies would persist, even if no penal law should be interposed to deter them? Should the Post Office Department string wires throughout the country, Smith predicted, it would attain the "highest approach to omniscience, within the limits of the Union, that human wants or human agency need aspire to."[72]

Kendall's position on federal control was complex. As a good Democrat, Kendall retained strong misgivings about governmental activism. The true object of government, Kendall postulated in 1843, was not to promote the happiness of the people, but to enable the people to promote their own happiness.[73] Instead of enacting new penal laws to stymie the private expresses, why not encourage the federal government to retrench its own establishments as fast as private enterprise advanced, and "content itself" with doing only that which the citizen "cannot effect for himself?"[74] Indeed, at one point, Kendall went so far as to propose that the Post Office Department abandon the railroad altogether as a means of conveyance, and rely exclusively on post riders to carry the mail.[75]

Yet Kendall also recognized that certain public projects fell within the legitimate domain of the federal government. As postmaster general in the 1830s, Kendall had endorsed various innovations in high-speed communication, including an elaborate Washington–New Orleans horse express. By far the most ambitious innovation to win Kendall's assent was an optical telegraph—modeled loosely on the French prototype of Claude Chappe—that Kendall hoped might one day connect the country's leading ports.[76] "That great public benefits will arise from the establishment of a line of [optical] telegraphs along our coasts, if not into the interior, there can be no doubt," Kendall declared in a public letter in February 1837. "The rapid diffusion of intelligence is of great importance in our busy country, and a portion of our abundant public funds cannot, in my opinion, be more usefully employed than in the attainment of that object."[77]

The awkwardness of Kendall's position was evident in a letter that he wrote in August 1845 to Morse's partner, Francis O. J. Smith. "One consideration" that favored a buyout, Kendall explained to Smith, was the " '*certainty*' " of a quick and substantial financial return. "If you and I and my principals can realize at once all of [the] wealth that the human heart ought to desire, it is better for us to take it, than to fight our way for years through difficulties and perplexities, however brilliant in imagination may be the prospective."[78]

By far the most determined Democratic champion of federal control was Polk's postmaster general, Cave Johnson, the administrator under whose direction the first commercial telegraph had been established in 1845. Johnson's support for federal control is often misunderstood. Well known as a fiscal conservative, Johnson conceded in his annual report for 1845 that, based on the revenue generated thus far by the Washington–Baltimore line, he did not believe the federal government could ever run the telegraph at a profit.[79] Johnson's gloomy fiscal assessment outraged Amos Kendall, who accused him of deliberately using his public office to depress the value of Morse's patent.[80] In the years after the Civil War, Johnson's prediction would be routinely cited as proof that federal administrators had stumbled badly in their first attempt to run the industry, and should not be given a second chance.

However wrongheaded Johnson's prediction may appear in hindsight, it is important to remember that it was the only caveat that he raised in what was, in fact, a broad-gauged appeal for federal control. "In the hands of individuals or associations," Johnson declared in the same report, the telegraph might become the "most potent instrument" the world ever knew to effect "sudden and large speculations—to rob the many of their just advantages, and concentrate them upon the few." To forestall such a catastrophe, Johnson regarded some kind of regulatory apparatus as imperative: "The use of an instrument so powerful for good or evil cannot with safety to the people be left in the hands of private individuals uncontrolled by law."[81]

Military exigency reinforced Johnson's commitment to federal control. Shortly after the start of the Mexican War, Johnson reported to Congress that a private consortium of New York editors headed up by Moses Y. Beach of the New York *Sun* had established a horse express in Alabama to transmit from Mexico newspaper clippings with military reports in advance of the mail. The proprietors of this express, Johnson conceded, violated no federal law, since the recently enacted post office law had specifically exempted newspapers from the postal monopoly. Still, Johnson hoped to supplant the horse express with a telegraph for the duration of the war, and took the trouble to secure from Kendall the patent rights for such a venture on the "most liberal terms."[82]

Johnson failed to secure congressional support for his wartime telegraph and, in 1847, the Washington-Baltimore line passed out of federal control. With the exception of a brief moment during the First World War, postal administrators would never again be able to plausibly contend that they could outpace private enterprise in the circulation of time-specific information on commerce and public affairs.

Popular support for federal control never disappeared altogether. With the expansion of the telegraph network, however, several once-potent criticisms of the new technology came to seem overblown. Once the new technology became a mundane reality, rather than a visionary dream, editors discovered it to be less threatening to ordinary commercial transactions than they had feared, and more useful in their daily operations than they had anticipated.[83] It was, for example, by no means incidental that the most searching critiques in the New York press of private enterprise in telegraphy antedated the extension of the first telegraph line to New York City.

Particularly important in legitimating private control of the new technology were the steady stream of public statements that Amos Kendall issued between 1845 and 1847. In these statements, Kendall enunciated the rules and regulations of Morse's Magnetic Telegraph Company and defended the patentees' right to a monopoly of Morse's patent. "Of one kind of monopoly I am in favor," Kendall declared in the Washington *Union* in September 1847, "a monopoly of a man's own property. . . . Patent rights are as much private property as printing presses."[84] To mollify the press, Kendall promised editors special rates for the circulation of news—a promise that Kendall's own long tenure as a newspaper editor rendered especially credible.[85] And to win over merchants, Kendall stressed that his company would guarantee equal access for anyone who could afford the regular fees, and dismiss any employee who manipulated its wires to promote a purely private speculation. To fault the new technology for encouraging insider trading, Kendall believed, was particularly unfair. Prior to the advent of the electric telegraph, Kendall reminded his critics, merchants had long maintained an optical telegraph between New York and Philadelphia for the benefit of *"speculators exclusively"*—and no one had complained. It would be impossible, Kendall added, to devise a set of administrative procedures that would preclude the possibility of speculative abuse. Still, the rules his company had devised would "place all men on equality, in the use of the telegraph"—even though, of course, they could not "make them equal in the sagacity, industry, and enterprise, which enables them to use it profitably to themselves."[86]

Beginning in the summer of 1846, criticisms of federal control began to find their way into the press. Led by *Niles's National Register* and the *Albany Evening Journal*, a small but influential number of journals raised questions about the effectiveness of public administration of the new technology and warned against the political dangers that might accompany federal control.[87] Private enterprise, they agreed, had thus far worked remarkably well. Just as competition had brought about major reforms in mail delivery, editorialized Jeremiah Hughes of *Niles*, so, too, it would spur technical innovation in telegraphy.[88] The commercialization of the new technology by the federal government was likely to prove very costly, warned the *Evening Journal*, and was in any event too complicated for public administrators to coordinate. Furthermore, unless Congress enacted laws as arbitrary as the laws prohibiting private competition in mail delivery, Morse's patent would in all likelihood be quickly superseded, and "individual enterprise" would drive the government into bankruptcy.[89] If any business could be safely left in the hands of the people, predicted the editor of the New York *Evening Mirror*—in articulating the emerging consensus—it was telegraphy: "It is free to all who choose to pay for the use of it, and thus far has been managed with admirable skill and discretion."[90] The case for federal control received a further blow when, shortly thereafter, several state legislatures, led by New York, passed laws to curb the most serious forms of potential abuse.[91]

Following the Civil War, champions and critics of telegraph reform would endlessly debate the significance of this early experiment in federal control. While industry insiders typically dismissed federal control as a bizarre and short-lived aberration, a few old-timers were candid enough to recall that, at the time, they had held a different view. Proposals for the regulation of the telegraph industry by the federal government, declared veteran telegrapher George Prescott in 1866, were "unwise, injudicious, and unnecessary." Yet, Prescott added, this had not always been his position:

> During the first half of my twenty years' service as a telegraph operator, I was strongly of the opinion that it would have been good policy for the government to own and control the telegraph lines, and that the public would have been greatly benefited thereby. The companies were then small and poor, the lines were badly constructed and worse supported; and all progress was prevented by the constant and unremitting competition of rival lines. There was no question but that one company could do the telegraphic business over any given territory much cheaper and better than two or more. There is a striking

analogy in this respect between the telegraph and the mail service, and no one will deny that one company can manage this service better than two or more.

Given the unlimited resources of the federal government, Prescott explained, he had taken it for granted that it was the only institution with the requisite means to promote the public good.[92]

By 1866, Prescott had changed his mind. Now that Prescott's employer, Western Union, had established a dominant position in the American telegraph industry, Prescott no longer doubted that a private enterprise could coordinate a nationwide network. At approximately the same time, Morse himself reached a similar conclusion. Western Union, Morse wrote Kendall in March 1866, was "becoming, doubtless, a *monopoly*, but no more so than the post office system, and its unity is in reality a public advantage if properly and uprightly managed."[93]

During the 1840s, large numbers of Americans participated in a broad-ranging discussion of national communications policy, the first such discussion in American history. Political engagement was high and the command of the issues impressive. Though the privatization of the postal system had influential champions, in the end, Congress buttressed the existing regulatory regime. Indeed, in 1851 Congress went so far as to authorize improvements in the level of mail delivery that were independent of their possible impact on postal finance. In an age in which historians have often dismissed governmental institutions as agents of change, here was one policy decision that dramatically broadened the mandate of the federal government.

In telegraphy, in contrast, deregulation prevailed.[94] Notwithstanding the explicit preference of Morse and the misgivings of a leading segment of the press, legislators declined to establish a regulatory regime that was in any way comparable to the regulatory regime that had long existed in mail delivery. Even in telegraphy, however, deregulation had its limits. The industry remained constrained not only by a congeries of state regulations but also by federal court rulings on patent rights, contracts, and eminent domain. Following the Civil War, reformers would once again agitate for federal control, catalyzing a popular movement for "postal telegraphy" that, in the early twentieth century, would shape the regulatory regime in the telephone industry.[95]

The enactment of legislation to promote the public welfare is central to what the founders of the American republic meant by political republicanism, and is among the most important of the legacies of the American Revolution. Not until the 1840s would a younger generation move beyond the founders and decisively challenge this shared consensus. For various reasons, these reformers rejected political republicanism and embraced the noninterventionist economic credo that has come to be known as economic liberalism. In transportation, banking, and telegraphy, federal regulation was almost ritualistically disparaged. For the first time in American history, it became common to characterize as private even those enterprises that were the most heavily dependent on the public largesse— such as, for example, the land-grant railroads in the trans-Mississippi West. In the process, the now-familiar idealization of private enterprise emerged. It was a genuinely new idea, an invented tradition popularized by critics of governmental expansion as a reaction to, and critique of, the prior expansion of the early American state. In mail delivery, in contrast, a regulatory regime that dated back to the 1790s retained enough popular support to endure. Postal deregulation was not without its defenders; yet, in the end, this was one market revolution that failed.

NOTES

1. Washington *Daily Union*, June 29, 1847.

2. New York *Journal of Commerce*, July 16, 1840, July 30, 1840.

3. Ibid., February 2, 1844.

4. Ibid., February 29, 1844, 14 March 14, 1844.

5. Washington *Daily Union*, June 29, 1847.

6. Ibid.

7. Ibid.

8. For a more extended critique of historical writing on the early American state, see Richard R. John, "Governmental Institutions as Agents of Change: Rethinking American Political Development in the Early Republic, 1787–1835," *Studies in American Political Development*, 11 (Fall 1997): 347–80.

9. The distributive character of public policy in the early republic is a theme of Richard L. McCormick's *Party Period and Public Policy: American Politics from the Age of Jackson to the Progressive Era* (New York, 1986), esp. 204–6.

10. E. J. Hobsbawm and Terence Ranger, eds., *The Invention of Tradition* (New York, 1984).

11. For a related discussion, see Rush Welter, *The Mind of America, 1820–1860* (New York, 1975), chap. 6.

12. These generalizations are based on an on-line search of "A Century of Lawmaking for the New Nation: Congressional Documents and Debates, 1774–1873," an electronic library that is part of the Library of Congress's American Memory project.

13. *House Journal*, December 2, 1806, 4681 (emphasis added).

14. To get some idea of the frequency with which Americans used the phrase "private enterprise" in the early republic, I conducted an electronic search of the large collection

of nineteenth-century machine-readable documents that are included in the "Making of America" electronic libraries maintained by the University of Michigan and Cornell University. Electronic searches must be used in conjunction with other, more traditional methods of historical inquiry, since, among other things, their utility is predicated upon the representativeness of the documents they include. Still, it is suggestive that in neither library is the phrase "private enterprise" at all common prior to the 1830s, while, in the period between the 1830s and the Civil War, the phrase rarely occurs more than once or twice in a single book or article. Had contemporaries invested the phrase with the thick layers of meaning that it has since come to acquire, one would have expected that it would have been more frequently invoked. In most instances, contemporaries used it merely to distinguish a government project from a project that lacked government support. Only rarely did they hail it as a distinctively American achievement, and almost never did they use it to characterize a business activity (such as, for example, textile manufacturing or blacksmithing) in which the government did not engage. Searches of the Lexus-Nexus and "Century of Lawmaking" electronic libraries generated similar results.

15. William Leggett, "Free Trade Post Office," New York *Evening Post*, March 23, 1835, in Leggett, *A Collection of the Political Writings of William Leggett . . .* , 2 vols., ed. Theodore Sedgwick (New York, 1840), 1:245.

16. "The Projected Ship Canal to Connect the Atlantic and Pacific Oceans," *United States Magazine and Democratic Review* 6 (November 1839): 423 (emphasis added).

17. Michael Kammen, "The Problem of American Exceptionalism: A Reconsideration," *American Quarterly* 45 (1993): 22–24; Thomas K. McCraw, "Business and Government: The Origins of the Adversary Relationship," *California Management Review* 26 (1984): 42–44.

18. Richard R. John, *Spreading the News: The American Postal System from Franklin to Morse* (Cambridge, Mass., 1995).

19. John Lauritz Larson, *Internal Improvement: National Public Works and the Promise of Popular Government in the Early United States* (Chapel Hill, 2001); Richard R. John and Christopher J. Young, "Rites of Passage: Postal Petitioning as a Tool of Governance in the Age of Federalism," in *The House and Senate in the 1790s: Petitioning, Lobbying, and Institutional Development*, ed. Kenneth R. Bowling and Donald R. Kennon (Athens, Ohio, 2002), 100–138.

20. John, *Spreading the News*, chap. 2.

21. Richard R. John, "Private Mail Delivery in the United States during the Nineteenth Century—A Sketch," *Business and Economic History*, 2d ser., 15 (1986): 131–43; Richard R. John, "James Webster Hale," *American National Biography*, ed. John Arthur Garraty and Mark C. Carnes (New York, 1999), 9:825–26.

22. William Harnden to J. W. Lawrence, March 25, 1841, in A. L. Stimson, *History of the Express Companies* (New York, 1859), 60.

23. *Congressional Globe, Appendix*, January 27, 1845, 266.

24. Charles Wickliffe, "Report of the Postmaster General," *Senate Document* 1, 28th

Cong., 2nd sess., serial 449, 1844, 667–73; Washington *Madisonian*, December 9, 1843, January 6, 1844, February 3, 1844.

25. James W. Hale, "History of Cheap Postage," *American Odd Fellow* 10 (1871): 183.

26. Lysander Spooner, *Who Caused the Reduction of Postage in 1845?* (Boston, 1849), 15.

27. Stimson, *Express Companies*, 150.

28. Boston *Morning Chronicle*, July 12, 1844.

29. James De Peyster Ogden to Charles Wickliffe, August 22, 1844, in "Report of the Postmaster General," *Senate Document* 1, 685. See also Boston *Daily Advertiser*, June 26, 1844.

30. *Senate Document* 215, 27th Cong., 3rd sess., serial 416, 1843, 1.

31. Baltimore *Sun*, March 19, 1844.

32. Ibid., January 8, 1845.

33. *New-York Daily Tribune*, October 3, 1843.

34. Ibid., April 24, 1844.

35. *Buffalo Commercial*, June 29, 1844, cited in Elliott Perry, *Pat Paragraphs*, ed. George T. Turner and Thomas E. Stanton (Takoma Park, Md., 1981), 305.

36. Washington *Daily National Intelligencer*, February 14, 1844.

37. New York *Journal of Commerce*, January 29, 1845. The Post Office Department did in fact establish such an express. Washington *Constitution*, February 22, 1845.

38. *Congressional Globe*, February 11, 1839, 184.

39. Ibid., March 22, 1844, 423.

40. Amasa Dana, *Speech of Mr. Dana, of New York, on the Post Office Bill . . .* (Washington, 1845), 5; *Congressional Globe*, February 25, 1845, 348.

41. *Congressional Globe*, January 22, 1844, 172.

42. Ibid., January 27, 1845, 196.

43. *New-Hampshire Patriot* (ca. 1845), cited in Joshua Leavitt, *Cheap Postage: Remarks and Statistics upon the Subject of Cheap Postage and Postal Reform in Great Britain and the United States* (Boston, 1848), 18.

44. *House Report* 731, 30th Cong., 1st sess., serial 526, 1848, 3–5.

45. *Congressional Globe*, January 19, 1849, 301.

46. Gerrit Smith, *Abolition of the Postal System . . .* (Washington, 1854).

47. Boston *Morning Chronicle*, September 12, 1845.

48. Barnabas Bates to Lysander Spooner, March 16, 1851, Lysander Spooner Papers, Boston Public Library.

49. Wayne E. Fuller, *The American Mail: Enlarger of the Common Life* (Chicago, 1972), 65.

50. *Congressional Globe*, January 14, 1851, 234–35.

51. Charles M. Ellis, "The Postal System Exclusive," *Massachusetts Quarterly Review* 10 (March 1850): 271–74.

52. James W. Carey, *Communication as Culture: Essays on Media and Society* (Boston, 1989), 201–30; Daniel J. Czitrom, *Media and the American Mind From Morse to McLuhan* (Chapel Hill, 1982), 8–14.

53. Samuel F. B. Morse to Levi Woodbury, September 27, 1837, *House Document* 15, 25th Cong., 2nd sess., serial 322, 1837, 31.

54. Samuel F. B. Morse to Francis O. J. Smith, February 15, 1838, *House Report* 753, 25th Cong., 2nd sess., serial 335, 1838, 8.

55. Morse to Smith, February 15, 1838, *House Report* 753, 8–9.

56. *New York Herald*, April 22, 1845.

57. *Morning Courier and New-York Enquirer*, April 21, 1845.

58. Philadelphia *Public Ledger*, October 31, 1845.

59. *Morning Courier and New-York Enquirer*, April 22, 1845.

60. New York *Journal of Commerce*, January 11, 1845.

61. New York *Journal of Commerce*, November 18, 1846.

62. Baltimore *Patriot*, November 14, 1845, May 21, 1846.

63. New York *Sun*, November 29, December 18, 1845, February 13, 1846, February 4, 1847; *New York Herald*, April 22, 1845; Baltimore *Sun*, November 15, November 23, 1844, December 9, 1845, December 17, 1846; Philadelphia *Public Ledger*, June 7, 1844, May 15, October 29, October 31, 1845.

64. Cited in Washington *Daily National Intelligencer*, June 18, 1846.

65. *Niles's National Register*, September 26, 1846.

66. Kendall to Smith, August 12, 31 (quote), September 1, December 4, 1845, Francis O. J. Smith Papers, Maine Historical Society.

67. Kendall to George W. Hopkins, January 17, 1846, Petitions, House Committee on the Post Office and Post Roads, RG 233, National Archives.

68. Petition of Baltimore merchants, January 11, 1847, ibid. See also Henry Rogers to Cave Johnson, October 26, 1846, Letters Received, Records of the Post Office Department, RG 28, National Archives.

69. Henry Clay to Alfred Vail, September 10, 1844, Vail Telegraph Collection, Smithsonian Institution Archives. Clay's letter was published in 1892 and in the following years was often cited by champions of telegraphic reform. Frank G. Carpenter, "Henry Clay on Nationalizing the Telegraph," *North American Review* 154 (March 1892): 380–82.

70. Absalom Chappell, "Report of the Committee on Ways and Means," March 3, 1845, *House Report* 187, 28th Cong., 2nd sess., serial 468, 1845, 3, 5, 6.

71. New York *Evening Post*, June 10, 1844; Philadelphia *Pennsylvanian*, June 13, 1844; Washington *Constitution*, April 21, 1845; Washington *Union*, December 24, 1846.

72. Francis O. J. Smith, "The Post-Office Department, Considered with Reference to its Condition, Policy, Prospects, and Remedies," *Merchants' Magazine and Commercial Review* 12 (February 1845): 144, 147–49.

73. *Kendall's Expositor* 3 (July 25, 1843): 242.

74. Ibid. 3 (November 25, 1843): 386.

75. Ibid. 3 (October 17, 1843): 343.

76. Samuel Reid to Martin Van Buren, January 6, 1837, Records of the Office of the Electro-Magnetic Telegraph, RG 28, National Archives.

77. Kendall to John M. Robinson, February 8, 1837, in Washington *Globe*, February 15, 1837.

78. Kendall to Smith, August 12, 1845, Smith Papers, Maine Historical Society.

79. Cave Johnson, "Report of the Postmaster General," December 1, 1845, *Senate Document 2*, 29th Cong., 1st sess., serial 470, 1845, 861.

80. Kendall to Hopkins, January 17, 1846, RG 233, National Archives.

81. Johnson, "Report," 861.

82. Cave Johnson to Dixon H. Lewis, June 4, 1846, *Senate Document 373*, 29th Cong. 1st sess., serial 476, 1846, 2. For a related discussion, see Menahem Blondheim, *News over the Wires: The Telegraph and the Flow of Public Information in America, 1844–1897* (Cambridge, Mass., 1994), 48–50.

83. Blondheim, *News over the Wires*, chap. 3.

84. Washington *Daily Union*, September 22, 1847. See also Washington *Daily Union*, January 30, 1846, August 2, 5, 17, 25, 31, 1847, September 3, 1847.

85. Baltimore *Patriot*, June 20, November 19, 1845; Boston *Daily Advertiser*, November 14, 1845; *Utica Daily Gazette*, November 29, 1845. See also *Morning Courier and New-York Enquirer*, November 25, 1845.

86. *New York Morning Express*, March 10, 1846.

87. *Niles's National Register*, July 4, September 26, December 19, 1846; *Albany Evening Journal*, December 14, 1846; New York *Journal of Commerce*, December 16, 1846.

88. *Niles's National Register*, December 19, 1846.

89. *Albany Evening Journal*, December 14, 1846.

90. New York *Evening Mirror*, December 15, 1846.

91. Tomas Nonnenmacher, "State Promotion and Regulation of the Telegraph Industry, 1845–1860," *Journal of Economic History* 61 (March 2001): 19–36.

92. *Telegrapher*, August 1, 1866, vol. 2, 169.

93. Morse to Kendall, March 19, 1866, Morse Papers, Library of Congress. I am grateful to Kenneth Silverman for this reference.

94. Richard R. John, "Recasting the Information Infrastructure for the Industrial Age," in *A Nation Transformed by Information: How Information Has Shaped the United States from Colonial Times to the Present*, ed. Alfred D. Chandler, Jr., and James W. Cortada (New York, 2000), 55–105.

95. Richard R. John, "The Politics of Innovation," *Daedalus* 127 (Fall 1998): 187–214.

I3

Popular Movements and Party Rule

The New York Anti-Rent Wars and
the Jacksonian Political Order

When he arrived in Sand Lake, a village in the foothills of the Tagkhanic mountains just east of Albany, Governor William Bouck felt a shock of dismay and anger. A crowd was waiting for him. Brightly colored banners and transparencies filled the village square with strange icons, pictures of Indians, and mottoes like "Down with the Rent" and "The Land is Mine, Sayeth the Lord." As the governor arrived, the celebrants began firing a six-pound cannon; between one and two thousand people crowded around his carriage, "in various ways demonstrat[ing] their high respect for their chief magistrate." At the edge of the crowd stood a hundred men dressed in pantaloons, calico gowns, and painted muslin masks. The men carried "swords, knives, bits of scythes, . . . threatening looking cheese knives, . . . clubs . . . muskets, . . . [and] pistols."[1]

The governor had expected his visit to be secret; the crowd's presence meant that news of his trip would get back to Albany, exposing him to political attacks for abetting lawless agrarians. The controversy would deepen the divisions between radical Democrats and Bouck's conservative wing of the party of Jackson. The people who greeted him were anti-renters, tenant farmers dedicated to destroying New York's leasehold estates and distributing the land among those who farmed it. More than a score of estates existed in New York, covering two million acres in the Hudson Valley and the surrounding hills, the Catskill piedmont, and the Mohawk and Susquehanna Valleys. Some 260,000 tenants— about a twelfth of New York's population—farmed on long-term leases in exchange for cash rents or payments in produce and labor. In 1839, tenants on the 750,000-acre manor of Rensselaerwyck began organizing to resist their landlords' demands. Sand Lake was on Rensselaerwyck; when the governor arrived there in August 1844, the movement was spreading rapidly to other estates. Within a year, it would claim between 25,000 and 60,000 supporters in eleven counties. Everywhere they organized, anti-renters initiated a rent boycott, began lobbying the legislature, and sought ways to challenge their landlords' titles in court. They also created bands of disguised men like those at the edge of the crowd in Sand Lake. These were the "Indians," who forcibly prevented lawmen from evicting tenants or seizing their personal property to cover their overdue rent.[2]

Bouck had come to meet with the anti-rent leaders. For three hours, he tried to work out a formula for settling the farmers' dispute with their landlords. In this he failed. But he did inform them that he had directed the sheriff of Rensselaer County not to serve any process against tenants without consulting the attorney general and the chief justice of the state supreme court. This order, all knew, would end prosecution of tenants for nonpayment of rent. After the meeting,, the anti-renters held a rally. The governor sat uncomfortably on the dais as the "Indians" displayed their horsemanship and as movement leaders urged the assembled farmers to resist the legal collection of rents "by all possible means."

From the vantage of the early twenty-first century, Bouck's meeting with the anti-renters seems downright bizarre. Many contemporaries were shocked at the governor's appeasement of a movement dedicated to resisting the laws of his state. But part of the strangeness of the meeting springs from the way historians of the antebellum United States have separated and compartmentalized popular movements and party politics. Movements like the anti-renters are the province of social history, which analyzes their roots in the structures of exploitation and the cultural traditions of the exploited; men like Bouck belong in political histories. Both sorts of history minimize or caricature the interplay between popular movements and party politics. Social historians either ignore party politics or depict politics as an arena in which popular demands were routinely co-opted and silenced. Most political historians fall into opposing sorts of errors. Many "new political historians" depict popular movements as marginal to the main story of partisan conflict, while neo-progressive political historians portray Bouck's Democratic Party as something of a popular movement itself, its platform and ideology a more or less unmediated reflection of the aspirations of urban wage-earners and frontier farmers. The first two groups portray popular movements and party politicians as exerting only minimal influence on one another, while the second sees an unproblematic continuity between the two.[3]

Bouck's meeting with the anti-renters, however, reminds us of both the striking differences between the political culture of party leaders and plebeian constituents *and* the mutual influence between them. Like most white, male, plebeian Americans, the anti-renters were enthusiastic participants in electoral politics and had made the ideas, rituals, and tactics of the Whigs and Democrats their own. There was much in the scene at Sand Lake that Bouck would have found familiar: the banners, illuminations, speeches, and songs were borrowed from Democratic ritual and visual culture. The "Indians" were another matter. Rooted in older traditions, they celebrated the savage and grotesque and dedicated themselves to making the laws unenforceable. Like other party politicians, Bouck found them foreign, repugnant, and politically dangerous. Still, there was no denying that the anti-renters were becoming a powerful force in New York's competitive political scene, and Bouck was courting them; his was an effort to forge an informal alliance between the insurgents and the conservative wing of the Democratic Party. Bouck's courtship held political dangers, however. Many members of his own party, as well as many Whigs, bitterly opposed the anti-renters as a threat to property rights and the sanctity of the law. The event at Sand Lake suggests that, far from being irrelevant to or easily assimilated to party politics, popular movements could sometimes have a complex and potentially destabilizing relationship to the politics of party and state.

The Anti-Rent Wars thus present an opportunity to reexamine the relationship between party politics and popular movements in antebellum America. And they open up a new avenue of inquiry into antebellum political history as a whole. For popular and reform movements were a central element in the politics of antebellum America. While most political historians see the transformation of American public life in the first half of the nineteenth century as centering on the achievement of nearly universal white male suffrage and the creation of mass-based, competitive parties, these changes were part of a much broader set of transformations. The early nineteenth century witnessed an explosion in the number of voluntary associations, rebellions, and reform movements outside the parties, many of which were explicitly political—that is, they sought to change or maintain the rules governing community life through collective, public means. A short list of such political, extra-party efforts includes the labor movement in its various guises (trade unions, Workingmen's parties, the ten-hour movement); urban crowd actions; rural rebellions and land reform movements; socialism, both Christian and "Utopian"; nativism; and a plethora of evangelical reform movements (Sabbatarianism, temperance, moral reform, opposition to capital punishment and to Indian removal, abolitionism, and Women's Rights—to name a few). Given their ubiquity and (in some cases) influence, to ignore the role of such movements in antebellum politics is much like writing about American politics after World War II without mentioning the civil rights, antiwar, and feminist movements. Yet this is what most historians of antebellum politics do.[4]

Far from being divorced from the main story of partisan conflict, many reform and plebeian activists offered a bold challenge to the way in which two-party politics was conducted. Reformers' criticism of party politics was twofold. They depicted politicians as corrupt in their policy decisions—as sacrificing the public good to the interests of liquor dealers, slave owners, land monopolists, or exploitative employers. And they offered blistering critiques of the very institutions, norms, behaviors, and attitudes structuring electoral life. To many evangelicals, party competition inspired activists to engage in "falsehood, slander, and bribes," incited the "low passions" of the "fickle multitude," destroyed Christian harmony, and diverted everyone's attention from spiritual matters. Partisanship, Horace Bushnell wrote, was "the worst form of papacy ever invented." For their part, urban labor leaders denounced the "wire pullers" and "designing political demagogues" whose search for partisan advantage led them to "batten down the rights and privileges of the laboring classes."[5]

Many reformers offered alternative ways of organizing public life. The labor movement pioneered the politics of class-based association and public appeal; evangelical reformers developed a sophisticated combination of press, publicity, and personal pestering that aimed at making public opinion hostile to sin. When reformers organized electorally, they sought to bring these other forms of public mobilization into the electoral arena, hoping thereby to transform and purify politics. Whether they shared the Workingmen's Parties' hope of ending economic parasites' control of political office through a producer-controlled political movement, embraced William Lloyd Garrison's dream of replacing all human political institutions with "the dominion of God, the control of an inward spirit," or worked with the Liberty Party to bring about a "political millennium," reformers of many stripes sought to remake politics and government according to the principles that underlay their own dissident political practices.[6]

But the relationship of many movements and rebellions to party politics was not merely oppositional; it was often dialectical. For all their disdain for partisan practices, reformers and plebeian activists often borrowed heavily from the methods and ideas of the parties. Few Americans felt greater repulsion at the idolatry of party than Charles Grandison Finney. Yet he called on his fellow evangelicals to emulate those politicians who "get up meetings, circulate handbills and pamphlets, blaze away in the newspapers, send ships about the streets on wheels with flags and sailors"—in an effort to "get all the people to . . . *vote in* the Lord Jesus Christ as the Governor of the Universe." In the cities, scores of Democratic activists courted the working-class and immigrant vote, keeping alive an ideological and programmatic give and take between their party and ethnic organizations and the labor movement. Labor leaders contributed to this interchange by serving as Democratic activists; party leaders rewarded their efforts by occasionally nominating them for office. Although it was never straightforward, the influence of reform and plebeian movements on the parties could sometimes be profound. The most dramatic example of this was, of course, abolitionism. But other examples abounded: nativists, temperance advocates, land reformers, trade unionists, and labor reformers all had a noticeable impact on party platforms and the careers of several politicians. One need look only at the career of Horace Greeley, whose message as a Whig spokesman was deeply influenced by labor reform, land reform, Fourierism, and the body reforms, to appreciate the impact that reform and plebeian initiatives could have on party politicians. And one need only consider the bitter conflict between Greeley and conservative Whigs to see that this influence had an important, though largely unexplored, impact on the parties.[7]

This essay offers an in-depth exploration of one instance of the dialectical relationship between the major parties and popular movements by examining the anti-renters' interactions with the Whig and Democratic Parties. As the meeting at Sand Lake suggests, party leaders and tenant militants belonged to separate but overlapping political subcultures, with different social ideals, conflicting political practices, and incompatible conceptions of democracy. Tenants were enthusiastic participants in the political culture of the second party system, and party spokesmen were their most influential political teachers. But the anti-renters were critical and selective pupils. Their stance toward the parties was one of selective appropriation, bricolage, and outrage at their instructors' failure to live up to their own principles. For their part, party activists neither faithfully echoed nor completely silenced the anti-renters' ideas and demands; they too selectively appropriated and reshaped their constituents' principles and policies. Examining this process of appropriation and reappropriation promises a more nuanced understanding of how Jacksonian democracy worked at the grass roots. It also promises to uncover a hitherto unexamined source of dynamism in the Jacksonian political order. The negotiation and conflict between party leaders and plebeian activists in the anti-rent district played a significant part in destroying the second party system in New York and in shaping the political order that replaced it.

Although it was an insurgent movement, the anti-rent campaign borrowed heavily from the Whig and Democratic Parties. Beginning in the 1820s, political parties replaced landlords as the main mediator between tenants and the government and drew virtually all adult white male tenants into the political process. Partisan conventions, rallies, and parades became a staple of community life, offering leasehold residents a chance to imbibe and affirm in songs, toasts, and banners the political messages of their parties. Voter participation on the West Manor of Rensselaerwyck in Albany County grew from 36 percent in 1822 to over 90 percent after 1828, while turnout in the main leasehold towns of Delaware County jumped from 30 percent in 1820 to over 85 percent in 1840. A smaller but significant number of tenants served as convention delegates or on electoral committees, thus gaining critical training in political organizing and mass mobilization.[8]

Once they broke with their landlords in 1839, anti-rent activists put this political training to new uses. Over 35 percent of anti-rent activists in Albany and Delaware counties (101 out of 285) had served as delegates at Whig or Democratic county conventions or had joined countywide partisan committees between 1828 and 1840. These militants borrowed their movement's structure and style from the major parties. Insurgents created anti-rent associations that oversaw a rent strike, coordinated legal challenges to the landlords, and educated and mobilized the tenantry. From 1844 on, they also established an anti-rent political organization, nominating candidates for local and state office. In both of these efforts, they copied the Whigs' and Democrats' pyramidal structure of local, county, and state associations, conventions, and electoral committees. They also appropriated the parties' calendar of rallies, dinners, picnics, and parades. But for the message conveyed in their speeches, songs, and toasts, anti-rent rituals and meetings were identical to those of the Whigs and Democrats.[9]

The anti-renters also drew on the anti-monopoly ideas of the Democrats, who enjoyed electoral majorities in most leasehold towns, and applied them to the monopoly of the soil. Just as Democrats denounced the Second Bank of the

United States and other chartered corporations as a new "aristocracy" elevated by government-bestowed privileges, so did anti-renters depict landlords as "an aristocracy encouraged and protected by law." Militants denounced the "court gifts" of land that had established leasehold estates and painstakingly reconstructed numerous frauds by which landlords had expanded their original grants. These grants, they argued, had been wrongly confirmed by a postrevolutionary legislature stacked with proprietors and their allies. Landlords' aristocratic privileges continued to be maintained through unequal laws that proscribed challenges to landlords' titles, allowed proprietors to exempt themselves from local property taxes, and tolerated their power of distress—the right (denied to other creditors) to seize and sell tenant's personal property for unpaid rent.[10]

Leasehold militants declared that these special privileges empowered landlords to "withhold from the people their dearest rights." Proprietors stripped tenants of the fruits of their labor—a fact that one Delaware County insurgent found "revolting to every principle of American liberty." They enjoyed control over the economic prospects of entire communities, making a mockery of the dignity and independence due each citizen: "These laboring men scarce breathe in [the landlord's] presence; his mandates are those of a Dictator; and thousands must plod their way yearly with trembling steps and enter the halls of his lordship, bending and bowing . . . to solicit the favor of enjoying *their* property." This artificial inequality of power endangered republican government, anti-renters maintained. Landlords' wealth enabled them to suborn legislators, while their power over tenants allowed each proprietor to "bend his fellow man to his own will, and mak[e] him subserve his own selfish, political or mercenary interests." These were the very evils that Democrats attributed to banking monopolies.[11]

Anti-renters united around three demands that aimed at ending landlords' special legal privileges: abolition of landlords' power of distress, taxation of rent incomes, and, most importantly, a "title-test" law which would permit tenants to defend themselves in suits for nonpayment of rent by challenging the validity of their landlords' titles. This final demand was formulated to serve a simpler and more audacious aim: to abrogate the title of the "pretended proprietors" and bestow legal possession of the soil upon its cultivators. Behind this aim lay a belief, at least as old as the Revolution, that republican freedom was attainable only in a society marked by universal, individual, freehold landownership. "In all free governments," the anti-renters of Delaware County declared, "it is essential that the people themselves be free. They cannot be free unless independent. . . . To be completely sovereign, they must individually be the lords of the soil they occupy." Anti-renters believed that universal landownership would make the expropriation of one man's labor by another impossible, thus ensuring the dignity, the equality, and the independent citizenship of all male producers. Beneath this equality remained the subordination of women and children. Militants sought to do away with "unnatural" class hierarchies, and to retain those based on the "natural" categories of sex and age. Women and children would be subordinate to male householders, who controlled their labor; the householders themselves, however, would meet one another in the marketplace and in politics as equals, without a superior class to expropriate the products of their labor or control their votes.[12]

With this critique of the leasehold system and this vision of utopia, lease-hold militants created a heretical Jacksonianism, one that linked the Democrats' egalitarian, anti-monopoly ideology to an older popular tradition that affirmed the right of every producer to land. Democrats were no stranger to ideas linking land and freedom. Drawing on a tradition that reached back to Thomas Jefferson and to the popular agrarian thought of the Revolutionary era, they insisted that "a well-educated, industrious and independent yeomanry are the safest reposi-tory of freedom and free institutions." But with important constituencies among urban employers, wage earners, and landlords, few Democrats could safely ar-gue, as the anti-renters did, that landless men were unfree. More concretely, the anti-renters sought to challenge their landlords' titles in court, and they de-manded that the legislature abrogate the common-law rule barring tenants from doing so. This demand flew in the face of the Jacksonians' reverence for vested rights and strict construction of the federal Constitution; most Democrats con-sidered the proposed law to be both unconstitutional and socially dangerous. Most importantly, the anti-renters directed the Jeffersonian tradition against existing concentrations of property, raising fears of an all-powerful state disturb-ing existing social relations and trampling on the rights of property. If successful, they might set a precedent that could be used against slave property; their movement thus posed a potential threat to intersectional harmony within both parties. Nor did it help that most landlords were Democrats.[13]

Thus the emergence of two-party democracy had a momentous and ironic outcome at the grass roots. To win support in the leasehold districts, the Whigs and Democrats offered tenants powerful social and political ideas and trained large numbers of estate residents as political organizers. The anti-renters turned these skills and teachings to uses that most Whigs and Democrats found threat-ening. In the process, both groups helped change the character of farmers' movements in the United States. Transformed by the revolution in electoral politics, New York's anti-renters were the first rural insurgents to build a sus-tained mass movement in the American countryside. Their movement provided a turning point between the local, violent, and easily crushed rural rebellions of the early republic and the sustained mass movements of the Grange and the Populists.[14]

Older traditions still carried enormous appeal for the anti-renters, however. Insurgents combined newer ways of doing politics with a tradition of mobbing, which originated in Europe and had been sustained in earlier leasehold rebellions. They also drew on the charivari—a highly ritualized crowd action in which the young men of a neighborhood, dressed in grotesque and terrifying disguises, treated newlyweds or people who had violated local mores with extravagant threats, mild assault, and the "rough music" of tin pans, drums, horns, horse fiddles, and catcalls. The anti-renters adopted these traditions to their needs, creating bands of "Indians" like those who greeted Governor Bouck at Sand Lake. These were groups of boys and young men, dressed in fantastic costumes—calico gowns and sheepskin masks adorned with paint, horses' tails, and ribbons, and complemented by a farcical oversupply of guns, swords, knives, and clubs.[15]

The Indians served two tactical purposes.[16] They intimidated and assaulted community members who paid rent, bought land, or otherwise gave support to the landlords. In this way, they ensured community support for the anti-rent movement. They also protected tenants who supported the rent boycott by halting any officer of the law who entered their area and subjecting him to an elaborate ritual of intimidation and humiliation.[17] In their recruitment of young men, their disguises, and their rituals of intimidation, the anti-rent "Indians" recreated the charivari and turned it to a new, political purpose.

They recreated the charivari in another way as well: by giving voice to a persistent corporatist and personalist strain in tenant culture. The anti-rent associations and parties spoke in the Whigs' and Democrats' universalistic (though racially and gender exclusive) language of natural rights. They championed principles of political economy that would apply to all white men. The Indians consistently supported the legislative aims of the associations. But they had another aim as well: to enforce local rules of behavior and punish the people who violated them. "Tribes" were organized by neighborhood, and each one focused primarily on its own community, working to ensure the economic security of specific individuals whom its members knew personally. The "Prophet" of a Rensselaer County tribe assured the "white brethren" who gathered to hear him that the Indians sought to protect "their neighbors . . . they were blood connexions of many who stood around them." These ersatz aborigines were equally personal in their treatment of enemies. The Albany County tribe, for example, immortalized one hated deputy sheriff's misdeeds and boasted of their thrashing of him in a song,

"The End of Bill Snyder." Anonymous letters bore witness to similar grudges. One threatened an up-rent hotel keeper with "TAR AN FEATHER" and "A DOSE OF PISTLS PILS" and closed with the telling line: "THE PUBLIC FEELING IS AGAINST YOU." With sentiments like these, the Indians perpetuated a locally oriented, corporatist tradition in which each community protected its own and enforced its own unwritten code of conduct.[18]

Whether participating in the rent boycott, thrashing lawmen, or voting for anti-rent candidates, leasehold militants acted on a conception of democracy that they had learned from the Democrats and had adapted to their own purposes: the unqualified sovereignty of the people. Militants believed that a single popular will existed, above the clash of personal, group, or local interests. This will, when not distorted by corrupt influences, always pointed to the best interests of a community. From this point of view, government appeared as nothing more than an extension of the will of the citizenry. George W. Lewis of Sand Lake summarized this view well: "The people rule in this country, and they can make any laws they are a mind to, . . . and it is a libel and an insult, upon the patriotism of the sons of '76, to tell them that they can't do the work."[19]

For most anti-renters, popular sovereignty implied the right of the people to overthrow any laws or institutions that injured the common good—including the federal and state constitutions. They thus ridiculed the reverence for vested rights and constitutional restrictions that led most lawmakers to oppose their demands. According to "Socrates," anyone who sought to "protect and defend the constitution of the State, however . . . shamefully it may encroach upon the constitution of the people" was "only fit to be the servile drudge of Patroonery." Many insurgents also defended citizens' right to break laws that violated natural law, defied the will of God, or offended the sensibilities of a sovereign people. L. H. Vermilia warned that the laws that enforced farm leases "never can, they never will, hereafter be enforced. It is useless to lay so much stress upon law and order, when injustice is so palpable as to be seen and felt in every man's household. That law and order ceases to become binding when the main feature of all law, equality, and the right of the people to govern themselves is broken down in a manner that would disgrace many a nabob of older countries."[20]

As they had done with their social vision, the anti-renters adapted the Democrats' ideals of popular sovereignty and put them to new uses. With this adaptation, leasehold militants turned the teachings against the teacher. Most anti-renters had been loyal Democrats until 1844. But in that year, Democrats in the legislature had joined with conservative Whigs to rebuff their demands, with little resistance from liberal Whigs. A few months later, the Indians killed two people. The leaders of both parties led a chorus of denunciation, and Governor

Silas Wright called out the militia. In the wake of these events, militants concluded that political leaders in both parties had betrayed their duties to a sovereign people. The people, they believed, had awakened to a galling wrong and demanded redress; the people's representatives, rather than bowing to their masters' will, "refused to give them any aid" and "thrust them into prison."[21]

In seeking an explanation for this betrayal, anti-renters unleashed a torrent of grievances against the Jacksonian political order. They celebrated one of the accomplishments of this order—the opening of the electoral process to most white men. But they saw the development of a distinct class of political leaders as a hindrance to popular sovereignty. A Delaware County correspondent declared that "the people" were held "in bondage" by "office-holding aristocrats" who kept them from "govern[ing] themselves." Insurgents also worried that men of wealth had come to dominate legislative halls, allowing them "to control and rule us" and to "make laws to suit themselves." So too had lawyers come to control the legislature, allowing them to draft "abstruse, dark, blind, and unintelligible" laws in order to force people to depend on their expertise. Current lawmaking, many anti-renters believed, was little short of a conspiracy among lawyers to "relieve" the farmer "of his purse." Worst of all, "money is felt at the ballot box." Because of this, "officers . . . will not dare to act contrary to the will of the landed aristocracy, for fear its influence, will not *return* them, to their cherished place of office."[22]

The anti-renters' political ideas and tactics confirm what most historians of the second party system have concluded: that partisan political culture occupied a central place in the cultural world of the Jacksonian rank and file. But New York's militants approached partisan politics with neither uncritical enthusiasm nor "engaged disbelief."[23] Instead, they took seriously what they had learned from the Whig and Democratic parties, reshaped their teachings and methods to address their own needs, and combined them with a creative adaptation of older political traditions. The result was an insurgent politics—one that would have been impossible without the liberating tendencies of the Jacksonian revolution, but which challenged the political system created by that revolution.

It is tempting to end the story here, with the creation of an insurgent political culture. But anti-renters and the major parties remained interdependent and dialectically intertwined. To build an effective political organization, the anti-renters needed the skills of lawyers, editors, lobbyists, and politicians—skills that only party and reform activists possessed. Luckily, party activists were highly receptive to initiatives from the political margins. Electoral competition in New York was fierce: between 1840 and 1846, no governor won office with as much as 53 percent of the statewide vote. A few thousand voters could determine who controlled the legislature and the governor's mansion. Party leaders therefore had an enormous incentive to win new constituencies over to their parties.[24]

This incentive was compounded by the factional bickering that plagued both parties. Although united in support of state action to aid both capitalist development and moral uplift, the Whig Party had from its origins included both reactionary champions of an organic, paternalist vision of society and former Anti-Masons who embraced democracy and sought to free society from ancient forms of bondage. These Whigs coalesced into conservative and liberal factions during the 1840s, as party leaders battled over the efforts of William Seward, Thurlow Weed, and their allies to embrace an antislavery platform, court the Catholic vote, and offer political assistance to the anti-renters. Democrats, too, broke into warring camps after 1843. Radicals (also known as Barnburners) defended their party's policy of limited government and laissez-faire economics against conservatives (dubbed "Hunkers" by their enemies), who sought to promote economic development through government-sponsored roads, canals, and corporate charters.[25]

These disputes created important openings for popular movements like the anti-renters. Factional competition within parties gave partisan activists an added incentive to win new supporters, for such allies could help them not only win elections, but wrest control of the party from their factional rivals as well. More important, factionalism made such alliances less costly by setting the potential supporters and opponents of popular movements into warring camps. All Whig landlords sided with the conservatives, leaving liberals free to offer cautious support to the leasehold militants. Similarly, Democratic landlords were uniformly radicals, allowing Hunkers to forge an alliance with insurgent tenants.[26]

A third factor encouraging alliances between party activists and popular movements was the ubiquity of political outsiders seeking entry to the corridors of power. As Horace Greeley observed, the emergence of mass-based, partisan politics had flooded the towns and cities of the nation with "a large class of young lawyers and aspirants" who were "more anxious to be on the winning than on the right side, and whose gaze is fascinated and fixed by the prospect of judgeships, seats in the legislature, &c. &c." The anti-renters found allies among precisely such outsiders. Some were ambitious young lawyers and editors just embarking on their careers; others were mature and accomplished Whig lawyers whose political prospects had been cut short by their support for the antislavery cause. Still others hailed from the National Reform Association, a land-reform organization based in the New York City journeyman's movement. To many of these allies, the Anti-Rent Wars provided an opportunity to serve a cause they believed in. For all, they presented an occasion to advance their careers and to win a new constituency to their organizations. Movements like the Anti-Rent Wars offered a well-organized cadre of local activists and several thousand votes—considerations that might secure a nomination, swing an election, and breathe life into a stalled political career.[27]

These allies played a complex role in the tenants' movement. They brought their skills as lawyers, editors, and lobbyists to the cause. They also brought their own ideas about political economy and political expediency, and they fought to bring tenants to their way of thinking. These leaders served as ideological middlemen between the anti-renters and the political parties or reform organizations to which they belonged. They sought to reshape tenants' thinking to conform to the broad programs and ideologies of their organizations. At the same time, they struggled to convince their organizations to champion the anti-renters' cause.

One such ally was Thomas Ainge Devyr, an Irish-born land reformer, Chartist, former radical Democratic editor, and founding member of the National Reform Association. Editor of the anti-rent *Albany Freeholder* in 1845 and 1846, Devyr worked to tie tenants' dream of a society composed of petty proprietors to the National Reformers' attack on a cornerstone of capitalist development: private property in land. He endorsed the tenants' belief that the landlords had no right to estate lands. But where most tenants made this claim on the basis of faulty paper titles, he denied the right of any man to possess more land than he and his family could till. "The Law of Nature and Nature's God," he argued, bequeathed to "every man who comes into this world . . . an equal right to the soil." He insisted that land was not a commodity but was God's gift to humanity, to be used, but never owned, by its cultivators.[28]

Where Devyr sought to tie the anti-renters' dream of universal proprietorship to an explicitly agrarian political economy, Whig and Democratic activists worked to convince tenants that widespread landownership would be the natural outcome of economic competition, social mobility, and the laws of the market. The main evil of the leasehold system, activists from both parties agreed, was that it stifled individual initiative, undermining productivity and economic progress. Robert Watson, a Democratic anti-rent legislator, argued that landlords' claim to the improvements tenants made on their farms destroyed the natural tendency of people to promote the public good by pursuing private gain. Rather than enriching their soil through careful cultivation, they "taxed it to the uppermost. . . . No works of utility, improvement, and of elegance will be constructed with an idea of being enlarged hereafter." Even more distressing was the fact that leasehold tenures divided ownership between landlords and tenants, hindering what a committee of the state assembly called "a free exchange of the lands." As a consequence, the committee complained, leasehold tenures "tend to restrain labor from seeking, through shifting employments, its most advantageous application, and to repress the disposition, the habit, and the opportunities of enterprise."[29]

Whig and Democratic anti-rent leaders endorsed the anti-renters' three legislative demands and their desire to distribute leasehold lands among those who farmed them. With the leasehold system destroyed, they believed, individual enterprise and the free flow of land and labor to their most efficient uses would best ensure a widespread distribution of land. According to Watson, young, landless men would work as laborers to accumulate the capital with which to begin farming on their own. These early years would instill industry, economy, and sobriety in a young man, for "every dollar he can spare will go to pay for his farm." Once he purchased a homestead, security of property would spur his energies, leading him to create wealth and develop the resources of the nation. Ira Harris, a Whig anti-rent legislator, also insisted that competition and social mobility in a market economy were the sole legitimate mechanisms for distributing land. "The real estate of a country," he said, "should be left free to center, where it sooner or later will, if competition and enterprise are left free to operate unobstructed, in the hands of the industrious and prudent. Every attempt to interrupt this natural course of things is contrary to the true interests of a *republican* community."[30]

Just as they worked to win the anti-renters over to new ideas about political economy, so too did Whigs, Hunkers, and National Reformers seek to change their conception and practice of politics. Thomas Devyr endorsed the tenants' vision of popular sovereignty, but insisted that lasting reform could never be achieved through defensive measures like those of the Indians. He hoped to convince his readers to forge a disciplined electoral alliance with urban workers, reformers, and western farmers. The Indians' violent resistance merely "kick[ed]" unjust laws aside "for a moment." A permanent solution to land monopoly, he insisted, could be achieved only "by a match of rifle-shooting at the ballot boxes."[31]

For their part, Whig and Democratic activists acted as missionaries from the party Church. They strove to replace the anti-renters' syncretic political culture with a strict adherence to the political rules of the parties. Men like Watson and Harris sought to convince tenants that democracy was not a process by which the people enforced their will unimpeded, but a cosmopolitan process of coalition building, of linking local movements and issues to state and national platforms, and of brokering between constituencies. Samuel Gordon, a Democratic supporter of the Delaware County militants, contended that the anti-proprietor struggle was "too narrow a platform to erect a political party on"; it was properly "a single ingredient in the democratic cauldron, in which the great and conservative elements of eternal right, truth and justice, are mingled to compound the greatest good to the greatest number."[32]

This conception of politics required a strict adherence to the Constitution and the rule of law. Watson, Harris, and their colleagues suffered frequent attacks from opponents in their own parties for their alliance with "lawless agrarians." These leaders knew too well the political costs of Indian violence and of tenants' disdain for constitutional protections to contracts and property. They sought to contain these costs by silencing such ideas and activities. Robert Watson strove to convince the anti-renters that the success of their cause depended on courting "public opinion" and state legislators; doing so required that they disband the Indians, show strict regard for the constitution, and disavow the "agrarian" ideas of the National Reformers: "We wish the legislature to understand distinctly, that we ask them to pass no law that will violate the constitution—that will rob a single individual of his rights, or that will in any manner impair the sacred rights of property. Let what will come, we feel that the laws and constitution of our country must be maintained."[33]

A single phrase—"let what will come"—spoke volumes. It revealed that for Watson, as for Whig anti-rent leaders, commitment to constitutionalism and the rule of law came before commitment to the aims of the anti-renters. Watson and Harris repeatedly affirmed their belief in the constitutionality of the insurgents' legislative demands. Theirs was a minority opinion, however; most lawmakers and judges considered the anti-renters' title-test bill to be unconstitutional. Thus Harris's statement that he would support all anti-rent measures that were consistent with "fair and constitutional legislation" begged the critical question: what if those measures were unconstitutional? Similarly, Watson made clear that if anti-renters were forced to choose between existing property rights and their desire for what they called "the homes of our fathers," tenants must choose the former: "If the landlords have title to this land, let them keep it." Most critically, party activists' demand that the Indians disband threatened to undermine the rent boycott and to subject thousands of tenants to eviction. Whig and Democratic anti-rent leaders thus affirmed the justice of tenants' wish to destroy the leasehold system and win ownership of their farms, but entreated them to be ready to give up those aims if they could not be won by legislative and constitutional means. Alexander Johnson, a Rensselaer County Whig, encouraged anti-renters to "imagine . . . a better state of society," but insisted that "we must for the time being—submit" to landlord rule.[34]

This debate over the boundaries of legitimate political action was decided in a series of conflicts on the ground. The first and fiercest conflict was over the Indians. In December 1844, the Indians of Rensselaer and Columbia counties killed two men. As *posses comitatus* marched on the leasehold towns and the governor called out the militia, anti-renters in several towns held "law and order" meetings and demanded that the Indians disband. The anti-Indian movement echoed their Whig and Democratic allies' defense of the constitution and the rule of law. "Our government," one meeting declared, "is a government of laws, constituted and emanating from the people." Resistance to law invited "anarchy and the establishment of arbitrary and despotic power."[35]

The Indians rejected these calls to disband, and public support for them remained high. To the braves and their supporters, existing laws were not the embodiment of the people's will, but the product of a conspiracy between landlords and politicians to perpetuate the former's unnatural power over tenants. The eagerness of elected officials to crush the Indians demonstrated that this conspiracy extended to the suppression of civil liberties:

> Freemen, arouse! These impish lords have caused
> The guardians of your rights, to stain your laws,
> (Which should be free and equal unto all,)
> With *damning blots*, of special legislation—
> To hold fair justice's scales with partial hand,
> And make it a *crime* for you, to *speak* your wrongs,
> Or nobly to repel them!

Under such circumstances, many argued, the Indians were the natural heirs to the Sons of Liberty—defenders of the people's liberty and "a natural, and necessary consequence of the wrong perpetuated upon the farmers, and attempted to be enforced by law."[36]

Most importantly, the braves refused to disband because the anti-renters' legislative strategy alone could not achieve their most cherished goal: the protection of specific kin and neighbors. A band of Rensselaer County vigilantes "declared in the most violent manner that they should prevent any arrests of their friends from being made until such time as the Legislature shall act in the matter. . . . The Indians swear that they will not allow their friends to be 'picked off.' " Similarly, the Albany County chief Yellow Jacket affirmed his tribe's "determination to watch over and protect the people of these counties, . . . *penal laws to the contrary notwithstanding*."[37]

Once arrayed against the might of the state, the Indians' defensive, localist, and personalist politics could not survive. On August 7, after eight months of escalating conflicts with lawmen, the Delaware County tribe shot and killed

Deputy Sheriff Osman Steele at a sheriff's sale in Andes. Sheriffs in three counties assembled enormous posses; Governor Wright again called out the militia. Hundreds of armed men swept through the leasehold towns of Delaware, Columbia, and Schoharie counties, searching houses, trampling crops, and arresting hundreds of suspected Indians. Faced with this show of force, the Indians disbanded, never to regroup.[38]

That left electoral politics. But here, too, the anti-renters and their leaders divided over strategy and aims. Beginning in 1845, Thomas Devyr sought to draw the anti-renters into a statewide electoral alliance with the National Reformers. The aim of this alliance, he declared, was to "regulat[e] LAND MONOPOLY" by "moderating down the scale of ownership" of the soil. Whig and Democratic activists, who wished to harness the tenants' movement to their own factions, moved quickly to squelch Devyr's campaign. Charles Bouton, the Democratic publisher of the *Albany Freeholder*, fired Devyr as editor. Alexander Johnson, the new Whig editor of the journal, urged the anti-renters to choose their candidates from the nominees of the major parties. "No party," Johnson warned, "can long be sustained in this country, with . . . but one measure for its object. But a body of men, comparatively few in numbers, may engraft a favorite measure upon one, or the other, of the two parties . . . and thus secure success for their cause." Devyr moved down the street and began publishing the *Anti-Renter*, a journal explicitly allied with the National Reformers. From the pages of his new paper, Devyr launched a vitriolic campaign against "political quacks" like Bouton, Harris, and Watson who, he said, sought to subordinate the tenants' movement to their parties and political careers.[39]

This rift among anti-rent leaders brought important ideological divisions among insurgents into the open. A significant minority of anti-renters supported Devyr and the land reformers. Over a dozen local anti-rent associations formally affiliated with the National Reform Association. Many more supported the radicals' ideas without joining their organization. Scores of letters to the anti-rent and National Reform press endorsed the notion that every citizen had a natural right to land. Numerous meetings demanded a constitutional limit to the size of individual landholdings and backed the reformers' call for the distribution of the public domain, in small lots, free of charge, to landless settlers. A majority, however, remained loyal to the notion of land as a privately owned commodity. "William Tell" defended the right of each man to hold any amount of land "accumulated through his own honest industry." Most tenants refused to take sides, however, and strove to force their battling leaders to bury their differences for the good of the movement.[40]

However divided in their conceptions of political economy, most anti-renters remained united in their political aspirations. Stunning victories in the 1845 elections gave militants an exhilarating sense of their power at the ballot box. At the same time, the suppression of the Indians and the legislature's continued failure to pass a title-test bill fueled their discontent with the Whigs and Democrats. In this context, increasing numbers of leasehold insurgents expressed the hope of creating a new politics of the people, built on the ashes of the existing parties. In January 1846, "H.M.S.," a long-time Democratic activist and one of the architects of the Albany militants' alliance with the Hunkers, rose in the county Democratic convention to denounce his fellow Jacksonians' efforts to reunite its feuding Hunker and Barnburner factions. The only hope for the republic, he argued, was to destroy both parties and unite the progressive elements of both. "I am sure the spirit of Seventy-Six still lives; and it only remains for our two great political parties to be sifted, and the virtuous part of both parties to unite their efforts to secure to ourselves equal rights, and to posterity a free soil."[41]

In the spring and summer of 1846, meetings throughout the leasehold district called for the anti-rent nominating convention to be held before the Whig and Democratic conventions and endorsed Ira Harris as the anti-rent candidate for governor. In addition to being enormously popular among anti-renters, Harris had the overwhelming support of liberal Whigs; tenant leaders doubtless hoped that their early endorsement of him would either compel the Whigs to nominate Harris or win numerous liberals over to an independent anti-rent party. Insurgents thus pronounced their desire to create an independent political organization which would, in one way or another, create a realignment in state politics. Harris, however, faced strident opposition from conservative Whigs, who promised to campaign against the Whig ticket if the party nominated him. Unwilling to divide his party or to run on a third-party ticket, Harris coordinated a campaign against his own nomination among the anti-renters. His supporters packed the critical Albany County nominating convention and, after the meeting adjourned, called a secret rump session to appoint delegates to the state nominating convention. Harris also successfully pressured the anti-rent state central committee to call the convention after the Whigs and Democrats had made their nominations. With the Democrats' renomination of the hated Silas Wright assured, this move paved the way for endorsing the Whig nominee.[42]

At the anti-rent convention, support for drafting Harris remained high, but Harris's supporters defeated the movement to nominate their leader. Instead, they fought to win the endorsement of John Young, the Whigs' nominee for governor. Young's stance on the anti-renters' demands was mixed. Although in 1845 he had helped ensure the passage of bills to abolish landlords' right of distress and to tax rent income, Young opposed the anti-renter's central demand: a title-test bill. Numerous delegates arrived determined to make an independent nomination. But Harris's supporters prevailed. After Young was nominated, seven delegates, all of them National Reform sympathizers, walked out. Several bolters joined with Liberty Party activists to call a "Free Soil" convention, where they nominated a slate of land reformers and abolitionists. Their ticket, however, had little money and only twelve days to campaign. Thomas Devyr, the Free Soilers' nominee for the legislature, barely mentioned the campaign in the *Anti-Renter*. Instead, he urged anti-renters to " 'choke off' the Junto" by voting against the regular anti-rent candidates. By campaign's end, he was publishing letters and reports that openly supported the Democratic slate. Faced with conservative outrage from within his own party at the anti-renters' endorsement of him, Young steadfastly avoided taking any stand on the leasehold controversy.[43]

Anti-renters were thus faced with an unhappy choice. The Free Soilers unreservedly endorsed their demands, but had no chance of winning and were doing their best to divide the movement. John Young, on the other hand, showed little enthusiasm for the anti-rent cause. Many tenants protested Young's nomination but voted for him anyway. In each of the five major anti-rent counties, Young and the other anti-rent nominees won in a landslide, defeating their running mates on the Whig and Democratic tickets by thousands of votes. Voters in four other counties gave the anti-rent slate more modest majorities. Young won by eleven thousand votes, with almost the entire margin of victory coming from anti-rent strongholds. The Free Soil Party made a disastrous showing, garnering fewer than one hundred votes in Albany County. In early December, Thomas Devyr, broke and despairing, closed the doors of the *Anti-Renter* and returned to his previous home in Brooklyn.[44]

The suppression of the Indians and the victory of John Young signaled a dramatic narrowing of what Iver Bernstein has called "the boundaries of the political." This narrowing, in turn, significantly constrained the practical options left to tenants. With the collapse of the Indians, the anti-renters' belief that the will of "the People" should trump unjust laws became a dead letter; so too did their attempt to enforce the unwritten rules of their communities in defiance of statute law end. On a more practical level, the suppression of the vigilantes left tens of thousands of tenants vulnerable to dispossession. Landlords issued a flood of ejection suits and distress warrants; in a handful of counties, tenants abandoned the movement and began to buy their landlords' interest in their farms.[45]

The election of 1846 proved equally decisive. John Young's victory spelled the defeat of the anti-renters' vision of democracy in which the will of "the People" trumped constitutions and dictated the actions of the state. It also signaled the defeat of many anti-renters' hopes for establishing in law every citizen's right to the soil. With the Indians demobilized and hope for a new party ended, the movement no longer held out the possibility of transcending the rules and limits of politics as defined by Whig and Democratic leaders. Henceforth, anti-rent spokesmen who won seats in the legislature or had access to party councils would consistently avoid demands that challenged constitutionalism, property rights, the sanctity of contracts, the rule of law, or the needs of their parties.

With these verities unchallenged, the anti-renters faced a political stalemate. The legislature continued to resist anti-rent demands for a title-test law. In 1848, at the suggestion of Governor John Young, it passed a resolution calling on the state attorney general to investigate the validity of landlords' titles and, if he found them wanting, to sue for recovery of their lands on behalf of the state. But as conservatives insisted and the resolution's supporters knew, the statute of limitation barred challenges to titles for land held peaceably for over twenty-one years. The effort to overturn landlords' titles was an assured failure, undertaken in bad faith. Under intense pressure from the anti-renters, the attorney general initiated suits against the major estates. With the leasehold controversy shunted off to the courts, the leaders of both parties forged an implicit treaty of nonintervention. At the 1848 Whig state convention, conservatives campaigned successfully to dump John Young from the party's ticket. To "loud applause," the conservative James Brooks told the convention that the anti-rent excitement was "a two-edged sword, and it would cut whoever touched it. . . . This discussion must stop, if we would have harmony." Brooks's proposal became unofficial policy among both Whigs and Democrats. Thereafter, few officials or candidates for office raised the leasehold issue, either to support or condemn the anti-renters.[46]

Faced with political stalemate and a campaign of legal prosecutions on the part of the landlords, anti-renters everywhere abandoned the movement. In 1851, the state supreme court dismissed the state's suits to recover landlords' estates. A year later, the *Albany Freeholder*, the last of five anti-rent newspapers, closed its doors. The state anti-rent executive committee ceased to meet, and militants everywhere ceased nominating candidates for office. The movement survived as a rump phenomenon in pockets of Albany, Rensselaer, and Otsego counties. Despite their firm belief that the proprietors had no valid claim to the soil, tenants struggled to pay their back rents and buy out their landlords; those without the means to do so left the region.[47]

Despite this defeat, the relationship between party leaders and anti-renters was not one of simple cooptation. In transforming the anti-rent movement, both parties were themselves transformed. In tandem with the growing crisis over slavery, the Anti-Rent Wars exacerbated divisions in both parties and helped bring about the collapse of the Whigs. In 1845, Barnburners and conservative Whigs in several counties broke with their regular party organizations, which had nominated anti-rent candidates, and created bipartisan "Law and Order" tickets in opposition to the tenants' movement. Opposition spread to the state Whig Party, where conservatives carried on a vitriolic campaign against the liberals' alliance with the anti-renters. When John Young won the anti-rent nomination for governor in 1846, conservative Whigs campaigned against him in the fall election. James Watson Webb's *New York Courier and Enquirer* denounced Young's lukewarm support for anti-rentism as "the most bare-faced attempt at LEGISLATIVE ROBBERY—the most manifest outrage on vested rights, that has ever been brought forward in any civilized community."[48]

Conservative outrage intensified between 1846 and 1850, as liberal Whigs forged ever-closer alliances with both the anti-renters and antislavery voters. After 1845, liberals staunchly opposed the territorial expansion of slavery, championed the civic equality of African Americans, and sought to defend black residents from slave catchers. In 1847, the anti-renters of Columbia hired William Seward, the undisputed leader of the liberals, as their lawyer in their effort to overturn the title to Livingston Manor. The next year, John Young proposed the resolution empowering the state attorney general to sue for recovery of leasehold estates, and liberals in the legislature passed the measure. Seward, acting as attorney for the Columbia County anti-renters, signed on as an assistant to the attorney general in the campaign to overturn landlords' titles. In 1849, Seward was elected to the U.S. Senate, and quickly emerged as a leader of the antislavery forces in that body, delivering a barrage of inflammatory speeches against the peculiar institution.[49]

These actions drove conservative Whigs into open rebellion. Backed by landlord money, they established a new newspaper, the *Albany State Register*, which sought to "purge" the party of the "abolitionism, antirentism, fourierism, and agrarianism" that they believed liberals like Seward, Greeley, and Harris espoused. By endorsing these causes, the *Register* warned, liberals threatened to "dissolve the Union of the States," "prostrate all law and order in the dust," and "resolv[e] . . . society into its original elements." That year, conservative "Silver-Grays" bolted the Whig convention; the most reactionary of them nominated a fusion ticket with the Hunkers, which they billed as the "Anti-Disunion Ticket. Anti-Abolition, Anti-Seward, Anti-Weed, Anti-Anti-Rent, Anti-Demagogueism." Although most participants in this revolt quickly rejoined the Whigs, their mutiny weakened the party beyond recovery. In 1854, most of the Silver-Grays abandoned the Whigs for the Know-Nothings; a year later, the remaining Whigs officially merged with the Republicans.[50]

Having helped destroy the second party system in New York, former anti-renters and their Whig allies played a significant part in creating the political order that replaced it. The very process of taming the movement forced activists like Ira Harris, Robert Watson, and Alexander Johnson to innovate, and their innovations had an enormous impact on the broader political order. In order to retain the support of tenants, these men had to absorb many of their ideas and push them in new, less dangerous directions. Watson and his colleagues fully endorsed the tenants' producerism and their desire for universal landownership. But they wedded these beliefs to ideas that had never before been articulated by anti-renters or party leaders in the leasehold district—a belief that social mobility would dissolve economic inequality and a faith in the distributive powers of a capitalist economy. They sought to tie producerism to a faith that equality, prosperity, and republican citizenship would best be preserved by the workings of the emerging capitalist economy. This was not entirely a new synthesis; the Jeffersonian Republicans voiced an early version of it during the 1790s. But it continued to be re-created in social and ideological conflict as entrepreneurs and political leaders justified capitalist social relations to audiences championing producers' rights. Less than a decade before the anti-rent conflict, urban master artisans had forged a similar synthesis to defend their new workshop practices from the challenges of an emerging labor movement. These ideas would soon become adopted, refined, and extended by leaders of the new Republican Party. In the process, they would become the ideological centerpiece of that party: its ideology of free labor.[51]

At the same time, Whig and Democratic activists knew that many tenants had come to endorse the National Reformers' belief that each citizen had a natural right to land. In a bid to win these tenants' loyalty, they began to take the radicals' ideas as their own. But they made those ideas safe for capitalism by applying them not to land already held by whites as private property, but to the vast public lands of the West. There, they argued, American citizens could claim their right to the soil. As Alexander Johnson wrote from Thomas Devyr's old office, "man has a certain 'inalienable right,' not only to 'life, liberty, and the pursuit of happiness,' but also to a sufficiency of the common elements, by God created *and not already appropriated* to render the first inalienable right operative." By 1846, every anti-rent spokesman and elected official agreed. These politicians were among the first party activists to outline what would become another element of the Republican Party program: the Homestead Act.[52]

Finally, Democratic and Whig anti-rent leaders came to endorse something like the leasehold militants' vision of the government as an extension of the will of the people. And they tied this vision to the Whigs' commitment to an activist state. An 1847 committee of anti-rent legislators endorsed the state's power to destroy unfree systems of property and labor. The legislature, the committee declared, had indisputable power "to terminate this manorial system by just and constitutional legislation." This awesome power should be guided by popular conceptions of justice and the interests of the many. Landlords, committee members acknowledged, had "a legal, abstract right" to protection from tenants' challenges to their title. But given that the majority of the people believed their titles to be fraudulent, such "technical impediments should not prevent a full investigation" of landlords' titles.[53]

Formulations like these affirmed the anti-renters' belief that constitutional and legal principles must give way before the people's sense of justice. Increasing numbers of anti-rent legislators thus began to articulate an idea that would be championed by the Radical Republicans of the postwar period: a vision of an all-powerful, democratic state, capable of transforming social relations at the bidding of a sovereign people. More generally, they, along with the Liberty Party, pioneered an idea at the center of the Radical Republicans' philosophy before the war: the power of the state to use all its constitutional powers to circumscribe or abolish an "unfree" form of property and system of labor.[54]

Although these ideological and programmatic innovations remained on the political margins during the Anti-Rent Wars, former anti-renters helped bring them into the Republican Party during the crisis of the Union. H. J. Munger, a Delaware County activist, recalled that in 1856, leasehold insurgents "united with the old Whigs and the Abolitionists and formed a new party under the name of the Republican Party." In Albany County, at least a quarter (27 out of 107) of the delegates from the anti-rent towns at Republican county conventions between 1855 and 1860 came from the ranks of former and current anti-rent activists. By 1860, the new party won a majority of voters in fifteen out of nineteen anti-rent towns in the core anti-rent counties of Albany, Delaware, Columbia, and Rensselaer. Only in Schoharie County did a majority of anti-rent towns remain in the Democratic camp. Perhaps most importantly, the former Whig allies of the insurgents—men like Ira Harris, William Seward, and Horace Greeley—enjoyed disproportionate influence in the new party, both statewide and nationally. With their former anti-rent supporters, these leaders helped win their party over to the ideas and policies that they had helped forge: an ideology of free labor that celebrated petty proprietorship, a commitment to a homestead act, and a taste for using the power of the state to transform social relations.[55]

The Anti-Rent Wars in no way "caused" the emergence of the Republican Party, in the leasehold district or elsewhere; the slavery controversy did that. Nor did they alone lead the new party to endorse a homestead act, a revised ideology of free labor, or a new conception of the state. Rather, they were one of the most influential of several social conflicts that provided the Republicans with the raw materials for their ideology and platform. William Gienapp, Michael Holt, and others have correctly argued that the Republicans found their main constituency among Yankees and other Protestants.[56] But these were not the only constituencies that the new party sought, nor were religion and culture the only commitments through which Republicans sought to appeal to Yankee voters. Critical to the party's strategy was tying their antislavery message to the experience, class interests, and reform commitments of a wide range of overlapping constituencies. Thus, in addition to appealing to the antislavery, nativist, and prohibitionist commitments of Yankee voters, they sought to appeal to the producerist sentiments of artisans and farmers (many of whom were New Englanders and their descendants) and to reconcile those sentiments to the economic liberalism championed by the manufacturers, bankers, and professionals in their ranks. They also endeavored to appeal to the class interests of land-hungry farmers and sought to recruit voters who had been swayed by the National Reformers' call for government recognition of every citizen's right to the soil. And they sought to win the support of diverse constituencies—abolitionists, labor reformers, textile and iron workers, National Reformers, and anti-renters—who looked to the state to abolish or reform existing social relations.[57] In doing so, they drew on the ideas and demands of these constituencies—often only after transforming them.

In the end, the relationship between rebellious tenants and their Whig and Democratic allies did not result in either simple cooptation or a simple victory for grass-roots demands. Instead, it transformed both popular and party politics. The Indians' corporatist and localist politics went down to defeat. So too did tenants' challenge to a specialized political class's control of politics and their hope of turning the government into an extension of the will of "the People." On the other hand, the anti-renters helped destroy the second party system in New York. They helped create a new party. They transformed their leaders' economic and social vision, helping make a new, producerist vision of capitalist development dominant in northern politics. They helped win a homestead act. And they helped convince their leaders to endorse the use of the state to end "unfree" relations of property and labor. Far from being a case of simple representation or simple cooptation, the Anti-Rent Wars unleashed a dialectic that helped usher in a new political era.

1. *Albany Atlas* (weekly edition), August 13, 1844; *Albany Argus*, August 12, 1844; *Young America*, August 17, 1844.

2. For overviews of the Anti-Rent Wars, see Henry Christman, *Tin Horns and Calico: A Decisive Episode in the Emergence of Democracy* (1945; reprint, Cornwallville, N.Y., 1978); David Maldwyn Ellis, *Landlords and Farmers in the Hudson Mohawk Region, 1790–1850* (Ithaca, 1946); Reeve Huston, *Land and Freedom: Rural Society, Popular Protest, and Party Politics in Antebellum New York* (New York, 2000). The estimate of the population of New York's estates comes from State of New York, *Messages from the Governors*, ed. Charles Z. Lincoln, 11 vols. (Albany, 1909), 4:408. Twenty-five thousand people signed anti-rent petitions in 1845; the movement's main newspaper, the Albany *Freeholder*, claimed fifty to sixty thousand supporters for the movement in that same year. *New York Assembly Documents* 1845, 247:1, cited in Charles W. McCurdy, *The Anti-Rent Era in New York Law and Politics, 1840–1865* (Chapel Hill, 2001), chap. 7; *Freeholder*, May 21, August 27, 1845.

3. One example of a new social historian who ignores party politics is Christopher Clark, *The Roots of Rural Capitalism: Western Massachusetts, 1780–1860* (Ithaca, 1990). For examples of new social historians who depict politics as a black hole for popular initiatives, see Sean Wilentz, *Chants Democratic: New York City and the Rise of the American Working Class, 1788–1850* (New York, 1984); Alan Dawley, *Class and Community: The Industrial Revolution in Lynn* (Cambridge, Mass., 1976). Progressive and neo-progressive historians of the Jacksonian era include Arthur M. Schlesinger, Jr., *The Age of Jackson* (Boston, 1946); and Charles Sellers, *The Market Revolution: Jacksonian America, 1815–46* (New York, 1991). The specific argument I cite here is Sellers's. Political historians who minimize the interaction between popular movements and political parties include Joel Silbey, *The American Political Nation, 1838–1893* (Stanford, 1991); Richard P. McCormick, *The Second American Party System: Party Formation in the Jacksonian Era* (Chapel Hill, 1966). My approach takes as its starting point the work of Harry Watson, Amy Bridges, and Ronald Formisano, who argue that party leaders appropriated and reshaped popular demands as part of their project of appealing to various constituencies and combining them into viable electoral coalitions. I wish to extend their analysis in two ways, however. I argue that this process of appropriation sometimes went both ways, with constituents appropriating and reshaping the ideas and methods of party leaders; and I suggest that this process could be fervently contested. See Harry Watson, *Jacksonian Politics and Community Conflict: The Emergence of the Second American Party System in Cumberland County, North Carolina* (Baton Rouge, 1981); Watson, *Liberty and Power: The Politics of Jacksonian America* (New York, 1990); Bridges, *A City in the Republic: Antebellum New York and the Origins of Machine Politics* (New York, 1984); Ronald P. Formisano, *The Transformation of Political Culture: Massachusetts Parties, 1790s–1840s* (New York, 1983).

4. The literature on reform and plebeian movements is voluminous; space allows only a sampling here. On the labor movement, see John R. Commons et al., *History of Labor in*

the United States, vol. 1 (New York, 1918); Wilentz, *Chants Democratic*; Dawley, *Class and Community*; Teresa Anne Murphy, *Ten Hours' Labor: Religion, Reform, and Gender in Early New England* (Ithaca, 1992). On evangelical reform, see Mary P. Ryan, *Cradle of the Middle Class: The Family in Oneida County, New York, 1790–1865* (New York, 1981); Robert H. Abzug, *Cosmos Crumbling: American Reform and the Religious Imagination* (New York, 1994); James Brewer Stewart, *Holy Warriors: The Abolitionists and American Slavery* (New York, 1976); Ellen Carol DuBois, *Feminism and Suffrage: The Emergence of an Independent Women's Movement in America, 1848–1869* (Ithaca, 1978); Nancy Isenberg, *Sex and Citizenship in Antebellum America* (Chapel Hill, 1998). On urban crowd actions, see Paul A. Gilje, *The Road to Mobocracy: Popular Disorder in New York City, 1763–1834* (Chapel Hill, 1987); Christine Stansell, *City of Women: Sex and Class in New York, 1789–1860* (New York, 1986); Leonard L. Richards, *Gentlemen of Property and Standing: Anti-Abolition Mobs in Jacksonian America* (New York, 1970). On rural rebellions, see Huston, *Land and Freedom*; Charles Brooks, *Frontier Settlement and Market Revolution: The Holland Land Purchase* (Ithaca, 1996); Paul Wallace Gates, *Fifty Million Acres: Conflicts over Kansas Land Policy, 1854–1890* (Ithaca, 1954). For a brilliant discussion of associational politics and public life in nineteenth-century American cities, see Mary P. Ryan, *Civic Wars: Democracy and Public Life in the American City during the Nineteenth Century* (Berkeley, 1997).

5. Richard Carwardine, *Evangelicals and Politics in Antebellum America* (New Haven, 1993), 11 (quotations) and 1–49; Aileen S. Kraditor, *Means and Ends in American Abolitionism: Garrison and His Critics on Strategy and Tactics* (New York, 1967), 11–32, 118–68; Wilentz, *Chants Democratic*, 236; Bridges, *City in the Republic*, 108.

6. Wilentz, *Chants Democratic*; William Heighton, *An Address to the Members of Trade Societies, and to the Working Classes Generally* (London, 1827), 24–28; Kraditor, *Means and Ends*, 11–32, 118–68; *Liberator*, December 15, 1837, reprinted in George M. Fredrickson, ed., *Great Lives Observed: William Lloyd Garrison* (Englewood Cliffs, 1968), 47–51 (quotation on 48).

7. The quotation is from Charles G. Finney, *Lectures on Revivals of Religion* (1835), quoted in Jeffrey L. Pasley, "Party Politics, Citizenship, and Collective Action in Nineteenth-Century America: A Response to Stuart Blumin and Michael Schudson," *Communication Review* 4 (2000): 43–44. On reform and plebeian activists' appropriation of party tactics, see Pasley, "Party Politics," 43–44; Silbey, *American Political Nation*, 205–8. On the give-and-take between working-class and immigrant organizations and the Democratic Party, see Bridges, *City in the Republic*, 83–124; Wilentz, *Chants Democratic*, 201–15, 227–37, 326–35, 383–86; David Montgomery, *Citizen Worker: The Experience of Workers in the United States with Democracy and the Free Market during the Nineteenth Century* (New York, 1993), 115–62; Montgomery, *Beyond Equality: Labor and the Radical Republicans, 1862–1872* (1967; reprint, Urbana, 1981), 208–15.

8. *Delaware Gazette*, July 9, 1828, October 10, 1832, July 9, 1834, September 23, 30, 1840, and 1820–40, *passim*; *Albany Evening Journal*, July 9, 10, 14, 15, August 25, 1840, and 1820–40, *passim*. Figures for voter participation before 1828 are from the First American Democratization Project files, American Antiquarian Society; my thanks to

Philip Lampi for allowing me access to these returns. Voting figures from 1828 onward are for president during presidential election years and for governor in other even years, and are from the *Delaware Gazette*, *Daily Albany Argus*, and *Albany Evening Journal*, 1828–40. The total number of eligible voters for 1820–24 was estimated by adding half the white males between the ages of 16 and 26 to all the white men over the age of 26 counted in the *Fourth Census of the United States, 1820*. Total voters for 1826–28 and 1836–38 were drawn from the *Census of the State of New York*, 1825 and 1835. Total voters for 1840 were estimated by adding 90 percent of the white men between the ages of 20 and 29 to all the white men listed as 30 and older in the *Sixth Census of the United States, 1840*. For a fuller discussion of both the deferential political culture on the estates before the 1820s and the emergence of a partisan political culture, see Huston, *Land and Freedom*, chaps. 1–2.

9. *Freeholder*, May 28, July 9, 16, September 3, October 8, 29, 1845, February 25, March 11, July 8, 15, December 2, 30, 1846. Anti-rent leaders' experience as party activists was ascertained by cross-tabulating the names of anti-rent activists with the names of delegates, nominees, and committees of correspondence listed in the reports of county Anti-Mason, Whig, and Democratic nominating conventions that preceded the November elections of each year, 1832–44. The Anti-Masonic and Whig conventions for Albany County are reported in the *Albany Evening Journal*. The Democratic conventions for Albany County are reported in the *Daily Albany Argus*; those for Delaware County are reported in the *Delaware Gazette*. Unfortunately, the Whig newspaper for Delaware County, the *Delaware Express*, has not survived for the 1830s and 1840s.

These figures greatly underestimate the actual number of party activists among the anti-rent leadership, for two reasons. First, no record of Whig conventions in Delaware County survives; those anti-rent activists who had served there are not counted. Just as important, many more activists were likely to have served the major parties on the town rather than the county level.

10. *Freeholder*, May 28, October 8, 1845; *Young America*, February 8, 1845. On the Democrats' critique of banking "aristocracy," see *Delaware Gazette* (Delhi, N.Y.), August 29, October 24, 1832, May 21, August 20, 1834, October 10, 1838; *Daily Albany Argus*, August 27, 1829, August 1, 28, October 15, 1832; John Ashworth, *"Agrarians" and "Aristocrats": Party Political Ideology in the United States, 1837–1846* (Cambridge, 1983), 43–47; Watson, *Liberty and Power*, 132–71.

11. *Freeholder*, May 28, July 9, August 13, 1845, March 25, April 1, 1846; *Anti-Renter* (Albany), October 4, 1845.

12. *Young America*, February 8, 1845; *Freeholder*, May 28, 1845. Quotation is in *Freeholder*, January 21, 1846. For a fuller discussion of the anti-renters' vision of utopia and the exclusions and evasions in that vision, see Huston, *Land and Freedom*, chap. 5.

13. Silas Wright, "Address to the New York State Agricultural Society," quoted in Ashworth, *"Agrarians" and "Aristocrats,"* 22 (quotation); *New York Assembly Documents*, 1844, No. 183. On the partisan loyalties of New York's landlords, see Huston, *Land and Freedom*, 71–72.

14. On the local, violent rural uprisings of the colonial era and the early republic, see Alan Taylor, *Liberty Men and Great Proprietors: The Revolutionary Settlement on the Maine Frontier, 1760–1820* (Chapel Hill, 1990); Taylor, "Agrarian Independence: Northern Land Rioters after the Revolution," in Alfred F. Young, ed., *Beyond the American Revolution: Explorations in the History of American Radicalism* (DeKalb, Ill., 1993); Edward Countryman, "Out of the Bounds of the Law: Northern Land Rioters in the Eighteenth Century," in Alfred F. Young, *The American Revolution: Explorations in the History of American Radicalism* (DeKalb, Ill., 1976). On such uprisings on New York's leasehold estates, see, for example, Sung Bok Kim, *Landlord and Tenant in Colonial New York: Manorial Society, 1664–1775* (Chapel Hill, 1978), 281–415; Irving Mark, *Agrarian Conflicts in Colonial New York, 1711–1775* (New York, 1940). On the modern, mass-based farmers' movements of the late nineteenth century, see Solon S. Buck, *The Granger Movement: A Study of Agricultural Organization and Its Political, Economic, and Social Manifestations, 1870–1880* (Cambridge, Mass., 1913); D. Sven Nordin, *Rich Harvest: A History of the Grange, 1867–1900* (Jackson, 1974); John D. Hicks, *The Populist Revolt: A History of the Farmers' Alliance and the People's Party* (Lincoln, 1961); Lawrence Goodwyn, *Democratic Promise: The Populist Moment in America* (New York, 1976).

15. On charivari on New York's estates, see Julia Hull Werner, "A Skimeton," *New York Folklore Quarterly* 20 (1964): 134–36; and from *American Notes and Queries* 1, see letter from C. L. Fernald, October 13, 1888, 288, and letters of Alice C. Chace, September 29, 1888, 263–64, and May 5, 1888, 8. On charivari in North America, see Bryan D. Palmer, "Discordant Music: Charivaris and Whitecapping in Nineteenth-Century North America," *Labour / Le Travailleur* 3 (1978): 3–62. The age of the Indians was derived from indictments in "Anti-Rent War Documents" (typescript), Delaware County Clerk's Office, Delhi, N.Y. On the vigilantes' disguises, see *Albany Atlas*, July 10, August 13, 1844; *Daily Albany Argus*, December 28, 1844; testimony of Isaac L. Burhans before the Delaware County grand jury, August 8–11, 1845, Acc. No. Test. 1, 2, p. 8, "Anti-Rent War Documents." For a full discussion of the ritual culture of the Indians, see Huston, *Land and Freedom*, chap. 5.

16. Appropriating an "Indian" identity also served critical ideological functions and conveyed complex racial, class, and gendered messages. See Huston, *Land and Freedom*, chap. 5.

17. *Albany Morning Atlas*, August 15, September 2, 1844; *Young America*, September 7, 14, 1844; Indictment, People vs. Jonas Piester and nine others, September 27, 1845, "Anti-Rent War Documents," 5:1; deposition of Abraham Decker, June 6, 1842, file 6211, Governor's Papers, William Seward Papers, Clements Library, University of Michigan; "Newspaper Clippings Relating to Anti-Rent Disturbances in New York State with Some Account of the Resulting Trial," New York State Library, Manuscripts Division, Albany, 16–17, 23, 39, 94.

18. "Tar and Feather Letter," Delaware County Historical Society, Delhi, N.Y.; *Daily Albany Argus*, June 23, 1841; *Albany Evening Atlas*, August 12, 1844; Christman, *Tin Horns and Calico*, 42–44, 326–27.

19. *Freeholder,* June 4, 1845.

20. Ibid., June 11, 1845, March 25, 1846.

21. *New York Assembly Documents* 1844, No. 183; *Journal of the Assembly,* 1844, 945; *Daily Albany Argus,* December 23, 25, 28, 31, 1844, January 1, 11, 1845; *Young America,* December 28, 1844, January 11, 14, March 22, 1845; New York (State), *Messages of the Governors,* ed. Charles Z. Lincoln, 11 vols. (Albany, 1909), 4:140, 149–50; *Freeholder,* May 6, 1846.

22. *Freeholder,* April 30, July 9, 1845, January 10, February 25, May 6, 1846, February 10, 1847.

23. For interpretations that stress the enthusiasm of the rank and file for party politics, see William E. Gienapp, "Politics Seems to Enter into Everything: Political Culture in the North, 1840–1860," in *Essays on Antebellum American Politics, 1840–1860,* ed. Stephen E. Maizlish and John J. Kushma (College Station: Texas A&M University Press, 1982), 14–69; Watson, *Jacksonian Politics and Community Conflict*; Watson, *Liberty and Power*; Silbey, *American Political Nation.* For the argument that popular attitudes toward party politics was marked by "engaged disbelief," see Glenn C. Altschuler and Stuart M. Blumin, "Limits of Political Engagement in Antebellum America: A New Look at the Golden Age of Participatory Democracy," *Journal of American History* 84 (1997): 855–85.

24. DeAlva Stanwood Alexander, *A Political History of the State of New York,* 3 vols. (New York, 1906), 2:45, 55, 89, 120.

25. Ibid., 2:47–64, 76–78, 83–85, 90–95, 112, 126; Ashworth, *"Agrarians" and "Aristocrats,"* 87–125, 136–70.

26. Horace Greeley to Schuyler Colfax, September 23, 1845, Horace Greeley Papers, New York Public Library; *Albany Evening Journal,* March 1845, in "Newspaper Clippings," *Albany Evening Journal,* reprinted in *Freeholder,* October 1, 1845; *New-York Tribune,* reprinted in *Freeholder,* August 27, September 17, December 17, 1845; Timothy Corbin, Jr., to William C. Bouck, July 13, 1844, Box 3, William C. Bouck Papers, Cornell University Archives, Ithaca; Burton A. Thomas to Bouck, August 5, 1844, Box 3, Bouck Papers; Thomas and William J. Potter to Bouck, August 12, 1844, Box 3, Bouck Papers; Bouck to A. Gallup, August 29, Box 1, Additional Bouck Papers, Cornell University Archives; Bouck to ——, August 7, 1844, Box 3, Bouck Papers; Timothy Corbin to Bouck, August 7, 1844, Box 3, Bouck Papers; *Albany Evening Atlas,* August 12, 1844; *Albany Weekly Atlas,* August 13, 1844; and *Daily Albany Argus,* August 13, December 21, 23, 28, 1844. For a fuller examination of landlords' political affiliations and of the Hunkers' and liberal Whigs' courtship of the anti-rent vote, see Huston, *Land and Freedom,* chaps. 2, 6.

27. Horace Greeley, *Why I am a Whig: Reply to an Enquiring Friend* (New York, n.d.), 3. My analysis here is based on biographical information on six reformers and party activists who allied with the anti-renters: Ira Harris, Robert D. Watson, Thomas Ainge Devyr, William H. Gallup, Calvin Pepper, and Samuel Gordon. On Harris, Watson, and Devyr, see the text and notes below. Gallup was a Whig editor in Schoharie County; he published the anti-renters' first newspaper, the *Helderberg Advocate.* Pepper was a Whig

lawyer, an abolitionist, and a land and labor reformer. He served briefly as clerk of the Albany County board of supervisors during the 1830s, but never again gained a political post—perhaps because of his commitment to controversial causes. Samuel Gordon, a Democrat, served as a district attorney, state assemblyman, and member of the U.S. House of Representatives during the 1830s and early 1840s, but found his political career cut short by his failure to win a series of personal rivalries with other members of the local Democratic Party. Entry for William H. Gallup, Manuscript Population Census, 1850, Schoharie County; *American Biographical Archive*, sheet 590, frame 215; Christman, *Tin Horns and Calico*, 55; George R. Howell and Jonathan Tenney, *Bi-Centennial History of the County of Albany, New York, from 1609 to 1886* (New York, 1886), 89; *Daily Albany Argus*, January 3, 1840, September 21, 1841; *Young America*, June 14, 1845; *Freeholder*, June 18, 1845.

28. Thomas Ainge Devyr, *The Odd Book of the Nineteenth Century*, 2 vols. (Greenpoint, N.Y., 1882), 1:45–46, 51–55, 77, 89, 92–93, 136, 147–49, 154–208; 2:25–43; *Biographical Dictionary of American Labor*, ed. Gary M. Fink (Westport, Conn., 1984), 185–86; *Freeholder*, April 23, 30, May 7, 14, June 4, 11 1845 (quotation on May 14).

29. *Freeholder*, May 28, June 4, 1845; *New York Assembly Documents* 1846, No. 156, 7–8.

30. *Freeholder*, August 20, 1845; Ira Harris, *Abolition of Distress for Rent: Remarks of Mr. Ira Harris of Albany, upon the Bill to Abolish Distress for Rent* (Albany, N.Y., 1946), 7.

31. *Freeholder*, May 28, July 23, 1845.

32. *Delaware Gazette*, reprinted in *Freeholder*, June 18, 1845.

33. *Freeholder*, May 28, July 23, 1845.

34. Ibid., May 28, June 4, July 9, December 24, 1845; January 21, 28, February 4, 1846; *Daily Albany Argus*, November 1, 4, 1844.

35. *Daily Albany Argus*, January 4, 6 (quotation), 8, 14, 20, 24, February 10, 1845; *Young America*, January 11, 18, February 15, 1845.

36. *Freeholder*, May 7, 28 (quotation), July 9 (quotation), 16, 23, 30, 1845; *Daily Albany Argus*, January 1, 14, 31, March 4, 10, 17, April 30, 1845; *Young America*, January 11, 18, February 1, 8, March 8, 15, May 3, 31, August 16, December 20, 1845; "Newspaper Clippings," 16–17.

37. *Daily Albany Argus*, January 13, 1845; *Young America*, August 16, 1845.

38. *Freeholder*, August 13, 27, September 3, October 1, 8, 22, November 5, 1845; *Delaware Gazette*, August 20, 27, September 2, October 15, 1845; "Newspaper Clippings," 7, 11, 27, 79, 109; Christman, *Tin Horns and Calico*, 182–203, 220–33.

39. *Freeholder*, May 28, July 9, August 6, 1845, July 29, September 2, 1846; *Young America*, May 24, 1845; *Anti-Renter*, January 31, June 6, 1846.

40. *Freeholder*, August 27, September 3, 10, 17, November 5, 1845, January 21, February 8, 25, April 8, August 26, October 14, October 1846; *Anti-Renter*, September 13, 1845, February 14, 21, 28, 1846; *Young America*, August 9, 23, 1845, February 21, 28, March 7, 1846, and 1845–46, *passim*; *Equal Rights Advocate* (Hudson, N.Y.), July 15, 1846.

41. *Freeholder*, April 9, 16, 30, November 12, 19, December 3, 1845, February 25, March 25, June 10, 24, 1846. The quotation is in *Anti-Renter*, January 17, 1846.

42. *Freeholder*, May 21, July 8, September 23, 30, 1846; *Equal Rights Advocate*, July 22, 1846; Horace Greeley to Schuyler Colfax, February 28, April 22, 1846, in Greeley Papers, New York Public Library.

43. *Equal Rights Advocate*, October 7, 21, 1846; *Freeholder*, September 2, October 14, 28, December 9, 1846; *Anti-Renter*, October 17, 1846; Christman, *Tin Horns and Calico*, 272–73.

44. *Freeholder*, November 25, December 16, 1846, January 6, 1847; *Equal Rights Advocate*, November 11, 1846; Devyr, *Odd Book*, 2:50–51.

45. *Freeholder*, September 10, 17, 1845; Alf Evers, *Woodstock: History of an American Town* (New York, 1987), 200–202; Iver Charles Bernstein, "Expanding the Boundaries of the Political: Workers and Political Change in the Nineteenth Century," *International Labor and Working-Class History* 32 (1987): 59–75.

46. *Messages from the Governors*, 4:411–12; *New York Assembly Documents* 1848, No. 126; *Journal of the Assembly of the State of New York*, 1848, 1014–15; *Journal of the Senate of the State of New York*, 1848, 575; *New York Daily Tribune*, September 16, 1848.

47. *Opinion of Hon. Judge Cady, in Supreme Court. The People of the State of New York, vs. George Clarke* (Albany, 1851); *Livingston Manor Case. Opinion of Mr. Justice Wright, in the Case of The People* agt. *Hermon Livingston. Supreme Court—Columbia County* (Hudson, 1851). On the collapse of the anti-rent movement, see G. Clarke to Campbell P. White, September 26, 1851, Campbell White Papers, New-York Historical Society, New York City; Ellis, *Landlords and Farmers*, 286–87; Huston, *Land and Freedom*, chap. 8. On tenant buyouts of landlords, see John Kiersted to Henry Overing, February 1, November 25, 1847, October 9, 1848, August 6, 1851, Kiersted-Overing Letters, Manuscripts Division, New York State Library; *Albany Freeholder*, September 8, 1847, November 20, 850; Roxbury Assessment Roll, 1864, Roxbury Town Clerk's Office, Roxbury, N.Y.; Evers, *Woodstock*, 200–202; David Murray, *Delaware County, New York: History of the Century* (Delhi, N.Y., 1898), 95–96; Caroline Evelyn More and Irma Mae Griffin, *History of the Town of Roxbury* (Walton, N.Y., 1953); Albert Champlin Mayham, *The Anti-Rent War on Blenheim Hill: An Episode of the '40s* (Jefferson, N.Y., 1906); J. H. French, *1860 Gazetteer of the State of New York* (Syracuse, 1860), 157n; Church and Tyler Rent Ledger, Rensselaerville and Westerlo, 1838–1890, Walter S. Church Business Records, Manuscripts Division, New York State Library.

48. *Freeholder*, November 12, 1845, February 25, April 15, 22, July 29, August 12, September 2, October 21, 1846; *New York Courier and Enquirer*, reprinted in *Equal Rights Advocate*, August 5, 21, October 21, November 25, 1846, and in *Albany Freeholder*, October 14, 1846; *New York Express*, reprinted in *Equal Rights Advocate*, October 21, 1846; *New York Tribune*, reprinted in *Freeholder*, November 11, 1846; *Albany Atlas*, November 3, 1846.

49. *Freeholder*, May 27, June 24, July 15, October 21, 1846, May 23, September 5,

1849, August 7, 1850; *Messages From the Governors*, 4:410–12; *New York Assembly Documents* 1848, No. 126; *Journal of the Assembly*, 1848, 1011–15; *Journal of the Senate*, 1848, 535; Alexander, *Political History*, 2:101–46; Glyndon G. Van Deusen, *William Henry Seward* (New York, 1967), 105–7, 110–11.

50. *Daily State Register* (Albany, N.Y.), March 27, October 1, 2, 7, 9, 18, 19, 21, November 1, 1850; *New York Daily Tribune*, September 18, 27, 30, 1850; *Freeholder*, November 6, 1850; Pell to White, March 21 [1850?], White Papers; De Alva Stanwood Alexander, *A Political History of the State of New York*, 3 vols. (New York, 1906), 3:153–58, 165–68, 175–79, 189, 198–204, 211–14. The quotations are in *Daily State Register*, March 27, October 2, 1850, and in *Freeholder*, November 6, 1850.

51. On the Jeffersonians' synthesis of producerist ideology and free-market political economy, see Joyce Appleby, *Capitalism and a New Social Order: The Republican Vision of the 1790s* (New York, 1984). On urban master artisans' free-laborism, see Wilentz, *Chants Democratic*, 271–86. On the Republicans' free labor ideology, see Eric Foner, *Free Soil, Free Labor, Free Men: The Ideology of the Republican Party before the Civil War* (New York, 1969), 11–39.

52. *Freeholder*, December 17, 1845 (quotation), January 28, June 24, 1846; *Equal Rights Advocate*, August 19, December 2, 9, 23, 1845; *Anti-Renter*, February 14, 1846; *Young America*, October 4, 1845.

53. *New York Assembly Documents* 1847, No. 162, 6–8.

54. Montgomery, *Beyond Equality*, 72–89; Foner, *Free Soil*, 115–23.

55. H. J. Munger, "Reminiscences of the Anti-Rent Rebellion" (typescript), New York State Historical Association archives, Cooperstown, N.Y.; Foner, *Free Soil*. Election data is from *Albany Evening Journal*, November 27, 1855, November 25, 1856, November 16, 1858, November 8, 1860; *Delaware Gazette*, November 19, 1856, November 17, 1858, November 21, 1860; Silbey-Benson New York Election Data, 1845–57. Many thanks to Joel Silbey and John Kern for allowing me to use this data. Lists of delegates and officers at Albany County Republican conventions were drawn from the *Albany Evening Journal*, 1855–60, and were compared to lists of anti-rent activists in Albany County drawn from the *Albany Freeholder*, 1845–52, the *Anti-Renter*, 1845–46, and anti-rent broadsides in the Broadside Collection, Albany Institute of History and Art, Albany.

56. William Gienapp, *The Origins of the Republican Party, 1852–1856* (New York, 1987); Michael F. Holt, *The Political Crisis of the 1850s* (New York, 1983); Paul Kleppner, *The Third Party System, 1853–1892: Parties, Voters, and Political Cultures* (Chapel Hill, 1979).

57. Foner, *Free Soil*, 11–72; Richard H. Sewell, *Ballots for Freedom: Antislavery Politics in the United States, 1837–1860* (1976; reprint, New York, 1980), 277–320, 343–65; Montgomery, *Beyond Equality*, 45–134; Montgomery, *Citizen Worker*, 132–34; Murphy, *Ten Hours' Labor*; Helene Sara Zahler, *Eastern Workingmen and National Land Policy, 1829–1862* (New York, 1941), 147–76; Robbins, *Our Landed Heritage*, 150–216; Alexander Saxton, *The Rise and Fall of the White Republic: Class Politics and Mass Culture in Nineteenth-Century America* (New York, 1990), 227–62.

14

Commentary

Déjà Vu All Over Again: Is There a New New Political History?

With man we enter history.
—Frederick Engels

*I define postmodern as incredulity
toward metanarratives.*
—Jean-François Lyotard

Since the 1980s, American political historians have been bemoaning their fall from grace.[1] Can the soul of American political history be saved? Is it possible to reconcile the tendencies within a profession that seems to focus entirely on race, class, and gender with the formerly important study of ordinary politics associated with the formal political system of elections, legislation, and administration? Is there a New New Political History rooted in cultural studies and postmodernism that will chart a new road to salvation? In line with the intent of this volume, I will limit my response to a discussion of some tendencies in the political history of the early republic—the turf originally staked out by the Society for Historians of the Early Republic. SHEAR was founded in 1977 by frustrated traditional political historians seeking a venue for their work, free from the shadow of social history.

My title is derived from that icon of American popular culture, Yogi Berra, and a discussion on the H-SHEAR listserv in early 1997. The discussion began with a post from Marion Nelson Winship, in which she alluded to the emergence of a "new New Political History." She was joined in this exchange by a number of young scholars, including the editors of this volume, and together they generated a list of historians who seemed to be working in this new genre. The end result was a session at the 1998 SHEAR meeting devoted to the subject, a session that was also the genesis of the present volume.

These discussions directed attention to the emergence of a new cultural history of politics of the early republic that was clearly related to the larger debate among historians over the "linguistic turn" of postmodernism and neo-Marxist critical theory. This discussion implied that the New New Political History might supplant the old "New Political History" of a generation ago. Sessions at the 2000 meeting of the Social Science History Association (SSHA) were related to this theme and the impact on political history of the linguistic or cultural turn in general. Because I was on the Council of SHEAR and on the program committee for the 2000 SSHA meeting that extended this discussion, the editors asked me to comment on the relationship of the New Political History to the essays presented in this volume.

For all its proponents' paranoia about their own marginalization, traditional political history is alive and well. It includes not only the immensely popular genre of political biography, such as the recent best-sellers on John Adams and Benjamin Franklin, but also such academically acclaimed efforts as the Oxford History of the United States and the series of presidential administration histories published by the University Press of Kansas. Of course, traditional political history has lost its dominant place within the profession, but it continues to draw more readers and acclaim (especially outside the academy) and has more practitioners than the "new" histories.[2]

THE NEW POLITICAL HISTORY

The New Political History was a product of the late 1950s and early 1960s. While often incorrectly associated with the conservative complacence of "consensus history," it had radical roots. The triumvirate most closely associated with inventing the New Political History is Lee Benson, Allan G. Bogue, and Samuel P. Hays. Benson was a Brooklyn Communist Party organizer, Bogue a Canadian socialist (or, as he prefers to be called, a "populist"), and Hays a Convinced Quaker and a conscientious objector during World War II. They were tuned in to the most interesting political currents of the day and focused on making history more analytical.

In the mid-1950s, under the influence of Paul Lazarsfeld, Benson embraced the social sciences and lectured historians on the need for better research designs and more systematic analysis. He turned from economic history to the study of voting behavior and explored ways that elections might be used by historians to examine past public opinion.[3] This led to his iconoclastic book, *The Concept of Jacksonian Democracy: New York a Test Case* (Princeton, 1961), which provided the model for much of the New Political History.

Benson's book involved explicit research design, the operationalization of concepts, and the logic of multivariate analysis. While it incorporated perhaps a dozen other major ideas and techniques drawn from the social sciences, *The Concept of Jacksonian Democracy* is best remembered (often only remembered) for its chapters on ethnocultural groups and religious groups and their effect on politics. These communities, Benson argued, provide the building blocs for major party coalitions and act as the agents of political change. Benson also believed that good, systematic political history would be the best way to study American culture.[4]

It was, however, Bogue who in 1967 coined the term, "New Political History."[5] In that essay, he mainly discussed historians who used a variety of forms of quantitative and behavioral analysis to examine various traditional questions in American political history. As it emerged in the 1970s, the core of the New Political History was made up of essays, monographs, and dissertations written by Bogue, Benson, and Hays and their students.[6] The New Political History later became associated primarily with younger scholars, such as Joel Silbey, Ron Formisano, and Paul Kleppner, who generally applied quantitative techniques and social theory to the analysis of elections and legislative behavior. Of course, there were others working in much the same vein, including Richard Jensen and Michael Holt, respectively students of C. Vann Woodward and David Donald. There was also a certain amount of cross-pollination from those influenced by Roy Nichols and Thomas Cochran. Most important was Richard P. McCormick, who provided some of the first systematic studies of voter turnout, applied social science theory to the study of political parties, and focused several of his students on legislative behavior. One must note as well the work of Thomas

Alexander and his students at the University of Alabama, who examined both voting and legislative behavior.

The New Political History has often been caricatured as the "ethnocultural school" devoted solely to electoral studies, but in fact it was and continues to be much broader. The quantitative study of American political history actually began with the collective biographies of political leaders rather than the analysis of either elections or legislative behavior. Collective biography was an old technique going back to Charles Beard's study of the Constitutional Convention. It continued to be applied to test hypotheses and to address common assumptions of traditional historians. In the 1950s, there was a great deal of discussion among traditional political historians about who were the Federalists and the Anti-Federalists, the members of the workingmen's parties, the abolitionists, the Progressives, and others.[7]

New Political Historians brought some much-needed analytical rigor to these debates. Hays, who had been examining the social basis of voting behavior in the Midwest as a means of better understanding the conflicts of ethnic, religious, and socioeconomic groups, focused his most influential work on political elites and municipal reform. He attacked the methodological weaknesses of Richard Hofstadter's study of Progressivism, and his colleagues took on other influential works.[8] Like Benson, Hays was primarily interested in decision makers (be they voters or party leaders) and the cultural context in which they acted. In this he used collective biography to examine the ideas and behavior of these reform groups in relation to their position in the social structure and how this affected policy making.[9]

Hays's influence led to more systematic studies by the New Political Historians and to their desire to look at the political elite of officeholders, bureaucrats, lobbyists, and other "influentials" at both the federal and state levels of government and eventually examine how these groups changed over time. In line with this interest in the behavior of elite decision makers, the New Political Historians turned to analyzing the roll call votes in Congress and state legislatures. But rather than just looking cursorily at the final votes on a few key measures, such as the vote for war in 1812 or that on the new charter for the Bank of the United States, the New Political Historians analyzed patterns of behavior that appeared in either all the votes or systematic samples of the roll calls. Alexander and Silbey introduced new methods taken from political science to examine the influence of sectionalism in the antebellum era. Bogue, who had been influenced by his colleague at Iowa, the British historian William O. Aydelotte, provided the model for future studies and directed numerous graduate students.[10] The New Political Historians used these techniques to answer questions about the development of parties in Congress and the state legislatures, partisan belief systems, and even the saliency of certain issues at different times and different levels of the political system.

Just as they were not only concerned with outcomes of legislation, they also were not simply interested in the outcomes of elections. One of the central ideas found in all New Political Histories is that elections have to be seen in sequence. They are not individual events, as historians had traditionally portrayed them. The New Political Historians thus rejected as well the "presidential synthesis" associated with traditional history and examined electoral behavior at national, state, and local levels.[11]

The crucial organizational device adopted from political science by the New Political Historians was the idea that American political history has been characterized by a series of party systems such as that suggested by Richard P. McCormick.[12] The political development of the United States can be described in terms of generation-long periods of stable or normal partisan conflict punctuated by periods of "critical realignment," during which the political agenda and the coalitional structure of the major parties was reoriented. A good deal of the New Political History was devoted to analyzing periods of realignment such as the 1850s and the 1890s, but this implied an understanding of the relevant characteristics of each of the stable periods as well. By focusing on parties and party systems, the New Political Historians were able to study the relationships between national and state politics, voters and the political elite, and the social structure and the political structure. The realignment model provided a way to approach political development and decay.[13]

The prospects for the New Political History looked good in the 1970s. Jobs were tight but departments were looking for people who could understand quantitative methods. Summer training programs in quantitative political history at the University of Michigan and the Newberry Library were doing well. There were clear books by historians on the use of computers and quantitative methods.[14] The Social Science History Association was formed in 1975, and its journal *Social Science History* provided a forum where the increasing number of New Political Historians could publish. In the 1970s and 1980s there was an infusion of a second wave of new Ph.D.s and vigorous debate within the ranks over methods.[15] Often these internal debates were much more bitter than the criticism the New Political Historians received from traditional political historians.

But this is not to say that even in its prime the New Political History dominated the writing of political history in the United States. Although there were exceptions, most of the New Political Historians, for personal reasons, dealt with the century from the 1820s to the 1920s. When Bogue polled political historians about the most important books written on American political history since World War II, only Benson made it into the top five. The others were by Arthur M. Schlesinger, Jr., C. Vann Woodward, and two by Richard Hofstadter. The New Political History never produced a textbook.[16] Nevertheless, by the late 1970s, the New Political Historians were dynamic, confident, and productive. They registered real achievements in their analysis of ordinary politics, and laid out an intellectual defense of their approach and methods.

From the beginning of the 1980s on, however, the New Political Historians were under attack in the profession. Traditional historians tended to argue that quantitative methods tended to make history bloodless, devoid of both emotion and ideas. Students often complained that the New Political History was political science, not history. The main line of criticism came from the left and particularly the new social (and labor) historians, some of whom found quantitative methods and the "ethnocultural interpretation" reactionary.[17] They charged the New Political Historians with trying to deny the importance of class conflict. While one or two of the New Political Historians had joint appointments, generally they functioned in history departments where they were often the only quantifier and in which they generally taught traditional period courses. Much of their work was published in a coterie of quantification-friendly history journals, including *Social Science History*, *Historical Methods Newsletter*, and *The Journal of Interdisciplinary History*,[18] or in journals devoted specifically to the social sciences. Yet they found that for promotion and legitimacy in their own departments they also had to publish in the major historical journals that were accepting fewer and fewer essays on political history. New positions generally went to social historians.

By the 1990s, the New Political History, like its practitioners, had aged without perpetuating a vigorous third generation of students. One of the second generation asked ironically, "Do Historians Count Anymore?" Another asked, "Is There an Audience for History with the Facts Left In?"[19] New Political Historians have continued to produce first-rate, prize-winning political history, but the authors of these books are, for the most part, the usual suspects.[20] Several new manuals on methodology, written by historians, have appeared, reasserting the value of quantitative methods.[21] A recent article in *Social Science History*, however, was entitled, "Everyone's Doing Congressional Historiography: Where Are the Historians?"[22]

WILLIAM G. SHADE

The announcement of a New New Political History might have been an occasion for celebration at the twenty-fifth anniversary meeting of the SSHA in 2000. But, alas, the New New Political History foreseen in the discussion on H-SHEAR reflected the linguistic turn—a new cultural history of politics more interested in texts and discourse than political behavior and policy making. It was seemingly more in line with Joyce Appleby's call for a response to the postmodern challenge and the need for "a more profound historical inquiry that [begins] with the assertion that our sense of reality is socially constructed."[23]

Of course, cultural history per se is hardly new. The New Political Historians were called "ethnoculturalists" and criticized for limiting the idea of culture to the folkways and worldviews of religious and ethnic communities and failing to acknowledge the culture of the working class. In fact, New Political Historians used the much broader concept of political culture, imported from the study of international politics, well before traditional political historians were at ease with it.[24] As Formisano has shown, both Bernard Bailyn and Richard Hofstadter used the term to describe the symbolic and subjective aspects of political behavior, the underlying beliefs, values, and assumptions that must be read between the lines.[25] But it is clear that the kind of cultural history Marion Winship had in mind grew from different seeds and produced a quite different fruit. Its language, concepts, and theories were derived from postmodern writers and, particularly, from the debate over postmodernism that has been most active in literary criticism and comparative literature. This cultural history comes out of an almost completely different and contrasting intellectual and philosophical stream than the positivist empiricism that underlay the original New Political History.[26]

During the 1990s there has been a vigorous debate over the impact of postmodernism on the writing of history. The formation of the Historical Society in 1998 was designed primarily to counter postmodernist influences. In some ways, the idea of postmodern history is an oxymoron since that perspective in its full-throated version—e.g., Jean-François Lyotard—generally undermines the legitimacy of both traditional history and social science history. (Perhaps the New Political History should be seen as an unindicted co-conspirator in the Enlightenment project.) Traditional history is the postmodernists' target and most are not familiar with the New Political History.[27]

I have a much narrower and more modest focus. Is there a New New Political History? The new generation of political historians writing about the early republic use different language and choose quite different topics to study than the New Political Historians did forty years ago. Most write as though they skipped a generation of scholarship, almost totally unaware of the New Political History, certainly not interested in it, and directing their revisionism at quite traditional histories. That may be because the New Political History did not produce a significant body of literature on the early republic before 1820, which is the specialty of most of the scholars who have so far been identified with this newest political history. Most of what the New Political Historians had written on the early period dealt with the development of political parties. In this they incorporated the work of several somewhat more traditional historians.[28] The most distinctive idea to come out of this collaboration was the discontinuous and incomplete development of parties during these years.[29]

For the most part, these recent historians of the early republic have gone off on their own without directly confronting earlier work other than to rail against the mammoth synthesis, *The Age of Federalism*, by Stanley Elkins and Eric McKitrick, and several recent (very popular) historical biographies. They tend to revise more by expanding the scope of "the political" and integrating cultural themes rather than by directly addressing either traditional studies or the work of the New Political Historians. Certainly the most active current of new scholarship in the political history of the early republic bears the influence of the contemporary intellectual world in which the postmodern debate represents a critical force. Surely everyone is aware of the impact of postmodernism and the debate over it on other aspects of history, particularly the social history of gender and race. Consequently new interpretations of this era could not be uninfluenced. Right now there is not enough published work to talk about a school of political history, but there is a feeling that something is going on.

Winship thought that the paragon of the New New Political History was David Waldstreicher, whose book *In the Midst of Perpetual Fetes: The Making of American Nationalism, 1776–1820*[30] and articles have won several prizes. He negotiates easily the linguistic turn and has internalized postmodern usages and key concepts. But his book is surprisingly comprehensible in traditional terms. While he stretches the concept of the political to include much more than traditional historians on African Americans, women, and symbolic popular activities such as toasts and parades, he focuses upon the quest for a national identity. In general his is a book about the invention of community, what once was called the rise of nationalism. Waldstreicher's methods are rather traditional, although he was clearly influenced in his understanding of nationalism by the English Marxist Eric Hobsbawm.[31]

When the discussion of the New New Political History first arose, most of the work associated with it was either in journal articles or unpublished. Now there is enough to assess the degree to which we are dealing with a new school of historical writing that is about to flower like the New Political History in the late 1960s and early 1970s. Along with Waldstreicher's, we now have several recent books that might be considered early representatives of a New New Political History: Joanne B. Freeman's *Affairs of Honor: National Politics in the New Republic*, Jeffrey L. Pasley's *"The Tyranny of Printers": Newspaper Politics in the Early American Republic*; and Saul Cornell's *The Other Founders: Anti-Federalism and the Dissenting Tradition in America, 1788–1828*.[32]

Comparing the perspectives, language, and methodology of these books and the essays collected here enables us to see the diversity of the scholars associated with the New New Political History. It also reveals the somewhat distant relationship of these scholars to postmodernism. Pure and simple, the people today writing revisionist political history of the early republic are not postmodernists and reflect relatively little "French" influence in their language and perspectives on history, certainly a good deal less than Waldstreicher.[33]

In the original discussion of the New New Political History, Freeman played a key role and was mentioned as one of the most important practitioners of the new genre, yet her focus and her conception of culture differs radically from the tendency of Waldstreicher to employ the postmodern language of literary criticism. Freeman's book is, however, a selectively iconoclastic view of the "Federalist Era" and the founding fathers. She begins with an anecdote about the confrontation of Alexander Hamilton with a mob when he was in the streets advocating the Jay Treaty. Freeman, however, is more interested in his response and that of the mob than with either what Hamilton had to say or what the mob may have collectively believed. Freeman is postmodernist in her concern for texts—even confrontations such as that mentioned above she treats as "text"—and individuals' emotions. Each of the chapters is associated with an individual and usually constructed around some text, often in the narrowest use of the term, such as William Maclay's diary or Thomas Jefferson's "Anas." Her sketches are narrow in focus and unbounded in interpretation. Yet all her interpretations center on the idea of honor, which she sees as *the* political culture of the founding generation.

Freeman interprets everything in relation to this honor culture. In the process she deals with things that appear in the usual texts about this period, although the balance is swayed toward the accentuation of the personal. In almost all cases the narrative is dominated by the personal conflicts between members of the governing elite. Other historians have noted the concept of fame, the politics of passion, and the deep strain of antipartyism, even paranoia, in the Republican ideology, but no one has focused upon honor so exclusively as Freeman. Instead of the code of honor being part of the political culture and affecting political behavior and consequently political structure, it—honor—is her sole subject. The code of honor shared by the political elite forms the entire content of her conception of the political culture of this generation of American politicians.

One never learns about anything the government ever did or how or if it was constructed. Do not send a student to this book to find out about the Whiskey Rebellion (not mentioned in the index) nor the Alien and Sedition Acts (treated briefly in several sentences in the introduction) or Hamilton's economic policy. Freeman has a long, interesting chapter that deals with the elections of 1796 and 1800, but never strays beyond the personal relationships of the contestants. In fact, gossip, rumors, and duels seem central to her interest, though in fairness her concern for extensive research in the primary sources sets her apart from some others who allow rumor and fiction to influence their views on the "character" of politicians in the early republic. Freeman writes extremely well and her discussions are engaging and her interpretations always interesting. She has a point. These were eighteenth-century men trying to come to terms with a new world of political discourse and emotion. Yet the focus seems to legitimate an approach as confessedly subjective and personal as she argues the politics of the founders were. In a way it is disarming, since she does not ask us to engage her argument, but like a good postmodernist, Freeman simply insists that was the way it was—at least for her.

No historian and particularly no traditional historian has ever denied the importance of personal relationships, or that even the most commonplace politician has an incredible ego-involvement in the meanest of offices. I have trouble wondering why Freeman, who was alive and politically aware in the last days of Richard Nixon, finds unusual the self-consumed politician who thinks for every second of his life that he is a man of honor. No, I am not suggesting that Nixon and Hamilton shared the same sense of honor. Nixon was more interested in fame than were any of the founders and wrote more books defending himself.

Freeman seems to believe that only the historiography of the founding generation has been dominated by the personal conflicts of the past. But that is where political history of the Jacksonian movement and the Progressive Era and the New Deal began. It is where all political history begins, or has since Thucydides and Plutarch. Forrest McDonald, the brilliant and eccentric historian of the early republic, agrees with Freeman both on her philosophy of history and that the personal relationships of the politicians were paramount to the history of these years. But McDonald deals with substantial issues and has given us the best description available of the Hamiltonian system.[34] Freeman seems not to care about policy at all and certainly seems to share none of the traditional interest in how this generation may have contributed to the modernization or democratization of the political process or to the creation of what we call ordinary politics. There is none of the ordinary in her book, and consequently ordinary people can neither share the political culture of the elite nor have a culture of their own.[35]

Along with Waldstreicher and Freeman, Winship's original list of New New Political Historians included a student of Bernard Bailyn, Jeffrey L. Pasley, whose book on the political activity of printers has subsequently appeared. It is hard to conceive of a book on relatively the same subject—"National Politics in the New Republic"—that could be so different from Freeman's on almost everything: focus, interpretation, method, and the concept of culture.[36] *"The Tyranny of Printers"* is certainly a welcome addition to the literature, but if anything its methodology and language are less influenced by postmodernism than any of the authors previously discussed.

Pasley traces the development of what he calls the "newspaper-based political system" of the United States from the 1790s into the 1830s. His emphasis is on the 1790s and the first decade of the nineteenth century. He depicts the emergence of a partisan press in relation to the professional development of political editors from artisan printers to middle-class editorialists and party leaders. By the mid-nineteenth century, a good number of politicians serving in Congress and state legislatures had careers that began as political printers. Pasley's emphasis is on the rise of the Republican press, first as the basis for an opposition to the Federalists, and then, after 1800, as the mouthpiece for the new, more democratic regime of the Jeffersonians. In this he convincingly argues that they opened up and took advantage of the public sphere to contest the administration's Hamiltonian and pro-British policies.

Pasley traces, in greater detail than we have had previously, the expansion of the political press and lesser-known Republican editors in the backcountry outside the major cities. Yet he pays little attention to the methodological concerns of the New Political Historians, such as the clear construction of concepts or the testing of hypotheses. This is most obvious in his unsystematic use of the term party and his modest reliance on quantitative analysis. Pasley, however, deals in a creative and stimulating fashion with ordinary politics—parties, voters, and the political elite of party managers and officeholders. His concept of the public sphere is limited to written rational discourse. His language is that of traditional history and his pro-Jeffersonian sentiments are those of a neo-Progressive historian. This book could have easily been written had there been no linguistic turn.

Saul Cornell's *The Other Founders* is yet a different book, although more like that of Pasley than those of Waldstreicher or Freeman. I have included it, although he was not mentioned in the H-SHEAR discussion of a New New

Political History, because Cornell is the one historian of the early republic who has written about the possible effects of the postmodern debate on history and he is comfortable with that language.[37] Also, his book—which is surely the best study of Anti-Federalist thought we have—focuses on texts. Cornell has done an excellent job of categorizing and explaining the various strands of Anti-Federalism. He has carefully charted the printings of various pamphlets and analyzed what he calls the "political sociology" of the various elements of Anti-Federalism.[38]

Cornell is an intellectual historian of politics, and his narrative involves a series of focused analyses of specific texts. The arguments, which he admirably reconstructs, are those of individuals and the context is their personal context, although his approach is nothing like that of Freeman. He believes that political acts have larger importance. While he uses his accounts of reprints to give an impression of distribution and relative weight of various arguments, he offers no real evidence on these matters. The essence of quantification for the New Political Historians was an attempt to systematically judge the relative importance of behaviors, ideas, and attitudes. This intent seems to be absent from the new work as are the quantitative methods.

Almost all the New New Political historians, and most of their generation, refer to and generally extol Jürgen Habermas's concept of "the public sphere" as an essential element of democracy.[39] They emphasize the role of a vibrant dissenting or opposition press. While I tend to disagree with their overly limited conception of the public sphere, my point here is that while Cornell argues that the Anti-Federalists and their heirs were precursors of Habermas, he goes little beyond this. He hardly embraces postmodernism. He has written an excellent intellectual history that is on the whole methodologically quite conservative. If there is any unity to this group of younger historians to which the H-SHEAR discussion drew attention, it is their use of Habermas—who is a critic of postmodernist nihilism—and their interest in the press and "print culture." Neither of these tendencies reflects postmodernism.

These scholars desire to celebrate the development of American democracy in the early national period without denying that restrictions were placed on women and blacks. Inherently critical of the system, they embrace it, actually more than the New Political Historians did. They choose to emphasize its potential for diversity and democracy. Traditional political history is too consensus-oriented for them, overly enamored with American exceptionalism, and too pro-Federalist, as seen in the current apotheosis of John Adams.

Interestingly, the cultural historian William C. Dowling, who has written about Federalist culture expressed in Joseph Dennie's "little magazine," the *Port*

Folio, complained recently about the pro-Jeffersonian bias of the present generation of scholars of the early republic.[40] Although it is not present in the essays in this book, the Federalists have received a lot of good press lately, because of their perceived sympathy toward blacks and women. While the most radical democrats could be found among the Republicans of the urban North, the southern Republicans were generally less democratic than their Federalist opponents when race and gender are taken into account.

An English professor at Rutgers University, Dowling has written a book that should be included in any discussion of the New New Political History, since it emphasizes its commitment to cultural history. But *Literary Federalism in the Age of Jefferson* differs in several ways from the books mentioned.[41] While he shows a close attention to "text," Dowling uses none of the postmodernist language one might expect. He does introduce the concept of the "public sphere," but in his hands it was a much more spacious arena. The public sphere is a metaphorical "space" without inherent content, and Federalist editor Joseph Dennie and his little magazine were active in it. Of course they were then dissenters and the Republicans the masters of the state. Finally, Dowling differs from the others in discussing in great detail and with nuance Federalist thought, or at least the thought of some Federalist intellectuals whom he takes very seriously. Interestingly, he builds upon the work of Joyce Appleby and her understanding of the Federalists as classical republicans.

Yet the main thrust of the writings discussed thus far as a potential New New Political History is generally humanist and methodologically traditional. There is, however, some evidence that all the advocates of the cultural history of politics do not completely ignore the social sciences and even quantitative methodology. Hidden in the footnotes of Waldstreicher's prize-winning essay on Abraham Bishop, written with Stephen R. Grossbart, there is a reference to the use of roll call analysis and Guttman scales to identify parties in the Connecticut legislature that begs for clarification. Similarly, Pasley does display a few charts and graphs and a collective biography of printer/politicians, and Andrew Robertson attempts to understand the voters' perceptions of the political system.[42] It is just the sort of thing that the New Political History brought to political history and that some advocates of the New New Political History generally eschew.

While these younger scholars share with other current cultural historians a quest for "meaning," they are strikingly traditional in their methods, if not their language and concepts. Their interests and methods, if not their interpretations, seem to me to most resemble a 1990s version of the work of those scholars associated with the American Studies movement in the 1950s—John William Ward, William Taylor, David Brion Davis, Marvin Meyers, Leo Marx, and

Henry Nash Smith.[43] At least this is what they seem to aspire to, and certainly it is proper to compare Waldstreicher's *In the Midst of Perpetual Fetes* to some of these earlier works that searched for "the American Character," since he is concerned with the origins of national consciousness. His book reads much more like the works of Smith, Ward, and Taylor than any of the New Political Histories, and his concerns, sources, and methods are quite similar to theirs. Waldstreicher's graduate school mentor David Brion Davis represents a personal link between the newest political historians presented here and the American Studies movement of the 1950s.

THE NEWEST POLITICAL HISTORY

Given the wide variety of approaches and perspectives presented in this volume, the editors wisely have steered away from claims that these essays represent a single historical approach that might represent a New New Political History. They all discuss "culture." But the use of the concept of culture in these essays and the ways the authors approach culture differs radically.[44] Thus, the editors opted for the term "newest political history," which does not claim the coherence of an emerging "school." They also do not set themselves up against the old New Political History. In fact, they do not have much to say about it. The focus of these essays' revisionism is the traditional political histories of the era and, in fact, a subset of them. While these writers seem disdainful of the Consensus historians, they definitely want to push the democratization of American politics back into the early republic.[45]

In their introduction, the editors of this volume set out their general views and several propositions that they believe are related to all the essays. What strikes me is that their response to traditional historians, who emphasize the great men and their personal traits, seems very much like the New Political Historians' rejection of the presidential synthesis and their desire to examine popular participation in American politics as a way to better understand the common man. Undoubtedly, there is some difference between some of these authors' definition of "the political" and that implicit in the work of the New Political Historians, but there are also various definitions of "the political" in the essays in this book. Its boundaries remain unclear. Perhaps the greatest strength of this collection is that it represents the diversity of younger historians' conceptions of political history. Certainly many of the younger generation are returning to the study of politics. They must, because the subject is too important to leave to the political scientists and the students of political development like Stephen Skowronek, Theda Skocpol, and Robert D. Putnam.[46]

WILLIAM G. SHADE

Both the authors of these essays and the New Political Historians wanted to examine politics as actually practiced. (Most of the New Political Historians were political junkies, as are some of the newest political historians, like Pasley, who was a journalist and now has his own blog.) To the New Political Historians this meant connecting the levels of the political system by examining the relationship between voters and the political elite. It meant studying the relationship between political behavior and the changing social and economic structures of the society. Benson and Bogue began their careers as economic historians, and Hays's best-known book is *The Response to Industrialism*. The voting behavior studies were all grounded in a context of economic and demographic change. The same is true of the studies of legislative behavior. The New Political Historians had much more affinity with the New Economic Historians and the demographers than with the New Social Historians because there was an easier methodological mesh. Richard John's essay here is an excellent use of the sources that New Political Historians exploited or opened up. Similarly, Saul Cornell's essay forces an understanding of state laws and courts that is congenial to the New Political Historians' perspective on the importance of federalism.

My own work with constitutional convention debates, as well as that of several New Political Historians, highlighted them as "sites of struggle" and "agents of change," in John's terms.[47] While one may study the statements of radical intellectuals who claim to represent the "people," as does Reeve Huston in his excellent essay on perhaps the greatest unstudied topic of American political history, one must realize that local newspapers, broadsides, and legislative and constitutional convention debates are about as close as we will get to the rational debate of the people. This is the public sphere. And the newest historians presented here agree. This certainly seems to be Jeffrey Pasley's argument. He is much more explicit about his editors than are the cultural historians who ascribe modern meaning to symbolic events. The main difference between the newest political historians and the aging New Political Historians involves most of the newest political historians' refusal to indulge in even modest quantification in their analysis of these sources.

When New Political Historians argued that the early republic lacked an institutionalized party system, their emphasis was on the analysis of its development and decline over time. The New Political Historians were keenly aware of the creative activity in politics of such groups as the militia, the Grange, and the Masons, as well as the most important voluntary organizations in American life, the churches. Building on Benson's work, Formisano brought both the Anti-Masons and the Masons back into view. In fact, the New Political Historians placed great stress on the politics of kith, kin, and neighborhood. They wrote about identity and campaign style, picnics and parades, although they did not detail these events as do the newest political historians, nor attach as much significance to them as does Pasley in his tale of the travels of the mammoth cheese. Finally, although there can be serious arguments about the meaning of political culture, the concept was brought into the study of American history by the New Political Historians, and they often used it to make comparative statements.[48] In relation to all these matters, Pasley, Robertson, and John in their essays extend the work of the New Political Historians by incorporating some lessons learned from the new cultural history.

While none of the New Political Historians wrote about the international dimension or cosmopolitan nature of politics in the early republic, few disagree with this perspective. I am sure that my colleagues welcome investigations like that presented in Seth Cotlar's stimulating essay. In fact, the New Political Historians wrote with an international understanding in mind. They were not trained in comparative literature, but rather comparative politics. Aside from American and British students of political development, Europeans, such as Stein Rokkan, Ralf Dahrendorf, Maurice Duverger, and Giovanni Sartori, were required reading.[49] But so were the classic writers of political sociology: Marx, Durkheim, Weber, Mosca, Micheals, and, most important, Ostrogorski.[50]

Today a number of the New Political Historians are interested in comparative history. It seems to me that most of the New Political Historians would agree that political culture in the 1790s was more cosmopolitan and international than historians of the decade have usually considered it to be. Most have focused on the construction of the government under the Constitution and when acknowledging the importance of foreign affairs, it was in ways that split the American elite and led to the formation of political parties. But the United States was still a new nation on the edge of Europe, questing to be a part of the cosmopolitan center. Andrew Cayton's essay reminds readers about the flexibility of borders and the limits of national identity well into the nineteenth century. It reflects the recent fascination with the Spanish American borderlands that were the focus of several expansionist schemes in the early national era.[51]

The New Political Historians singlehandedly revived the sophisticated study of nativism in the 1850s by treating it as something more than another chapter in the history of bigotry in America.[52] They gave political meaning to both temperance and woman suffrage. Their emphasis on ethnicity and the cultures of immigrant groups logically forced a concern with their European and Asian roots, as well as the folkways of older subcultures within the country and its regions. The New Political Historians also aided the integration of American religious history into political history.[53]

There are differences other than interpretation between the New Political Historians and the newest political historians presented here. Most New Political Historians will find the methods of the newest historians of the early republic insufficiently systematic and fatally undertheorized.[54] This is not simply a matter of quantification, although I would defend the necessity to use statistical techniques. *The Concept of Jacksonian Democracy* relied on no sophisticated statistical manipulation to make Benson's argument. He calls for the clarification of concepts and the logic of behavioral analysis. This forced historians to consider a different kind of thinking about their arguments. The methodologies presented here are all quite old-fashioned, even if some of the interpretative schemes are unconventional. They not only do not like quantification, but also reject the entire literature of American and British political science. Other than the excellent theoretical essay by John Brooke, which easily could have appeared in either *Social Science History* or the *Journal of Interdisciplinary History*, most of the newest political historians show little of the methodological self-awareness or statistical concern that was commonplace among the New Political Historians. There is little explicit modeling and very infrequent use of quantitative analysis.[55] In fact, these newest historians of politics seem to want to throw off such intellectual straitjackets and emphasize interpretation rather than analysis.

Another important difference between the work of New Political Historians and that presented here involves the focus on questions of race and gender. This does not mean that they ignored either racism or the role of women. In fact, New Political Historians produced one of the best studies of racism and American politics, as well as the seminal study of women in nineteenth-century American politics.[56] These works, however, emphasized ordinary politics and suggested that the study of African American or women's political activity should be seen in terms of the ways in which ordinary politics restricted their alternatives and provided the conditions for both failure and success.[57]

Certainly students of twentieth-century politics working in the tradition of the New Political History have either incorporated black voters and black leaders into their work or focused specifically upon racial questions.[58] The current generation of political historians influenced by the New Social History has emphasized identity politics and looked at the activities of African Americans and women from the perspective of the disadvantaged groups. Some of this can be seen in the essays by Rosemarie Zagarri and Richard Newman, although both are more of interest for their interpretations, which plow new ground, than for their methodological inventiveness. The essays of Nancy Isenberg, Albrecht Koschnik, and David Waldstreicher, however, draw upon some of the insights of cultural history to expand the political realm in ways unforeseen by the New Political Historians and make important additions to our understanding of American political history.

Thus, the essays in this volume often represent quite different ways of doing history, but extensive study of these subjects is refreshing for political historians of all sorts and signals that the fortunes of American political history are beginning to turn. As long as the newest political historians desire to extend the boundaries of political history and to encompass the findings that were put forward by the New Political History, they will receive encouragement from both the old New Political Historians and traditionalists. Waldstreicher's proclaimed desire to reconcile the political culture approach and the culture of politics approach seems admirable. Brooke's attempt to use Habermas to integrate the newest political history with the best previous studies of ordinary politics is strikingly innovative and worthy of much further development and demonstration. Above all, the energy and engagement of the newest political historians represented in this book provides hope for the revitalization of American political history.

NOTES

1. Joel H. Silbey, "The State and Practice of American Political History at the Millennium: The Nineteenth century as a Test Case," *Journal of Policy History* 11 (1999): 1–31; Mark Leff, "Revisioning U.S. Political History," *American Historical Review* 100 (1995): 829–53; and Steven M. Gillon, "The Future of Political History," *Journal of Policy History* 9 (1997): 240–55.

2. Lee Benson presented a devastating critique of traditional political history in "Research Problems in American Political Historiography," in *Common Frontiers of the Social Sciences*, ed. Mirra Komarovsky (Glencoe, 1957), 113–83, 418–21. Arthur M. Schlesinger, Jr., debated with Benson the value of social-scientific history in "The Humanist Looks at Empirical Social Research," *American Sociological Review* 27 (1962): 768–71.

3. Lee Benson, *Toward the Scientific Study of History* (Philadelphia, 1972), and Lee Benson, *Turner and Beard* (Glencoe, 1960).

4. See Ronald P. Formisano, "The Invention of the Ethnocultural Interpretation," *American Historical Review* 99 (1994): 453–77.

5. Allan G. Bogue, *Clio & the Bitch Goddess: Quantification in American Political History* (Beverly Hills, 1983), collects his essays and provides a general history of the New Political History.

6. Robert P. Swierenga, ed., *Quantification in American History: Theory and Research* (New York, 1970); Joel H. Silbey and Samuel T. McSeveney, eds., *Voters, Parties, and Elections: Quantitative Essays in American Popular Voting Behaviour* (Lexington, Mass., 1972); Lee Benson et al., *American Political Behavior: Historical Essays and Readings* (New

York, 1974); William O. Aydelotte, ed., *The History of Parliamentary Behavior* (Princeton, 1977); and Joel H. Silbey, Allan G. Bogue, and William H. Flanigan, eds., *The History of American Electoral Behavior* (Princeton, 1978), illustrate the New Political History at the time, both in the essays and the extensive bibliographies.

7. Forrest McDonald, *We the People: The Economic Origins of the Constitution* (Chicago, 1958); Walter Hugins, *Jacksonian Democracy and the Working Class: A Study of the New York Workingmen's Movement, 1829–1837* (Stanford, 1960); David Donald, *Lincoln Reconsidered* (New York, 1960); Richard Hofstadter, *The Age of Reform* (New York, 1955).

8. See Samuel P. Hays, *American Political History as Social Analysis* (Knoxville, 1980). Benson similarly attacked McDonald, while his student Gerald Sorin revised Donald in *The New York Abolitionists: A Case Study of Political Radicalism* (Westport, Conn., 1971). Hays was also a contributor to David S. Landes and Charles Tilly, eds., *History as Social Science* (Englewood Cliffs, N.J., 1971).

9. While one of the criticisms of the New Political History is that it involved only studies of voting behavior and failed to address policy making, the first books of Benson, Bogue, and Hays were about policy making, as was my *Banks or No Banks: The Money Question in the Midwest, 1832–1865* (Detroit, 1972).

10. Thomas B. Alexander, *Sectional Stress and Party Strength: A Study of Roll Call Voting Patterns in the United States House of Representatives, 1836–1860* (Nashville, 1967); Allan G. Bogue, *The Earnest Men: Republicans and the Civil War Senate* (Ithaca, 1981); and Joel H. Silbey, *The Shrine of Party: Congressional Behavior, 1841–1852* (Pittsburgh, 1967). See also William O. Aydelotte, *Quantification in History* (Menlo Park, N.J., 1971).

11. Thomas C. Cochran, "The 'Presidential Synthesis' in American History," *American Historical Review* 53 (July 1948): 748–59.

12. Richard P. McCormick, *The Second American Party System: Party Formation in the Jacksonian Era* (Chapel Hill, 1966); Richard P. McCormick, "New Perspectives on Jacksonian Politics," *American Historical Review* 65 (1960): 288–301.

13. William Nisbet Chambers and Walter Dean Burnham, eds., *The American Political Systems: Stages of Political Development* (New York, 1967).

14. Edward Shorter, *The Historian and the Computer: A Practical Guide* (Englewood Cliffs, N.J., 1971); Charles M. Dollar and Richard J. Jensen, *Historians Guide to Statistics: Quantitative Analysis and Historical Research* (New York, 1971).

15. J. Morgan Kousser, *The Shaping of Southern Politics: Suffrage Restriction and the Establishment of the One-Party South, 1880–1910* (New Haven, 1974); Allan J. Lichtman, *Prejudice and the Old Politics: The Election of 1928* (Chapel Hill, 1979); Richard L. McCormick, *From Realignment to Reform: Political Change in New York State, 1893–1910* (Ithaca, 1981); Ballard C. Campbell, *Representative Democracy: Public Policy and Midwestern Legislatures in the Late Nineteenth Century* (Cambridge, Mass., 1980); Dale Baum, *The Civil War Party System: The Case of Massachusetts, 1848–1876* (Chapel Hill, 1984); Margaret Susan Thompson, *The "Spider Web": Congress and Lobbying in the Age of Grant* (Ithaca, 1985); and Philip R. VanderMeer, *The Hoosier Politician: Officeholding and Political Culture in Indiana, 1896–1920* (Urbana, 1985). Kleppner, Formisano, Silbey, Jensen,

Shade, Holt, and Allswang all produced "second" books, and the essays in Paul Kleppner et al., *The Evolution of American Electoral Systems* (Westport, 1981), synthesized much of the work of the New Political Historians.

16. The closest thing was Robert Kelley's *The Cultural Pattern of American Politics: The First Century* (New York, 1979).

17. The New Political Historians were interested in religious history. They all cited Gerhard Linski, *The Religious Factor* (New York, 1961), and Rodney Stark and Charles Y. Glock, *American Piety: The Nature of Religious Commitment* (Berkeley, 1968).

18. Essentially I have used direct citations in some of the above listed volumes, the methodology used, participation in the SSHA, and publication in the journals mentioned to categorize those I have associated with the New Political History. The New Political History was only a part of the more general movement toward social science history that effected students of Europe and Latin America and the other social science disciplines, particularly economics and the New Economic History. For a traditional critique by a cultural historian, see Jacques Barzun, *Clio and the Doctors: Psycho-History, Quanto-History & History* (Chicago, 1974).

19. John F. Reynolds, "Do Historians Count Anymore? The Status of Quantitative Methods in History, 1975–1995," *Historical Methods Newsletter* 31 (1998): 141–48; and Paula Baker, "Is There an Audience for History with the Facts Left In?," unpublished paper presented at the Organization of American Historians annual meeting, St. Louis, Mo., March 2000.

20. Paul Kleppner, *Continuity and Change in Electoral Politics, 1893–1828* (Westport, Conn., 1987); Paul Goodman, *Towards a Christian Republic: Antimasonry and the Great Transition in New England, 1826–1836* (New York, 1988); Allan G. Bogue, *The Congressman's Civil War* (New York, 1988); Joel H. Silbey, *The American Political Nation, 1838–1893* (Stanford, 1991); Peter J. Argersinger, *Structure, Process, and Party* (Armonk, N.Y., 1992); Paul Bourke and Donald Debats, *Washington County: Politics and Community in Antebellum America* (Baltimore, 1995); Robert R. Dykstra, *Bright Radical Star: Black Freedom and White Supremacy on the Hawkeye Frontier* (Cambridge, Mass., 1993); Ballard C. Campbell, *The Growth of American Governance: Governance from the Cleveland Administration to the Present* (Bloomington, 1995); William G. Shade, *Democratizing the Old Dominion: Virginia and the Second Party System, 1824–1861* (Charlottesville, 1996); and Michael F. Holt, *The Rise and Fall of the American Whig Party: Jacksonian Politics and the Onset of the Civil War* (New York, 1999). Additions to the ranks of the New Political Historians included William E. Gienapp, *The Origins of the Republican Party, 1852–1856* (New York, 1987); Randolph A. Roth, *The Democratic Dilemma: Religion, Reform, and the Social Order in the Connecticut River Valley of Vermont, 1791–1850* (New York, 1987); John F. Reynolds, *Testing Democracy: Electoral Behavior and Progressive Reform in New Jersey, 1880–1920* (Chapel Hill, 1988); Kenneth J. Winkle, *The Politics of Community: Migration and Politics in Antebellum Ohio* (New York, 1988); Daniel W. Crofts, *Reluctant Confederates: Upper South Unionists in the Secession Crisis* (Chapel Hill, 1989); Robin Einhorn, *Property Rules: Political Economy in Chicago, 1833–1872* (Chicago, 1991); Paula Baker, *The*

Moral Frameworks of Public Life: Gender, Politics and the State in Rural New York, 1870–1930 (New York, 1991); and Lex Renda, *Running on the Record: Civil War-Era Politics in New Hampshire* (Charlottesville, 1997).

21. Loren Haskins and Kirk Jeffrey, eds., *Understanding Quantitative History* (New York, 1990); Konrad H. Jarausch and Kenneth A. Hardy, *Quantitative Methods for Historians: A Guide to Research, Data, and Statistics* (Chapel Hill, 1991); and Thomas J. Archdeacon, *Correlation and Regression Analysis: A Historian's Guide* (Madison, 1994).

22. Barry Friedman, "Everyone's Doing Congressional Historiography: Where Are the Historians?" *Social Science History* 24 (2000): 333–48. The study of American political history has blossomed among political scientists. There are now over 600 members of the politics and history group of the American Political Science Association and it has its own newsletter, *Clio*.

23. "The Power of History," *American Historical Review* 103 (1998): 1–14. See also her *Inheriting the Revolution: The First Generation of Americans* (Cambridge, Mass., 2000).

24. Examples include Paul Kleppner, *The Third Electoral System, 1853–1892: Parties Voters and Political Cultures* (Chapel Hill, 1979); Jean H. Baker, *Affairs of Party: The Political Culture of Northern Democrats in the Mid-Nineteenth Century* (Ithaca, 1983); and Ronald P. Formisano, *The Transformation of Political Culture: Massachusetts Parties, 1790s–1840s* (New York, 1983). Baker's first books were very much like those of the New Political History. Her cultural history of partisan politics in *Affairs of Party* and "The Ceremonies of Politics: Nineteenth-Century Rituals of National Affirmation," in *A Master's Due: Essays in Honor of David Herbert Donald*, ed. William J. Cooper, Jr., Michael F. Holt, and John McCardell (Baton Rouge, 1985), 161–78, have influenced the writers in this volume.

25. Ronald P. Formisano, "The Concept of Political Culture," *The Journal of Interdisciplinary History* (2000): 393–426.

26. Although there are few examples of thoroughly postmodernist history in the historical literature related to the early republic, the work of Joanne Pope Melish reflects heavy influence of postmodernism. See "The 'Condition' Debate and Racial Discourse in the Antebellum North," *Journal of the Early Republic* 19 (1999): 651–72; and *Disowning Slavery: Gradual Emancipation and 'Race' in New England, 1780–1860* (Ithaca, 1998). A recent attempt to reorient the argument by a historian of the early republic is Richard D. Brown, "Microhistory and the Post Modern Challenge," *Journal of the Early Republic* 23 (2003): 1–20.

27. Elizabeth Fox-Genovese and Elisabeth Lasch-Quinn, eds., *Reconstructing History: The Emergence of a New Historical Society* (New York, 1999); Chandra Mukerji and Michael Schudson, eds., *Rethinking Popular Culture: Contemporary Perspectives in Cultural Studies* (Berkeley, 1991); Keith Windschuttle, *The Killing of History: How Literary Criticism and Social Theorists Are Murdering Our Past* (New York, 1996); Joyce Appleby, Elizabeth Covington, David Hoyt, Michael Latham, and Allison Sneider, eds., *Knowledge and Post Modernism in Historical Perspective* (New York, 1996); and Keith Jenkins, ed., *The Postmodern History Reader* (New York, 1997). A left-wing critique is Bryan D. Palmer, *Dissent into Discourse: The Reflection of Language and Writing of Social History* (Philadelphia, 1990).

28. Rudolph M. Bell, *Party and Faction in American Politics: The House of Representatives, 1789–1801* (Westport, 1973); John Hoadley, *Origins of American Political Parties, 1789–1803* (Lexington, Ky., 1986); Ronald L. Hatzenbuhler and Robert L. Ivie, *Congress Declares War: Rhetoric, Leadership, and Partisanship in the Early Republic* (Kent, 1983), used quantitative analysis to study roll call voting in Congress and typify the New Political Historians. Sidney H. Aronson, *Status and Kinship in the Higher Civil Service: Standards of Selection in the Administrations of John Adams, Thomas Jefferson, and Andrew Jackson* (Cambridge, Mass., 1964), and Whitman H. Ridgway, *Community Leadership in Maryland, 1790–1840: A Comparative Analysis of Power in Society* (Chapel Hill, 1979), studied elites and appointments. David A. Bohmer, "The Maryland Electorate and the Concept of a Party System in the Early National Period," in *The History of American Electoral Behavior*, ed. Joel H. Silbey, Allan G. Bogue, and William H. Flanigan (Princeton, 1978), 146–73, is an excellent study of voters based on poll books. Manning Dauer, Noble Cunningham, David Hackett Fischer, William N. Chambers, Paul Goodman, Lisle Rose, Carl E. Prince, Richard Beeman, Richard H. Buel, Jr., Linda Kerber, James M. Banner, Norman Risjord, and James Broussard studied party development. Of these, only Chambers was associated with the New Political Historians. He and Dauer were political scientists. Fischer and Risjord (in his later articles and second book) showed an affinity for the New Political History. Goodman, particularly in his articles, such as "Social Status and Party Leadership: The House of Representatives, 1797–1804," *William and Mary Quarterly*, 3d ser., 25 (1968): 465–74, and his later work seemed to move into the New Political Historians' camp. Buel, Kerber, and Banner were associated with the "Republican synthesis," as were Gordon Wood, Roger H. Brown, Richard Hofstadter, Drew McCoy, Lance Banning, and Joyce Appleby (as a critic). Ironically, Bogue noted that the term "new political history" could have been used with equal justice to characterize the work of these historians (*Clio & the Bitch Goddess*, 115).

29. The limits of the institutionalization of political parties during the early national period has been carefully analyzed by Ronald P. Formisano: *Transformation of Political Culture*; "Deferential-Participant Politics: The Early Republic's Political Culture, 1789–1840," *American Political Science Review* 68 (1974): 473–97; "Federalists and Republicans: Parties Yes—System No," in Kleppner et al., *Evolution of Electoral Systems*, 33–76. See also James Sterling Young, *The Washington Community, 1800–1828* (New York, 1966); Daniel Sisson, *The American Revolution of 1800* (New York, 1972); James Roger Sharp, *American Politics in the Early Republic: The New Nation in Crisis* (New Haven, 1993), which refers to the Federalists and Republicans of the 1790s as "proto-parties"; Roy F. Nichols, *The Invention of American Political Parties* (New York, 1967); and Richard P. McCormick, *The Presidential Game: The Origins of American Presidential Politics* (New York, 1982).

30. (Chapel Hill, 1997).

31. E. J. Hobsbawm, *Nations and Nationalism since 1780: Programme, Myth, Reality* (Cambridge, Eng., 1990). Ironically, Waldstreicher has been criticized for ignoring class: Andrew R. L. Cayton, "We Are All Nationalists, We Are All Localists," *Journal of the Early Republic* 18 (1998): 521–28.

32. Freeman's book was published in New Haven in 2001; Pasley's in Charlottesville, also in 2001; and Cornell's in Chapel Hill in 1999.

33. Even Waldstreicher has been criticized for not being sufficiently postmodernist: see Ronald Schultz's review of *In the Midst of Perpetual Fetes* for H-SHEAR (December 1, 1998). Waldstreicher was Holt's student at the University of Virginia. He was also influenced greatly by his reading of Formisano and Jean Baker (personal communication).

34. See McDonald's works covering the same chronological ground and same major figures as Freeman's book does: *The Presidency of George Washington* (Lawrence, Kans., 1974); *The Presidency of Thomas Jefferson* (New York, 1976); and *Alexander Hamilton: A Biography*.

35. Simon P. Newman, *Parades and the Politics of the Street: Festive Culture in the Early Republic* (Philadelphia, 1997), can be considered a typical new cultural history and yet presents a totally different world of politics of the 1790s. He reflects English neo-Marxist history represented by Raymond Williams, E. P. Thompson, and Eric Hobsbawm rather than the primarily French postmodernism (or poststructuralism) of Lyotard, Michel Foucault, and Jacques Derrida.

36. Compare reviews of the two books in the *Washington Post National Weekly Edition* (October 29–November 4, 2001), 33–34, by Pauline Maier (on Freeman) and Richard N. Rosenfeld (on Pasley).

37. Saul Cornell, "Early American History in a Postmodern Age," *William and Mary Quarterly*, 50 (1993): 329–41.

38. Here my complaint is that he did not go further. He might have tried to revise the quantitatively oriented Jackson Turner Main: *The Antifederalists: Critics of the Constitution* (Chapel Hill, 1961); and *Political Parties Before the Constitution* (Chapel Hill, 1973). New Political Historians who have written on the Confederation period are Van Beck Hall, *Politics without Parties* (Pittsburgh, 1968); H. James Henderson, *Party Politics in the Continental Congress* (New York, 1974); and Owen S. Ireland, *Religion, Ethnicity, and Politics: Ratifying the Constitution in Pennsylvania* (University Park, Pa., 1995).

39. The early republic historian who has discussed "the public sphere" at greatest length is John L. Brooke. See "Ancient Lodges and Self-created Societies: Voluntary Association and the Public Sphere in the Early Republic," in *Launching the "Extended Republic": The Federalist Era*, ed. Ronald Hoffman and Peter J. Albert (Charlottesville, 1996), 273–380; and "To Be 'Read by the Whole People': Press, Party, and Public Sphere in the United States, 1789–1840," *Proceedings of the American Antiquarian Society* 110 (2002): 41–118. These essays and Brooke's earlier book, *The Heart of the Commonwealth: Society and Political Culture in Worcester County, Massachusetts, 1713–1861* (New York, 1989), as well as his publication in *The Journal of Interdisciplinary History*, might mark him as a New Political Historian. Habermas was brought up in the Frankfurt School and was thus at one time a devotee of social science. See Rolf Wiggershaus, *The Frankfurt School: Its History, Theories and Political Significance* (Cambridge, 1995).

40. See his review of Doron Ben-Atar and Barbara B. Oberg, eds., *Federalism Reconsidered*, and Donald R. Kennon, ed., *A Republic for the Ages* in *The Journal of American History*

87 (2000): 656–57. The Ben-Atar and Oberg volume includes essays by Cayton, Wald-streicher, and Zagarri. See also the somewhat different recent cultural histories that show little postmodern influence: Marshall Foletta, *Coming to Terms with Democracy: Federalists Intellectuals and the Shaping of American Culture* (Charlottesville, 2001); Jonathan D. Sassi, *A Republic of Righteousness: The Public Christianity of the Post Revolutionary New England Clergy* (New York, 2001); and Louis P. Masur, *1831: Year of Eclipse* (New York, 2001).

41. William C. Dowling, *Literary Federalism in the Age of Jefferson: Joseph Dennie and the Port Folio, 1801–1811* (Columbia, 1999).

42. David Waldstreicher and Stephen B. Grossbart, "Abraham Bishop's Vocation; or, The Mediation of Jeffersonian Politics," *Journal of the Early Republic* 18 (1998): 617–58; Pasley, *Tyranny of Printers*; Andrew W. Robertson, *The Language of Democracy: Political Rhetoric in the United States and Britain, 1790–1900* (Ithaca, 1995).

43. On this highly creative moment in American historiography, see Hennig Cohen, ed., *The American Experience: Approaches to the Study of the United States* (Boston, 1968); Hennig Cohen, ed., *The American Culture: Approaches to the Study of the United States* (Boston, 1968); Stanley Coben and Lorman Ratner, eds., *The Development of an American Culture* (Englewood Cliffs, N.J., 1970).

44. For an illustration of the wildly different understandings of "culture" in the history profession see Lawrence E. Harrison and Samuel P. Huntington, eds., *Culture Matters: How Values Shape Human Progress* (New York, 2000). For further discussions of the problem over the past generation see Clyde Kluckhohn, "The Concept of Culture," in *Culture and Behavior: Collected Essays of Clyde Kluckhohn* (New York, 1962); Robert K. Berkhofer, "The Culture Concept;" and William H. Swell, Jr., "The Concept(s) of Culture," in Victoria E. Bonnell and Lynn Hunt, eds., *Beyond the Cultural Turn: New Directions in the Study of Society and Culture* (Berkeley, 1999), 35–61.

45. The First Democracy Project, which has been consistently supported by the New Political Historians, will yield a wonderful source that will permit much more sophisti-cated analyses of the politics of the early republic. None of the New Political Historians denied the existence of Pasley's "newspaper parties" or that in various places there were the high turnouts and consistent behavior that Robertson cites. The differences are conceptual and technical.

46. These scholars associated with bringing the state back into political science are all involved in the SSHA alongside the New Political Historians. Like Charles Tilly, who coined the phrase, they look for "large structures." Tilly, a former president of the SSHA, also said that history was too important to leave to the historians. One of the historians in this volume who has been influenced by these writers is Richard R. John. See his excellent essay, "Governmental Institutions as Agents of Change: Rethinking American Political Development in the Early Republic, 1787–1836," *Studies in American Political Development* 11 (1997): 347–80.

47. Shade, *Banks or No Banks*, and *Democratizing the Old Dominion*.

48. Ronald P. Formisano, "The Concept of Political Culture," *Journal of Interdisciplinary History* (2000): 393–426.

49. An extensive bibliography would be out of place, but illustrative of this influence are Joseph LaPalombara and Myron Weiner, eds., *Political Parties and Political Development* (Princeton, 1966), and Stein Rokkan, *Citizens, Elections, Parties: Approaches to the Comparative Study of the Processes of Development* (New York and Oslo, 1970). In this connection, William Nisbet Chambers, *Political Parties in a New Nation: The American Experience, 1776–1809* (New York, 1963), might be considered the New Political History's synthesis for the early republic, although it has been criticized by other New Political Historians.

50. M. Ostrogorski, *Democracy and the Organization of Political Parties* (New York and London, 1902), defined the questions that are still relevant today. In the 1960s there was a brief edition in paperback edited by Seymour Martin Lipset. Lipset's many books, including *Political Man: The Social Basis of Politics* (New York, 1960), and *The First New Nation: The United States in Historical and comparative Perspective* (New York, 1963), had a tremendous impact on the New Political Historians, although they criticized him and found his history rather thin.

51. Traditionally the borderlands have been the province of those who teach Latin American history such as Amy Turner Bushnell, David J. Weber, and James Brooks, authors of superb recent studies. For evidence that historians of the United States are being drawn into this finally, see Jeremy Adelman and Stephen Aron, "From Borderlands to Borders: Empires, Nation-States, and the Peoples in Between in North American History," *American Historical Review* 104 (1999): 814–41.

52. In *The Concept of Jacksonian Democracy*, Benson drew upon the work of John Higham and Oscar Handlin to insist upon the agency of the Irish Catholics in the culture wars of the 1840s.

53. See Mark A. Noll, ed., *Religion and American Politics: From the Colonial Period to the 1980s* (New York, 1990).

54. Richard Biernacki, "Method and Metaphor after the New Cultural History," in Bonnell and Hunt, *Beyond the Cultural Turn*, 62–92, particularly 80–82, raises questions of the matter of theory and its relation to method that were and are central to the New Political Historians.

55. Among social historians there have been those who have taken a distinctly social science approach and participate in the SSHA and cooperate with the New Political Historians. The conflict is with others, particularly the labor historians influenced by E. P. Thompson, who lean toward cultural history in its British Marxist form, but consider quantitative and social science approaches as suspect on ideological grounds.

56. Dykstra, *Bright Radical Star*; Paula Baker, "The Domestication of Politics: Women and American Political Society, 1780–1920," *American Historical Review* 89 (1984): 620–47, and *Moral Frameworks of Public Life*. See also Kousser, *Shaping of Southern Politics*; Phyllis F. Field, *The Politics of Race in New York: The Struggle for Black Suffrage in the Civil War Era* (Ithaca, 1982); Ronald P. Formisano, "The Role of Women in the Dorr Rebellion," *Rhode Island History* 51 (1993): 89–104; and Ronald P. Formisano, "The 'Party Period' Revisited," *Journal of American History* 86 (1999): 93–120. My own work on women's history consists of an anthology of essays: Jean E. Friedman, William G. Shade,

and Mary Jane Capozzoli, eds., *Our American Sisters: Women in American Life and Thought*, 4th ed. (Lexington, Mass., 1987); twenty-one entries in A. H. Zophy, ed., *Handbook of American Women's History* (New York, 1990); and " 'A Mental Passion': Female Sexuality in Victorian America," *International Journal of Women's Studies* 1 (1978): 13–29.

57. Silbey, "State and Practice of American Political History."

58. John Allswang, *A House for All Peoples: Ethnic Politics in Chicago, 1890–1936* (Lexington, Mass., 1971); John Allswang, *The New Deal and American Politics: A Study in Political Change* (New York, 1978); Ronald P. Formisano, *Boston against Busing: Race, Class, and Ethnicity in the 1960s and 1970s* (Chapel Hill, 1991); Dale Baum, *The Shattering of Texas Unionism* (Baton Rouge, 1999); and J. Morgan Kousser, *Colorblind Injustice: Minority Voting and the Undoing of the Second Reconstruction* (Chapel Hill, 1999). My contributions to African American history are William G. Shade and Roy C. Herrenkohl, eds., *Seven On Black: Reflections on the Negro Experience in America* (Philadelphia, 1969); Willis F. Dunbar and William G. Shade, "The Black Man Gains the Vote: The Centennial of 'Impartial Suffrage' in Michigan," *Michigan History* 56 (1972): 42–57; and William R. Scott and William G. Shade, eds., *Upon These Shores: Themes in African-American Experience 1600 to the Present* (New York, 2000), which includes my essay, " 'Though We Are Not Slaves, We Are Not Free': Quasi-Free Blacks in Antebellum America."

Contributors

John L. Brooke, Humanities Distinguished Professor of History at the Ohio State University, is completing a manuscript entitled "Columbia: Civil Life in the World of Martin Van Buren's Emergence, 1776–1821."

Andrew R. L. Cayton is Distinguished Professor of History at Miami University in Oxford, Ohio. His most recent books are *Ohio: The History of a People* (2002) and, with Fred Anderson, *The Dominion of War: Liberty and Empire in North America, 1500–2000* (forthcoming).

Saul Cornell is Associate Professor of History and Director of the Second Amendment Research Center of the John Glenn Institute at the Ohio State University. He is the author of *The Other Founders: Anti-Federalism and the Dissenting Tradition in America, 1788–1828* (1998).

Seth Cotlar is Assistant Professor of History at Willamette University in Salem, Oregon. He is currently finishing a book on the rise and fall of transatlantic radicalism in the early republic. His article, "Joseph Gales and the Making of the Jeffersonian Middle Class," appeared in James Horn, Jan Ellen Lewis, and Peter Onuf, eds., *The Revolution of 1800: Democracy, Race, and the New Republic* (2002).

Reeve Huston teaches history at Duke University in Durham, North Carolina. He is the author of *Land and Freedom: Rural Society, Popular Protest, and Party Politics in Antebellum New York* (2000), which won both the Dixon Ryan Fox prize of the New York State Historical Association and the Theodore Saloutous Prize of the Agricultural History Society. He is currently at work on a study of conflicts between party leaders, plebeian activists, evangelical reformers, female and black activists, and Indian leaders over the meaning and practice of "democracy" between 1815 and 1840.

Nancy Isenberg is co-holder of the Mary Frances Barnard Chair in Nineteenth-Century American History at the University of Tulsa. She is author of *Sex and Citizenship in Antebellum America* (1998) and co-editor, with Andrew Burstein, of *Mortal Remains: Death in Early America* (2002). She is currently working on a biography of Aaron Burr.

Richard R. John is Associate Professor of History at the University of Illinois at Chicago, where he specializes in the cultural and institutional history of the United States. He has written widely on topics in the history of American communications and is the author of *Spreading the News: The American Postal System from Franklin to Morse* (1995). He is currently completing a history of American telecommunications between the 1830s and the 1910s.

Albrecht Koschnik teaches early American history at Florida State University. His publications include "The Democratic Societies of Philadelphia and the Limits of the American Public Sphere, circa 1793–1795," *William and Mary Quarterly* (2001). He is currently completing a manuscript dealing with voluntary associations, partisanship, gender, and the public sphere in Philadelphia between the American Revolution and the late 1830s.

Richard Newman teaches African American and environmental history at the Rochester Institute of Technology. He is the author of *The Transformation of American Abolitionism* (2002) and the forthcoming *Black Founder: Richard Allen and the Early Republic*. He is the co-editor of *Pamphlets of Protest: Early African American Protest Writing, 1790–1860* (2001) and the forthcoming *Palgrave Environment Reader*. He is also an educational consultant to the Strong Museum in Rochester, New York.

Jeffrey L. Pasley is Associate Professor of History at the University of Missouri's main campus in Columbia. He is author of *"The Tyranny of Printers": Newspaper Politics in the Early American Republic* (2001), which won the Association for Education in Mass Communication and Journalism's best history book award for 2002.

Andrew W. Robertson is Associate Professor of History at Lehman College and the Graduate Center of the City University of New York. He is the author of *The Language of Democracy: Political Rhetoric in the United States and Britain, 1790–1900* (1995). He has been Principal Investigator of the First Democracy Project at the American Antiquarian Society. He is currently at work on a book about early republican political culture and voting, "The Second American Republic, 1787–1825."

William G. Shade is Professor Emeritus of History at Lehigh University in Bethlehem, Pennsylvania. He has taught at five universities in the United States and in Ireland, England, and Russia, where he most recently served as Nikolay V. Sivachev Distinguished Chair in American History at Moscow University. He has written over forty articles and authored or edited thirteen books, including *Democratizing the Old Dominion: Virginia and the Second Party System, 1824–1861* (1996), which won the Avery O. Craven Prize of the Organization of American Historians in 1997.

David Waldstreicher is Professor of History at Temple University in Philadelphia. He is the author of *In the Midst of Perpetual Fetes: The Making of American Nationalism, 1776–1820* (1997), which won the Jamestown Prize of the Omohundro Institute of Early American History and Culture, and most recently of *Runaway America: Benjamin Franklin, Slavery, and the American Revolution* (2004).

Rosemarie Zagarri is Professor of History at George Mason University in Fairfax, Virginia. She is the author of *A Woman's Dilemma: Mercy Otis Warren and the American Revolution* and other books and articles on the early republic. She is currently completing a study of women and politics during the early national period.

Index

Antebellum era, 186

Anticlericalism, 275

Anti-Federalists, 252, 257, 258, 267, 305; and right to bear arms, 259–61; and Dissent of the Minority, 259–62; and fears of being disarmed, 261, 264; criticism of Constitution, 264–65

Anti-Jacobinism, 65, 276–77, 287–88, 290, 292, 295; British, 286, 295

Anti-Jacobin Review, 274

Anti-Masonic Party, 366, 401

Anti-rent/anti-renters: and American Revolution, 17–18; and threat to state legitimacy, 237; and social history, 356; and electoral politics, 357; and second party system, 360; and leasehold militants, 362; and former Democrats, 364; and political activists, 367; and collapse of Whigs, 375; and Republican emergence, 378

Antislavery, 7

Appleby, Joyce O., 5, 393, 399

Aristocracy, 361

Aristotle, 167

Arkansas Territory, 307, 311

Arms, right to bear: in founding era, 255–59; Federalists' view of, 257–58; Anti-Federalists' dissenting views on, 259–62; and right of revolution, 262–65; changing interpretations of, 265–67. *See also* Second Amendment

Articles of Confederation, 253

Artisans, 44

Atheism, 276

Atlantic world, 211

Augusta County, Va., 65, 74

Austin, Moses, 307

Austin, San Felipe de, 321

Austin, Stephen F.: early life, 307; and Mexican independence, 314; as patriarch, 318–20; favors Texas independence, 323

Aydelotte, William O., 390

Ayuntamientos (local councils), 322

Bache, Benjamin Franklin, 278

Bailyn, Bernard, 7, 393

Baker, Jean H., 57

Baker, Paula, 234

Baltimore, 69, 168, 339, 344

Baltimore *Patriot*, 342

Baltimore *Sun*, 335, 342

Bancroft, George, 236

Bank of St. Louis, 307

Bank of the United States, 294, 306, 360, 390

Baptists, 32, 34, 36, 37, 47, 221

Barbour, James, 59

Barker-Benfield, George, 234

Barlow, Joel, 253

Barnburners, 366, 372, 375

Barruel, Abbé Augustin, 284, 288

Bates, Barnabas, 338

Bavarian Illuminati, 284

Beach, Moses Y., 346

Beard, Charles, 390

Beckley, Maria, 114

Bennet, James Gordon, 341

Bennington, Vt., 115

Benson, Lee, 236, 388

Berkeley County, Va. (now W.Va.), 65

Berkshire County, Mass., 31, 42, 45, 46

Berlandier, Jean Louis, 317

Bible Tract Societies, 193

Biddle, Nicholas, 168, 173

Bill of Rights, 260, 265

Binney, Horace, 164

Bishop, Abraham, 85, 278

Black Abolitionist Papers, 192

Blackstone, Sir William, 218

Blennerhassett, Harmon, 146, 150

Bloomfield, Joseph, 138

Blount, William, 308

Blumin, Stuart M., 17, 236–37

struction of, 362. *See also* Second
Amendment
Constitutional history, 15, 251–52; of
race and gender, 252
Constitutionalism: popular, 253; plebian,
253–54; and anti-renters, 369, 370
Consumption, clothing, 79, 81, 87, 89–
90, 92
Continental Army, 115, 232
Continental Congress, 331
Cope, Thomas, 90
Cornell, Saul, 10, 395, 397–98
Cosmopolitanism, 16, 287
Cotlar, Seth, 16, 237, 402
Courting, 60; of disparate political inter-
ests, 66
Coushatta Nation, 311, 316
Couverture, 60
Covington, Ga., 336
Coxe, Tench, 257, 261–62
Craft, Ellen, 93
Creek Nation, 311
Criollos, 312–13, 314
Critical Period, 7
Crowd actions, 358. *See also* Riots
Cult of domesticity, 119
Cultural history/historians: and political
history, 2, 3, 5, 252; and newest politi-
cal history, 208, 210; and terms and
practice of consent, 212; as Burkeans,
225–26, 236; and persuasion, 238
Cultural persuasion. *See* Persuasion
Cultural politics, 9–10, 11
Cultural studies, 10, 226
Culture, 4, 226
Cunard, Samuel, 332
Custis, Nelly Parke, 109
Cutler, Manasseh, 35

Dahrendorf, Ralf, 402
Danbury, Conn., 37
Dandyism, 131, 141, 142, 151

Davis, Cornelius, 285, 286, 287
Davis, David Brion, 399
Davis, Natalie, 62
Davis, Susan, 61
Dawley, Alan, 13
Declaration of Independence, 40, 111,
217
Deference, 15, 166; and electioneering,
57, 60–65, 66, 67, 72, 73, 75; and par-
ticipation, 57–58; defined, 58–59;
African American, 182, 185–91, 192,
193
Deferential-participant culture, 57
Deism, 275
Delaware, 168
Delaware County, N.Y., 360, 361, 368,
370, 371, 377
Delaware Nation, 311, 317
Delaware River, 168
Deliberation, 208–11, 220, 225–30, 232,
236, 237–38
Deliberative political function, 58–59
Democracy, 4, 5, 45, 49, 182, 224, 263,
276, 295, 362; radical, 275, 293; British,
276
Democratic Party, 94–95, 344; as popular
movement, 357
Democratic politics, 167
Democratic radicals, 275, 293; British,
276
Democratic-Republican Party, 38, 39, 84,
107, 110, 111, 117, 135, 237, 292
Democratic-republican societies, 236
Democratization, 4, 5, 12, 95, 97, 236,
278, 280, 305
Democrats, 17, 237, 345, 356–78; radical,
356; and anti-renters, 360, 362; and
evils of banking, 361; and egalitarian-
ism, 362; and natural rights, 363; Barnburners and Hunkers, 366; and landownership, 367; reuniting factions of,
372

Dennie, Joseph, 32, 398–99

Deregulation. *See* Federal government

Devyr, Thomas Ainge, 367, 371, 373, 376

De Witt, Green, 318

Dinmore, Richard, 109

Discourse, 210, 211, 231, 238; of domesticity, 119

Disfranchisement, black, 49, 180

Dissent, 229

Dobson, Richard, 289

Domesticity, cult of, 119

Donald, David, 389

Don Quixote, 142

Dorr War, 237

Douglas, Charles, 306

Douglass, Frederick, 92, 93, 95, 197

Dowling, Wiliam C., 398–99

Duane, William, 294

Duels, 145, 171–72

Dunmore, Lord, 83

Du Pont de Nemours, E. I., 86

Durkheim, Émile, 402

Duverger, Maurice, 402

Duwali, 311

Dwight, Timothy, 282–83, 284, 285, 288

Easton, Hosea, 191

Eaton, Daniel Isaac, 294

Eaton, Peggy, 235

Electioneering, 61, 74–75; rituals of, 57, 68; mass politicking, 58; and treating, 66; participant, 66, 68, 72

Electoral competition, 365

Elkins, Stanley M., 2, 8, 394

Ellis, Charles M., 338

Ellis, Joseph J., 1, 2

Ellis, Markman, 235

Emancipation, British, 199

Embargo, 112, 113, 114, 169

Emmons, Nathaniel, 288

England, 130; Stuart Restoration in, 231

Enlightenment, 182, 208, 223

Eppes, John W., 62

Ethnic interests, 68, 359

Ethnoculturalists, 236. *See also* New political history/historians

Evangelical Christianity, 305

Everett, Edward, 193

Factions, 118

Federal government, 331; and regulation, 328–30, 332, 336, 348–50; and deregulation, 330–31, 341–42, 350; as regulatory regime, 332, 349; and postal deregulation, 337–39

Federalism (form of government), 258; states' rights version of, 262–63

Federalism/Federalist Party, 8, 10, 252, 267; and press, 32, 42; and Mammoth Loaf, 36; and clergy, 39–40; and George Washington, 41; women mocked by, 47; and electioneering ritual, 65–72; and voter turnout, 74; "court" style of, 84; and women's partisanship, 108, 110–14, 117, 118, 121, 124; and Burr, 134, 136, 145; and dandyism, 141; and young men, 159, 161; military organizations of, 162, 165–66, 168–70, 281; political organizations of, 165–68; symbolic appropriation of Washington, 166, 169, 171, 172–73; appropriation of American Revolution, 170–71, 172; gendered language of, 173; and African Americans, 186, 191; and "counter-revolution" (1798), 237; and print influence, 252; celebration of Constitution, 253; and state militias, 257; and right to bear arms, 257–58, 261–62, 267; and mobocracy, 265; defeated in 1800, 275; cultural offensive of, 276, 293; and "Jacobinism," 279; oratory of, 280–86; and "society," 292; decline of, 305

Ferguson, Adam, 215

Festivals, 57, 62, 63, 71, 75

Hall, Prince, 184, 189

Hall, Timothy, 221

Hall, Willard P., 338

Hallock, Gerald, 329, 336, 338, 341

Haltunnen, Karen, 235

Hamilton, Alexander, 14, 107, 133–36, 142, 395, 396

Hamilton, William, 183, 189, 190, 194, 195

Hamiltonians, 8, 79

Harnden, William, 332

Harrington, James, 58

Harris, Ira, 368, 369, 371–73, 376, 377

Harrisburg, Pa., 199

Harrison, William Henry, 14, 123

Hartford, Conn., 63

Harvard College, 289

Haskell, Thomas, 235

Haswell, Anthony, 115

Hawkins, Joseph H., 308

Hay, George, 147

Hays, Samuel P., 389

Henry, Patrick, 258

Hewitt, Nancy, 234

Hidalgo y Costilla, Miguel, 314

"Hidden transcript" of protest, 188

Hillhouse, Rebecca Woolsey, 112

Historical Methods Newsletter, 392

History of the Book in America, 221, 222–23

Hobbes, Thomas, 215

Hobsbawm, Eric, 331, 394

Hofstadter, Richard, 7, 117, 392, 393

Holidays, 39, 40, 42, 43, 49, 57, 188

Hollander, Ann, 144

Holt, Michael, 378, 389

Holton, Woody, 14

Homer, 167

Homestead Act, 376

Hopkins, Lemuel, 136

Horton, James, 180

Horton, Lois, 180

Houdon, Jean-Antoine, 266–67

Household, 306, 320

House of Representatives, U.S., 168, 308

Howe, Daniel Walker, 237

Hudson Valley, 356

Hughes, Jeremiah, 343, 347

Hume, David, 218, 226

Humphreys, David, 85

Hunkers, 366, 368, 372

Hunt, Lynn, 219

Huston, Reeve, 11, 17, 18, 232, 401

Identity, 76

Ideology, 5, 7, 122, 313

Illinois, 237; General Assembly of, 335

Illuminati, 44; Bavarian, 284

Immigrants, 48, 359

Inclusion, 180

Independence Day, 111

India, 219

Indians. *See* Native Americans

"Indians": whites masquerading as, 232, 355–57, 363–65, 369–70, 373

Industrial Revolution, 92

Institutional studies, 16

Interests: courting, 66–67; propertied, 66–67; party, 68; religious and ethnic, 68

Internal improvements, 366

Invented tradition, 331, 350

Inversion, 60–64, 72

Iowa, University of, 390

Irving, Peter, 138, 139, 145

Irving, Washington, 148

Isaac, Rhys, 6, 83

Isenberg, Nancy, 10, 14, 234, 403

Issues, political, 59, 65, 331

Jackson, Andrew, 14, 235, 305, 308, 314, 323, 338

Jackson, James, 37

Jacksonian democracy, 360

Jacksonianism/Jacksonians, 3, 7, 10, 17, 182, 191, 193, 236, 362

231; civil society and, 233; reform and, 235; and atheism, 295; in Texas, 323

Rensselaer County, N.Y., 356, 363, 369, 370, 374, 377

Rensselaerswick, N.Y., 356, 360

"Republican Court," 235–36

Republicanism (ideology), 4, 7, 8, 83, 224, 258; political, 349–50

Republican Party (founded 1854), 376; Radical Republicans, 377; social movements' relationship to, 378

Republican Party (Jeffersonian), 8; and newspapers, 32; and societies, 39; and celebratory politics, 40, 41, 71; and competition, 46, 65, 66, 67; electioneering of, 68, 69, 70, 72; and women, 108; and women partisans, 111–18, 121; Burr and, 130, 134, 137, 145, 148; and young Federalists, 166, 167, 168, 169, 173

Revolution, right of, 262–65

"Revolution of 1800," 34, 45, 49

Reynolds, Maria, 137–38

Rhetoric, 74, 88, 131; and voting, 58; and ritual, 58, 70. See also Oratory; Persuasion

Rhode Island, 32; Dorr War in, 237

Richmond, Va., 66, 114, 117, 145, 181

Richmond Enquirer, 112

Richmond *Virginia Argus*, 66, 69

Richmond *Virginia Gazette*, 148

Right of revolution. See Revolution, right of

Right to bear arms. See Arms, right to bear

Riots, 232, 237, 263, 358

Ripley, Sally, 116, 117

Rituals: electioneering, 57–58; and rhetoric, 58, 70; inversion, 60–64, 72; political, 251

Rives, Julia Cabell, 117

Robertson, Andrew W., 12, 236, 399, 402

Robertson, David, 149

Robison, John, 284, 288, 289

Rockingham County, Va., 66

Rokkan, Stein, 402

Role reversal, 62–63, 74–75. *See also* Inversion

Roman Catholics. *See* Catholicism/Catholics

Roman republic, 213

Rose, Willie Lee, 233

Rousseau, Jean-Jacques, 133, 217, 218, 220, 222, 227, 281

Roxbury, Mass., 119

Rudé, George, 232

Ruggles, David, 192, 193, 198–99

Rush, Benjamin, 260

Rush, Jacob, 186

Rusticus, 182–83

Rutledge, John, Jr., 135

Ryan, Mary P., 57, 234

Sabbatarians, 193, 358

Saltillo, Mexico, 319

San Antonio, Tex., 308

Sandifer, Marmaduke, 321

Sand Lake, N.Y., 355–56, 363, 364

San Jacinto, Battle of, 323

Santa Anna, Antonio Lopez de, 324

Sartori, Giovanni, 402

Satire, 48, 131

Saucedo, José Antonio, 319

Savannah, Ga., 181

Schlesinger, Arthur M., Jr., 236, 392

Schoharie County, N.Y., 371, 377

Schuyler, Philip, 134

Scott, James, 188

Scott, Joan, 108

Second Amendment, 254; and Dissent of the Minority, 260; and scholarship, 267. *See also* Arms, right to bear

Second Great Awakening, 221

Second party system, 359–60, 376

and Embargo, 112–14; and patriotism, 114–15, 118, 120; as mediators, 119, 120; "female politicians," 122; Burr and, 131, 141; and reform, 233–35; and persuasion and deliberation, 234–35; and "Republican Court," 235–36; and individual rights, 256; and "Rights of Women" satire, 291; and evangelicalism, 305; loss of influence of Cherokee women, 310; and women's rights, 358
Wood, Gordon S., 3–5, 7, 10, 222
Woodbury, Levi, 328–30, 344
Woodward, C. Vann, 389, 392
Woodward, William, 184
Woolman, John, 92
Working class, 359
Workingmen's parties, 358

Wrentham, Mass., 288
Wright, Silas, 365, 371

Xenophobia, 283

Yankees, 378
Yellow fever, 184–85
Yellow Jacket, 370
Young, Alfred F., 6, 222
Young, John, 372–73, 374, 375

Zagarri, Rosemarie, 13, 237
Zaret, David, 223
Zavala, Lorenzo de, 316
Zboray, Mary, 237
Zboray, Ronald, 237
Zuckerman, Michael, 89